Studies of Organized Crime

Volume 14

Series Editor
Dina Siegel
Willem Pompe Institute, Utrecht University, Utrecht, The Netherlands

This series will publish theoretically significant books in two primary areas. One is the political economy of organized crime and criminality whether at the transnational, national, regional, or local levels (focus on financial crime, political corruption, environmental crime, and the expropriation of resources from developing nations). The other is human rights violations, particularly in Third World countries. Manuscripts that cover either historical or contemporary issues of the above, utilizing qualitative methodologies, are equally welcome. In addition, we are particularly interested in publishing the work of sophisticated junior scholars.

More information about this series at http://www.springer.com/series/6564

Georgios A. Antonopoulos
Editor

Illegal Entrepreneurship, Organized Crime and Social Control

Essays in Honor of Professor Dick Hobbs

Springer

Editor
Georgios A. Antonopoulos
Teesside University
Middlesbrough, UK

ISSN 1571-5493
Studies of Organized Crime
ISBN 978-3-319-31606-2 ISBN 978-3-319-31608-6 (eBook)
DOI 10.1007/978-3-319-31608-6

Library of Congress Control Number: 2016933781

Printed on acid-free paper

This Springer imprint is published by Springer Nature
The registered company is Springer International Publishing AG Switzerland

Introduction

This volume honours Dick Hobbs, emeritus professor of sociology at Essex University and visiting professor at the University of Western Sydney. This volume has been assembled in recognition of his achievements as an outstanding scholar and teacher.

Dick Hobbs was born in East London in 1951 and has had a long and distinguished scientific career. In 1977 Hobbs obtained a Bachelor in Education from Preston Polytechnic, and in 1982 he earned an M.Sc. in Sociology from the London School of Economics. In 1986 he completed his doctoral studies at the University of Surrey with a thesis entitled *Doing the Business: Entrepreneurship, the Working Class and Detectives in the East End of London*, which was published 2 years later (Hobbs, 1988) and has become one of the classic ethnographic studies on criminal entrepreneurship and a prime example of *haute criminologie*. The particular work won him (in 1989) the prestigious *Philip Abrams Prize*, a prize awarded by the British Sociological Association for the best book published by a new author. *Doing the Business*, a sociological/criminological masterpiece, was the result of research on the connections between crime, political economy and working-class culture.

From 1985–1988 and while he was completing his doctoral studies, Hobbs worked as a research fellow at Oxford University and later as visiting lecturer at Reading University. In 1989, and for 1 academic year, he worked as lecturer in sociology in the Polytechnic of Central London before joining the University of Durham as lecturer in sociology in 1990. Throughout these years, Hobbs also worked as part-time lecturer in other institutions such as Ealing College of Higher Education and Brunel University. In Durham, Hobbs spent 15 years moving up the academic ranks before moving to the London School of Economics for 5 years. In 2011, Hobbs was appointed full professor at Essex University where he also served as director of the Essex Criminology Centre.

Apart from the extremely influential books, edited collections, chapters in volumes and journal articles he produced, Hobbs has conducted research and authored reports for the Home Office, the Howard League and the European Commission. His funding pedigree would be (in fact is) envied by colleagues who are now pestered to obtain external funding, and it is worth saying that Hobbs' sociological and criminological contribution has not been limited to academia. A rather 'hidden' aspect of Hobbs' work is his regular contributions to local and national radio and television (such as programmes and documentaries), as well as a series of obituaries to senior British 'underworld' figures to *The Independent*.

Among the many awards he has won, including the aforementioned *Philip Abrams Prize* (1989), the *Radzinowicz Prize* (2003), and the *Outstanding Publication Award* by the International Association for the Study of Organized Crime (IASOC) (2014) for *Lush Life* (Hobbs, 2013), Hobbs has also won the University and Colleges Union's *Life Changer Award* for 'changing people's lives through education', which is an honour that many in academia are not aware of. Despite his standing in the field, however, Hobbs was never impressed with academic titles and honours; he has always been much more interested in substance, advancing criminological and sociological research and knowledge, and helping his students become better at what they do.

During his career, Dick Hobbs has selected several areas of research with an emphasis on the role of the 'glocal' political economy in shaping crime and deviance. Most of these areas are in some way or another connected to the concept of 'organized crime', including criminal entrepreneurship, 'transnational'/local crime, drug smuggling and drug markets, cigarette smuggling (Hornsby and Hobbs, 2007), bouncers (Hobbs et al., 2003), policing of 'serious' and 'organized' crime, and the links between the so-called underworld and the upperworld, which are put forward in this collection. Hobbs' efforts have always been geared towards overcoming orthodox, unsubstantiated accounts on 'organized crime' through offering a deep and thick description of phenomena produced by an exemplary application of the ethnographic method, and exposing 'organized crime's' normality and 'unremarkability' (Antonopoulos & Papanicolaou, 2014), and its embeddedness in the local community.

His enthusiasm for the ethnographic method has been such that has influenced colleagues internationally and many of his students, primarily research students, who continue the tradition and to whom Hobbs' impact has been indelible. His colleague in his Durham years, James Sheptycki (this volume), calls Dick Hobbs 'the Clifford Geertz of British criminology' and this characterization is accurate and justified. His East London background and his natural immersion in the field allowed Hobbs to be a pioneer in 'organized crime' studies, although he probably does not identify himself as either a 'pioneer' (see below) or an 'organized crime' scholar. His background also allowed him to not only present a side of London that does not feature in sightseers' guides and travel agencies' brochures[1] but also

[1] For an interesting sightseer's guide to *criminal* London see Hollington and Hollington (2013).

introduce to the reader many of 'the chaps' (Hobbs, 1988: viii) such as 'Mr. T', 'Harry the Fish', 'Tony the Phone' and many others who are now immortalized through his work.

His stance has never been that of an arrogant and distant intellectual looking down on the real world from the ivory tower. Hobbs is proud of his working-class background, he is open about the various manual and clerical jobs he did before the start of his bright academic career, and is certainly not one of the kind of people that he describes in the first paragraph of his latest masterpiece, *Lush Life* (Hobbs, 2013). In July 2014 he took me around various places in the East End where *Doing the Business* was set and for a stroll down Blossom Street in Spitalfields where *Nichols & Clarke*, a sanitary ware company and one of Hobbs' former employers, was located. 'Researchers', he noted during our stroll, 'should bring their biography to the research table'. Given his academic success and international recognition his humility is striking. When I announced to him that I would like to edit his *liber amicorum*, he did not see the point in such an endeavour and in fact on two occasions he even tried to prevent me from working on the project!

An avid story teller (just spend 10 min with him in a pub and you will be inundated by interesting anecdotes from the British 'underworld' ranging from unorthodox extortion practices, extinct transgressive communities in the 1960s East End to—perhaps too—personal information about iconic criminal figures), Hobbs possesses a number of appealing personal qualities that most certainly proved handy during his research. This is why Hobbs has been loved, respected and admired by colleagues and students alike, and there were numerous examples of that: from a 'Dick Hobbs appreciation society' in Facebook run by Durham university students to seminar discussions about how 'Lock, Stock and Two Smoking Barrels' could have been better staged had Guy Ritchie read *Doing the Business* and *Bad Business* (Hobbs, 1995) or the enthusiasm with which colleagues invited to contribute a chapter for this volume responded, to mention just a few.

I am one of the people who have been heavily affected by Hobbs in more than one way: his enthusiasm about the subject, his incessant curiosity, his practical research-related advice, his motivating harshness when reading drafts of my thesis chapters (see also Winlow, 2001), and the first opportunity given to me to 'teach' undergraduates. When I firstly met Hobbs in person in 2001 in order to be interviewed for a Ph.D. place at the University of Durham (and having read and been enthused by *Doing the Business* at that point), I thought to myself that 'if I ever become "half-as-cool" as him', I would consider myself successful. Some 15 years later I still have not made it (the notion of 'cool' also being as vague as this of 'organized crime'). But I am proud to say, and I am sure this is the case with the other students of Hobbs some of which feature in this collection, that I have been taught by a man and academic of such high quality, humility, and integrity. The authors of the contributions and the editor of the volume not only wish to contribute to the themes put forward in this collection but would also like to emphasize their huge appreciation for Dick's scientific work.

The Contributions

Following this introduction, this collection comprises nineteen chapters along four parts:

- *Part I—'Organized crime': Theoretical perspectives, structures and empirical manifestations* (Chaps. 1–8).
- *Part II—Criminal Finances* (Chaps. 9 and 10).
- *Part III—Dealing with 'Organized Crime'* (Chaps. 11–17).
- *Part IV—Dick Hobbs' Influence on Theory and Methods* (Chaps. 18 and 19).

Part I—'Organized Crime': Theoretical Perspectives, Structures and Empirical Manifestations

In Chap. 1 *Letizia Paoli* attempts to identify the most relevant promoting factors of organized crime. Initially, the author pays some attention to the problems of defining 'organized crime'. Organized crime is a phenomenon (or a set of phenomena) that is very loosely and vaguely defined (officially and unofficially), and it can include diverse *collectivities* and *activities*. Paoli focuses on the macro-factors or general determinants for both 'criminal organizations' (with a focus on contexts such as Italy, China, Japan, Russia) and schemes that provide illegal goods and services, which operate in a hostile environment formed by their very illegality. In this way, Paoli attempts at highlighting the limits and possibilities for government interventions against manifestations of organized crime. As the author notes, '*the overall goal of organized crime control policies should be clear: envisaging interventions that can reduce the total harms resulting from both the organized crime phenomena and the policies aiming to control these phenomena…*' (Paoli, this volume).

Chapter 2 by *Klaus von Lampe* discusses patterns of relations among criminals that are not centred around the commission of profit-making or perform quasi-governmental functions by controlling and regulating the behaviour of criminals, but on a broad range of *associational* criminal structures. These structures perform the core functions of creating and reinforcing social bonds between criminals, provide channels for privileged communication between and among criminals, foster mutual support, and establish and enforce rules that increase security and predictability in a chaotic environment full of risks. The author proposes a fourfold typology to break down the category of associational criminal structures into subcategories. Von Lampe's proposed typology is based on two criteria: *formalization* ('*the degree to which the behaviour and the relations within an organisation are explicitly specified independently of the individual characteristics of those occupying positions in the organisational structure*') and *legality* ('*the degree to which structures originate in and constitute legal entities*').

In Chap. 3 *Mike Levi* examines the organization of long firm fraud from the early nineteenth century to the Second World War on the basis of his archival research of the manuscripts of cases at London's Central Criminal Court and the Law Reports. 'Long firm', as a term, was commonly used from the late 1860s onwards, although it connoted a type of *individuals* rather than a type of *activity*. 'Long firmers' tended to be professional *commercial* criminals, and it is interesting to note that there was very little overlap between long firm fraudsters and 'traditional' criminals. The historical examples offered by Levi highlight that there is '*a whole spectrum of organisational formats ranging from the loner who pawns the few goods he is able to get to the syndicated crime model*' as well as a whole spectrum of organizational sophistication and scale with various *modi operandi* reflecting conditions, developments, trends and growth in legal national and international trade long before the internet was present to facilitate fraud.

Chapter 4 by *Toine Spapens* presents an overview of organized crime structures and activities occurring in North Brabant in the Netherlands from 1648 onwards. The particular province was notorious for being the home of numerous rural gangs in the Seventeenth and Eighteenth Centuries, and from 1830 to 1962 for the smuggling of various commodities such as salt, coffee, chocolate and pepper among many others. Smuggling in the particular area included schemes of different scale, degrees of organization and sophistication, involving a wide variety of actors from the 'underworld' and the 'upperworld' taking advantage of the 'criminogenic asymmetries' (Passas, 1999) offered by borders. The author also focuses on activities thriving in the 1970s North Brabant, relatively recent developments and trends in organized crime in the area, as well as measures against organized crime. In the concluding section, Spapens looks into some possible theoretical explanations that offer leads for further research: criminal opportunities, networks, social exclusion, and lack of effective countermeasures.

Kenny Monrose in Chap. 5 offers an account of the inner workings of a street economy, as this is put forward by the participants themselves, and highlights how this form of entrepreneurship helped to sustain many young black men in Thatcherite Britain. The context of this account is Newham's '*Frontline*' in London, a location that was developed as a result of social exclusion of black people as well as racial discrimination, and was frequently characterized by all types of social problems and crime, although, naturally, it also provided a number of unique legal functions. In the process, Monrose introduces the reader to the limited opportunity structures for Afro-Caribbean people in (pre-Thatcherite and) Thatcherite Britain as well as the 'blues party' and the 'shubeen' (an illegal party which was also a venue for illegal gambling) whose '*subterranean and seamy character… was exploited to maximum benefit by those who facilitated them, by the introduction of their entrepreneurial nuance and skill*' (Monrose, this volume).

Anna Sergi and *Nigel South* in Chap. 6 look into the strategies and interests of the Calabrian mafia, 'ndrangheta, in activities affecting the environment with a specific focus on the abuse/misuse of EU structural and innovation funds for environmental innovation projects allocated to the region of Calabria in the South of Italy. The authors identify a link between the choices of Calabrian 'ecomafia clans' with the criminal opportunities offered by European regional environment-related policies as well as emphasize the local aspect of 'ndrangheta business. As Sergi and South (this volume) suggest '*though the 'ndrangheta clans are highly effective in their transnational businesses, their local dimension, through conditioning of the private and public sectors in Calabria, is fundamental for their prosperity and longevity*'. Importantly, the authors highlight the convergence of interests between (eco)mafia clans in Calabria and the political sphere which creates a space of negligent governance that includes—among other—the management and absorption of EU funds.

Chapter 7 by *Anton Kojouharov* and *Atanas Rusev* offers a detailed account of the illegal and predatory moneylending landscape and business in Bulgaria, a context in which a number of factors have affected the development of the alternative (and informal) credit markets and their—often—extortionate ends. The authors use data from in-depth interviews with law enforcement officers, experts on the topic and convicted offenders as well as open Bulgarian sources. They offer a concise review of definitions of relevant terms and present a typology of moneylenders. Four types of moneylenders classified by their registration status—legal or illegal—and by their basic characteristics are identified: *legal market oriented* (formal financial institutions); *illegal market oriented* (benevolent moneylenders); *illegal predatory* (classic loan sharks); *legal predatory* (certain fast-credit companies, pawn shops). Kojouharov and Rusev also offer an overview of the clientele of moneylenders including criminals, gamblers, the poor and lower middle class people as well as legal businessmen affected by the economic crisis.

Chapter 8 by *Anqi Shen* and *Georgios A. Antonopoulos* provides the findings from a study on the role of females in criminal entrepreneurial activities in the post-1978 reform era China. The particular chapter relies primarily on empirical data drawn from a recent, wider qualitative study on women and crime in China for which 26 incarcerated female offenders were interviewed by the first author at a female prison in the southeast region of the country in 2013. The study shows that women, commonly motivated by economic incentives, play a variety of roles in various criminal markets in China. A typology of these roles is provided. The participants are involved in illegal markets as criminal leaders, business partners, supporters, occasional entrepreneurs, or investors. Apart from taking a gender-sensitive approach, the authors also consider the issue of social class, the participants' personal conditions, overall social changes in China, and their interplay in the women's involvement in illegal markets.

Part II—Criminal Finances

In Chap. 9 *Friedrich Schneider* aims at providing an account of the financial flows of transnational crime and tax fraud in OECD (Organization for Economic Co-operation and Development) countries. The author offers a number of methodological remarks about money laundering and the estimations of laundered money globally and by top destinations of 'dirty money'. In addition, Schneider provides a preliminary review of the available empirical findings of the proceeds of transnational 'organized crime' worldwide and for a number of developed countries (such as the United States, Australia, the Netherlands and Italy). On the basis of proceeds, globally, tax fraud constitutes by far the biggest share of all ('organized') illegal activities (66 %). In terms of illegal markets and other empirical manifestations of 'organized crime' in particular, and according to the available evidence, the drug market is the biggest business followed by counterfeiting, human trafficking and oil smuggling. The proceeds from all other 'organized criminal activities' are much lower.

Chapter 10 by *Petrus van Duyne*, *Jackie Harvey* and *Liliya Gelemerova* addresses the issue of proportionality in the global anti-money laundering (AML) regime. The authors examine the evidence on crime-money 'threat', critically review attempts to produce this evidence as well as the measures against the alleged 'threat' and costs, and look into efforts related to the regulated sectors. 'Money laundering' is a technical construction, a fuzzy term exploited by the 'threat assessment industry' for political and financial objectives, the volume of the 'threat' of money laundering remains largely unspecified, there are assumptions underlying models which 'might' be true, and independent empirical evidence is difficult to find. In addition, the AML policies entail significant financial and political costs to society, costs that are not addressed from a proportionality perspective. The authors also highlight that '*at the work floor the experienced proportionality balance between threat and measures is different from the one conveyed at policy making and political level*'.

Part III—Dealing with 'Organized Crime'

In Chap. 11 *Filippo Marco Espinoza* and *Georgios Papanicolaou*, on the basis of archival and other historical sources, offer an exploration of the socio-political context of smuggling and of official responses towards it during the period of the Italian Administration of the Dodecanese between 1912 and the beginning of World War II. The authors situate historically the phenomenon of smuggling in the Dodecanese, document the Italian Administration's policy and practice towards smuggling in the Dodecanesian archipelago, and offer a reflection on its implications for contemporary debates on 'organized crime'. As the authors note, '*illegal markets and the forms of social organisation that sustain them cannot be narrowly approached as a technical matter of crime prevention and suppression but rather as social practices and strategies, which are rooted in historically given conditions, reflect particular economic, social and political interests, and may thus be symbiotic with or antagonistic to other social practices and strategies, particularly those promulgated by the state*' (this volume).

Paul Larsson in Chap. 12 focuses on the processes whereby biker groups in Norway have been selected for attention by the police and media as a 'threat'. The author pays attention to two specific periods: 1992–1997 and 2011–2015. The chapter analyses the central role of biker groups in the process of defining and making sense of the concept of 'organized crime' in Norway. According to the author, bikers served as 'suitable enemies' in this process, initially in 1992 when Rowdies in the city of Trondheim became a chapter of Hells Angels and later in 2011 when '1 % clubs' got re-labelled as '*criminal* 1 % clubs' and were identified as integral elements of the 'serious organized crime' scene in the country. As Larsson succinctly puts it, '*[i]n this process of giving meaning to the term organized crime, a term that felt foreign and un-Norwegian, the biker groups, especially Hells Angels and Bandidos, played an essential role as "role models*"' (this volume).

In Chap. 13 *Cyrille Fijnaut* highlights the local dimension of organized crime by means of a detailed account of a municipal policy against organized crime in inner-city Amsterdam. The platform for this municipal policy is a report on organized crime problems in central Amsterdam in the late 1990s within the context of a Dutch parliamentary commission (Van Traa commission) into the abuse of police investigative methods in the country. The particular report identified that a number of professional criminals and organized crime groups fully or partly controlled important aspects of the economy in central Amsterdam. The municipal policy that has been implemented includes—among other—the monitoring of real estate purchases in Amsterdam's Red Light District and the application of a zoning plan for the inner city. The author of the chapter provides a description of the various phases in the development of the particular municipal policy and discusses the possibilities offered by the policy as well as its logistical complications.

Since the 1990s, Greece has been frequently represented as an important context for human trafficking for sex and in fact in some official and unofficial accounts as the centre of trafficking in Europe. Chapter 14 by *Paraskevi S. Bouklis* looks into the Greek anti-trafficking developments on the basis of her empirical research conducted on the Greek anti-trafficking mechanisms as well as on analysis of media representations of trafficking in women. Greek anti-trafficking, which mostly had a legal basis with an anti-'organized crime' rhetoric and sentiment, borrows integral components from the crime control industry and the victims' industry, and has mobilized numerous strategies and practices that Bouklis examines in the chapter. As the author suggests, within the increasing financialization and neoliberalization of the world economy, the trafficking victims' industry is an exemplary set of domain expansion efforts '*which are not always validated and, in their claim-making (in)capacity, initiatives have been accused of direct participation in trafficking*' (Bouklis, this volume).

In recent decades scholars have shown an interest in the relationship between organized religion and 'organized crime'. In Chap. 15 *Gary Armstrong* and *James Rosbrook-Thompson* focus on the role of religion in Serious Youth Violence (SYV)/gang interventions in contemporary East London. The research described was based on an ethnography (2011–2013) in the London Borough of Newham, a diverse setting that, according to police intelligence, contains known youth gangs, some of which are 'violently active'. In the chapter, the authors examine the work of a Pentecostal Christian charity, *Teaching Against Gangs* (TAG), and the ways in which its founder draws on Christianity in persuading young (predominantly black) men to turn their backs to gang life, a life pervaded by threatened and actual violence. According to Armstrong and Rosbrook-Thompson (this volume) '*[t]he TAG programmes concomitantly promoted the development of leadership skills, seeking ways out of the "gang mentality", "breaking the chains" of anger and addressing past hurts/emotional pain and family dysfunction*'.

Brendan Quirke in Chap. 16 considers the experiences of two relatively new member states, the Czech Republic and Romania, in their effort to establish effective anti-EU fraud structures. In his endeavour, Quirke conducted interviews with government officials in the Czech Republic and Romania as well as with Czech academics. In addition, he undertook a review of secondary materials such as European Commission reports and government documents. The author examines the specific problems the Czech Republic and Romania have encountered and the ways they adopted to overcome them. Of specific interest here is the context regarding Czech and Romanian applications to join the European Union, and the wider political, social and economic circumstances in the particular countries. Existing problems of corruption, difficulties in establishing relevant structures, lack of investigatory experience, support offered by OLAF and the European Commission etc. are examined. Lessons for future accessions of countries such as those in western Balkans are also highlighted.

In Chap. 17 *Nicholas Dorn*, focusing on the financial market crises from 2007 onwards and the misconduct that was publicized, suggests that there is a need for a governance shift from past- and present-focused *regulation* to future-orientated *policy*. Four regulatory modes placed on a 'public–private' continuum (reflecting ownership of regulation and visibility) are discussed; however, as the author suggests, it is the debates on *policy* that attempt at answering fundamental questions about the financial market and how to transform it. What is also proposed in this chapter is that the financiers constitute a 'risk class', '*a sub-set of the elite, with which it shares a general position of privilege, yet within which it is differentiated by its particular relationship to risk*' (Dorn, this volume). The question with which this chapter concludes is whether the analysis of public and private manifestations of regulation can be taken into a future-aware, 'risk class' analysis, and touches upon policies: suppression, a 'polluter pays' principle, and 'right-sizing' of finance.

Part IV—Dick Hobbs' Influence on Theory and Methods

In Chap. 18 *Steve Hall* and *Simon Winlow* offer an account of Dick Hobbs' legacy of ethnography from its early days of exploring crime, political economy, entrepreneurship and the working class in the East End of London to his latest effort dealing with global 'organized' crime and its 'glocal' nodes. The authors discuss Dick Hobbs' multi-faceted contribution and the effect of his forceful and extremely rich descriptive accounts. As they put it in their chapter: '*the richness of his data and the honesty of its presentation allowed him to make… intellectual connections in a convincing manner, which he did far more effectively than most other ethnographers. For this reason alone his work is a beacon for the younger generation to follow....*'. Moreover, the authors suggest that Hobbs' work will continue to be a source of inspiration not only for the younger generation of criminologists but also for the new ultra-realist programme in criminological research.

Chapter 19 by *James Sheptycki* celebrates the ethnographic approach to understanding the sociology of crime and policing. This chapter, which reflects on recent fieldwork undertaken in an intelligence unit in Toronto police department, is grounded in some preliminary observations about the politics of policing gun-crime in the particular city and places it in the context of the ethnographic tradition. The chapter considers a number of practical and ethical issues that are of interest to ethnographers and reflects upon the dilemmas of doing ethnographic criminological research. Sheptycki also contextualizes his discussion by reference to the author's own biography and an appreciation of Dick Hobbs whom he considers '*one of those important scholars who helped to create and sustain the conditions for people who believe that the answers to the most general questions—why? how? what?—are to be found in the fine details of lived life*' (this volume).

Middlesbrough, UK Georgios A. Antonopoulos

References

Antonopoulos, G. A. & Papanicolaou, G. (2014). *Unlicensed capitalism, Greek style: Illegal markets and 'organized crime' in Greece*. Nijmegen: Wolf Legal Publishers.

Hobbs, D. (1988). *Doing the business*. Oxford: Oxford University Press.

Hobbs, D. (1995). *Bad business*. Oxford: Oxford University Press.

Hobbs, D. (2013). *Lush life*. Oxford: Oxford University Press.

Hobbs, D., Hadfield, P., Lister, S. & Winlow, S. (2003). *Bouncers: Violence and governance in the night-time economy*. Oxford: Oxford University Press.

Hollington, K. & Hollington, N. (2013). *Criminal London: A sightseer's guide to the capital of crime*. London: Aurum.

Hornsby, R. & Hobbs, D. (2007). A zone of ambiguity: The political economy of cigarette bootlegging. *British Journal of Criminology, 47*(4), 551–571.

Passas, N. (1999) Globalisation, criminogenic asymmetries, and economic crime. *European Journal of Law Reform, 1*, 399–423.

Winlow, S. (2001). *Badfellas: Crime, tradition and new masculinities*. Oxford: Berg.

Contents

Contributors

Georgios A. Antonopoulos School of Social Sciences, Business and Law, Teesside University, Middlesbrough, UK

Gary Armstrong College of Business, Arts and Social Sciences, Brunel University, London, UK

Paraskevi S. Bouklis Open University, Milton Keynes, UK

Nicholas Dorn Institute of Advanced Legal Studies, University of London, London, UK

Petrus van Duyne Tilburg University, Tilburg, The Netherlands

Filippo Marco Espinoza Scuola di Dottorato in Studi Umanistici, University of Trento, Trento, Italy

Cyrille Fijnaut Tilburg Law School, Tilburg University, Tilburg, The Netherlands

Liliya Gelemerova University of Manchester, Manchester, UK

Steve Hall School of Social Sciences, Business and Law, Teesside University, Middlesbrough, UK

Jackie Harvey Newcastle Business School, Northumbria University, Newcastle, UK

Anton Kojouharov Center for the Study of Democracy, Sofia, Bulgaria

Klaus von Lampe Department of Law, Police Science and Criminal Justice Administration, John Jay College of Criminal Justice, New York, NY, USA

Paul Larsson The Norwegian Police University College, Oslo, Norway

Mike Levi School of Social Sciences, Cardiff University, Cardiff, UK

Kenny Monrose School of Law and Social Sciences, University of East London, London, UK

Letizia Paoli School of Law, University of Leuven, Leuven, Belgium

Georgios Papanicolaou School of Social Sciences, Business and Law, Teesside University, Middlesbrough, UK

Brendan Quirke Business School, Manchester Metropolitan University, Manchester, UK

James Rosbrook-Thompson Department of Humanities and Social Sciences, Anglia Ruskin University, Cambridge, UK

Atanas Rusev Center for the Study of Democracy, Sofia, Bulgaria

Friedrich Schneider Department of Economics, Johannes Kepler University of Linz, Linz, Austria

Anna Sergi Department of Sociology, University of Essex, Colchester, UK

Anqi Shen School of Social Sciences, Business and Law, Teesside University, Middlesbrough, UK

James Sheptycki Faculty of Liberal Arts and Professional Studies, York University, Toronto, ON, Canada

Nigel South Department of Sociology, University of Essex, Colchester, UK

Toine Spapens Department of Criminal Law, Tilburg University, Tilburg, The Netherlands

Simon Winlow School of Social Sciences, Business and Law, Teesside University, Middlesbrough, UK

About the Editor

Georgios A. Antonopoulos obtained his doctorate from the University of Durham in 2006. He is currently Professor of Criminology at the School of Social Sciences, Business and Law of Teesside University. His teaching and research interest include the criminality, criminalization and victimization of minority ethnic groups, qualitative research methods, and 'organized crime'/illegal markets. He is an associate of the *Cross-Border Crime Colloquium*, associate editor of the journal *Trends in Organized Crime* (published by Springer), and member of the editorial boards of the journals *Global Crime*, *Journal of Financial Crime*, *Journal of Money Laundering Control* and the *British Journal of Criminology*. In 2009 he won the European Society of Criminology *Young Criminologist Award*. In 2014 he was executive director of the *International Association for the Study of Organized Crime* (IASOC).

Part I
'Organized Crime': Theoretical Perspectives, Structures and Empirical Manifestations

Chapter 1
Towards a Theory of Organized Crime: Some Preliminary Reflections

Letizia Paoli

Introduction

We owe Dick Hobbs some of the most insightful and lively analyses of professional and organized crime (e.g., Hobbs, 1988, 1995, 2013; Pearson & Hobbs, 2001). In his latest book *Lush Life*, Dick Hobbs (2013) has also magisterially shown how the term "organized crime" has since the 1990s been misused by skillful moral entrepreneurs and politicians to signify the growing popular concern for crime and the increasing insecurity of our late modern societies, and to justify far-reaching legal and institutional reforms at both the national and international level.

Given the public concern about organized crime and the vast array of legal and institutional reforms adopted to control it, it is important to reflect upon the determinants of organized crime. Without a better understanding of these determinants and the causal models linking them to the different forms of organized crime, in fact, policy interventions risk selecting unrealistic goals or even obtaining counterproductive results. Yet this avenue has not been systematically pursued. Even though research on organized crime has greatly expanded over the past 25 years, most studies are descriptive, tend to focus on specific phenomena and/or are often circumscribed to single national or even subnational contexts, reflecting the difficulties of the empirical data collection (see Hobbs & Antonopoulos, 2014, for a review of the research methods used). As a result, comparative research has remained very limited (see Paoli and Fijnaut, 2004 for an isolate case) and no systematic attention has so far been given to the causes of organized crime (for an overview of recent research, see Paoli, 2014b).

This chapter is to a large extent based on material from Paoli (2013) and Paoli (2014a).

L. Paoli (✉)
School of Law, University of Leuven, Leuven, Belgium
e-mail: Letizia.Paoli@law.kuleuven.be

G.A. Antonopoulos (ed.), *Illegal Entrepreneurship, Organized Crime and Social Control*, Studies of Organized Crime 14, DOI 10.1007/978-3-319-31608-6_1

In this chapter, I intend to start identifying the most relevant promoting factors of organized crime on the basis of the existing literature and my own work. I focus, in particular, on macro-factors or general determinants, which can be defined in accordance with Wikström, Oberwittler, Treiber, and Hardie (2012) as "causes of the causes." I do not consider here situational or individual factors nor do I claim to be exhaustive or even systematic. My contribution is meant to be an invitation to launch a systematic reflection on the crucial issue of the "causes" of organized crime.

The Definitional Conundrum

Looking for an *explanans*—in our case, the determinants of organized crime—presupposes a clear definition of our *explanandum*, that is organized crime itself. Alas, despite its policy relevance, organized crime remains still today an unclear and contested concept. As Mike Levi puts it, organized crime is like the psychiatrist's Rorschach blot, whose "attraction as well as … weakness is that one can read almost anything into it" (2002: 887). Even the official definitions of organized crime are very loose and vague. For example, the 2000 UN Convention on Transnational Organised Crime defines the key concept of "organised criminal group" as a *"structured group of three or more persons, existing for a period of time and acting in concert with the aim of committing one or more serious crimes or offences established in accordance with this Convention [i.e., punishable by a maximum deprivation of liberty of at least four years], in order to obtain, directly or indirectly a financial or other material benefit."* (UNODC, 2000). This means that anything from the Italian Cosa Nostra to a gang of thieves, from Al Qaida to a youth clique or a drug trafficking network can be considered an "organised criminal group" according to the UN text (Paoli & Vander Beken, 2014).[1]

De facto, both the scientific and policy discourses have oscillated between two different understandings of organized crime, so much so that it is still unclear if organized crime is to be understood as sets of actors engaging in crime or sets of criminalized activities. At one extreme, organized crime is said to consist of long-lasting criminal organizations with a well-defined collective identity and subdivision of work among its members (Reuter, 1983; Paoli, 2003)—with protection rackets considered the quintessential function of such organizations (e.g., Schelling, 1971; Gambetta, 1993). At the other extreme, organized crime is equated to a set of criminalized activities, primarily the provision of prohibited goods and services (e.g., Van Duyne, 1997; Edwards & Levi, 2008; Hobbs, 2013).

Originating from the now discredited alien conspiracy theory, the former view is enthusiastically embraced by the media and the policy-makers seeking to justify draconian measures. Although it is rejected by most scholars, such understanding is

[1] The recent shift of emphasis from organized to serious crime in the EU policy debate does not contribute to conceptual clarity (Dorn, 2009). In fact, the term "serious crime" is left undefined and merely associated with a list of offenses (Paoli, Adriaenssen, Greenfield, & Conickx, 2015).

corroborated by the existence of a few large-scale and long-lasting criminal organizations worldwide, which I have termed elsewhere "mafia-type criminal organizations" (Paoli, 2002b). These are primarily the Sicilian Cosa Nostra and Calabrian 'Ndrangheta, the Italian-American La Cosa Nostra, the Chinese Triads, the Japanese Yakuza, and the post-Soviet *vory v zakone* (thieves-in-law).

The second view, which is now dominant in the scientific understanding of organized crime, is most clearly exemplified by the criminal activities listed as typical of organized crime in the Organized Crime (Threat Assessment) Reports produced at regular intervals by Europol (2013) and national law enforcement and governmental agencies (e.g., the UK Serious and Organized Crime Agency[2] and German Bundeskriminalamt). In this second paradigm, depending on the authors and agencies, the identification of organized crime with the provision of illegal goods and services can be complete (e.g., Van Duyne, 1997) or merely partial (e.g., Edwards & Levi, 2008; Hobbs, 2013).[3] Prohibited psychoactive drugs (e.g., heroin, cocaine, and cannabis) are the best-known examples of illegal goods but, in addition to them, this category also includes goods produced and traded in violation of specific regulations: human beings, if trafficked for the purposes of sexual exploitation or forced labor; cigarettes, alcohol, and gasoline, if exchanged without paying excise and other taxes; diamonds, wood, and other natural resources, if extracted illegally or sold outside the legitimate channels. The category of illegal services is also broad, as it ranges from gambling (in those jurisdictions in which it is still prohibited; see Spapens, 2014) to paid sex (in jurisdictions where prostitution itself or its exploitation is prohibited) and the facilitated entry into a country, in the case of human smuggling. We will use these two ideal-typical views of organized crime as starting points of our analysis.

The Determinants of Criminal Organizations

A comparative analysis of the major mafia-type criminal organizations indicates that a single general factor played a preponderant role in their rise: the weakness of the local government authorities. There is a consensus among the scholars who have carried out research on the Southern Italian mafia since the early 1960s that the origins of the mafia phenomenon in the second half of the nineteenth century cannot be understood unless the forms and pace of the state-building process in Southern

[2] Currently National Crime Agency.

[3] Organized crime official reports and scholarly studies (e.g., Edwards & Levi, 2008) also often include different forms of "illegal transfers" (e.g., robberies, extortions, embezzlement, and frauds). Unlike the provision of illegal goods and services, these transfers do not create value but merely transfer it from one person to another. Not least for this very reason, though, the harm they generate is more evident than the harms accruing from the provision of illegal goods and services (see Paoli, Greenfield, & Zoutendijk, 2013 for an assessment of the harms associated with cocaine trafficking in Belgium). Due to length restrictions, these forms of predatory crimes are not discussed here.

Italy are taken into account. In Charles Tilly's words (1988: xxi), the mafia is "an outgrowth of the particular form that the process of state formation took in Italy." That is to say, the mafia developed because the national system of power expanded without fully subordinating local systems of power. Indeed, it was obliged to actually rely on these systems—constituted by landlords who wanted to maintain their role as feudatory and mafia organizations—if it wanted to govern at all in the larger areas of southern Italy. A vicious circle was consequently set in motion, one which has been described very clearly by Henner Hess (1973: 25): "The chronic weakness of the state resulted in the emergence of self-help institutions and the exclusive power positions of informal groups made it impossible for the state to win the loyalty of the public, while its resultant weakness again strengthened the family, the clientele and *mafioso* positions."

Likewise, the Heaven and Earth Society (*Tiandihui*), the Chinese "secret society" out of which modern Triads derive, was founded around 1760 in the Fujian province—an area characterized by continuous turmoil, recurrent cycles of rebellion and sustained feuding among the local lineages in the absence of a strong government power (Murray, 1994: 6–21). *Hui*, secret societies, developed in other parts of Southeast China as well, which was then a distant border area and had been unsettled by the transition from the Ming to the Qing dynasty. Founded on fictive blood relationships and distinguishing themselves from other informal institutions through their readiness to use violence, secret societies catered to the needs of marginalized, often young men, whose ranks had increased due to population growth and the increased commercialization fostered by foreign trade (Ownby, 1993).

The ancestors of the modern Yakuza groups—that is, the itinerant bands of Japanese roadside gamblers (known as *bakuto*) and peddlers (*tekiya*)—are known to have been active since the Middle Ages to provide protection to their members. Long tolerated by Japanese government institutions, yakuza groups were able to substantially expand their size, economic and political power in two phases in which the Japanese government was particularly weak: the first half of the nineteenth century and after Japan's defeat in the Second World War (Hill, 2003). Founded in Stalinist prisons in the 1930s, *vory v zakone* and other Russian crime groups have gained unprecedented political power and control over economic resources after the implosion of the Soviet Union in 1991 (Volkov, 2014).

State weakness as the key determinant of mafia-type criminal organizations is mirrored in what is regarded as the quintessential function of such organizations: the provision of protection. Gambetta (1993: 1) has gone as far as defining the Sicilian mafia as "a specific economic enterprise, an industry that produces, promotes and sells private protection" 1992: i. While Gambetta's analysis can be criticized for his one-sided emphasis on protection and his denial of the multifunctionality of mafia-type organizations,[4] he must be credited with having rediscovered the

[4] Founded on premodern status and fraternization contracts, mafia-type organizations have historically been used by their members to achieve a plurality of goals and to accomplish a variety of functions. As Dian Murray puts it, the members of the first Chinese secret societies "originally organized for one purpose, sometimes found themselves mobilized for different ends, and simulta-

political dimension of Southern Italian mafia organizations that had been neglected in the studies conceptualizing mafia groups as illicit enterprises (e.g., Catanzaro, 1991). Although mafia bonds have been exploited over the decades and centuries for a plurality of different aims, the provision of protection and, more generally, the exercise of political functions remain the typifying activities of mafia-type criminal organizations, so much so that they can be considered as political communities that are not fully institutionalized. These groups act as political bodies toward their own members, but throughout their history they have been struggling—with varying degrees of success—to force their own primordial legal order onto the entire population of their territory and to endow it with legitimacy. They have never succeeded, however, in neutralizing all the rival centers of power (Paoli, 2003; see also Hill, 2003 and Volkov, 2014).

While criminal groups posing as proto-states rose in several parts of premodern Europe (e.g., Egmond, 2004), most of them were swept away by the consolidation of modern state structures. The current mafia-type organizations have survived in contexts in which government structures have remained weak or a considerable portion of them have been willing to enter into pacts with mafia-type organizations. At least up to the mid-twentieth century, for example, Italian government authorities came to terms with the representatives of mafia power and de facto delegated to the latter the maintenance of public order over wide areas of western Sicily and southern Calabria, where the authority of the central government was scarce and even the personal safety of state officials was in danger. As the Parliamentary Anti-Mafia Commission finally acknowledged in 1993, *"in practice, the relationships between the institutions and mafia took place, for many years, in the form of relationships between two distinct sovereignties: neither would attack the other, as long as each remained within its own boundaries... The state attacked only when the Cosa Nostra attacked and after that it would go back to the cohabitation"* (Commissione Parlamentare d'inchiesta sul fenomeno della mafia e sulle altre associazioni similari, 1993).

In Japan as well, Yakuza bosses have held close ties with members of the political establishment and specifically the Liberal Democratic Party (LDP), which came into power in 1955 and remained the party of government for all but three of the subsequent 64 years. Until the end of the 1960s these ties were, according to Hill (2014) and other scholars he quotes, systemic and were not greatly concealed. In 1952, for example, yakuza were called upon by senior conservative politicians to protect the Diet building against left-wing protestors trying to prevent the passage of the Subversive Activities Bill. Only since the 1970s have these ties started to be seen as inappropriate and, whenever they have come to light, they have sometimes led to the premature end of the careers of the involved politicians. This does not mean, however, that they are no longer cultivated. According to an informant quoted by Hill (2014), at least six cabinet ministers in a recent LDP government had yakuza links.

neously involved in activities where the distinctions between 'legal' and 'illegal', 'protection' and 'predation', or 'orthodox' and 'heterodox' blurred" (1994: 2). Only by sacrificing empirical evidence it is possible to single out an encompassing function or goal that can characterize mafia-type criminal organizations throughout their lives.

Exploiting the weakness of the state and, at the same time, their own privileged contacts with corrupt politicians and civil servants, mafia-type criminal organizations have traditionally increased their legitimacy by providing income and other non-material advantages to their associates and a variety of services for the general population, such as civil-service jobs, a pension benefit or impunity for their supporters or votes for befriended politicians. Additionally, in Italy, Japan, Russia, and Chinese communities all over the world, they have occasionally controlled the workforce and carried out "dirty work" for colluding companies and landowners—for example, by protecting them from ordinary criminals or by breaking strikes or other forms of protests. Further, mafia-type organizations have supplied goods and services for which there is, despite their official prohibition, a public demand. It is through the latter function that mafia-type organizations become involved in the criminal activities being considered exemplary of the alternative understanding of organized crime—thus creating a partial overlapping between the two views. Contrary to what is often maintained however, mafia-type organizations are far from controlling illegal markets worldwide and indeed, according to a plurality of independent researchers, their "market share" has in recent years further declined (Paoli, 2014b and specifically Hill, 2014; Volkov, 2014; Chin, 2014).

The relevance of political protection for the survival of mafia-type organizations also emerges from the analysis of the cases in which these groups have been weakened or dismantled. In China, Triad groups were swept away by the Communist regime that took over in the 1949, and survived only outside mainland China and specifically in Hong Kong and Macao, where they were tolerated by the local government authorities (Chu, 2005). The strengthening of the Russian government structures in the first decades of the twenty-first century and specifically, the increased efficiency of Russian courts have also considerably reduced the demand for the protection and mediation provided/imposed by the local organized crime groups and reduced the latter's control of legitimate markets (Volkov, 2014).

The Determinants of Criminal Activities

It is almost a platitude to note that public demand constitutes the main determinant for the provision of illegal goods and services. The evidence for such a statement is most compelling in the case of illegal drugs. Considerable research has been carried out on the topic, and many scholars agree that drug production can be eventually pushed by a successful upstream intervention from one location to another but it will not be reduced in its global dimension as long as there is not a corresponding decline in demand. The illegal drug industry is like a balloon: when it is "squeezed" or curbed in one location, it tends to "bulge" or reemerge in another location (e.g., Friesendorf, 2007; Paoli, Greenfield, & Reuter, 2009).

The so-called "balloon effect" applies not only to production but also trafficking. In exceptional circumstances, law enforcement agencies of contemporary democratic governments have been able to stop traffickers from using certain locations for their drug shipments. Such successful interventions, however, have been possible only on islands—particularly the Caribbean—that are easy to control (e.g., 100 % searches on all air passengers boarding at Curacao International Airport in the early 2000s). It has turned out to be impossible to replicate such successes with democratic means in any large country with many border crossings. Moreover, even when they have been successful, as in the case of the Dutch police in Curacao, these interventions have led to the shifts of drug trafficking routes to other countries—the Dutch police's measures in Curacao unintentionally contributed to the emergence of Western Africa as a cocaine transhipment venue (UNODC, 2007: 6).

Despite the ultimate powerful role of demand, it would be unjustified to conclude that political conditions have no impact on illegal markets. For example, they play a key role in determining the location of production of opiates (specifically, heroin) and cocaine. In their book on the world heroin market, Paoli et al. (2009) conclude that the location of opium poppy cultivation depends heavily on the role of governments, because after meeting some basic climatic and socioeconomic needs, effective illegality—that is, the degree to which the prohibition on opiate production and trafficking are effectively enforced—constitutes a major determining factor. All else being equal, cultivation tends to concentrate in countries with no effective enforcement of opium prohibitions and with local government or quasi-government tolerance or support for opiate production and trade. Afghanistan and Burma, the world's two leading opium producers, most clearly illustrate this principle. Mutatis mutandis, the same analysis seems also to fit cocaine. Like opium, coca, the plant that gives rise to cocaine, grows in only a few relatively poor countries, although technically speaking it could grow in many other countries and has historically been grown in Java, Taiwan, and Bengal. None of the three major coca-growing countries, i.e., Colombia, Peru, and Bolivia, strictly enforces prohibitions on cultivation in growing regions.

The draconian measures occasionally imposed by authoritarian governments and quasi-state authorities also vividly demonstrate the impact that government decisions can have, at least in the short-term, on illegal markets. In less than twelve months from the start of the twenty-first century, the Taliban regime in Afghanistan achieved what most scholars and policy makers had thought to be impossible: namely, it cut Afghanistan's illicit opium production by over 90 % from peak levels, amounting to a 65 % reduction in world production. The Taliban ban was lifted when the Americans invaded Afghanistan after 9/11; since then opium production in Afghanistan has returned to, and surpassed, previous record-breaking levels (UNODC, 2015). Most experts agree that, even if the Taliban had remained in power, the opium ban would have not been sustainable in the long run. The recent experience in Burma, where opium production started to increase again since 2006 after having been squashed by the Wa and other quasi-government authorities in the Shan State, seems to confirm that prediction. It also exemplifies the balloon effect, as opium cultivation largely moved from the areas controlled by the quasi-state authorities to neighboring regions formally administered by the Burmese government (UNODC, 2010).

In at least one case, the draconian measures of an authoritarian government have also achieved long-term, lasting change. The radical and concerted opium suppression campaign by the new Communist-led regime in the early 1950s eliminated opium consumption and production in China, then still by far the largest market in the world. Much like the bans of the Taliban regime and Wa authorities, such a campaign entailed degrees of coercion that no democratic government can rightfully employ (Zhou, 2000). Moreover, the coercive measures of the Communist government may not have been the only determinant of the illegal market change. Without downplaying the achievement of the Communists' anti-drug crusade, Dikötter, Laarmann, and Zhou (2004: 208–209) convincingly argue that medical and social variables were at least as important as the political factors in the long-term decline of narcotic culture. Penicillin began to be sold in the 1940s as the first antibiotic capable of treating a whole range of diseases that had been previously managed with opiates. The social status of opium was already on the decline in the 1930s: by then social elites had begun to consider opium smoking morally reprehensible and old-fashioned, and started to praise abstinence instead. As in Java (Rush, 1985), tobacco smoking progressively superseded opium smoking.

Totalitarian regimes have also been able to prevent the integration of their countries into international illegal markets. Most Western illegal drugs, for example, were unavailable in Russia until the implosion of the Soviet Union in 1991. (A variety of locally produced illegal psychoactive drugs were nonetheless consumed; see Paoli, 2002a). The bulkier the product is, the higher the chances of control. The Iron Curtain effectively deprived 400 million people of their right of free movement—and "protected" them from falling prey to human trafficking and smuggling.

The chances of controlling illegal markets are, however, much more limited for democratic governments committed to the rule of law and market economy. As long as these are not willing to resort to authoritarian border and law enforcement methods or to disrupt legitimate trade by, say, inspecting every container crossing their national borders, it will be almost impossible for them to stop illegal market flows. Indeed, these can be regarded as the price we need to pay for democracy and market economy. Much like the informal economy, of which they are part, illegal markets constitute a "normal," unavoidable component of all modern state societies (Portes, Castells, & Benton, 1991: 299).

Contemporary governments have even less leverage than their predecessors over illegal—and legal—market flows as a result of economic globalization and deregulation. The diminution of state-enforced restrictions on exchanges across borders—the core trait of globalization—has accelerated the interconnections between previously separate domestic legal and illegal markets and increased the mobility of goods, capital, and human beings. At the same time, economic liberalization has reduced the ability of governments to withstand and regulate market forces and has unintentionally facilitated the sectors of the global economy that remain criminalized (Andreas, 2002). For illegal entrepreneurs it has become easier than ever to move drugs and other illegal commodities from producing to consuming countries, to repatriate profits, to establish business partnerships with foreign counterparts and even to operate in foreign countries themselves.

If the prospects of controlling global illegal market flows are quite bleak, the in-depth analysis of the world heroin market by Paoli et al. (2009) suggests that government authorities, even in democratic societies, are not powerless vis-à-vis organized crime activities. One of Paoli et al.'s (2009) main conclusions is that the strictness of governments' enforcement of prohibitions—in other words, the degree of effective illegality to which opiates (i.e., opium and its derivatives, including heroin) are subject—is the most important single factor to shape how the opiate/heroin market is organized in a particular country and the behavior of its producers and traffickers. It impacts, in particular, the size, organization, and operating methods of enterprises that produce or traffic illicit opiates.

These findings tie in well with a growing body of literature on organized crime in Western countries that shows that the great majority of illegal exchanges in Western countries are carried out by numerous, relatively small and often ephemeral enterprises. In other words, "disorganized crime" (Reuter, 1983), rather than organized crime understood in terms of large-scale stable criminal organizations, predominates on the illegal markets of Western countries, reflecting the constraints deriving from the enforcement of prohibitions. These constraints have to do with the fact that illegal market entrepreneurs are obliged to operate both without and against the state.

First, since the goods and services they provide are prohibited, illegal market actors cannot resort to state institutions to enforce contracts and have violations of contracts prosecuted. Nor does the illegal arena host an alternative sovereign power to which a party may appeal for redress of injury. As a result, property rights are poorly protected, employment contracts cannot be formalized, and the development of large, formally organized, long-lasting companies is strongly discouraged (Reuter, 1983).

Second, all illegal market actors are forced to operate under the constant threat of arrest and confiscation of their assets by law enforcement institutions. Participants in criminal trades will thus try to organize their activities in such a way as to assure that the risk of police detection is minimized. Incorporating illegal transactions into kinship and friendship networks and reducing the number of customers and employees are two of the most frequent strategies illegal entrepreneurs employ to reduce their vulnerability to law enforcement moves (Reuter, 1983; see also Bouchard & Morselli, 2014).

Due to the threat of police intervention, either in terms of seizing assets or imprisoning participants, the planning time horizons of illegal entrepreneurs are likely to be much shorter than those in legal markets. Since an illegal enterprise can hardly be sold as the entrepreneur ages, he is likely to divert an increasing share of his profits to legal assets which can be passed on to his heirs.

Finally, since they are operating against the state, illegal enterprises are prevented from marketing their products. They cannot create their own brand image and try to bind customers to it. Strong economies of scale, however, are associated with advertising and the advantages linked to the nationwide marketing of one's own products have long been recognized as a very important factor in the rise of modern large-scale corporations. Illegal enterprises, however, are by definition excluded from the possibility of exploiting these advantages because, by doing so, they would obviously attract law enforcement attention and damage their own businesses. For the same motives illegal enterprises in Western countries resort sparingly to violence; as Pearson and Hobbs (2001: 42) put it, "violence and killings attract police attention and leave traces, as well as attracting retaliation. Violence is therefore strictly 'bad for business.'"

For all the above reasons, it is unlikely that large, hierarchically organized enterprises will emerge to mediate economic transactions in the illegal marketplace of countries with effective governments. The factors promoting the development of bureaucracies in the legal portion of the economy—namely taking advantage of economies of scale of operations and specialization of roles—are outbalanced in the illegal arena by the very consequences of product illegality. Even mafia-type organizations are subjected to the constraints deriving from the illegal status of products and, when they deal in drugs or other illegal products, they do not operate as monolithic productive and commercial units. On the contrary, their members frequently set up short-term partnerships with other mafia members, or even non-members, to carry out illegal transactions. The average illegal market actors in Western countries are not interested in, or capable of, exercising a quasi-political power similar to that of mafia-type organizations. As Europol (2003: 10) recognizes: "politically, few OC groups pose a direct threat to Member States." Most organized crime groups active in the richest Western countries are simply too small and ephemeral to be able to exercise such political power.

The situation can look radically different in countries with lax or no enforcement of official prohibitions. Paoli et al.'s (2009) analysis of the world heroin market, for example, concludes that opiate enterprises can become large and stable, and assume bureaucratic characteristics, if they are closely linked via corrupt ties to, or coincide with, a powerful state or quasi-state authority. Under conditions of lax or non-enforcement, opiate enterprises may form oligopolies or even monopolies, if powerful and engaged state or quasi-state authorities back them up. The extent of violence and bribery also depends on the strength and involvement of state or quasi-state authorities. Violence may be high, if the supporting state or quasi-state authority is weak; it may be low, if the state or quasi-state authority is strongly institutionalized and directly involved in the drug trade.

This model also predicts that for countries that have become accustomed to lax or non-enforcement, a shift toward strict enforcement may imply a worsening of drug-related corruption, violence and instability in the interim. What happened in Afghanistan during the first two decades of the twenty-first century clearly demonstrates the potential for worsening conditions: powerful drug producing and trafficking organizations have used all available means to oppose state efforts to enforce prohibition more rigorously and fight for the "right" to continue their established businesses.

Illegality and enforcement seem to have similar effects on the size and operating methods of cocaine and cannabis trafficking enterprises as they have on opiate-related firms. For example, large and stable cocaine trafficking organizations having no qualms about openly challenging state sovereignty have consolidated in countries lacking consistent enforcement of prohibitions, such as Colombia and Mexico (e.g., Medel & Thoumi, 2014; Thoumi, 2014). Presidents Fox and Calderon's determined fight against Mexican drug cartels plunged the country into an unprecedented spiral of violence. Mutatis mutandis, the model of varying effective illegality seems to be applicable to the enterprises producing and dealing with synthetic drugs and other illegal goods and services.

Concluding Remarks and Policy Dilemmas

From a bird's eye view, the chapter seeks to identify the main macro-determinants of the two main forms of organized crime identified in the literature, that is, mafia-type criminal organizations and the provision of illegal goods and services. In doing so, it shows the limits but also the possibilities of government interventions. The bad news is that democratic governments committed to the rule of law and market economy have limited control over illegal market flows.

The good news is: (1) Mafia-type organizations consolidate only in contexts characterized by a persistent state weakness and can survive only if the government is unable to exercise its core functions and has poor legitimacy or its representatives are willing to come to terms with the mafia groups; (2) Governments can substantially influence the risks assessments and actual behaviors of enterprises that produce or traffic illegal opiates and, possibly, other illegal products. If they can enforce prohibitions with sufficient rigor, they can reduce the violence, corruption and instability associated with illegal markets. The advantages of the strict enforcement of prohibitions, though, must be balanced against the social and financial costs of such enforcement to avoid unnecessarily curbing civil liberties, causing unintended harm and further burdening state coffers. In the case of opiates, for example, strict enforcement reduces the harms of opiate production and trafficking within the current drug control regime. After considering the costs and unintended consequences of prohibition itself, though, one might well have to conclude that the total harms of opiate production, trafficking, consumption, *and* policies can be better reduced by alternative policy regimes.

The US war on drugs of the past three decades, for example, may have helped keep the US drug market relatively "disorganized," but has failed to reach its main goal of reducing drugs availability (Reuter & Trautman, 2009). Through its interdiction, moreover, it has helped spread the problem of drug production and trafficking to a number of Latin American countries, has created endless opportunities for corruption and violence in both the USA and abroad, and unintentionally contributed to the destabilization of several, already weak Central American and, more recently, West African countries (e.g., OAS, 2013). Of the world's eight most murderous countries, seven lie on the cocaine-trafficking route from the Andes to the USA and Europe. Honduras, for example, a small Central American country of eight million people, records each year more than 7000 murders. In the European Union, with a population of 500 million, the figure is under 6000 (The Economist, 2013).

Even in the USA itself, moreover, the US war on drugs has produced huge social and financial costs. It has played a key role in the phenomenal increase of the US prison population (Zimring, 2010). Nowadays drug convictions account for almost half of American prisoners in federal prisons and 17 % of those under state jurisdiction (Carson & Golinelli, 2013: 3). Twenty-five and 33 % of the adults on probation and parole, respectively, also had a drug charge as their most serious offense (Maruschak & Bonczar, 2013: 17 and 19).

While no country can legitimately aspire to host large-scale, powerful criminal organizations or a large number of drug addicts, preventing such developments needs to be traded off with the costs and unintended consequences of the policies adopted to reach such goals and the goals of more generic crime control and health policies. The case of gambling is particularly enticing: this activity was once considered a quintessential activity of the Italian-American mafia and other US crime groups (e.g., Reuter, 1983). However, its progressive decriminalization and regulation have subtracted sources of revenues for illegal players and opened up the market for legitimate businesses, with no major rise in gambling addiction (Spapens, 2014).

Policy interventions to control whatever form of organized crime should, in other words, be inspired by the realization of the governments' limits and potential for harm. They should also be checked—both ex ante and ex post, that is, prior to and after enactment—for their appropriateness and effectiveness. Ex post, special attention should be given to the policy's unintended consequences, as these are difficult to fully anticipate in advance. Alas, whereas legal scholars and policy analysts usually scrutinize proposed bills and other policy documents for their respect of basic human rights principles and other constitutional norms, much less research has so far been carried out on the effects, including the unintended consequences, of the policy measures adopted. Such research is often not supported by government agencies: these often seem not to be interested in knowing ex post if the policies they adopted out of faith, ideology or in reaction to an emergency, are really working or not.

The evaluation of organized crime control measures is also hampered by the imprecise knowledge we still have of the many phenomena related to the umbrella concept of organized crime. As we have no precise measure of the extent of many organized crime problems, it is impossible to say if an intervention has led to a 10 % reduction of those problems or not. The evaluation of organized crime control measures is also hindered by the umbrella concept of organized crime itself. No single researcher or even team of researchers has the capability to assess the impact of policies targeting such a broad spectrum of problems ranging from Cosa Nostra or mafia-type organizations to human trafficking, from thieves' gangs and youth gangs to money laundering, from illegal drug trafficking to cybercrime in a national or, even worse, in an international context. The policy assessment, as the study of the underlying organized crime phenomena, can only be done for a specific criminalized activity, group, or local context. In other words, organized crime might well have been a catchy umbrella concept to raise the public's and policy-makers' attentions but because of its imprecision, conflicting definitions and multiple referents, it is neither an adequate research nor a policy-making concept.

Despite these uncertainties, the overall goal of organized crime control policies should be clear: envisaging interventions that can reduce the total harms resulting from both the organized crime phenomena and the policies aiming to control these phenomena, drawing from the realization that both organized crime actors and activities *and* the related policies cause harms and that bad policies may even inadvertently create opportunities for organized crime.

References

Andreas, P. (2002). Transnational crime and economic globalization. In M. Berdal & M. Serrano (Eds.), *Transnational organized crime and international security. Business as usual?* (pp. 37–52). Boulder, CO: Lynne Rienner.

Bouchard, M., & Morselli, C. (2014). Opportunistic structures of organized crime. In L. Paoli (Ed.), *Oxford handbook of organized crime* (pp. 288–302). New York: Oxford University Press.

Carson, E. A., & Golinelli, D. (2013). *Prisoners in 2012: Trends in admissions and releases, 1991–2012*. Washington, DC: US Department of Justice Bureau of Justice Statistics.

Catanzaro, R. (1991). *Il delitto come impresa. Storia sociale della mafia*. Milan: Rizzoli.

Chin, K.-L. (2014). Chinese organized crime. In L. Paoli (Ed.), *Oxford handbook of organized crime* (pp. 219–233). New York: Oxford University Press.

Chu, Y. K. (2005). Hong Kong triads after 1997. *Trends in Organized Crime, 8*, 5–12.

Commissione Parlamentare d'inchiesta sul fenomeno della mafia e sulle altre associazioni similari. (1993). *Relazione sui rapporti tra mafia e politica con note integrative*, doc. XXIII, no. 2, XI Legislature. Rome: Camera dei Deputati.

Dikötter, F., Laarmann, L., & Zhou, X. (2004). *Narcotics culture. A history of drugs in China*. Hong Kong: University of Chicago Press.

Dorn, N. (2009). The end of organized crime in the European Union. *Crime, Law and Social Change, 51*, 283–295.

Edwards, A., & Levi, M. (2008). Researching the organization of serious crimes. *Criminology and Criminal Justice, 8*, 363–388.

Egmond, F. (2004). Multiple Underworlds in the Dutch republic of the seventeenth and eighteenth centuries. In C. Fijnaut & L. Paoli (Eds.), *Organised crime in Europe: Concepts, patterns and policies in the European Union and beyond* (pp. 77–107). Dordrecht: Springer.

Europol. (2003). *European Union organised crime report*. Luxembourg: Office for the Official Publications of the European Communities.

Europol. (2013). *SOCTA 2013: EU serious and organised crime threat assessment*. 's-Gravenzande: Deventer.

Friesendorf, C. (2007). *US foreign policy and the war on drugs: Displacing the cocaine and heroin industry*. London: Routledge.

Gambetta, D. (1993). *The Sicilian mafia: The business of private protection*. Cambridge: Harvard University Press.

Hess, H. (1973). *Mafia and mafiosi: The structure of power*. Farnborough: Saxon House.

Hill, P. (2003). *The Japanese mafia: Yakuza, law and the state*. Oxford: Oxford University Press.

Hill, P. (2014). The Japanese Yakuza. In L. Paoli (Ed.), *Oxford handbook of organized crime* (pp. 234–253). New York: Oxford University Press.

Hobbs, D. (1988). *Doing the business: Entrepreneurship, the working class and detectives in the East of London*. Oxford: Oxford University Press.

Hobbs, D. (1995). *Bad business: Professional crime in modern Britain*. Oxford: Oxford University Press.

Hobbs, D. (2013). *Lush Life. Constructing organized crime in the UK*. Oxford: Oxford University Press.

Hobbs, D., & Antonopoulos, G. A. (2014). How to research organized crime. In L. Paoli (Ed.), *The Oxford handbook of organized crime* (pp. 96–111). New York: Oxford University Press.

Levi, M. (2002). The organization of serious crimes. In M. Maguire, R. Morgan, & R. Reiner (Eds.), *The Oxford handbook of criminology* (3rd ed., pp. 878–913). Oxford: Oxford University Press.

Maruschak, L. M., & Bonczar, T. P. (2013). *Probation and parole in the United States, 2012*. Washington, DC: US Department of Justice Bureau of Justice Statistics.

Medel, M., & Thoumi, F. E. (2014). Mexican drug "cartels". In L. Paoli (Ed.), *The Oxford handbook of organized crime* (pp. 196–218). New York: Oxford University Press.
Murray, D. (1994). *The origins of the Tiandihui. The Chinese Triads in legend and history*. Stanford, CA: Stanford University Press.
OAS (Organization of American States). (2013). *The drug problem in the Americas*. Washington, DC: OAS.
Ownby, D. (1993). Chinese hui and early modern social order: evidence form eighteenth century southeast China. In D. Ownby & M. Somers Heidhues (Eds.), *Secret Societies reconsidered: Perspectives on the social history of modern South China and Southeast Asia* (pp. 34–67). Armonk, NY: East Gate Book.
Paoli, L. (2002a). The Development of an illegal market: Drug consumption and trade in post-Soviet Russia. *British Journal of Criminology, 42*(1), 21–39.
Paoli, L. (2002b). The paradoxes of organized crime. *Crime, Law and Social Change, 37*(1), 51–97.
Paoli, L. (2003). *Mafia brotherhoods: Organized crime, Italian style*. New York: Oxford University Press.
Paoli, L. (2013). Searching for the determinants of organized crime. *Behemoth, 6*(1), 10–26.
Paoli, L. (2014a). Introduction. In L. Paoli (Ed.), *The Oxford handbook of organized crime* (pp. 1–11). New York: Oxford University Press.
Paoli, L. (Ed.). (2014b). *The Oxford handbook of organized crime*. New York: Oxford University Press.
Paoli, L., Adriaenssen, A., Greenfield, V. A., & Conickx, M. (2015). *Shouldn't we be serious about serious crime?* working paper.
Paoli, L., & Fijnaut, C. (2004). General introduction. In C. Fijnaut & L. Paoli (Eds.), *Organised crime in Europe: Concepts, patterns and policies in the European Union and beyond* (pp. 1–19). Dordrecht: Springer.
Paoli, L., Greenfield, V. A., & Reuter, P. (2009). *The world heroin market: Can supply be cut?* New York: Oxford University Press.
Paoli, L., Greenfield, V. A., & Zoutendijk, A. (2013). The harm of cocaine trafficking. Applying a new framework for assessment. *Journal of Drug Issues, 43*(4), 407–436.
Paoli, L., & Vander Beken, T. (2014). Organized crime: A contested concept. In L. Paoli (Ed.), *The Oxford handbook of organized crime* (pp. 13–31). New York: Oxford University Press.
Pearson, G., & Hobbs, D. (2001). *Middle market drug distribution*. London: Home Office Research, Development and Statistics Directorate.
Portes, A., Castells, M., & Benton, L. A. (1991). Conclusions: The policy implications of informality. In A. Portes, M. Castells, & L. A. Benton (Eds.), *The informal economy: Studies in advanced and less developed countries* (pp. 298–311). Baltimore, MD: John Hopkins University Press.
Reuter, P. (1983). *Disorganized crime: The economics of the visible hand*. Cambridge, MA: MIT Press.
Reuter, P., & Trautman, F. (Eds.). (2009). *A report on global illicit drugs markets 1998–2007*. Luxembourg: European Communities.
Rush, J. (1985). Opium in Java: A sinister friend. *Journal of Asian Studies, 44*(3), 549–560.
Schelling, T. (1971). What is the business of organized crime? *American Scholar, 40*(Autumn), 643–652.
Spapens, T. (2014). Illegal gambling. In L. Paoli (Ed.), *The Oxford handbook of organized crime* (pp. 402–418). New York: Oxford University Press.
The Economist. (2013, February 23). Towards a ceasefire: Experiments in legalisation are showing what a post-war approach to drug control could look like. *The Economist*.
Thoumi, F. E. (2014). Organized crime in Colombia: The actors running the illegal drug industry. In L. Paoli (Ed.), *The Oxford handbook of organized crime* (pp. 177–195). New York: Oxford University Press.
Tilly, C. (1988). Foreword to *The Mafia of a Sicilian village, 1860–1960: A study of violent peasant entrepreneurs,* by A. Blok. (pp. i–xxi). New York: Polity.

UNODC. (2000). *United Nations Convention Against Transnational Organized Crime*. Vienna: UNODC.

UNODC. (2007). *Cocaine trafficking in Western Africa: Situation report*. Vienna: UNODC.

UNODC. (2010). *South-East Asia opium survey 2010*. Vienna: UNODC.

UNODC. (2015). *2015 World drug report*. New York: UNODC.

Van Duyne, P. (1997). Organized crime, corruption, and power. *Crime, Law, and Social Change, 26*, 201–238.

Volkov, V. (2014). Russian mafia: Rise and extinction. In L. Paoli (Ed.), *The Oxford handbook of organized crime* (pp. 159–176). New York: Oxford University Press.

Wikström, P. O., Oberwittler, D., Treiber, K., & Hardie, B. (2012). *Breaking rules: The social and situational dynamics of young people's urban crime*. Oxford: Oxford University Press.

Zhou, Y. (2000). Nationalism, identity and state building: The anti-drug crusade in the People's Republic, 1949–1952. In T. Brook & B. Tadashi Wakabayashi (Eds.), *Opium regimes: China, Britain and Japan, 1839–1952* (pp. 380–404). Berkeley, CA: University of California Press.

Zimring, F. E. (2010). The scale of imprisonment in the United States: Twentieth century patterns and twenty-first century prospects. *The Journal of Criminal Law and Criminology, 100*(3), 1225–1246.

Chapter 2
The Ties That Bind: A Taxonomy of Associational Criminal Structures

Klaus von Lampe

Introduction

In his book "Lush Life" Dick Hobbs argues that "(s)erious crime should be understood in terms of interlocking networks which are (…) expressed as amalgams of family, neighbourhood, region, nationality, and which merge with purely instrumental commercial coalitions" (Hobbs, 2013: 103). Two recurring themes in the study of organised crime are encapsulated in this quote. The first theme is the social embeddedness of criminal structures (Kleemans & van de Bunt, 1999). Criminals do not act and interact in a social vacuum (Van Duyne, 1996: 344), "(t)hey are outside the law but inside society" (Hobbs, 1995: 13). The second theme is the interplay of functionally distinct structures that define the organisation of crimes and criminals. The distinction that Dick Hobbs makes is that between "commercial" networks centred on profit-making criminal activities and networks that are inherently social in nature but nonetheless shape and facilitate profit-making criminal activities. In particular, he stresses the importance of family and neighbourhood—"familial and highly localized allegiances"—for providing an organisational context for criminal "firms" as "the primary unit of organization of serious criminality" (Hobbs, 1995: 114).

There is a broad range of scholarly work that in one way or other contextualises profit-oriented co-offending structures with a view to their overlap with non-economic, social ties. Ianni and Reuss-Ianni (1972), for example, examined how an Italian-American family clan in New York, the "Lupollo family", gave coherence and meaning to various licit and illicit business activities. In a subsequent study of criminal structures among African Americans and Puerto Rican and Cuban immigrants in

K. von Lampe (✉)
Department of Law, Police Science and Criminal Justice Administration,
John Jay College of Criminal Justice, New York, NY, USA
e-mail: kvlampe@jjay.cuny.edu

G.A. Antonopoulos (ed.), *Illegal Entrepreneurship, Organized Crime and Social Control*, Studies of Organized Crime 14,
DOI 10.1007/978-3-319-31608-6_2

the New York area, Francis Ianni found "two forms of behavioural organisation" in crime networks which he labelled "associational networks" (Ianni, 1975: 293) and "entrepreneurial networks" (Ianni, 1975: 307). Associational networks are constituted by close personal ties formed in childhood gangs or in prison. The purpose of associational networks is not the commission of profit-making crime. Instead they play a role in fostering mutual trust among criminals, promoting a basic criminal code of conduct and in shaping criminal reputations (Ianni, 1975: 293–298). In the case of entrepreneurial networks, in contrast, individuals come together "largely for mutual profit, and their dependence upon each other is related entirely to advancing that profit" (Ianni, 1975: 307). A similar distinction of economic and social structures was made by Patricia Adler (1985) in her analysis of drug importers and wholesalers in Southern California. In her ethnographic research she found business structures—partnerships, groups and supplier-customer relations—embedded in "friendship networks, social affiliations with other drug world members that had business overtones" and "a larger circle of acquaintances which was composed of dealers and smugglers the individual knew socially, yet with whom he or she had no business dealings" (Adler, 1985: 63). Like Hobbs and Ianni, Adler saw illegal entrepreneurial structures emerge from underlying social relationships, namely friendship networks within the drug world but also kinship ties (Adler, 1985: 66–67).

From a different angle, Mark H. Haller looked at the roles performed by the Italian-American Cosa Nostra and also arrived at a differentiation of entrepreneurial and associational structures. Studying the Philadelphia family under the leadership of Angelo Bruno, Haller concluded that Mafia families do not have the character of business enterprises because "members (and their associates) are involved in independent legal and illegal activities that are their own and from which they derive income" (Haller, 1992: 2). The functions that the Bruno family served, Haller argued, were of a different nature, including that of a fraternal organisation which provides "male bonding and social prestige for members", that of a businessmen's association which provides "members with contacts and mutual assistance" and that of an association which sets and enforces rules among members similar to the self-governance of lawyers through the Bar Association (Haller, 1992: 2–3; see also Paoli, 1998).

Entrepreneurial and associational structures have been found to overlap and merge to different degrees. Dick Hobbs emphasises both entrepreneurial and associational characteristics in his depiction of the traditional criminal firms "based upon family ties and neighourhood dispositions" (Hobbs, 2013: 105). Crimes may be committed "on behalf of the family enterprise" or members may "engage in a range of individual projects" where the firm serves as a "brand, a rhetorical device that encapsulates the entrepreneurial activities of family members and their close associates" (Hobbs, 2001: 552).

In other research, the empirical relation between associational and entrepreneurial structures ranges from full separation to full integration. Ianni, for example, saw associational networks and entrepreneurial networks "as characteristic stages of development in black and Hispanic organised crime networks" (Ianni, 1975: 311) with entrepreneurial networks representing "the highest stage of organised crime network development" (Ianni, 1975: 312), implying that associational and entrepreneurial structures not only are separate entities, they may not even have a parallel existence (see also Densley, 2012). In the case of Mafia families, associational and entrepreneurial structures are largely depicted as analytically and empirically distinct but intrinsically linked phenomena (see for example Anderson, 1979; Gambetta, 1993; Haller, 1992; Paoli, 1998; Reuter, 1983; Schelling, 1971). In the case of the Southern Italian mafia associations the greatest level of integration of associational and entrepreneurial structures appears to be reached when "illicit activities are sometimes run by the heads of the single families and the profits divided more or less equally between the affiliates" (Paoli, 2003: 144). An even further overlap of associational and entrepreneurial structures seems to exist where illegal enterprises form the centre of social interaction of participants. Anqi Shen, for example, in her study of female involvement in crime in modern China characterises illegal gambling operations in the context of so-called "black-society style criminal organisations" (BSSCO) as "a semi-working environment somewhere between a social club and a business setting" (Shen, 2015: 44) that provides "a sense of belonging, self-worth, status, and perhaps also an imaginary welfare support and protection" (Shen, 2015: 45).

There is a growing recognition that "looking beyond offender's immediate co-offenders [is] key to understanding success in making money out of crime or in avoiding detection" (Bouchard & Ouellet, 2011: 85) and that there is a "need to include different types of criminal (co-offending and institutional associates) and kinship associations when analyzing deviant networks" (Malm, Bichler, & Van De Walle, 2010: 53). However, there is no clear notion, let alone a consensus on how to delineate and conceptualise this sphere that surrounds co-offending structures. Concepts such as those of network core and periphery (Malm et al., 2010), of strong and weak ties (Morselli, Tremblay, & McCarthy, 2006), or of manifest and latent ties (von Lampe, 2003) capture the fact that there are gradations in cohesiveness and frequency of interaction between criminals, yet as such these concepts contribute relatively little to a better understanding of the nature of the ties that bind criminals outside of co-offending structures. A more fruitful approach in this respect appears to be the consideration of different functions that the ties connecting criminals may serve. Ianni's distinction between entrepreneurial and associational networks is one such differentiation, the distinction between illegal enterprise and illegal governance another (Varese, 2010). But arguably this is as far as current conceptualisations go. In particular, there does not seem to be a coherent conceptual framework with which to order the terrain populated by such phenomena as Hobbs' family firms, Adler's friendship networks or Haller's fraternal organisations. The purpose of this chapter in honour of Dick Hobbs is to propose a tentative classification that may mark a first step in this direction.

Criminal Structures and Associational Criminal Structures

The starting point of the following discussion is a conceptualisation of criminal structures that is broader than the notion of co-offending networks and seeks to encompass all the myriad ways in which criminals interact and are connected with other criminals. A criminal structure according to this view can be defined as "an arrangement of relationships between criminals that have an impact—directly or indirectly—on the commission of crime" (von Lampe, 2016: 93). The definition applies to three functionally distinct types of criminal structures alluded to above (see also von Lampe, 2003: 16; 2016: 101–104). There are first of all entrepreneurial criminal structures. As indicated, these are configurations that serve economic functions in the sense that they are geared toward generating material benefits through criminal activities. Then there are associational criminal structures, the focal point of this paper. Associational criminal structures serve social functions. Their contribution to profit-making crime is only indirect, for example by facilitating the collaboration of criminals through the creation of a common basis of trust. The third functional type of criminal structures are those that perform quasi-governmental functions by controlling and regulating the behaviour of criminals, for example by providing mechanisms for the non-violent resolution of conflicts between illegal entrepreneurs in a particular territory or market (Reuter, 1983).

Even though these three types are not necessarily empirically distinct, it is important to distinguish them analytically in order to avoid comparing apples and oranges. What sets associational criminal structures apart from entrepreneurial and quasi-governmental structures is their inward orientation. Entrepreneurial and quasi-governmental structures are defined by collaborative ties that are oriented towards interaction with the outside world, be it customers of illegal goods and services, victims of predatory crimes or subordinates to illegal governance. Associational criminal structures, in contrast, are defined first and foremost by the social bonds that connect their members and by the demarcation of members from non-members. Associational criminal structures are also the more permanent and more static element in crime networks as opposed to the more dynamic and more flexible networks that characterise illegal businesses and illegal markets. It is one of the main contentions made here that there are highly diverse relational patterns among criminals that fit this mould, including mafia families, biker gangs, peer groups, friendship networks and possibly entire criminal subcultures.

Common Features of Associational Criminal Structures

The concept of associational criminal structures as used here is a further elaboration of Francis Ianni's concept of associational networks which stresses the non-economic nature of some of the ties that connect criminals. The term "associational" refers to the quality and function of social ties; it does not necessarily imply the existence of an association in the sense of a delineable organisational entity. The concept of associational criminal structures is also more encompassing than the word "criminal" suggests. The focus is not narrowly on configurations that are criminal per se, formed by criminals for criminal purposes. The concept of associational criminal structures also includes configurations that are rooted in legitimate society, for example outlaw biker gangs that are officially registered clubs. They do not conflict with the law by their mere existence, their collective actions may also be within the bounds of the law and they may have among their ranks law-abiding citizens. Yet at the same time they function as associations of criminals with respect to the members that are breaking the law (Barker, 2007).

As discussed elsewhere (von Lampe, 2016: 172–182), associational criminal structures provide benefits for criminals in essentially four different ways. They create and reinforce social bonds, they facilitate communication, they promote mutual support, and they establish and enforce a code of conduct among their members and thereby increasing predictability and security in an environment that is chaotic and full of risks.

Bonding

Associational criminal structures as understood here are patterns of relationships that connect offenders through social bonds that are affectionate rather than instrumental in nature. They instil a sense of belonging based on perceived commonalities of their members, respectively perceived differences between members and non-members. Outlaw motorcycle gangs, for example, construct their identity around a shared defiance of mainstream society, and an adherence to particular notions of masculinity and brotherhood and a hedonistic lifestyle centred on motorcycling (Barker, 2007; Quinn & Koch, 2003).

The bonds that define associational criminal structures can be an original product of the formation of or recruitment into an associational criminal structure. However, it is arguably more common to see pre-existing social relationships, namely family, friendship and community ties, constituting the building blocks of associational criminal structures. In that case, social bonds are transformed and reinforced rather than established in the first place. For example, in the case of the Sicilian Mafia, the Italian-American Cosa Nostra and especially the Calabrian 'Ndrangheta there is a strong overlap between associational structures and blood families (Paoli, 2003: 30–31). At the same time, the obligations that come with membership in a mafia association go beyond the obligations linked to familial ties and, in fact, they may conflict with the allegiance of a member to his blood family to the extent that the killing of a relative, when deemed necessary by the mafia association, has to be accepted "without showing any resentment or sorrow" (Paoli, 2003: 79).

Belonging to an associational criminal structure means sharing a common bond, perhaps based on shared characteristics, experiences, interests or values. At the same time, belonging to an associational criminal structure implies a distinction between insiders and outsiders, members and non-members, suggesting that members possess certain qualities which non-members are lacking. Membership in an associational criminal structure, therefore, conveys some sense of exclusivity even where there is no formalised membership. For example, in the case of friendship networks among drug traffickers (Adler, 1985) or in the case of charismatic underworld figures that are surrounded by a clientele of less influential criminals (Albini,

1971) one can expect to find some shared notion of where the line is drawn between insiders and outsiders. Take Dick Hobbs' account of the "City Arms" pub where status differences between "full-time villains" and strata of less well-respected criminals were reflected in the spaces that each group occupied in the bar room (Hobbs, 1989: 142–143). However, the notion of exclusivity is arguably most salient where membership is clearly defined. This is true for Italian mafia-type associations and the Italian-American Cosa Nostra as well as for other fraternal associations with formalised membership such as the post-Soviet Thieves in Law (*vory-v-zakone*) or the Hell's Angels outlaw motorcycle gang, all of which are highly selective by their own standards in the recruitment and admission of new members and portray themselves as elites in their respective spheres. Prospective members have to undergo a lengthy process of screening, testing and schooling, and those accepted will tend to consider membership an important personal achievement, typically resulting in an enhanced social status within their subcultural milieu or even within larger parts of society (Barker, 2007: 73; Haller, 1992: 2; Lombardo, 1994: 300; Paoli, 2003: 152; Varese, 2001: 175).

The sense of belonging is further amplified where formal membership is attained through initiation rituals and where the association itself and membership in the association are shrouded in secrecy, characteristics that are shared by secret societies such as the Italian mafia-type associations or the Chinese triads (Paoli, 2003; Chu, 2000). The rite of initiation and the shared secret of the inner workings of the association demarcate a world separate from and in many respects in opposition to legitimate society (Paoli, 2003: 18; Simmel, 1950: 359). At the same time, relationships within this world are typically modelled after those found in the legitimate spheres of society, namely kinship. Criminal associations commonly frame internal structures in quasi-familial terms as those between brothers, between father and son or between uncle and nephew (Chu, 2000: 19; Hill, 2003: 67–68) and assume that the ritual kinship ties formed by the initiation into the association create a level of commitment and trust similar to that of natural family bonds (Paoli, 2003: 76).

Irrespective of ideas of "brotherhood" and "family" that could be discounted as pure ideology, there are various ways in which associational criminal structures can promote mutual trust. To the extent that membership is homogeneous, solidarity and trust may emerge from a sense of likeness (Paoli, 2003: 52). Continuous interaction among members is also likely to generate trust, namely, through the formation of affectionate bonds and a growing sense of predictability of the others' behaviour where this is not already the foundation from which associational criminal structures are built. Members of mafia-type organisations, for example, typically spend considerable time socialising with other members, although this may be confined to smaller groups ("crews") within larger mafia families (see Pistone, 1989; Ulrich, 2005), whereas outlaw motorcycle gangs such as the Hell's Angels hold regular weekly meetings and organise a host of other social events at the level of chapters, the basic organisational unit, and even at national and international levels (Barker, 2007). To the extent associational criminal structures select members according to their assumed worth as criminals, trust can emanate from the expectation that these individuals have proven their reliability and trustworthiness. Importantly, this expectation may not only be shared by members but also by outsiders. In these instances, trust is based on the assumption that members of a particular associational criminal structure can generally be trusted (Skarbek, 2014: 77; von Lampe & Johansen, 2004: 170).

Communication

Associational criminal structures can be viewed as forums for the relatively secure exchange of criminally relevant information. Communication among members is secure to the extent that individual members can have confidence in the reticence of the other members. This is a matter of mutual trust as well as of the adherence to and enforcement of a code of conduct, discussed further below, that emphasises secrecy. The facilitation of communication within associational criminal structures has implications in at least two important respects, the commission of crimes and the promotion and reinforcement of a criminal ideology (see Quinn & Koch, 2003: 287–288).

Associational criminal structures provide privileged communication channels for the sharing of information that is relevant for successfully carrying out illegal activities, for example information about potential co-offenders, crime opportunities, and know-how. The communication within associational criminal structures will also strengthen, directly or indirectly, a positive self-image as criminal and will promote norms and values that justify or even glorify criminal conduct and a criminal life-style and ultimately "make crime easier (less inhibited) and more attractive" (Thrasher, 1963: 265).

Mutual Support

The bonds that tie individuals together in an associational criminal structure almost by nature establish a commitment to mutual support. There is an unspoken or explicit obligation to come to the aid of other members when needed. Letizia Paoli, drawing on Weber and Sahlins, has argued that in the case of mafia-type associations the initiation marks a "status contract" and a "contract of fraternization" that subject members to a "regime of generalized reciprocity", which means that members have to lend support to other member "with no expectation of short-term rewards" (Paoli, 2003: 17).

Mutual support can come in various ways and can translate into different kinds of benefits for members. However, it is important to note that conceptually and empirically, belonging to an associational criminal structure does not translate into an obligation to participate in or otherwise support specific criminal endeavours of other members. Associational criminal structures are confined to the role of "nurturing and generating deviant collaborations" (Hobbs, 2001: 550) while members are generally free in their decision to choose co-offenders. Even in the case of mafia-type associations, members “are in no way obliged to select their partners from within the mafia community” (Paoli, 2003: 5; see also Chu, 2000: 87).

An important aspect, potentially even the main *raison d'être* for some associational criminal structures is protection against threats from other criminals. When criminals associate and band together in “mutual protection associations” (Quinn, 2001: 384) they can find strength in numbers in a chaotic and hostile environment where no recourse to the police and the courts is available to protect property rights and personal safety. In this respect, belonging to a recognisable collective of criminals creates a “protective cloak of association” (Hobbs, 2013: 160).

Associational criminal structures may also provide protection against law enforcement, for example through the sharing of corrupt ties to law enforcement officials, through help with the intimidation of witnesses, support for fugitive and incarcerated members and their families, and by way of financial aid to cover legal costs. Support may be lent directly by one individual member to another or in an organised way where the associational criminal structure provides a framework for the pooling of resources. However, not all associational structures and not even all formal criminal associations actually do provide such services. For example, a study in the USA found that “there is little evidence that spouses and families of organized crime members or associates are taken care of in any systematic way, if husbands are imprisoned” (Edelhertz & Overcast, 1993: 135). On the other hand, collective mutual support does not hinge on formal organisation. Informal networks, such as friendship groups or entire underworld milieus, may serve a similar function by raising funds on an ad hoc basis (Fordham, 1972: 115; Kerner, 1973: 214).

In some cases, material support for individual members is institutionalised in a communal fund to which members and sometimes also non-members make contributions in the form of entry fees, membership dues or payments on special occasions (Anderson, 1979: 35; Paoli, 2003: 48, 86). This is perhaps best exemplified by the Thieves in Law, a criminal association that came into existence in the Soviet Gulag system and that is organised around a communal fund (*obshchak*) (Serio, 2008: 160; Volkov, 2002: 58). The *obshchak* is set up inside a particular correctional facility, in a particular territory or by a particular group of Thieves. Reportedly, there now also exists a national *obshchak* with a volume of several hundred million US dollars (Shalikashvili, 2009: 34; Skoblikow, 2006: 51; Sobolev, Rushchenko, & Volobuev, 2002: 84). The use of funds is authorised by membership meetings for the benefit of individual members, for example to cover medical, legal and funeral expenses or to bribe law enforcement and prison officials (Skoblikow, 2006: 51; Sobolev et al., 2002: 86; Volkov, 2002: 58).

Code of Conduct

One basis upon which associational criminal structures are commonly built is a code of conduct, a set of shared behavioural norms. It is hard to imagine that there could be the kind of bonding and mutual support characteristic of associational criminal structures without such normative consensus. The question is more how unique and how encompassing the norms and values are that are shared by the members. In the case of mafia-type associations they may "constitute a separate legal order" (Paoli, 2003: 120). Some of the rules may be specific to a particular associational structure, some may be adopted from a larger subcultural context, and some may represent a universal code of conduct that simply reflects the imperatives of associating under conditions of illegality. There are striking similarities between the traditional codes of conduct of such geographically and culturally disparate associations such as the Sicilian Mafia, Chinese triads, Japanese yakuza groups and also underground movements like the French Resistance during World War II (Chu, 2000: 3; Cressey, 1969: 171; Hill, 2003: 73). As Donald Cressey has pointed out, these organisations survive under illegality by essentially abiding by the same set of rules that include "(1) extreme loyalty to the organization and its governing elite, (2) honesty in relationships with members, (3) secrecy regarding the organization's structure and activities, and (4) honorable behavior which sets members off as morally superior to those outsiders who would govern them" (Cressey, 1969: 171). These rules protect, first of all, the existence of an associational structure, and where an internal hierarchy exists, they protect in particular the interests of the leadership. Directly or indirectly, however, the rules also benefit the individual members, namely by making the behaviour of those they interact with and rely on more predictable and thereby reducing the complexity of the reality they face (Haller, 1992).

Rules Primarily in the Interest of the Association as Such

The norms and values that govern associational criminal structures can be roughly grouped with respect to their functions with some mainly pertaining to and benefiting the associational criminal structure as such and some primarily benefiting individual members. The main function of some rules, it seems, is to define an associational criminal structure as a separate entity with distinct qualities. For example, some criminal associations have established rules that forbid members to make their livelihood from anything other than crime (Hartmann & von Lampe, 2008: 112; Paoli, 2003: 125; Serio, 2008: 152). Similarly, there are commonly rules in place that mandate members not to seek assistance from or to collaborate with the government in any form, especially not in matters of security and justice. In the Sicilian Mafia, for example, according to one turncoat, "it is a fundamental rule for every man of honor never to report a theft or crime to the police" (cit. in Gambetta, 1993: 119; see also Paoli, 2003: 109). These rules set an associational criminal structure apart from legitimate society but also lift its members above the ranks of less determined criminals.

Other rules stipulate how members should behave in order to be honourable, and by implication, what is required of members in order to uphold and strengthen the reputation of the associational structure (Decker, Bynum, & Weisel, 1998: 408; Gambetta, 1993: 120). Some elements of the code of conduct are derived from the broader social context. In the case of Italian mafia-type associations, for example, behavioural rules are variations of conservative norms and values centred on masculine honour and sexuality and on family morality (Travaglino, Abrams, Randsley de Moura, & Russo, 2014). Mafiosi are supposed "to lead an irreproachable family life" (Gambetta, 1993: 120; see also Paoli, 2003: 74). Mafiosi are also expected to "live an outwardly modest life" (Cressey, 1969: 216) and to "conceal their own importance, and to minimize any signs of their power" (Paoli, 2003: 111). The context specificity of some of these rules becomes apparent when one looks at other associations of criminals that have rather different ideas about proper behaviour, namely outlaw motorcycle gangs. Their codes of conduct, for the most part, emphasise such things as promiscuity and aggressive machoism and stress the importance of riding a motorcycle regularly (Barker, 2007; Quinn & Koch, 2003).

A third type of rules seems to aim primarily at sustaining associational criminal structures. Some of these rules apply mostly to formal criminal associations and pertain to the participation of members in group activities and to the continuous support of the association, namely by paying membership dues. Members of outlaw motorcycle gangs, for example, commonly are obliged to attend regular meetings and to participate in other club-related events (Barker, 2007). Rules on how to behave on these occasions supplement the more basic rules, such as the Hell's Angels rule "No using dope during a meeting" (Barger, 2001: 46).

Obligations of secrecy can also be understood as rules that protect the continued existence of associational criminal structures. Not disclosing privileged information reduces the threat of outside interference from law enforcement and from other criminals (Reuter, 1983). However, there are important variations in the scope of what is considered privileged information that is subject to the code of secrecy. In one extreme, associational criminal structures are organised as secret societies and their very existence is meant to be kept a secret (Gambetta, 1993: 121; Paoli, 2003: 108). In the other extreme, the existence of associational criminal structures is propagated and members openly display symbols such as tattoos, pins or patches that make their membership status visible to outsiders (Barker, 2007; Hartmann & von Lampe, 2008).

The code of silence overlaps with rules against cooperation with the authorities and not to inform on other criminals. Sometimes the impression is given, especially in journalistic accounts, that this is something specific to mafia-type associations and their code of omertà. Omertà is a concept that originates in Sicilian culture and is linked to "the idea of a true man" who is supposed to protect his honour, his property and his family through his own efforts (Hess, 1996: 109). In contrast, silence and non-cooperation with the government are principles that are traditionally recognised in criminal circles, including inside prisons, and more generally in marginalised segments of society (Albini, 1971: 267–269; Cressey, 1969: 176; Ianni, 1975: 306–307; Sutherland, 1937: 10; Taylor, 1984: 149; Thrasher, 1963: 142).

Rules of secrecy may be flanked by rules against behaviour that increases the risk of a member disclosing sensitive information. In the Sicilian Mafia, for example, members are obliged to exercise "stringent self-control and self-discipline" and they must refrain "from getting drunk or using drugs" (Paoli, 2003: 111). Likewise, information concerning the mafia group must not be put in writing (Paoli, 2003: 112). In a similar vein, some associational criminal structures prohibit involvement in certain types of crimes, partly because they are deemed dishonourable and partly out of concern that they may attract increased law enforcement attention (Haller, 1992: 4). In the case of mafia-type associations, for example, more or less strictly enforced prohibitions have existed against direct involvement in drug trafficking and kidnapping for ransom (Anderson, 1979: 37; Haller, 1991: 6; Paoli, 2003: 125), and against violence directed at law enforcement officials and ordinary citizens (Lombardo, 2013: 164).

The code of silence can be viewed as a specific expression of a more general principle of unequivocal loyalty towards the associational structures and its individual members. Another manifestation of this principle is absolute obedience to the leadership in the case of hierarchically structured criminal associations (Cressey, 1969: 168; Hill, 2003: 72). Indeed, former Mafia boss Joseph Bonanno in his autobiography mentioned "obedience to one's superiors" first in a list of duties of a mafioso (Bonanno, 1983: 77).

Rules Primarily in the Interest of Individual Members

While some norms primarily benefit and protect associational criminal structures as such, other norms appear to protect first and foremost the interests of individual members. Two basic rules need to be mentioned in this respect, the obligation to provide mutual support and the corresponding obligation not to harm other members. This latter principle is translated into a number of different rules that apply to most if not all associational criminal structures. One important rule prescribes honesty in dealings with other members. "The rule of truth", Gambetta explains with regard to the Sicilian Mafia, "is said to be even more important than the notorious rule of silence" (Gambetta, 1993: 122). In addition, there are more specific rules that address typical conflict scenarios and are designed to avoid or resolve disputes among members. A member is usually not allowed to physically assault another member (Abadinsky, 2013: 59; Hill, 2003: 72; Decker et al., 1998: 407), or in the case of the Hell's Angels, only according to rules that limit the risk of serious injury: "Any fights between members will be STRICTLY one onto one, no rings are to be worn, no weapons to be used, no kicking when a guy is down" (cit. in Detrois, 2012: 234). Personal property of other members must also be respected (Decker et al., 1998: 407), as well as, in the case of male dominated or all-male associational structures, the wives or girlfriends of another member (Barker, 2007: 48; Chu, 2000: 3; Hill, 2003: 73; Skarbek, 2014: 118). In addition, an obligation commonly exists to respect the business interests of members and not to enter into direct competition with one another (Anderson, 1979: 71; Edelhertz & Overcast, 1993: 113; Haller, 1991: 6–7; Sutherland, 1937: 12).

Enforcement of Internal Rules

Complementary to the existence of rules are mechanisms for the enforcement of rules. In their most developed forms, associational criminal structures like the Sicilian Mafia and Italian-American Cosa Nostra or the Thieves in Law have a quasi-judicial system in place which, notably, not only maintains internal discipline but also serves a governance function that extends to non-members (Reuter, 1983; Volkov, 2002). Responsibilities and procedures for responding to violations of internal rules are formalised to some degree (Cressey, 1969: 207–211) with senior members charged with settling disputes among members and meting out punishment for transgressions against the code of conduct (Haller, 1992). However, internal discipline can also be enforced in non-hierarchical criminal associations such as the Thieves in Law were internal governance is exercised by the membership collectively in meetings that have absolute authority over individual members (Serio, 2008: 155; Sobolev et al., 2002: 91–92). In less developed associational criminal structures such as friendship networks, responses to rule violations are more informal, involving members on an ad hoc basis, and may not go beyond a "reaction of disapproval" (Weber, 1968: 34).

Depending on whether the violated norms primarily protect the associational criminal structure as such or the interests of the individual members, the system of rule enforcement can take on the form of criminal justice or civil justice or a combination of the two. Criminal justice responses come in the form of punishment that is meted out for wrongdoing against common interests, whereas civil justice applies to the resolution of conflicts between members as parties of equal status. Typical forms of punishment that associational criminal structures use include fines, temporary suspension of membership, expulsion, humiliation, corporal punishment, and death (Barker, 2007: 92–93; Chu, 2000: 34; Paoli, 2003: 128–129). Typical civil justice measures are orders to desist from inappropriate behaviour, to financially compensate the wronged member, or to show gestures of reconciliation (Cressey, 1969: 210; Maas, 1997: 172–173).

A Typology of Associational Criminal Structures

In the preceding section it has been argued that associational criminal structures constitute a distinct pattern of relationships among criminals defined by a set of core functions that are essentially social in nature. In this section a typology is proposed with which the various manifestations of associational criminal structures can be grouped into more homogeneous subcategories as a basis for further theorising and research. The proposed typology rests on two criteria, formalisation and legality. Formalisation refers to the degree to which the behaviour and the relations within an organisation are explicitly specified independently of the individual characteristics of those occupying positions in the organisational structure (Scott, 1981: 15).

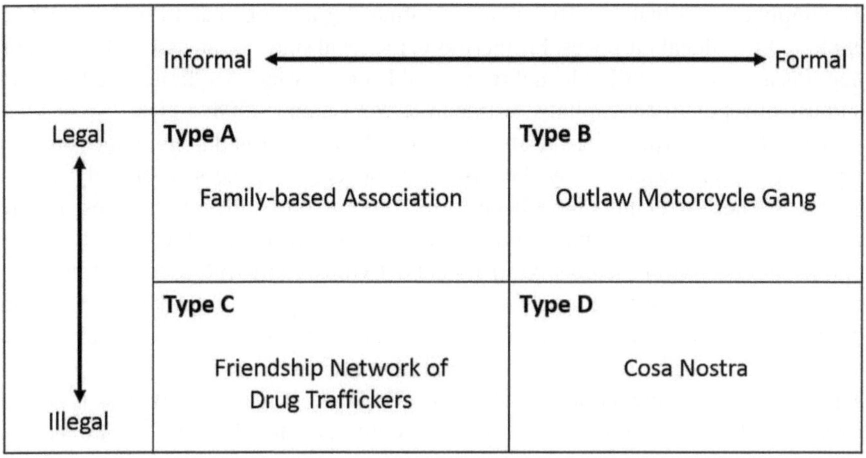

Fig. 2.1 A typology of associational criminal structures

Legality, for the purpose of the present discussion, pertains to the degree to which structures originate in and constitute legal entities. The combination of both dimensions leads to the differentiation of four types of associational criminal structures (Fig. 2.1).

The first two types of associational criminal structures are represented by relational patterns that are rooted in legitimate society and may have retained some degree of legality, even to the point that they have a dual nature as criminal and as non-criminal structures. Some of these structures resemble formal organisations and some are informal collectives.

Associational criminal structures that have some footing in legitimate society and at the same time show no formalisation (Type A) are arguably best exemplified by natural families that provide cohesion and status to members who engage in criminal activities. This seems to apply at least to some of the "family firms" described by Hobbs (1989, 2001, 2013) as well as to, for example, Arabic-speaking family clans that are powerful players in the German underworld (Henninger, 2002; Kamstra, 2014). These "family-based associations" (Hobbs, 2013: 97), to the extent they overlap with the underlying kinship unit, are inherently legitimate structures simply because natural families as such cannot be subject to criminalisation. Their recruitment patterns are also rooted in mechanisms that by nature are legitimate in that membership is primarily attained through birth or marriage. However, it seems that some individuals not related by blood can also gain "an allegiance to such a firm" (Hobbs, 2013: 105) in a more conventional sense through mutual recognition of a status of affiliate (see Hobbs, 2013: 161).

The second type of associational criminal structure that has a footing in legitimate society but in contrast to family-based associations shows a high level of formalisation (Type B) is perhaps best represented by those outlaw motorcycle gangs that hold a legitimate status as officially registered associations or foundations and that protect their club insignia as registered trademarks (Barker, 2007: 132).

The implication is that the efficiencies of formal organisation can to some extent be exploited for illegal purposes. Furthermore, the legal status of an association means that it is an easily identifiable and recognisable entity which facilitates the build-up and use of reputational capital (Hartmann & von Lampe, 2008: 134).

The other two types of associational criminal structures captured by the fourfold typology are characterised by their rooting and embeddedness in entirely illegal contexts. These structures have been formed in pursuit of illegal purposes. In one case (Type C), associational criminal structures are informal patterns of relations that have emerged in the context of illegal activities, represented, for example, by the friendship networks of drug traffickers described by Patricia Adler (1985). One typical pattern was that of "circles" of drug dealers who socialised on a daily basis, thereby promoting mutual trust and facilitating the exchange of information about suppliers and customers (Adler, 1985: 70–71). These structures may be difficult to identify and delineate for criminals and law enforcement alike, but they are far less ambiguous targets for law enforcement than the family-based associations of Type A. In the other case (Type D), associational criminal structures have been formed by criminals for criminal purposes and show a high degree of formalisation. One example is the Italian-American Cosa Nostra with its formalised membership and formal hierarchical order, including the ranks of ordinary member ("soldiers") and mid-level "lieutenant" and the leadership ranks of "boss", "underboss" and "consigliere" (Cressey, 1969: 112–115).

It goes without saying that there are other dimensions across which associational criminal structures vary and that are not captured by this fourfold typology. For example, there are variations in the degree of vertical differentiation and in the importance attached to the use of violence. In both respects the Thieves in Law constitute a deviant case with their flat hierarchy and a code of conduct that does not particularly emphasise the use of violence (Serio, 2008: 165; Varese, 2001: 155–157; Volkov, 2002: 57).

Conclusion

Starting with the notion that there is more to criminal networks than co-offending structures, this chapter seeks to systematise some of the patterns of relations that connect criminals and that are not directly geared towards the commission of profit-making crimes. The focus is on associational criminal structures as opposed to entrepreneurial criminal structures and quasi-governmental criminal structures. Two main points are made in this discussion, first that a broad range of structures are similar in that they perform the same set of functions fostering, for example, bonds of trust and mutual support, and second, that these structures can be meaningfully grouped within a fourfold typology based on the criteria of legality and formalisation. As a result, some salient similarities and differences are highlighted between phenomena described in the empirical organised crime literature such as family-based associations of criminals, outlaw motorcycle gangs, friendship networks of drug traffickers and mafia-type associations. It is argued that these phenomena represent functional equivalents with respect to the bonding of offenders and that they have to be taken into consideration when analysing and assessing criminal networks. Future research should examine what implications variations in the legality and formalisation of associational criminal structures have with respect to their resilience and their impact on profit-oriented crime and illegal governance.

References

Abadinsky, H. (2013). *Organized crime* (10th ed.). Belmont, CA: Wadsworth.

Adler, P. A. (1985). *Wheeling and dealing: An ethnography of an upper-level drug dealing and smuggling community*. New York: Columbia University Press.

Albini, J. (1971). *The American mafia: Genesis of a legend*. New York: Meredith Corporation.

Anderson, A. G. (1979). *The Business of organized crime: A Cosa Nostra family*. Stanford, CA: Hoover Institution Press.

Barger, R. 'Sonny'. (2001). *Hell's Angel: The life and times of Sonny Barger and the Hell's Angels Motorcycle Club*. London: Fourth Estate.

Barker, T. (2007). *Biker gangs and organized crime*. Newark, NJ: Matthew Bender.

Bonanno, J. (1983). *A man of honor*. New York: Simon and Schuster.

Bouchard, M., & Ouellet, F. (2011). Is small beautiful? The link between risks and size in illegal markets. *Global Crime, 12*(1), 70–86.

Chu, Y. K. (2000). *The triads as business*. London: Routledge.

Cressey, D. R. (1969). *Theft of the nation: The structure and operations of organized crime in America*. New York: Harper & Row.

Decker, S. H., Bynum, T., & Weisel, D. (1998). A tale of two cities: Gangs as organized crime groups. *Justice Quarterly, 15*(3), 395–425.

Densley, J. A. (2012). The organisation of London's street gangs. *Global Crime, 13*(1), 42–64.

Detrois, U. (2012). *Höllenritt: Ein deutscher Hells Angel packt aus* (5th ed.). Berlin: Ullstein.

Edelhertz, H., & Overcast, T. D. (1993). *The Business of organized crime: An assessment of organized crime business-type activities and their implications for law enforcement*. Loomis, CA: The Palmer Press.

Fordham, P. (1972). *Inside the underworld*. London: George Allen & Unwin.

Gambetta, D. (1993). *The Sicilian mafia: The business of private protection*. Cambridge, MA: Harvard University Press.

Haller, M. H. (1991). *Life under Bruno: The economics of an organized crime family*. Conshohocken, PA: Pennsylvania Crime Commission.

Haller, M. H. (1992). Bureaucracy and the mafia: An alternative view. *Journal of Contemporary Criminal Justice, 8*(1), 1–10.

Hartmann, A., & von Lampe, K. (2008). The German Underworld and the Ringvereine from the 1890s through the 1950s. *Global Crime, 9*(1&2), 108–135.

Henninger, M. (2002). ‚Importierte Kriminalität'und deren Etablierung. *Kriminalistik, 56*(12), 714–729.

Hess, H. (1996). *Mafia & Mafiosi: Origin, power and myth*. New York: New York University Press.

Hill, P. B. E. (2003). *The Japanese mafia: Yakuza, law, and the state*. New York: Oxford University Press.

Hobbs, D. (1989). *Doing the Business: Entrepreneurship, the working class, and detectives in the east end of London*. Oxford: Oxford University Press.

Hobbs, D. (1995). *Bad Business: Professional crime in modern Britain*. Oxford: Oxford University Press.

Hobbs, D. (2001). The Firm: Organizational logic and criminal culture on a shifting terrain. *British Journal of Criminology, 41*(4), 549–560.

Hobbs, D. (2013). *Lush life: Constructing organized crime in the UK*. Oxford: Oxford University Press.

Ianni, F. A. J. (1975). *Black mafia: Ethnic succession in organized crime*. London: New English Library.

Ianni, F. A. J., & Reuss-Ianni, E. (1972). *A Family Business: Kinship and social control in organized crime*. New York: Russell Sage.

Kamstra, S. (2014). Berlin im Griff der OK? *Der Kriminalist, 46*(7–8), 18–26.

Kerner, H.-J. (1973). *Professionelles und organisiertes Verbrechen: Versuch einer Bestandsaufnahme und Bericht über neuere Entwicklungstendenzen in der Bundesrepublik Deutschland und in den Niederlanden*. Wiesbaden: Bundeskriminalamt.

Kleemans, E. R., & van de Bunt, G. H. (1999). The social embeddedness of organized crime. *Transnational Organized Crime, 5*(1), 19–36.

Lombardo, R. M. (1994). The social organization of organized crime in Chicago. *Journal of Contemporary Criminal Justice, 10*(4), 290–313.

Lombardo, R. M. (2013). *Organized crime in Chicago: Beyond the mafia*. Urbana, IL: University of Illinois Press.

Maas, P. (1997). *Underboss: Sammy the Bull Gravano's life in the mafia*. New York: HarperCollins.

Malm, A., Bichler, G., & Van De Walle, S. (2010). Comparing the ties that bind criminal networks: Is blood thicker than water? *Security Journal, 23*(1), 52–74.

Morselli, C., Tremblay, P., & McCarthy, B. (2006). Mentors and criminal achievement. *Criminology, 44*(1), 17–42.

Paoli, L. (1998). Criminal fraternities or criminal enterprises? *Transnational Organized Crime, 4*(3–4), 88–108.

Paoli, L. (2003). *Mafia Brotherhoods: Organized crime, Italian style*. New York: Oxford University Press.

Pistone, J. D. (1989). *Donnie Brasco: My undercover life in the mafia*. New York: Signet.

Quinn, J. F. (2001). Angels, Bandidos, Outlaws, and Pagans: The evolution of organized crime among the big four 1% motorcycle clubs. *Deviant Behavior, 22*(4), 379–399.

Quinn, J., & Koch, D. S. (2003). The nature of criminality within one-percent motorcycle clubs. *Deviant Behavior, 24*(3), 281–305.

Reuter, P. (1983). *Disorganized crime: The economics of the visible hand*. Cambridge, MA: MIT Press.

Schelling, T. C. (1971). What is the business of organized crime? *The Journal of Public Law, 20*(1), 69–82.

Scott, W. R. (1981). *Organizations: Rational, natural, and open systems*. Englewood Cliffs, NJ: Prentice-Hall.

Serio, J. D. (2008). *Investigating the Russian mafia*. Durham, NC: Carolina Academic Press.

Shalikashvili, M. (2009). *"Diebe im Gesetz": Eine kriminelle Organisation im deutschen Jugendstrafvollzug?* Berlin: Wissenschaftlicher Verlag Berlin.

Shen, A. (2015). *Offending women in contemporary China: Gender and pathways into crime*. Basingstoke, UK: Palgrave Macmillan.

Simmel, G. (1950). *The sociology of Georg Simmel, translated, edited, and with an introduction by Kurt H. Wolff*. Glencoe, IL: The Free Press.

Skarbek, D. (2014). *The social order of the underworld: How Prison Gangs Govern the American penal system*. Oxford: Oxford University Press.

Skoblikow, P. A. (2006). Über kriminelle ("diebische") Traditionen und Normen bei der Beilegung von Streitfällen in Russland Anfang der 1990-er Jahre. *Kriminalistik, 62*(1), 46–54.

Sobolev, V. A., Rushchenko, I. P., & Volobuev, A. F. (2002). *Organized criminal groups in Ukraine: Traditional and typical (sociological essay)*. Kharkov: National University of Internal Affairs.

Sutherland, E. H. (1937). *The professional thief: By a professional thief*. Chicago, IL: The University of Chicago Press.

Taylor, L. (1984). *In the underworld*. Oxford: Basil Blackwell.
Thrasher, F. M. (1963). *The Gang: A study of 1313 Gangs in Chicago*, abridged edition. Chicago, IL: University of Chicago Press.
Travaglino, G. A., Abrams, D., Randsley de Moura, G., & Russo, G. (2014). Organized crime and group-based ideology: The association between masculine honor and collective opposition against criminal organizations. *Group Processes and Intergroup Relations, 17*(6), 799–812.
Ulrich, A. (2005). *Das Engelsgesicht: Die Geschichte eines Mafia-Killers aus Deutschland*. München: Deutsche Verlags-Anstalt.
Van Duyne, C. P. (1996). The phantom and threat of organized crime. *Crime, Law and Social Change, 24*(4), 341–377.
Varese, F. (2001). *The Russian mafia: Private protection in a new market economy*. Oxford: Oxford University Press.
Varese, F. (2010). What is organized crime? In F. Varese (Ed.), *Organized crime: Critical concepts in criminology* (Vol. I, pp. 1–33). London: Routledge.
Volkov, V. (2002). *Violent entrepreneurs: The use of force in the making of Russian capitalism*. Ithaca, NY: Cornell University Press.
von Lampe, K. (2003). Criminally exploitable ties: A network approach to organized crime. In E. C. Viano, J. Magallanes, & L. Bidel (Eds.), *Transnational organized crime: Myth, power and profit* (pp. 9–22). Durham, NC: Carolina Academic Press.
von Lampe, K. (2016). *Organized crime: Analyzing illegal activities, criminal structures and extra-legal governance*. Thousand Oaks, CA: Sage.
von Lampe, K., & Johansen, P. O. (2004). Organised crime and trust: On the conceptualization and empirical relevance of trust in the context of criminal networks. *Global Crime, 6*(2), 159–184.
Weber, M. (1968). *Economy and society: An outline of interpretive sociology*. New York: Bedminster.

Chapter 3
Globalisation, Locale and Bankruptcy Fraud: A Historical Exploration

Mike Levi

Introduction

> *For as much as many light-hearted and evil disposed persons not intending to get their living by truth according to the laws of this realm, but compassing and devising daily how they may unlawfully obtain and get into their hands and possession money, goods, chattels, and jewels of other persons for the maintenance of their unthrifty living, and also knowing that they being lawfully convicted thereof according to the laws of this realm, shall die therefore, have now of late falsely and deceitfully contrived devised and imagined privy tokens and counterfeit letters in other names unto divers persons, their special friends and acquaintances for the obtaining of goods, cattels and jewels into their hands and possession, contrary to right and conscience.*
>
> 34 & 35 Hen. VIII, C. 4, 1543

Modern discussions on economic crimes largely ignore or are ignorant of any historical perspective. From the comments of most police, politicians and media, we might assume that transnational fraud and economic crimes are purely contemporary phenomena, and if we add the word 'cyber' in front, the world is utterly transformed for the first time into one vulnerable to depredation from anywhere in the globe. The latter point is reasonable: the Internet is a technological innovation that has had a transformative effect on the cheapness, ease and scale of fraudulent attempts which can reach into our daily lives. But it will be argued here that the difference is one of degree rather than of kind and we should not forget that compared with international shipping, rail and horse, the invention of the telegraph had more effect than the Internet on money transfers and laundering.

Dick Hobbs' work has been based around the disruption of conventional wisdom about 'organised crime', and I will here revisit part of the history of fraud, focusing on my empirical work, at the boundary between white-collar and organ-

M. Levi (✉)
School of Social Sciences, Cardiff University, Cardiff, UK
e-mail: Levi@Cardiff.ac.uk

G.A. Antonopoulos (ed.), *Illegal Entrepreneurship, Organized Crime and Social Control*, Studies of Organized Crime 14, DOI 10.1007/978-3-319-31608-6_3

ised crime. In doing so, I make passing reference to some good recent but broader historical studies of white-collar crime (Locker & Godfrey, 2006; Shore, 2015; Taylor, 2013; Wilson, 2014) as well as to some that are less analytically good (Robb, 1992), before returning to the contemporary. Note that white-collar crime is a term that covers a wide range of criminal acts and victim-offender relationships in space and time, and historical exegesis depends on what subset of financial crimes we are analysing. Thus, Wilson (2014) asserts that the criminalisation and trial of frauds really began with the 1850s, but as the opening quote and some illustrations in this chapter demonstrate, fraud has a much older bankruptcy (with civil imprisonment), criminalisation and prosecution history: what was newer (and was her focus) was the association with the joint stock company, whose growth generated a larger set of criminal and concealment opportunities, and a wider socio-economic scale of victims than had been possible before. This even affected the exploitation of institutional trust for lower level commercial credit frauds such as those described here.

Fraud is not just a crime of affluence, but even though modest sums from large numbers of poor people can be ripped off to provide a profitable source of income; the rise of classes of potential victims with funds to invest and lose is an important component of situational opportunities for fraud. Thus the Conservative government's intriguing decision to allow those over 55 to free up their pension funds from the poor returns offered by insurance products—symbolised by the UK Work and Pensions Minister Steve Webb's well-cited soundbite in March 2014 that savers were entitled to blow their pension pots on a Lamborghini if they wanted to—predictably generated a rise in fraud victimisation as well as a significant rise in saver confusion and consumption (Select Committee, 2015), as foreseen by this author and several consumer fraud newspaper columnists and BBC radio programmes such as *You and Yours*, when the proposals were announced. If only the Lamborghinis they thought they were going to buy were real! As I noted (Levi, 2008, originally 1981), one can translate *laisser faire* as "liberty to be 'done'".

My PhD predated Hobbs' entry into academia, and involved studying the organisation and control of 'long-firm fraud', a curious term, sometimes mistakenly referred to as 'long term fraud', which is inaccurate since most such frauds are relatively short in duration. In essence, it means running one or more businesses with the initial or subsequent aim of defrauding creditors. Thus, it is actually a subset of the broader category of bankruptcy/corporate insolvency frauds, some of which start out as scams from the start, others develop into frauds because the owner/outsiders develop a taste for more money than the business can provide; and in other cases still, the owners cannot bear to call a halt to the business even though it *should be* clear to them (and intermittently may be) that it cannot pay for the goods it has ordered: these I termed respectively pre-planned, intermediate and slippery-slope frauds, reflecting the degree of conscious criminality and the stage at which the 'rational choice' happened. It also prefigured contemporary interests in outsider and insider crimes, and the role of professional 'enablers'—in this case, Insolvency Practitioners and Company Formation Agents—as part of the ecosystem of criminality.

Long-Firm Fraud in the Nineteenth Century

It is not clear why the term 'long' is attached to the firm: evidence points to goods ordered from a distance, but long also meant false in Elizabethan times. The first trace of the term that I was able to find is in the *Manchester Guardian* (1858), which reports a criminal case at the Salford Police Court involving a number of people called 'the long firm', who carried on what the magistrate termed a 'system of rascality' in which associates ordered goods on credit for which they did not pay. The victim in court was a female partner of someone connected to them who had been given a black eye by a member of the long firm, and she testified about members of the gang cheating each other: so no honour among fraudsters. The assailant was fined ten shillings and asked for time to pay, which was refused because the magistrate said they had heard 'about the value of your promises of payment and we shall keep you here till you pay. We do not give credit here.'

The second mention was on 2 January 1869, in a periodical called *The Orchestra*. The article refers to the doings of the "long-firm", a body of phantom capitalists who issue large orders to supply an infinite variety of goods'—including musical instruments—and the term appears in several late nineteenth century dictionaries. The *Oxford English Dictionary* quotes Ogilvie (1882) as having defined the 'long firm' as 'that class of swindlers who obtain goods by pretending to be in business at a certain place and ordering goods to be sent to them, generally from persons at a distance, without any intention of payment'. The *Daily News* (20 September 1886) referred to one case as follows:

> *This was the usual case of what is termed long-firm swindling. The prisoner pretended to carry on business in the city, and ordered goods of all descriptions, which were never used for legitimate purposes but which were immediately pawned or otherwise disposed of.*

In France, the *bande noire* was the term given to the fraudsters, but there have been no parallel studies of the phenomenon outside the UK. So as Shore (2015, Ch. 6) also notes in her excellent historical study of London's criminal underworlds, 'long firm' was in fairly common use from the late 1860s onwards, though it was defined as a class of *individuals* rather than as a class of *activity*. She notes that fraud prosecutions at the Old Bailey rose from 2.27 % of prosecutions in the 1840s to 7.44 % of prosecutions in the 1870s and 10.27 % by the 1890s.

Decades before cases were available online, I set myself the laborious task of going through the (printed) manuscripts of cases at London's Central Criminal Court, the Old Bailey and the Law Reports. The first criminal prosecution resembling a long-firm fraud found in the historical cases in England was *R. v. Hevey, Beatty and McCarthy* (1782), 168 ER 218. Beatty had been in business previously as a ballast-heaver; Hevey was an insolvent debtor who had been liberated from the King's Bench Prison during the riots of 1780; and McCarthy was a poor man who had absconded from St Giles. They used a phoney place of business to get goods on credit for which they did not pay. They set up two business houses, one of which was a counting house (an early form of bank or discount house). They had 500 bills of exchange printed, and Hevey would offer them in payment for the goods he purchased, suggesting to vendors that they check the validity of his bills with the counting house. When vendors went to the counting house, they would observe Beatty hard at work there, apparently carrying out the duties of a clerk, and he would assure them of the bona fides of Hevey's bills. Then, before the bills of exchange matured, the parties would abscond. They were convicted, but only after they had obtained considerable quantities of rum, brandy, watches and other merchandise.

Similar frauds (although on a far larger scale) were operated by one Richard Coster (Pelham, 1841). Coster was a man of poor origins, who dealt in horses and apples as well as receiving stolen goods. In 1810, he started a business in Bristol as a general agent and discounter of bills of exchange, and in that same year he was acquitted on a charge of obtaining goods by false pretences. He later moved to London, where he worked as a job-broker and clerk. In 1825, by destroying all the evidence against him, he succeeded in obtaining another acquittal, this time on charges of conspiracy to defraud and obtain bills of exchange by false pretences. (His partner was less fortunate, being sentenced to transportation.) He became a Freemason under a false name (presumably for social and legal protection as well as status) and, under different names in different premises, he owned a feather-bed factory, a wharf and businesses dealing in bills of exchange, bullion and coral, all of which changed their addresses frequently.

Coster used the (naturally) excellent references from his beneficially owned other genuine trading firms to obtain goods on credit from home and abroad. In this way, he obtained the entire stock of a celebrated German wine-grower, a large quantity of Dublin stout (beer) and a large stock of timber, as well as general merchandise. The combination of physical distance and false names minimised the risks of detection and active prosecution, particularly at an age of poor and erratic communications. Showing that problems of relating scams to natural persons and proving the connections is not confined to the internet age, Pelham (1841: 371) points out

> *The number of his aliases and the impossibility of identifying his person, secured him from the consequences of arrest, for in no transaction did he ever appear personally to complete the terms of his contract, or to give any security for repayment. All this was done through the medium of agents, whom he had bound to himself by some ties of more than ordinary firmness, and who acted either as principal or agent, as purchaser or referee, as the necessities of the case might require their employment. To these persons, who were mostly decayed tradesmen, he behaved with little generosity. They were retained at salaries ranging from ten to twenty shillings per week, according to the extent of their usefulness; and he scrupled not, whenever an opportunity presented itself, to cheat them out of their stipulated share of the plunder which he might procure.*

In contemporary times, this might well be described as 'organised crime', and the agents as enablers. Not only did Coster specialise in long-firm frauds but he also sent forged notes in payment when required in advance of delivery. In the end, one of his men fell into a trap set for him and was arrested when picking up some goods sent to an alias. Coster was discovered to be the 'brain' of the scheme and, unfortunately for him, the letter ordering the goods was found to be in his handwriting: an early illustration of forensic analysis by visual inspection. Two of his subordinates were induced to give evidence against him, and on 16 April 1833 he was sentenced to transportation for life.

The general pattern of long-firm swindling during the nineteenth century is well attested by the cases tried at the Old Bailey in London. Prior to 1850, almost all the cases prosecuted fell into two categories.

1. The business would operate normally, except that the firm would go bankrupt—a large number of bills of exchange remaining unpaid—and the proceeds of the sale of goods would not be declared at the bankruptcy examination for the benefit of the creditors but would be secreted away by the bankrupt, and he (since they were almost all male) would be charged with concealing part of his estate in bankruptcy from the creditors. Although it is difficult to tell, it appears that these cases were not 'pre-planned' frauds from their inception, but rather they were reactions of traders to the ruin which bankruptcy was expected to bring in its wake.
2. A trader planning fraud would claim some renowned market for the goods he wished to purchase on credit, for example, in 1836 one man claimed that the goods were urgently required overseas by Admiral Sir John Byng. Depending on the commercial competence and contacts of the fraudster, the goods would then be sold off through normal channels or be pawned for cash, never to be collected. Indeed, fraudsters frequently were caught pledging the goods they had just bought or with the pawn tickets in their jackets. Having pawned them, the fraudster would try to find a buyer for them and, if successful, would redeem them. Fredur (1879) provides an intriguing guide to some aspects of this background organisation, but applying Hobbs-like scepticism to his journalistic claims, there is no way of verifying whether his description of long firms as organised by a centralised organisation—the Long Firm—is valid nationally, even if was valid locally. It appears more likely that there is a whole spectrum of organisational formats ranging from the loner who pawns the few goods he is able to get to the syndicated crime model that Fredur espouses.

The comparative rarity of prosecutions for long-firm fraud before 1850 is evidenced by the fact that out of 3475 cases tried at the Old Bailey during 1836 (a randomly selected year), only two were long firms. One cannot deduce that long firms themselves were uncommon then, for many may have remained undetected or unprosecuted, but the examination of all the prosecuted cases reveals that the most common frauds in this period were 'short cons'. A servant would come into a shop or warehouse and take goods on the pretext that they were for his master. The goods would then be pawned immediately. Or a man (gender intentional) would bring to a wholesaler or manufacturer, customers of good repute, show them around, and subsequently would get goods on credit on the false pretence that they were for his clients, whereas in fact they were for himself. In many of these cases, reference is made to the person having been driven to crime by extreme poverty.

After 1850, prosecutions for long-firm fraud became far more common than they had been hitherto, and they received some public comment. For example, in his history of the lives of the urban poor in London, Mayhew (1862: 388–390) states

> *Large quantities of goods are sent from the provinces to parties in London, who give orders and are entirely unknown to those who send them, and fictitious references are given, or references in town connected with them ... A considerable traffic in commercial swindling in various forms is carried on in London. Sometimes fraudulently under the name of another well-known firm; at other times under the name of a fictitious firm.*

These long firms were not confined to London, for Mayhew discusses in detail one carried out at Droylesden, near Manchester. Shore (2015) mentions long-firm fraud cases in the 1860s in Birmingham, Derby, Liverpool, Manchester, Nottingham and Wolverhampton, and significant clusters around Manchester.

My study of the transcripts of all cases tried at the Old Bailey 1850–1872 reveals that, during that period, 80 people were convicted of involvement in long-firm frauds. In addition, ten were acquitted of such involvements: one of these was an accused conspirator, but the other cases were dismissed on the grounds that no criminal offence had been proved to have been committed. This is connected with the legal difficulties encountered by prosecutions under the False Pretences Act 1757, the sort of difficulty that has bedevilled fraud prosecutions subsequently (Levi, 1993). In some instances, long-firm frauds are carried out in the kind of abstract setting mentioned above by Mayhew. In others, however, they operate by means of the abuse of *personal* trust. For example, supposedly independent agents would 'set up' suppliers to sell goods to swindlers who—unknown to the suppliers—were their confederates. One of the earliest such cases prosecuted was tried in 1852. Henry Keene, who had worked for a large corn firm, went to a corn-factor whom he knew and told him that he would recommend him to some good customers, who would buy his flour. In evidence, the factor said:

> *I told him to bring no customers but those he knew; he said he would bring me none but the very best. I met him soon after in the corn-market, and he recommended Jerrard to me. I asked if he was a man of property and trustworthy; and he said 'yes' he had known him for many years and he had always paid uncommonly well.*

Jerrard came along to see the factor later with a prosperous-looking man called Nicholls, who said that he would lend Jerrard £50 to pay for some goods. In fact, they both ran bakers' shops, which used the flour and oats that they obtained on credit. Jerrard said he would pay for the goods the next week and when he could not be found—he was actually in jail for civil debt—Nicholls said that payment had nothing to do with him. Keene was later arrested in Gloucester, doing a similar swindle under a different name. (Organised fraudsters were mobile centuries before the internet was invented.)

It was discovered later that the goods invoiced to Jerrard had been sent on to Nicholls, the driver having been given a substantial tip to keep his mouth shut, and that the oats had been sold to a dealer in the Old Kent Road for 80 % of their invoice value. Keene had at one time rented a shop at Maidstone for a week, installed an accomplice under the name '0. Watkins & Co.', and ordered two chaff machines from a firm in Reading, asking them to be forwarded to Paddington station for collection. The police stated in court that there was a team of 14 arrant swindlers working together on various projects, which rivals present-day teams of fraudsters who order goods or stolen identities.

Of a slightly less sophisticated, but still of professional nature, was the fraud carried out in the same year by Henry Gerhardt and Thomas Hogg. They used each other as referees, having rented premises and represented to the suppliers that they were going to improve them, and got ale, boots, flour and groceries on credit. They used false names, since as one supplier stated when asked if it was on Hogg's representation that he had given Gerhardt credit (necessary to prove fraud by false pretences):

> *No, I would not have given credit unless I had had that character—I would not have given Gerhardt credit if I had known his name was Gerhardt—certainly not, because that name was well known to me, as having appeared frequently before me in the 'Trade Protection Circular', in the Swindler's List.*

This also shows the growth of commercial trade protection bodies and lists as a crime reduction mechanism. Gerhardt had previously been sentenced in 1847 to 12 months' imprisonment for fraud. His practice was to pay for a small amount, and then to 'pay' for the larger order with a bill of exchange, which was valueless. The 'lure' for suppliers was even larger orders in the future: 'He should want rather a large amount, but as he was going to alter and beautify the premises, he should want but a small quantity now'. In some cases of this period more complex situations occurred, in which people who had traded—to all appearances legitimately—for some time were accused of fraud. In one case, a textile merchant who had been trading for 2 years resold goods for 50–66 % within days of purchasing them. When a creditor who had known him for some years went to see him about a renewed bill, he said:

> *You shall be made right tomorrow, but the fact is, I am going to make a smash of it—I said 'Indeed, and to what amount?'—he said 'It will be such a smash as has not occurred in London for some time, it will be at least £10000; it is a bad job, and I shall start off for Australia, for I shall never face my friends again.'*

Since the creditor in question was not in fact paid, we cannot assume his evidence was truthful, but the timing of goods purchased was certainly well thought out. Indeed, where extended credit by bills of exchange at 3 months is given, the losses can be easily compounded by placing large orders before the previous bill is due.

Some individuals sought to exploit apparent loopholes in international law to escape conviction. For example, for 20 years, Messrs. Braun and Kortoske acted as an intermediary purchaser of textiles for a Canadian firm, English businesses being unwilling to trade direct with foreigners. Then, in 1861, they suddenly set up their own Canadian business, and supplied it with £36,000 of goods that year, comprising large amounts from existing suppliers and £12,000 from 62 new suppliers. One man, who lost £1000 was more cautious than some:

> *1860 was the first time we dealt with them as commission agents, and the goods were all paid for—I had no more difficulty, when I first went, in selling the goods than I have with anyone else—I found no greater readiness to buy goods until the end of August—I went one day and they gave me an order for 30 pieces of black cloth, which I never solicited—I then began to be cautious and never sold them any more because they were bought in a very loose manner, such as no man, who meant to pay for the goods, would have done .... I had gone to them for, I think, ten years, but I could never sell them any goods till 1861.*

After lengthy wrangles in court, the prosecution was allowed to proceed on one count, the rest being bad in law, and the accused were convicted. Braun was recommended to mercy by the assignees, on the grounds that he was acting under Kortoske's influence and he was given 2 months imprisonment, Kortoske receiving 12 months. This *modus operandi* was common in the 1860s, reflecting the growth of international trade.

Changes in commercial structure between the mid-nineteenth century and today are also mirrored in the organisation of fraud. The abuse of personal trust was manifested in two main ways: in deliberate conspiracies between a supposedly impartial agent and a long-firm, the former recommending the latter to his contacts; and in the exploitation by a fraudster of an agent's or a supplier's personal trust in him. The latter sometimes had extremely tragic consequences, for agents were driven into bankruptcy or even suicide when they used their good names to obtain goods for fraudsters whom they believed to be honest.

There were many other cases of international long-firm frauds in the latter half of the nineteenth century. One ingenious pair of fraudsters engaged (apparently) in trade between England and Australasia obtained goods from both countries on Bills of Exchange which were dishonoured, and also money from the shippers of goods from the discounting of invoices for goods which were never delivered.

Rollo Reuschel (1895), the London correspondent of the German newspaper *Koelnische Volkszeitung*, gives us a fascinating perspective on the ambience of long-firm fraud, which he must have been obsessed by uncovering and which must have found a ready audience for, or he would not have been given the liberty and time to write about the phenomenon in German and in English. Reuschel (1895: 25) states that

> *Twice a year, the London sledge-drivers hold their 'International Congress', and the worthy proprietors of the leading long firms decide upon their common action for the coming season. From time to time they visit Germany too in order to get connections. Their honest mien, their manners and appearance, their liberality in spending money on good dinners and champagne, dazzle their chosen victims, who do not wake from their trance until they are caught by a heavy loss, that their amiable visitor and customer, the proprietor of 'that leading London firm', was nothing more or less than-a German sledge-driver [the translation from the German colloquial term schlittenfarer].*

The implication here is that long-firm fraudsters are fairly loosely organised into a federated body, in a crude parallel of the modern conception of American syndicates and Glenny's (2009) construct of *McMafia*. There is no doubt as to which is the strongest nodal link in the chain of fraud (Reuschel, 1895: 6):

> *A most important person is the 'sharper', usually a 'respectable City firm', exporting goods to Australia, India, the Cape, and other British colonies. He is nothing better than a receiver of stolen property, who disposes of the goods obtained by fraud from the manufacturers by the sledge-drivers. The sharpers are very careful to conduct their shady business in such a manner as not to come into conflict with the law. Whatever they pay for the goods, and if it be the tenth part only of the real value, they always insist on getting a receipt for an amount representing the current market price of the commodity they buy, and they never make a payment in the presence of witnesses. They remain thus always on the safe side and, never being betrayed by the thieves, enjoy undisturbed the fame of most respectable firms.*

The practice was for all the goods bought from any one long-firm fraud to go to one 'sharper', who would extract as low a price as possible.

The crucial role played by the 'sharper' makes his position both the most profitable and the safest in what we might now term the long-firm fraud script. Reuschel does not tell us whether the 'sharpers' originated the long-firm frauds, or merely took their goods. They were not in legal terms 'fences' because until the Theft Act

1968 (now superseded by the Fraud Act 2006) it was not a crime merely to buy goods knowingly from a long firm. Provided that the 'sharpers' did not conspire with long-firm fraudsters to *obtain* the goods, or to commit a bankruptcy offence, they were safe from any form of criminal liability. One particularly interesting feature of the organisation of long-firm frauds at that time was the role played by two prominent firms of trade protection agents, who acted to manage references and complaints for those who paid them off.

One such case involved German swindlers called Lehnert and Opitz who, though had separate entrances in different streets, were in fact connected by doors to each other's rooms. The agents charged low fees and wrote long florid reports, and they were well patronised as agents for French, German and Swiss trade protection societies. Lehnert would be paid by the organiser of a long-firm fraud, and in exchange would give his firm good references and would 'cool the marks out' (Goffman, 1952) when the firm failed. His technique was very clever. For example, the following is his reply to a credit inquiry:

> *This firm exists since last year and is exporting goods of all kinds to East India. The proprietor, B. Arnold, is said to have been there with the following firms [named], who have sent him as their buyer to Europe. He is said to draw from each of the firms a salary of £400 per annum and 2 % commission. 'The person enquired of is a capable man who understands his business. He had his bank account at the City Bank, Fore Street. B. Arnold have paid until now. Payments are made according to the terms usual in the East, that is cash against shipping documents, and as regards any eventual credit, it is strongly advised to insist upon these terms.*

This advice cleverly combines what is obviously an excellent reference with a recommendation not to give credit which Lehnert knew would be disregarded. By this method, he can later claim that he was right all along. His custom was that just before the smash of a 'friendly' long firm, he would warn manufacturers that the firm was totally rotten, and without funds. In this way he would gain the reputation of being well-informed (as indeed he was). He was often given the task of pursuing the malefactors and, after a long and (for the creditors) expensive search, would declare himself frustrated, and suggest that there was no point in throwing good money after bad. In his capacity as London agent for 23 credit bureaux in Germany and Austria, he was able to supply a 'sucker-list' to the long firms, since he knew the customers of those agencies to whom he supplied reports. (There are analogies in the ways that 'boiler room' investment frauds and other predators pass on lists of marks to their successor firms and sell them to others.)

Lehnert's techniques of doing business were highly profitable for him and for his associates. For example, one Martin Zucher swindled merchants in Russia, Germany, France and Hungary out of eggs, and even the Russian Consul-General could not get them to pay up—an early example of the politicality of cross-border pursuit of crime and suspects. He also got vegetables from Croatia, hams and sausages from Germany, wine from Italy, salad oil and bicycle bells. He had paid Lehnert, so when creditors employed him to look for the offender, he told them that the man had gone to the south of France with terminal galloping consumption, as tuberculosis was then called. (In reality, the only rapid consumption was that of the foodstuffs and their proceeds.) However, Lehnert did not pay Zucher his share of the proceeds from the sale of bicycle bells, and in retaliation, Zucher did not pay him 'protection' for his next long firm. Consequently, this did not prosper, because Lehnert gave him bad references. They then made up and he was given good references. A similar thing happened with another long-firm merchant. Lehnert further distinguished himself in villainy by taking the then large sum of £75 for giving evidence in Dresden that a German was a swindler. As a consequence, the man was sentenced to 12 years' penal servitude.

The success of this brilliant scheme was threatened by media expose—an early case of the impact of investigative journalism—so, with characteristic verve, Lehnert first used a rival German newspaper to try to discredit the journalist and, when that failed, got Opitz to prosecute Reuschel for libel, in the manner later popularised by some elite fraudsters such as the late Robert Maxwell. The libel action was dismissed, however, and the paper took out a private prosecution against the pair for conspiracy to defraud. Lehnert jumped bail and fled, but Opitz was sentenced to 8 months' hard labour.

Arnstein, having organised a successful long firm in cigars, set himself up as a Professor of Music at a fictitious college. He advertised for violins in German newspapers, saying that he would pay good prices, but when violins were forwarded, he would not pay up. Many of the hapless creditors complained to the Consulate, but in order to prosecute, the plaintiff had to come to England personally, and this meant more cost, which they were reluctant to undertake. In Germany, the Public Prosecutor would have taken over the case and the expense would have been borne by the general body of taxpayers. Most German creditors found it difficult to understand why this was not the case in England. This is a classic illustration of the problem of 'tragedy of the commons', the failure to act collectively for the common good because it is not in the interest of any one individual, and it is a persistent theme in the non-pursuit of economic crime to the present.

In this selection of cases from amongst the many, I have attempted to characterise the major methods by which long-firm frauds were organised in the middle of the nineteenth century. Although the organisation of criminality—crime scripts—can be deduced, it is more difficult to assess the relationships between criminals at this time. Some defendants are stated by the police to be part of a gang of swindlers, but little of the background organisation appears in the trial transcripts. Then, as now, the shadowy figures who may instruct the 'front men' and who 'fence' the goods escaped criminalisation. To one creditors' representative was stated:

> *The chief of the London police is quite willing to help, but one of the victims must appear personally as plaintiff. Characteristic are the words of the Commissioner of Police; he knew, he said, Arnstein a long time, and the police knew Arnstein to be everything else, but not 'a clean potatoe'.*

The instruments he obtained from these long-firm frauds were used in the legitimate Colleges of Music which he and his associates ran. In general, the method used by most long-firm frauds was simply to write to firms abroad on smart headed notepaper, preferably with the backing of Lehnert, asking for goods. Since trade was bad in Germany, and the manufacturers there believed that London was paved with gold, they contributed to their own victimisation by their own lack of due diligence on counterparties. On occasions, however, the long-firm merchant would do the buying abroad, or set up a mark for some confederates in England, whom he would recommend as people in a large way of business. Reuschel propounded his own lay theory about why people went into long firming:

> *It is sad that the greatest part of these long firm swindlers are Germans ... To a certain extent the cause might be found, perhaps, in the abundance of educated men in Germany, who are unable to find a suitable occupation; to do a common labourer's job they are too lazy, and thus they turn to sledge-driving* (Reuschel, 1895: 120).

The actual *process* by which they got into long-firm fraud varied considerably. First, there were those who arrived penniless, gravitated to the beer-houses in the City Road which the German community, and especially the long-firm community, frequented. They would thus join the guild of the Knights of Industry, as Reuschel ironically calls them. Then, there is a further group:

> *The greatest pleasure to the heart of a veteran sledge-driver is to receive into the heart of the guild a clerk who fled in the company of his master's cash box and who trembles at the sight of his own shadow. They are the genuine material from which sledge-drivers are made, and they form the aristocracy of the German vagabonds in London* (Reuschel, 1895: 20).

The last group of recruits arrive as a consequence of what he terms 'the Export Swindlers of the German Empire' (Reuschel, 1895: 74). German manufacturers want to sell abroad. However, rather than test the market at their own expense: 'Their scheme is to look for, and to find an agent possessed of a few thousand marks, and offer a commission of 2–3 %, that he, at his own expense, may lay the foundations for a future "world-renowned firm"' (Reuschel, 1895: 74). They mark up the prices by 15 %, which they think the English can afford, and all they pay him until his half-yearly commission is due is postage expenses. They then offer him goods in lieu of his commission, and he finally has to accept this, even though he may have worked hard to build up a connection. In order to live, the agent has to sell goods quickly, at a loss, and does so again to survive, until he cannot extricate himself. At that point, the greedy manufacturers find out their mistake, but the long-firm guild has another member. Thus, German firms laid the situational opportunities and pressures for their own victimisation.

When someone did a successful long-firm fraud, his cover was 'blown', and he would thenceforth have to employ 'front men' as clerk for him, if he wanted to stay in the same line of business. What more often happened, however, was that the fraudsters would open up one company after another, using different names and often dealing in different goods, so that they would not be recognised. The only people whom they could not afford to 'turn over' were the 'sharpers' for, otherwise, they might not be able to sell their goods from the next long firm. The valuable role of the 'swag man' in commercial life, especially in textiles, has continued up till the present. The greater part of the goods ordered by long firms came from abroad, since the English firms were too smart to be victimised, and also because the risk of prosecution was so small, the victims being loath to lose still more money by coming to England. Reuschel (1895: 113) states:

> *In England, credit is not so easily given and obtained as in other countries. But here, as elsewhere, the small manufacturers and the beginners are far more disposed to open a credit to customers than old-established firms in a large way of business, who have greater experience, and who may dare to demand from new customers cash at the first, second, and third transaction.*

Thus far, the actual frauds themselves that I have mentioned have been fairly crude affairs, although the background organisation which protects them and which buys their 'gear' is very well organised. However, some of the frauds were highly sophisticated, and I should like to describe one in some detail, for it demonstrates a degree of international criminal cooperation which would be the envy of many latter-day villains.

A German fraudster called Listmann came to Naples in 1885, and set up business as a commission agent. He employed as his travellers two other Germans called Ernest and Arfest Schreck; with excellent genuine references from two very well-accredited German manufacturers, they began to order large quantities of goods. The first orders were paid for in cash, without trouble, and then came the 'ramp'. Listmann wished to start credit transactions, and this is done on the Continent by means of bills of exchange. He did not have the organisation in Italy to generate fraudulent bills of exchange, so he utilised a London connection for this purpose.

In London every long-firm swindler possessed rubber stamps and Indian ink, and would endorse or accept any bill of exchange, for any amount, for a commission of two shillings and six pence per £100 accepted (0.00125 %). With the aid of these worthless bills of exchange, Listmann bought at least £32,000 of goods from Germany and France in the space of some 40 days, a huge amount in contemporary terms. He claimed, when ordering the goods, that they were for the most renowned firms in Naples, and gave their genuine names and addresses. However, he also bribed postal officials in Italy to intercept the mail of those firms, and when the 'letters of advice' from forwarding agents were sent, they were instead given to Listmann and, with the assistance of bribed customs officials and railway clerks, the goods never reached their destination. The Neapolitan firms did not even know that the goods had been ordered until the fraud 'broke'.

By mid-May 1886, the bills were soon to become due, and the villains arranged through a Hamburg solicitor to notify creditors that a creditors' meeting would be held on 23 May. This was in fact a delaying tactic and, when the day came, neither they nor their solicitor was there. By the time the Public Prosecutor issued a warrant, all three had long before left the country.

The fraudsters did, however, have one problem. Cash transactions were the exception in the Italian trade, and although they had sold a lot of their goods at 60 % below cost, Listmann usually had to sell to his own customers at the same 3–6 months bills that he had given himself. Not wanting to lose the benefit of this extra cash, he hit upon a scheme. While he went to Buenos Aires and Ernest Schreck went to London, Arfest was sent to Germany, where he obtained a job as a bank clerk on a small salary. With the help of a third person, Arfest got the bills discounted through a leading firm in Altona. At the last moment before he was to join Listmann in South America, Arfest Schreck was arrested in Germany. With him were four savings books with £3000 in credit, £700 in sovereigns and bank notes, and many boxes of goods. He was imprisoned for this, but after 2 years he was released, because he had become 'mentally diseased', whereupon he joined his brother in England.

Meanwhile, the legal tangles over the bankruptcy were so drawn out that the creditors eventually accepted an agreement with the Schrecks that they would keep only 7000 marks of the money seized, and would withdraw their action against them. At this point there is a tie-in with the London long-firm scene, for Ernest set up in London, but not under Lehnert's protection, so in a reference given in 1889 Lehnert described him as an 'arch-swindler'. Having learned better, Schreck paid his percentage to Lehnert, so by 1891 he had suddenly become 'an excellent man of business … respectable and diligent'.

One of the respectable German firms which had given references for the Neapolitan fraud suggested to a German manufacturer that he appoint Schreck's firm as his London agent. After he had been swindled he met, apparently by chance, none other than Opitz who had been sent to Germany by Lehnert for that purpose, since he had heard that the manufacturer was going to prosecute Schreck. Opitz offered his help in tracing and prosecuting the swindler so, needless to say, no prosecution was ever instituted. The German finally accepted Lehnert's advice to accept £100 in full and final settlement of his claim for £380.

By the late nineteenth century international long-firm frauds had become so advanced that they were becoming a source of diplomatic concern. An article in *The Standard* (date unknown) commented that

> *The Austrian Consul-General in London having informed the Vienna Chamber of Commerce that Austrian merchants have repeatedly incurred heavy loss by giving credit to long firms in England, the Chamber has issued a notice warning traders of the risk of opening accounts with foreign customers, without first obtaining satisfactory information respecting their position.*

However, it is clear that given Lehnert's strategy, reasonable diligence in obtaining credit references was not a sufficient condition for the prevention of fraud.

During the nineteenth century there developed a clearly identifiable 'long-firm subculture', bound together in part by common national origin (in the case of the Germans) but by no means all immigrants. In these respects, long-firm fraud was more 'organised' than it has been at any time since, even in the supposed heyday of English 'syndicated crime' during the 1960s. For all this, however, there is no evidence that Lehnert exercised any centralised financing, organisation and 'fencing' functions in the manner of the great thief-taker and crime-organiser Jonathan Wild (Howson, 1970). His continued existence depended upon his ability to make money for others rather than on any physical muscle he had to back up his situation: in terms of the roles popularised in Gay's *The Beggars' Opera*, he was more a cunning Peachum than the dangerous robber MacHeath.

Gender and Long-Firm Fraud

Fredur (1879) discusses female long-firm fraudsters, and Reuschel (1895: 56) mentions a rare case of female emancipation in long-firm fraud. In this case, a businessman in Germany was ruined by a long-firm fraud, and brought his wife to England to see if he could salvage anything. His wife ran off with the long-firm merchant and he died. When her new husband was forced to flee to Australia, she did a long-firm fraud herself, and shipped the goods off to Australia. After that the firm closed down. Her gender rendered it difficult for her to secure another office, and she had to associate herself with a former colleague of her husband. This man died the following year but his wife, an Englishwoman, had also profited by his instruction. The two ladies went into partnership, and they engaged a disgraced clergyman as manager. However, her husband did not like this situation, and returned to London, where he established the women as 'sharpers', and their firm became semi-legitimate:

> *All goods are bought at 10 % of their value. No goods are sold in London; all is forwarded to Australia, and thus the stolen property cannot be traced. The police has no cause to interfere, as the ladies are always able to produce receipts showing that the goods were bought from 'a firm' at the proper market price, and the firm remains highly respected in the City to this day.*

Shore (2015) notes that there were seven females convicted of long-firm frauds in the period 1874–1920.

Long-Firm Fraud in the Twentieth Century to the Second World War

No information of a comparably detailed nature about the long-firm underworld between the late nineteenth century and the 1960s appears to exist. One must be content, therefore, with the somewhat more limited perspective that one can glean from the literature and from trials at the Old Bailey. During the period 1898–1910, 21 people were convicted and 6 acquitted in long-firm fraud trials at the Old Bailey. The cases appeared to fall into two main categories:

1. 'Intermediate' frauds, occurring mainly in the context of the bad business conditions which existed at the turn of the century;
2. 'Professional swindlers', who traded for very brief periods before going bankrupt.

The case of Lewis Solomons, who went bankrupt for £5000 in 1904, provides a good example of intermediate fraud. He had traded honestly for 20 years, and had always paid promptly until his bankruptcy. He was a boot manufacturer, and sold all the leather he bought on credit to a convicted fraudster and bankrupt, whose wife traded as a boot manufacturer in the East End of London.

An example of the second category, that is, of the professional swindler, is described below. In 1901, Charles Frederick Matusch and Richard Harvey were accused of conspiring with other in a series of long-firm frauds. They had six companies, all of which were properly registered. However, some of them traded from the same address and supplied each other with good trade references. On occasions they used false names and accommodation addresses (such as lodging houses). Once, they even traded in the name of a respectable firm, but used their own address. The trial proved that they had obtained at least £2500 in goods comprising pianos, paper, typewriters, cigars, wine, spirits, bicycles and furniture.

When the police arrested Matusch, they found with him a letter addressed to 'Mr Anderson, GPO, Poste Restante, Stoke', in which 'Anderson' was asked to come to London immediately and tell him what had happened, that they were all in danger, but he should try to get the warrants against them withdrawn. They sent off the letter, but informed the Staffordshire police, who arrested Harvey when he picked up the letter. They found on him a loaded six-shooter, indicating a preparedness to use violence. However, by the time the police got to the others, they had escaped already and were never captured. After their conviction, the police stated that Matusch had been engaged in frauds since 1893, and that Harvey had been similarly occupied since 1897. Matusch was sentenced to 5 years penal servitude, and Harvey to 18 months hard labour.

In 1901, there was a similar instance of systematic swindling, which led to sentences of 8, 6, 5 and 3 *months* respectively for four brothers who had run different long firms from different addresses over a period of at least 6 years. So in spite of the frauds being against licit business, the penalties were not high. Before the Pallash brothers were sentenced, a police inspector observed

> *Information was laid against them at Highgate Police Court on two occasions, but there was difficulty about getting the witnesses up from the country, and the evidence was not sufficiently strong to succeed .... In another case, we laid the facts before counsel, but were advised to take no action in consequence of the loose way in which the (supplier) did their business.*

Here, too, there are themes which are familiar to those who seek to prosecute international frauds today. This case also draws our attention to the social reaction component in fraud which has remained implicit hitherto. The invocation of the criminal justice process depends on decisions that are made by victims, police and prosecutors about what action should be taken. It also depends on the perception that what has happened is a criminal offence: in this case, a fraud rather than an 'ordinary' trading loss. In a few cases, tradespeople took action against long-firm fraudsters on the apparent grounds of general public interest rather than direct personal offence. For example, in the case of R. *v. Sheen and Keeling*, tried at the Old Bailey in 1862, a witness stated that he had known the accused to have been trading under different names since May 1860. At his suit, Keeling had been imprisoned by the Insolvent Court in 1860 for a debt of £40, and had served 7 months' imprisonment. In the present case, he had told a detective that they were engaged in swindles:

and he stopped numbers of goods that had been delivered there, and some hams—I did not do that on my own responsibility, but upon information—I am an upholsterer, but I considered it my duty as a tradesman to interfere with hams or anything else I saw them getting—I have made it my business to cheek these people wherever I could, because they sold the goods three days after they got them—I have thought it my duty when they were trading under a fictitious name to give information to the police, to prevent the public being defrauded.

However, there must have been many cases where no similar action was taken. In so far as the availability of civil imprisonment for debt immortalised by Dickens may have affected the decision to prosecute, the Old Bailey cases may not be representative of long-firm frauds as a whole.

Another factor of importance is the cost of prosecution to victims and to government. Until 1869, when the Debtors Act (32 and 33 VIC., C. 62) was passed, long-firm fraud prosecutions were private matters, paid for by the victims. Thereafter, the state took on the burdens of prosecution in cases where it appeared to the Bankruptcy Court that conviction was probable. In 1879, the Prosecution of Offences Acts (42 and 43 VIC., C. 22) brought into existence the role of the Director of Public Prosecutions, and this extended further the 'public interest' aspect of the decision to prosecute. It seems likely that state-financed prosecutions may have led to an increase in the rate at which long-firm frauds were prosecuted, and so too did the rising number and expertise of detectives.

Although the Old Bailey transcripts that I was able to access then ceased by the First World War, there is clear evidence that long-firm frauds were a 'significant social problem' during the 1920s. For example, at the end of a trial at the Old Bailey in 1929, Sir Henry Dickens pronounced that

I have given fair warning that anyone convicted of long firm fraud will go to penal servitude. I have tried a good many of these cases, and I am getting tired of them. Statistics show that losses to traders through long-firm frauds amounted to £28 million, and generally the largest sufferers were people in the textiles trade. The judges are determined to put down that class of offence. (From the archives of Dun & Bradstreet Ltd; source unknown.)

There is extensive discussion of long-firm frauds by Moore, who states that

By far the heaviest losses incurred by supply houses have been in respect of long firms ... The swindling firm itself is 'long'. That is, there are confederates dotted about the place who name each other as referees when seeking credit, and thus weave a web in which wholesalers and manufacturers have been caught and 'bled white' times without number (Moore, 1933: 85).

Moore distinguishes the 'long firm' from the 'bogus retailer' on the grounds that the latter forges his references. Long-firm merchants, on the other hand, operate as follows: 'A good account is established by one of the gang to start with. Duly paying his bills, he becomes, in time, a "reference"' (Moore, 1933: 85). The 'reference' then is used by the other members of the gang in a concerted series of frauds. Moore (1933: 86) refers to industry self-policing and adds that:

There have been numerous exposures of heavy sentences passed on such rogues, immediately after the War especially. On the whole, successful big-scale long-firm swindles are not so numerous as they were. This is due no less to closer co-operation among supply firms

themselves than to vigorous police action. Suppliers were compelled to realise that their own independent action in taking up references could never give them more than inadequate protection, owing to the subtlety of the long-firmer's methods. It was seen that counter-methods of equal subtlety would have to be employed, for these swindlers know how to play their cards to get a 'good mark' with the very best houses in the trade and even with the most vigilant status-inquiry offices. The long-firmers, it was argued, presumably did not suddenly blossom forth as swindlers, but in all likelihood would have an antecedent somewhat dubious history. They were probably hardened tricksters, experienced in this field, and the need, therefore, was to build up a record of such individuals, a register in which would be entered every black mark recorded against any such person, together with details as to aliases and the like; a valuable record which any supply house which 'had its doubts' might consult. The textiles trades have been perhaps the worst sufferers, and after the War, the preliminary move came from them ... As a result, the would-be long-firmer now finds the road, in the textile trade at any rate, much thornier than it was a decade back ... It is not uncommon for a wholesaler or manufacturer to consult the [Textile Trades] Association, and to learn out of hand that the individual about whom information is sought is known to the officials under half a dozen aliases, as having operated in perhaps as many different branches of trade and parts of the country, and as one, possibly, who has served several terms of imprisonment. One comment needing to be made is that this excellent preventive system is, as yet, far from complete. The fuller co-operation of other branches of the trade, besides drapery and the like, is needed. When this has been secured, the long-firm swindle should become very difficult ... except in cases where individuals make absolutely their first appearance as cheats from a respectable environment, so that nothing is known against them.

Moore makes no mention of long firms in the second edition of his book, so one may presume that they were no longer perceived as a major commercial problem by the end of the 1930s, perhaps the result also of the Great Depression making credit harder to obtain for the licit and the illicit alike.

Conclusions

In the preceding pages, I have sought to set out some of the most salient features of the organisation and techniques of long-firm fraud from the early nineteenth century to the Second World War. The cases that I have quoted reveal that there have been long-firm frauds both of considerable sophistication and of considerable crudity during all the periods concerned. Similarly, in every period, there has been a wide spectrum of modes of organisation, from the sole trader who carries out a 'one-off long firm to the groups of 'professional swindlers' who act in concert to carry out a series of systematic frauds. There is no evidence that long-firm frauds nationally have ever been integrated within a single organisational format. It is noteworthy, however, that there is very little indication of overlap between long-firm fraudsters and 'traditional' property or violent criminals. In so far as the long firmers were 'professional criminals', they tended to be 'professional *commercial* criminals', eschewing other forms of predatory crime, unless they turned to the latter subsequently. Shore (2015: 140) thoughtfully concludes from her rigorous examination of court and media records:

A close consideration of a set of long--firm frauds has enabled insight into the structure of this type of fraud and the characteristics (in relation to age and occupation) of the individuals involved. Hence, the importance of cross-class readings of crime has been highlighted here. In particular, from the later nineteenth century, the involvement of clerks, commercial travellers and agents suggests that lower-middle-class and aspirational Mr Pooters were to be increasingly implicated in crimes of this type.

There were some large London fraud gangs in the 1860s such as that run by a middle-aged former coffee house keeper in Southwark George Bristowe, which probably intimidated witnesses (Shore, 2015: 134). But although the nineteenth century saw increasing conceptions of crime as 'organised' and 'professional', the exclusive concentration on commercial crime distinguishes these persons from many of those who turned to long-firm fraud a century later during the 1960s, who worked collaboratively under the aegis of the Kray and Richardson gangs (who employed the threat and practice of torture techniques to keep them in line). However the older pattern re-emerged subsequent to the 1970s (Levi, 2008: Preface), and especially since the Global Financial Crisis of 2008–2010 made credit harder to obtain anyway, both for businesspeople and for individuals (see Levi, 2013; Levi & Smith, 2011, for more general analysis of the effects of the crisis on fraud). So this credit squeeze makes it hard for any outsiders to come in and scam businesses, though taking over existing firms or their existing proprietors, using them as tools of fraud remain possible.

However, some caveats should be applied on the interpretation of these data. The very first media report mentioning the long firm referred to a network in Manchester, and Shore (2015) gives further regional examples; but cases tried at the Old Bailey or those in the expatriate German community are unlikely to be representative of those in the country as a whole. Different patterns of organisation and of technique may have been observable elsewhere. Furthermore, the criminal cases represent only those about which enforcement decisions have been taken: despite the investigative journalism efforts of Reuschel and the nationwide research of Shore (2015), our understanding remains partial and tentative of how many or what kind of long-firm frauds remained unprosecuted during these periods. Consequently, it would be most unwise to extrapolate observations about officially defined fraud and to apply them to 'actual', but not officially defined, long-firm frauds. Inferences about the latter category are difficult enough to make when examining contemporary commercial conduct: the problem is greater still when we try to separate out the 'real fraud' component from the 'social definition and reaction' component in historical essays.

Finally, though Great Britain was an imperial power with a huge global reputation for affluence and a reasonable one for commercial integrity (see the magisterial history by Kynaston, 2012), it would be puzzling if long-firm frauds were an exclusively British phenomenon: what about other great trading empires such as the Netherlands, or more extractive but still large trading empires such as those of Belgium, France, Portugal and Spain? Whether the criminal and commercial records exist elsewhere to examine this phenomenon are beyond my knowledge, but this does raise questions about the transfer of techniques and cultural practices which, as some of the cases discussed here demonstrate, revealing interesting insights into the growth and transfer (or absence thereof) of criminal methodologies in different legal and cultural contexts that are raised by Varese's (2011) work on the Mafia as well as by Hobbs' own stress on the importance of embedding professional crime in its local environment and his serial critiques of the metaphor of 'organised crime' and its misuse. What this study (and the more contemporary research in Levi, 2008) has shown is that many frauds are 'organised enough' to be successful: however it is generally only when gangsters become involved in their commission that the label of 'organised crime' is attached to financial crimes. Yet why is that label not applied to many elite scandals such as the LIBOR rate-fixing and other price-fixing conspiracies which meet the somewhat nebulous criteria of organised crime (see also van de Bunt, 2010)? Is it because despite the efforts to shift the term socially upwards to apply to accountants, lawyers and real estate agent 'crime enablers', we have been conditioned to think of 'organised crime' as a product of the wholly criminal underworld and find it too difficult to liberate ourselves from that dominant *gestalt*?

References

Extraordinary disclosures at the Salford Police Court: "The long firm" exposed. (1858, March 17). *Manchester Guardian*.

Fredur, T. (1879). *Sketches from shady places*. London: General Books.

Glenny, M. (2009). *McMafia: Seriously organised crime*. London: Vintage.

Goffman, E. (1952). On cooling the mark out: Some aspects of adaptation to failure. *Psychiatry, 15*(4), 451–463.

Howson, G. (1970). *Thief-taker general: The rise and fall of Jonathan Wild*. London: Hutchinson.

Kynaston, D. (2012). *City of London: The history, distilled from original four volumes*. London: Vintage.

Levi, M. (1993). *The investigation, prosecution, and trial of serious fraud*. Royal Commission on Criminal Justice Research Study No. 14. London: HMSO.

Levi, M. (2008). *The Phantom capitalists: The organisation and control of long-firm fraud* (2nd ed.). Andover: Ashgate.

Levi, M. (2013). Financial crimes and the global financial crisis. In P. van Duyne, J. Harvey, G. A. Antonopoulos, K. von Lampe, A. Maljevic, & J. Spencer (Eds.), *Human dimensions in organised crime, money laundering and corruption* (pp. 201–228). Oisterwijk: Wolf Legal Publishers.

Levi, M., & Smith, R. (2011). *Fraud vulnerabilities and the global financial crisis*. Trends & issues in crime and criminal justice no. 422. Canberra: Australian Institute of Criminology.

Locker, J. P., & Godfrey, B. (2006). Ontological boundaries and temporal watersheds in the development of white-collar crime. *British Journal of Criminology, 46*(6), 976–992.

Mayhew, H. (1862). *London labour and the London poor*. London: Griffin, Bohn.

Moore, M. C. (1933). *Frauds and swindles*. London: Gee & Co.

Pelham, C. (1841). *Chronicles of crime*. London: Reeves and Turner.

Reuschel, R. (1895). *The knights of industry: Revelations about foreign long-firms in London*. London: Author.

Robb, G. (1992). *White-collar crime in modern England: Financial fraud and business morality 1845–1929*. Cambridge: Cambridge University Press.

Select Committee. (2015). *Pension freedom guidance and advice*. London: House of Commons.

Shore, H. (2015). *London's criminal underworlds, c. 1720–c. 1930: A social and cultural history*. London: Palgrave.
Taylor, J. (2013). *Boardroom scandal: The criminalisation of company fraud in nineteenth century Britain*. Oxford: Oxford University Press.
Van De Bunt, H. (2010). Walls of secrecy and silence. *Criminology & Public Policy, 9*(3), 435–453.
Varese, F. (2011). *Mafias on the move: How organized crime conquers new territories*. Princeton, NJ: Princeton University Press.
Wilson, S. (2014). *The origins of modern financial crime*. London: Routledge.

Chapter 4
North Brabant: A Brief History of a Hotbed of Organised Crime

Toine Spapens

Introduction

Since the 1980s, studies of street crimes such as robberies have made clear that these were often concentrated in specific spatial areas. Sherman, Gartin, and Buerger (1989), for example, analysed 323,000 calls to the Minneapolis police and found that 50 % originated from only 3 % of the places in the city. Studies show that the members of organised crime networks also seem to be concentrated in specific areas. The Italian mafia for example has its heartland in the regions of Campania, Calabria, Sicily, and to a lesser extent Apulia (Dickie, 2013). In Spain, the region of Galicia is considered a hot spot of organised crime (van de Bunt, Siegel, & Zaitch, 2014). Organised crime in Lithuania appears to be concentrated in the Kaunas region (Rawlinson, 2001). A number of years ago the Dutch police found that gangs of Polish car thieves operating in the Netherlands almost always came from the Wroclaw area (KLPD, 2005a). In the Netherlands itself, the province of North Brabant is generally seen as a hotbed of organised crime.

Of course, we can immediately question whether it is indeed possible to assess the scale of organised crime activities in specific areas, and thus whether the examples above are in fact hotbeds of different or specific types of organised crime or merely have an image problem. As far as North Brabant is concerned observations show that specific types of serious and organised crime do occur there more often. The majority of synthetic drug laboratories uncovered in the Netherlands in the past 25 years were found in the southern part of the country. The number of professional cannabis nurseries has also been disproportionally high in the south, ever since indoor cultivation methods became fashionable in the Netherlands. The same applies to organised vehicle theft and the theft of commercial vehicles and loads.

T. Spapens (✉)
Department of Criminal Law, Tilburg University, Tilburg, The Netherlands
e-mail: a.c.spapens@tilburguniversity.edu

G.A. Antonopoulos (ed.), *Illegal Entrepreneurship, Organized Crime and Social Control*, Studies of Organized Crime 14, DOI 10.1007/978-3-319-31608-6_4

From 1830 to the 1960s, what were sometimes well-organised groups, engaged in large-scale smuggling back and forth across the Belgian border. Further back in history, rural gangs operated in the area. The names of some of the families appearing in criminal records of the seventeenth and eighteenth centuries are familiar to modern-day police officers investigating ecstasy production, for example. All of this seems to indicate that North Brabant does indeed have more serious and persistent problems than most other parts of the Netherlands.

Why organised crime "meso networks" seem to concentrate in certain areas is a highly intriguing question.[1] To answer this question, a group of academics based in North Brabant will be investigating this topic over the next few years from criminological, economic, sociological, cultural and historical perspectives. The scope of this chapter is, of course, far more limited. Here, I present a brief overview of the types of illegal activity occurring in North Brabant from 1648 until now that we would define as serious and organised crime by today's standards. In the concluding section, I look into some possible theoretical explanations that offer leads for further research.

The Rural Gangs (1648–1830)

The history of North Brabant has not been free of armed conflict. The province was one of the principal battlegrounds of the Dutch War of Independence (1568–1648), and both the Spaniards and the Dutch left a trail of great harm and destruction there. This was caused not only by the fighting as such, but also because both warring parties purposively displaced inhabitants and destroyed houses and crops to deny the other party access to food, housing and other necessities (Adriaenssen, 2007). Following the Peace of Münster, which ended the War of Independence, Spain handed over "State Brabant" to the Republic of the Seven United Netherlands. However, State Brabant, whose territory roughly equals the present-day Province of North Brabant, was not considered an integral part of the Republic. Instead it was treated more like a colony and exploited by the imposition of heavy taxes and other charges. In 1715, State Brabant also became a buffer zone between the Republic and the Austrian Netherlands (the territory of present-day Belgium). This implied that foreign troops were occasionally garrisoned there requiring food and lodging from the population, and that it sometimes saw renewed armed conflict. This happened

[1] In earlier work, I introduced the term "meso network" to distinguish between criminal groups ("micro networks") and the entire world community of persons who engage in organised crime ("macro network"). Of course, the macro network is a theoretical rather than a practical concept. Although no formal barriers exist for persons who want to establish criminal relations, and Dutch drug traffickers for example maintain such relations all over the world, most members of organised crime groups do not maintain global relations. Generally, however, at the meso level they do have criminal contacts outside the scope of their criminal group and this allows them to cooperate with or even switch from one group to another (Spapens, 2012).

for example in 1747, when the French occupied parts of Brabant during the Austrian war of succession and captured several cities, such as Bergen op Zoom.

Understandably, these developments did not contribute to the prosperity of the inhabitants, who were relatively poor to begin with. North Brabant's sandy soils yielded poorer harvests than other parts of the Netherlands, and in those days much of the province was still heavily forested and thinly populated. Finally, the competent authorities held little legitimacy with the population. For example, during the latter days of the War of Independence the Dutch built a citadel in the city of 's-Hertogenbosch not with the aim of defending it but to repress possible uprisings.

How this situation promoted the development of sometimes large and well-structured rural gangs is unknown, but such gangs clearly operated in North Brabant and also used it as a staging place to commit crimes in Holland, present-day Belgium and the German Rhineland. One example is the White Feather Gang, which between 1720 and 1726 had its lair in the Ravensbos, a remote forest situated outside the village of Kaatsheuvel near the present Efteling amusement park. This group was well organised and consisted of 200–300 persons, including women and children. Most of them were described as "heathens" from Eastern Europe (Grootswagers, 1983). The White Feather Gang had a military structure and was very well armed, which suggests that it also comprised laid-off mercenaries or deserters from the armies stationed in the area. The location of the gang's camp was particularly interesting, because it was situated at the border of three jurisdictions: the Baronie of Breda, the Meijerij of 's-Hertogenbosch, and Holland. The group made sure not to commit crimes in the area where it resided and instead raided the Republic, taking advantage of the excellent infrastructure provided by tow canals and tugboats (*trekschuiten*) that connected the towns in Holland to move quickly from one place to another. The gang took the stolen goods to their camp and divided them amongst the members or sold them (Egmond, 1989). The local population and some corrupt officials also profited by procuring stolen goods at reduced prices. In return, the local notables put little effort into disrupting the gang's activities. Any counteraction would require showing up in strength, and such a presence would, of course, be quickly detected, for instance by innkeepers who acted as paid informers for the criminals. However, this does not imply that the White Feather Gang operated with impunity. In 1726, after numerous complaints from jurisdictions in Holland, the authorities sent a military force to the Ravensbos and arrested some 60 members of the group, including its leader Swarten Johannes (Black John). He was sentenced to death in September 1726. Other important members also ended on the gallows, and in 1727 the gang ceased to exist (Grootswagers, 1983).

Another example worth mentioning is the hamlet of "the Heike" (now the village of Sint Willebrord). In the eighteenth century, it was the home of a number of families involved in serious crimes. The core of one gang consisted of three brothers, Machiel, Cornelis and Marijn Jansse Jaspers. Between 1756 and 1760, the Jaspers Gang stole cattle and beehives and committed burglaries and violent crimes, and its members wrote letters to farmers threatening to burn down their farmhouses unless they paid a ransom (*brandbrieven*). It took until 1763 before Machiel was convicted (Pisters & van Riemsdijk, 1996: 99).

Just like the Ravensbos, the Heike was situated on the border of multiple jurisdictions, in this case the Baronie of Breda and the Markiezaat of Bergen op Zoom. It was also close to the border of the Austrian Netherlands. The location of the hamlet provoked arguments between the reeves of neighbouring jurisdictions as to which one should take action against the criminals who found refuge there. It must be noted that, as in the case of the Ravensbos, it was only possible to safely enter the Heike by force. That was a costly affair for the local authorities and something they were only willing to do when arrests needed to be made. Consequently, the Heike developed into a judicial no man's land. The 175 inhabitants, divided into some ten families who often intermarried, had acquired a serious criminal reputation by the end of the eighteenth century. The hamlet was known as *Schooiersheike* (Scallywag Heike) or *Kleijn Amsterdam* (Little Amsterdam) (Pisters & van Riemsdijk, 1996).

Rural gangs were equally active in other parts of North Brabant. They committed burglaries and armed robberies and were often formed ad hoc from a network of beggars, peddlers, rag merchants and other people living on the edge of society (van den Eerenbeemt, 1970). At the end of the eighteenth century, some local gangs developed into larger criminal groups, such as the Great Dutch Gang, which formed around 1789 and comprised at least 56 men, for the most part Jews. They were particularly active from 1794 to 1796 but dissolved after a number of key members were apprehended (Egmond, 1986). Factors that help explain banditry in the south of the Netherlands include the social exclusion and marginalisation of substantial numbers of Jews and Gypsies who had fled repression in Eastern and Southern Europe (Egmond, 1994: 117–168, 240–241; Egmond, 2004: 99–101).

The examples of the Heike and the White Feather Gang have shown that gangs took advantage of the borders between jurisdictions. At the end of the eighteenth century, the Netherlands numbered no less than 200 independent jurisdictions in which the courts were competent to handle all types of criminal cases and to impose every penalty, including the death sentence (Egmond, 1989: 17). Although judicial cooperation was not uncommon, there was no systematic investigation of gangs that operated across boundaries. However, this situation changed radically at the end of the eighteenth century. In 1795, the unity of the State was declared and, after ratification of the Constitution of 1798, the days of local self-governance in judicial matters were over (Haarman, 1922: 17). Furthermore, the French annexed Holland in 1810 and introduced their *Code Pénal*. The police were transformed into an independent institution and—specifically in the south of the Netherlands (which then included Belgium)—the regime formed Gendarmerie units and tasked them with maintaining public order in the countryside. In the new situation, it took the Gendarmerie only a few years to wipe out the large gangs completely (Fijnaut, 2012). These results, however, did not mean that Napoleon's police gained popularity. Their main task was not to protect the people against crime but to protect the regime against adversaries. To this purpose they did not hesitate to abuse their powers, make unlawful arrests and search people's houses at will, and employed secret agents as well (Haarman, 1922). Consequently, the population generally mistrusted and hated the police and was reluctant to seek help or report crimes.

Smuggling Across the Dutch-Belgian Border (1830–1962)

The Netherlands regained its independence from France in 1814 and the United Kingdom of the Netherlands was formed the following year. Only 15 years later, in 1830, the Kingdom's southern provinces seceded and became the independent state of Belgium. The border between the two countries soon offered interesting opportunities for smuggling, and there was no shortage of persons willing to grasp them. In the final quarter of the nineteenth century, for example, a kilo of salt was ten cents cheaper in Belgium than in the Netherlands, and there was hardly a grain of salt to be found in the Dutch border towns that had not been smuggled (Spapens & Willemsen, 2002).

During the First World War, when the Germans occupied Belgium and the Netherlands remained neutral, an electric fence and military patrols were not enough to stop the smugglers, who focused on petroleum, coffee, chocolate and pepper. During the Second World War, after the liberation of the south of the Netherlands in the autumn of 1944, goods such as liquor, tobacco, silk stockings, motorcycles and tyres were smuggled in from Belgium. Cattle, agricultural products, oysters and shrimp went in the opposite direction (Spapens & van Oirschot, 1988: 104). The war would continue in the Netherlands until May 1945, and until then the frontline that ran roughly along the old border between State Brabant and Holland hardly moved. Throughout this time, Allied forces personnel garrisoned in North Brabant enthusiastically participated in smuggling activities. After the war, in the 1950s, butter became the smugglers' object of choice to traffic to Belgium. On the return trip they carried cigarettes, particularly the then popular brand of Chesterfields (Haenen & Buddingh, 1994).

Returning to 1830, the Heike quickly developed into a key smuggler's den, although smuggling activities were common along the entire border. Both the men and women of the village took part in this, and they were involved in poaching and theft as well (Schreurs, 1947). In the border area, the trade in legitimate and smuggled goods was completely intertwined and many of the inhabitants played some part in the smuggling activities. Most were "mules" who carried goods across the border in a rucksack. The organisers of the shipments remained largely in the background. Criminals living in the Heike were able to engage in large-scale smuggling because they also had shady contacts in cities such as Rotterdam, The Hague and Amsterdam (Schreurs, 1947). Although this has not yet been the object of historical research, we can assume that these "obscure elements" were the main contacts for selling the smuggled goods. In addition, during the First World War a large section of the Dutch field army was garrisoned in North Brabant. Many soldiers participated in the smuggling activities and because they came from all around the country, this will undoubtedly have furnished the men from the Heike with useful new contacts to whom they could supply goods.

After the Second World War, the battle between the smugglers and government customs officers intensified. The size of the shipments increased and so did the financial risks. There was no shortage of firearms available, and criminals were not afraid to use them against pursuers. They also used trucks and cars fitted with armoured plating to break roadblocks (Spapens & van Oirschot, 1988).

Opportunities for smuggling came to an abrupt end when Belgium, the Netherlands and Luxemburg formed a customs union, which became effective in 1962. Border controls were lifted and although price differences continued to exist, from then on individual customers could simply drive to the neighbouring country, buy goods that were cheaper and bring them back home.

The 1970s: Predatory Crime, Illegal Alcohol and Amphetamine

The effect of the Benelux Economic Union on criminal opportunities merits more in-depth criminological research. Judging from what happened in my own family, most of the persons who carried goods across the borders in rucksacks simply accepted that the opportunity to earn some extra money had ceased. The key persons in the smuggling network, however, looked for other markets. Those who sell smuggled goods ultimately need customers who want to buy the product. In the case of consumer products, it is usually far more effective and less risky to return them to the regular market instead of selling them under the table. So the hardcore criminals in North Brabant turned to large-scale theft and apparently built up a network with contacts from their smuggling days to fence the stolen goods. In addition, vehicle crime developed into an important activity from the 1960s onwards. Last but not least, new markets for illegal alcohol and amphetamine appeared.

Predatory Crime

In the 1960s and 1970s, criminal groups of travellers started to attract attention. One example was the "Kempen Gang", which numbered about 50 members of various families living in trailer camps in North Brabant. The gang committed approximately 200 burglaries of commercial properties as well as armed robberies. Just as in the smuggling era, they rammed police blockades, shot at pursuers and strewed the roads with caltrops to avoid apprehension. In 1979, a police action involving 160 officers at three trailer camps led to the arrest of the leading gang members, with main suspect Toon P. being sentenced to a prison term of 12 years.

With the exception of a small community of Gypsies, most of the travellers were Dutch nationals who traditionally worked in itinerant occupations. In the 1960s, the government chose to concentrate them in some 50 large trailer camps, most of them located in remote areas (Khonraad, 2000). The camps were overcrowded, lacked amenities and were plagued with mass unemployment. Not surprisingly, most travellers developed an aversion to the authorities, and the situation contributed to increasing and more serious criminal behaviour. In response, the authorities closed the large camps in the 1980s and relocated the inhabitants to numerous small camps with between five and twenty "trailers", but also to normal houses.[2] Although the travellers' community now numbers a mere 30,000 persons, their involvement in organised crime remains disproportionally high, particularly in the south of the Netherlands.

The 1960s also saw a rise in vehicle theft. A study of large-scale criminal investigations in the south of the Netherlands reveals that between 1992 and 1996, vehicle crime came second after narcotic drugs (Moerland & Boerman, 1999: 40). The research shows that all sorts of companies operating in the lower segment of the car market, such as used car dealers and scrapyards, were linked to the criminal groups and sometimes even owned by members. These companies greatly facilitated thieves, for example by delivering wrecks that matched stolen cars and using them to pretend that they had repaired the total loss (Moerland & Boerman, 1999: 149). Some thieves appeared to specialise in construction vehicles, and the theft of mini excavators was and still is endemic. Heavy equipment is shipped to Africa, for instance (Spapens, 2008: 139).

To this day, criminal groups in North Brabant specialise in large-scale theft, for example from distribution warehouses. In addition, a 2007 study revealed that the risk of commercial vehicles and cargo being stolen in the European Union is highest in the Netherlands (van den Engel & Prummel, 2007: 6). Within the Netherlands, the Rotterdam–Venlo transport axis has the highest incidence of stolen lorries, trucks and loads (Kuppens, de Vries-Robbé, van Leiden, & Ferwerda, 2006). The thieves specifically target cargo of high value that is easy to sell on the stock lots market, such as razor blades and washing powder, but also cigarettes, liquor and coffee. For a number of years the Dutch police operated a team of detectives who uncovered a substantial network of persons fencing the stolen goods; its members sometimes ordered specific loads to be stolen and "invested" in them together (Spapens, 2008).

Illegal Alcohol

In the 1960s, other criminal groups started to focus on the large-scale production of illegal alcohol (Spapens & Horsten, 1990). Until then, this had mainly been a problem in Belgium but that changed when the Belgian authorities began to crack down on illegal alcohol distillers after a methyl alcohol scandal resulted in several deaths. Increased penalties drove some Belgian distillers to set up shop in the Netherlands. Dutch criminals then professionalised the business further and increased the volume. The first illegal distillery was discovered in 1968 and within 10 years another 65 had followed. Almost 90 % of these were located in the south of the Netherlands

[2] The word 'chalet' is more appropriate to describe a modern-day trailer. Although some wheels are fitted to the structure to comply with the legal definition of a trailer, it can only be moved with a low loader.

(Spapens & Horsten, 1990). Alcohol production gradually ceased in the late 1960s. Heavier penalties in the Netherlands resulted in a shift of production back to Belgium. The Dutch Fiscal Intelligence and Investigation Unit also successfully disrupted production by making it almost impossible to procure large distillation columns.

Amphetamine

Another novelty in the 1970s was amphetamine production. Until 1976, amphetamine was not included in the Dutch Opium Act. Instead, it was sold in pharmacies and doctors prescribed it to patients who wanted to lose weight (Gonsalves & Verhoog, 1999: 170). In neighbouring countries, however, amphetamine was already a controlled drug. Consequently, the Netherlands was an important source country for legal amphetamine. In 1967, for example, German amphetamine trafficker Kalle Pauksch settled in the south of the Netherlands and began to supply Sweden with the product. Several Dutchmen who worked as couriers for Pauksch were apprehended. In 1972, under severe pressure from Sweden, the Dutch authorities apprehended and extradited Pauksch. He was quickly succeeded by Dutch criminals. After amphetamine became illegal in 1976, they also set up illegal laboratories. According to estimates by the Dutch police, the Netherlands developed into one of the world's biggest amphetamine producers in the 1980s (KLPD, 1993). In the early 1990s, most of the intercepted shipments were destined for Scandinavia, the UK, Germany and Belgium (Weijenburg, 1996: 132). In the mid-2000s, a shortage of the precursor chemical BMK resulted in a temporary drop in the number of laboratories discovered by the police. When the "cooks" started to use Apaan as an alternative, amphetamine production increased again (see below).

Drug Trafficking

Apart from amphetamine, criminal groups based in North Brabant also turned their attention to other drug markets in the 1970s, starting with hashish and marijuana. These drugs had become increasingly popular from the second half of the 1960s, starting with young people in the major cities, and students in particular (Cohen, 1975; de Kort, 1994). Increasing demand also attracted the traditional criminal underworld, for example in Amsterdam, where some members had the means to invest in larger shipments. In 1974, the Dutch police, assisted by the navy, intercepted the fishing vessel "Lammie" carrying a shipment of over 3000 kilos of hashish. Investigations revealed that some well-known members of the Amsterdam Red Light District underworld had organised the transport (Middelburg, 2000).

In the second half of the 1970s, criminals from North Brabant who also had money to invest as well as the necessary smuggling experience and eager customers in neighbouring countries, began to cooperate with traffickers based in Amsterdam who at the time had better access to suppliers in Lebanon, Pakistan and other important source countries (Tweede Kamer, 1996: 20). Not unimportantly, the southerners also had a sufficiently violent reputation to make their business partners think twice about cheating them. Their close relationship became clear when Klaas Bruinsma was shot in the car park of the Amsterdam Hilton in 1991. Bruinsma led a criminal group trafficking hashish and marijuana which had developed into one of the largest groups in the Netherlands in the 1980s. At the time of his murder, the Hilton hotel bar was a meeting point favoured by assorted criminals and shady business persons. On the evening of Bruinsma's murder, his friend Koos R., a "traveller" from North Brabant and a known drug criminal, was also present and witnessed the shooting (Middelburg & van Es, 1994: 28).

From the 1970s onwards, the criminal landscape of North Brabant started to diversify with the arrival of newcomers, particularly from Turkey, Morocco, Surinam and the Dutch Antilles. These countries were also source and transit countries for heroin, hashish and cocaine, respectively, and members of the existing criminal underworld quickly developed relationships with persons in the immigrant communities who were willing to break the law.

Ecstasy Production

As explained above, the Netherlands was already a source of amphetamine in the 1960s. From the early 1990s onwards, the country also became an important producer of ecstasy and cannabis. Once again, criminal groups originating in the south played key roles. The case of ecstasy essentially repeats the history of amphetamine trafficking. Ecstasy, or MDMA, quickly gained popularity in the second half of the 1980s, with the United Nations adding it to its list of controlled psychotropic substances in 1986. In the Netherlands, however, MDMA remained legal until 1988 because there were no indications of widespread use. That was absolutely not the case in the UK, however, where ecstasy-fuelled "raves" soon gained momentum. It did not take British dealers long to find out that they could procure excellent quality MDMA *legally* in the Netherlands. By the time ecstasy was finally included in the Dutch Opium Law, "house parties" and the demand for party pills had exploded in the Low Countries as well. Production followed and the Dutch police discovered three laboratories as early as 1988 and 1989 (Weijenburg, 1996: 139).

The first illegal manufacturers were trained chemists. The result was ecstasy of excellent quality soon favoured by customers from all over the world (Husken & Vuijst, 2002). Illegal production began in the Amsterdam area but the centre of gravity quickly shifted to the south and the Belgian border region (Spapens, 2006). For example, between 1998 and 2003 the police annually dismantled between 34 and 43 laboratories, almost all operated by criminal groups from North Brabant and Limburg (KLPD, 2005b: 62).

Why the Netherlands and the south in particular became the heartland of ecstasy production is difficult to determine. One possible explanation is its experience with the manufacture of amphetamine, although in practice all sorts of ecstasy "cooks" appeared, ranging from professional chemists and pharmacists to amateurs who had once set to work guided by a simple recipe and were lucky enough not to perish during the learning process. Producing ecstasy is not "rocket science", however, and it is easy to find the required knowledge, hardware and chemicals in any industrialised country. A better explanation may, therefore, lie in the contacts with foreign wholesale buyers that the southerners apparently had or succeeded in developing. In the end, there is no point in manufacturing millions of pills if you cannot sell them.

The flow of Dutch ecstasy pills were a growing annoyance to the authorities in other countries from the mid-1990s onwards. The pressure from France and Germany in particular started to affect the Netherlands' reputation and the authorities therefore established a special Synthetic Drugs Unit in 1997. Apart from taking investigative action, its task was to show that the Netherlands was indeed taking ecstasy seriously. The former head of the unit once told the author of the current chapter that he gave presentations all over the world to this end, and because these visits also required him to attend official lunches and dinners, he had to order a larger-sized uniform three times.

Not surprisingly, given the massive task placed before them, the 48 staff members of the Synthetic Drugs Unit were unable to rein in ecstasy production to any substantial degree. On the contrary, production grew in the second half of the 1990s when the USA became a major destination country. Of course, the US authorities were not amused. During an official visit to the White House in September 2000, President Bill Clinton personally lectured Dutch Prime Minister Wim Kok about the apparent incompetence of the Dutch authorities when it came to tackling ecstasy production and trafficking. Unprepared for this reception and being notoriously bad tempered himself, Kok immediately summoned all procurators-general and chiefs of police to his office upon his return to the Netherlands and angrily demanded action (Spapens, 2006).

The result was the multifaceted plan "Colluding against ecstasy". It included stricter inspections at harbours and airports and the mounting of six specialised "XTC teams" with the police, comprising more than a hundred extra detectives. Furthermore, almost all regular investigations of organised crime were directed towards synthetic drug production. In 2001, for instance, 88 % of all large-scale drug investigations concerned synthetic drugs (Meijer et al., 2003). The Synthetic Drugs Unit focused specifically on imports of the precursor chemicals PMK and BMK, which mostly came in from China. This time, the efforts were not without effect: the "top ten" producers and traffickers were arrested and convicted to sentences ranging up to 14 years (Spapens, 2006). In addition, the police arrested several persons who custom-built the reaction vessels necessary for large-scale production, and a Chinese criminal group that imported PMK.

However, the most effective results by far were achieved quietly on the diplomatic front. The Chinese authorities agreed to shut down the production of precursor chemicals for which there was no legitimate use, and producers in the Netherlands soon faced serious shortages of PMK and BMK. By 2007, ecstasy production had virtually ceased. Producers tried to switch to safrole and sassafras oil, but these precursors are also difficult to obtain. Although ecstasy is once more becoming increasingly popular, the police have uncovered only a small number of laboratories, although some of these were high-capacity production facilities. The story is otherwise for amphetamine, however. As explained above, the "cooks" found a cheap and easily available alternative in Apaan. Amphetamine production has been rising again for the past few years, and laboratories and dumped chemical waste are found almost every week, especially in the Tilburg area.

Cannabis Cultivation

Finally, cannabis cultivation became a new criminal opportunity at about the time when ecstasy started booming. Crucial to this trend were indoor growing techniques introduced in the early 1990s. Some 5 years later, much of the cannabis used in the Netherlands was home grown. The authorities welcomed this development because they assumed that the growers were mostly idealists and small-scale operators, whereas criminal groups controlled most of the cannabis imports. In practice, however, the importers very rapidly started growing cannabis as well. As early as 1992, the police uncovered a nursery of 80,000 plants in North Brabant. In 1994, they found 323 nurseries, 31 % of which were located in the south of the Netherlands (Weijenburg, 1996: 184–185). In 1998, police intelligence showed that all known organised crime groups in one of the three police regions in North Brabant had switched from ecstasy production to cannabis cultivation or combined the two activities (Gooren & Rebel, 1998).

Although ideological growers whose primary goal is to grow cannabis of the highest quality do exist, most growers are only in it for the money and care less about quality. A 2007 study of the world behind cannabis cultivation showed how a network had developed consisting of different types of growers, ranging from those who ran their own professional nurseries to persons who only provided space and let others build and operate the plantation. The network also comprised specialist facilitators, such as electricians, persons who built plantations and organised teams of cutters, and specialists in drying the buds (Spapens, van de Bunt, & Rastovac, 2007). However, organised criminal groups control the buying, selling and export of wholesale amounts of cannabis and also often run their own large plantations. Their pivotal role is underlined by the fact that, according to estimates, 54–93 % of Dutch cannabis is sold to foreign buyers (van der Giessen, Van Ooyen-Houben, & Moolenaar, 2014).

When compared to the importation of drugs and synthetic drug production, cannabis cultivation is much more labour intensive. In 2012, a key figure in the cannabis network in the Tilburg area decided to cooperate with the police after his fellow criminals had started to threaten him and demand financial compensation for the loss of several nurseries to thieves and the police. He identified sixty different criminal groups in the Tilburg area and estimated that 2500 persons were involved in cannabis-related activities on a daily basis (RIEC Zuidwest et al., 2013).[3] The cannabis network, therefore, resembles the large-scale smuggling operations of the 1940s and 1950s. Similar to the heyday of smuggling, many people play modest roles, with a much smaller number of seasoned criminals controlling the market.

Recent Developments

Over the past 5 years, worries about the undermining effects of organised crime in North Brabant have increased. Clearly, ecstasy and cannabis in particular have furnished many criminals with substantial amounts of money. This they tend to spend on luxury goods, clothes, jewellery, cars and holidays (RIEC Zuidwest et al., 2013). They usually also store cash in hidden places in their houses, or bury it in small plastic barrels. In August 2012, for example, the police found €800,000 in cash while searching 15 different houses.

Criminals also invest money in real estate and businesses, however. One managed to buy up 74 private homes in the city of Eindhoven over a period of 6 years with an estimated value of €12 million. Another, a cannabis grower, bought a horse riding school and was arrested just before its planned opening by the mayor. Criminals also increasingly engage in charity and in sponsoring sports clubs. In the previous example, the cannabis grower's wife announced in the local newspaper that she would be organising special events at which handicapped children would be allowed to ride horses for free.

Another important development is that criminals try to infiltrate local politics, for example to influence the debate about drug policy, but also to favour their legitimate business undertakings in the municipality. Others are less subtle and turn to violence against local authorities if they interfere with their business. One notorious example is an attack on the town hall of Waalre in 2012, in which the building was set on fire and destroyed. A police investigation showed that the motive of the attack was probably a conflict between the local authorities and travellers about illegal edifices built at the local trailer camp. In several other municipalities, mayors had to be put under 24-h police protection, albeit temporarily, because of threats from the criminal underworld.

Finally, criminals nowadays seem less inclined to stay under the radar. Of course, most persons involved in organised crime are known to the authorities as well as to the local community, not in the least because they usually convert their houses into small fortresses with heavy-duty roller shutters, alarms, floodlights and CCTV cameras. In the past few years, however, many have also become visible members of outlaw motorcycle gangs such as Satudarah and "No Surrender". It is not clear, for

[3] The informer did not give a precise definition of the Tilburg area. The city itself and the adjacent village of Goirle have about 250,000 inhabitants. If the surrounding area is included, that figure rises to approximately 400,000.

instance, why Satudarah—originally a motorcycle club of doormen of Moluccan descent established in 1990—opened its ranks a few years ago to criminals from the travellers' community and admitted them as fully fledged members almost without a trial period. Today some 20 % of members do not even have a licence to drive a motorcycle (DLIO, 2014).

The authorities long took a relatively lenient approach to these developments. Cracking down on cannabis cultivation was, and by some accounts still is, considered problematical because it is viewed as the logical if undesired outcome of Dutch drug policy. Why put a lot of effort into combatting cannabis cultivation when we allow the sale of the same product in coffee shops? Successful criminal investigations had little effect because the key members of groups that operated nurseries with thousands of plants or exported several hundreds of kilos of cannabis per week were rarely sentenced to more than 2–4 years in prison, of which they only needed to serve two thirds (Spapens et al., 2007). Police officers noticed that during their prison terms, the "bosses" simply delegated tasks to their wives or a trusted "deputy" and kept running the business from jail.

Although studies showed that organised criminal groups play a pivotal role in the cannabis network, change came only very gradually (Cf Bovenkerk & Hogewind, 2003; Spapens et al., 2007). It came as a shock when a public prosecutor revealed during a seminar that between 2000 and 2005 at least 25 murders in the southern criminal underworld were cannabis-related (*Parool*, 2007). This by no means led to immediate changes, however. It was only after 2011 that the authorities took a different approach, particularly in response to the increasing violence against local administrative authorities. This gave rise to fears that the south of the Netherlands was becoming a "Sicilian state". In response, the authorities set up a taskforce to coordinate a multi-agency approach to the problems. They now target criminals and their activities not only through the criminal law but increasingly through administrative and fiscal measures, as well as any other creative interventions fit to disrupt criminal business processes. For example, in the case of the criminal who bought a large number of houses in Eindhoven, the police ran a small-scale investigation showing that he had falsified papers to acquire substantial mortgages. As a result, the banks revoked his loans and blacklisted him. He rented most of his property to students and the municipality began regular inspections of compliance with safety regulations. Not surprisingly, the inspections revealed numerous shortcomings and the owner was instructed to make improvements, backed by orders for administrative penalties to the tune of €1 million. His lawyer wrote to the mayor to complain that these actions, which of course were reported in the local press, had devastated his client's reputation and business, and that he could now not show his face anywhere. The letter was pinned to the wall of the taskforce's office as a mission accomplished trophy.

In 2014, however, it became clear that the authorities had been premature in thinking, as they did in 2012—in the midst of budget cuts at the public prosecutions office and a complex police reorganisation—that the taskforce would need only 2 years to drastically reduce cannabis cultivation. What is more, the rise in amphetamine production had added to the problems. Growing pressure on the national government resulted in the continuation of the taskforce and the assignment of 75 extra police officers to North Brabant, tasked specifically with combatting organised criminals and their activities that undermine society's integrity. At present, however, the effects of these additional efforts remain unclear.

Conclusion

From a theoretical and practical viewpoint, we can explore many different explanations for the historical observations presented above. Below I briefly mention four of them: criminal opportunities, networks, social exclusion and lack of effective countermeasures.

A common way to approach organised crime is from the opportunity perspective (Cf. Paoli, 2014). In North Brabant, one opportunity did indeed follow another from 1648 onwards. The rural gangs took advantage of the borders between jurisdictions, and ceased to exist as soon as the French occupiers centralised prosecution and established Gendarmerie units. In 1830, the Belgian border caused a shift to large-scale smuggling that continued until 1962. The criminal underworld then continued to rely on its contacts with persons who could deposit goods that were not entirely "clean". From the 1970s onwards, narcotic drugs gradually developed into the primary money maker. Once again, opportunities to sell the product to foreign customers appear to explain large-scale imports as well as indigenous production of alcohol, synthetic drugs and cannabis.

Second, from a network perspective we could hypothesise that the Brabant criminal underworld succeeded in developing a network of criminal relations mainly in the neighbouring countries of Scandinavia and the UK that enabled them to deposit all sorts of smuggled and, later, stolen and illegally produced goods. In the 1970s, drug trafficking further expanded the network to Lebanon, Pakistan, China, the USA, Australia and other countries. At present, we still know little about how such contacts have developed, and more importantly, whether and how key members of the North Brabant meso network succeed in monopolising them.

Third, social exclusion has facilitated the emergence of criminal groups in the area at different levels. In the seventeenth and eighteenth centuries, these groups consisted of immigrants from Eastern and Southern Europe and other groups living on the edge of society (see also Fijnaut, 2014: 64). In the twentieth century, the marginalisation of travellers explains in part why members of this community started to commit increasingly serious crimes.

Fourth, organised crime usually thrives in areas where the administrative authorities and law enforcement are weak (van de Bunt et al., 2014). This was certainly the case during the period of the large rural gangs. Although North Brabant became an equal part of the Netherlands in 1814, and the legitimacy of the authorities has not been contested as such, some believe that its regional culture is still more anti-authoritarian than usual and this could provide for an environment that facilitates criminals (Tromp, 2015). Although law enforcement certainly has not been weak, it is true that, as a rule, the Dutch police's criminal investigation departments are understaffed and were long hindered by organisational fragmentation (Fijnaut, 2012). Furthermore, cannabis cultivators in particular have had little to fear from the investigative authorities. However, the government has always responded to situations that got out of hand.

Clearly, comparative research will be necessary to explore these and other possible explanations in more depth, not only within the Netherlands by contrasting North Brabant with areas that seem to be less affected by organised crime, but also by comparing the province to "hotbeds" in other parts of Europe and beyond.

References

Adriaenssen, L. (2007). *Staatsvormend Geweld: overleven aan de frontlinies in de Meierij van Den Bosch*. Tilburg: Stichting Zuidelijk Historisch Contact.

Bovenkerk, F., & Hogewind, W. (2003). *Hennepteelt in Nederland: het probleem van de criminaliteit en haar bestrijding*. Utrecht: Willem Pompe Instituut voor Strafrechtswetenschappen.

van de Bunt, H., Siegel, D., & Zaitch, D. (2014). The social embeddedness of organized crime. In L. Paoli (Ed.), *The Oxford handbook of organized crime* (pp. 321–339). Oxford: Oxford University Press.

Cohen, H. (1975). *Drugs, druggebruikers en drug-scene*. Alphen aan de Rijn: Samson.

Dickie, J. (2013). *Mafia republic*. London: Hodder & Stoughton.

DLIO. (2014). Outlawbikers in Nederland. Woerden: Nationale politie.

van den Eerenbeemt, H. (1970). *Van mensenjacht en overheidsmacht. Criminogene groepsvorming en afweer in de meierij van's-Hertogenbosch, 1795–1810*. Tilburg: Stichting Zuidelijk Historisch Contact.

Egmond, F. (1986). *Banditisme in de Franse Tijd; Profiel van de Grote Nederlandse Bende, 1790–1799*. Amsterdam: De Bataafsche Leeuw.

Egmond, F. (1989). Georganiseerde misdaad en de overheid in het verleden: Nederland tijdens de 17e en 18e eeuw. In C. Fijnaut (Ed.), *Georganiseerde misdaad en strafrechtelijk politiebeleid* (pp. 11–22). Lochem: J.B. van den Brink.

Egmond, F. (1994). *Op het verkeerde pad. Georganiseerde misdaad in de Noordelijke Nederlanden 1650–1800*. Amsterdam: Uitgeverij Bert Bakker.

Egmond, F. (2004). Multiple underworlds in the Dutch Republic of the Seventeenth and Eighteenth Centuries. In C. Fijnaut & L. Paoli (Eds.), *Organised crime in Europe* (pp. 77–107). Dordrecht: Springer.

van den Engel, A., & Prummel, E. (2007). *Organised theft of commercial vehicles and loads in the European Union*. Brussels: European Parliament.

Fijnaut, C. (2012). *Het nationale politiekorps*. Amsterdam: Uitgeverij Bert Bakker.

Fijnaut, C. (2014). Searching for organized crime in history. In L. Paoli (Ed.), *The Oxford handbook of organized crime* (pp. 53–95). Oxford: Oxford University Press.

van der Giessen, M., Van Ooyen-Houben, M., & Moolenaar, D. (2014). *De export van in Nederland geteelde cannabis: een schatting van de omvang en een bespreking van de mogelijkheden en beperkingen van het onderzoek*. The Hague: WODC.

Gonsalves, R., & Verhoog, G. (1999). *Mr. Gonsalves memoires*. Amsterdam: De Arbeiderspers.

Gooren, W., & Rebel, J. (1998). *Trendkaart Veiligheidsatlas georganiseerde criminaliteit in de politieregio Brabant-Noord*. Tilburg: IVA.

Grootswagers, K. (1983). *De historie van het Loonse kerkdorp Kaatsheuvel*. Breda: Uitgeverij Brabantia Nostra.

Haarman, J. W. (1922). *Geschiedenis en inrichting der politie in Nederland*. Samsom: Alphen aan den Rijn.
Haenen, M., & Buddingh, H. (1994). *De danser*. Amsterdam/Antwerp: De arbeiderspers.
Husken, M., & Vuijst, F. (2002). *XTC smokkel*. Amsterdam: Uitgeverij M.
KLPD. (1993). Synthetische Drugs. Zoetermeer: Korps Landelijke Politiediensten, Divisie Centrale Recherche en Informatie.
KLPD. (2005a). Eindrapportage van het Project Polaris. Driebergen: Korps Landelijke Politiediensten, Dienst Nationale Recherche.
KLPD. (2005b). Criminaliteitsbeeldanalyse synthetische drugs 2002–2004. Driebergen: Korps Landelijke Politiediensten, Dienst Nationale Recherche.
Khonraad, S. (2000). *Woonwagenbewoners, burgers in de risicomaatschappij*. Utrecht: Uitgeverij Jan van Arkel.
de Kort, M. (1994). A short history of drugs in the Netherlands. In E. Leuw & I. Haen Marshall (Eds.), *Between prohibition and legalization. The Dutch experiment in drug policy* (pp. 3–22). Amsterdam: Kugler.
Kuppens, J., de Vries-Robbé, E., van Leiden, I., & Ferwerda, H. (2006). *Zware jongens op de weg. Een onderzoek naar georganiseerde diefstal in de wegtransportsector*. Arnhem: Advies- en Onderzoeksbureau Beke.
Meijer, R., Grapendaal, M., van Ooyen, M., Wartna, B., Brouwers, M., & Essers, A. (2003). *Geregistreerde drugscriminaliteit in cijfers*. Zoetermeer/The Hague: Korps Landelijke Politiediensten/WODC.
Middelburg, B. (2000). *De Godmother*. Amsterdam/Antwerp: Uitgeverij L.J. Veen.
Middelburg, B., & van Es, K. (1994). *Operatie Delta*. Amsterdam/Antwerp: Uitgeverij L.J. Veen.
Moerland, H., & Boerman, F. (1999). *Georganiseerde misdaad en betrokkenheid van bedrijven*. Deventer/Antwerp: Gouda Quint/Kluwer Rechtswetenschappen.
Paoli, L. (Ed.). (2014). *The Oxford handbook of organized crime*. Oxford: Oxford University Press.
Parool. (2007, 13 December). Veel geweld in hasjhandel grensstreek. Het Parool.
Pisters, L., & van Riemsdijk, M. (1996). Criminaliteit en Strafrechtspleging in Stad en Land van Breda, 1700–1795. *Jaarboek De Oranjeboom, 49*, 65–116.
Rawlinson, P. (2001). Russian organised crime and the Baltic states: Assessing the threat. Economic and Social Research Council, Working Paper 38. London: ESRC
RIEC Zuidwest, Integraal Afpakteam, Tilburg University. (2013). Integraal Appèl. Oosterhout/Breda/Tilburg.
Schreurs, A. (1947). *Het Kerkdorp St. Willebrord (het Heike)*. Utrecht: Dekker en Van de Vegt.
Sherman, L. W., Gartin, P. R., & Buerger, M. E. (1989). Hot spots of predatory crime: Routine activities and the criminology of place. *Criminology, 27*, 27–55.
Spapens, P., & Willemsen, M. (2002). *Tilburgs kookbuukske*. Liempde: Kempen uitgevers.
Spapens, P., & van Oirschot, A. (1988). *Smokkelen in Brabant*. Hapert: De Kempenpers.
Spapens, P., & Horsten, P. (1990). *Tappen uit een geheim vaatje, de geschiedenis van de illegale alcoholstokerijen in Nederland*. Hapert: De Kempenpers.
Spapens, T. (2006). *Interactie tussen criminaliteit en opsporing*. Antwerp/Oxford: Intersentia.
Spapens, T. (2008). *Georganiseerde misdaad en strafrechtelijke samenwerking in de Nederlandse grensgebieden*. Antwerp/Oxford: Intersentia.
Spapens, T. (2012). *Netwerken op niveau*. Tilburg: Prima Print.
Spapens, T., van de Bunt, H., & Rastovac, L. (2007). *De wereld achter de wietteelt*. The Hague: Boom Juridische uitgevers.
Tromp, J. (2015, April 18). Brabanders knappen hun vuiltjes zelf wel op. De Volkskrant.
Tweede Kamer. (1996). Vergaderjaar 1995–1996. 24072, nr. 17, The Hague: Sdu uitgevers.
Weijenburg, R. (1996). *Drugs en drugsbestrijding in Nederland*. The Hague: VUGA.

Chapter 5
'Struggling, Juggling and Street Corner Hustling': The Street Economy of Newham's Black Community

Kenny Monrose

Introduction

> Why don't you just fuck off to where you come from. So I did - I got on the 58 bus back to Forest gate (Smitty).

The front line in Forest Gate, Newham, East London will be debated here for the following reasons. Firstly, and most importantly for the purposes of this *liber amicorum*, this is an area Dick Hobbs is well acquainted with. He was born, raised and schooled in Newham, and spent some years as a dustman, and school teacher in Forest Gate. Therefore, it is my wish that this piece can in some way add an additional dimension to his celebrated publication record, as the inner workings of Newham's black community is not something which is hugely visible in his work. This is of course no surprise, and it is not difficult to see why, since minority populations by their very nature are insular in character, and are often suspicious to difference. Hobbs' early work mentions that the innovative nature and entrepreneurial spirit of the denizens and dwellers of East London is often informed by ethnic succession:

> Like Chicago's 'Little Hell', East London has functioned as an area of first settlement for generations of immigrants. Like its American counterpart the East End's isolation and reliance upon the whims of the market place take over from more traditional social forces, such as religion and the family, and by absorbing those characteristics appropriate to the market, a culture has been created that is a hybrid of various ethnic groups, yet still retains an essential identity that is not Jewish, Irish, West Indian, or Asian but is that of the East End (Hobbs, 1988:140).

Skulduggery as Hobbs defines it, often lies at the epicentre of the adapted behaviourisms adopted by East Enders. Within numerous accounts, Hobbs happens upon

K. Monrose (✉)
School of Law and Social Sciences, University of East London, London, UK
e-mail: K.Monrose@uel.ac.uk

G.A. Antonopoulos (ed.), *Illegal Entrepreneurship, Organized Crime and Social Control*, Studies of Organized Crime 14,
DOI 10.1007/978-3-319-31608-6_5

a number of mischievous characters. For example, in *Doing the Business* (1988) he spends time with an affable and extremely shrewd character known only as '*Jacko*' who after taking possession of an extendable ladder without the owners permission, and realising that it cannot be used for burglary, decides to utilise the device to make *a straight pound note,* and becomes a window cleaner. In East London this type of adaptive wisdom is common. The day-by-day entrepreneurial dexterity of East End characters such as '*Jacko*' is not unusual—anything and everything has the propensity for negotiation. The continuity and prevalence of the entrepreneurial spirit throughout East London, as we will see, is not only applicable to the 'indigenous' white working class that Hobbs chiefly comments on, but is of equal significance to black and minority populations, who were unable to forge access to the traditional lumpen options that were open to white working class men.

The data used within this chapter is from a relatively recent PhD thesis which examined the lifestyles and life histories of African Caribbean men in East London (Monrose, 2013). The methods used to unpack the associated complexities and intersectionality related to identity, gender and ethnicity highlighted in the study, were reliant on the application of a number of semi-structured interviews, and both formal and informal exchanges.

Newham- A Cold Sore on the Mouth of the Thames

> These properties are in an advanced state of dilapidation and decay. Hastily constructed for easy profit during the building boom of the Victorian and Edwardian era, housing here suffers from all sorts of defects. Normal Victorian houses were built with at least a slight damp proof to protect them, but many of the homes in Newham don't even have that: the top structures have gone, timbers were undersize and back additions were built with half brick, and not whole bricks. This is an east end phenomenon; you will never see it anywhere else in London (Newham Monitoring Project, 1984: 7).

Areas where the newly arrived immigrants settled, had very little public housing available. In Newham for example, the housing stock was depleted by 60 %, due to the blitz which took place during the war. The influx of an increased population, and an already ravaged housing stock meant that cramped living conditions were common. In addition, the local government housing sector often refused to house black people, for it might cause a level of resentment amongst the established white tenants:

> Nobody wanted to live next door to blacks Ken, that was the worst thing that could happen to you and your family (Taxi Terry).
>
> There are too many stinks of foreign cooking. You can say I'm racist if you like. The lifts are filthy because of their spitting and urine, and they leave rubbish everywhere (Dench et al., 2006:173).

Tied to difficulties of accommodation, was the matter of employment. Hobbs (1988) and Downes (1966), stress that historically the economy of the East End of London, particularly the boroughs of Newham and Tower Hamlets, where a significant number of blacks had become residents, relied heavily on the industry provided by the docks. The docks acted as the gateway to the wealth of the nation, as it was here that commodities and raw materials transported from the commonwealth arrived. The sheer expanse of the docks meant that a considerable workforce was necessary to keep it functioning in an effective manner. To be a dock worker during the post war years was considered a lucrative career, which upon entering, was regarded as employment for life. However dock work, was reserved primarily for white men, whose heritage lay in the local community. Therefore, the newly arrived blacks found it difficult to secure work here. Instead many were employed in the numerous factories and foundries situated *around* the docks, in companies such as Fords, Tate & Lyle and Fray Bentos (Benyon, 1974). By the late 1970s life in Britain became increasingly politically charged, particularly with reference to race and immigration (Gilroy, 1987; Solomos, 1988). Resentment of black presence increased to unprecedented heights, and with this we witnessed the re-emergence of extreme right-wing political groups such as the National Front and British Movement, who used the perceived threat of *'the coloureds taking over'* to gain support.

Preston (2007) suggests that at the core of the inequalities within British society lies the class structure. One of the more significant institutions to reflect these inequalities is the education system (Drew, 1995). Educational governance in Newham mirrored wider issues of social class and divisions of labour which were evident throughout society (Willis, 1977). Habitually students in Newham were unable to unfasten the cultural capital needed to successfully navigate the regimes which exist within schools, by virtue of not possessing the accepted linguistic code, accent and familiarity of *high culture*. This was significantly relevant to black students, who were instead encouraged to focus on lifestyle, sport and music, opposed to life chances, life skills and academic excellence:

> The obstacles confronting the West Indian child in the British classroom are tremendous, and are the chief cause of the notoriously slow progress he makes. Mainly because of his mutilating colonial heritage, the West Indian child is severely handicapped and cannot make the tremendous adjustment necessary to remedy the deficits in his socio-cultural background, which he must do if he is to take full advantage of the educational opportunities open to him in his new metropolitan environment. It is unrealistic to think, for example, that unaided -without sympathy, compassion and the provision of extra special facilities to facilitate the transaction—the young west Indian can overcome all short comings of his inferior educational upbringing and colonial origin and suddenly respond to the considerably different and more demands made on him by the British school system (Pryce, 1979: 120).

Parents who were economic migrants, and experienced the harshness of Caribbean paucity, saw an English education as a means by which their cherished children could escape the biting poverty that they had to endure. The reality however was somewhat different from this idealistic flight of fancy. What resulted in schools between black students and white teachers was a tempestuous '*us and them*' relationship (akin to politicians and police), or as defined by Fanon, as the relationship between the coloniser and the *'other'* (Fanon, 1967). The lasting perception of the British educational system for blacks in Britain was one of an institution in place to oppress, fragment and subjugate them:

> Teachers said I was rubbish. All the guys I hung around with were told the same thing as me. Papers, television, books, comics, police- whatever, they all said you were rubbish. So what do you end up thinking? (Fire).

By the 1980s the demography of Newham had shifted dramatically with the increased influx of black and Asian families, and as a result the local education authority could no longer sustain its unofficial colour bar, and restricted entry to its flagship, overwhelmingly white schools. This move proved unpopular among teachers who had been employed in these colour exclusive schools, and who it is alleged, were unhappy about *having* to teach an increased number of *ethnic* pupils (Newham Monitoring Project, 1991). As a result 'white flight' took place within the education sector, with senior teaching staff vacating their posts within the borough. Moreover, the south of the Newham, close to the docks (East Ham South, Canning Town, West Ham, Custom House and North Woolwich) began to develop a notorious reputation as an extreme right-wing stronghold, with racially motivated attacks commonplace, and even incidents of cross burnings taking place on the West Ham memorial grounds during the 1980s:

> No parent was happy to send a child to a school in the south of the Borough, for here the National Front was becoming organised (Newham Monitoring Project, 1991: 137).

Thatcher, Thatcher the Milk Snatcher

> People are really afraid that this country might be rather swamped by people from a different culture. The British character has done so much for democracy, our land has done so much throughout the world, that if there is any fear that it might be swamped, people are going to react and be rather hostile to those coming in (Margaret Thatcher, World on Action, Granada TV, 1978).

Even before her appointment as the British Prime Minister in May 1979, Margaret Hilda Thatcher was already courting controversy. As Secretary of State for education from 1970 to 1974, she was responsible for revoking free milk for children of infant and primary school age, an act which singled her out for extreme criticism. However, this was to be the beginning of a series of hard-line legislative measures which was to litter her three terms, and 11 year premiership. Her legacy will be remembered by many for the sheer number of violent civil disorders that the country witnessed under her watch. In addition, the new powers that Thatcher had given to the police, changed the face of British policing beyond all recognition. With Thatcher as Prime Minister the fabled golden age of British policing ended (Newburn, 1990). Community policing and policing by consensus was curtailed particularly within notorious urban environs such as Newham. With her implementation of target hardening, and deployment of military trained personnel into key positions of police authority, the cohesive and co-operative relationship between communities and law enforcement was destined to break down. The police were no longer a service in place to *serve* the public. Under Thatcher, they became a quasi-military organisation, in place to keep the working class subservient. One of the results of the militarization of the police was the inevitable criminalisation of black communities. In 1987 Metropolitan Police Commissioner Kenneth Newman outrageously insisted that areas inhabited by 'ethnics' should be policed as if policing terrorists[1]:

> There is one thing that policing terrorism has in common with policing ethnic ghettoes. Policing activities must be accomplished by social and economic measures, and the policies of the police and civil administration must be coordinated with a coherent strategy (Metropolitan Police Commissioner Newman 1987 cited in Rose, 1992: 37).

Numerous social maladies fouled Thatcher's tenure, but the so called race riots during her first term had huge ramifications which changed not only the face of race relations in Britain, but the manner in which police work was conducted. It was not only Liverpool and Lambeth that the exploitation of the notorious *sus law*[2] flourished, closer to home in Newham the infamous police initiative was frequently misappropriated:

> There were snatch squads all up and down Upton Lane then. One minute you could be trodding down the street minding your own business, and the next thing you know you were in the back of a meat wagon (Dave).

Britain was in economic decline by 1981 and Thatcher's Britain being economically depressed made stark reading. Although the country saw a fall in population, there was evidence of both housing shortages and high unemployment. Black communities felt the brunt of this. Black working youth at this time occupied the same labour market position as their parents, if they managed to secure any employment status at all, causing a huge level of disenchantment as the promises of integration, and the attempts at assimilation failed:

> It was a ticking time bomb for a generation of kids born in the UK. They were supposed to do better than their mums and dads, and were about to put themselves on the white collar market having been advised at school that they should view themselves as British, and at home that once they had an education doors would swing smoothly open (Bradley, 2000: 255).

Additionally, recreational facilities and social spaces were also restricted for black youths, meaning that the only few public places where black youth felt safe to gather and congregate, went on to be labelled as *Frontlines*, and frequently characterised as locations for all manner of social ills, such as drug dealing, prostitution and illegal activity. Black eateries, parties and even places of worship were often raided regularly by police, on so called '*coon hunting*' expeditions, and blanket stop

---

[1] Metropolitan Police Commissioner, Sir Kenneth Newman's, occupational history lay in having spent several years as chief of operations in the Royal Ulster Constabulary, through some of its more turbulent times. It, therefore, came as no surprise that some of the operational tactics he implemented whilst in command of the Met were based on his experiences in Northern Ireland. Newman was responsible for bringing plastic bullets to the streets of London, and also held office when CS gas was deployed for the first time outside of Northern Ireland. He was clearly an advocate of militarised and a heavy handed notion of policing.

[2] In 1824 the Vagrancy Act was introduced as a measure to deal with specific problems in England following the Napoleonic wars.

and search tactics adopted by the police on society's powerless, disenfranchised underclass further added to their perceived sense of alienation (Solomos, 1988):

> Locations where unemployed youths-often black youths-congregate: where the sale of and purchase of drugs, the exchange of stolen property and illegal drinking and gaming is not unknown. The youth's regard these symbolic locations as their territory, police are viewed as intruders, the symbolic authority, they equate with the criminal rookies of Dickensian London (Rose, 1992: 65).

The Development of the Blues, Shubeen and Front line

> Hey little girl don't forget that we've got a date. I'll be at the gate at precisely quarter to eight. So put on your best dress and don't be late. Yes, I would appreciate if you have some faith. We gonna have nice time tonight. We gonna rub this ya music tonight. We gonna have nice time tonight. We love tight (late night blues) Out of sight (late night blues). 'Nice time', Don Carlos, 1980, pirate records.

The blues party[3] and the shubeen[4] were an integral part of black British life from the early 1960s and are crucial to the understanding of the development of the front line, and the importance such venues served. The blues party was crucial in terms of the promotion of cultural solidarity and expression. In its original guise, the blues party was an informal gathering which took place within a selected domestic residence, typically at the extremity of the working week, away from the confines and rigours of a *West Indians* life in Britain. The sounds for the blues party originally surrounded the legendary Blaupunkt 'blue spot' radiogram which was an integral feature of the Caribbean home (McMillan, 2009; Samra & Fingers, 2014). Over time the sound system took over from the radiogram. (Sound system culture and the importance of it in black British culture is spoken about in-depth elsewhere, see Henry, 2006; Bradley, 2000; Back, 1988). A number of respondents who attended these events remarked on the meaning they held:

> All roads led to the blues dance. It was our thing. It was safe. It was an extension of our front room, and the vibes was always nice. There was a guy called *Chicken the thunderstorm* who would keep a blues all around East (London) it used to be ram, his dances were bad man……As the song says Girls like sand to match everyman, and music like dirt for your monies worth. There were loads of other sounds from the area. King original, Sledgehammer, Chappie Dread, and Jah youth, but Chicken was the one (Eric).

The impact of 'raving' (blues party or shubeen attendance) within black British life is not fully appreciated by those outside of the black British experience. For example, Harvard Professor Henry Louis Gates Jnr, an African American, upon a visit to Britain fails to appreciate the true significance of 'raving'. His sojourn to Britain relays an experience of night spent in what he calls *going blues*, noting the atmosphere therein was not one of celebration, jubilation and jollification which he

[3] A house party. The name is derived from the use of the 'blue spot' Blaupunkt radiogram.

[4] An illegal party which charges an entrance fee and sells alcohol, and is a space for illegal gambling; also known as a *push in*.

expected, but one of escape, where he is surrounded by uptightness and harsh expressions:

> Everybody was smoking Ganja: You could get high just from breathing. But what always struck me was how joyless it all seemed: nobody spoke or even laughed. Expressions were hard, affectless (Gates Jnr, 1997, in Owusu, 2000: 170).

Gates Jnr's perception is accurate in that blacks in Britain were discontented and victims of unrelenting social pressure. However, his assessment that these occasions are joyless remains questionable:

> Raving... I miss them day's bro. There was a session going on every weekend, and it gave us a place to meet up have fun and relax (Jerry).

Distinguished British record producer and musician Dennis Bovell adds: "A blues was the only place you could get a girl. Reggae dancing was full embrace, and if you were young and living at home, that was your only chance to spend a night in someone's arms" (in Spencer, 2011). The experience of the blues for Gates Jnr, as an observer of black British culture, are just that, an observation of one not touched by the lived realities of black British life. The blues was considered a safe space for black people who lived in communities where an invisible colour bar existed. Over time the blues party was transformed into the shubeen. The subterranean and seamy character of the shubeen was exploited to maximum benefit by those who facilitated them by the introduction of their entrepreneurial nuance and skill. Unlike a blues party, the full capacity of the building was used for the shubeen. Furnishings were removed, carpet displaced, a bar area was erected, and a gate charge administered. Additionally, and more importantly the shubeen provided a designated section for gambling. Marketing for the shubeen was normally unnecessary, as its location was firmly established. The shubeen typically began in the early hours, and it was not unusual for them to continue until the afternoon:

> I used to go out in my Farah's and Gabicci, but wear my football kit underneath so I was ready for Sunday football over Wanstead flats (Fire).
>
> You didn't have to know the door number of the shubeen - it was where the windows shook (George).

Life on the Line-the Street Bazaar

> You gonna mourn me on the front line; they got me living on top of my existence. Oh appreciating my resistance.
>
> (Eddy Grant, Living on the front line, 1979, Mercury Records)

Due to the well-documented accounts of over policing and criminalisation that beset black communities across Britain at the time, shubeens were subjected to regular police incursions and raids leading to the closure of prominent sites which in some cases caused tittle-tattle in high places; the John Profumo MP affair is one such example. However, as is common within the experience of marginalised groups, novel and innovative transformation soon took place. The blues and the shubeen, which was previously limited to a few rooms or an isolated building, now centred on a small public space; colloquially know as *the line* in the parlance of participants. These pocket-sized spaces attracted a large number of energetic young men that enabled *the line* to become a significantly robust and buoyant market place for black males to congregate and feel safe:

> The traditions of anti-colonialism dormant in the first generation of immigrants are resuscitated in the youth of the second generation. Thus areas such as Railton Road in Brixton or St Paul's in Bristol represent the toehold of colonial people fighting back against imperialism. The front line is a colony within the host country. The culture that has grown up there is the vanguard of Afro-Caribbean culture, it is a culture of survival which every now and then breaks out into open resistance (Lea & Young, 1984: 119).

The north stretch of Upton lane Forest Gate in the 1980s was regarded as the front line of Newham, both by the police and community members:

> This was our thing. No white people could be part of this- yeah they could buy stuff but never able to sell on our spot- it was our thing. Yeah there may have been a couple of stray white girls hanging around here and there but that was it-no white man or paki man could come around here (Jones).

South of the main A118 trunk road, had a high number of black residences. Many of the homes were owner occupied premises of families who had arrived to Britain in the 1950s. Like most economic migrants from the Caribbean, these were respectable and hard-working families, who were often involved with the church, and looked with scorn upon unlawful activity which could potentially lead to engagement with the police (Monrose, 2013). Therefore, sons were cautioned in no uncertain terms, to avoid the iniquitous faces and places on *the line*.

Despite the well-meaning but meagre provisions made by the church, state appointed leisure facilities for young people in Newham was lacking, particularly after the abolition of the GLC (Greater London Council) in 1986. As a result public space became fertile ground for a front line to develop. *Chester's* established itself as one of the most prominent spots on *the line* where the core of the socially excluded and disadvantaged black men gravitated. So strong was the reputation of *Chester's*, it soon drew people in from well beyond the boundaries of Forest Gate and Newham, and attracted individuals from black communities all over London, and sometimes beyond. Its popularity was due to its surroundings which provided all the necessary components for a street-based marketplace. *Chester's* formed part of a small retail holding, close to a bus stop and a mini cab office, phone box, sweet shop, and café. Behind the building was a warren of alleys, where deals of all kind would take place. Internally, Chester's was equipped with a pool table, chill out area and most importantly a gambling room. *Rapid* spent a number of years doing business from *Chester's*, describes what it was like:

> It was a place to meet up and do deals. It had a pool table, a little room to gamble in if that was your thing, and if you wanted a smoke you could. You have to remember Ken at the time all the government resources weren't going to the black community, we weren't getting anything. Chester's provided us with a place to hang out and do our thing, and gave us the opportunity to make a lot of money; it was an important place for so many reasons. People like to say that it was all bad, but it wasn't,—there was a lot of love there. We were happy for each other to be making a bit of money (Rapid).

As expressed by *Rapid, the line* was a place of importance where males felt free to display the varying forms of black masculinities and be at ease. This can be compared to Anderson's ethnography of street corner men in South Chicago (Anderson, 1999; 1976), and Pryce's (1979) work in Bristol, both of which examine the unique lifestyles of black men.

The Presentation of Black Masculinities

As I have stated elsewhere, the manner in which the black macho is staged can be adequately defined as a pictogram for powerlessness (Monrose, 2013). To be seen making money was vital to life on *the line*, and within the skill of being a good earner, lay the presentation of an image needed to not only to secure status among peers, but to reclaim the highly sought after notions of respect from wider society. These are prominent factors for those actively involved with doing deals on the *line*. *Dave* here speaks of an older highly favoured doyen who frequented the line, who he and other youths looked up to with an admiring gaze:

> He was my role model; we all looked up to him. The money, the jewellery, the clothes, even the way he walked. I wanted to be like him. If someone asked me what I wanted to be when I grew up I would say him. This guy always had a wad of cash on him, a big wad. There were a few people like that who made a lot of money. These guys drove E-type jags, Mercedes sports, Saabs; there was even someone who had a black Rolls Royce (Dave).

To carve out niche and earn good money on the line however was not an easy task, in fact *Blacker* states that it was onerous work, and not a vocation for those not willing to put in maximum effort:

> Being on that front line and being in Chester's was serious graft. There wasn't any time for skylarking, it serious business that was going on in there (Blacker).

Rapid adds

> I was all over the place working. One minute I'd be in Chester's the next I'd be down the road somewhere else hustling money. It wasn't like how it is nowadays with all that gang postcode madness. Everyone was free to make money where they could, and people around you were happy for you, if you were doing well.

However, although lucrative, hustling proved to be an incredibly precarious form of behaviour that was far from risk free. This was a world where reputation alone rules, and being perceived as unpredictable and dangerous is often crucial. Anderson (1976, 1999) maintains that the code and ethics dictated by *black street corner men,* demand particular displays of masculinity. For example, being able to fight or possessing a reputation to be able to manage one's self physically, is a primary tool in the hustler's amour in order to garner heightened level of social kudos. Even for those not proficient in unarmed/armed combat, the subcultural structure of urban street life demands that this form of masculine posturing at the very least is showcased:

> There are guys who were from good families and were good at school, but just wanted to be known for something...anything. I guess they didn't feel respected enough anywhere else so they came here to try and get stripes. They weren't bad really, just impressionists, and did stupid things to get attention. These are the ones that got into the most trouble. It got to the point that you just don't see them anymore (Jones).

Police harassment and monitoring was an ever present occupational hazard, which was no surprise due to the type and volume of criminality that was taking place. Whilst the police had their methods of scrutiny and surveillance of *the line*, participants boasted of how practiced and proficient they became to avoid capture:

> The police thought they were smart, but we had skills to spot them. There was this car, I'll never forget it. A blue Ford Sierra it was, registration number C** HEV. It was supposed to be unmarked but we knew it well (Dave).
>
> We watched everything and had our own little codes when we do our runnings. Unmarked cars? You could always tell if it was the bull [police] a mile off because of the little aerial on the back windscreen (George).

Increased proactive policing, harsher penal guidelines, and target hardening introduced by the Thatcher government, clamped down on any suspicion of illegal activity, targeting black communities through the length and breadth of the country, which meant the closure of popular spots such as *Chester's* . For the younger and more aspiring youths, *the line,* despite being devoid of the spots, remained a location where they began to gather and openly hawk all means of illegal wares including so called 'hard drugs'. No longer was the hustling that took place on *the line* discrete, but was now overt and audaciously displayed. This caused activity to spill into nearby residential streets and prompted an outcry from local residents, and the inevitable heavy handed response from the police:

> This was the times that coppers walked about on their own; this copper was trying to fuck with a youngster. Well the youngster wasn't having it and boxed him up and the next thing we knew his hat fell off—that was it, you can't knock a copper helmet off. He was on the radio and calling for reinforcements. In a flash it was like a riot... helicopters, meat wagons, all sorts. Loads of us got nicked (Dave).

The older more seasoned of the participants, saw the writing on the wall, and either pooled their resources together and set up their own legitimate places, or decided to superannuate from the adoptive hustler lifestyle:

> I was doing armed robberies, burglary, fencing and shit like that for a long time. I suddenly realised what a lengthy sentence would mean. At the time Maggie was handing out ten year sentences like jelly tots. Black guys like us were getting 10 or 15 for crap. I didn't want to be away from my family for that long, so I stopped; simple as that (K).

Conclusion

> *When a community is under siege, it must look inward to itself for hidden resources that might provide ammunition or sustenance* (Hobbs, 1988:175).

Front lines had a profound influence on black British life. The negative subtext of these locations is both well-known and well-documented. However, there still remain factors that remain silent. Firstly it must be remembered that these locations developed as a result of social exclusion and marginalisation, in a period when black people were considered as destabilising British society and regarded as police property. These spaces despite their criminal elements, allowed young blacks to feel safe, in what was a very racially prejudiced time. The solidarity which existed in these enclaves is something which is left unspoken, and as respondents stated, financial gain between participants was celebrated as they were happy to see their contemporaries *make a raise*, within a society which had blocked them from doing so. Unlike their parent's generation, this assembly was more forward thinking in terms of forging and establishing a foothold in British society. Money, skills and resources, which were cultivated by virtue of working *the line*, was amassed to set up businesses such as radio stations, promotion companies, and restaurants, which proved to be incredibly popular. The innovative techniques and cultural contributions that denizens of *the line* possessed also influenced popular culture. For example the acid house scene of the 90s as well as modern festival events, were heavily influenced by creativity of the doyens from *the line*. Black cultural identity layered with the complexities arising from being British, Afro-Caribbean, working class, and an East Ender, fused into an intricate and convoluted cultural compendium, which at the centre lies the spirit of enterprise and entrepreneurship that is a common thread in Hobbs' work on the East London.

References

Anderson, E. (1976). *A place on the corner*. Chicago, IL: University of Chicago.

Anderson, E. (1999). *Code of the streets: Decency, violence and the moral life of the inner city*. New York, NY: Norton.

Back, L. (1988). Coughing up fire: Sound systems in South-East London. *New Formations, 5*, 141–52.

Benyon, H. (1974). *Working for ford*. London: Allen Lane & Penguin.

Bradley, L. (2000). *Bass culture: When reggae was king*. London: Penguin.

Dench, G., Gavron, K., & Young, M. (2006). *The new east end: Kinship, race & conflict*. London: Profile Books.

Don Carlos, *Nice time, 1980, Pirate Records*.

Downes, D. (1966). *The delinquent solution*. London: Routledge & Kegan Paul.

Drew, D. (1995). *'Race', education and work: The statistics of inequality*. Aldershot: Avebury.

Eddy Grant, *Living on the frontline, 1979, Mercury Records*.

Fanon, F. (1967). *Black skin white masks*. New York, NY: Grove Weidenfeld.

Gilroy, P. (1987). *There Aint no black in the union jack: The cultural politics of race and nation*. London: Hutchinson Education.

Henry, W. (2006). *What the deejay said*. London: Nu Beyond.

Hobbs, D. (1988). *Doing the business*. Oxford: Oxford University Press.

Lea, J., & Young, J. (1984). *What is to be done about law and order?* Harmondworth: Pluto.

Margaret Thatcher. (1978). *World in Action, Season 14, Episode 11, Broadcast 2030 30/1/78*, Granada Television.

McMillan, M. (2009). *Front room: Migrant aesthetics in the home*. London: Black Dog publications.
Monrose, K. (2013). *It's not as simple as ABC: A qualitative study of African-British Caribbean men.* Unpublished doctoral thesis, Department of Sociology, University of Essex, Colchester, UK.
Newburn, T. (1990). *Keeping in touch: police-victim communication in two areas.* Research Study 116. London: HMSO.
Newham Monitoring Project. (1984). *Annual Report.* London: Newham Monitoring Project.
Newham Monitoring Project. (1991). *Annual Report.* London: Newham Monitoring Project.
Owusu, K. (2000). *Black British culture & society: A text reader*. London: Routledge.
Preston, J. (2007). *Whiteness and class in education*. Dordrecht: Springer.
Pryce, K. (1979). *Endless pressure*. Harmonworth: Bristol Classics.
Rose, J. (1992). *A climate of fear: The murder of PC Blakelock and the case of the Tottenham three*. Bloomsbury: Sale.
Samra, M., & Fingers, A. (2014). *Sound system culture: Celebrating Huddersfield's sound systems*. London: One Love Books.
Solomos, J. (1988). *Black youth, racism and the state: The politics of ideology and policy*. Cambridge: Cambridge University Press.
Spencer, N. (2011). Reggae: The sound that revolutionised Britain. *The Guardian*, January 30.
Willis, P. (1977). *Learning to labour*. London: Saxon House.

Chapter 6
'Earth, Water, Air, and Fire': Environmental Crimes, Mafia Power and Political Negligence in Calabria

Anna Sergi and Nigel South

Introduction and Methods

The involvement of organised crime reaches into many aspects of public services, from waste disposal to construction and maintenance. This often results in corruption, pollution and completed or semi-completed projects that are inadequate or even dangerous. Ruggiero and South (2010) have described such illegal services as 'dirty collar crime' and Walters (2013: 281; see also Szasz, 1986) observes that this kind of criminal enterprise has flourished as a result of 'lax implementation and enforcement' of rules and law and that today, this is 'an insight pertinent to southern Italy's procurement of waste contracts and lack of regulatory oversight'. The focus of this chapter is Calabria, where a system of unruly order operates in the interests of the 'ndrangheta and local elites to maintain weakness in regulatory oversight, contract compliance and environmental safeguards.

This chapter uses the latest reports from the Italian NGO Legambiente on environmental-mafia (ecomafia) crimes in Italy as well as in Calabria. This is combined with a qualitative reading of the data provided by OpenCoesione, an online interactive portal that collates news and progress of European-funded projects in each Italian region, according to sector. In addition to these sources and to other reports and documentation available from both EU and Italian law enforcement agencies and institutions (especially Anti-mafia operations and reports), five interviews with key participants in Calabria were carried out: two with Anti-mafia prosecutors, one with a Legambiente representative for the Calabrian Region, one with a Judge and one with an Anti-mafia Investigator; all provided valuable commentary, overviews and analysis.

A. Sergi (✉) • N. South
Department of Sociology, University of Essex, Colchester, UK
e-mail: asergi@essex.ac.uk; n.south@essex.ac.uk

G.A. Antonopoulos (ed.), *Illegal Entrepreneurship, Organized Crime and Social Control*, Studies of Organized Crime 14, DOI 10.1007/978-3-319-31608-6_6

Background: Calabria and the 'Ndrangheta

The Calabrian region is one of the 20 regions of the Italian Republic. It has a population of less than two million people in five provinces (Cosenza, Catanzaro, Reggio Calabria, Vibo Valentia and Crotone). According to both national data (ISTAT, 2013) and European elaborations (European Commission, 2015), Calabria has a very weak industry, very slow growth, very low GDP with very high unemployment rates. Within the European Union Regional Policy, Calabria is placed in Objective 1 of the Structural Funds as the region's GDP per capita is below 75 % of the EU average. Objective 1 is the Convergence Objective and aims at accelerating economic development in the identified depressed areas through development funds and social funds (European Commission, 2015). As underdevelopment, economic depression and unemployment are notoriously both causes and effects of organised crime, especially mafia-type organised crime, in certain territories (Arlacchi, 2010; Gambetta, 1993; Paoli, 2003; Varese, 2011), it is not surprising that in Calabria we find what Italian authorities consider the strongest, most connected and wealthiest Italian mafia (DNA, 2015). The clans belonging to the Calabrian 'ndrangheta—which, according to Anti-mafia investigators and prosecutors, is today a very flexible organisation—enjoy territorial autonomy, as well as the protection coming from a common brand (DDA, 2014; DNA, 2015).

As every mafia-type organisation in Italy, the 'ndrangheta—which we refer to by one single name to indicate a structure of power based on intimidation and having a long-term criminal plan—possesses a very strong political dimension. With the control of the territory, from the smallest to the biggest criminal and economic opportunity, the clans in the region often act as alternative governance players (Sergi, 2015a) and are the main, sometimes the only, investors (Arlacchi, 2009, 2010). On the other side, the governing class has often been unable to effectively deal with the most pressing tasks and requirements for development and innovation, while, at the same time, being often involved in public scandals of corruption and mafia proximity (Ciconte, 2013; Sergi, 2015a). Mafia scholars have identified the power vacuum—the persistent and constant inability of the governing class to effectively manage the politics of the region—as a framework to explain the mafia-politics nexus also in Sicily (Arlacchi, 1986, 2010; Gambetta, 1993). However, the 'ndrangheta clans have proved to be very active also in politics outside of Calabria (Sciarrone, 2014); this mirrors in the high number of proceedings for the dissolution of town councils for mafia infiltration also in the North of Italy (Mete, 2009).

As a qualified minority of Calabrian society, the 'ndrangheta is today a mafia-type criminal system supported by social prestige and embedded in society. As with any other mafia, the clans of the 'ndrangheta are concerned with financial gains and interests, but are also social structures with strategic goals (Sciarrone, 2010, 2011), which require their involvement and proximity with both political and entrepreneurial figures in the territory, the so called 'grey area' of mafia power (Ciconte, 2013; Mete, 2011). The 'ndrangheta clans share the same characteristics of the more general mafia typology whose power is

> *largely based on exercising violence, whether actual or threatened, and on exploiting traditional cultural codes and manipulating social relationships in order to establish mutual exchanges in political and economic circles* (Sciarrone & Storti, 2014: 41).

In this framework, which already denotes a strong link between the criminal clans and their territory, mafia clans in Calabria sit next to the governing class when they are not the governing class themselves (Sergi, 2015a) while pursuing a number of illegal activities, extortion racket primarily at the local level (Asmundo, 2011; Paoli, 2003; Ruggiero, 2010) and drug trafficking nationally and internationally (Sergi and Lavorgna, 2016; DNA, 2015; Gratteri & Nicaso, 2015; Sergi, 2015b). The origins of the 'ndrangheta as we know it today are quite recent. While forms of mafia power have been recorded in the region since Italy's post-unification, until the 1990s, the Calabrian mafia has been completely shadowed by a stronger Sicilian Cosa Nostra. This, however, does not mean that the criminal clans were not active prior to 1990s. In fact during 1970s and 1980s they were engaged in violent feuds and were accumulating money asking for ransom in dozens of kidnappings (Casaburi, 2010; Ciconte, 1992, 2011; Sergi, 1991). After the 1990s the alliances and the structures have changed while the wealthiest families have heavily invested in the drug trade with the money they had collected through kidnappings and extortion (Ciconte, 2011; Forgione, 2009), benefiting as well from the massive Anti-mafia action, which weakened Sicilian Cosa Nostra.

As of today, district and national Anti-mafia prosecutors sustain the existence of a very strong centralised organisation in the area around the capital city Reggio Calabria, where the clans, the '*ndrine*, maintain a very high degree of autonomy (Commissione Parlamentare Antimafia, 2008; DNA, 2014). Various Anti-mafia operations, such as Operation *Crimine* in 2010, have enriched the picture of the 'ndrangheta both locally and nationally. As described by the national Anti-mafia prosecutors (DNA, 2014: 109):

> *It is therefore confirmed (...) that when we refer to the 'ndrangheta, we talk about an organisation having a group of shared prescriptions, unitary structures recognised by affiliates (these structures, by the way, receive economic contributions from all the 'horizontal' structures of the association), and, finally, common instruments to resolve conflicts and produce regulations for all associates.*

At the national and international levels, clans of the 'ndrangheta have been using their family ties and deep territorial bond to increase their influence in the north of Italy (Lavorgna, 2015; Sciarrone, 2014) as well as in Europe (Europol, 2013; Sciarrone & Storti, 2014) or around the world, such as Australia (Sergi, 2015b), the United States and Latin America (Sergi and Lavorgna, 2016; Gratteri & Nicaso, 2015; Sergi, 2015c). In the past two decades, authorities, scholars and journalists have been paying an increased degree of attention to the 'ndrangheta, its movements abroad (Varese, 2011), its globalised markets (Calderoni, 2012) and its structure. This growing attention, while positively provoking a long overdue response to the phenomenon, has often shifted away the attention from the local dimension within Calabria itself, where the 'ndrangheta is born, lives, breathes, prospers and always returns. In order to understand how the criminal clans act in the Calabrian territory, how they interact with local, national, European economies and investors, it is necessary to understand the power they derive from their social and personal networks. While on one side it is the drug trade the main activity to contribute to the wealth of the clans, on the other side, also the drug trade would not be as successful as it is if not for the control over the territory. More than half of the cocaine shipped to Italy arrives through the Calabrian port of Gioia Tauro (DNA, 2014: 128). Other local activities, such as extortion, procurement of public contracts, fraud schemes in construction contracts, usury, embezzlement and exploitation of European funds (DNA, 2014, 2015) contribute to this mafia's profits and confirm the bond with the Calabrian territory as a whole. In brief, even though the 'ndrangheta clans are highly effective in their transnational businesses, their local dimension, through conditioning of the private and public sectors in Calabria, is fundamental for their prosperity and longevity.

European Governance, Regional Development and the Environment in Calabria

The European Union manages regional policies, their instruments and procedures in a decentralised manner through national and regional governments. Regional policies within the EU mirror and comply with various EU policies related, generally, to growth, development, support for innovation, information society, transparent administration, state aid, transportation and obviously good governance. Within EU policies, therefore, structural funds are a means of enabling regions to obtain '*greater levels of convergence with the EU in terms of economic prosperity, social welfare, quality of democracy and efficiency in providing public services*' (Greco & Cretu, 2011: 66). As stated, the Calabrian Region is one of the regions that fits within the EU Convergence Objective as

> [*t*]*he regional innovation system is weak and characterised by low R&D* [research and development] *investment. All indicators show a very limited innovation capacity with respect to both Central-Northern and Southern Italian regions* (European Commission, 2015).

EU Structural Funds are supported by four programmes:

1. The European Regional Development Fund (ERDF) for infrastructure and investment, generating jobs and SMEs;
2. The European Social Fund (ESF) for training, social integration and employment;
3. The European Agricultural Guidance and Guarantee Fund (EAGGF, Orientation section) for rural development and aid to farms;
4. The Financial Instrument for Fisheries Guidance (FIFG) for the adaptation of the fisheries sector;

Support to regions in Objective 1 is the main priority of the European Union's Cohesion Policy. As stipulated by article 158 of the EU Treaty, the Union works to 'promote harmonious development' and aims particularly to 'narrow the gap between the development levels of the various regions'.

Particularly, in Calabria, the relevance of EU Structural Funds to support innovation policy is crucial. More than 75 % of the overall Research, Technological Development and Innovation (RTDI) budget comes from these funds (European Commission, 2015), which essentially means that if the structural funding system does not work and is not effective, the region will never reach any of its strategic goals for growth and good governance. Regional innovation policies have been working with various principles, ranging from cooperation, internationalisation, development of private-public clusters and creation/growth of high-tech enterprises. The priority is definitely '*the creation of an innovation friendly environment able to support, create and attract new business*' (European Commission, 2015). The website of the European Union for the Calabrian Region notes that this includes, among other things, a concentration of resources in:

- Transport and Logistics, Cultural Heritage, Life Sciences, Agro-industry and ICT (which were already financed in the previous programme period).
- Renewable Sources and Energy Efficiency, Environment, Advanced Materials and Manufacturing Systems, Resources and Marine Environment (which are being financed ex-novo in the programme period 2007–2013).

The peculiar situation of Calabria, with its very weak political class and very strong entrepreneurial criminal system, necessarily affects the way funds are allocated, received and used. As noticed by Greco and Cretu (2011: 73),'*structural funds' management causes important changes in the domestic institutional structure, favouring the redistribution of powers at regional and local levels and represents a determinant factor for better governance at subnational level*' in Calabria. The region is underdeveloped when it comes to economic growth, and research constantly highlights the scarce productivity and high dependence on public expenditure when compared to other Italian regions (Ciani & DeBiase, 2015; Svimez, 2015). Some of the structural weaknesses of the regions are certainly made worse by the presence of both mafia groups and a negligent governing class (Sergi, 2015a). The convergence of interests between mafia clans and the political class does create a shared space of negligent governance that also includes the management and absorption of EU funds and effectively hinders innovation.

According to Legambiente (2015), there were 22 open investigations on corruption in relation to the environment in Calabria in May 2015. Legambiente's aggregation of data in 2015 also reveals that roughly 10 % of the total national illegal actions against the environment are committed in Calabria; Calabria ranks in the top five regions for the number of illegal activities against the environment committed overall. Even though these data are impressive, Legambiente warns, and the prosecutors confirm (DNA, 2015), that this is not the true extent of environmental crimes in Calabria. The presence of ecomafias—criminal clans proactively involved in environmental investments, frauds and illegal activities—is much higher than is officially reported. For example, the Legambiente Report for 2015 says that in

Calabria there are neither effective policies to handle and prevent waste nor procedures to contrast illegal activities linked to waste dumping. Existing policies focus on enlarging older dumps or opening new ones without really investing in recycling, for example. This is where criminal clans find their ideal business for an easy profit, while the governing class benefits from the lack of compliance around environmental issues that would instead require serious efforts and monetary investment from local authorities.

As it is often the case with 'ndrangheta clans, their involvement in business does not need to be strategic or even direct. Frauds and misuse of EU funds have been often at the centre of scandals in the media, especially when it comes to investments related to the environment, such as infrastructure (Freeman, 2012). However, although it seems that politicians or mafia clans are blamed for different scandals equally, the interactions between the two parties, and the involvement of 'ndrangheta clans in political choices related to investment concerning the environment, as well as the acquiescence or active involvement of the governing class in environmental crimes, still remains to be fully understood.

Environmental Investments and Deviance in Calabria

Investments and Funds

Illegal acts that harm the environment in Calabria are of different types. Calabria has amazing natural resources but still maintains secluded and untouched territories where controls are weak and there is a lack of care and preservation. According to Legambiente (2015), in 2014 in Calabria there were 555 offences against the environment, almost 10 % of national offences, 578 people were under investigation but only one had been arrested and 201 confiscation orders issued.

This section will first look at the area of Reggio Calabria, as the most interesting case to analyse qualitatively for what concerns structural funds, negligent governance, environmental crimes and mafia power. This specific focus allows an easier approach to smaller data. In fact, the city of Reggio Calabria, which is at the same time the largest city, with the highest mafia density (Calderoni, 2011, 2014; Sergi, 2015a) and the administrative capital of the Region, registers 2.5 % of the national total of crimes against the environment just by itself. The link between this figure and the involvement of criminal clans is easily grasped, but not easily proved, as most of the times a negligent political class contributes to the illegal activity by action or omission. The data provided by OpenCoesione, a portal on the use and allocation of structural funds in Italy, reveal that just for the area of Reggio Calabria there is a total investment of 1.1 billion Euros, with 2.872 open and monitored projects. In particular, protection and innovation activity related to the environment in Calabria is the second highest-ranking category of intervention and allocation of structural funds, following Transport (OpenCoesione, 2015). The 133.800.857 Euros currently invested within the Environment classification covered 22 projects in the area in 2013–2014 alone. Overall, the projects in the Environment sector can be categorised as below:

Element affected	Water	Air	Fire	Earth
No. of Projects	16	1	1	4
Examples of Projects	Optimisation, management and/or strengthening of drainage and depurative/ purification systems	Realisation of Meteorological Radar to prevent risks and handle emergencies	Realisation of an experimental system to monitor and prevent fires in woodlands	Unauthorised rubbish dumping
	Recovery and salvage on the coast			Support for separate collection of rubbish

By contrast, the Energy sector is among the lowest ranked for funding. In the Energy classification, which receives 16.403.521 Euros, we find 13 projects in Reggio Calabria. These 13 projects labelled under the category Energy are almost equally split in two sub-categories: six projects relate to renewable energies and seven relate to the maintenance, innovation and creation of installations to support the performance and development of buildings with different objectives.

A number of issues arise from a preliminary qualitative analysis of these 35 projects. It can be noticed, for example, how most of the projects are late in terms of completion dates, while others are officially on-going but have not yet started. Others have not received any portion of the funding allocated yet, which is a sign of problems in the allocation procedures. These considerations can be extended to further analysis of projects in Calabria. Four specific areas of intervention on the environment for both protection and innovation can be identified as examples where investments are prone to 'going bad': (1) the pollution of waters; (2) the multiple interests over renewable energies; (3) the irregularities in waste cycles; (4) the ageing of infrastructure more generally. This is visible not only for the area of Reggio Calabria but also for the whole region. In terms of numbers, in the last fund injection for 2007–2012, Calabria had 10.5 billion Euros invested in total, for a total of 33.449 projects (OpenCoesione, 2015). The Environment received 1.242.714.039 Euros for a total of 1.164 projects across the region, while the Energy sector received 476.738.968 Euros for a total of 1.032 projects overall.

A Closer Look

The pollution of Calabrian waters is one of many sad stories related to the environment in the region and in general in the South of Italy. In particular, pollution of the waters includes negligent or missing depuration processes, unauthorised dumping at sea, sewers directly connected to the sea, and oil spilling. In its report on water for 2013–2014, Legambiente (2014) counted 406 illegal activities at sea in Calabria (12 % of the national sum) with 461 people under investigation and 137 confiscation orders issued. Clearly, it is not only individual acts that fly below the radar because, more often than not, the violations also come from public and private buildings, i.e. hospitals, prisons, hotels, factories. Moreover, when it comes to depuration of waters, the stakes are even higher. On the one hand, all cases relate to malfunctioning and irregularities of depuration plants and infrastructure, which means that sewage ends up directly discharged into the sea. On the other hand, this malfunctioning is a structural problem of the whole drainage system in the region, which has attracted structural funds for projects of innovation and intervention, often not allocated due to lack of political will or adequacy of companies and contractors to carry out the projects (Legambiente, 2015). OpenCoesione reveals that in 2015 there were 35 open projects in the whole region allocated from Structural Funds 2007–2013 solely for water depuration and improvement of drainage systems across the region, including a few in the area of Reggio Calabria. A closer look at these projects shows that most of them have been discontinued and the end date of the project has passed without a new date being announced or publicised. As indicated by one of the investigating judges in one of the most affected areas with polluted sea and shores in Calabria:

> [*w*]*ith all the difficulties to handle and manage the projects, basically everything is done through bribes or at least in the vision of gain; the politician needs to see a clear profit of any sort or he/she won't proceed.*

Moving to the second area of investment, renewable energies are today a very lucrative and growing business in Calabria. When looking at the number of projects in the region we see how Calabria in theory invests in both wind power (68 open projects) and photovoltaic (416 open projects); this is because the region is geographically inclined and privileged, as is the rest of Southern Italy, in developing these technologies. In general, the economic benefits of an installation that produces electric energy from renewable sources, especially wind and photovoltaic, are linked to both the acquisition of state incentives and the sale or self-consumption of the energy once generated. In both wind power and photovoltaic sectors, there are multinational and large companies both domestic and foreign that compete for investments. In these sectors, and especially in Calabria, the biggest risk is that the very complex bureaucracy required to have the projects assigned—and the general lack of control over the projects once underway—might create opportunities for criminal infiltration, money laundering and general lack of compliance (Caneppele, Riccardi, & Standridge, 2013). Safeguarding investments in renewable energies while also protecting the environment means: avoiding infiltration or laundering of proceeds of crime through energy projects; preventing criminal networks from tampering with tenders and contracts; detecting corrupt relationships and the exchange of favours aimed at avoiding compliance or the granting of (false) authorisations and falsification of controls on projects. Renewable energies are, for Legambiente, the sector where frauds are more likely to go undetected (Legambiente, 2014). More importantly, as the interests involved are political, economic and criminal, the risks associated with illegal activities related to renewable energies are also associated with the negligent application of procedures and controls on wind farms or on photovoltaic plants, which could then represent a hazard for the environment, workers and communities. As declared by a Legambiente analyst in Calabria:

> *Both traditional and more modern installations for renewable energies are often built with lots of promises, but then you realise that they have been built where they shouldn't have been built. Someone has deposited false declarations. This 'someone' is close to the clan, is a mediator who knows how to exploit the funds and how to get the technical support needed to declare false measurements.*

When it comes to area 3, waste cycles, according to Legambiente (2015), Calabria has been neglected by the media over the past few years while the neighbouring region, Campania, has been at the centre of attention with scandals related to local authorities and to the clans of the Camorra infiltrating and directing the waste business. However, in Calabria problems with waste are not only present but also potentially very dangerous. The Parliamentary Inquiry Commission on illegal activities connected to the waste cycle has more than once reprimanded Calabrian choices:

> *Waste recycling is slow to start notwithstanding a substantial injection of financial resources from the EU to the Calabrian region. (...) [Calabria is] totally lacking those implantations, which, on the basis of latest evolution in technology applied to industries, guarantee the correct disposal of urban waste* (Commissione Parlamentare, 2011: 36).

At the same time, in Calabria there is another dimension, particularly worrisome, which relates to waste: radioactive materials, especially those disposed of at sea. Calabria has been at the centre of national and international news in recent years (BBC, 2009) for the so-called *navi dei veleni*, ships of poison, sunken vessels of nuclear and radioactive materials (allegedly 30) in the sea around both Calabrian coasts, never officially found but whose locations are suspected and investigated. The involvement of the 'ndrangheta in these matters has been announced by investigators on various occasions but never really proven as this became a matter of national security. As observed by the first Anti-mafia prosecutor who worked on the case:

> *The same channels used for trafficking arms became the channels of illegal waste, of whatever type. First in some African countries, such as Somalia, then South Africa, then in Latin America, especially Panama. But then in Calabria, as the state does not have any idea of how to control the territory, they clearly had a free zone. The control of the territory in Calabria secured the operations on land, then they just had to buy old vessels, have them under insurance, fill them with any type of waste they were given, drown them at sea, get the insurance money and walk away free, as to drown vessels at sea is virtually not a crime. How could that be picked up?*

The ships of poison, as well as other activities linked with toxic waste and illegal waste disposal, are all linked to the lack of interventions and controls over drainage systems, to the pollution of water and to the reclamation of contaminated land. In brief, the issues around illegal and toxic waste dumping are issues of control of the territory as well as slackness in control and policing from authorities. As the special parliamentary commission for the waste emergency in Calabria in 2011 pointed out, in Calabria there are structural problems that make waste collection cumbersome. These are the problematic geographical distances of certain municipalities isolated from others, the mountains and territories associated with earthquake risks, and the lack of appropriate plant and infrastructure, for example; these are also the areas where European funds have been mostly allocated. Notwithstanding the injection of funds, these problems are today the same as they were in 1999 when the national government declared the state of emergency in Calabria for waste disposal and appointed an external Commissioner (Commissione Parlamentare, 2011). There are, in addition, problems that are linked with the 'ndrangheta clans especially in the area of Reggio Calabria but also examples where corporations outside Calabria worked with mafia clans to handle hazardous waste hidden in trucks left in common dumps in Calabria (DNA, 2015). The interest of mafia-type groups of the area in the waste management and disposal business was a historical opportunity unlikely to be missed, according to the Parliamentary commission in 2011, because essentially it only requires money to invest without any other specialisation. The consequences, in terms of harm to the environment and health, are not part of mafia's risk analysis for their investments and their operations can be flexible, even 'lending' territory in the region to other criminal clans, such as the Camorra clans, which have been working with the Calabrians in disposing of waste illegally in both regions (Commissione Parlamentare, 2011; DNA, 2015).

Importantly, the cycle of waste management and disposal, the interests around renewable energies, and the pollution of waters are all essentially linked to a more general point, which is point 4, the ageing and weak status of infrastructure in Calabria. As will be argued, this is the point of intersection between mafia power and negligent governance that epitomises the situation in Calabria. As described, funds are allocated to build, maintain and strengthen drainage systems and to reclaim lands. They are also allocated to maintain old and to construct new plant and installations for renewable energies. Finally, funds are allocated to support waste collection through new systems and to enlarge and strengthen existing dumps. Eventually, these projects depend on the capacity of the construction sector to work well and efficiently. As indicated by the Parliamentary Commission on the illicit activities linked to the waste cycle in Calabria in 2011, 'ndrangheta clans have always been attracted to the 'cement cycle', involving the construction sector, which includes unauthorised excavations, illegal activities against the landscape related to construction, and frauds against public administration for the construction of public works. This interest in constructions has been particularly visible in the sagas of road construction, especially the A3 motorway Salerno—Reggio Calabria, which has been a scandal at the centre of various investigations and international reports (Donadio, 2012).

In 2003–2004, Anti-mafia Operation *Arca* established that since the 1990s some of the main clans in the area had a system in place to secure control of subcontractors, through extortion and direct or indirect administration, in order to benefit from public and structural funds over the building of the motorway. Between 2007 and 2010, an EU anti-fraud investigation demanded that Italy should repay £307 million to the EU when '*more than 381 million euros was lost through fraud, fake contracts and ghost road works*' (Waterfield & Squires, 2012). The investigation found the highest levels of corruption involving all levels of public offices in the region. Moreover, Operation Arca has also brought to the attention of the authorities how, amongst other things, sub-contractors had used the motorway for other purposes. Under the major road trajectories the authorities have unearthed non-hazardous and hazardous waste as filling materials. The defence force 'Carabinieri' has advanced the hypothesis that through this system the clans have buried toxic and/or radioactive waste too but that in this they are probably acting for others (Commissione Parlamentare, 2011). As encapsulated in the words of one of the Anti-mafia prosecutors who worked on the 'ships of poison':

> *Yes, the 'ndrangheta has control over the territory. Undisputed. But in these matters, in environmental issues let's say, waste, renewable energies, dumping of toxic materials at sea, they are an ignorant monster. It is clear to see that they are the investors or the 'cleaners', but there is obviously someone else, the masonry, politicians in Italy or even abroad, they are behind this.*

Last but not least, the existence of old and unfit infrastructures relates back to the costs of maintenance of old and new plant and infrastructure, for example, for renewable energy projects—which, as noted, also require specialist knowledge and are therefore expensive. Similarly, the existence of unauthorised dumps and the lack of controls over the dumping of waste at sea depend on the extended use of drainage and waste collection and disposal systems that are old, overfilled and would need expensive investments to be updated and made fit for purpose. As noticed by one Investigator:

> *Reality is that these systems, in order to comply with the requirements of the law for the protection of the environment, do cost a lot and require specialism. So on one side you need and welcome mafia money, but there is no 'influencing' of public funds necessarily. Controls and compliance cost a lot. But also expertise costs a lot. If you are in the business, you don't necessarily ask where the expertise comes from.*

Innovation and Protection of the Environment in Calabria: Between Mafia Power and Negligent Governance

To scholars and any interested and careful observer, Calabria appears to be a peculiar region where, in a relatively small geographical area, what can be seen is the mutually advantageous cohabitation of mafia clans, lazy public administrators, corrupt public officials and politicians, all at the expense of a community of people that seem passive and unaware of their misfortunes (see also Ruggiero & South, 2010). As the EU injects money to restructure, innovate and promote convergence, the funds expended in Calabria, specifically but not only in the Environment and Energy sectors, seem to make little difference or at the very least feed suspicions of corruption or even fraud. The innovation that the EU wishes to support is resisted in Calabria. Even when the projects do reach a successful visible end point without delays or scandals, the delivered projects are deficient.

When it comes to the Environment and the protection of natural resources, Calabria suffers from both the pressure and density of mafia power, as well as from the negligence of the political class in implementing controls and allocating funds from the convergence schemes. It is not news that political power in Southern Italy is highly defective (Gambetta, 1993; Sciarrone, 2011) as well as that 'ndrangheta clans in the region are involved in political and financial decisions and are strong because of their will and ability to acquire and use power (Paoli, 2003; Sergi, 2015a). It can be argued that there is a systematic interpenetration between mafia interests and malpractices or omissions at the political and administrative levels in Calabria. It is, again, not news that some members of the public administration have known ties to the clans and are more or less directly subject to mafia influence while members of clans have often participated in public administration at their convenience. When it comes to the use of money, especially the injection of funds from the EU for convergence purposes, it seems that the line between mafia and political/administrative negligence is totally permeable. This is very visible in a preliminary analysis of the projects within the Environment or Energy categories. The normative complexity in these sectors has facilitated and never solved the existence of conflicts over competences among public bodies in the region. These conflicts, on one side, slow down procedures of control and due diligence, on the other side open up projects and opportunities to specialist figures, the *intermediaries* or *facilitators* (Legambiente, 2015), individuals or even companies, who work for the clans and know how to twist the regulations in their favour due to the cumbersome nature of bureaucracy as well as the technicalities of the projects. Intermediaries are able to acquire lands and obtain authorisations very quickly in a world of murky connections and shadowy dynamics (Legambiente, 2015).

A Green Perspective on Organised Crime in Calabria

The kind of opportunism and exploitation responsible for environmental degradation in Calabria can also be considered from the point of view of a now substantial body of work that adopts a 'green' perspective to examine the criminological, legal, cultural and public health consequences of environmental crimes and harms (see e.g. South & Brisman, 2013). As Walters (2013: 281) notes, one leading NGO in this field, the Environmental Investigation Agency, has suggested that '*environmental crime is currently one of the most profitable forms of criminal activity*' and that it is therefore '*no surprise that organised criminal groups are attracted to its high profit margins*'. In response, an environmentally aware criminology can contribute to an interdisciplinary approach to both public policy and environmental activism in ways that may help to formulate new conceptions of offending and regulation.

With regard to the occurrence of environmental harm and crime, Lynch and Stretesky (2014) have described how certain forms of economic and social structure can produce '*zones and patterns of ecological/environmental disruption*' or '*ecological disorganisation*' (157), both urban and rural (168). In this process, capitalism plays a significant role in creating hazards, pollution and toxic wastes that require disposal. In general, in seeking solutions to the problems created, capital will seek to externalize the costs and find the least expensive responses (Lynch & Stretesky, 2014: 169). Developing this analysis further, Stretesky, Long, and Lynch (2013) have applied a perspective from ecological Marxism to the damaging and exploitative cycles of contemporary capitalist growth economies. The idea of the 'treadmill of production' (Gould, Pellow, & Schnaiberg, 2004) is usually employed in analysis of the interplay of the private sector, the state, and labour and consumers, resulting in ecological disorganisation. However the role of environmentally destructive activities pursued by organised crime groups in contributing to ecological disorganisation is also significant. Until now this point does not seem to have been considered in relation to this analytic approach. In essence, the processes underpinning the treadmill of production and ecological disorganisation involve 'ecological withdrawals' and 'ecological additions'. The former will generally involve extraction of raw materials and resources from the environment, and the latter refers to the resulting waste, toxicity and pollution emitted or burned off into the atmosphere, disposed of in the waters of rivers and seas, or deposited and buried in the earth.

Stretesky et al. (2013) use the treadmill of production framework to show how corporate capital profits from the exploitation and misuse of the resources of the natural world. In a parallel way, although the profiteering of organised crime groups and corrupt political classes differs from that of corporate capital in some respects, the most fundamental feature can be seen as common. This is that the logic of accumulation of wealth and power is shared not only across corporate interests but also by mafia groups and by the local ruling class. Both of the latter are involved in servicing—while simultaneously exploiting—the system of opportunities that accompanies initiatives designed to stimulate further economic growth. As many discussions of organised crime have shown, the entrepreneurial criminal is in many respects a mirror of the legitimate entrepreneur (Ruggiero & South, 2010). In this case, criminal enterprises benefit directly from inefficient and poorly managed legitimate opportunities. Thus, considered from the point of view of the treadmill of production thesis, the profit and power achieved by 'ndrangheta clans and ruling elites depend substantially upon the control and misuse of EU structural and innovation funds directed at processes of ecological 'withdrawals' and ecological 'additions'.

Conclusion

In Calabria, the normative complexity of the environment sectors, together with the weak management of plant and infrastructure, and the missing implementation of control, not only dissipates structural and innovation funds but also highlights the lack of a proactive political class that favours illegality and mafia interference. Decision-making processes, specific technical choices and accountability are complex anywhere and everywhere in these sectors, but in Calabria in particular they are complicated in ways that also enable fluidity of operations and for control and profit to move from the legal to the illegal. Both criminal clans and administrators, for different reasons and motives, move within a shared area of sleaze, malpractice, corruption and fraud. The infiltration in, and the interferences with, structural funds does not appear to occur solely as a result of any rational plan of criminal clans to secure investments and money, but it is enabled and allowed by the propensity of the ruling class of administrators to incentivise the entrance of mafia into these investments through corrupt behaviours, unethical decision-making and lazy controls. As noted above, the logic of accumulation of wealth and power is shared both by mafia groups and by the ruling class that should fight them. As demonstrated in recent studies about the political nexus of 'ndrangheta clans in Calabria, for investments and use/abuse/misuse of structural and innovation funds, mafia clans and political negligence *concur and collude* regarding the nature of governance quite successfully (Sergi, 2015a).

This however does not mean that the boundaries between the legal and the illegal are completely done away with. Mafia infiltration in environmental investments and management of resources has also brought the inclusion of 'eco-mafia aggravation' into the latest environmental crime legislation of May 2015. Article 452-octies of law 68/2015 provides a charge of aggravation and sentences where mafia-type criminal organisations (as defined in article 416-bis of the penal code) are found '*to commit any of the crimes against the environment…or acquire management or control of economic activities, licences, authorisations, contracts or public services for the environment*'. Moreover, if in these criminal activities, there is the ascertained participation of public officials whose functions relate to the environment, the sentences are harsher. This demonstrates, once again, how the picture is clear to the authorities, which note that mafia crimes occur alongside the likelihood that administrators, public officials and politicians might have facilitated and/or participated in this criminal activity.

References

Arlacchi, P. (1986). *Mafia business. The mafia ethics and spirit of capitalism*. New York, NY: Verso.

Arlacchi, P. (2009). *Mafia, peasants and great estates. Society in traditional Calabria*. Cambridge: Cambridge University Press.

Arlacchi, P. (2010). *La mafia imprenditrice. Dalla Calabria al centro dell'inferno*. Milano: Il Saggiatore.

Asmundo, A. (2011). Indicatori e costi della criminalita' mafiosa. In R. Sciarrone & Fondazione Res (Eds.), *Alleanze nell'Ombra: Mafie ed economie locali in Sicilia e nel Mezzogiorno* (pp. 49–66). Roma: Donzelli.

BBC. (2009). Mafia 'sank ships of toxic waste', *BBC News Europe*, 16 September 2009. Retrieved October 11, 2015, from http://news.bbc.co.uk/1/hi/world/europe/8257912.stm.

Calderoni, F. (2011). Where is the mafia in Italy? Measuring the presence of the mafia across Italian provinces. *Global Crime, 12*(1), 41–69.

Calderoni, F. (2012). The structure of drug trafficking mafias: The 'Ndrangheta and cocaine. *Crime, Law and Social Change, 58*(3), 321–349.

Calderoni, F. (2014). Mythical numbers and the proceeds of organised crime: Estimating Mafia proceeds in Italy. *Global Crime, 15*, 138. doi:10.1080/17440572.2014.882778.

Caneppele, S., Riccardi, M., & Standridge, P. (2013). *Green energy and black economy: Mafia investments in the wind power sector in Italy*. Milano: Università Cattolica di Milano – Transcrime.

Casaburi, M. (2010). *Borghesia mafiosa. La 'ndrangheta dalle origini ai giorni nostri*. Bari: Dedalo.

Ciani, E., & DeBiase, G. (2015). *European structural funds during the crisis: Evidence from Southern Italy*, Temi di Discussione, Working Papers No. 1029, Banca d'Italia. Retrieved from https://www.bancaditalia.it/pubblicazioni/temi-discussione/2015/2015-1029/index.html?com.dotmarketing.htmlpage.language=1.

Ciconte, E. (1992). *'Ndrangheta: Dall unità a oggi* (2nd ed.). Roma: Laterza.

Ciconte, E. (2011). *'Ndrangheta*. Soveria Mannelli: Rubbettino.

Ciconte, E. (2013). *Politici (e) malandrini*. Soveria Mannelli: Rubbettino.

Commissione Parlamentare. (2011). Attività ciclo rifiuti.

Commissione Parlamentare Antimafia. (2008).

DDA. (2014). *Relazione semestrale. II Semestre*. Rome: Direzione Investigativa Antimafia.

DNA. (2014). *Relazione annuale sulle attività svolte dal Procuratore Nazionale Antimafia e dalla Direzione Nazionale Antimafia nonché sulle dinamiche e strategie della criminalità organizzata di tipo mafioso*. Rome: Direzione Nazionale Antimafia.

DNA. (2015). *Relazione annuale sulle attività svolte dal Procuratore Nazionale Antimafia e dalla Direzione Nazionale Antimafia nonché sulle dinamiche e strategie della criminalità organizzata di tipo mafioso*. Rome: Direzione Nazionale Antimafia.

Donadio, R. Corruption Is Seen as a Drain on Italy's South. *New York Times*, 12 October 2012. Retrieved from http://www.nytimes.com/2012/10/08/world/europe/in-italy-calabria-is-drained-by-corruption.html?pagewanted=all&_r=0.

European Commission. (2015). Calabria Region, Profile. Retrieved October 11, 2015, from https://ec.europa.eu/growth/tools-databases/regional-innovation-monitor/base-profile/calabria.

Europol. (2013). *Threat assessment. Italian organised crime*. Europol, The Hague. Retrieved October 11, 2015, from https://www.europol.europa.eu/.../italian_organised_crime_threat_0.pdf.

Forgione, F. (2009). *Mafia export. Come Cosa Nostra, 'Ndrangheta e Camorra hanno colonizzato il mondo*. Milano: Dalai Editore.

Freeman, C. (2012). Making a killing on contracts: How Italy's Mafia has plundered EU building funds, *The Telegraph*, Europe 20 October 2012. Retrieved October 11, 2015, from http://www.telegraph.co.uk/news/worldnews/europe/italy/9622553/Making-a-killing-on-contracts-how-Italys-Mafia-has-plundered-EU-building-funds.html.

Gambetta, D. (1993). *The Sicilian mafia: The business of private protection*. Cambridge, MA: Harvard University Press.

Gould, K. A., Pellow, D. N., & Schnaiberg, A. (2004). Interrogating the treadmill of production: Everything you wanted to know about the treadmill but were afraid to ask. *Organization and Environment, 17*(3), 296–316.

Gratteri, N., & Nicaso, A. (2015). *Oro bianco*. Milano: Mondadori.

Greco, R., & Cretu, G. (2011). European governance and regional development: The management of the structural funds in Calabria. *Cooperazione Transfrontaliera, Sviluppo Locale e Ambiente, XX(1)*.

ISTAT. (2013). *L'Italia del censimento. Struttura demografica e processo di rilevazione*. Retrieved from http://www.istat.it/it/files/2013/01/Calabria_Volume.pdf.

Lavorgna, A. (2015). La 'ndrangheta migrante si espande a Nord-Est. *Giornale di Storia Contemporanea, 18*(1), 123.

Legambiente. (2014). *Ecomafia 2014*. Napoli: Marotta e Cafiero Editori.

Legambiente. (2015). *Ecomafia 2015*. Napoli: Marotta e Cafiero Editori.

Lynch, M. J., & Stretesky, P. B. (2014). *Exploring green criminology: Toward a green criminological revolution*. Aldershot: Ashgate.

Mete, V. (2009). *Fuori dal comune*. Roma: Bonanno.

Mete, V. (2011). Scioglimenti, dati in rete contro il silenzio. *Guida agli Enti Locali – Il Sole 24 Ore, 15*, 20–23.

OpenCoesione. (2015). *Regione calabria. Tutti i progetti*. Interactive Portal. Retrieved October 11, 2015, from http://www.opencoesione.gov.it/territori/regioni/calabria-regione/.

Paoli, L. (2003). *Mafia brotherhoods: Organized crime, Italian style*. New York and Oxford: Oxford University Press.

Ruggiero, V. (2010). Who corrupts whom? A criminal eco-system made in Italy. *Crime, Law and Social Change, 54*(1), 87–105.

Ruggiero, V., & South, N. (2010). Green criminology and dirty-collar crime. *Critical Criminology, 18*(4), 251–262.

Sciarrone, R. (2010). Mafia and civil society: Economico-criminal collusion and territorial control in Calabria. In J. L. Briquet & G. Favarel-Garrigues (Eds.), *Organized crime and states. The hidden face of politics* (pp. 173–196). New York, NY: Palgrave Macmillan.

Sciarrone, R. (2011). Mafie, relazioni e affari nell'area grigia. In R. Sciarrone & Fondazione Ras (Eds.), *Alleanze nell'ombra. Mafie ed economie locali in Sicilia e nel Mezzogiorno* (pp. 3–47). Roma: Donzelli.

Sciarrone, R. (Ed.). (2014). *Mafie del Nord. Strategie criminali e contesti locali*. Roma: Donzelli.

Sciarrone, R., & Storti, L. (2014). The territorial expansion of mafia-type organized crime. The case of the Italian mafia in Germany. *Crime Law and Social Change, 61*, 37–60.

Sergi, P. (1991). *La 'Santa' violenta*. Periferia: Cosenza.

Sergi, A. (2015a). Mafia and politics as concurrent governance actors. Revisiting political power and crime in Southern Italy. In P. C. van Duyne, A. Maljević, G. A. Antonopoulos, J. Harvey, & K. von Lampe (Eds.), *The relativity of wrongdoing: Corruption, organised crime, fraud and money laundering in perspective* (pp. 43–70). Oisterwijk: Wolf Legal Publishers.

Sergi, A. (2015b). The evolution of the Australian 'ndrangheta. An historical perspective. *Australian and New Zealand Journal of Criminology, 48*(2), 155–174.

Sergi, A. (2015c). Calabrian mafia extends its international reach. *Jane's Intelligence Review*. (August), 41–44

Sergi, A., & Lavorgna, A. (2016). *'Ndrangheta. The glocal dimensions of the most powerful Italian Mafia*. London and New York: Palgrave Macmillan.

South, N., & Brisman, A. (2013). *Routledge international handbook of green criminology*. London: Routledge.

Stretesky, P. B., Long, M., & Lynch, M. (2013). *The treadmill of crime: Political economy and green criminology*. Abingdon: Routledge.

Svimez. (2015). *Rapporto Sull'Economia del Mezzogiorno. SVIMEZ Associazione per lo sviluppo dell'industria nel Mezzogiorno*. Bologna: Il Mulino.

Szasz, A. (1986). Corporations, organised crime and the disposal of hazardous waste. *Criminology, 24*(1), 1–27.

Varese, F. (2011). *Mafias on the move: How organized crime conquers new territories*. Princeton, NJ: Princeton University Press.

Walters, R. A. (2013). Eco mafia and environmental crime. In E. O'Brien (Ed.), *Crime, justice and social democracy: International perspectives* (pp. 281–294). Basingstoke: Palgrave.

Waterfield, B., & Squires, N. (2012). Italy repays £307 million to EU after road project 'mafia corruption' exposed. *The Telegraph*, 5 July 2012. Retrieved October 11, 2015, from http://www.telegraph.co.uk/news/worldnews/europe/italy/9376202/Italy-repays-307-million-to-EU-after-road-project-mafia-corruption-exposed.html.

Chapter 7
Sharks in Sheep's Clothing: Modalities of Predatory and Illegal Lending in Bulgaria

Anton Kojouharov and Atanas Rusev

Introduction

The market for illegal or unlicensed money lending has been growing steadily in Europe in the last several years, particularly after the onset of the global financial crisis (Ellison, Dignan, Forster, & Whyley, 2010; Policis, 2005). Although currently there is no adequate data for the size or trend of illegal money lending in Bulgaria, experts have long asserted that the conditions of the financial market in Bulgaria, most importantly the access to credit, remain favourable for an upward prevalence of unlicensed money lending practices (CSD, 2013). Moreover, using the growth of the consumer credit market, consumer credit demand and consumer indebtedness as indicators, we may posit an assumption for growth valid for the Bulgarian illegal lending market. The above factors have been recognised as important drivers in shaping the characteristics of the illegal money lending sector and its upward trend (Kempson & Whyley, 1999).

The problem with illegal money lending becomes even more exacerbated and relevant in periods of financial crises. This is the case because many businesses in need of financial services and products to sustain and/or grow operations may find themselves excluded from the legitimate sector and may resort to alternative sources in the informal market. The same can be applied to individual consumers who have been refused by the formal financial market. Although, as our research will come to identify, not all illegal money lenders may be doubtlessly related to organised crime, most do have dubious and questionable origins of their funds. Still, many organised crime groups in Bulgaria deal in or have dealt in loan sharking. Illegal money lending has long been associated with money laundering techniques used by organised crime groups (OCG). Such loans are given in accordance with furthering their ultimate goal,

A. Kojouharov (✉) • A. Rusev
Center for the Study of Democracy, Sofia, Bulgaria
e-mail: anton.kojouharov@csd.bg; atanas.rusev@csd.bg

G.A. Antonopoulos (ed.), *Illegal Entrepreneurship, Organized Crime and Social Control*, Studies of Organized Crime 14, DOI 10.1007/978-3-319-31608-6_7

which is to acquire possession of the collateral left by the debtor, which has a particular legalising value for them. OCG have been identified to make substantial use of legitimate business structures to launder the proceeds of their crimes and anchor themselves in formal business (Europol, 2008; Masciandaro, 2001).

Research has revealed an additional dimension to illegal money lending that further underscores its importance as a separate research topic. Some loan sharks provide loans to other criminals and experts have uncovered solid evidence pointing to diversification and specialisation of money lenders (Abadinsky, 2010). Illegal money lenders may opt to deal only with legitimate businesses, regular individuals or gamblers. Others venture into funding criminal entrepreneurs. Although currently under-researched, the role of loan sharks as providers of start-up capital for various illicit activities may provide valuable insight into the intricate puzzle of the underground and criminal financial universe.

A number of factors have fuelled the development of the alternative and informal credit markets generally and the extortionate ends of them in particular. These include: the growth in demand for credit, and for forms of credit that cannot be met by mainstream credit companies; lack of information especially for vulnerable consumers; and lack of more suitable alternatives for those who are most vulnerable (Kempson & Whyley, 1999). Statistics have shown that a confluence of indebtedness, disadvantage, reduced availability and high costs of credit are producing the circumstances where a substantial number of people have few options but to borrow from dubious sources (Policis, 2005). It is widely argued that the critical risk factor for resorting to loan shark services is potential victims' access to formal high cost credit (Policis, 2005).

Still, the above paints a rather simplistic picture of illegal money lending as an offshoot of organized crime. The flow of money often appears to outline a reality of intricate convergences of legal and illicit funds through legal and illegal businesses, some of which may not be readily associated with organised crime. Moreover, it has been previously noted that money can flow the opposite direction as well, since sometimes the profits from lawful businesses are also used for loan sharking (Albanese, 2007).

Illegal money lending has not traditionally enjoyed a particularly high political salience in Bulgaria. In addition to a lack of regulatory clarity (see Petrov, 2010) and political commitment to understand and tackle the problem, another reason for its almost wholly under-researched status is that illegal money lending is inherently peculiar and difficult area for adequate qualitative research. At its simplest, it involves a financial transaction that serves the mutual interests of the participants and as such it remains underground unless circumstances change significantly to force one side to break the bond. Interest in the topic has mostly been generated through increased media reporting of stories of debtor victimisation in recent years, particularly since the onset of the global financial crisis.

Apart from isolated and generally scarce publications on the jurisprudential and historic aspects of usury, no comprehensive study has been produced to describe in more detail the illegal lending market in Bulgaria.[1] Therefore, the main aim of this paper has been exploratory and inquisitive in paving a way

[1] For a legal discussion on usury, see Petrov (2010); for a historical account, see Avramov (2007).

towards filling in the void in the research on the subject. Our preliminary findings indicate a departure from classical views and theories on loan sharking. The illegal money lending reality in Bulgaria appears interlaced by a rich tapestry of legal, grey and illicit money streams flowing through and inter-connecting a diverse typology of licit and shadow entities, regular businesses and individuals, as well as organised crime. In the following part we explain how we collected the data for the present study. We then offer a concise review of definition of terms and state of the art in some of the pertinent literature, followed by an attempt to present a tentative typology of illegal and predatory lenders. Next we provide a concise overview of some of the more prolific clientele of quick and illegal loans, which have been identified in our research. We conclude with some points of discussion and guidelines on further research.

It should be noted from the inception that because of the lack of previous research on the Bulgarian market, reference points are at times made with findings from reports on other markets. This is intended both to set reference for comparison and to attempt placing the Bulgarian market within a larger research context. It is, therefore, important to caution that findings have generally shown that profiles of illegal lenders and their clients, as well as types of loans and modus operandi, are to a large degree contingent on contexts and their characteristics may differ in response to factors such as access to credit, level of public indebtedness and weight of the regulatory framework, among other things. For example, in the United Kingdom, findings differ significantly in a number of features (e.g. types of borrowers). This is a consequence of a wider availability of legitimate financial products to high-risk borrowers, who would be excluded from the formal financial systems in most of continental European countries (Ellison, Collard, & Forster, 2006).

Methodology and Limitations

This study is based on a number of semi-structured in-depth interviews conducted over the first half of 2014. Interviewees included one representative from the Ministry of the Interior (MoI) and four from the State Agency for National Security (SANS). The study aimed a balanced national account of illegal money lending and as such the law enforcement involvement included representation in four of Bulgaria's largest cities—Bourgas, Varna, Sliven and Blagoevgrad. The interview schedule was part of a larger, EU-funded project—FINOCA—in which MoI and SANS were involved as partners. The remit of FINOCA was to investigate the sources and modalities of the financing of criminal enterprises.

Interviews were also conducted with three convicted felons in the Pazardjik prison and one in Sofia's Kremikovci prison. After access was granted by the MoI, the prison interviewees volunteered to share their experiences; therefore the motivation and truthfulness behind their involvement remains speculative. Consequently, a sense of caution should always be exercised when taking into consideration criminal testimony (Table 7.1).

Table 7.1 List of interviewed sources

Source	Description
BG-SL1	SANS representative in Sliven
PR-SF1	Prison inmate in Sofia, Kremikovci
BG-BS1	SANS representative in Bourgas
BG-BL1	MoI representative in Blagoevgrad
PR-PZD4	Prison inmate in Pazardjik
PR-PZD7	Prison inmate in Pazardjik
PR-PZD1	Prison inmate in Pazardjik
BG-VR1	SANS representative in Varna
BG-PK1	SANS representative in Pernik

The increased level of media coverage of illegal money lending and debtors' victimisation has also been taken into consideration. An analysis of online media is provided in order to compare, corroborate and, where pertinent, fill in the gaps in our research. Searches were performed on Google indexed Bulgarian language media outlets using keywords 'лихвари' (loan sharks), 'лихварство' (loan sharking), 'бързи кредити' (fast credits[2]) separately and each combined separately with keywords 'насилие' (violence), as well as 'бързи кредити' (fast credits) also combined with 'незаконен' (illegal). The selected timeframe encompassed the period between 2007 and 2013 in order to include developments from the onset of the financial crisis until the present. Overall 52 articles were analysed (see Fig. 7.1).

A Sea of Terms: Defining the Problem

The field of illegal money lending has rarely been interrogated independently outside the larger scope of organised crime activities. It has been widely established, especially in the leading literature on loan sharking in the 1960s and 1970s, that illegal money lending is closely associated with mob-style criminal activities (Goldstock & Coenen, 1978, 1980; Haller & Alviti, 1977; Kaplan & Matteis, 1968; Mayer, 2012). Indeed, this feature of loan sharking has attracted some academic attention, namely as a proxy of acquiring a more comprehensive insight into the nature of organised crime as it identifies how illicit profits are employed in both money laundering and generating additional criminal profits, thereby sustaining and expanding the criminal enterprise (Albanese, 2007).

Terminology is often affixed within the context of the phenomena it aspires to define. The terms usury, predatory lending, loan sharking, illegal money lending and underground/shadow financing are meant to describe different but related developments with one overlapping element as a common denominator—devi-

[2] The phrases 'quick loans', 'quick credit', 'fast loan', 'fast credit', 'easy credit', 'easy loans' are in this chapter intended to mean one and the same thing. Therefore, they will be used interchangeably.

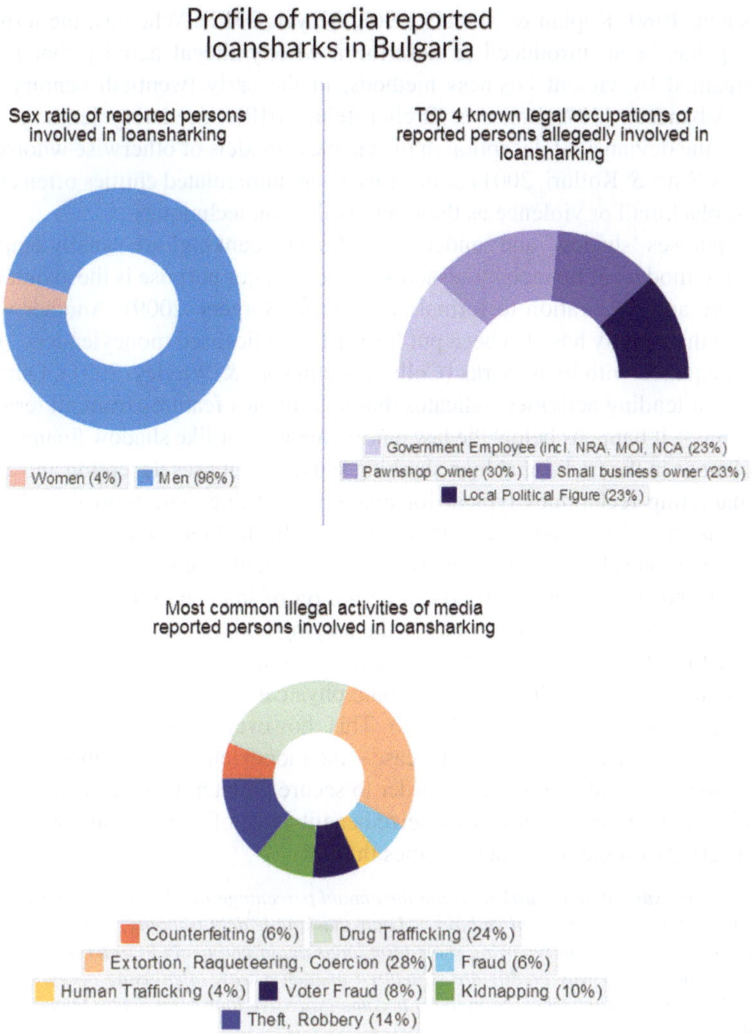

Fig. 7.1 Profiles of media reported loan sharks. *Source*: Analysis of media reports published in Bulgarian online media 2007–2014 ($n=52$)

ancy—which, at times, proves ambiguous in attempting to adequately frame a phenomenon. Apart from its marketable sounding catchiness for a long time the American term 'loan sharking' had been more or less the norm since a large volume of the illegal lending literature has traditionally stemmed from the United States.

For almost a century now the term loan sharking has referred to imagery of organised crime-related thugs infamous with their violent collection methods. Originally describing an American urban reality, this phenomenon has mostly been associated with the activities of mafia-like structures, while little academic effort has been put forward to interrogate the problem more centrally in itself (Goldstock

& Coenen, 1980; Kaplan & Matteis, 1968; Mayer, 2012). Whereas, the term loan sharking has been introduced to describe a wholly illegal activity that is often accompanied by violent business methods, in the early twentieth century urban USA (Albanese, 2007; Baker & Breitenstein, 2010), 'predatory lending' refers rather to the deviancy of deception in the business models of otherwise wholly legal activities (Carr & Kolluri, 2001) or in cases where unregulated entities often employ threats, blackmail or violence as their debt collection techniques.

The phrases 'shadow' and 'underground finance/banking' are usually employed to point to models of financial transactions whose major purpose is the avoidance of disclosure and declaration to formal authorities (Borgers, 2009). Another way of labelling the activity has also been put forward—'unlicensed moneylenders', which is often equated with loan sharks (Collard, Kempson, & Whyley, 2001). Our probe into illegal lending activities indicates that it combines features from all terms and definitions—it happens below the law enforcement radar like shadow finance; it can be violent as in the traditional loan sharking sense; and it uses deception and aggressive marketing techniques typical for predatory lending. The term illegal money lending is therefore used in a somewhat umbrella fashion, while usury/usurious practice and loan sharking may be used interchangeably for stylistic purposes.

Haller and Alviti (1977) propose a definition of loan sharking focusing on the initial part of the transaction process—the levying and agreement of interest. They stipulate that 'loan sharking is defined as the lending of money at an illegal rate of interest and without holding claim to some physical possession of the borrower as collateral' (Haller & Alviti, 1977: 128). This, however, proves impractical, as our data indicates, since that is rarely the case—the moneylenders are rather meticulous in their methods and techniques in order to secure collaterals. Even Roma lenders, operating in deprived communities, seize benefit cards of their clients for collateral. Mayer (2012), on the other hand, argues that:

> *the real measure of loan-sharking is not the annual percentage rate lenders charge, but the length of time expensive debt endures… Loan-sharking is debt trapping; it is a predatory practice that consists in renewing short-term loans again and again in order to maximize fee income. In this way credits are structured in such a way, often using deception and fraud, that presumably short-term loans became expensive long-term debts* (Mayer, 2012: 838).

Other authors seem to support the entrapment-like relationship between creditor and debtor as central in defining illegal money lending. According to the Personal Finance Research Centre (Ellison et al., 2006: 61):

> *Illegal lenders seek to control their victims primarily in order to create an ongoing income stream over a continually extended term, essentially for as long as it can be sustained. They, therefore, obfuscate both the cost of the loan and the terms on which it is made, through a range of mechanisms.*

Therefore the term *predatory debt trapping* is well suited to describe the predominant features of today's illegal money lenders regardless of context. However, as Mayer (2012) argues, if we make debt duration the measure of loan sharking, rather than the application of violence to collect the debt, then today's payday lending is loan sharking. This, however, is not entirely unfounded for the Bulgarian context, since a number of organised crime-related entities have been known to hold legal payday loan operations maintaining their extortionate, fraudulent and often violent methods of coercion and collection. In this way, the loan shark aims to prolong the debt perpetually because the high interest payments are extremely profitable and because it can be both costly and risky to switch clients frequently (Mayer, 2012). This is the typical business model of every loan shark, violent or not (Mayer, 2012). An interrogation of the operations of a Chinese illegal moneylender in the Netherlands confirms that debt trapping is a preferred business technique—out of 120 identified illegal money lending clients only 32 were one-time customers, while over half have taken out more than two loans (Soudijn & Zhang, 2013).

Most authors identify two major groups of illegal moneylenders in distinguishing between non-violent payday-like moneylenders with dubious legality and mob-related violent loan sharks (Goldstock & Coenen, 1980; Haller & Alviti, 1977; Mayer, 2012). This proves somewhat too narrow a definition for the contemporary Bulgarian illegal money lending reality. A number of cases have been registered in recent years where debtors have become victims of violent collection methods of otherwise fully legitimate loan companies (Savateva & Radkova, 2013; Trud Online, 2014). Such developments have contributed to the challenge of properly defining the phenomenon in Bulgaria, as convergences of legality and criminality appear to be endemic and rooted in the local context. Still, according to some research, violent moneylenders are rather the exception (Mayer, 2012) while others have argued that 'most relationships between illegal lenders and their customers are based on fear and intimidation with lenders seeking to control their customers with a range of coercive practices' since such methods increase the likelihood of collection while decreasing the likelihood of reporting to authorities (Ellison et al., 2006: 7).

Several arguments may be put forward supporting the mostly non-violent nature of illegal money lending: (1) hiring muscle can be expensive and risk exposure; (2) injuring a debtor may prevent him/her from working and returning the loan; (3) when a loan shark has a reputation for violence it is expected that he/she will be a choice of last resort compared to other less or non-violent competitors; (4) most illegal moneylenders will have secured a collateral whose value greatly exceeds that of the loan. Nevertheless, violence might have a positive disciplining effect, particularly in case a loan shark has a widely defaulting clientele.

Studies have repeatedly pointed out that loan sharks are not in the 'muscle' business but in the credit business, and thus 'they lend money to customers whom they expect will pay off and eventually return as customers again' (Albanese, 2007: 109). Moreover, it is argued that as a whole the loan shark is not after the customer's business (Albanese, 2007). Our interviews, however, indicate that many lenders use deliberate deceptive techniques in convincing their clients to pawn disproportionately large collaterals, such as real estate property, as well as movables and valuables, with the intent of eventually acquiring the ownership. Reports of illegal lenders with dozens of properties are not uncommon. What is more significant is that some loan sharks do participate in the debtors business, especially in case of criminal entrepreneurship in smuggling excise goods as investors.

Persons in organized crime, especially leaders, usually isolate themselves from direct involvement in loan sharking by delegating to trusted associates (Albanese, 2007). Our research shows that the role of non-members is often played by professional or expert financiers who are usually also involved in serious financial schemes such as VAT fraud. There is some indication that these experts are involved in illegal money lending as well, since they are usually entrusted with some portion of the OCG financial reserves to launder and/or yield additional profits.

The contradicting positions on the centrality of violence in the debtor-creditor relationship may be explained with the difference in client profiles. For example, in the United Kingdom where the financial market services even the highest risk clients, researchers have found that aggression and violence is commonly being used, resultant from many debtors exhibiting a chaotic lifestyle and being involved with drugs or and/or suffer from mental health problems (see Ellison et al., 2006). No such in-depth study is available for Bulgaria in order to provide some basis for reference and comparison. Although our research indicates that one particular type of clients that stand out is the gambling addict, extreme marginalisation among loan shark clients outside the Roma communities, is not observed.

Plenty of Fish in the Ocean: Loan shark Diversity

Our data confirms the view that illegal money lending tends to be often a crime of opportunity. In general, loan sharks come from a wide array of personal, ethnic and professional backgrounds. They may or may not be connected with organised crime groups and their initial source of criminal investment may not always be of illegitimate origin. However, it must be duly noted that the prevailing expert opinion is that loan shark funding, whether initial or re-investment, is overwhelmingly a product of the grey or illegal economy, regardless of noted exceptions whereby legitimate funds are being used to finance illegal lending.

Data from the conducted interviews suggests that successful loan sharks are proactive in targeting and acquiring customers. Many set up pawnshops in close proximity to places of gambling, from where it is expected that they receive regular business. Some loan sharks make arrangements with casino owners or employees in assisting with customer acquisition. In some cases loan sharks work directly with casino owners, who instruct their employees to direct clients on where they can acquire quick loans. In others, a lower level loan shark, usually working with funds lent by a higher level lender or often his boss, frequents the casinos and gambling halls in his territory to find potential customers, usually gambling addicts and people performing poorly at the games (BG-BL1, BG-SL1, BG-PK1).

Apart from word of mouth, acquiring customers very often is a product of the social skills of the loan shark. Illegal lenders are often described as extremely sociable, friendly and even charismatic (BG-BL1). They utilise deception to draw in their potential victims and even be perceived as friends, close acquaintances or someone who is providing a valuable favour. It is perhaps this particular feature of a loan shark's profile that explains their immensely diverse professional and personal backgrounds: among reported and alleged loan sharks orchestra musicians and military personnel have been identified (see Paunov, 2014).

As indicated by our media analysis (see Fig. 7.1), the presence of government employees among alleged illegal lenders, presupposes an intersection of corruption and other in-office offenses with criminal opportunism. Some reported loan sharks seem to have a background in local politics and the state administrative apparatus, including former and acting staff from customs, revenue agency and the police. It has been established that former and current customs and revenue officers do collude and cooperate with OCG for smuggling and VAT fraud, respectively (PR-PZD7, BG-SL1, BG-BS1, BG-VR1). However, to what extent extortion, corruption and abuse of public office are involved in generating funds invested in illegal money lending is a matter of further research and analysis.

The researched loan sharking landscape has generally been observed to include four types of money lenders classified by their registration status—legal or illegal, and by their basic characteristics as per literature review and data from interviews. A tentative typology is presented in Table 7.2. The data from the conducted interviews and media analysis call for an important differentiation between *legal market oriented* lenders and *legal predatory* lenders. On the one hand, there are the formal banking and non-banking financial institutions, including fast-loan companies that do not engage in deviant or irregular practices. On the other, there are a handful of fast-loan businesses that, regardless of alleged ties with organised criminal structures, appear to base their business models around debt trapping, extortionate credit and aggressive collection techniques. Where such businesses have alleged connection with underground figures, they appear as a legitimate extension of the criminal structure, complete with office infrastructure, commercial websites, marketing and sales structures. In this respect, their mimicry of legitimacy is only exposed when punitive 'brigades' are tasked with collection. In some sense, the legitimate money lending structure outsources debt collection to its criminal counterpart.

Table 7.2 Loan shark typology

	Characteristics			
Status of money lender	Ties with organised crime	Aggressive collection methods	Extortionate interest rates	Debt Trapping
Illegal—market oriented (benevolent moneylenders)	No	No	Yes	Yes
Legal—market oriented (formal financial institutions—banks)	No	No	No	No
Illegal—predatory money lenders (Roma and classic loan sharks)	Yes	Yes	Yes	Yes
Legal—predatory money lenders (certain fast credit companies, pawnshops)	Yes/no	Yes/no	Yes	Yes

Whereas, as per interviews conducted, there is clear connection with organised crime in the modus operandi and structure of *illegal predatory* lenders, no such association may be proposed for the *illegal benevolent* money lenders. The collected data suggest that benevolent loan sharks tend to operate independently and non-violently. As expected, the most notable common denominator in the characteristics of legal predatory lenders and illegal ones are the impending debt trapping techniques applied to ensure a perpetual state of indebtedness (see Table 7.2).

The Illegal Predator: A Classic Tale with a Contextual Twist

Illegal lending is rarely the only criminal or underground activity of loan sharks. The conducted interviews indicate that in many cases loan sharks have begun their career with proceeds from other crimes that they have committed or have been a party to (BG-SL1, BG-BS1, BG-BL1, BG-PK1). Globalisation, exploits of regulatory gaps and the use of internet technology exacerbate the process of criminal network branching and diversification. In this respect the opportune criminal intent seizes the opportunity to engage in a new field of illegal activity based on the circumstance of the current environment, the prospect and promise for profit and a basic risk assessment of market entry.

Individual loan sharks who have entered the illegal lending business may have made a profit from crimes committed with own resources or as part of an OCG. Noteworthy in such cases is that, regardless of whether an individual or group effort, the structure or group of the predicate offense may not be a factor in the consequent newly endeavoured loan sharking activities. A typical such case is a criminal who has made a profit from another criminal activity, such as fraud and trafficking (the latter usually associated with OCG structures), which has resulted in some 'free' capital, usually in the vicinity of tens of thousands of Bulgarian leva (BGN). Lending in such cases may first start among the closest of friends and is initially not intended as a way of usual and continual activities. Yet, as rumour spreads and more persons approach the potential loan shark for money, the clear and present opportunity triggers the criminal mind to realize this lucrative potential and expand his activities into loan sharking.

As some interviews suggest, new opportunistic loan sharks may not always be aware of the competition and/or the average rates given at certain neighbourhoods or on certain thresholds of amounts of money being lent (PR-PZD7). In such scenarios, the new player on the bloc is duly approached by fellow loan sharks, usually in an aggressive manner, and threatened if the offered rates are below the city/neighbourhood average. Once the rates have been compromised, the new loan shark is left to operate without further harassment.

Trust is often perceived as the paramount factor in any business relationship. This is especially true in the criminal world. Therefore, when a criminal activity or organisation is expanding its scope and structure, it proceeds in doing so with trusted and tested people. Quite often long-term friendships, extended family and previous criminal dealings are the basis and source for recruiting new members of OCG geared towards expansion.

A loan shark, who has risen above the mid level, necessarily functions in the capacity and structure of an organized criminal group. The head of the group is the person with the financing, while below him are the street 'money' dealers that handle customer interaction. Some organisations employ a 'right hand', who is usually a trusted person, who assesses the risk of loan takers and advises the boss. Apart from them, the group typically includes the 'collectors', who are employed mostly on a permanent basis and are deployed when a customer defaults on payment. In addition, certain groups work closely with lawyers, notaries and private court executors, who in some instances are complacent with the criminal activity and receive a percentage of the transactions (PR-SF1, PR-PZD1, PR-PZD7, Fig. 7.2).

Sufficient data is lacking at this point of the research to determine whether OCGs necessarily seek to engage in and/or upscale loan sharking. Moreover, where upscaling has been the case, it is not certain whether money lending is viewed as part of a growth strategy of the criminal enterprise or whether it is a case of a more natural filling in on the small credits vacuum created by the financial and cultural context. Nevertheless, one model of loan shark upscaling, as described by one of the respondents, may be directed towards increasing the amounts of the loans and enlarging customer base, which may also require some geographic expansion, i.e. in different neighbourhoods or in different cities. There are cases, for example, wherein a loan

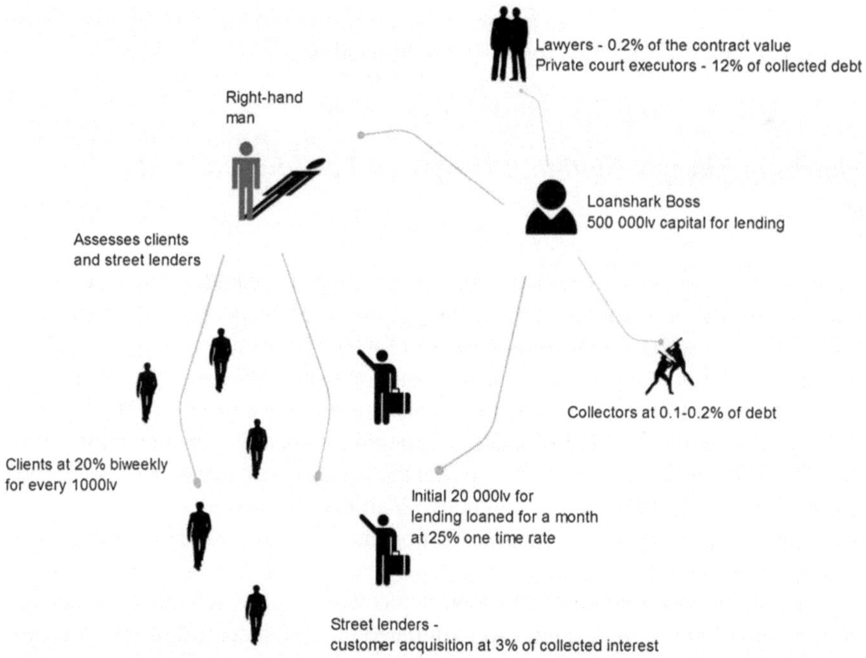

Fig. 7.2 An illegal lending OCG (PR-PZD1, PR-PZD4, PR-PZD7, PR-SF1)

shark from southern Bulgaria lends to an entity in northern Bulgaria (BG-SL1). Despite the reported competition on the city level, such discrepancies—where an illegal lender from one city provides services to a customer in another—is explained by the fact that most clients, especially those turning over larger transactions, are attracted through acquaintances and established relationships. In many cases, the 'right-hand' man in the loan sharking scheme plays the role of the broker in acquiring new business. Therefore, clientele acquisition is governed by the factors of trust and personal recommendations and is less influenced by convenience (BG-BS1).

A second upscaling model has been proposed by two interviewees. It includes the recruitment of street-facing money lenders, whereby the OCG leader lends a certain amount to a newly recruited operative recommended by the right-hand man or another trusted relation. These intra-OCG loans may reach to tens of thousands of leva. The street lender then proceeds to acquire new customers and becomes a loan shark himself as, after he has repaid the full amount, he continues to work for the loan shark ring-leader (PR-PZD7, BG-BL1).

It seems that some criminal entrepreneurs tend to exploit any opportunity for diversification, regardless of their main criminal activities (BG-PK1, Fig. 7.1). A profitable OCG has, on the one hand, accumulated the necessary financial resources, and on the other, it has developed the prerequisite structure and human resources to endeavour into the field of loan sharking. Among the identified backgrounds of loan sharking OCG are trafficking, fraud (including VAT fraud), and excise goods smuggling (PR-PZD7, BG-SL1, BG-BS1, BG-VR1). In most cases the criminal proceeds designated for financial crimes, including illegal lending and VAT fraud, are not managed by the criminal boss per se, but are entrusted into a closely related/connected individual within the group—the right-hand man.

Sharks in Sheep's Clothing: Predatory Lending Under the Veil of Legality

Until 2014, continued deregulation and lax rules for non-banking financial institutions created the necessary conditions for the consumer financing gap to be filled by fast credit/payday loan organizations, many of which have dubious reputation. Until recently, a non-banking financial institution could be established by obtaining a license from the Bulgarian National Bank and a proof of a deposit of 250.000 lv. As of May 2014, there were 261 officially registered non-banking financial institutions and 26 credit unions/cooperatives who deal in providing fast consumer loans (BNB, 2014). Some of these companies, although legitimately registered, employ aggressive loan sharking methods of debt collection and trapping, and they are connected to suspicious and underground figures.

Pawn shops have provided some loan sharks with a convenient cover-up activity, at least until 2009, when changes were initiated to tighten control over particularly their lending operations. Pawn shops naturally attract persons in need of temporary or other financial relief, and are conveniently located next to casinos and gaming halls. In some towns and cities the largest and most popular pawnshops are next to the local hospital (BG-BS1). As of the end of 2012, the number of registered pawn shops in Bulgaria stood at 1179, according to data from the National Revenue Agency (Kyuchukov, 2013).

It can be argued that the lax legislation regulating the non-banking financial sector, the high cost of formal credit and the increased demand for consumer loans have all converged to create favourable conditions for the infiltration of shadow and/or criminal structures in the formal financial system. The cost of credit is a vital indicator that weighs in the overall access to financing and it may be logically expected that the higher the cost of credit, the more likely for the loan seekers to rely on alternative sources for funding. The cost of consumer credit in Bulgaria is one of the highest in the EU. In 2009 the interest rate for a 1 year consumer loan stood at 15.45 % against an EU median of 7.54 % (Reigfner, Clerc-Renaud, & Knobloch, 2010). In addition, Bulgaria is the poorest country in the EU, whereby workers receive the lowest wages in the Union, while at the same time Bulgaria has one of the highest household indebtedness in Europe (Reigfner et al., 2010). These are also important push factors that drive clients to resort to the services of fast-loan companies, as most of them only require personal identification and do not conduct background credit checks or due diligence.

The size and prevalence of the grey economy, particularly in income-concealing activities such as 'envelope wages', also play a decisive role in pushing customers to newly established fast-loan companies. About 13.8 % of employees in 2013 are considered to have received a part of their wages undeclared (CSD, 2013). This means that there is a considerable portion of Bulgarians who may have the means to repay a loan but are excluded from the formal banking sector, as they are unable to present proof of income. The high risk of providing credit to already indebted or financially compromised individuals is then often mitigated by employing loan shark type methods of collection, including harassment, threats, extortion and, in extreme cases, violence. Thus, the demand for credit, the high cost of legitimate financial services and loose provisions regulating entry into the non-banking financial sector create conditions for convergence of legitimate facades with criminal substance in the fast-loan market.

Pawn shops have traditionally been an additional instrument for fronting unlicensed and illegal money lending practices. Until 2009 pawn shops had been allowed to use real estate for collateral and charge uncapped interest rates. Moreover, pawn shops are instrumental in money laundering schemes thus combining the convenience of attracting clients in need of loans and concealing the criminal proceeds from the law enforcement radar. As a result of the regulatory changes some loan sharking activities shifted to fast-loan companies, which to a certain degree had also been used to legalize illegal lending activities. In recent years the market for fast small household loans has experienced significant growth, especially in the period 2004–2008 (BNB, 2014).

A series of changes to curb illegal lending and over-indebtedness have been initiated since 2009. The latest such amendment was made in the Consumer Credit Act, which no longer excludes loans under 200 euros from its provisions, thereby preventing fast credit business to levy extortionate interest on loans of up to 200 euros (Consumer Credit Act, 2010). In 2009 regulations were passed that tightened control over pawnshops, especially their loaning business. Previously uncapped, or capped at significantly high levels, interest rates were restricted to 3 % per month. In addition, pawn shops could no longer loan against real estate collateral. Despite the new restrictive regulations, the conducted interviews have shown that alleged illegal money lenders still operate pawn shops as either a cover-up business, money laundering purposes or both (BG-SL1, BG-BS1). The new regulations shifted some loan sharking activities to assume the form and appearance of the so-called okazion shops—second-hand goods shops—that operate on the principle of a pawn shop but are not regulated as such (BG-SL1).

Sources indicate that in towns and cities of southern Bulgaria, elements associated with a prominent criminal syndicate manage a portion of their criminal proceeds through loan sharking. Whereas, in other areas, organic sustained growth of loan sharks is more widely the norm (PR-SF1, PR-PZD1). The loan sharking activities may be completely illegitimate, flowing through the already established and functioning OCG methods, structures and human resources. However, very often a loan sharking OCG utilizes or rather exploits weaknesses in the legislation, whereby it employs tools and mechanisms which are used to cover up illegal operations, attract customers and launder the proceeds. Pawn shops, credit unions—particularly in the northern part of the country—and financial institutions offering quick consumer loans are reported to be the most widely utilized businesses (BG-VR1).

Most of the aggressive and violent collection methods which have been observed involving legally registered fast-loan companies are with those allegedly functioning as 'branches' of OCG (BG-SL1; BG-BS1; Savateva & Radkova, 2013). Upon defaulting by the debtor fast credit companies' punitive 'brigades' commence threatening phone calls, intimidation visits to the workplace and/or home and may, in some cases, resort to physical violence. Still, however, debt trapping techniques appear prevalent in some fast-loan companies, including such where criminal connection may not be established. The most common technique used to trap the debtor to either prolong the state of indebtedness or to create a situation where he/she is made contractually obliged to pay additional fees, is obfuscation of the terms and conditions of the loan contract (see Judgement No. 272, 2011; Judgement No. 2218, 2012; Table 7.3).

The Toothless Shark: Urban Myth or Reality

The secretive and mutually beneficial nature of the relationship between the lender and his/her clients makes it difficult to ascertain with confidence the prevalence of violence in loan sharking. On one hand, our research shows that physical harm is inflicted almost exclusively in cases where a defaulted debtor is subject to legal action by the loan shark (e.g. seizure of collateral, court execution of a promissory note). Many such cases have involved loan sharking

Table 7.3 Popular debt trapping techniques

In illegal money lenders
– The loan shark makes herself/himself 'unavailable' at the time of due repayment, thus causing the debtor to default on payments schedule, therefore inflicting additional fees and interest (BG-SL1, BG-BS1, BG-BL1).
– The loan shark uses deceptive means, e.g. the client may be tricked into believing that they are signing two identical copies of a promissory note, while in fact they are two different documents for an identical amount, therefore doubling the initial amount of the loan (BG-BL1).
In legal predatory money lenders
– The client is led to believe that they are signing an application for credit, whereas they are in fact signing a credit contract. Often the document is presented with incompletely filled in fields, in which values on the parameters of the credit, such as interest rates, are added at a later stage without the knowledge of the debtor (Offnews, 2013).
– Upon defaulting on payments the client is coerced into signing a supplementary agreement to the credit contract, authorising the creditor to impose fees and interest in breach of the regulations governing consumer loans (Marinova, 2015).
– The fast credit company may refuse to accept and/or acknowledge early repayment of the loan and levy additional taxes and fees (Judgement No. 2218, 2012).
– Credit parameters are absent or obfuscated in the loan contract (Judgement No. 272, 2011).

methods used in collection activities by legitimate fast-loan companies, especially in recent years when this business sector expanded rapidly. At the same time, however, few loan sharks have been convicted based on victim testimony, as most debtors fear retribution if they cooperate with the authorities (BG-SL1). Nevertheless, there is some evidence pointing to the existence of the 'benevolent' type of a loan shark. This person may be a local businessman who has acquired significant amounts of cash from various sources, including legal businesses. Such figures are perceived as benefactors, as they usually provide loans to people in need. They are well known and respected in their immediate community for their financial assistance for the needy (BG-BS1).

Loan sharking is a relatively simplistic and—to a large extent—opportunistic activity having one basic prerequisite: available cash funds. Therefore, the scope of individuals and backgrounds that may potentially become involved in loan sharking is considerably wide. Research indicates that there are no particular spheres of legal business activities that are prone to becoming sources of illegal lending. In one reported case a loan shark boss owns two cafes/restaurants, a sewing factory and a cheese-making facility (PR-PZD4). Other legitimate sources include sale of real estate, particularly in the period prior to the collapse of real estate market.

Respectively, legal businesses being managed in conjunction with loan sharking are utilized in the money laundering process. Very often investment flows in both legitimate and underground directions, supporting both illegal lending and legal businesses, are needed both for profit *and* for cover-up and money laundering purposes. At least some loan sharks invest in precious metals, currency and real estate (PR-PZD4). The most widely used business areas connected with laundering the proceeds of loan sharking are pawnshops, sports-betting franchises, cafés and restaurants, fitness facilities, EU funds in agriculture, and insurance.

The Clientele

Both interviews and media analysis confirm the general view that illegal money lending intensifies during an economic downturn. Moreover, the pool of customers seems to become wider and more diversified in terms of both individuals and businesses. Our research indicates that, although customers may come from all walks of life, there are groups that appear particularly vulnerable and prone to resorting to the services of illegal lenders and shady fast-loan companies. Some of the social groups that had been identified as particularly active in taking out loans include criminals, gamblers, the poor and lower middle class, as well as businessmen affected by the economic crisis.

The Criminal

The prevalence of criminals borrowing from illegal lenders in order to finance their illicit activities is ambiguous at best. Accounts from criminals involved in smuggling, fraud and trafficking reveal a general reluctance to deal with loan sharks outside of their own OCG, since they are perceived as 'crooks' (PR-PZD7; PR-SF). In the instances in which a criminal does take a loan from a loan shark, it is almost exclusively a one-time deal (PR-PZD7). These are mostly targeted loans for a particular transaction e.g. purchase of goods to be smuggled, including cigarettes and other excise goods. In such cases, the interest rate charged is specifically negotiated and is usually higher, and the term of the loans is much shorter. This is the case because, in the case of smuggling cigarettes, a truckload of the merchandise is usually sold in a few days, after which the debtor can repay the loan shark. Therefore, financial relationships between criminals and loan sharks tend to be incidental and short term.

The Gambler

Persons with gambling addiction and related problems have been identified on several occasions to be especially targeted by loan sharks (PR-PZD7; PR-SF, BG-BS1). One scenario involves complicity on the part of the gambling facility owner, whereby a commission would be received upon successful loan referral. The mechanism for luring in potential loan shark clients is straightforward—the dealer is instructed to offer the client an opportunity to take a loan and continue to gamble with a view to potentially recover losses. Once the client agrees the loan shark or a representative takes over the transaction. Our data shows a high prevalence of gamblers using illegal money lending services (PR-PZD7; PR-SF, BG-BS1).

A proxy indicator of the connection between loan sharking and gambling may be sought in the location preference for pawn shops, which have been traditionally associated with illegal lending. In many cities and towns, pawn shops are conveniently located in close proximity to casinos and gambling halls.

The Heavily Indebted/Working Poor

Our data indicates that the widest and most persistent customer base for loan sharks and dubious quick loan companies are the poor and lower middle class people. These are individuals and families that experience significant financial difficulties in meeting basic needs such as paying monthly bills and taxes. Because this social stratum cannot afford to set aside funds for savings, the occurrence of an unexpected event that requires financial commitment may sway them towards the services of a loan shark. Such events often include medical emergencies, urgent domestic repairs, etc. (BG-SL1, BG-BS1, BG-BL1, BG-PK1)

Previous research into illegal money lending and loan sharking has established that cultural and economic context determines the characteristics of both supply and demand. For example in developed credit markets which have stricter regulatory systems (France, Germany and Japan) illegal lenders focus on middle income, credit-impaired borrowers, who—in states with looser financial regulations—like the United Kingdom, are targeted by sub-prime lenders (Ellison et al., 2006). Consequently the profile of the average client of illegal lending in the United Kingdom is female with children, aged 30–40 (Ellison et al., 2006), which is not the case in other contexts (see Soudijn & Zhang, 2013), where most debtors appear to be men. Access to finance and the level of rigidity of the financial regulatory system may shape the profile of the debtors and creditors contingent on context; however, their relationships and the modus operandi of the illegal lender display close similarities across states.

Generally, it appears that in more strictly regulated financial markets, apart from the delinquents, recidivists and gambling addicts, the pool of illegal money lending clients is expanded to include representatives from low- and low/mid-income levels who do not necessarily share any deviant background. This, in turn, may be speculated to allow a more business-like functioning of the lender-debtor relationship as some studies have suggested (see Soudijn & Zhang, 2013).

Loan sharking is said to occur mostly in deprived areas (Ellison et al., 2006). Although this holds true for Bulgaria, particularly in Roma communities all of which can be classified as deprived micro-communities (OSI, 2008), a significant part of the observed cases of illegal lending do not fall within this framework. Rather, illegal lending is often resorted to on an incidental basis by low income persons—to cope with steep medical expenses and urgent purchase of household items, among others.

An emergent issue with illegal money lending in deprived and marginalised communities is that it carries a political stain. In some communities it has been observed that loan sharking plays an additional role in creating dependencies which then can be exploited by the creditor for personal, criminal and/or political purposes (Silke, 2000). In Roma communities loan sharking is a lucrative option for local leaders as it increases the amount of influence they can exercise in their communities. If an individual owes money to a money lender, it makes that individual more vulnerable to pressure, which is used to push debtors to participate in criminal activities and/or influence political events, e.g. arranged voting in elections.

The Businessmen in Trouble

It is not uncommon for legitimate businessmen to rely on loan sharking services (BG-BS1, BG-BL1). However, this may be understood as a last resort measure as usually businessmen in financial trouble tend to seek loans from fellow businessmen, associates and acquaintances. The financial and real-estate crisis of 2007 put tremendous financial strain on realtors and builders as many declared bankruptcy and ceased operations. The business and marketing model for much of the construction industry, for example residential buildings, presupposes a risk of defaulting on bank loan payments or insolvency on the part of the constructor. A builder may start construction with only part of the funds needed for finishing the project. This is possible since many sales are being concluded before a residential unit is completed, i.e. the buyer pays bellow market price, as construction is still ongoing, while the seller procures the much needed funds to finish the whole building. With the onset of the financial and real-estate crisis, property prices and sales plummeted, leaving many construction sites unfinished and properties undeveloped. It is not uncommon that a builder resorts to illegal lenders in order to finish a project, therefore minimising damages.

Another business sector that appears prone to financial difficulties is the food-and-drink establishments with a seasonal character in turnover and economic performance, especially those on the Black Sea resort areas. Owners of such establishments have been known to reach for informal lending sources to refurbish a café, restaurant or night club before the holiday season. Such businesses usually deploy various tax avoidance schemes, e.g. non-issuance of fiscal notes, declaring false expenses, etc. Therefore, their officially declared profit is usually unrealistically low, potentially presenting an obstacle if submitted to a bank in a loan application process. In such scenarios, a small business owner may rely on funding from a loan shark as a last resort (BG-BS1, BG-BL1).

On the other hand, an increasing demand for credit is also seen as a factor driving small businesses to illegal and/or dubious sources of financing. According to an EU-wide study, 70 % of small and medium-sized entrepreneurs rely mainly on financing by own means for starting up a business (EIF, 2009).

In addition, local research reveals that 51 % of small businesses do not use any type of bank financing (Jordanova, 2014), while 23 % of small businesses have never applied for a bank loan (Mitkova, 2014). Perhaps more importantly, as one EU study concludes, 'the existing micro-financing schemes do not cover the potential demand of potential and existing micro enterprises; a financing gap of about €110 million can be assumed during the coming years' (EIF, 2009: 15). As such, illegal and dubious sources appear resilient in providing financing for growth and sustainability of small businesses, regardless of the condition of the economy.

Summary and Conclusion

This study has provided a valuable first interrogation of the illegal lending in Bulgaria. The general assumption that loan sharking is typically associated with OCG has been confirmed to be valid as most OCGs deal in money lending. Still, not all illegal money lending is run by OCGs per se; rather the market appears to include self-starters financing their activities through criminal and grey activities—not necessarily associated with OCG—and legal business owners who venture into loan sharking in order to seize an opportunity for increasing profits. In addition, loan sharks in Bulgaria appear to have been naturally stratified into several levels depending on the amounts they can loan out, whereby transfer of clients between them is not uncommon. Our research further indicates that most common illegal money-lender approach is that of predatory debt trapping, often involving deceptive tactics. In many cases loan sharks appear to be after the collateral.

Perhaps most noteworthy is the convergence of legal instruments and illegal methods in the modus operandi of money lenders. Exploiting regulatory weaknesses, many shady and outright criminal structures have penetrated the legitimate fast-loan sector for the purpose of both money laundering and profit-making. Although operating a legitimate business, these organisations often employ methods typical of the mob-style loan shark, including deception, coercion, threats and violence. What is more alarming, however, is the trend in legitimate fast-loan companies, for which no ties with OCG may be ascertained, which employ deceptive and often illegal debt trapping tactics and intimidating collection methods.

Finally, illegal money lending in Bulgaria, whether wholly criminal or disguised as a legitimate business, enjoys a noteworthy resilience that is anchored in the local cultural and economic context. It intensifies both during periods of economic growth as demand for credit increases and in times of financial crisis as individuals and businesses, pressed by cash shortage, reaching out to informal sources of financing. In addition, criminal entrepreneurs at times resort to illegal money lenders in order to start up illicit activities. As such, illegal money lending in Bulgaria has far-reaching impact on individuals, businesses and the criminal world, which makes it a topic that requires a more comprehensive policy-relevant research.

References

Abadinsky, H. (2010). *Organized crime* (9th ed.). Belmont, CA: Wadsworth.

Albanese, J. (2007). *Organized crime in our times* (3rd ed.). Newark, NJ: Matthew Bender.

Avramov, R. (2007). *Communal capitalism: Reflections on Bulgarian economic past* (Vol. 1). Sofia: Centre for Liberal Strategies.

Baker, D., & Breitenstein, M. (2010). History repeats itself: Why interest rate caps pave the way for the return of the loan sharks. *Banking Law Journal, 127*, 581.

Borgers, M. (2009). Regulating and combating underground banking. *Criminal Law Forum, 20*, 97–111.

Bulgarian National Bank (BNB). (2014). *Registry of Financial Institutions (pursuant Art. 3, para 2 of the Credit Institutions Act)*. Retrieved May 22, 2014, from http://bnb.bg.

Carr, J., & Kolluri, L. (2001). *Predatory lending: An overview*. Chicago, IL: Fannie Mae Foundation.

Center for the Study of Democracy (CSD). (2013). *The hidden economy: Policy brief no 37*. Sofia: Center for the Study of Democracy.

Collard, S., Kempson, E., & Whyley, C. (2001). *Tackling financial exclusion: An area-based approach*. Bristol: The Policy Press.

Consumer Credit Act. (2010). State Gazette, Issue No. 18 of 5 March 2010.

Ellison, A., Collard, S., & Forster, B. (2006). *Illegal lending in the UK – Research report*. London: Personal Finance Research Centre.

Ellison, A., Dignan, T., Forster, R., & Whyley, C. (2010). *Interim evaluation of the national illegal money lending projects*. London: Department for Business, Innovation and Skills.

European Investment Fund (EIF). (2009). *Executive summaries of evaluations studies on SME access to finance in EU Member States/Regions carried out by EIF in the Context of the JEREMIE (Joint European Resources for Micro to Medium Enterprises) Initiative from 2006 to 2008*. Brussels: ESF.

Europol. (2008). *OCTA 2008: EU organised crime threat assessment*. The Hague: European Police Office.

Goldstock, R., & Coenen, D. (1978). *Extortionate and usurious credit transactions: Background materials*. Ithaca, NY: Cornell Institute on Organized Crime.

Goldstock, R., & Coenen, D. (1980). Controlling the contemporary loanshark: The law of illicit lending and the problem of witness fear. *Scholarly Works*. Paper 273.

Haller, M., & Alviti, J. (1977). Loansharking in American cities: Historical analysis of a marginal enterprise. *The American Journal of Legal History, 21*(2), 125–156.

Jordanova, T. (2014). 51% от малките фирми не теглят кредити [51% of small firms do not take loans]. *Trud Online*. Retrieved May 22, 2014, from http://www.trud.bg.

Judgement No. 2218 in 2012, Ruse Regional Court.

Judgement No. 272 of 18 July 2011 in Cassation Administrative Case No. 194, Sliven Administrative Court.

Kaplan, L., & Matteis, S. (1968). The economics of loansharking. *The American Journal of Economics and Sociology, 27*(3), 239–252.

Kempson, E., & Whyley, C. (1999). *Extortionate credit in the UK: A report to the DTI*. London: Personal Finance Research Centre.

Kyuchukov, S. (2013). Заложните къщи двойно повече от пицариите. [Pawnshop twice as many as pizzerias] *Standard News Online*. January 15. Retrieved May, 2014, from http://www.standartnews.com.

Marinova, E. (2015). КЗП забрани на фирма за бързи кредити да иска незаконни лихви [CPC banned a fast credit company from levying illegal interest rates]. Retrieved September 22, 2014, from www.investor.bg.

Masciandaro, D. (2001). In offense of usury laws: Microfoundations of illegal credit contracts. *European Journal of Law and Economics, 12*(3), 193–215.

Mayer, R. (2012). Loan sharks, interest-rate caps, and deregulation. *Washington and Lee Law Review, 69*, 807–848.

Mitkova, I. (2014). Половината от малките и средните фирми не използват кредити. [Half of SMEs do not take out loans]. *Sega Online*. Retrieved May 22, 2014, from http://www.segabg.com.

Offnews. (2013). Прокуратурата *проверява за измами с бързи кредити, БНБ и КЗП също под лупа* [The prosecution probing for fraud with fast credits, BNB and CPC also under scrutiny], Retrieved May 12, 2015, from www.offnews.com.

Open Society Institute (OSI). (2008). *Ромите в България: Информационен справочник*. Sofia: OSI.

Paunov, R. (2014). Музикант на съд за лихварство [Musician to be tried for loansharking]. *24 Chase Online*. Retrieved May 22, 2014, from www.24chasa.bg.

Petrov, V. (2010). Приложно поле на наказателната отговорност за кредитиране от физически лица [Applicability of the punitive provisions for loaning to natural persons]. *Икономически алтернативи, 3*, 134.

Policis. (2005). *Economic and social risks of consumer credit market regulation. A comparative analysis of the regulatory and consumer protection frameworks for consumer credit in France, Germany and the UK*. London: Policis. Retrieved from www.policis.com.

Reigfner, U., Clerc-Renaud, S., & Knobloch, M. (2010). *Study on interest rate restrictions in the EU*. Zentrum für Europäische Wirtschaftsforschung GmbH (ZEW, Mannheim). Retrieved May 22, 2014, from http://ec.europa.eu/internal_market/finservices-retail/docs/credit/irr_report_en.pdf.

Savateva, D. and Radkova, S. (2013). 20 мутри в ареста за рекет, жертви правят курбан [20 thugs arrested, victims celebrate], *24 Chasa Online*. Retrieved May 22, 2014, from www.24chasa.bg.

Silke, A. (2000). Drink, drugs, and rock'n'roll: Financing loyalist terrorism in Northern Ireland—Part two. *Studies in Conflict and Terrorism, 23*(2), 107–127.

Soudijn, M., & Zhang, S. (2013). Taking loan sharking into account: A case study of Chinese vest-pocket lenders in Holland. *Trends in Organised Crime, 16*, 13–30.

Trud Online. (2014). Професия лихвар - малки присъди, огромни печалби [Profession loan-shark – Small sentences, huge profits]. *Trud Online*. Retrieved May 2, 2014, from www.trud.bg.

Chapter 8
Women in Criminal Market Activities: Findings from a Study in China

Anqi Shen and Georgios A. Antonopoulos

Introduction

Although organised crime is considered a predominantly male-dominated terrain, there is substantial evidence across contexts regarding the involvement of women (see Landesco, 1936; Block, 1980; Siegel, 2014; Fiandaca, 2007). Several studies have focused exclusively on and documented the role of females in various manifestations of organised crime such as, for example, the drug markets in some contexts (e.g. Dunlap & Johnson, 1992a, 1992b; Dunlap, Johnson, & Manwar, 1994; Dunlap, Johnson, & Maher, 1997; Miller, 2001; Denton, 2001; Anderson, 2005; Kostakos, Antonopoulos, Maspero, & Grammatikakis, 2010; Grundetjern & Sandberg, 2012; Fleetwood, 2014). These works trace the careers of female drug entrepreneurs, and the interesting combination of personal qualities, career choices in the market, strategies and the general socio-historical contingencies. In the last two decades or so, an increasing number of academic studies have also focused on women's role in transnational organised crime settings (e.g. Zhang, Chin, & Miller, 2007; Kleemans, Kruisbergen, & Kowenberg, 2014) and within various organised crime structures such as the Italian mafias (see for example Jamieson, 2000; Fiandaca, 2007; see also articles in a special issue of *Trends in Organised Crime* published in 2014). As Arsovska and Allum (2014: 2) suggest, *"we can conclude that women are no longer passive actors as once believed or perceived; yet the question remains as to the extent of their active engagement and involvement in criminal activities"*.

While the presentation of the relevant studies mentioned above is not by any means exhaustive, there is still a need to collect further international evidence to

A. Shen (✉) • G.A. Antonopoulos
School of Social Sciences, Business and Law, Teesside University, Middlesbrough, UK
e-mail: Anqi.Shen@tees.ac.uk; G.Antonopoulos@tees.ac.uk

G.A. Antonopoulos (ed.), *Illegal Entrepreneurship, Organized Crime and Social Control*, Studies of Organized Crime 14, DOI 10.1007/978-3-319-31608-6_8

better understand female involvement in transnational manifestations of organised crime (Siegel, 2014). We would argue that further evidence is also needed to construe female participation in local criminal markets (see Hobbs, 1998; Siegel, 2012) beyond standard accounts of victimisation and coercion of females into these markets (see, for example, Gay, 2005; Townsend & McVeigh, 2009), particularly of the sexual exploitation of females by "organised criminals" (Mahan, 1998). This chapter investigates the roles of females in criminal market activities in the post-1978 reform era in China, and is based mainly on interviews with incarcerated women convicted of a variety of criminal market activities.

A few initial points are due here. Firstly, criminal market activities refer to profit-driven crimes that more or less require organisation and co-operation with others. There is sufficient evidence to suggest that some criminal market activities, such as manufacturing and/or selling counterfeit goods, organising others for prostitution and even child trafficking, are not typically recognised as "organised crime" in China. In this context, only large-scale "criminal organisations", which are believed to pose a serious threat to socialist market economy and social stability, are defined as "organised crime" and are thus targeted (Broadhurst, 2012; Trevaskes, 2010; Xia, 2006). In China, "organised crime" is institutionally defined and is reserved for only one particular type of criminal organisation specified in the criminal code. Mainly considering the local socio-legal setting, we generally avoid using the term "organised crime" in this chapter. Instead, the term "criminal market activities" is adopted to refer to the offences involving the female offenders examined in this study—leading or participating in criminal groups that primarily run illegal gambling schemes, organising others for prostitution, drug trafficking/drug dealing, and trafficking in children and women.

Secondly, we admit that some of the criminal activities examined in this study here do appear on the surface to be "individualistic crimes" (Steffensmeier, 1983) which involve one female offender who acts independently in the criminal trade. However, all the criminal market activities showed a recognisable degree of organisation and co-ordination of persons. Participants were involved in different types of criminal market activities across various levels of organisation, networking and complexity of criminal operations.

Thirdly, it is worth noting that the notion of "criminal market activities" in this study does not precisely match what is typically understood as such in China. The term is used interchangeably with the "crimes of undermining the socialist market economic order" specified in Chapter 3 of the Chinese criminal code. These crimes include crimes violating company law, offences in relation to the financial market, counterfeiting currency, financial fraud, tax offences and intellectual property offences.

The remainder of this chapter is structured along four sections. It begins with some essential background information on women and criminal markets in China. This is followed by a short methodology section and a presentation of the empirical findings on the range of roles females play in the criminal markets in the particular context. Finally, we offer a discussion of our findings in the concluding section.

Women and Criminal Markets in China: A Sociocultural Background

Criminal market activities presumably did not exist in China until the reform era started in 1978, when the market economy was introduced. Under the state-planned economy, there was a general shortage of supplies, prices were tightly controlled by the state, and enterprise and market activities outside the state control were ideologically regarded as the "tail of capitalism" and criminalised under a politicised view of law (Saich, 2015). For example, selling surpluses over the commune's target in countryside or profiting from buying cheap and selling at a higher price in urban settings was a criminal offence that could be sentenced harshly. Black markets were heavily policed and there was little, if any, room for "organised criminal activities". Two decades or so after the reform, criminal markets have flourished under the free market economy. With money becoming a major drive in social life in post-Mao Chinese society as a whole, women, just like men, have become active players in the money-generation processes.

Women were active players during Mao's era when a radical notion of feminism was promoted to encourage women to actively participate in the public workforces so as to boost productivity (Bailey, 2012; Rofel, 1999; Yan, 2009). Accordingly, gender equality within the family was also promoted in order to free up women from traditionally defined domestic roles within the home and to allow them to join the socialist production processes (Verdery, 1996). It can be argued generally that gender equality in the Maoist era appeared largely in terms of allocation of work and obligations (Shen, 2015). Whilst emancipation of women, although limited in the above sense, was a distinct social phenomenon in Maoist China there is no sufficient evidence to suggest that in that period female criminality surged and became a serious social concern as those who take the emanicipation approach (see Smart, 1977; Box & Hale, 1983) would expect. However, female crime is seen as rising (statistically speaking) since the reform era started (see Shen & Winlow, 2013).

In the reform era, men and women have been institutionally encouraged to participate in entrepreneurial activities, to establish businesses and pursue individual wealth. Along with encouraging money-creation, the Party-state has been strategically stimulating mass consumption in order to expand the domestic market and ultimately to speed up economic growth. Consequently, during the late 1980s and early 1990s, consumption and possession gradually replaced political symbols as the path toward defining one's value and social status (Yan, 2009). In other words, material consumption has become symbol of social status and recognition. According to *China Brief* (Ni, 2012), social changes in recent decades have inevitably reshaped the mindset of Chinese women, especially the younger ones, turning them into more ambitious consumers than their sisters in the pre-reform eras. Women are particularly targeted by consumer goods retailers and service providers, which compete to launch promotional campaigns to boost female consumption. The feminine consumer culture stimulates the motivation and ambition of women to participate in market activities.

In this process, however, Chinese women are facing two inequalities—social inequality and the gendered inequality: as women, their behaviour is still restricted by the traditional gender code. For example, the main qualities associated with the private sector include the ability to take risks, to mix with a wide array of people, to travel and make contacts, and these are regarded as male attributes (Wylie, 2004). In fact, the private sector and particularly entrepreneurialism are seen as inherently masculine spaces (Rofel, 1999). In this context, women are inherently disadvantaged even before embarking on a market activity. At the same time, China's increasingly deepening social inequality means that different segments of the female population have different experiences, with (so-called) "urban underclass", migrant and rural women being in worse conditions compared with their middle-class counterparts (see Goodman, 2004). For the female members of the marginalised social groups, social networks are constrained to those who are similarly situated at the margins of the mainstream Chinese society.

The number of women operating in criminal markets in China is unknown for two major reasons. Firstly, official crime statistics relating to female offenders are not readily available in the country (Shen & Winlow, 2013), let alone any figures indicating the scale of women's involvement in the criminal markets. Like elsewhere, criminal offences associated with the criminal markets were assumed to be committed by men historically (Steffensmeier, 1983; Vigil, 2008).

Secondly, crime is categorised fairly differently in China compared to many western systems. For example, the offence of organising others for prostitution and other offences in relation to the sex trade are usually recognised to be "sex offences"—along with offences typically committed by women using female sexuality as a resource for criminal gain. Thus, even if sometimes patchy statistics may be available, they rarely have comparative analytical value. However, despite a lack of official statistics, it is reasonable to believe that women are not shy performing in the criminal markets given the current socio-economic climate in the country and the willingness of women to participate in entrepreneurial activities. Evidence does show that female offenders, largely driven by economic incentives, are willing to take their chances in criminal markets, although their reasons for seeking monetary gain via criminality may vary from poverty to material and leisure consumption to moving up on the ladder of social status (Shen, 2015). It is in this cultural and socio-economic context that the role of females in criminal market activities in China is examined.

Methodological Notes

Our empirical data are drawn from a separate study on women and crime in China (see Shen, 2015). Twenty-six (26) incarcerated female offenders were interviewed by the first author at a female prison in the southeast region of the country in 2013. In that study, the primary aim was to look at the impact of the traditional gender norm and neoliberal policy and practice on Chinese women in general and female

Table 8.1 Number of participants by type of offence

Type of offences	Number of participants
"Black-Society Style Criminal Organisations"	4
Organising others for prostitution	9
Trafficking in children	10
Trafficking in women	2
Drug trafficking/drug dealing	1
Total	26

offenders in particular. In this chapter, we focus only on the role that women play in criminal markets. The bulk of the data are derived from semi-structured interviews (Table 8.1).

An interview protocol was used in order for the data collection to be systematised although this was not slavishly followed and the participants were free to introduce issues that they wanted or thought were relevant to the topic of the interview. The females' narratives about their entry, involvement and role in a criminal market, as well as about other relevant issues, reflected their own interpretations of their situations, their lives and the criminal markets they were involved in. In the text, we offer examples of female criminal entrepreneurs and excerpts from the interviews conducted with these participants, and in order to protect their anonymity, which was promised to them prior to the interview, we use fictitious initials to present them (e.g. TCY).

We have endeavoured to corroborate our primary dataset with information from secondary sources such as news reports. In this chapter, supporting evidence also comes from our previous empirical research on organised crime in the same socio-economic context (see Shen, Antonopoulos, & von Lampe, 2010; Shen, Antonopoulos, & Papanicolaou, 2013), which were based on Chinese open sources.

This type of study has its limitations. As reflected upon by almost all researchers who have conducted interviews with "organised criminals" and/or illegal entrepreneurs (e.g. Zhang & Chin, 2004), there are issues of generalisability and one can never be absolutely confident about validity. Nevertheless, "cross-checking" and "member checking" significantly contribute towards eliminating untruthful accounts. In addition, there is the issue of representativeness of the sample (Hobbs & Antonopoulos, 2014). The world of "organised crime" is a very complex and diverse terrain, and we are fully aware that due to our small sample of convicted women who may be the least successful entrepreneurs and possibly influenced by the institutional setting, only tentative conclusions can be drawn.

Finally, there is a possibility that the open sources are biased against the least successful female entrepreneurs, and may also be presenting the issues relating to the actors in a sensational and morally charged manner. Although China is hardly an exception to the sensational manner in which crime is treated in official and media accounts, Zhong (2009: 109) has already argued that official, media and even academic accounts in China "are replete with language of strong moral flavour, in line with the strongly moralistic quality of the whole society". However, we note here that we have not adopted our sources' representations of the female actors involved in the illegitimate businesses, but rather only use the purely "technical" information to make inferences.

Findings: Women's Role in Illegal Markets

Previously, just as with the legitimate business sector, the criminal trade was regarded as "the working world" that was preserved for men (Beare, 2010) and women were at best positioned at the periphery or margins of business. Our data shows that the Chinese female offenders who participated in this study were either involved in the criminal markets independently or with others, and that their activities in the criminal markets share certain common characteristics with the legitimate entrepreneurial activities—most notably risk-taking motivated by unpredictable financial rewards. The according to our data, the role of females could be broadly divided into several categories which are discussed below in turn.

"Leaders"

Prior to her arrest, TCY was leading an established criminal group, which primarily ran illegal gambling and related services such as loan sharking. WXJ was holding a leading position in a hotel complex that provided illegal sex services. The independent female sex work organisers such as CL, YL and LLL were operating independently but their daily business activities inevitably involved high level organisation and co-ordination with entertainment facilities and a variety of individuals in the sex trade, and thus in a loose sense they were organising these transactions. Sufficient evidence from the interviews shows that the female criminal "leaders" were clearly money-driven, rather than power-seeking, they were pursuing money commonly for consumption power, social status and individual freedom that were closely associated with wealth.

Prior to forming and leading the group, TCY, a divorced woman in her mid-thirties, was living a financially comfortable and relatively stable life. She failed a number of attempts to become rich and respected in the legitimate markets but realised her dream in the criminal markets. TCY was a powerful boss, who was supported by a group of "friends" (key associates) to run an "underground" gambling den. She also hired a group of male rural migrants to protect her illicit business operations. Being a female crime boss, TCY apparently had a number of distinct qualities—personal abilities, managerial skills and experiences, and networks in both the criminal circles and the legal sphere—all of which were prerequisites of a successful business leader in the criminal and legitimate markets. Additionally, although not physically involved, she had no problem to authorise violence, when she felt it was necessary to protect her means of money-generation, as she explained:

I used migrant workers to kan-chang-zi for me. Kan-chang-zi involves preventing local hooligans from disrupting gambling operations, interfering in disputes between gamblers, collecting commissions from both winners and losers, and enforcing loans and interests.

Previous studies suggest that female criminal bosses, such as Xie Caiping, who was convicted of leading a notorious criminal group that ran 80 gambling and opium dens for a period of four years (Broadhurst, 2012), tend to have connections with local officials who often act as "protection umbrellas" for organised criminals (see Wang & Antonopoulos, 2015). Here, TCY had "contacts with the local police" and an obscure "influential friend". It is reasonable to assume that the "friend" was somehow connected with the local authorities and also the criminal circles given that she commented on the "good *guanxi*" (social networks) that she had locally where her illegal gambling business operated. This is not surprising as the criminal-official nexus is typical in the context of the relatively well-established crime groups in China (see for example Xia, 2006; Wang, 2014). TCY made it clear in the interview that leading a criminal group to run the gambling den was entirely money-driven and money had indeed meant freedom and status to her:

I must say the gambling den made me a successful woman. I had my own expensive cars and large apartments in the city... and I was able to gamble in Macao's casinos. What else could I do to get all these?

Most of the women who played a leading role in transactions in their respective markets, were commonly knowledgeable about their trades, independent and determined to succeed in money-making. At the same time, they were typically adventurous and, when seeing an opportunity, they grabbed it despite potential risks. Their income may be high but unstable, which depends on a combination of factors and many demands, as a female sex work organiser, YL, remarked:

I worked out different methods to ensure payment was made by clients to xiaojie (female sex workers) and commissions were made by xiaojie to me... Organising xiaojie was costly and uneasy... I eventually enrolled an MBA course to enhance my managerial knowledge and skills and I found it was useful.

YL's involvement in the sex market becomes understandable if her life story is considered as a whole. The 30-year-old migrant woman had previously made many attempts to find respectable jobs and establish legitimate businesses but failed. Her goal was one day to run a car sale business and she was financially preparing for it herself via organising others for prostitution. In fact, what YL did apparently is a normal course of action for any self-made entrepreneur. Thus, like business women in the mainstream Chinese society (see Wylie, 2004), female entrepreneurs in the criminal markets are also pushed to develop knowledge, techniques and interpersonal skills.

In our dataset, this category of female leaders was typically found among sex work organisers who organised others, usually young women, for prostitution and in this criminal market women seem to have left their male counterparts behind for a number of reasons. The first reason is the very nature and conditions of this particular market. The sex industry in China is barred and streetwalking is a very risky activity exposed to law enforcement. Therefore, the sex trade runs hidden in the legitimate entertainment businesses facilities. Sex workers are largely rural migrants who are easily persuaded to sell their bodies to make quick money (Liu, 2012; Zheng, 2014). An illicit service sector has been naturally formed, in which individuals act to bring sex workers and their clients together in a variety of settings. In this illegitimate business sector, female organisers have advantages, as CL noted:

> *Xiaojie preferred women to organise work for them. My xiaojie followed me because... I understood them. As a woman myself, I knew exactly what they wanted, and what they tried to avoid.*

Likewise, both YL and LLL also had a number of *xiaojie* who were their "friends". This, in fact, is not surprising. When examining the role of Chinese female smugglers in the transnational context, Zhang et al. (2007) found that females were often active players who tended to be seen as care givers, as being more attentive than men to issues relating to female hygiene, heath and safety, and thus were preferred by illegal migrants. In some markets, such as the sex trade and human smuggling, women appear to bring some unique advantages to the business compared to men (see Steffensmeier & Terry, 1986), and one of them is that some of them had already been sex workers or had worked in the industry and were considered "insiders". One of our interviewees, CL, was even asked by several female sex workers to be their organiser.

Secondly, the sex trade in China does not seem to be so profitable as to attract the involvement of "serious" organised criminals (see Chin & Finckenauer, 2012). Evidence suggests that sex work organisers are usually incorporated in entertainment companies that offer both legitimate and illegitimate services, and tend to use the sex trade to attract wealthy clients to consume extremely high-priced food and drinks, hire private rooms, and ask for other related, possibly illicit, services (see for example *Xinhua News,* 2015). Independent sex organisers may organise sex workers for large-scale entertainment establishments or use their venues to facilitate transactions between sex workers and their clients (Shen, 2015). Thus, even the legal economy facilitates opportunities for independent female sex organisers, such as several of our participants here, to operate in the sex trade and be relatively protected within the confines of legal establishments.

Thirdly, in China, as in other contexts, social stigma is attached to prostitution and the sex industry as a whole (see Shen, 2015). An interview with the son of a former criminal group leader in Henan province in an earlier study on organised crime in China (Shen, 2013) suggests that the "criminal gangland" in certain regions of mainland China tends to attach shame to those being involved with prostitution, and "gangs" which are engaged in prostitution are often looked down by the "real" gangsters who prefer "brotherhood", strength, physical power, intimidation and bribery to gain money and reputation. Therefore, generally, for "serious organised criminals", running prostitution is *"shang-bu-liao-tai-mian"* ("cannot be put on the table to talk about")—something that is not considered honourable and worthwhile. The interviews which this chapter is relied on also revealed that Chinese male sex work organisers felt "inconvenient" to personally go between female sex workers and their clients, and this perhaps indicates, interestingly, a gender barrier for men to engage in the sex trade in the Chinese context.

Business Partners

Business partners here refer to women who play an equal role with men in criminal operations. According to our data, this category of female entrepreneurs usually includes female intimate partners of male entrepreneurs (see also Siegel & Blank, 2010; Mullins & Wright, 2003). Typically, they met their intimate partners in the same social circuits, which men and women were similarly situated in, they shared similar social backgrounds, life conditions, norms and values, and they worked together. An example is 53-year-old YGY who was given the suspended death penalty for a relatively small drug smuggling scheme along with her lover and another two male associates of his. YGY described herself as a business partner of these men:

> *I had always been a businesswoman. Initially, I made some money from buying second-hand clothes from Guangzhou and selling them in Chongqing. Then I opened a hot pot restaurant but closed it down after I got married... then I divorced... Soon I met my boyfriend who was smuggling drugs with two friends... Four of us worked together and had meals together almost every day... you would have to deal with them, wouldn't you? All of us were sentenced to death but my sentence and that of one of our friends were suspended... I can survive without any man. I am an able person and hard working. I was successful before... I was not a big drug dealer as I made not much money from it...*

On some occasions criminal business partnerships are formed within legitimate businesses between and among individuals who are partners in legal businesses or via opportunistic and/or existing individual connections (mostly relatives, friends and acquaintances) as LLN, a 24-year-old entrepreneur in the sex trade, noted:

> *I made a friend in a karaoke bar; he was a floor manager there. He suggested that I should organise some xiaojie for them... I found four girls who were my middle school friends who wanted to do this. I hired a minibus and the owner was a male friend of mine, and I had another friend who helped me rent rooms. We stayed there together until we were caught.*

In the child trafficking business, the female partners tended to rely on only one or two layers of personal contacts—mainly sisters, sisters-in-law, cousins and acquaintances from the same village or known at work (see also Shen, 2015). Therefore, the findings in this study seem to support those in different cultural contexts (see for example Steffensmeier, 1983; Kleemans et al., 2014) pointing to the fact that the circle of contacts of women in the criminal world tends to be more intense interpersonally.

Supporters

Supporters here are meant to include ordinary female group players and those women in intimate couples who have "an independent position from a man: they worked together but the relationship was one sided" (Siegel & Blank, 2010: 440). Supporting women are either recruited by leaders/organisers to participate in a criminal market scheme (Shen, 2015) and also, as in other contexts (see, for example, Hübschle, 2014), more often they first enter the criminal markets through a relationship with a man who was already actively involved in illicit businesses (see Siegel & Blank, 2010). Female supporters do not split the profits of the business as is the case with female business partners; they either receive a salary or a payment or they do their work—sometimes unwillingly—simply to facilitate the business of "their men". In the present study, WFL appeared to be a "financial manager" for her boyfriend's illegal business (see also Soudijn, 2010)[1]:

> *I collected money from clients and also distributed proceeds among us [several associates who worked together with WFL and her boyfriend]. My boyfriend said that it was easier for a woman to do this sort of things.*

In addition to handling money, WFL was also responsible for marketing the business locally through a variety of channels. Another supporter, CAL was mainly housekeeping for the "family business", in her words, which was operated by a criminal organisation led by her husband:

> *After I was retired, I was always there to help look after the company, say, preventing people stealing raw materials from our warehouses and chasing debtors... My husband did not discuss business with me but that's ok.*

WJ, who got unwillingly involved in a scheme to help her husband organise *xiaojie* for prostitution, also played a house keeping role (see Anderson, 2005). She was responsible for cleaning, cooking as well as taking sex workers to their clients: *"My husband said it was not convenient for a man to go everywhere with female prostitutes. This was why he insisted that I come with him or he would divorce me"*.

Similar to the members of mafia associates who were expected to refer to women belonging to their affiliate's family as "sisters" (Paoli, 2003; see also Longrigg, 1998), the wives or female intimate partners of male leaders in the criminal world were referred to as *"da-sao"* ("wife of the oldest brother") or *"lao-ban-niang"* ("wife of the boss"). However, unlike what was observed in the US context (see Steffensmeier, 1983), in China a woman close to a male leader did *not* seem to automatically obtain authority through him. Rather, she may still be subjected to restrictions and may have to earn respectability by observing the traditional gender norms. Moreover, unlike female supporters of intimate partners in legitimate enterprises, their counterparts in the criminal markets did not seem to be aware of all of their husbands or male partners' businessactivities, and were not involved in any decision-making, as CNX remarked:

> *Since I started being with my boyfriend I stopped socialising with other friends... I rarely joined them [the male partners] when they were talking about business. I did not gamble, drink alcohol, or take drugs... No one in the group made a sexual joke about me like they did to other women. It was at the trial when I first heard that they [the male associates] were involved in forced trading, kidnapping, false imprisonment.*

[1] An interesting example of a female being involved in the financial management of illegal business involves a mistress of a public official being reportedly sent to study law in a university in Beijing to develop her counter-investigation skills and also manage his proceeds of bribery (*World Journal*, 2015).

Of course, not all women who play a supplementary role in criminal enterprises have a relationship with male players or leaders and emotionally depended on them. Our data shows that "ordinary" female supporters seem to have played a similar role to that of male supporters. LFM was an example and, as an "ordinary" supporter, she was not involved in decision-making; her job was mainly collecting debts for her group. Occasionally, she was involved in physical violence along with her male associates when a debtor refused to pay (see Denton & O'Malley, 1999). However, this case is rather atypical in the sense that the females' direct involvement in violence was very rare in this study despite that some had tolerated, accepted or even authorised violence exercised by the men. In the Chinese criminal world, just as in the mainstream society, women are still restricted by the traditional gender stereotypes (see Goodman, 2004).

Occasional Entrepreneurs

This category of female criminal market actors is typically found among female child traffickers who are often opportunistic, one-off criminal entrepreneurs, with no careful planning or a long term objective. Among the ten convicted female child traffickers we interviewed, nine had no previous convictions whilst 69-year-old JLY was convicted of sheltering others for prostitution ten years prior to the interview. Thus, as Shen et al. (2013) have also observed, child traffickers do not usually have a long history of involvement in human trafficking or other type of offending.

Among the ten child traffickers, nine were illiterate and one was a primary school dropout; all participants were either residing in remote areas of rural China or migrants originally from those areas. The brief socio-demographic snapshot seems to suggest a group of "amateur" female entrepreneurs who are unlikely to be sophisticated, calculated, powerful organised female human traffickers, such as those present in different geographic and cultural settings (see for example Arsovska & Begum, 2014; Iacono, 2014; Kelly, 2007; Mancuso, 2014; Siegel & Blank, 2010). Often, in their business there were plentiful opportunities to obtain children who were subsequently sold or "given away" for money, as GDX explained:

> *My manager [in a factory where she worked as a migrant worker] wanted an additional child but under the one-child policy he could not have one. When he heard that in our hometown sometimes babies were abandoned, he approached me asking whether I could find one for him... I rang a lao-xiang (acquaintance) and told her that someone wanted to adopt a child... Half-a-year later, the lao-xiang said that she got one from her relatives for me.*

Evidence shows that in the child trafficking business obtaining children to sell does not seem to require particular knowledge, techniques, skills, and experiences. However, although the child business may be a comfortable zone for the uneducated, inexperienced female entrepreneurs to gain access to, given that some of them might even sell their own children[2] or children from their immediate social environment, it was hard for them to succeed and gain much but criminal convictions as a consequence, as PGM illustrated:

> *I was illiterate and had never left home before. I was scared of going with the baby on my own, so I asked my cousin to go with me. She was also illiterate... At the railway station, when I saw the uniformed policemen, I became very nervous. They probably saw that I was nervous and came to ask me... They arrested me.*

Along with police detection, the uneducated, inexperienced rural female entrepreneurs might also be victimised themselves in criminal markets. For example, QMC—a 58-year-old illiterate female child trafficker—was tricked by two male criminals on her way home, and subsequently robbed of all her illicit proceeds from selling a baby boy. The occasional female entrepreneurs in this dataset were themselves members of vulnerable and disadvantaged groups. They were keen to gain a little extra cash by means they thought to be manageable, and an easy access to children. Thus, irrespectively of their socio-economic status, women in China are not always "blocked access" (Steffensmeier, 1983) to criminal market activities. However, easy entry does not automatically enable "good" performance in the criminal world. Here, there is a clear lack of ability among female child traffickers to operate "successfully" in the criminal markets, similarly to being unable to achieve successes in the legitimate businesses, as a result of the overall social marginalisation and exclusion.

Investors

As in the legitimate markets, some people may choose to invest in criminal markets without actually participating in them (see Antonopoulos & Hall, 2015). In this dataset, YX was involved in the sex trade as an investor:

> *I had some spare money and was looking for investment opportunities. A friend of mine persuaded me to invest in a hotel in which sexual services were provided. I gave her 80,000 yuan... Neither of us was involved in managing it. I knew there were xiaojie there, but I never said anything.*

YX was convicted of organising others for prostitution as an owner of the hotel which ran sex services, although she was also running a small but highly successful legitimate beauty salon at that time and financially she did not have to take risk. Again, this was a rather atypical case and investors seem to be women who own legal enterprises generating sufficient income that can be invested in illegal markets.

---

[2] A relatively recent child trafficking case involved 37 babies the vast majority of whom were sold by their own parents to others involved in child trafficking (Ng, 2015). Moreover, according to another recent Chinese TV report (JSTV, 2015), among 133 reported child trafficking incidents, 67 perpetrators were actually the parents of trafficked children (see also Yang, 2012).

Conclusion

This chapter set out to investigate the role of females in the criminal markets in China. We found that women operating in the Chinese criminal markets could be group *leaders*, *business partners*, *supporters* (including ordinary group players and supplementary players in the husband's or intimate partner's schemes), *occasional entrepreneurs*, and *business investors*. Unlike their counterparts in other settings (Siegel, 2014), the female criminal entrepreneurs here operated locally. Rather than seeking impact or pursuing political objectives, the Chinese women participating in criminal enterprises were largely, if not solely, motivated by economic incentives for different personal reasons. Our findings are in line with research on the same subject in geographical contexts, something that indicates the dynamism of the role of women in the criminal markets (see, for example, Cayli, 2015) and also recognises that their role, position and gendered performance in criminal market activities should be understood in its historical and cultural contexts. At the same time, we also claim that there are other dimensions should also be examined, such as social class and personal conditions and abilities, as well as women players' willingness to develop knowledge, techniques and interpersonal skills.

Although there is undeniable overall gender inequality in China, at an individual level, our study shows that it is the human and social capital one possesses, rather than gender *per se*, that very often seems to be more dominant in determining the involvement, the role and success in the criminal markets. Opportunities linked to personal connections forged by geographical/physical and socio-demographic proximity (Kleemans et al., 2014) or opportunities provided through one's employment in a legal business are crucial, since these legal businesses act as a platform upon which *legal* relationships between and among actors transform into *illegal* ones (see Kleemans & van de Bunt, 1999; 2008). What von Lampe (2007) calls "social microcosm" of illegal entrepreneurs is of critical importance for participation in a trading scheme and for success: it can often act as non-monetary capital for the female entrepreneurs (and the business altogether) in a hostile environment in the illegal markets.

We have also found that the nature of the market itself and specific conditions in a market may be important to women as an entry factor, as well as to the level and the pattern of a woman's involvement in a criminal market (Zhang et al., 2007). The sex trade, for instance, is a terrain for more trusting and smoother relationships between and among female entrepreneurs and sex workers. In addition, the sex trade does not offer sufficient profits that warrant involvement for male, "serious organised criminals", and there are cultural variables relating to the sex trade that do not appear to be appealing for male entrepreneurs. Thus, an opportunity that allows female criminal entrepreneurs to operate in the sex trade and succeed in it is created.

Finally, it is important to recognise that criminal market activities in China—and by extension female participation in them—are an intrinsic part of the general culture and economy that is shaped by China's pro-market turn. In post-1978

China, the "open door" policy and economic reforms made profit and economic development a national movement (Liu, 2005). The economic reform facilitated the emergence of criminal markets in a variety of ways. Primarily, it introduced a new ethos of entrepreneurship. Deng Xiaoping's saying, "be the cat white or be the cat black, it is the clever cat that will catch the mouse", is indicative of the mentality instilled, emphasising success regardless of the approach. In turn, the increasing political emphasis on market forces has promoted a blurring of the legal and the illegal sector. In this context, women are not distinguished from men when considering their participation in criminal market activities and, although they are structurally constrained, some are highly competent, connected and situated in the "right" criminal market, namely a market that does not violate gender expectations and one full of structural prospects. They are thus able to succeed, just as they would in the mainstream economy (Chen, 2008; see also Grundetjern & Sandberg, 2012).

References

Anderson, T. L. (2005). Dimensions of women's power in the illicit drug economy. *Theoretical Criminology, 9*(4), 371–400.

Antonopoulos, G. A., & Hall, A. (2015). The Financial Management of the Illicit Tobacco Trade in the United Kingdom. *British Journal of Criminology*. doi:10.1093/bjc/azv062.

Arsovska, J., & Allum, F. (2014). Introduction: Women and transnational organised crime. *Trends in Organised Crime, 17*, 1–15.

Arsovska, J., & Begum, P. (2014). From West Africa to the Balkans: Exploring women's roles in transnational organised crime. *Trends in Organised Crime, 17*, 89–109.

Bailey, P. (2012). *Women and gender in twentieth-century China*. London: Palgrave.

Beare, M. (2010). *Women and organised crime*. Report No. 013. Ottawa: Research and National Coordination Organised Crime Division, Law Enforcement and Policy Branch, Public Safety.

Block, A. (1980). Searching for women in organised crime. In L. H. Bowker (Ed.), *Women and crime in America* (pp. 192–213). New York: Criminal Justice Press.

Box, S., & Hale, C. (1983). Liberation and female criminality in England and Wales. *British Journal of Criminology, 35*(23), 35–45.

Broadhurst, R. (2012). Black societies and triad-like organised crime in China. In F. Allum & S. Gilmour (Eds.), *Routledge handbook of transnational organised crime* (pp. 157–170). London: Routledge.

Cayli, B. (2015). Codes of commitment to crime and resistance: Determining social and cultural factors over the behaviours of Italian Mafia women. *Deviant Behaviour*. doi:10.1080/01639625.2014.977206.

Chen, M. (2008). Entrepreneurial women: Personal wealth, local politics and tradition. In D. S. G. Goodman (Ed.), *The New Rich in China: Future rulers, present lives* (pp. 112–125). London: Routledge.

Chin, K.-L., & Finckenauer, J. O. (2012). *Selling Sex Overseas: Chinese women and the realities of prostitution and global sex trafficking*. New York: New York University Press.

Denton, B. (2001). *Dealing: Women in the drug economy*. Sydney: UNSWP.

Denton, B., & O'Malley, P. (1999). Gender, trust and business: Women drug dealers in the illicit economy. *British Journal of Criminology, 39*(4), 513–530.

Dunlap, E., & Johnson, B. (1992a). Structural and economic changes: An examination of female crack dealers in New York City and their family life. Presentation at the annual meeting of the *American Society of Criminology*, New Orleans, November.

Dunlap, E., & Johnson, B. (1992b). Who they are and what they do: Female dealers in New York City. Presentation at the annual meeting of the *American Society of Criminology*, New Orleans, November.
Dunlap, E., Johnson, B., & Manwar, A. (1994). A successful female crack dealer: Case study of a deviant career. *Deviant Behaviour, 15*, 1–25.
Dunlap, E., Johnson, B., & Maher, L. (1997). Female crack sellers in New York City. *Women and Criminal Justice, 8*(4), 25–55.
Fiandaca, G. (2007). *Women and the Mafia*. New York: Springer.
Fleetwood, J. (2014). Keeping out of trouble: Female crack cocaine dealers in England. *European Journal of Criminology, 11*(1), 91–109.
Gay, R. (2005). *Lucia: Testimonies of a Brazilian drug dealer's woman*. Philadelphia, PA: Temple University Press.
Goodman, D. S. G. (2004). Why women count: Chinese women and the leadership of reform. In A. E. McLaren (Ed.), *Chinese women* (pp. 19–41). London: Routledge.
Grundetjern, H., & Sandberg, S. (2012). Dealing with a gendered economy: Female drug dealers and street capital. *European Journal of Criminology, 9*(6), 621–635.
Hobbs, D. (1998). Going down the 'glocal': The local context of organised crime. *Howard Journal of Criminal Justice, 37*(4), 407–422.
Hobbs, D., & Antonopoulos, G. A. (2014). How to research organised crime. In L. Paoli (Ed.), *The Oxford handbook of organised crime* (pp. 96–117). New York: Oxford University Press.
Hübschle, A. (2014). Of bogus hunters, queenpins and mules: The varied roles in women in transnational organised crime in Southern African. *Trends in Organised Crime, 17*, 31–51.
Iacono, E. L. (2014). Victims, sex workers and perpetrators: Gray areas in the trafficking of Nigerian women. *Trends in Organised Crime, 17*, 110–128.
Jamieson, A. (2000). Mafiosi and terrorists: Italian women in violent organisations. *SAIS Review of International Affairs, 20*(2), 51–64.
JSTV. (2015). Explore: Are human traffickers sentenced harshly or not in China? Assessed June 19, 2015, from http://www.jstv.com/n/nc/pdxw/201506/t20150618_15814279.shtml
Kelly, L. (2007). A conductive context: Trafficking of persons in Central Asia. In M. Lee (Ed.), *Human trafficking* (pp. 73–91). Cullompton: Willan.
Kleemans, E., & van de Bunt, H. G. (1999). The social embeddedness of organised crime. *Transnational Organised Crime, 5*(1), 19–36.
Kleemans, E., & van de Bunt, H. G. (2008). Organised crime, occupations and opportunity. *Global Crime, 9*(3), 185–197.
Kleemans, E., Kruisbergen, E., & Kowenberg, R. (2014). Women, brokerage, and transnational organised crime: Empirical results from the Dutch organised crime monitor. *Trends in Organised Crime, 17*, 16–30.
Kostakos, P., Antonopoulos, G. A., Maspero, A., & Grammatikakis, G. (2010, June 2–5). The role of women in 'organized crime' in Greece. Presentation at the John Jay College international conference *Societies in Transition: Balancing Security, Social Justice and Tradition*, Marrakesh, Morocco.
Landesco, I. (1936). The woman and the underworld. *Journal of Criminal Law and Criminology, 26*, 901–912.
Longrigg, C. (1998). *Mafia women*. London: Vintage.
Liu, J. (2005). Crime patterns during the market transition in China. *British Journal of Criminology, 45*, 613–633.
Liu, M. (2012). Chinese migrant women in the sex industry: Exploring their paths to prostitution. *Feminist Criminology, 7*(4), 327–349.
Mahan, S. (1998, March). Women's place in organised crime. Paper presented at the annual *Academy of Criminal Justice Sciences* meeting, Albuquerque, New Mexico.
Mancuso, M. (2014). Not all madams have a central role: Analysis of a Nigerian sex trafficking network. *Trends in Organised Crime, 17*, 66–88.
Miller, J. (2001). *One of the guys*. New York: Oxford University Press.

Mullins, C. W., & Wright, R. (2003). Gender, social networks and residential burglary. *Criminology, 41*, 813–840.

Ni, V. (2012). Consumption trends and targeting China's female consumers. *China Briefing*. Accessed June 16, 2015, from http://www.china-briefing.com/news/2012/03/08/consumption-trends-and-targeting-chinas-female-consumer.html

Ng, N. (2015). Chinese police rescue 37 babies in trafficking bust. Accessed June 19, 2015, from http://edition.cnn.com/2015/01/14/china/china-child-trafficking-bust/

Paoli, L. (2003). *Maria Brothers*. New York: Oxford University Press.

Rofel, L. (1999). *Other Modernities: Gendered yearnings in China after socialism*. Berkeley, CA: University of California Press.

Saich, T. (2015). *Governance and politics of China* (4th ed.). London: Palgrave.

Shen, A. (2013). Perception of organised crime: An exploratory study of British university students and Chinese university students at home. Paper presented at the annual conference of the British Society of Criminology, 1-4 July, University of Wolverhampton.

Shen, A. (2015). *Offending women in contemporary China: Gender and pathways into crime*. London: Palgrave.

Shen, A., Antonopoulos, G. A., & von Lampe, K. (2010). The dragon breathes smoke: Cigarette counterfeiting in the People's Republic of China. *British Journal of Criminology, 50*, 239–258.

Shen, A., Antonopoulos, G. A., & Papanicolaou, G. (2013). China's stolen children: Internal child trafficking in the People's Republic of China. *Trends in Organised Crime, 16*(1), 31–48.

Shen, A., & Winlow, S. (2013). Women and crime in contemporary China: A review essay. *International Journal of Comparative and Applied Criminology, 38*(4), 327–42.

Siegel, D. (2012). Mobility of se workers in European cities. *European Journal on Criminal Policy and Research, 18*, 255–268.

Siegel, D. (2014). Women in transnational organised crime. *Trends in Organised Crime, 17*, 52–65.

Siegel, D., & Blank, S. (2010). Women who traffic women: The role of women in trafficking networks – Dutch cases. *Global Crime, 11*(4), 436–447.

Smart, C. (1977). *Women, crime and criminality – A feminist critique*. London: Routledge and Kegan Paul.

Soudijn, M. (2010). Wives, girlfriends and money laundering. *Journal of Money Laundering Control, 13*(4), 405–416.

Steffensmeier, D. (1983). Organizational properties and sex-segregation in the underworld: Building a sociological theory of sex. *Social Forces, 61*, 1010–1032.

Steffensmeier, D., & Terry, R. (1986). Institutional sexism in the underworld: A view from the inside. *Sociological Inquiry, 56*, 304–323.

Townsend, M., & McVeigh, T. (2009, September 6). Gangsters prey on young women to smuggle cigarettes. *The Observer.*

Trevaskes, S. (2010). *Policing serious crime in China: From 'strike hard' to 'kill fewer'*. Oxon: Routledge.

Verdery, K. (1996). *What was Socialism and what comes next?* Princeton, NJ: Princeton University Press.

Vigil, J. D. (2008). Female gang members from East Los Angeles. *International Journal of Social Inquiry, 1*(1), 47–74.

von Lampe, K. (2007). Criminals are not alone: Some observations on the social microcosm of illegal entrepreneurs. In P. van Duyne, A. Maljevic, M. van Dijck, K. von Lampe, & J. Harvey (Eds.), *Crime business and crime money in Europe* (pp. 131–156). Nijmegen: WLP.

Wang, P. (2014). Extra-legal protection in China: How guanxi distorts China's legal system and facilitates the rise of unlawful protectors. *British Journal of Criminology, 54*(4), 809–830.

Wang, P., & Antonopoulos, G. A. (2015). Organized crime and illegal gambling: How do illegal gambling enterprises respond to challenges caused by their illegality in China? *Australian and New Zealand Journal of Criminology*. doi:10.1177/0004865815573874.

World Journal. (2015). Official sent mistress to university studying law to gain counter-investigation knowledge and skills. Accessed June 18, 2015, from http://www.worldjournal.com/3193446/chapter

Wylie, C. (2004). Femininity and authority: Women in China's private sector. In A. E. McLaren (Ed.), *Chinese women – Living and working* (pp. 42–64). London: Routledge.

Xia, M. (2006). Assessing and explaining the resurgence of China's criminal underworld. *Global Crime, 7*(2), 152–175.

Xinhua News. (2015). *Huang-jia-yi-hao* (the Royal No 1 Nightclub in Zhengzhou) did not rely on prostitution to make huge profit. Accessed June 18, 2015, from http://news.xinhuanet.com/legal/2015-06/05/c_127882307.htm

Yan, Y. (2009). *The individualisation of Chinese Society*. Oxford: Berg.

Yang, M. G. (2012). *Research on the correction systems for women in China.* Nanjing: Nanjing University Press.

Zhang, S., & Chin, K.-L. (2004). *Characteristics of Chinese human smugglers*. Washington, DC: US Department of Justice.

Zhang, S. X., Chin, K.-L., & Miller, J. (2007). Women's participation in Chinese transnational human smuggling: A gendered market perspective. *Criminology, 45*(3), 699–733.

Zheng, T. (2014). Prostitution and human trafficking. In L. Cao, I. Y. Sun, & B. Hebenton (Eds.), *The Routledge handbook of Chinese criminology* (pp. 197–208). Oxon: Routledge.

Zhong, L. Y. (2009). *Communities, crime and social capital in contemporary China.* Cullompton, Devon: Willan Publishing.

Part II
Criminal Finances

Chapter 9
The Financial Flows of Transnational Crime and Tax Fraud in OECD Countries: Some Empirical Facts

Friedrich Schneider

Introduction

Over the last two decades, the growth of the world economy was quite high and improved the economic well-being all over the globe, but this development was accompanied by some negative developments too. Two of them are (1) proceeds from international organized crime and (2) proceeds from financial and tax fraud, both of which rose remarkably over this period. In this paper, I will deal with two questions:

1. From which sources do international crime organizations get their proceeds, and what do we know about their size and development?
2. How large are the proceeds from financial and tax fraud?

Hence the main focus lies on providing a detailed knowledge about the size of the proceeds of international crime and the ones from financial and tax fraud. An attempt is also made to give a preliminary answer of the origin of both types of criminal proceeds (questions 1 and 2). An analysis of the financial proceeds and their sources is important in order to reduce this illegal income. Hence, my paper will try to meet two objectives: (1) to widen the knowledge of this subject and (2) to enhance the understanding of the main issues relating to transnational crime. The body of literature on transnational crime is huge and diverse and quite often descriptive; hence in this paper only those contributions, which contain the latest and (hopefully) reliable figures, are summarized.[1]

[1] See for example Unger (2007), Walker and Unger (2009), Masciandaro (2004, 2005, 2006), Schneider (2010, 2011, 2013), UNODC (2010), D'Souza (2012) and Pickhardt and Prinz (2012).

F. Schneider (✉)
Department of Economics, Johannes Kepler University of Linz, Linz, Austria
e-mail: friedrich.schneider@jku.at

G.A. Antonopoulos (ed.), *Illegal Entrepreneurship, Organized Crime and Social Control*, Studies of Organized Crime 14, DOI 10.1007/978-3-319-31608-6_9

This paper is structured as follows: section 2 provides some methodological remarks about money laundering and section 3 gives a review of the empirical findings and on the types of transnational crime (including cybercrime) proceeds. In section 4 some conclusions and policy recommendations are drawn.

Money Laundering: Some Methodological Remarks

It is obvious, that "crime money" or "dirty money" is laundered. This has the purpose to make dirty money appear legal (compare Walker, 1999, 2007). There are many methods of money laundering; in Table 9.1 according to Unger (2007) and Walker (2007) the 12 most common methods are shortly explained. Which of these methods is chosen depends on the type of crime activity and on the institutional arrangements in a country where the criminal money is "earned". For example, in the drug business method 8, business ownership, is quite often used.[2] In the drug business and in big cities, quite reasonable amounts of cash are earned by drug dealers in a lot of different places, which they infiltrate into cash intensive operations such as restaurants, which are especially well suited for money laundering purposes.

Unger (2007) estimates the amount of laundered money and its top 20 destination countries; these figures are shown in Table 9.2. In this table two estimates are presented, one by Walker (1999, 2007) and one by the IMF. The Walker figure of 2.85 trillion USD is much larger than the IMF figure with 1.50 trillion USD (both figures are for the year 2005). Walker's figures have been criticized as being too high which was one reason why the IMF estimates are shown, too.

Table 9.2 clearly demonstrates that two thirds of worldwide money laundering was done in the first 20 countries listed. One should realize that most of these countries are highly developed and have quite sizeable legal/official economies, which makes them highly attractive for reinvesting the laundered proceeds. What is also amazing is, that there are only a few small countries and/or offshore countries (OFCS) and tax heavens among them (Cayman Islands, Vatican City, Bermuda, and Liechtenstein).[3] The majority of countries that attract money laundering flows are economically big players. The United States has the largest worldwide share of money laundering of almost 19.0 %, followed by the Cayman Islands (4.9 %), Russia (4.2 %), Italy (3.7 %), but also smaller countries like Switzerland (2.1 % of worldwide money laundering), Liechtenstein (1.7 %), and Austria (1.7 %) are attractive. If one takes the lower IMF value for Austria, Switzerland, and the United Kingdom, roughly 5.5 % of the total amount is laundered, which comes close to roughly 10 % of official GDP of these three countries. However, it needs to be emphasized that it is not clear whether this money is "only" laundered in these countries or remains in these countries; it may well leave these countries after the laundering process.

[2] Compare Schneider (2004) and Masciandaro (2004).

[3] Compare also Masciandaro (2005, 2006), Zdanowicz (2009), Reuter and Truman (2004), and Walker and Unger (2009).

Table 9.1 The methods of money laundering

1.	Wire transfers or electronic banking	The primary tool of money launderers to move funds around in the banking system. These moves can conceal the illicit origins of the funds or just place the money where the launderers need them. Often the funds go through several banks and even different jurisdictions.
2.	Cash deposits	Money launderers need to deposit cash advances to bank accounts prior to wire transfers. Due to anti-money-laundering regulations they often 'structure' the payments, i.e. break down large to smaller amounts. This is also called 'smurfing'.
3.	Informal value transfer systems (IVTS)	Money launderers need not rely on the banking sector, other transfer providers, such as the Hawala in Hindi are readily available to undertake fund transfers. These systems consist of shops (mainly selling groceries, phone cards, or other similar items), which are also involved in transfer services. IVTSs enable international fund transfers, as these shops are present in several jurisdictions.
4.	Cash smuggling	Money launderers might mail, Fedex, or simply carry cash with them from one region to another, or even to different jurisdictions.
5.	Gambling	Casinos, horse-races, and lotteries are ways of legalizing funds. The money launderer can buy (for 'dirty' cash) winning tickets—or in the case of casinos chips—and redeem the tickets or the chips in a 'clean' bank check. Afterwards, the check can be easily deposited in the banking sector.
6.	Insurance policies	Money launderers purchase single premium insurance (with dirty cash), redeem early (and pay some penalty) in order to receive clean checks to deposit. Longer term premium payments might make laundering even harder to detect.
7.	Securities	Usually used to facilitate fund transfers, where underlying security deals provide cover (and legitimate looking reason) for transfers.
8.	Business ownership	Money might be laundered through legitimate businesses, where laundering funds can be added to legitimate revenues. Cash-intensive operations, such as restaurants, are especially well suited for laundering.
9.	Shell corporations	Money launderers might create companies exclusively to provide cover for fund movement without legitimate business activities.
10.	Purchases	Real estate or any durable good purchases can be used to launder monies. Typically, the item is bought for cash and resold for clean monies, like bank checks.
11.	Credit card advance payment	Money launderers pay money in advance with dirty money, and receive clean checks on the balance from the bank
12.	ATM operations	Banks might allow other firms to operate their ATMs, i.e. to maintain and fill them with cash. Money launderers fill ATMs with dirty cash, and receive clean checks (for the cash withdrawn) from the bank.

Source: Accounts by Unger (2007) and Walker (2007)

In general, Table 9.2 demonstrates how substantial the amount of laundered money is and that two thirds of these funds are concentrated in only 20 countries.

Bagella, Busato, and Argentiero (2009, p. 881) apply a two-sector dynamic general equilibrium model to measure money laundering for the United States and

Table 9.2 The amount of laundered money and top 20 destinations of laundered money, year 2005

Rank	Destination	% of worldwide money laundering	Walker estimate 2.85 trillion USD Amount in billion USD	IMF estimate of 1.5 trillion USD worldwide Amount in billion USD
1.	United States	18.9	538,145	283,500
2.	Cayman Islands	4.9	138,329	73,500
3.	Russia	4.2	120,493	63,000
4.	Italy	3.7	105,688	55,500
5.	China	3.3	94,726	49,500
6.	Romania	3.1	89,595	46,500
7.	Canada	3.0	85,444	45,000
8.	Vatican City	2.8	80,596	42,000
9.	Luxembourg	2.8	78,468	42,000
10.	France	2.4	68,471	36,000
11.	Bahamas	2.3	66,398	34,500
12.	Germany	2.2	61,315	33,000
13.	Switzerland	2.1	58,993	31,500
14.	Bermuda	1.9	52,887	28,500
15.	Netherlands	1.7	49,591	25,500
16.	Liechtenstein	1.7	48,949	25,500
17.	Austria	1.7	48,376	25,500
18.	Hong Kong	1.6	44,519	24,000
19.	United Kingdom	1.6	44,478	24,000
20.	Spain	1.2	35,461	18,000
	SUM	67.1	1,910,922	1,006,500

Source: Unger (2007, p. 80)

the EU-15 macro areas over the sample 2000:01-2007:01 at a quarterly data basis. Their time series are generated through a fully micro-founded dynamic model, which is appropriately calibrated to replicate selected stochastic properties of the two economies (legal and illegal). Their model has a short run perspective. Bagella et al. (2009, p. 881) get the following results: First their simulations show that money laundering accounts for approximately 19.0 % of the GDP measured for the EU-15, while it accounts for 13.0 % in the US economy, over the sample 2000:01-2007:04. Second, the simulated money laundering appears less volatile than the corresponding GDP. As regards the EU-15 macro area, the simulated statistics suggest that money laundering volatility is one-third of the GDP volatility; for the US economy, the same statistics produce a figure of two-fifths. Considering these estimates I admit that they are quite high and I have some doubts how plausible these large figures are.

In another study, Walker and Unger (2009, p. 821) again undertake an attempt to measure global money laundering and/or the proceeds from transnational crime. They criticize the traditional and often used methods such as case studies, proxy variables, or models for measuring the crime economy, arguing that they all tend to overestimate money laundering. They present a theoretically orientated model, which is a gravity one and which makes it possible to estimate the flows of illicit funds from and to each jurisdiction in the world. This "Walker Model" was first developed in 1994, and was updated in 2008/2009. The authors elaborate that their model belongs to the group of gravity models which have recently become popular in international trade theory. The authors argue that the original Walker Model estimates are compatible with recent findings on money laundering. Once the scale of money laundering is known, its macroeconomic effects and its impact of crime prevention, regulation and law enforcement, and the scale of money laundering and transnational crime can also be measured. Walker and Unger (2009, pp. 849–850) conclude that their model still seems to be the most reliable and robust method to estimate global money laundering, and thereby the important effects of transnational crime on economic, social, and political institutions. Rightly they argue that the attractiveness of the distance indicator in the Walker model is a first approximation, but is still not theoretically satisfactory.

A better micro-foundation for the Walker Model will be needed. A micro-foundation means that, the behavior of money launderers is analyzed, and in particular what makes them send their money to a specific country. Hence, Walker and Unger (2009, p. 850) conclude that an economics of crime micro-foundation for the Walker Model would mean that, similarly to international trade theory, behavioral assumptions about money launderers should be made. Their gravity model can be seen as a reduced form or outcome of a rational calculus of sending the money to a certain country and potentially making large profits. Using their model in Table 9.2, the amount of laundered money and the top ("most" attractive) 20 destinations of laundered money is shown for 2005. The U.S. ranks number one, followed by the Cayman Islands and Russia. With 18.9 % of worldwide money laundering, the U.S. has by far the biggest share, followed by the Cayman Islands with 4.9 %.

Transnational Crime Proceeds[4]

Worldwide Figures

"Dirty" money from crime is earned through various underground activities, like drug, weapons, and human trafficking. How much crime money in all its forms can be observed?[5] The most widely quoted figure for the extent of money laundering criminal proceeds has been the IMF consensus range of 2.0–5.0 % of global GDP in 1998 (compare IMF, 2010).

---

[4] For a detailed analysis see Schneider (2005, 2008a, 2008b, 2009, 2011, 2013), Schneider and Windischbauer (2008), Schneider, Dreer, and Riegler (2006), and Takats (2007).

[5] Smith (2011) estimates that this amount is 1.5 trillion USD per year. However, these estimates are more guestimates, because no clear sources are given and, even more importantly, the procedure of calculation is not shown and critically discussed.

Table 9.3 FATF estimate of worldwide money laundering (1988–2005)

Estimation of laundered crime proceeds		
Year	In bn USD	As a percentage of global GDP
1988	340.00	2.0
1996	1100.00	3.5
2005	2300.00	3.0

Source: Data from IMF (2010) and FATF (2007)

Table 9.4 IMF estimates of laundered money, worldwide (1996–2009)

Estimation	Minimum	Mid-point	Maximum	Increase in %
IMF estimates of money laundered as a percentage of global GDP	2	3.5	5	–
Estimate for 1996 in billion USD	600	1100	1500	–
Estimate for 2005 in billion USD	900	1500	2300	36.0
Estimate for 2009 in billion USD	1200	2000	2900	33.0

Source: Data from OECD Observer, Paris, various years

In Tables 9.3 and 9.4 the FATF estimates and the IMF estimates of worldwide money laundered for a similar period are provided (FATF 1988–2005, IMF 1996–2009). Considering first the FATF estimate, the amount of worldwide money laundering is 2.0 % of global GDP in 1988, increased to 3.5 % in 1996, and decreased again to 3.0 % in 2005. The IMF estimate has a range of between 2.0 and 5.0 % of Global GDP over the period 1996–2009. In absolute terms the worldwide money laundered increased by 36.0 % from 1996 to 2005 and by 33.0 % from 2005 to 2009, which is quite a big increase. These FATF or IMF figures are more or less in a similar range.

In Table 9.5, the FATF estimates of global amounts of laundered money up to the year 2009 are shown. Here the key focus lies on drugs and for this a calculation of the total amounts laundered from all criminal proceeds.

Table 9.5 also shows some newer FATF data, again for the drug market for the year 2003. For the year 2003, the FATF estimate of the total amounts laundered (from all criminal proceeds) is 880 billion or 2.4 % of world GDP. Extrapolated to the year 2009, the calculation reaches 1.4 trillion USD.

In Table 9.6 money laundering by region is shown over the period 2000–2005. North and South America have by far the biggest share with 37.8 % in 2000, which remains more or less constant up to 2005, with 37.7 %. Then follows Asia Pacific with a modest increase from 29.7 % in 2000 to 31.5 % in 2005. Europe showed a slight decrease; it was 27.8 % in 2000 (of all money laundered proceeds) which declined to 26.0 % in 2005.

In Table 9.7 the cross-border flows of global "dirty money" in trillion USD are shown over the period 2000–2005 on a worldwide basis. This includes tax fraud money and all money which leaves a country due to some criminal reason. Table 9.7 shows, that the overall amounts of dirty money laundered varies between 1.1 and 1.6 trillion USD and increases to 1.7–2.5 trillion USD in the year 2009. This is quite a large sum which means a range between 2.9 and 4.3 % of the world GDP. The

Table 9.5 Updated FATF model of global amounts laundered

Estimate of drug sales in key markets (1988)	124 bn USD
As a percentage of global GDP (1988)	0.8
Estimate of drug sales in key markets (UNODC estimate for 2003)	322 bn USD
As a percentage of World GDP	0.9
Assumed proportion that is laundered (initial FATF estimate)	66–70 %
Estimate of amounts laundered related to drugs (2003)	220 bn USD
Proportion in % of global GDP (2003)	0.6
Estimated proportion of drugs in total amounts laundered (initial FATF estimate)	25.0 %
Estimated total amounts laundered in 2003	880 bn USD
As a percentage of GDP	2.4
Extrapolated to global GDP in 2009	1.4 trillion USD

Sources: Data from IMF (2010) and UNODC (2005)

Table 9.6 Annual money-laundering by region, billion USD (2000–2005)

Region	2000		2002		2005[a]	
America	313	37.8 %	328	38.3 %	350	37.7 %
Asia-Pacific	246	29.7 %	254	29.7 %	292	31.5 %
Europe	230	27.8 %	234	27.3 %	241	26.0 %
Middle East/Africa	38	4.6 %	40	4.7 %	44	4.7 %
Total	827	100.0 %	856	100.0 %	927	100.0 %
In % of GDP	2.7		2.6		2.0	

[a]Projection

Source: Celent (2002)

Table 9.7 Cross-border flows of global 'dirty money' (*including tax evasion*) in trillion USD, shown as a percentage of average GDP over the 2000–2005 period

	2000–2005			Extrapolated to 2009		
Variable	Low trillion	High trillion	In % of GDP 2000–2005	Low trillion	Mid-point trillion	High trillion
Overall amounts laundered	1.1	1.6	2.9–4.3	1.7	2.1	2.5
of which criminal component	0.3	0.5	0.9–1.5	0.5	0.7	0.9

Sources: Data from Baker (2005) and World Bank (n.d.)

classic criminal component lies only between 27.0 and 31.0 % of the total dirty money. Hence, one clearly realizes that capital flight and tax fraud money is by far the biggest proportion of dirty money.[6]

In Table 9.8 the different types of proceeds of transnational crime (time range 2003–2009) are shown. Here we have a clear-cut result. Drugs are the biggest

[6]Compare also Pickhardt and Prinz (2012).

Table 9.8 Proceeds of transnational crime (time range 2003–2009)

Kind of crime	Billion USD	In % of total proceeds	Sources
1. Drugs	320	50	UNODC (2005) (data refer to 2003)
2. Counterfeiting	250	39	OECD, Magnitude of Counterfeiting and Piracy of Tangible Products, Paris, 2009
3. Human trafficking	31.6	5	P. Belser (ILO), Forced Labor and Human Trafficking: Estimating the Profits, 2005
4. Oil	10.8	2	GFI estimate based on Baker, 2005 (quantities) and US Energy Information Administration (prices: 2003–2010)
5. Wildlife	7.8–10	1.4	GFI estimate based on Francesco Colombo, "Animal Trafficking—A Cruel Billion-Dollar Business," Inter Press Service, September 6, 2003; Coalition Against Wildlife Trafficking, World Wildlife Fund
6. Timber	7.0	1.1	GFI estimate for 2009 based on Wood Resources International, OECD, Paris, various years
7. Fish	4.2–9.5	1.1	GFI estimate for 2010, based on Norwegian national advisory group against organized IUU-fishing (FFA) and United Nations Food and Agriculture Organization
8. Art and cultural property	3.4–6.3	0.8	GFI estimate based on Interpol, International Scientific and Professional Advisory Council of the United Nations Crime Prevention and Criminal Justice Programme
9. Gold	2.3	0.4	GFI estimate based on estimates from UNODC, 2010 and other sources on illegal gold trade in DRC, South Africa and Peru
10. Human organs	0.6–1.2	0.1	GFI estimate based on United Nations
11. Small arms and light weapons	0.3–1.0	0.1	GFI estimate based on Small Arms Survey and UNODC
12. Diamonds and colored gemstones	0.9	0.1	GFI estimate for 2009 based on UN, Kimberley Process: Rough Diamond Statistics and US Geological Survey
Total 1.–12. (midpoint estimates)	645	100.0	
Total 1.–12. Rounded	650		
In % of global GDP in 2009	1.1		
In % of average global GDP, 2000–2009	1.5		

Source: data from Global Financial Integrity (2011) and author's elaborations

business with 50.0 %, followed by counterfeiting with 39.0 %, human trafficking with 5.0 %, and oil with 2.0 %. The proceeds from all other crimes are much lower. In total we have here a sum of 650 billion USD which amounts to 1.1 % of global GDP.

Finally, in Table 9.9 the various "estimates" or guestimates of worldwide turnover of organized crime in billion USD are shown. Table 9.9 clearly shows a huge range and it is left to the reader to make his or her own judgment of plausibility. A median of all estimates is 1900 billion USD for the year 2009 and the average is 2100 billion USD in 2009 or 3.6 % of world GDP. The confidence interval lies between 1600 and 2600 billion USD or 2.7–4.4 %.

Table 9.9 Estimates of worldwide turnover of organized crime, billion USD, as a percentage of GDP

Origin/study	Year	Volume in bill USD (worldwide)	As a percentage of global GDP
M. Schuster	1994	500–800	0.9–3.0
International Monetary Fund and Interpol	1996	500	1.6
UN estimates	1994/1998	700–1000	2.4–3.4
S. Kerry	1997	420–1000	1.4–3.3
J. Walker	1998	2850	9.5
National Criminal Intelligence Service	1998	1300	4.3
	2001	1900	5.9
	2003	2100	5.6
I. Takats (2007)	2005	600–1500	1.3–3.3
J.D. Agarwal and A. Agarwal (2006)	2005	2000–2500	4.4–5.5
Global Financial Integrity (2011) (estimate for transnational crime)	2000–2009	650	1.5
J. Walker (based on J. Walker and B. Unger) (2009)	2001	1000	3.4
F. Schneider (University of Linz)	2001	800	2.5
	2002	960	2.9
	2003	1200	3.2
	2004	1400	3.3
	2005	1500	3.3
	2006	1700	3.4
Tentative estimate[a]	2009[a]	2000	3.4
Median of all estimates	2009[b]	1900	3.3
Inter-quartile range of all estimates	2009[b]	1500–2400	2.6–4.1
Average of all estimates	2009[b]	2100	3.6
Confidence interval of mean (95 %)	2009[b]	1600–2600	2.7–4.4

[a]Tentative estimate, assuming that Schneider's proportion of turnover of organized crime expressed as a percentage of GDP remained unchanged over 2006–2009 period

[b]Extrapolated to global GDP in 2009

National Crime Proceeds

In Table 9.10 the estimated earnings from criminal activities are shown over the period 1965–2010 for the United States. In absolute figures, one observes a strong increase from 49 billion USD in 1965 to 1043 billion USD in 2010. If one standardizes these figures as a percentage of GDP, one observes a modest increase up to the year 2000; it was 6.8 % in 1965 and 8.0 % in 2000, then it decreased to 7.0 % in 2010. If one considers the ratio of criminal income as percentage of total illicit income (criminal plus financial and tax fraud income), one realizes that classical criminal income ranges between 29.0 % in 2000 and a maximum of 49.0 % in 1985. This clearly shows that financial and tax fraud is again by far the largest crime figure in the U.S..[7]

In Table 9.11 the figures for Australia are shown. Table 9.11 demonstrates that fraud, drugs, and shop lifting are the three biggest types of crime. In total the criminal proceeds in Australia reached 10.9 billion Australian dollars or 7.1 billion USD and are in a range between 1.5 and 2.8 % of Australian GDP.

Table 9.12 shows the crime proceeds for the Netherlands. Again, the remarkable result shows that 73.0 % of all crime proceeds come from financial, social security, and tax fraud, followed by drugs with 12.4 % and illegal workers with 3.1 %. In the Netherlands, the range of the crime proceeds is between 11.0 and 19.0 billion euros which amounts to 2.6–4.3 % of official GDP.

Table 9.10 Estimated earnings from criminal activity[a] in the United States, billions of current USD (1965–2010)

	Tax evasion included		Criminal income (*tax evasion excluded*)		
Year	Estimated criminal income	In % of GDP	Estimated criminal income	In % of GDP	Ratio of criminal income in total illicit income
1965	49	6.8	18	2.5	37 %
1970	74	7.1	26	2.5	35 %
1975	118	7.2	45	2.7	38 %
1980	196	7.0	78	2.8	40 %
1985	342	8.1	166	4.0	49 %
1990	471	8.1	209	3.6	44 %
1995	595	8.0	206	2.8	35 %
2000	779	8.0	224	2.3	29 %
2010[b]	1043	7.0	300 (235–350)	2.0 (1.6–2.3)	29 %

[a]Criminal activities included: trafficking in illicit drugs, human trafficking, burglary, larceny-theft, motor vehicle theft, robbery, fraud, arson, non-arson fraud, counterfeiting, illegal gambling, loan sharking, and prostitution. Tax evasion crimes included federal income, federal profits, and excise tax evasion

[b]Tentative UNODC estimate based on previous estimates and trends derived from new drug and crime data

Source: data from Reuter and Truman (2004) and author's elaboration

[7] See also Pickhardt and Prinz (2012).

Table 9.11 Estimated criminal proceeds in Australia, million AUD (1998 and 2003)

Illegal activities	2003 (Revised estimates)		Mid-point estimates in % of GDP	
	Min	max	1998	2003 (rev.)
1. Fraud	3000	3500	1.8	0.4
2. Drugs	2000		0.2	0.3
3. Theft			0.3	
4. Shoplifting	1020	2460		0.2
5. Car theft	654			0.1
6. Stealing from persons	545			0.1
7. Other theft	659			0.1
8. Burglaries (breaking and entering)	1193		0.2	0.2
9. Assaults	979		0.1	0.1
10. Homicide	323		0.0	0.0
11. Property damage	510		0.2	0.1
12. Robbery and extortion	37		0.0	0.0
Total 1.–12. in million AUD	10,920	12,860	2.8	1.5
Total 1.–12. in million USD	7100	8300		
In % of GDP	1.4	1.6		

Sources: Data based on Walker (2007), Walker and Unger (2009) and author's elaboration

Table 9.12 Estimated unlawful earnings in the Netherlands, million EUR (2003)

Type of crime	Proceeds of crime, million €	Proceeds of crime Mid-point estimates in % of total
1. Financial, social security and tax fraud[a]	7735–15,450	73.3
2. Drugs	1960	12.4
3. Illegal workers	490	3.1
4. Prostitution	460	2.9
5. Theft	345	2.2
6. Burglary	340	2.1
7. Fencing	190	1.2
8. Illegal gambling	130	0.8
9. Illegal copying	90	0.6
10. Computer-crime	26	0.2
11. Violent offences	6	0.0
12. Other offences	187	1.2
Total 1.–12. in million EUR	11,959–19,674	
Total 1.–12. in million USD	13,500–22,300	
As a percentage of GDP	2.6–4.3	

[a]Based on the assumption that between 5 and 10 % of the total amounts were discovered and reported

Source: data from Unger (2007) and author's elaborations

Table 9.13 Estimates of the income and profits of organized crime in Italy (2009)

Income	In billion EUR	
1. Trafficking drugs	60.00	
2. Trafficking in human beings	0.87	
3. Arms trafficking	5.80	
4. Smuggling	1.20	
Subtotal trafficking 1.–4.		67.87
5. Protection racket	9.00	
6. Loan sharking (usury)	15.00	
Subtotal 'predatory activities' 5.+6.		24.00
7. Theft and robbery	1.00	1.00
8. Procurement	6.50	
9. Agro-crime	7.50	
10. Games and gambling	2.50	
11. Counterfeiting	6.50	
12. Illegal construction	2.00	
Subtotal—illegal economic activities 7.–12.		25.00
13. Ecomafia/agromafia	16.00	16.00
14. Prostitution	0.60	0.60
15. Financial gains	0.75	0.75
Total income in bn EUR 1.–15.	135.22	135.22
Total income in bn USD 1.–15.		188.58
Total income in % of GDP		8.9

Source: data from SOS SOS Impresa (2010) and author's elaboration

Finally, in Table 9.13 the crime proceeds of Italy are shown. Crime proceeds from drugs are by far the largest with 60.0 billion euros, followed by ecomafia/agromafia-related activities with 16.0 billion euros, and loan sharking with 15.0 billion euros. Total income of crime proceeds is 135.0 billion euros or 8.9 % of the Italian GDP, which is a quite high figure.

Costs and Proceeds of Cybercrime: The latest Development in International Organized Crime

According to Anderson et al. (2012), in the last 10–15 years, cybercrime originates primarily from white-collar crimes. In the year 2007 the European Commission defined cybercrime in the following way[8]:

1. Traditional forms of crime such as fraud or forgery, though committed over electronic communication, networks, and information systems;
2. the publication of illegal content over electronic media; and
3. crimes unique to electronic networks.

[8] This definition is taken over from Anderson et al. (2012, p. 3); compare also Levi and Suddle (1989) as well as Levi (2009a, 2009b).

Today, cybercrime takes many forms, like online banking fraud (phishing) or fake antivirus, computer programs. In a first systematic paper Anderson et al. (2012) try to give a survey in measuring the cost of cybercrime and/or the criminal proceeds from some types of cybercrime.[9] Cybercrime is a rather new development and is certainly becoming more and more important. What type of cybercrime costs can one observe? Anderson et al. (2012) state the following four:

1. Costs in anticipation of cybercrime, such as antivirus software, insurance, and compliance;
2. costs as a consequence of cybercrime, such as direct losses and indirect costs, such as weakened competitiveness as a result of intellectual property compromise;
3. costs in response to cybercrime, such as compensation payments to victims and fines paid to regulatory bodies; and
4. indirect costs such as reputational damage to firms, loss of confidence in cyber transactions by individuals and businesses, reduced public-sector revenues and the growth of the underground economy.

These types of costs are shown in Fig. 9.1, where Anderson et al. (2012) try to analyze the costs of cybercrime and also some criminal revenues. From Fig. 9.1 one clearly realizes that criminal revenues or criminal proceeds can be derived from the direct losses of cybercrime. Direct losses (or proceeds of national or transnational criminal activities) include

1. money withdrawn from victim accounts;
2. stolen software; and
3. faked financial transactions.

What does one know about the costs (and partly proceeds of criminal activities) in the cybercrime area? Anderson et al. (2012) provide an interesting table (Table 9.14) about a first estimation of the costs (and partly proceeds) of the category of cybercrime.

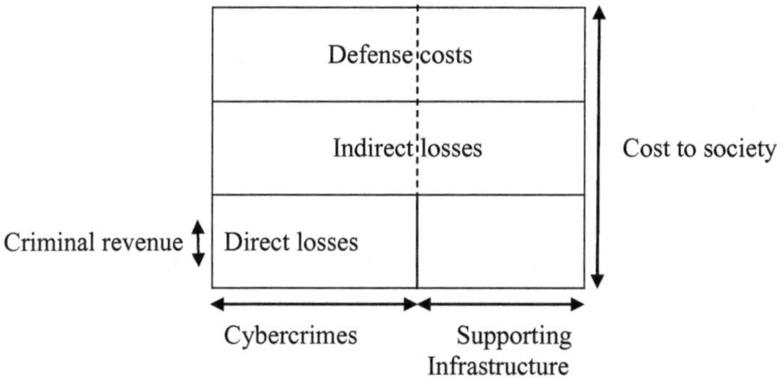

Fig. 9.1 Framework for analyzing the costs of cybercrime. *Source*: Anderson et al. (2012)

[9] Compare also Taylor (2011), Van Eeten and Bauer (2008).

Considering the four cost components (cost of genuine cybercrime, cost of transnational cybercrime, cost of cybercriminal infrastructure, and cost of traditional crimes becoming "cyber") in Table 1.14, one clearly realizes that no. 4 "Cost of crime against public institutions (welfare tax fraud)" becoming "cyber" is by far the largest part covering 67.5 % of all costs of cybercrime, which amounts to a sum of 150.2 billion USD on a global estimate. If one further turns to the global estimate, one realizes that the cost of "genuine cybercrime" on a worldwide basis is 3.5 billion USD or 1.6 % of the total cost of cybercrime. The 3.5 billion USD can also be seen as the large part of the proceeds of genuine cybercrime activities. If one considers no. 2 "Cost of transitional cybercrime" one realizes that it amounts to 44.2 billion USD or 19.8 % of the total cost of cybercrime. With 24.8 billion USD the cost of cybercriminal infrastructure is quite sizable; it amounts to 11.9 % of the total cost. As already said the costs of traditional crimes becoming cyber are 150.2 billion USD, the largest part of the cost of cybercrime. Again this could at least partly be seen as criminal proceeds of cybercrime activities in these areas, especially tax fraud. In general Table 9.14 clearly demonstrates that the cost and proceeds of cybercrime activities are sizable. In the future they will certainly rise because the use of electronic networks for crime activities becomes more and more attractive.

Summary and Conclusions

In this chapter an attempt is made to review the literature of the finances of international organized crime with a strong focus on estimations of the volume of the finances of transnational crime. This paper comes to the following preliminary findings:

First, to get an estimate of the extent and development of the amount of the financial means of transnational crime over time is very difficult. On a worldwide basis and in 2009 1.4 trillion USD (or 2.5 % of world GDP) coming from all types of crime is estimated to be laundered (see IMF, 2010). These figures are preliminary with a quite large margin of error, but give a clear indication of how important money laundering and the turnover of transnational crime nowadays is.

Second, tax fraud and/or illegal cross-border capital flows are by far the biggest share of all illegal transactions reaching 66 % of all illegal capital flows/proceeds. From these preliminary results one can draw three conclusions:

1. The revenues of transnational crime are extremely difficult to estimate. They are defined differently in almost every country, the measures taken against them are different and vary from country to country, and it is not at all clear which part of these revenues from transnational crime stays in a country with the consequence of a severe double counting problem.
2. To fight against transnational crime is difficult, too, as there are no efficient and powerful international organizations which can effectively do this job.[10]
3. Tax fraud and/or other illegal cross-border capital flows should be the prime target for governments and a rigorous fight against tax heavens should have high priority.

[10] Some fist attempts have been made, like the FATF, or some office of the UN; compare e.g. UNODC (2004, 2005), FATF (2004, 2005) and FATF-GAFI (2005, 2006); see also D'Souza (2012).

Table 9.14 An estimation of the various cost components (partly proceeds) of cybercrime

Type of cybercrime	UK estimate (in bn USD)	Global estimate (in bn USD)	Reference period	Criminal revenue	Direct losses	Indirect losses	Defense cost
1. Cost of genuine cybercrime							
Online banking fraud							
– Phishing	0.016	0.32	2007	x?	x?		
– Malware (consumer)	0.004	0.07	2010	x▼	x▼		
– Malware (businesses)	0.006	0.20		x▼	x▼		
– Bank tech. countermeasures	0.050	1.00	2010				x?
Fake antivirus	0.005	0.10	2008–2010	x▲	x▲		
Copyright-infringing software	0.001	0.02	2010	x▲	x▲		
Copyright-infringing music etc.	0.007	0.15	2011	x▼			
Patent-infringing pharma	0.014	0.29	2010	x			
Stranded traveler scam	0.001	0.01	2011	x▼			
Fake escrow scam	0.010	0.20	2011	x▼			
Advance-fee fraud	0.050	1.00	2011	x▼			
SUM of 1.	0.164 (0.9 %)	3.50 (1.6 %)					
2. Cost of transitional cybercrime							
Online payment card fraud	0.21	4.20	2010		(x)		
Offline payment card fraud							
– Domestic	0.11	2.10	2010		x▼		
– International	0.15	2.94	2010		x▼		
– Bank/merchant defense costs	0.12	2.40	2010				x▼
Indirect costs of payment fraud							
– Loss of confidence (consumers)	0.70	10.00	2010			x?	
– Loss of confidence (merchants)	1.60	20.00	2009			x?	
PABX fraud	0.19	4.96	2011	x▲	x▼		
SUM of 2.	3.07 (6.7 %)	44.20 (19.8 %)					
3. Cost of cybercriminal infrastructure							

(continued)

Table 9.14 (continued)

Type of cybercrime	UK estimate (in bn USD)	Global estimate (in bn USD)	Reference period	Criminal revenue	Direct losses	Indirect losses	Defense cost
Expenditure on antivirus	0.17	3.40	2012				x▲
Cost to industry of patching	0.05	1.00	2010				x?
ISP clean-up expenditures	0.00	0.04	2010			x?	
Cost to users of clean-up	0.50	10.00	2012			x?	
Defense costs of firms generally	0.50	10.00	2010				x?
Expenditure on law enforcement	0.02	0.40	2010				x▲
SUM of 3.	1.24	24.84 (11.9 %)					
4. Cost of cybercrime from fraud against public inst.							
Welfare	1.90	20.00	2011	x▲	(x)		
Tax fraud	12.00	125.00	2011	x?	(x)		
Tax filing fraud	–	5.20	2010	x▲	(x)		
SUM of 4.	13.90 (75.7 %)	150.20 (67.5 %)					
SUM of 1.–4.	18.37 (100 %)	222.70 (100 %)					

Estimating costs and scaling: Figures in boldface are estimates based on data or assumption for the reference area. Unless both figures in a row are bold, the non-boldface figure has been scaled using the UK's share of world GDP unless otherwise stated in the main text. Extrapolations from UK numbers to the global scale should be interpreted with utmost caution. A threshold to enter this table is defined at $10 m for the global estimates
x: included, (x): partly converted; with qualifiers x▲ for likely over-estimated, x for likely▼ underestimated, and x? for high uncertainty
Source: Anderson et al. (2012, p. 24) and author's own calculations

References

Agarwal, J. D., & Agarwal, A. (2006). Money laundering: New forms of crime, and victimization. Paper presented at the *National Workshop on New Forms of Crime* and *Victimization*, Department of Criminology, University of Madras, India.

Anderson, R., Barton, C., Böhme, R., Clayton, R., Van Eeten, M. J. G., Levi, M., … Savage, S. (2012). Measuring the cost of cybercrime. Paper presented at the 11th *Workshop on the Economics of Information Security (WEIS),* Berlin, Germany, June 25–26.

Bagella, M., Busato, F., & Argentiero, A. (2009). Money laundering in a microfounded dynamic model: Simulations for the U.S. and the EU-15 economies. *Review of Law and Economics, 5*(2), 879–902.

Baker, R. W. (2005). *Capitalism's Achilles heel – Dirty money and how to renew the free-market system*. Hoboken, NJ: John Wiley and Sons.

Belser, P. (2005). *Forced labor and human trafficking: Estimating the profits*. Geneva: ILO.
Celent, C. (2002). *Anti-money laundering: A brave new world for financial institutions*. Retrieved from http://www.celent.com/reports/anti-money-laundering-brave-new-world-financial-institutions.
Colombo, F. (2003). *Animal trafficking – A cruel billion-dollar business*. Washington, DC: World Wildlife Fund.
D'Souza, J. (2012). *Terrorist financing, money laundering and tax evasion: Examining the performance of financial intelligence units*. Boca Raton, FL: CRC Press.
FATF. (2004). *Report on money laundering and terrorist financing*. Paris: FATF.
FATF. (2005). *Report on money laundering and terrorist financing*. Paris: FAFT.
FATF. (2007). *Financial system abuse*. Paris: FATF.
FATF-GAFI. (2005). *Third mutual evaluation report on anti-money laundering and combating the financing of terrorism*. Paris: FATF.
FATF-GAFI. (2006). *Third mutual evaluation report on anti-money laundering and combating the financing of terrorism*. Paris: FATF.
Global Financial Integrity. (2011). *Transnational crime in the developing world*. Retrieved from http://www.gfintegrity.org/storage/gfip/documents/reports/transcrime/gfi_transnational_crime_web.pdf.
IMF. (2010). *Financial system abuse, financial crime and money laundering - Background paper*. Washington, DC: IMF.
Levi, M. (2009a). *Money laundering risks and e-gaming: A European overview and assessment*. Cardiff: Cardiff University.
Levi, M. (2009b). Fear of fraud and fear of crime: A review. In S. Simpson & D. Weisburd (Eds.), *The criminology of white-collar crime* (pp. 84–109). New York, NY: Springer.
Levi, M., & Suddle, M. (1989). White collar crime, shamelessness and disintegration: The control of tax evasion in Pakistan. *Journal of Law and Society, 16*(4), 489–505.
Masciandaro, D. (2004). *Global financial crime: Terrorism, money laundering and offshore centres*. Aldershot: Ashgate.
Masciandaro, D. (2005). Financial supervisory unification and financial intelligence units. *Journal of Money Laundering Control, 8*(4), 354–371.
Masciandaro, D. (2006). Offshore financial centres and international soft laws: Explaining the regulation gap. Paper presented at the Second Annual Conference of the Italian Society of Law and Economy, Rome, Italy.
Pickhardt, M., & Prinz, A. (Eds.). (2012). *Tax evasion and the shadow economy*. Cheltenham: Edward Elgar.
Reuter, P., & Truman, E. (2004). *Chasing dirty money – The fight against money laundering*. Washington, DC: Institute for International Economics.
Schneider, F. (2004). The financial flows of Islamic terrorism. In D. Masciandaro (Ed.), *Global financial crime: Terrorism, money laundering and offshore centres* (pp. 97–126). Aldershot: Ashgate.
Schneider, F. (2005). Shadow economies around the world: What do we really know? *European Journal of Political Economy, 21*(3), 598–642.
Schneider, F. (2008a). *Turnover of organised crime and money laundering: Some preliminary empirical findings. Discussion Paper*. Linz: Department of Economics, University of Linz.
Schneider, F. (2008). Money laundering from revenues from organised crime: Some preliminary empirical findings. Paper presented at the Conference *Illicit Trade and Globalization*, Venice National University, San Servolo, Italy, July 14–15.
Schneider, F. (2009). Die finanzströme von organisierter kriminalität und terrorismus: Was wissen wir (nicht)? *Vierteljahreshefte zur Wirtschaftsforschung, 78*(4), 73–87.
Schneider, F. (2010). Turnover of organized crime and money laundering: Some preliminary findings. *Public Choice, 144*, 473–486.
Schneider, F. (2011). The financial flows of transnational crime: Some preliminary empirical results. In G. A. Antonopoulos, E. Kooijmans, A. Maljevic, & K. von Lampe (Eds.), *Usual and unusual organizing criminals in Europe and beyond: Profitable crimes from underworld to upperworld* (pp. 215–232). Apeldoorn: Maklu.

Schneider, F. (2013). The financial flows of transnational crime and tax fraud in OECD countries: What do we (not) know? *Public Finance Review, 41*(5), 677–707.

Schneider, F., Dreer, E., & Riegler, W. (2006). *Geldwäsche: Formen, Akteure, Größenordnung – Warum die Politik machtlos ist*. Wiesbaden: Gabler.

Schneider, F., & Windischbauer, U. (2008). Money laundering: Some facts. *European Journal of Law and Economics, 26*(4), 387–404.

Smith, D. (2011). *Black money: The business of money laundering*. Retrieved from www.economywatch.com.

SOS Impresa. (2010). *XII Rapporto – Le mani della criminalità sulle imprese*. Retrieved from http://www.sosimpresa.it/userFiles/File/Documenti4/Rapporto_2009.pdf.

Takats, I. (2007). A theory of "Crying Wolf": The economics of money laundering enforcement. Paper presented at the conference *Tackling Money Laundering*, University of Utrecht, Utrecht, The Netherlands, November 2–3.

Taylor, J. (2011). Overseas cyber-crimewave taking £600m a year from the taxman, *The Independent*, December 3.

Unger, B. (2007). *The scale and impacts of money laundering*. Cheltenham: Edward Elgar.

UNODC. (2004). *World drug report*. Vienna: UNODC.

UNODC. (2005). *World drug report*. Vienna: UNODC.

UNODC. (2010). *The globalization of crime: A transnational organized crime threat assessment*. Retrieved from https://www.unodc.org/documents/data-and-analysis/tocta/TOCTA_Report_2010_low_res.pdf.

Van Eeten, M., & Bauer, J. M. (2008). *Economics of malware: Security decisions, incentives and externalities*. Technical Report OECD STI Working Paper 2008/1. Paris: OECD.

Walker, J. (1999). How big is global money laundering? *Journal of Money Laundering Control, 3*(1), 64–85.

Walker, J. (2007). Measuring global money laundering. Paper presented at the conference *Tackling Money Laundering*, University of Utrecht, Utrecht, Netherlands, November 2–3.

Walker, J., & Unger, B. (2009). Measuring global money laundering: The walker gravity model. *Review of Law and Economics, 5*(2), 821–853.

World Bank. (n.d.). Macroeconomic indicators. Retrieved from http://data.worldbank.org/indicator.

Zdanowicz, J. (2009). Trade-based money laundering and terrorist financing. *Review of Law and Economics, 5*(2), 854–878.

Chapter 10
The Monty Python Flying Circus of Money Laundering and the Question of Proportionality

Petrus van Duyne, Jackie Harvey, and Liliya Gelemerova

> I'm sorry to have kept you waiting, but I'm afraid my walk has become rather sillier recently.
>
> Monty Python's Flying Circus: The Ministry of Silly Walks[1]

Introduction: Proportionality and Global AML Policy

One does not need to be a moralist to recognize the moral function of the state as an actor protecting against harm. Since times immemorial this has given the responsible authorities huge powers that seem to have a built-in justification: "We act for the common good" which implies serving and protecting society against harm. And what is harm to society? Naturally, that depends on the two sides of the equation: society and harm. Though this appears a self-evident truth, looking closer the truth value soon evaporates as both concepts prove to be ill-defined and, therefore, boundless. In particular, the concept of harm has no boundaries. What does it encompass? Physical safety, war, public disorder, and health seem to be sufficiently delineable, but as soon as one addresses aspects other than (physical) health and harm,

[1] Monty Python's Flying Circus ran on BBC TV from 1969 to 1974. This quotation is taken from: http://www.telegraph.co.uk/comedy/comedians/monty-python-s-25-funniest-quotes/ (accessed 9/10/2015).

P. van Duyne
Tilburg University, Tilburg, The Netherlands
e-mail: Petrus@uvt.nl

J. Harvey (✉)
Newcastle Business School, Northumbria University, Newcastle, UK
e-mail: jackie.harvey@northumbria.ac.uk

L. Gelemerova
University of Manchester, Manchester, UK
e-mail: lilygel1@yahoo.com

G.A. Antonopoulos (ed.), *Illegal Entrepreneurship, Organized Crime and Social Control*, Studies of Organized Crime 14, DOI 10.1007/978-3-319-31608-6_10

boundaries become faint and inconsistent, if not arbitrary. And so are the related policies pursued to fend off alleged threats to such ill-defined aspects of the common good.

This sounds abstract, but has hard and tangible consequences. History abounds with examples of rulers who took their task of protecting society against harm so boundlessly that the cure was worse than the alleged threat, in particular, when spiritual values were at stake. One does not need to go as far as the Spanish Inquisition, which protected society against the threat of heresy, to recognize the effects of "boundless protection". Indeed, there are sufficient examples of lofty societal protection policies that to the degree in which they lack proper limitations, drift to an all-encompassing implementation and in due course become insensitive to the principle of *proportionality*. More recent examples can be found in regard to certain aspects of the global policies of drugs (ab)use, organized crime, and terrorism in which we find a constant shifting and blurring of the boundaries of implementation (Hobbs, 1998; Ruggiero, 2003; Van Duyne & Levi, 2005) wherein a serious threat presentation justifies extraordinary "serious" laws. Thus, in the UK the *Proceeds of Crime Act* (2002) and the *Serious Crime Act* (2007) enable the courts to impose heavy inroads against individual freedoms through restrictive conditions around work, travel, and finances for those involved[2] even in the absence of conviction. This is amplified by the state of technique, which allows the state an ever increasing (and intrusive) monitoring of citizens, all for the general good encompassing any kind of (un)safety. Technique is neutral and knows no balancing against other interests.

This balancing of interests matters. Policies that entail (financial and political) costs to society must be addressed from a proportionality perspective. This is the more important if such policies demand special additional efforts or intrude into human and citizens' rights and liberties. By its nature, criminal law policy has such an intrusive character which must therefore be balanced according to the principle of proportionality, even if this balancing sometimes slips into ritual formulations (Christoffersen, 2009; Jacobs, 1999). The principle of proportionality should not only play a role in criminal policy, but also in adjacent regulatory policies. One such adjacent field is the global anti-money laundering policy, of which the criminal and regulatory components are strongly connected. For this reason the focus of this chapter is to examine the role of the proportionality principle in the field of Anti-Money Laundering (AML).

Elements of Proportionality and AML Policy: Twin Scales

The concept of proportionality permeates the whole legal sphere but for practical application is clearly in need of operationalization: it supposes a clear equilibrium, which is not *a priori* given. This also applies to the field of AML

[2] Through application of serious crime prevention orders.

policy: operationalization of the concept is difficult although no one pleads to declare it irrelevant. However, making the proportionality principle concrete in its application cannot be achieved by a sweeping general formula. Instead, we have to look at elements in the AML policy that at first sight are relevant for determining proportionality. For each element we have to ask the question: "Can it be specified sufficiently for a proportionality equation?" We can also use the metaphor of the balance with two scales which must be filled concretely for properly weighing one against the other. For example, the threat of money laundering must be balanced against the countermeasures. This is a many faceted issue requiring a step-by-step analytical and empirical process, albeit, without subsequent guaranteed success.

The Crime-Money (and Laundering) Threat Side of the Balance

The term "money laundering" is a technical construction but not a neutral one. As early as 1998, Van Duyne indicated that it was exploited for political ends and provided with emotional meanings by what he termed the "threat assessment industry" (Van Duyne, 1998, p. 359; see also Verhage & Ponsaers, 2009). This is particularly the case if it is connected with the concept of "(transnational) organized crime" (Van Duyne & Nelemans, 2011). Thus we see enshrined in the supranational regulations statements that money laundering (and terrorist financing) "shakes the very foundations of our society."[3] Threat is indeed the first and most important relevant element to consider for balancing: politically it is the most mentioned reason for AML policy.

More important, the threat of crime-money is also a better candidate variable for a proportionality equation than a general moral imperative, such as "crime should not pay." A moral statement expresses an absolute or dichotomous value about an act such as law breaking: it is there or not. A threat is, in principle, a *scalable* phenomenon for "putting on the scales" of a balance. While this sounds simple, problems arise in determining exactly what should be added to the scales. That should be a solvable puzzle as every insurance expert knows: on one scale is the harm, on another the financial compensation. However, even an insurance comparison of two similar threats makes clear that nothing is self-evident. For example, New Orleans (USA) and the Western Netherlands both consist of lowlands and are always threatened by flooding. How to convert that threat proportionally into another variable: the size of the protecting dikes? That requires weighing other interests. The authorities of the two areas found two relevant but different "weights": value of physical assets versus value of human lives. In New Orleans protective dikes were constructed in proportion to the value of protected assets, which entailed that mainly poor neighborhoods (considered low valued assets) were flooded with loss of life of

---

[3] Directive 2005/60/EC 26th October 2005 (p. 1) on the prevention of the use of the financial system for the purpose of money laundering and terrorist financing, available from http://eur-lex.europa.eu/legal-content/EN/TXT/?uri=celex:32005L0060 (accessed 19/10/2015).

(mainly poor) citizens. In the Netherlands the threatened interest is the human life which implies dikes of an equal defense quality for all. Indeed, nothing is self-evident: the same water and potential flooding, but different threats and responses. Does this also apply to the AML policy?

Almost 30 years ago IMF Managing Director Camdessus stated that the threat of money laundering was "2 to 5 percent of global GDP … probably [as] a consensus range."[4] Underlying evidence for this "consensus range" was not provided, nor was it clear between whom such consensus existed. Notwithstanding such absence of facts, Tanzi (1996) and Quirk (1996) of the same Institute hastened to provide some substantiation. But where did that threatening crime-money come from? To provide a proxy-variable for money-generating crime they resorted to the crime-data from Interpol though seemingly without judging its (un)reliability for this purpose. Next they used a broad definition of money laundering, which is tantamount to the (hypothetical) sum of transactions in the shadow economy, particularly if tax crimes are included (Gelemerova, 2011).

This was an approach which conveniently fitted into the statement of the IMF hierarchy. Given the authority (and power) of the IMF it was adopted by the UNODC. In its report, the UNODC estimated the amount of crime-money (proceeds) at US $2.6 trillion in 2009 of which US $1.6 trillion would be "available" for laundering (UNODC, 2011). The term "available," a phrase with unspecified meaning, was adopted from the 1990 FATF report.[5]

Many academics eagerly jumped on the bandwagon or aligned themselves with the IMF-led mainstream, and have commented upon the justification for the anti-money laundering regime to protect society, the financial industry, and the economy against profit driven crime and connected laundering, albeit sometimes with a skeptical voice (Alldridge, 2003; Arnone & Borlini, 2010; Blickman, 2010; Bosworth-Davies, 2008; Gelemerova, 2011; Harvey, 2004; Levi & Maguire, 2004; McCarthy, van Santen, & Fiedler, 2014; Unger, 2007; Van Duyne, Soudijn, & Kint, 2009).

It should be observed that there are few independent empirical sources: as a matter of fact there is much "reference recycling." The FATF (1990) report uses United Nations sources for estimations (qualified by the FATF in that report as "of doubtful reliability" (p. 5)) while the UNODC (2005) uses again the FATF 1990 estimates as a source. There are also no independent sources used which are outside the "IMF consensus" while it is apparent that nobody knows how this consensus emerged. Walker and Unger (2009, p. 823) note that the figure is a complete guess and that it has not been replicated "even by academics doing intensive studies within the Fund." Despite this, Walker and Unger accept the IMF approach and most of the assumptions underlying this guessing "consensus." Others have drawn attention to the reliance that has and continues to be placed on what, therefore, amounts to

[4] A copy of the speech is available at http://www.imf.org/external/np/speeches/1998/021098.htm (accessed 20/10/2014).

[5] The FATF report was even more careful and used the formulation: "could be available for laundering" (FATF, 1990, p. 5). This subjunctive plus the undetermined phrase "available" was soon converted into the indicative mode: is being laundered.

inaccurate or flawed data: "Most literature on money laundering effects is pure speculation, or it is based on figures that are either wrongly cited, misinterpreted or just invented" (Barone & Masciandaro, 2011, p. 118; see also Blickman, 2010; Schneider & Windischbauer, 2008).

The attempt by the UNODC (2011, p. 79) to arrive at a more sophisticated estimation is marred by its heavy reliance on the "IMF consensus," the maintenance of which seems to be a holy task, while it is loaded by an accumulation of assumptions. For example, that money "available for laundering" would have an income threshold of €18.000[6] (to be discussed below). Below that threshold, money would simply be spent without laundering (though, according to the definition of the Council of Europe this is technically laundering too). Based on our prior research on more than 150 organized crime cases (Meloen, Landman, De Miranda, Van Eekelen, & Van Soest, 2003; Van Duyne, Kouwenberg, & Romeijn, 1990) and of confiscation and asset recovery databases (Harvey, 2014; Harvey & Lau, 2009; Van Duyne, de Zanger, & Kristen, 2014; Van Duyne et al., 2009), we can state that this is an unrealistic assumption. Based on a preliminary research on criminal money management (Van Eekelen, 2000), researchers at the Dutch Criminal Intelligence Unit decided to set the threshold for research on crime-money at €450,000 (at that time 1,000,000 Dutch guilders) for the simple reason that below this level there is little, if any, interesting laundering activity to be observed. The upper limit of such expenses was randomly set at the median of the GDP (the 50 % point): criminal income above that median was considered to be laundered. This has no empirical basis: it is a recurrent finding that criminal income distribution has a median of around €5000 (Van Duyne & Soudijn, 2010). In addition, the seepage of money due to criminal lifestyle which requires no laundering activities is substantial (Meloen et al., 2003; Van Duyne, 2003). Given these findings it may be more realistic to set the laundering threshold at between €100,000 and €500,000.

Though the word "available" is easily overlooked (perhaps because it is so common: it is one of the most frequent words in the UNODC (2011) report, occurring 168 times), it is important because it should be a key word in the threat operationalization. As discussed above, the first FATF (1990) report mentioned that "50 to 70 % [of proceeds] could be available for laundering" (p. 5). By its meaning this implies a division between laundered and not (yet) laundered money. This is important as it raises the question of what is threatening: laundered or *un*laundered money, with the latter then divided into available or launderable and not-available or non-launderable crime-money? It can be argued that one subset can be excluded from the scales of the threat balance: *laundered money*. By its nature it is already within the financial system and therefore has become a (taxable) part of the official GDP. One may not like it morally, but practically it poses no more financial threat than other recorded financial assets: due to successful laundering it is accountable, "traceable" and taxable.

What about the "*un*laundered" monies? Leaving aside whether unlaundered criminal money can technically exist in the first place (hiding proceeds is also

[6] For the year 2009.

laundering, according to the Council of Europe definition), the global dangers coming from proceeds hoarded in socks, mattresses and pillows or from the daily livelihood expenses trickling into the upperworld economy need to be specified. Criminal revenues, whether laundered or hoarded, have always slipped into the licit economy. Historical economic research should bring that to the surface: models must be tested on established historical data, not on the daydreams of scenarios. For example, how were the criminal revenues from bootlegging during the Prohibition era integrated into the US economy and what financial threats could be identified in the 1920s and 1930s?[7]

This short exposé leaves us with an unanswered question: the volume of the threatening phenomenon remains unspecified and we have a concept "available" that remains undefined. This scale of the proportionality balance appears to be filled with assumptions, unspecified concepts with fuzzy delineations and recycled argumentations. In short, collective hunches elevated to an "IMF consensus" as is discussed in the next section.

A Critical Survey of Attempts to Produce Evidence

The previous section does not bode well for the various attempts that have been made to give empirical substance to the threat side of the AML policy. Empirical studies are scarce and can roughly be divided into two groups: economists who are more or less consensus following or within the consensus range, and behavioral researchers who primarily test the assumptions of the consensus against observations carried out at the micro level using data from criminal files, law enforcement databases, or fieldwork.

Within Economic Models

In the absence of observable data, economists have tended to resort to construction of hypothetical models. The model has two important aspects: its basis and assumptions. The basis is formed by the definition of the phenomenon: "Money laundering is the process by which illicit source moneys are introduced into an economy and used for legitimate purposes" (Walker, 1995, p. 1). This definition has an enormous range of application as it also covers mere spending of crime-money (including tax crime) if that spending is for legitimate purposes.[8] Oddly, using crime-money for

[7] After the repeal of the Prohibition in 1933 many bootleggers, like Joseph P. Kennedy, the father of President Kennedy (Kessler, 1996), dropped out, settled their IRS problems and went into the newly legitimate liquor trade (Abadinsky, 1994, pp. 94–95).

[8] There are many definitions of money laundering, summarized by Busuioc (2007). Although, in many studies it is not clear what definition is being used: mentioning a definition at the beginning does not guarantee that the authors adhere to it and will not implicitly broaden its circle.

illegitimate purposes, like buying a boat intended for smuggling and paying the "criminal" crew, would not be laundering. The point of the hidden or "hoarded" monies remain untouched and is qualified as (self)laundering in most jurisdictions. Another part of the basis of the model concerns the estimated percentage laundered per type of crime, mostly 80%: methodologically debatable (no proper account of the respondents) and empirically unrealistic (Reuter, 2013, p. 227; Walker, 1995). With so much uncertainty in the basis we conclude that the validity of the model cannot be stronger than that of the basis. Unfortunately, a high degree of followership can be observed if judged by the direct acceptance of the assumptions and statements of the IMF, World Bank, and FATF, part of which find their way into economic models (Unger et al., 2013; Walker & Unger, 2009). These models stagger from the first step onwards mainly due to lack of empirical underpinning. Despite these inadequacies, both the model and findings were reused in the UNODC 2011 Report. This report, prepared by Thomas Pietschmann (Research Officer, STAS) and John Walker (Consultant), also made use of related estimates from Walker (1995) and Walker and Unger (2009).[9]

It should be noted that definitional fuzziness is also a characteristic of the UNODC Report (2011). The problem of defining is mentioned, but no formal operational definition (money laundering= ...) is proposed. There is no proper analysis of demarcation issues by which we mean: clarifying what is *excluded* from the set of laundering. In none of these studies is there an unambiguous choice for a particular operational definition or a proper specification of key concepts such as "available" (or "launderable").

As noted above, a rather *ad hoc* demarcation line has been drawn in the UNODC (2011) report whereby the median threshold of criminal income was set at €18,000 dividing (assumed/available) laundering and not-laundering. We will later see how plausible this is. Another approach mentioned in the report would be to subtract an approximated amount of money needed for consumption from the gross domestic product figures. "Amounts earned above such per capita consumption expenditure would be available for money-laundering" (UNODC, 2011, p. 81). Note again the added unspecified adverbial phrase of "available for" which easily slips towards the indicative "is." One can call this *indicative bias*: sliding from the subjunctive modus of "may," "might," and "could" to the indicative modus of "it is" (see Van Duyne, 1993; Van Duyne, Groenhuijsen, & Schudelaro, 2005).

Such an indicative bias can also be observed in the report of ECOLEF, drafted by the Utrecht School of Economics in which the phrase "available for laundering" also plays an important role. "Available" crime-monies are presented as a percentage of the GDP, which looks almost real. In the end the "results" are ranked according to an "actualized %" of laundering threats (="available"), though we are still within a hypothetical model which remains based on a defective definition and

[9] The methodology employed was reviewed by an "external reference group" that included Prof. Dr. Friedrich Schneider from Johannes Kepler University of Linz and Prof. Dr. Brigitte Unger from Utrecht University (UNODC, 2011, p. 2).

shady estimations as far as the alleged proceeds are concerned. Within the proposed models it looks convincing but as soon as one looks for independent empirical evidence, the model coverage becomes shallow and incoherent.

Outside the Consensus Models

There is more between heaven and earth than consensus models. What matters in the end is that the outcomes of a model are tested against "data on the ground": assumption against refutation. To this end Ferwerda (2013) has listed the presumed effects of money laundering on the economy, of which he found 25 in the literature (the "consensus"), and tried to find empirical evidence for each of them. Using a large variety of (open) sources, the author had to admit that for most effects independent evidence was lacking, an observation that had also been provided by Reuter (2013). Worse, for many of the stated effects, pretenses of evidence had been made without any trace. Ferwerda quotes Barlett (2002) who stated: "It is clear from available evidence," though without any reference to that alleged evidence. Nevertheless, Barlett, who discussed the effect of laundering on distortion of consumption, investment, savings, imports and exports, income and employment, demand for money, interest and exchange rates, corruption, reputation, and increase in crime, got away with this unsubstantiated statement and was (and still is) widely quoted.

Concerning the almost "self-evident" effect, the furthering of crime because of laundering, Ferwerda observed a measurement problem: laundering as a criminal act is counted in addition to the predicate offense. That entails that the independent variable of "laundering" is also counted in the dependent variable "prevalence of crime," making nonsense of the whole measurement exercise. More than a decade earlier Reuter and Greenfield (2001) came to the same conclusion. It is clear that it is time to move away from this large figure circus and its attendant overreliance on numbers that are "scientifically doubtful" (Schneider & Windischbauer, 2008, p. 117; see also Van Duyne & De Miranda, 1999; Reuter & Truman, 2005; Reuter & Greenfield, 2001).

Alldridge (2003), citing Van Duyne (1998), observes that if the amounts of crime-money had been near the sums estimated, the impact would surely have been noticeable, which it is not. We do not conclude that the inflow of crime-money in certain markets, such as the real estate market, has not had any effect. There is recurrent "anecdotal evidence" (widely spread over time and space) that crime-money investment in real estate had inflationary effects (Morocco: De Mas, 2001; Colombia: Keh, 1996). However, in what way do the effects of these crime-money flows differ from other money flows, e.g., originating from migrant labor savings or financial windfalls from the oil or minerals extraction industry (Van Duyne & Levi, 2005)? If badly managed oil money leads just as much to an unbalanced economy as the in- and outflow of crime-money, other and more relevant questions have to be raised.

For our objective to give meaning to the "proportionality balance," the outcomes of this surveillance look bleak. The *evidence* scale of the threat balance is "loaded" with unspecified concepts, assumptions underlying models which "might" be true but which are nevertheless presented in the indicative modus of "is."

This is a dilemma: despite this empirical fuzziness we cannot dispense with the concept of proportionality, but we cannot make it sharper either. Perhaps we should leave the scale of threat and the evading evidence as it is—"within brackets"—and accept that for most policy makers and their constituencies, the mere semblance of evidence is already sufficient as justification for what they are willing to put on the other scale: the accumulated efforts of the fight against money laundering.

The Effort Side

Leaving the threat scale for a while "within brackets" does not imply that the proportionality principle is no longer relevant. As a matter of fact it emerges all the time and in every measure that is taken to counter the threat of laundering: after all, these efforts are also presented as being in balance to the "threat" whatever its lack of precision. Nevertheless, it is equally difficult to draw up an exhaustive list of measures and convert these into something measurable such as money spent in fighting money laundering. So we will look at the bits and pieces that are available. To that end we turned to the reported efforts of the FATF and its sister organizations and to their documents of such effort: the Mutual Evaluation Reports (MERs). From there we turned to the regulated sectors to find out whether there are reliable data about their efforts.

Mutual Evaluations: Much Effort and Little Coherence

Since its establishment in 1989, the FATF has regularly issued "Recommendations" to the national authorities to act against money laundering. The aim of the FATF is to have these Recommendations translated into legal and regulatory frameworks and implemented across the globe. In order to prevent a noncommittal attitude, this has to be supervised. One can say that this constitutes a top-down effort in which the FATF and its "sisters," the FATF Style Regional Bodies (FSRBs), play a prominent role.[10] How is this role fulfiled and how much effort does it demand?

The FATF proclaims its objective as being to set standards and promote an effective implementation of measures against laundering.[11] That does not go for free. As the FATF is in essence a "policy making body"[12] and (in theory) not a kind of

[10] The FSRBs are: Asia/Pacific Group on Money Laundering (APG); Caribbean Financial Action Task Force (CFATF); Eurasian Group (EAG); Eastern and Southern Africa Anti-Money Laundering Group (ESAAMLG); FATF Latin America (GAFILAT); GIABA; Middle East and North Africa FATF (MENAFATF); Council of Europe (Moneyval).

[11] FATF website http://www.fatf-gafi.org/about/ (accessed 24/9/2015).

[12] FATF website http://www.fatf-gafi.org/about/ (accessed 24/9/2015).

Table 10.1 Summary of the mutual evaluation report process

Purpose of MER	Assessment of formal compliance with recommendations and assessment of effectiveness of implementation. Rating for each Recommendation as Compliant (C); Largely Compliant (LC); Partially Compliant (PC); and Non-Compliant (NC); Not Applicable (NA).
Assessment team	Appointed by FATF Secretariat from FATF members, associate members, FATF-style regional bodies or international organizations with observer status.
Skills	The team will include experts in law, law enforcement, and financial regulation with expertise in AML/CFT and includes a member of FATF secretariat. They will not necessarily have country specific knowledge
Scope of review	Institutional framework; AML/CFT laws, regulations, and guidance including both law and regulatory enforcement; assessment of effectiveness of the system to deter ML and CFT
Documentation	FATF Methodology for Assessing Compliance with the FATF 40+9 and a Handbook for Countries and Assessors.
Approach	Pre-visit completion of a questionnaire, team visit for a period of 1–2 weeks comprising meetings with government officials and with private sector; post visit drafting of the report in consultation with officials within the country. The report is tabled at and further discussed at one of the Plenary meetings when the ratings can be amended and once consensus is reached, the report is published. Within 2 years the inspected country has to report back to the plenary on progress made in addressing identified deficiencies.

Source: Adapted from Chaikin (2009: 242-244); see also Levi and Gilmore (2002: 346), Halliday, Levi, and Reuter (2014: 27).

global inspectorate, it has no budget for supervising the implementation of its own Recommendations. This task is ceded to the Member States to evaluate their own money laundering policy against the 40 Recommendations plus special Terrorist Financing Recommendations (as modified from 1990, 1996, 2003, and 2012), using for each Recommendation a simple four point "measuring rod," running from noncompliance to full compliance, which are summed to a final score. The stated purpose is to evaluate whether members have "effectively" built up their controls and systems to prevent criminal abuse of the financial system.

Simple enough, but each review is expensive to execute, involving a team of four to six "experts" with legal, financial, and law enforcement expertise and two members of the FATF/FSRB Secretariat, IMF or World Bank, protracted visits, meetings, and copious reports taking up to a year to complete with follow-up responses from the reviewed nation occurring over several years (See Table 10.1).

This mechanism of mutual evaluation results in the production of as many MERs as there are Member States. It focuses on outputs (in particular STRs/SARs,[13] convictions, and asset recovery) and ignores the costs associated with any system (Chaikin, 2009, pp. 242–244; Sharman, 2008, p. 641). The third evaluation round is just now drawing to a close and the fourth evaluation round has already commenced.

[13] Suspicious transaction reports/Suspicious activity reports.

There has been little critical interrogation of this expensive area of the AML framework that sees a "one size fits all" approach across multiple countries of different sizes, levels of development, and thus relative financial sophistication. We find the absurdity of Vanuatu (266,937 souls) drafting its AML legislation as "a word for word copy of the UN model" right down to provision for nonexistent complex financial derivatives (Sharman, 2008, p. 642). It looks like an example of what Van Duyne (2009, p. 1) calls: a "compulsive excessive regulatory disorder." It is also instructive that Levi and Gilmore (2002) pointed to the differential application in standards whereby the rules and sanctions are enforced more firmly against smaller states than against the USA.

We found three prior studies that have looked at compliance with individual Recommendations (attributing a numerical score to the compliance ratings) extracting information from individual country MERs, each of which has focused on a sample of countries. Arnone and Padoan (2008) and Johnson (2008) independently looked at the degree of compliance by Recommendation for samples of 20 and 16 countries using a four point constant interval linear scale. Ferwerda (2009) took another approach. Arguing that the assessment of the degree of compliance was influenced by the resources available to the country being assessed (with more expected of more developed countries), he proposed an alternative scoring system ranging across a 5 point scale that he applied to a sample of 17 countries. However, as there was no independent verification of his scoring, it too is open to criticism. Johnson (2008) looked at average levels of compliance before (from the self-assessment approach) and after 2003 (third round of mutual evaluation) and concluded that there was a reduction in levels of compliance. However, as different groups undertook the different evaluations, these remain as interpretation rather than findings. One consistent observation from these studies was that there was overarching criticism of the MER reports with inconsistency in layout, in underlying quality, and in overall size (Arnone & Padoan, 2008; Ferwerda, 2009; Halliday, Levi, & Reuter, 2014).

We decided to take more detailed stock of the outcomes of the third evaluation round by selecting a large sample (about 90 reports) in the hope of being able to gain a better view on the effort side. To our knowledge no other studies have attempted to analyze such a large sample.

MERs are not for the faint hearted: the quality and readability varies widely. As noted in Table 10.1, the mutual evaluation is not a free exercise: after thorough preparation the targeted country is visited for an on-site inspection of about 10 days by between 4 and 11 evaluators (average six) who issue a report of up to 650 pages (average 222 pages) in length. From the 90 reports that we reviewed, there was much variation and little consistency. So, for example, Uganda (rated by Transparency International a lowly 2.7 corruption TI-index[14]) was reviewed in June

[14] TI refers to Transparency International Corruption Perceptions Index. Although not a measure of money laundering, this is mentioned in the reports and is used here as an external indication of the susceptibility to laundering. The values reported are for 2005 and 2006, the start of the third round of evaluations.

2005 under the auspices of the ESAAMLG[15] by a team of four evaluators. Their deliberations resulted in a slim volume of 82 pages despite the fact the average compliance rating (against the Recommendations) was 1.2 and modal compliance rating merely 1. Contrast this with France: (with a general corruption rating of 7.4 by TI), reviewed in February 2011 under the watchful gaze of the FATF by seven evaluators. They proudly produced a veritable tome of some 664 pages even though their modal and average compliance judgements were 3 and 2.9, respectively. Smaller jurisdictions with a relatively low crime rate, e.g., Denmark, or small financial markets such as Moldova (299 pages and seven evaluators) or geographically remote such as Vanuatu (four staff spending 12 days) appear to require as much or more energy of the evaluators than larger countries. All this is a major effort in terms of traveling and staff and has been estimated to cost some US $300,000 per evaluation (Halliday et al., 2014, p. 49). Looking at it from the perspective of proportionality it was often "much ado about nothing" and certainly not about a money laundering threat.

The subjective nature of assessment has resulted in the evaluation of compliance with recommendation rules (inputs). Even this cannot be measured consistently. No matter the number of times it is used, referred to, and apparently "measured," one review team's conclusion about what effective compliance can be is very different from that of another. This implies that the phrase "partially compliant" can embrace such a range of responses it almost requires its own mini-calibration. Similarly, many of the reports assess "compliant" simply on the basis of control being present: box ticking wise. Effectiveness (outputs) seemed to be of subordinate concern. Incidentally the evaluators deplore the leniency of the (Scandinavian) courts and urge for a more repressive policy, apparently not realizing that in democratic constitutions judges are independent. Consistent with the surreal comedy that was the trade-mark of the *Monty Pythons Flying Circus* television show, we observe comments such as this from the Danish MER: "The criminalization of the financing of terrorism by Denmark is fully compliant, but Greenland and the Faroe Islands have not yet adequately criminalized the financing of terrorism, terrorists, and terrorist organizations." (Special Recommendation II, p. 58[16]) So the rating is reduced to "Partly Compliant" irrespective of the extremely limited potential for criminal or terrorist infiltration of the small economies of either Greenland (population 56,000) or of the Faroe Islands (population 49,000).[17]

The effort in terms of time and money does not end with the drawing up of the MERs. This tabular representation of the MER formula shown in Table 10.1 implies a closed end process that is complete at least within two years of the report being accepted. As discussed below, this is in fact far from the end of the matter as for

[15] ESAAMLG: Eastern and Southern Africa Anti-Money Laundering Group.

[16] MER available at http://www.fatf-afi.org/media/fatf/documents/reports/mer/MER%20Denmark%20full.pdf (accessed 25/9/2015).

[17] Denmark which, according to the ECOLEF report (Unger et al., 2013, p. 281) has the lowest "threat level," is nevertheless reproached by the FATF for not having criminalized self-laundering.

many jurisdictions the resulting follow-up can go on for many years. All reports must be reviewed by two or more reviewers after which (with comments and annotations of the evaluated country) it is presented to the FATF for the next Plenary Session or at the Plenary of one of the FATF regional-style bodies. This is (frequently) a place of "shame and blame." Countries with flaws in their system or its implementation get "homework" and have to submit follow-up reports till the Plenary is satisfied and the country can be relieved of its reporting duties. Countries that persistently fall short are subject to a visit by a "High Level Mission" (a kind of severe FATF Headmaster) effectively demanding compliance.

Dependent on the approach of the FATF-style regional organization, monitoring, and follow-up homework continues more or less frequently bearing little relation to the size of country, complexity of financial sector, or apparent vulnerability to criminal infiltration or indeed original evaluation. We looked into the follow-up procedure (or its absence) for a selection of countries. From this it can be observed that the Caribbean FATF (CFATF) is the most assiduous in the post evaluation follow-up requirements that are placed upon individual countries. The CFATF requires twice yearly reports of many Member States. But the CFATF also took the decision at its El Salvador Plenary in May 2015 that all Members who had not exited the third round follow-up process should simply be allowed do so by November 2015. For other countries reviewed under the auspices of Asian/Pacific Group (APG) nothing further appears to have been warranted or if it was, it is not then publically disclosed. MONEYVAL appear to execute the most thorough of procedures including revisits and reassessments by the "high level mission" leading to further long reports.

Countries persisting in their unrepentant noncompliance may in the end be "put into the corner" as a "high risk and non-cooperative jurisdiction."[18] This is not an inconsequential qualification: financial institutions transacting with these countries without enhanced due diligence may be sanctioned. Threat of international blacklisting (a now discontinued term) as sanction, refutes the idea of "soft law" (Stessens, 2000). It is a verdict without appeal and as such it is debatable whether these aspects of the work of the FATF heed the principle of proportionality.

Proportionality and the Flying Circus of observers

In addition, we looked at the expense side of the *social* efforts of the FATF. The procedure of mutual evaluation is not the only "tool" to maintain some kind of global socio-political coherence. Visiting each other, not only to conduct (and observe) MERs but also attending (as member and observer) the various (frequent) regional plenary sessions, training, and updating workshop sessions or typology workshops is an ongoing social activity. The intensity of these social activities is not

[18] The relevant countries are: Iran, North Korea, Algeria, and Myanmar. The latter two have taken steps towards improving their AML/CFT regimes, but the FATF Plenary thinks it is insufficient, particularly where it concerns terrorist financing. FATF Public Statement—26 June 2015.

to be underestimated: it is not only a matter of one FATF, but of a further eight FATF Style Regional Bodies (FSRBs). The FATF itself currently comprises 34 member jurisdictions and 2 regional organizations. The eight regional "FATF-*ies*" are its associate members, while there are observers from about 30 organizations represented in the plenary FATF meetings or other events such as typology workshops.

The phenomenon of *observership* is difficult to assess, but should not be underestimated, particularly not because of its quantity. There are some 93 institutions visiting the organizational events of both the FATF and FSRBs as observers. Three FSRBs have even more observers than Member States. The FATF, the IMF, World Bank, Interpol, and the United States have observer status in five or more FSRBs. To this should be added the *Egmont Group of Financial Intelligence Units* of 151 member FIUs, of which the events are (potentially) attended by 19 observers, comprising mainly a selection from the 93 observing institutions. As these are global social relationships which imply a lot of traveling, one can imagine that the maintenance of bonds between so many sister organizations and visiting observing relatives entails quite an expensive *Flying Circus*.

We are not the first to ask about the cost of this circus. Harvey (2011) drew a spectacular blank in her attempts to access budgetary information from the FATF and FSRBs; despite e-mail requests no information was provided. A similar blank wall was presented to our more recent enquiries (2015). Only three FSRBs presented any type of financial statement in their annual report and only the Asia and Pacific Group (APG) provided a breakdown of the annual budget of US $ 3.2 million for the fiscal year 2014–2015 of which US $ 640,144 is to cover travel expenses for their Executive Secretary and 13 staff. The FATF itself has a budget line for traveling of almost US $ 300,000. Similar budgetary information from other FSRBs or countries is not available. Nevertheless, even if it is not the case that "all visit all," it is plausible to assume some sort of a multiplier for the sum of these socio-institutional costs.

Costs: Budgets and Staff

The MERs also provide us with some information about efforts in terms of staffing and budgets of a large number of the FIUs within our sample: in 32 cases a budget was mentioned. These data must be treated with utmost caution: not only because they can be outdated, but also because their meaning can be ambiguous unless the law enforcement backgrounds are taken into account. For example, Russia and Lithuania have FIUs with respectively 550 and 450 employees while the size of their economies obviously varies enormously. However, according to the report on Lithuania, "the AML regime is mostly used for the detection of other crimes" which the evaluators criticize as "unacceptable," though without explaining what is wrong with such a use.[19] The massive effort of Russia is rather to be compared with that of

[19] This provides an example of the "meddlesomeness" of the FATF: financial investigation should serve to counter money laundering as well as crime-for-profit.

the USA FIU, which has a staff of 522 (2006) of which 107 are analysts. Whether these can be directly compared is problematic: the USA, having a bigger economy, a larger population, and a longer AML-tradition, produced 1075 money laundering convictions in the reporting year (not including convictions at state level) against 118 in Russia in the same year. The latter concern both "stand alone" (25) and "self-laundering" (93) convictions. There were 532 convictions with money laundering as "aggravating circumstances." A separate table "Cases containing FIU material" mentioned 95 convictions as FIU related.[20] This is the only clear reference to a connection between law enforcement output and FIU efforts.

Otherwise it is difficult to interpret the expenses/effort data of the MERs meaningfully without knowing the individual setting of the FIUs. For example the FIUs in Germany (2010, budget unknown) and Thailand (2007, budget US $4,100,000) have 245 employees each, but Germany produced 766 prosecutions and 608 convictions against 12 prosecutions and no convictions in Thailand. One may wonder how effective the Thai effort is, compared to that of Germany. However, in Germany the number of staff only concerns the FIUs at state (Länder) level, while at the central (BKA) level, FIU functions are embedded in a special section on Joint Financial Investigation.[21] Indeed, comparing FIUs, whether using effort (input in staff, budget) or output numbers (prosecutions or convictions) is fraught with *caveats*. For example, the FIU of China has 80 staff and that of Romania 90 staff. However, there are regionally about 300 full time employees of the Peoples' Bank of China and a further 7000 part-time, who perform FIU functions. Despite this difference, the outcome in terms of conviction is the same: one conviction for money laundering in each country (2006).[22]

The MERs do not comment on the apparent or perceived reputation of individual countries. However, we were surprised that the numbers appeared at odds with the "reputation" of a country, e.g., its significance as a financial center, without the evaluators taking this into consideration. For example, the British Virgin Islands is perceived as one of the "hotspot" offshore centers (Van Koningsveld, 2015), together with the Cayman Islands or Luxembourg. So one might reasonably expect that this would be reflected in a substantial workload and corresponding size of the FIU staff. However, these three FIUs have a staff of six (BVI and Cayman Islands) or seven (Luxembourg) with an average modest workload input of 178 suspicious transaction reports and 6 convictions.[23]

Overseeing our intermediary stock taking of the MERs from the perspective of efforts to be put into the scale to counterbalance the laundering threat, looks like

---

[20] MER Russia, pp. 39 and 61.

[21] MER Germany, 2010, p. 112; MER Thailand, 2007; pp. 85 and 97.

[22] MER Romania, 2008, p. 58; MER China, 2007. The Chinese statistics are somewhat non-transparent because 26 persons were convicted pursuant to art. 349 CC which covers hiding, transferring, etc., narcotic drugs *or* their pecuniary gains which implies that both or only one condition needs to be fulfilled producing unreliable ML statistics.

[23] The authors of the ECOLEF report notice that Luxembourg (highest average income in the EU) was slightly more "threatened" (according to the report) than other EU Member States.

"much ado about nothing." When we go beyond the individual member state's efforts and include the efforts and connected expenses of the Flying Circus of the FATF and FSRBs and weigh this subsequently against the quality of the output, it is difficult to consider this as a display of efficiency. The readability of the reports is generally low and quantitative core information is often difficult to find efficiently. The redundancy is high and the internal coherence often low. We already commented on the difficulty of how the evaluators can give any rating of efficiency and effectiveness of a country's performance in the absence of proper statistics. For example, the FIU in the Seychelles has no statistics but is found to be partially compliant. In this case the evaluators should have suspended their opinion, which did not happen. Another example is the phenomenon of corruption. In many reports corruption is mentioned as a problem, with specific reference to the TI corruption perceptions index but without sufficient analysis of the functioning of the government and the judiciary and of how corruption ties to laundering. See for example, countries such as Russia, China, Greece, or Bosnia-Herzegovina. The point about bribe laundering as a reason to file an STR to the FIU gets lost.[24] If there is so much bribery, where are the related STRs? While the FATF meddles with the criminalization of self-laundering (usually minor cases), we find no sign of the FATF's concern for the absence of meaningful FIU statistics on bribe laundering.

Concluding our search on the FATF efforts as something to put into the scale of the hypothetical proportionality balance, we find mainly a lot of fuzziness going together with a continuous deployment of much energy and expenses, but we find many indications that much of that energy has just dissipated.

Efforts related to the regulated sectors running the gauntlet between profit making and compliance

In order to better understand the proportionality of the AML regime and its effectiveness, the UK House of Lords held a hearing in 2008 which resulted in a two-volume report published in 2009. In its evidence to the same enquiry, The Law Society (2009) stated that

> The mutual evaluations conducted by FATF do not consider the costs actually borne by the private sector in meeting their compliance obligations. The mutual evaluations also do not quantify the scale of the criminal economy in the relevant jurisdiction or the actual overall results in impacting or preventing criminal activity achieved through the anti-money laundering regime in that jurisdiction.

The main costs are incurred by or on behalf of the regulated sectors. This is doubly plural: not only is the financial sector involved, but also designated non-financial businesses and professions (DNBPs). In addition, there are costs of supervision. Banks, credit institutions, stock brokers, casinos, but also lawyers, notaries, real estate brokers, car dealers, art dealers, auction houses, and other traders in valuables

[24] The statistics of "corruption mentioning" of these countries is also remarkable: Russia—68; China—27; Greece—15; and Bosnia-Herzegovina—73.

have to be supervised.[25] That does not go for free: supervising such an extensive and ramified field to check compliance of sometimes complicated "Recommendations" (meaning "demands") requires extra staff or a dilution of existing task performance. This creates "resource tensions." The ECOLEF Report (Unger et al., 2013, p. 114) mentions various arrangements to spread the burden of AML/CFT supervision across institutions.

This already indicates that this side of deployed efforts is difficult to assess as supervisory energy seeps at all sides through the regulated sector. The ECOLEF research team differentiates between five types of supervisory architecture:

- *The FIU model*: main agent and end responsibility;
- *The external model*: public administrative and government authorities;
- *The internal model*: own professional organs of supervision;
- *The hybrid model I*: a combination of internal and external authorities with end responsibility shared among the supervisors involved;
- *The hybrid model II*: responsibility shared between external, internal authorities, and the FIU.

With the exception of the first modality, there are always more supervisory institutions involved as each distinct business area requires its own supervisor (for example, one for the banks, one for the casinos, the notaries, etc.). In short, a lot of effort is deployed by numerous institutions to watch over compliance. How much does this cost? Unfortunately, when it comes to financial accountability hardly anybody can supply any breakdown except that AML/CFT supervision alone is for most supervisors not a full-time ongoing task.

Apart from the expenses of the supervising institution(s) it is in the regulated sectors where the real work is carried out and where consequently most of the expenses are incurred. If we want to find data to answer our proportionality question we have to look at these multiple work floors of bankers, accountants, realtors, and other entrepreneurs and professionals running the gauntlet between doing business and complying with recommendations: a "minefield" for which they never asked (Gelemerova, 2009; Verhage, 2009b, 2011).

Unfortunately, no answers from these frontlines are forthcoming. Focusing on the financial sector we find a combination of "data opacity" and occasionally more detailed references to the costs of compliance. Costs data are fragmented across the various parts of the regulated sector and across jurisdictions with the implication that it is not known how much globally is spent on compliance. There have been attempts, particularly among the larger audit and risk management firms, to collect costs data. These firms have also undertaken surveys to identify trends and determine changes in costs. However, they face the challenge of banks that are not necessarily able and/or willing to provide specific details of AML related costs. It may be difficult to single out compliance costs because many reporting entities, particularly banks, execute their anti-fraud and AML activities within the same unit and by the

[25] Together they form the category of Designated Non-financial Businesses and Professions (DNBP).

same persons. This results in combined costs which are difficult to keep apart. There are also expenses which are also inherently difficult to capture such as the *risk* avoidance costs: declining to take a customer on board because the account manager notices something unusual, which may be a risk, or because this potential customer is outside the bank's desirable risk parameters, i.e., its "risk appetite." As banks are encouraged to operate "risk based," it may be a rational conduct on the side of account managers to avoid any risk which also implies lost opportunities to make money. To complicate things, there are also saved future compliance costs in this de-risking. Such cost factors are difficult to identify.

When clients are taken on board, there are a number of mandatory activities: due diligence (perhaps in an enhanced form) and reporting suspicious or (depending on the country) even unusual activities. Carrying out due diligence costs staff time, in particular in cases of a politically exposed person (PEP), but this can also be cost saving in cases where a risky client is turned down for valid reasons (one usually cannot fully know).

The costs that are easier to recognize and measure as compliance costs (in general as well as client specific) would include the following:

1. Administrative costs at any stage of compliance, e.g., in relation to obtaining KYC documents;
2. legal costs, e.g.; legal fees for the preparation of contract clauses relating to AML and related complaince, e.g. sanctions, and anti-corruption assurance;
3. investment in technical products and software to assist compliance;
4. investment in staff: this includes salaries, training, and conference attendance to be part of the community of stakeholders.

But with such a typology we still do not have a cost estimate, because that requires insight into the budgets allocated by financial (and other regulated) institutions to perform these tasks. Here we face a double impediment. Big financial institutions which have a separate compliance department are likely to have a specified budget which may reveal a part of the compliance costs, namely those within that budget unit. Compliance interwoven with other financial service activities will remain invisible. In addition, such budgets will usually not be made public or a clear breakdown will not be available, because it constitutes "corporate sensitive information."

Surveying the various reports on the costs of the AML regime, we first note that respondents from the financial sector could not be presented as suitable suppliers of costs data of their own branch. This is not only caused by the opaque situation mentioned above but also is due to unwillingness. Specific costs, such as staff extension or buying new IT equipment must have a price tag. If not precise, then at least a "ball park" indication. So the reports mention IT costs as a generally acknowledged "main cost driver" but do not produce a market conforming estimate.

One of the earlier reports we inspected for data on compliance costs was commissioned by the municipal government for the City of London and carried out in 2005 by consultancy firm *Z/Yen* (Yeandle, Mainelli, Berendt, & Heal, 2005).

Apart from data from open sources, the findings in the report derived from interviews with 386 employees from the financial service sector of which 105 are from the international sector. The countries compared were: the UK and the US mainly with Germany, Italy, and France occasionally added. When it comes to estimation, the unexplained "best estimates" pops up, which works as follows: if there is a range between two estimates, the next "best estimate" is then the midpoint between the extremes. Is that an average or a median? There is no mentioning of a supposed underlying frequency distribution. These estimates are nothing but expressed opinions. If we substitute the word "estimate" for "opinion," all statements about "best estimates" become tautologies about "best opinions." It illustrates the extent to which we are deceived by a specific "AML congregation" language. We remind the reader of what we remarked earlier about the "indicative bias": slipping from "may be" to "is."[26]

The New Zealand Ministry of Justice commissioned *Deloitte* to assess compliance costs of its AML requirements (Ministry of Justice, 2008). The report provides a detailed account per financial industry branch and denoted non-financial sectors of (a) start-up and (b) on-going (estimated) expenses. It remains fairly independent in judging the reasonableness of estimates as given by respondents, adding its own adjustments. Thus, the provided estimates of start-up costs and on-going costs of NZ $227.6 million and NZ $128.2 million per year were adjusted to what the rapporteurs thought more plausible: NZ $111.8 million and NZ $42.7 million per year, respectively. Nevertheless, with only 32 interviewees spread over 15 targeted sectors, the empirical basis is too small for further extrapolations.[27] Deloitte's observed the need to moderate the claims of the interviewees, who may not have verified or validated their cost statements, points at serious *caveats* that form part of all these estimation surveys: *interviewees are unreliable estimators if they must consult their memory*. Still, they are treated like oracles. The lack of certainty appears to arise from the fact that clear figures (if available) are rarely disclosed.

A report by consultants of *Europe Economics* in 2009, on behalf of the European Commission, aimed to study the effects of five measures of the Financial Services Action Plan, among them the third AML Directive.[28] For the study, 78 firms were interviewed from across the EU classified as: Banks and financial conglomerates; asset managers; investment banks, and financial markets. Though the many tables suggest some exactness, nothing is further from the case. Again the "best estimate

[26] Other aspects not discussed here concern the severity of the anti-laundering measures, which were considered to be *dis*proportional by the UK interviewees.

[27] Deloitte, (2011) gave a stiff disclaimer at the end of the introduction (p. 4) of which the last sentence read: "We provide no assurances that the cost estimates will remain relevant beyond the date of this report and accept no accountability or responsibility for any changes to these estimates which might be occasioned when the final anti money laundering regulatory requirements become available."

[28] Directive 2005/60/EC of the European Parliament and of the Council of 26 October 2005 on the prevention of the use of the financial system for the purpose of money laundering and terrorist financing.

methodology" is based on "quantifying the impact of the Directives into a series of steps and thought experiments … which we hoped to be, in large part, intuitive" (Europe Economics, 2009, p. 124). Otherwise the whereabouts of the outcomes are a mystery "since in many cases the numerators and denominators would not be exactly comparable" (Europe Economics, 2009, p. 50). So we find tables with averages and medians without absolute clarity as to the total sample size or underlying frequency distributions. There is also a further big uncertainty: the absolute total of the 2007 operating expenses, which is the ultimate denominator of the proportions of one-off and on-going costs of the separate measures. These are interview based without indication of other independent sources. Perhaps the report is the best "intuitive thought experiment" we came across.

KPMG (2014)—"named Global AML firm of the year 2014"—elaborated on the global costs of compliance. The research tool consisted of a questionnaire to which 317 persons responded, all in knowledgeable positions within the financial industry, spread worldwide. Among other things, they were asked to give an estimate of the increase in compliance costs: "How much has total investment in AML activity increased compared to three years ago?" This is a difficult question: it supposes knowledge of two points in time plus a judgment: knowledge of the present AML specific expenses and those 3 years earlier (which is the 100%) about which subsequently a comparative estimate must be made in percentages with broad and unequal ranges (KPMG, 2014, p. 13: 25–50%; 50–100%, and >100% increase). No specific numbers are asked concerning identifiable compliance actions that are not interwoven with ongoing compliance activities (sunk costs): for example the acquisition of new monitoring tools or outsourcing of certain tasks. These are distinctive costs which must be budgeted. If they cannot be disclosed because of being "business sensitive," then that should have been mentioned as part of the methodological accountability.

Surveying these findings from the regulated sectors, based on the above discussed reports, there is an objective and a subjective outcome. In objective terms there are no concrete data to determine the sum of the efforts as a proportionate counterbalance to alleged money laundering threats. Subjective data abound, mainly indicating that most interviewees think that the expenses of compliance are steadily increasing. But to what end and what are the objectives? There is no clear answer to this question except the answer which is most frequently mentioned in the literature: "to avoid being sanctioned by the supervisors," which is felt as the real threat. It is therefore, good to close this section with a few opinions of interviewees on effectiveness worth quoting:

> The current requirements are a completely disproportionate response to money laundering—there are far too many reports, far too much wasted time and far too much bureaucracy—and you can quote me on that!
>
> A London based accountant (Yeandle et al., 2005, p. 31).

This complaint does not stand alone: inefficient bureaucracy may go hand-in-hand with the *institutional* success of the global FATF-regime which may be taken for the ultimate aim. In response to this state of affairs the regulated industry responds with its own cost-effectiveness of doing the minimum:

> The idea of customer identification is clearly sensible but the actual customer identification process that most banks employ is simply not effective—it is a box ticking exercise
> MLRO at a UK-based retail bank (Yeandle et al., 2005, p. 42).[29]

Discussion and Conclusions

> Customer: "Not much of a cheese shop really, is it?"
> Shopkeeper: "Finest in the district, sir."
> Customer: "And what leads you to that conclusion?"
> Shopkeeper: "Well, it's so clean."
> Customer: "It's certainly uncontaminated by cheese."
> Monty Python's Flying Circus: the Cheese Shop

In this chapter we addressed the global AML regime from the perspective of proportionality, a principle inherent in any justification of regulatory or criminal law action. Despite its ubiquitousness it is a difficult concept to operationalize best captured by the metaphor of balance with a pair of scales. In our field one scale is to be "filled" with the "threat against" and the other scale with the "weight of the state," a shorthand for all countermeasures. By their nature both are composites making operationalization far from easy. Still, this principle remains indispensable and also in the field of money laundering the task of specifying what has to be placed in the two scales must be taken seriously: for each measure proposed, the proportionality question relating to the threat has to be addressed.

Our *tour d'horizon* of what can be put into the scale at the "threat side" proved to be disappointing in its yield. On the one hand we find a "self-quotational" reality of a stakeholders trinity: the IMF/World Bank, the United Nations, and the FATF, around which we find a host of interested beneficiaries: supporting economists, researchers, and consultants confirming the "consensus." In Van Duyne (2011) this was qualified as a kind of *congregation of believers*. Within this congregation, one meets a repeated depiction of serious money laundering threats as a justification for the "heavy" global AML regime as it developed over the past four decades. However, as soon as one applies the basics of the empirical discipline, the underpinning of these threats proves to be quicksand: bad methodology with scattered islands of "anecdotal evidence" preventing one from sinking away. The estimates are crude and reflect more belief than knowledge. For example, the proposed threshold of criminal income of €18.000 above which laundering is assumed finds no support in the reality of criminal money management. Nevertheless, they are considered "best estimates."

---

[29] Similar quotations appearing in academic papers (Favarel-Garrigues, et al., 2011; Harvey & Lau, 2009; Verhage, 2009a).

Looking at the conceptual coherence we find an abundance of fuzziness. This concerns not only the core concept of laundering itself, but also the second most frequent concept suggesting an empirical meaning: "available for laundering." As far as the looming threat is concerned: it looks like a persistent bad-weather forecast of (financial) heavy weather but which in the past 25 years never came true. Looking at the proportionality balance we must conclude that there is not much that is solid to put into the "threat scale."

Subsequently we looked at the "weight of the state": the sum of the (international) legal and institutional countermeasures. That is very wide and therefore we had to be selective in our approach. Because the MERs (efforts and contents) cover all recommended measures as well as some other cost aspects of the FATF and FSRBs, we studied a large sample of them.

The MERs testify an unparalleled institutional global success, irrespective of proportionality: no government or regulated sector can shirk the FATF authority. But given the stick of "non-compliance" it can wield, one can no longer speak of informal power or "soft law." Likewise one should not take the word "Recommendation" as implying something one may take into consideration. The IMF, lurking behind the FATF, is unambiguous about this: "For the purposes of assessing compliance with the FATF Recommendations, the word should 'has' the same meaning as 'must'." (IMF & World Bank, 2004, p. 78). Woe betide the country which challenges this claim: it risks being put into *the* noncompliance corner.

But with that success come the expenses—ultimately passed onto ordinary customers (e.g., of banks) and taxpayers– and with that the connected proportionality question: does this whole regime counter the threat of laundering in a proportional way? First we have the extensive mutual evaluation circus which at the average costs "in excess of $300,000" (Halliday et al., 2014, p. 49) per turn does not go cheap. But do we have for this price a real "quality instrument"? The findings of our survey as well as that of Halliday et al. (2014) point at a negative answer: despite its unwieldy volumes, the MERs lack in many regards coherence and are difficult to compare. Most evaluators use a box ticking methodology without questioning whether certain recommendations are of any relevance for the evaluated jurisdiction. Indeed, for a number of countries, some recommendations may have come from another planet.

In addition, the whole bureaucracy surrounding the application of the MERs as well as the FATF and FSRBs should be questioned according to its proportionality. We observed a dense network of observers frequenting each other's Plenaries, workshops, and seminars. Some FSRBs have even more observers than member states. The Monty Pythons Flying Circus may indeed be no exaggerated metaphor.

It is interesting to observe that another dimension creeps into the reports: maximum repression devoid of any tempering proportionality. Evaluators frequently criticize countries that have in general a lenient sentencing culture, as well as for laundering offenses: no "dissuasive punishments." In their unbounded zeal the evaluators seem to forget that a basic constitutional principle of a democracy is the independence of the judiciary. Exerting pressure on lenient countries may be interpreted as an intrusion of sovereignty. The same applies to the phenomenon of "self-laundering" on which evaluators (and the FATF) keep harping when they evaluate countries where, for carefully weighed reasons, (forms of) self-laundering are not criminalized, actually an option left open by the 1990 Council of Europe Convention.[30] Nevertheless, it is mentioned as a shortcoming. But how important is the phenomenon of self-laundering financially? Apparently important enough that encroaching on a countries' sovereignty is considered proportional to its "threat."

Subsequently we surveyed the evidence presented by the regulated sectors. Where the FATF, its sister organizations and all the ongoing supervision and maintenance of networks do not seem to reflect much proportionality in relation to the money laundering threat, for the regulated sectors the proportionality issue is different and much sharper. Here we find enterprises at the front line who are burdened with new tasks and extra expenses. They are distant from shadowy threats wrapped in evaporating macro estimates of biblical dimensions at IMF and FATF level. Their AML tasks in terms of the office equipment and staff costs must be directly proportional to the threat they tangibly experience. And what does this amount to? In the first place the supervisors' authority to sanction lack of compliance (Gelemerova, 2011; Harvey & Lau, 2009; Levi & Maguire, 2004); then, of course, risky persons who may harm the institution and finally their reputation. The reputational risk is perhaps most frequently mentioned in the many warnings of the national supervisors and authorities. However, to what extent is this again a product of the official prayer wheel? The history of "secrecy havens" like Switzerland or Liechtenstein shows that savers do not run away from banks that launder, but rather from banks that lose their money (Harvey & Lau, 2009).

These considerations and statements from interviews indicate that at the work floor the experienced proportionality balance between threat and measures is different from the one conveyed at policy making and political level. This difference must be realized to prevent a top-down blaming of the work floor for all kinds of shortcomings. Before such brow-beating downwards, serious flaws should first be exposed at the level of the self-centered Flying Circus from which policies are imposed rife with fuzzy concepts and looming threat images that have not yet come true.

References

Abadinsky, H. (1994). *Organised crime*. Chicago: Nelson-Hall Publishers.

Alldridge, P. (2003). *Money laundering law*. Oxford: Hart publishing.

Arnone, M., & Borlini, L. (2010). International anti-money laundering programs. Empirical assessment and issues in criminal regulation. *Journal of Money Laundering Control, 13*(3), 226–271.

[30] The 1990 Council of Europe Convention No 141 on Laundering, Search, Seizure, and Confiscation of the Proceeds from Crime (the Convention, which became known as the Strasbourg Convention, was adopted in September 1990, opened for signing on 8 November the same year, and entered into force on 9 January 1993).

Arnone, M., & Padoan, P. (2008). Anti-money laundering by international institutions: A preliminary assessment. *European Journal of Law and Economy, 26*, 361–386.

Barlett, B. (2002). *The negative effects of money laundering on economic development*. Countering money laundering in the Asian and Pacific Region. Project No. 5967. Available at: http://www.afp.gov.au/~/media/afp/pdf/m/money-laundering-02.pdf.

Barone, R., & Masciandaro, D. (2011). Organized crime, money laundering and legal economy: Theory and simulations. *European Journal of Law and Economics, 32*(1), 115–142.

Blickman, T. (2010). *Countering illicit and unregulated money flows money laundering, tax evasion and financial regulation*. Amsterdam: TNI.

Bosworth-Davies, R. (2008). The influence of Christian moral ideology in the development of anti-money laundering compliance in the west and its impact, post 9-11, upon the South Asian Market. *Journal of Money Laundering Control, 11*(2), 179–192.

Busuioc, E. (2007). Defining money laundering. Predicate offences—The Achilles' heel of anti-money laundering legislation. In B. Unger (Ed.), *The scale and impacts of money laundering*. Cheltenham: Edward Elgar.

Chaikin, D. (2009). How effective are suspicious transaction reporting systems? *Journal of Money Laundering Control, 12*(3), 238–253.

Christoffersen, J. (2009). *Fair balance: Proportionality, subsidiarity and primarity in the European convention on human rights*. Amsterdam: Brill.

Deloitte. (2011). *Final study on the application of the anti-money laundering directive*. Brussels: Deloitte.

Duyne, P. C. van. (1993). Implications of cross-border crime risks in an open Europe. *Crime, Law and Social Change, 32*, 99–111.

Duyne, P. C. van. (1998). Money-laundering: Pavlov's dog and beyond. *The Howard Journal of Criminal Justice, 37*(4), 395–374.

Duyne, P. C. van. (2003). Money laundering policy. Fears and facts. In P. C. van Duyne, K. Von Lampe, & J. L. Newell (Eds.), *Criminal finances and organising crime in Europe*. Nijmegen: Wolf Legal Publishers.

Duyne, P. C.van. (2009). Serving the integrity of the Mammon and the compulsive excessive regulatory disorder. *Crime, Law and Social Change, 52*(1), 1–8.

Duyne, P. C. van, & Miranda, H. de. (1999). The emperor's cloths of disclosure: Hot money and suspect disclosures. *Crime, Law and Social Change, 3*, 245–271.

Duyne, P. C. van, de Zanger, W., & Kristen, F. H. G. (2014). Greedy of crime-money. The reality and ethics of asset recovery. In P. C. van Duyne, G. A. Antonopoulos, A. Markovska, K. von Lampe, J. Harvey, & A. Maljevic (Eds.), *Corruption, greed and crime money. Sleaze and shady economy in Europe and beyond*. Nijmegen: Wolf Legal Publishers.

Duyne, P. C. van, Groenhuijsen, M. S., & Schudelaro, A. A. P. (2005). Balancing financial threats and legal interests in money-laundering policy. *Crime, Law and Social Change, 43*(2–3), 117–147.

Duyne, P. C. van, Kouwenberg, R., & Romeijn, G. (1990). *Misdaadondernemingen. Ondernemende misdadigers in Nederland*. Arnhem: Gouda-Quint.

Duyne, P. C. van, & Levi, M. (2005). *Drugs and money. Managing the drug trade and crime-money in Europe*. London: Routledge.

Duyne, P. C. van, & Nelemans, M. D. H. (2011). Transnational organised crime: Thinking in and out of Plato's cave. In F. Allum & S. Gilmour (Eds.), *Handbook of transnational crime*. London: Routledge.

Duyne, P. C. van, & Soudijn, M. R. J. (2010). Crime-money in the financial system: What we fear and what we know. In M. Herzog-Evans (Ed.), *Transnational Criminology Manual* (Vol. 2). Nijmegen: Wolf Legal Publishers.

Duyne, P. C. van, Soudijn, M., & Kint, T. (2009). Bricks don't talk. Searching for crime money in real estate. In P. C. van Duyne, S. Donati, J. Harvey, A. Maljevic, & K. von Lampe (Eds.), *Crime, money and criminal mobility in Europe*. Nijmegen: Wolf Legal Publishers.

Europe Economics. (2009). *Study on the cost of compliance with selected FSAP measures*. Available at: http://ec.europa.eu/internal_market/finances/docs/actionplan/index/090707_cost_of_compliance_en.pdf.

Favarel-Garrigues, G., Godefroy, T., & Lascoumes, P. (2011). Reluctant partners?: Banks in the fight against money laundering and terrorism financing in France. *Security Dialogue, 42*(2), 179–196.

FATF. (1990). *Financial action task force on laundering*. Paris: FATF.

Ferwerda, J. (2009). The economics of crime and money laundering: Does anti-money laundering policy reduce crime? *Review of Law and Economics, 5*(2), 903–929.

Ferwerda, J. (2013). The effects of money laundering. In B. Unger & D. van der Linde (Eds.), *Research handbook on money laundering*. Cheltenham: Edward Elgar.

Gelemerova, L. (2009). On the frontline against money-laundering: The regulatory minefield. *Crime, Law and Social Change, 52*(1), 33–56.

Gelemerova, L. (2011). *The anti-money laundering system in the context of globalisation: A Panopticon built on quicksand?* Nijmegen: Wolf Legal Publishers.

Halliday, T., Levi, M., & Reuter, P. (2014). *Global surveillance of dirty money*. London: Centre on Law and Globalisation.

Harvey, J. (2014). Asset recovery substantive or symbolic. In C. King & C. Walker (Eds.), *Dirty assets: Emerging issues in the regulation of criminal and terrorist assets*. Aldershot: Ashgate.

Harvey, J. (2004). Compliance and reporting issues arising for financial institutions from money laundering regulations: A preliminary cost benefit study. *Journal of Money Laundering Control, 7*(4), 333–346.

Harvey, J. (2011). Money laundering phantoms, imagery and facts. In G. A. Antonopoulos, M. Groenhuijsen, J. Harvey, T. Kooijmans, A. Maljevic, & K. von Lampe (Eds.), *Usual and Unusual Organising Criminals in Europe and Beyond: Profitable crimes, from underworld to upperworld: Liber Amicorum Petrus C. van Duyne* (pp. 81–104). Antwerp/Portland: Maklu.

Harvey, J., & Lau, S. (2009). Crime-money, reputation and reporting. *Crime, Law and Social Change, 52*(1), 57–72.

Hobbs, D. (1998). Going down the 'Glocal': The local context of organised crime. *The Howard Journal of Criminal Justice, 37*(4), 407–22.

IMF, & World Bank. (2004). *Twelve-month pilot program of anti-money laundering and combating the financing of terrorism (AML/CFT) assessments*. Available at: https://www.imf.org/external/np/aml/eng/2004/031004.pdf.

Jacobs, F. G. (1999). Recent developments in the principle of proportionality in European community law. In E. Ellis (Ed.), *The principle of proportionality in the laws of Europe*. Oxford: Hart Publishing.

Johnson, J. (2008). Third round FATF mutual evaluations indicate declining compliance. *Journal of Money Laundering Control, 11*(1), 47–66.

Keh, D. I. (1996). *Drug money in a changing world: Economic reform and criminal finance*. Vienna: UNDCP.

Kessler, R. (1996). *The sins of the father*. New York: Warner Books.

KPMG. (2014). *Global anti-money laundering survey*. London: KPMG.

Levi, M., & Gilmore, B. (2002). Terrorist finance, money laundering and the rise and rise of mutual evaluation: A new paradigm for crime control? *European Journal of Law Reform, 4*(2), 337–364.

Levi, M., & Maguire, M. (2004). Reducing and preventing organised crime: An evidence-based critique. *Crime, Law and Social Change, 41*(5), 397–469.

Mas, P. de. (2001). De poreuze noordkust van Marokko. *Justitiële Verkenningen, 5*, 72–86.

McCarthy, K., Santen, P. van, & Fiedler, I. (2014). Modelling the money launderer. *International Review of Law and Economics*. doi:10.1016/j.irle.2014.04.006.

Meloen, J., Landman, R., Miranda, H. de, Eekelen, J. van, & Soest, S van. (2003). *Buit en besteding*. Zoetermeer: Elsevier Overheid.

Ministry of Justice. (2008). *New Zealand: Assessment of business compliance costs of the indicative anti-money laundering regulatory requirements*. Wellington: Ministry of Justice. Report by Deloitte.

Quirk, P. (1996). *Macroeconomic implications of money laundering*. Washington, DC: IMF. IMF Working Paper WP/96/66.

Reuter, P. (2013). Are the estimates of the volume of money laundering either feasible or useful? In B. Unger & D. van der Linde (Eds.), *Research handbook on money laundering*. Cheltenham: Edward Elgar.

Reuter, P., & Greenfield, V. (2001). Measuring global drug markets: How good are the numbers and why should we care about them? *World Economics, 4*, 159–173.

Reuter, P., & Truman, E. M. (2005). Anti-money laundering overkill?: It's time to ask how well the system is working. *The International Economy* (Winter), 56–60.

Ruggiero, V. (2003). Global markets and crime. In M. Beare (Ed.), *Critical reflections on organized crime, money laundering and corruption*. Toronto: Toronto University Press.

Schneider, F., & Windischbauer, U. (2008). Money laundering: Some facts. *European Journal of Law and Economics, 26*(4), 387–404.

Sharman, J. (2008). Power and discourse in policy diffusion: Anti-money laundering in developing states. *International Studies Quarterly, 52*(3), 635–656.

Stessens, G. (2000). *Money laundering: A new international law enforcement model*. Cambridge: Cambridge University Press.

Tanzi, V. (1996). *Money laundering and the international financial system*. Washington, DC: International Monetary Fund.

The Law Society. (2009). *Money laundering and the financing of terrorism—Memorandum by the Law Society of England and Wales*. Available at: http://www.publications.parliament.uk/pa/ld200809/ldselect/ldeucom/132/9030404.htm.

Unger, B. (2007). *The scale and impacts of money laundering*. Cheltenham: Edward Elgar.

Unger, B., Addink, H., Walker, J., Ferwerda, J., den Broek, M. van, & Delaenu, I. (2013). *Project ECOLEF The economic and legal effectiveness of anti-money laundering and combatting terrorist financing policy*. Brussels: European Commission.

UNODC. (2005). World Drug Report, Vol. 1: Analysis, UN publications. Retrieved from https://www.unodc.org/unodc/en/data-and-analysis/WDR-2005.html.

UNODC. (2011). *Estimating illicit financial flows resulting from drug trafficking and other transnational organized crime*. Vienna: UNODC.

Eekelen, J. van. (2000). *De neerslag van het misdaadgeld. Motregen, onweersbui of zondvloed?* Tilburg: Universiteit van Tilburg.

Koningsveld, T. J. van. (2015). *De offshore wereld ontmaskerd*. Zeist: Uitgeverij Kerckebosch.

Verhage, A. (2009a). Compliance and AML in Belgium: A booming sector with growing pains. *Journal of Money Laundering Control, 12*(2), 113–133.

Verhage, A. (2009b). Between hammer and anvil? The anti-money laundering complex and its interaction with the compliance industry. *Crime, Law and Social Change, 52*(1), 9–32.

Verhage, A. (2011). *The anti money laundering complex and the compliance industry*. London: Routledge.

Verhage, A., & Ponsaers, P. (2009). Power-seeking crime? The professional thief versus the professional launderer. *Crime, Law and Social Change, 51*, 399–412.

Walker, J. (1995). *Estimates of the extent of money laundering in and through Australia*. John Walker Consulting Services, Available at: http://www.criminologyresearchcouncil.gov.au/reports/200304-33.pdf.

Walker, J., & Unger, B. (2009). Measuring global money laundering: The Walker gravity model. *Review of Law and Economics, 5*(2), 820–853.

Yeandle, M., Mainelli, M., Berendt, A., & Heal, B. (2005). *Anti laundering requirements: Costs, benefits and perception*. London: Z/Yen. City Research Series (no. 60).

Part III
Dealing with 'Organized Crime'

Chapter 11
Smuggling in the Dodecanese Under the Italian Administration

Filippo Marco Espinoza and Georgios Papanicolaou

Introduction

This chapter offers an exploration of the socio-political context of smuggling in the Dodecanese in the era of the Italian occupation and then Administration (1912–1943), particularly between 1924, when the region formally came under Italian rule, and the beginning of the Second World War.[1] Beyond a contribution to the developing field of the historical study of the region during this particular period, a closer look at the policies of the Italian colonial regime towards smuggling raises a series of interesting questions for the study of the political economy of illegal markets. It is often the case today that the alarmism of official discourses on organised crime leaves little margin for a sober consideration of the complex relationship between illicit economic activity and the official policies and efforts to suppress that activity. In this light, illegal markets, clandestine flows of goods and services and the forms of social organisation that sustain them are typically approached and understood as a grave and unmitigated threat to social and political order and the state's fiscal and political interests more particularly. Our examination of the Dodecanese under the

[1] Work for this project is supported by a British Academy Small Research Grant (SG132031). We would also like to thank Ioannis Papageorgiou (Rhodes Centre for Historical and Social Research-Rhodes Project), and Irene Toliou, Director of the Greek General State Archives of the Dodecanese, for their generous support of our work. We would also like to extend our gratitude to the participants of the Rhodes Project SCE workshop 'Aspects of fascist expansionism in the Aegean: Rhodes at the centrestage', Rhodes, 28 June 2014, for the lasting inspiration and stimulating comments they have offered us on that wonderful day.

F.M. Espinoza
Scuola di Dottorato in Studi Umanistici, University of Trento, Trento, Italy
e-mail: Filippo.espinoza@unitn.it

G. Papanicolaou (✉)
School of Social Sciences, Business and Law, Teesside University, Middlesbrough, UK
e-mail: g.papanicolaou@tees.ac.uk

G.A. Antonopoulos (ed.), *Illegal Entrepreneurship, Organized Crime and Social Control*, Studies of Organized Crime 14, DOI 10.1007/978-3-319-31608-6_11

Italians, however, offers compelling reasons to question the wisdom of drawing such an *absolute* line of demarcation between the (under)world of clandestine economies and the (upper)world of state interests and policies. Despite its ambitious and serious intention to establish a colonial regime that would act as a showcase of the achievements of the metropolis, the Italian Administration of the Dodecanese not only approached the smuggling activities of local populations as a *relative* threat to the social order it sought to establish; it also understood illicit economic activity as a tool in the service of its vital and long-term interests in the region.

Our chapter, in tune with other contributions to this volume, is primarily intended as a rejoinder to contemporary debates on organised crime, advancing the idea that what is called 'organised crime' can be fully understood as an issue only within a political economy framework (Block & Chambliss, 1981). In other words, illegal markets and the forms of social organisation that sustain them cannot be narrowly approached as a technical matter of crime prevention and suppression but rather as social practices and strategies, which are rooted in historically given conditions, reflect particular economic, social and political interests, and may thus be symbiotic with or antagonistic to other social practices and strategies, particularly those promulgated by the state.

We offer here a selective overview of our investigation of smuggling in the Dodecanese during the Italian rule, an effort which has made extensive use of archival and documentary sources and is itself inscribed within a wider programme of research on the history of the Italian Administration. Given our aim, we only touch upon questions concerning the extent to which the Italian Administration can be viewed as a typical colonial pacification project or the extent to which it deviates from other Italian colonial projects; nor do we delve on the significance of the Administration's relations with metropolitan Italy's fascist regime, except in so far as they are of import for situating the former's approach to smuggling. Rather we focus on the Administration's policies towards smuggling as responses to the economic and political problems and opportunities this activity presented, particularly the first 6 years of the Italian rule during which illegal markets were for all practical purposes openly tolerated by the authorities.

The remainder of this chapter is organised in three parts: the first part situates historically the phenomenon of smuggling in the region of the Dodecanese, whereas the second part documents the Administration's policy and practice towards the prevalent and persistent reality of smuggling in the Dodecanesian archipelago. The concluding discussion codifies the results of our inquiry and offers a reflection on its implications for contemporary debates on organised crime.

Situating Smuggling in the Economic Life of Late Nineteenth to early Twentieth Century Dodecanese

The chapter in Dodecanesian history, which we examine, begins with the landing in Rhodes of an Italian force under General Giovanni Ameglio in early May 1912. The occupation of the Dodecanese was completed within the same month and was only intended as secondary, temporary pressure front in the Italo-Turkish war of 1911, the main theatre of which had been Libya. The occupation was, however, to last throughout the 1910s, well beyond the conclusion of the Tripolitanian war with the Treaty of Ouchy in October 1912, until 1924, when the region was formally annexed to Italy following the Treaty of Lausanne.

The Italians thus came to succeed the Ottoman Empire in the possession of a region whose history was punctuated by geography, demography and politics. The Dodecanese or Southern Sporades are spread over an area of 275,000 km^2 between Crete and Anatolia. Patmos is the northernmost island, the southernmost being Kastellorizo. The other islands are Agathonisi, Lipsos, Kalymnos, Nisyros, Tilos, Halki, Symi, Kasos, Karpathos, Rhodes and Astypalea. The largest islands are Rhodes (1412 km^2), Kos (282 km^2) and Karpathos (277 km^2), with no other island being larger than 100 km^2. Dominated by mountains, the Dodecanesian landscape is inhospitable and does not lend itself well to farming (Desio, 1924). Located at the south-eastern Aegean Sea, close to the most arid area of the Mediterranean, the islands receive no precipitation for half of the year (May to October), while during the winter they are exposed to strong winds and violent storms.

Historically, the scarcity of water and arable land has represented an insurmountable obstacle to agricultural development. During the Ottoman times, limited, subsistence agriculture was the rule across the region, even though the two largest islands, Rhodes and Kos, which have the 85 % of arable land in the region, did develop an agricultural economy depending heavily on fresh fruit and vegetables that could be traded in other parts of the Eastern Mediterranean. Other common crops, mostly destined for local consumption, were cereals and also olives, grapes and tobacco. Yet even in Rhodes, farming was limited to the northern coast, the rest of the island being mountainous (Arca Petrucci, 2010). The archipelago had lived under a constant threat of famine and emigration was endemic in older times. Even well into the nineteenth century, developments in chemistry and agricultural engineering had not been introduced to the region perpetuating the extreme backwardness of the systems already in place. As a result the yield was always uncertain (Vannutelli, 1909). Rural populations lived in extreme poverty, characterised by low consumption, surplus labour, land scarcity, backwardness and traditionalism. Leprosy, malaria and typhoid fever threatened the lives of people, living conditions were unhealthy, and nutrition was poor and deficient in protein.

The position of the archipelago, found at the intersection of the main nautical routes between Europe, Egypt and the Levant, and also the fact that most of the smaller islands offer good landing approaches, encouraged the development of activities related to the sea. Fishing and sponge trading had been practiced since the ancient times but, overall, the potential for seafaring had remained limited until the nineteenth century. As pirates and privateers prevailed throughout the modern age in the Aegean sea, the fear of raids and pillaging had forced people to concentrate only in fortified towns, like Rhodes, Kos and Astypalea, or on the heights. Thus, only Rhodes and Kos had been major seaports until the nineteenth century. The Town of Rhodes, in particular, had been an important commercial and strategic node in the region, featuring two small ports, Mandraki (Port of the Galleys) and Port of Commerce (Porto Colonna), as well as a natural bay, Akandia, which, during the first two centuries of Ottoman rule, were more than sufficient to cater for nautical and seafaring needs.

With the development of steam navigation and the opening of the Suez Canal in the second half of the nineteenth century, the region gained a renewed economic significance and islands specialising in fishing and sponge trading (Kalymnos, Symi, Halki and Kastellorizo) were able to tap into this development. During this period, the demand for sponges grew significantly at an international scale, due to this material's domestic and industrial uses (Mastrolia, 2003). The Dodecanesian merchants could rely on emigrant villagers and a distribution network, which extended across the principal European ports. Even the most barren islands of the archipelago (Stefenini & Desio, 1928) benefited from these developments and the blossoming of this industry boosted businesses more generally. As a result, the economic expansion made possible noticeable improvements in the living standard of the population as well as a significant increase in population numbers. General Ameglio commented in 1913 that

> *the population currently is double of what was a century ago; and [...] the municipalities[,] with the money collected for various taxes or by voluntary fundraising among the natives dwelling abroad[,] were able to equip their islands with free schools, public pharmacies, and even construct with their own means public works of some significance, such as the docks of Kalymnos, Symi and Nisyros* (Ameglio, 1913).

The development of economic activity across the region in the last few decades of the Ottoman rule also benefited from the relative decline of the ports of Rhodes, which were in poor condition and poorly maintained, inadequate to accommodate modern ships. These latter were forced to anchor in open waters thus making embarking and disembarking extremely difficult during the winter. Between November and April maritime trade was carried out only occasionally, and maritime and commercial activities were scarce. So the development of Rhodes itself was relatively curtailed, with industry limited to a few small factories, fairly insignificant from an economic perspective (Jaja, 1913). According to Ameglio (1913), the decline in commercial traffic could also be attributed to the development of the port of Izmir, which, before the Italian occupation catered almost completely for the commercial needs of the population.

The overall pattern of economic activity was also reflected in the demography of the region. An analysis of data relating to population density by Alexis Franghiadis (2009) showed that in the late Ottoman period, smaller islands such as Kastellorizo, Symi and Kalymnos had a population density exceeding 200 inhabitants per square kilometre. In contrast, the most peripheral as well as the main islands, including Rhodes, which was the most populated one and hosted the main urban centre of the region, the capital Town of Rhodes, did not exceed a population density of 50 inhabitants per square kilometre. The distribution of both population and growth encouraged the appearance of ancillary businesses and industries, such as small factories, coastal shipping, shipbuilding and tobacco. These activities helped generate alternative income in the periods during which activities related to the sponge fishing ceased, and created employment opportunities for those who could not work in the fisheries sector. The overall sense of growth in the region was unmistakable:

> *In the off-season the women made cigarettes from imported tobacco, many of which were smuggled into Greece. With their wealth, settlers from Calymnos bought farms on the mainland, and sold European goods in Budrum and up the gulfs. There were similar settlers from Cos. [...] Like Calymnos also, Symi had farms and small settlements on the mainland and on the peninsula of Cnidus to the north, where there are both cattle pastures and plantations of olives and almonds. [...] there was a flourishing yard for building sponge-trading boats and small vessels, and for prompt and skilful repairs [...] In modern times [Cos] established a lucrative trade in fresh fruit and vegetables with Egypt, carried till recently in its own spacious and speedy sailing vessels* (Myres, 1941: 147).

Yet the fates of the archipelago depended on nineteenth century economic developments as much as they depended on the political regime to which the islands were subject. Following his conquest of the region in 1522, Suleiman the Magnificent granted the Dodecanese a regime of privileges consisting in ample administrative and fiscal autonomy, which was largely retained by the Ottoman authorities until the *tanzimat* reform period of the mid-nineteenth century (Inalcik & Quataert, 1997). That the Dodecanese have been often called 'privileged islands' originates precisely from the introduction of this particular regime. The islands, with the exception of Rhodes and Kos, enjoyed complete self-government, consisting in authorities elected by the local communities on a yearly basis (known as *demogeronties*). The *demogerontia* exercised complete administrative authority over local affairs, including the collection of taxes locally, part of which funded government expenses and public works. The tax obligation of each island to the Ottoman authorities only consisted in a lump tribute paid in two installments yearly, while the Ottoman authorities retained a modicum of representation in the form of the local *sumpasha*, an official, who was nevertheless prohibited from "any intermeddling with the affairs of the Dodecanesians" (Zervos, 1919: 53). Given the composition of the population, these local institutions, particularly in the late Ottoman period, were effectively controlled by the landlords inland and the urban bourgeoisie of Greek origin (Doumanis, 1997: 24).

The global change of the nineteenth century, beyond entwining the Ottoman economy in the general boost of international trade, also entailed an increased European influence on Ottoman institutions, leading to major restructuring undertaken during the *tanzimat* reform period between 1839 and the end of the first constitutional era in 1878 (Inalcik & Quataert, 1997). In the process, the Dodecanesian islands were reorganized administratively into a singular province (*vilayet*) and were thus brought under the uniform administrative framework of the Empire introduced at that time. The Ottoman authorities, however, were unsuccessful in abolishing the privileges of the islands as their attempts on several occasions were met with considerable local resistance (Doumanis, 1997: 29). The political conditions that had been conducive to those islands' growth remained largely intact until at least 1881, when the Empire ceded partial control of the collection of a series of taxes and duties to the Ottoman Public Debt Administration (OPDA), an organisation that superintended the servicing of Ottoman public debt to European creditors. The coming of the Ottoman Public Debt Administration involved the introduction of a series of monopolies and therefore the collection of the corresponding taxes and duties on tobacco, salt, alcohol, and even the license fee for fishing that was also required for sponge fishing. Local resistance to these developments proved increasingly futile, and, ultimately, the implementation of radical reform programme of the Young Turks brought all privileges to an end in July 1909 and also involved the collection of taxes and duties by the Ottoman authorities without exception or exemption (Alhadeff, 1927).

We are now able to situate the vibrancy of smuggling within the ebb and flow of Dodecanesian life on the eve of the Italian occupation. To be sure, the geopolitical changes in the Aegean had given scope to a lucrative smuggling activity directed towards the newly established Greek state earlier in the nineteenth century. As mentioned previously, the exemptions enjoyed by the privileged islands had encouraged the growth of a local tobacco industry that drew raw material from local sources or from the Anatolian mainland and, often clandestinely, advanced the final product abroad. The legacy of this activity proved lasting:

> *A minor industry of Kalymnos is the cutting of tobacco for cigarettes, which employs some hundreds of the women. The tobacco is grown in Kos, Samos or further afield, and comes simply to be cut and shipped elsewhere. The industry is now quite an open one; but it seems to have originated in days when a good deal of smuggling went on between the islands under Turkey and those included in the Greek kingdom* (Myres, 1920: 337).

Following the establishment of the Ottoman Public Debt Administration and the introduction of a monopoly on tobacco, the scope of this business became considerably larger, as the clandestine flows could now target markets in the Turkish mainland as well as the non-privileged islands. In fact, because the OPDA was controlled by the Ottoman Empire's European creditors, the Ottoman authorities themselves had little interest in suppressing the activity. At the same time, the eventual ebb of the sponge trade encouraged the islanders to exploit more actively the advantages of the local ship-building industry and to turn more actively to the transportation of goods between Egypt and the southern coast of Anatolia. Islands like Kastellorizo ultimately abandoned sponge trading altogether (Doumanis, 1997: 18). In this context, the clandestine tobacco industry grew to an extent that smuggling was practiced virtually in plain daylight: in 1922, in Kalymnos alone there were 30 tobacco workshops, each one employing between 10 and 400 people and contributing to an overall annual production of 60 m cigarettes (Guidoni, 1922). As one of the military commanders of the Dodecanese, Vittorio Elia, commented later on, "under the Ottoman regime, smuggling constituted the only and true profession of Calymnos, Symi and Chalki, that specialised in this industry" (Elia, 1918b).

The Italian occupation beginning in the turbulent 1910s was thus to be confronted with a genuine riddle—not merely with a problem of economic decline and clandestinisation, but rather with a puzzle rooted deeply in questions of local government and international politics. To this we turn in the next section.

Smuggling and the Administration of 'Italy's Aegean Islands'

Given the region's objective strategic position in the eastern Mediterranean, the Italian occupation of the Dodecanese appears to have been preponderantly a move to exert additional pressure on the Ottomans during the Libyan war. Whether in the spring of 1912 the Italians had a genuine intention to annex the islands is a moot point. From an economic perspective, the Dodecanese's value was highly questionable and, at any rate, the composition of its preponderantly ethnic Greek population did not lend itself well to the Italian colonialist imaginary (Labanca, 2002: 180). To be sure, the same desire for colonial expansion that underpinned the Libyan war animated the Italian elites' ambitions towards the eastern Mediterranean. Italy had been present in developments in the Ottoman Empire firstly as early as 1881 as a party in the Ottoman Public Debt Administration and then later on by joining the supervision of the agreement between Turkey and Greece on the issue of the Cretan State (Bosworth, 1996: 52). At the time of the Libyan War, the islands could at best be viewed vaguely as a foothold towards the establishment of an Italian zone of influence in Asia Minor, an idea that enjoyed some currency among Italian business and political circles at the time. In the context of the negotiations to end the Libyan war, however, the Italians appeared reluctant to hold on to the islands with their priority being to gain full control of Libya, or advance their foreign policy goals in Albania (Bosworth, 1970; Doumanis, 1997: 34).

Yet as the war in Libya turned out to be the prelude to the Balkan wars of 1912–1913, and, eventually, to the Great War, so the international situation surrounding Italy's occupation of the Dodecanese changed. At the end of the Balkan wars Italy was still in possession of the islands, having cunningly used them as a bargaining tool in the period that intervened between the Treaty of Ouchy and the Treaty of Bucharest in July 1913. The redrawing of the borders in the Balkan peninsula and the acceleration of the Ottoman Empire's disintegration had amplified the scope for Italian gains and, in fact, with the 1915 Treaty of London Italy was promised full possession of the islands and a sphere of influence in Asia Minor in exchange for entering the war on the side of the Entente (Bosworth, 1970). The 'temporary' occupation of the Dodecanese was to last for almost a decade until the Treaty of Lausanne in 1923 formally awarded the region to Italy but with the latter's sight firmly set on Anatolia in anticipation of a further disintegration of the newly established Republic of Turkey, the islands came to be understood as an important lever for the pursuit of Italy's unsettled ambitions on the Turkish mainland.

This international context is important because it provides, in our view, some important clues to understanding the approach of the Italian Administration of the Dodecanese towards illicit economic activity in the region. Bold as this suggestion may be, an approach recognising this impact of this context on the Administration's grip on illicit markets and economic activity would result in a modification of conventional periodisations of Italy's possession of the Dodecanese. A conventional periodisation based on the general 'domestic' Italian policy in the Dodecanese roughly recognises three general periods (a) the 'temporary' occupation between 1912 and 1924; (b) the period of Mario Lago's 'modernising' governorship 1924–1936; and (c) the properly 'fascist' administration under Cesare De Vecchi after 1936 (Doumanis, 1997). Yet when the international political context of the *Possedimento* is taken into account as a factor underpinning Italian policy, it is possible to insert an additional period under Mario Lago lasting between 1924 and 1928, at which point Italo-Turkish relations were normalised following the signing of the Neutrality and Reconciliation treaty by the two countries (Barlas, 2004).

The significance of this context firstly becomes noticeable in the immediate consequences of the Italian occupation and the outbreak of the First World War on the region's economic life. Italy's entry in the war on the side of the Entente and the Ottoman Empire's siding with the Central Powers prolonged the devastating effects of the Italo-turkish war on the islands' economic life. As Turkey severed communications with the islands, the latter were deprived of goods, such as meat, poultry, vegetable and fresh fruit, which were sourced from the Anatolian Coast and on which they depended (Myres, 1920: 337). Sponge fishing and trading, which had been a significant source of income of the region, continued to decline. After the revolution of the Young Turks in 1909, the introduction of direct taxation and conscription directed the activity to sponge grounds in the Libyan sea and depleted the workforce employed in the trade. In the 1910s the establishment of the Italian monopoly on sponge fishing in Libya excluded Dodecanesians from those waters; later on between 1915 and 1919, the activity was altogether banned and many sponge fishers had to migrate (Myres, 1941). More generally speaking, the severance of the region's relations and exchange with Asia Minor meant that the former's position on what just a few years earlier had been the busiest route between Egypt and Greece suddenly became a lot less significant for commerce.

It appears, therefore, that developments on the international plane had an objective impact on the economic life of the region independently of developments on the domestic setting of the region, that is, of the policies of the Italian occupation. These latter, beyond the containment of Greek irredentism that the Italian occupation itself ignited in the first place, were cautious and largely respectful of the islands' status quo in matters of local government and taxation (Pignataro, 2011). Although the Italians did progressively erect an administrative bureaucracy to superintend local affairs, wartime Dodecanese existed after all in a sovereignty limbo, and the Italians continued to view the islands as a stepping stone towards further penetration in Anatolia. In fact, the deteriorating economic conditions confronted the Italians with a problem of a different order, which regarded the very sustenance of the Dodecanesian population. The islands were never self-sufficient in basic supplies, including food. With the major local routes from Asia Minor, the Black Sea and Greece cut-off or severely restricted, acute shortages began to be felt and as early as the first months of 1915 the Italian military command was required to organise supply lines from metropolitan Italy and, increasingly during the later stages of the war, via the port of Alexandria (Elia, 1918a). Nevertheless, the shortages were never resolved. As famine made itself cruelly felt and foodstuffs and other basic goods such as lamp oil became scarce and excessively expensive, the Italians resorted to a system of rationing which, beyond adding to the general discontent, also encouraged smuggling (Tsirpanlis, 1998).

Whether the Dodecanese recovered subsequently from the immense economic and social damage it suffered during the Great War is highly uncertain. The restoration of the islands supply and trade lines with the Anatolian coast, following the Armistice of Mudros in 1918, and the partitioning of the Ottoman Empire with the Treaty of Sèvres, proved temporary. The new Republic of Turkey raised again barriers to trade akin to the wartime ones, this time against a Dodecanese that was brought formally under Italian sovereignty, following the 1922 Treaty of Lausanne. This was a situation that persisted throughout the 1920s. Reflecting on the situation retrospectively in 1928, the journalist Vittorio Gayda commented that

> *commerce of the archipelago suddenly ceased for four important reasons essentially: (a) the prohibitive tariffs of the new Turkey, (b) the concentration of customs services and all their operations in Smyrna and Adalia, with the suppression of all the intermediary services like that of Scalanova [Kuşadası, Aydin], which served more directly the economic contact between the islands and the mainland, (c) the suspension of foreign transport services and therefore of Italian ones to the turkish coast, and (d) an insurmountable suspicion of the strictest kind against all attempts at peaceful Italian commercial expansion* (Gayda, 1928: 148).

Gayda was unambiguous about the inevitable consequences for the local economic life:

> *Under the pressure of these four negative elements but, above all, of the increasing distrust and resistance of the Turkish authorities, the commerce of the Dodecanese has been driven back from the Turkish coast, and, therefore, it has been cut off from its vital base. There is no more commerce except contraband. Defying storms and the darkness of the night in order to survive, Greek and Turkish sailors lease their boats and sails towards the coast, furtively loading and unloading goods with the complicity of the indigenous population* (Gayda, 1928: 149).

Yet from a political perspective there was no doubt that the 1920s were a new era in Dodecanesian history. Coinciding with the rise to power of Mussolini in Italy, the annexation of the islands opened up the prospect of a more intensive and extensive programme of embedding Italian sovereignty in them, and, ultimately, of building a showcase and an '*ubi consistam*' of Italian power in the Levant (Lago, 1924). To this end, the *Possedimento* was brought under a regime that differentiated it from both the Italian metropolis and the Italian colonies in Africa, in so far as the royal decree of 28 August 1924, which established it, awarded extensive powers and autonomy to the figure of the *Governor of the Italian Islands of the Aegean* (Pignataro, 2013). The appointed governor, Mario Lago, a career diplomat, who possessed strong connections within the Italian bourgeoisie, thus enjoyed substantive autonomy vis-à-vis the Italian government in Rome and was answerable directly to the Italian Ministry of Foreign Affairs. He was also granted almost complete control over the Dodecanese, with full legislative, executive and fiscal powers, and even powers extending into the domain of the judicial function: in a sense, the exercise of Italian sovereignty was delegated to the office of the governor (Alhadeff, 1927: 123). This political autonomy was so wide and *ad personam* to such an extent that Lago's successor in 1936 remarked that "the possedimento was ruled by [such] patriarchal systems as if it were a private company more or less" (De Vecchi, 1936: 243).

Equipped with such autonomy and powers the regime undertook an extensive 'modernising' effort. This on one hand involved projects underpinned by the colonialist logic of pacification centered on the maximisation of economic exploitation, and, on the other, projects animated by the political and cultural visions of ascending fascism. A programme of major public works resulted in the development of modern water supply, road, telegraph and telephone networks, new public buildings, restoration of monuments, archaeological excavations; later on, there were plans to develop the islands as a destination for tourism (Martinoli & Perotti, 1999). Importantly, the Italians undertook to reorganise or develop a series of local industries, such as tobacco, mineral extraction, forestries and local crops by establishing companies such as TEMI or CAIR. The effort also extended to establishing control of inter-island transport at the exclusion of local operators. Particularly in agriculture and forestry, the regime's modernising effort consisted in the development of new 'model' settlements, supported by especially established scientific agencies to support development and to increase production in these sectors (Doumanis, 1997; Pignataro, 2013).

There is no doubt that the regime's colonialist intentions were serious and ambitious, all the more because the Dodecanese provided Italy with an opportunity to develop a colony of a 'new' type, in which the predominantly white local populations would be assimilated into fascism's social vision (Labanca, 2002: 180). In reality, however, the colony's financial position remained precarious, since it never ceased to depend on generous subsidies from the central government in Rome. It is also a moot point whether it developed at any point an economic significance beyond the trade flows to and from the Italian mainland, and the Possedimento's overall balance of trade throughout the Italian era remained "greatly passive" (Crivellari, 1935). According to Doumanis, "the Rassegna Economica Delle Colonie, a contemporary Italian journal with up-to-date economic statistics, showed consistent negative trade balance figures. Between 1928 and 1932, the tonnage of imports outweighed exports ten-fold" (Doumanis, 1997: 47). In the 1920s, tension with Turkey continued to define the region's economic situation. The latter not only forced the Italians to abandon their more ambitious plans, such as the development of Rhodes into a free port and thus an influential commercial node in the eastern Mediterranean. It also brought them to accept the realities of local economic life, which was squeezed through the clashing rocks of Italian colonialist programmes and severance from its natural interchange with the Anatolian Coast.

In this context, smuggling not only continued to flourish but it also came to be seen by the authorities as a necessity. Reporting to Rome as early as September 1924, Governor Mario Lago remarked:

> *[T]he reopening of the east coast is a matter of life or death for the commerce of Rhodes [...] The local effects of this crisis are intuitive. A large part of the Dodecanesian population that used to live on the Anatolian trade, currently suffers from the darkest poverty. Rather, in order to survive, it throws itself into riskier smuggling. Naturally, even though they know it is not the Italian regime's fault that such disaster has befallen them, the Dodecanesians do not hold a high opinion of our authority. Which helps create a widespread mood, if not of hostility, at least of distrust, very harmful to the order of our regime. Smuggling becomes every day more organised in almost regular form with the collaboration of the Turks from the coast, who suffer from the uneconomical situation created by the Turkish government as much as our subjects. This government does not encourage smuggling, but neither does it apply itself to repressing it. Is it ever possible that the government of the islands offer to be the gendarme on Turkey's behalf and force these people to starve to death? I have many times stated that I consider the leaner regular trade preferable to the richest smuggling. I was thus always sincerely prepared to adopt measures of close collaboration between the authorities of the islands and the authorities of the coast aimed at eliminating all customs fraud. But to do so, it is necessary that the government of Ankara decide to revoke the measures taken in hatred of Italy and of the Dodecanesians and to allow free play to economic laws* (Lago, 1924).

It then appears that, from the viewpoint of the islands' authorities, the prevalence of smuggling and the under-enforcement of the customs regime went beyond the obvious difficulties posed by the extensive coastline or the lack of sufficient number of law enforcement officers, either of the Carabinieri or the Guardia di Finanza (Cecini, 2014).

It was also not a problem related to the complexity or the weaknesses of the customs regime itself: in fact, the relative leniency of that legislative regime, which until the 1930s punished customs offences with fines that would often be minimal or conditional ones, arguably provided an additional tool to the regime's tolerant stance to an activity that presented a 'natural' solution to a predominantly political problem of government. The strictly fiscal interests of the regime tied to customs enforcement were thus seen as subordinate to questions of maintaining order and upholding the regime's legitimacy among the local population. These in turn were instrumental to the equally political purpose of sustaining Italy's foothold towards further economic penetration into Anatolia, a region which was still viewed as geopolitically unsettled and thus as a long-term goal for Italy's expansionist ambitions throughout the 1920s.

The archival sources from Rhodes often suggest that law enforcement officials were quite aware of both such political exigencies and of the regime's stance towards smuggling, allowing a twofold interpretation of that situation. On one hand, officials would often support the petitions or appeals for leniency submitted by those convicted of smuggling offences, precisely on grounds of poverty or inability to pay the fine. On the other hand, the case may have been that no direct damage was inflicted on the regime's fiscal and wider economic interests, to the extent that smugglers would smuggle to Greece and Turkey goods produced and legitimately acquired in the Italian territory. For example, reporting in 1936 on individuals involved in smuggling activities, the commander of the Carabinieri noted that

> *in the past [the first individual] has exercised effectively and notoriously, on a large scale, the smuggling of alcohol and other goods at the expense of Greece and Turkey, an activity which was seen favourably by the [Italian] government of the time, also because it did not do any harm to our treasury, as he had always declared the merchandise which bought in order to smuggle it subsequently. … [the other individual] managed to attain a solid financial position, particularly with profits he made by exercising, as is well known to us, the smuggling of cigarette paper in our favour and at the expense of Greece and Turkey* (Grassini, 1937).

This second idea lends itself well to an understanding of why the toleration of smuggling by the Italian authorities continued to some extent into the 1930s. The normalisation of Italo-Turkish relations with the conclusion of the Neutrality and Reconciliation treaty in 1928 also coincided with the consolidation and modernisation of Italian customs legislation. The latter also brought about changes in the framework of sanctions against smuggling, doubling the amount of statutory fines and upgrading it to a criminal offence punished with a custodial sentence of 1–5 years. It also introduced aggravating circumstances such as armed smuggling, conspiracy to commit smuggling by three or more persons, or smuggling with the use of counterfeit documents or bribery and corruption of officials. Attempt, complicity and the reception of smuggled goods also became punishable offences by the Gubernatorial Decree 121 of 3 June 1930 (Istituto Coloniale Fascista, 1932: 690–691). So the change in the circumstances of the international political environment in the direction Lago was advocating in 1924 also brought about changes aimed at curbing smuggling. However, the regime in the Dodecanese still left leeway to take individual circumstances of the locals into account by means of pardons and amnesties. Additionally, smuggling still represented an opportunity for local economic interests to retain a channel of access to markets on the Turkish coast. By that time these interests had been integrated to some extent into the Italian economic modernisation programme and the production circuits that programme had engendered—for example, the individual mentioned in the Carabinieri report above was among the members of the local business elite in Patmos and in turn had relations with prominent commercial actors in Rhodes. At any rate, whether the Italian toleration to smuggling also involved a strategy to coopt those local economic and social elites would be an interesting and plausible research hypothesis.

The end of Mario Lago's governorship and his replacement by the ardent fascist Cesare de Vecchi in 1936 brought about a thorough change in the regime's policy towards local conditions. In the intervening period between his arrival and the outbreak of the Second World War, De Vecchi implemented policies which were directly in tune to the metropolitan regime's approaches and were directly aiming towards full Italianisation and political domination of the Dodecanesian population—inevitably, policies coloured by intensive repression of political dissidence. De Vecchi's 'domestic' policies in the Dodecanese and the subsequent crackdown on smuggling should be understood, again, in a twofold perspective. Firstly, from an economic viewpoint, on the eve of the Second World War, about 70 % of the region's produce went to Italy, while about 75 % of the imports came from Italy, including the large quantities of construction materials used in the public works (Myres, 1941: 154). Therefore, the Administration had a greater interest in strictly enforcing customs legislation. Secondly, this development must be viewed also in the context of international developments and the opening of a new war theatre in east Africa with the Italian invasion in Ethiopia in 1935. From that point forward and into the Second World War, smugglers were also seen as a potential military threat due to their intimate knowledge of the waters and of the coast. In 1935, for example, the Italian consulate in Piraeus, Greece, reported back to the Ministry of Foreign Affairs that

> *an officer of passport controls of the English consulate of Athens turned to known smugglers of Piraeus in order to find out whether they would be prepared, eventually, to take up the responsibility of transporting clandestinely weapons and war material, various supplies, and to carry out acts of espionage in the Dodecanese [...] The above mentioned smugglers have replied that more useful than themselves are, for the Dodecanese, the Dodecanesian smugglers resident in Piraeus and suburbs, who know perfectly all the islands of the Aegean* (Ministero degli Affari Esteri, 1935).

Conclusion

Our case study of Dodecanesian smuggling during the era of the Italian Possedimento shows how the regime's enforcement approach varied over time, for reasons well beyond any immediate considerations of law and order or crime suppression. Rather, the formulation of that approach had been contingent on a double confrontation. As aspiring colonialists, the Italians were firstly confronted with the reality of local conditions that were firmly rooted in the region's economic, social and political history; as fledging imperialists, secondly, they had to defend their newly acquired territorial gains from the shifts and turns of the very same world power games that brought them to the region in the first place.

Our analysis understands the policy of the regime towards smuggling as 'tolerance' of smuggling. While the official line of prohibition and sanctioning of smuggling had been naturally prescribed by the law, the archival and other historical sources offer compelling indications that the Italian authorities understood smuggling as a political necessity as much as the local populations understood smuggling as a necessity of economic life. This latter vitally depended on supply and trade routes extending beyond the porous borders of the region. The severing of those routes meant life on the verge of extreme poverty and famine. It is not the case, of course, that particular individuals did not take up the obvious opportunities to exploit and make fortunes out of their fellow islanders' plight. Some of them undoubtedly did, but these trajectories, much more than personal aberrations (Hobbs, 2013), were contingent on the wider historical conditions and socio-economic structure.

Our point is that the newly established authorities of these barren islands were very much part of that structure: for them, smuggling was not an unequivocal threat, but rather it presented both a threat and an opportunity: a threat, in so far as the activity of the local population in the vibrant clandestine markets of the region inflicted risks and losses to the regime's fiscal health; yet an opportunity nevertheless, in as much as these clandestine markets acted as a cushion of sorts, absorbing social tensions that posed a threat to the political stability of the newly established and geopolitically precarious Italian rule on the region. Our political economy analytical perspective would also interrogate the use of this opportunity as going beyond a mere strategy of political pacification of an abstract local population. Our material raises valid and interesting questions regarding the significance of illegal markets and smuggling in the articulation of local elites and the Italian regime into new networks of economic and social power in the region.

While we recognise the limitations that are inherent in a work in progress and the gravity of the tasks lying ahead, our account as it stands is already, at a bare minimum, a cautionary tale. Drawing from an unlikely historical context in the study of illegal markets, we can join those voices (e.g., Hobbs, 1998; van Duyne, 1996) that argue against the dominant current tendency to approach illicit economic activity and 'organised crime' as devoid of historical context and separate from power relations that traverse social and political hierarchy in its entirety.

References

Alhadeff, V. (1927). *L'ordinamento giuridico di Rodi e delle altre isole Italiane dell'Egeo*. Milano: Istituto Editoriale Scientifico.

Ameglio, G. (1913). *Contributo monografico per lo studio politico ed economico dell'isola di Rodi*. Rhodes: Tipo-litografia del Comando della 6a Divisione Speciale.

Arca Petrucci, M. (Ed.). (2010). *Atlante geostorico di Rodi. Territorialità, attori, pratiche e rappresentazioni (1912–1947)*. Rome: Gangemi.

Barlas, D. (2004). Friends or foes? Diplomatic relations between Italy and Turkey, 1923–36. *International Journal of Middle East Studies, 36*, 231–252.

Block, A. A., & Chambliss, W. J. (1981). *Organising crime*. New York, NY: Elsevier.

Bosworth, R. J. B. (1970). Britain and Italy's acquisition of the Dodecanes, 1912–1915. *The Historical Journal, 13*(4), 683–705.

Bosworth, R. J. B. (1996). Italy and the end of the Ottoman Empire. In M. Kent (Ed.), *The Great Powers and the end of the Ottoman Empire* (2nd ed., pp. 51–72). London: Frank Cass.

Cecini, G. (2014). *La Guardia di Finanza nelle isole italiane dell'egeo 1912–1945*. Rome: Gangemi Editore.

Crivellari, Q. (1935). *Commercio dei cambi. [Report of Crivellari to the Ministry of Foreign Affairs, Telespresso n. 16780, dated 20 April 1935]. Direzione Generale Affari Commerciali, Egeo 1930–1935 (category 28, file 'Questioni finanziarie')*. Rome: Diplomatic Historical Archive of the Ministry of Foreign Affairs.

De Vecchi, C. (1936). Report of the second Italian governor, De Vecchi, to the Italian Foreign Minister, Ciano, on the situation in the Dodecanes on the assumption of his duties. In L. Divani & P. Constantopoulou (Eds.), *The Dodecanese: The long road to union with Greece. Diplomatic documents from the Historical Archives of the Ministry of Foreign Affairs* (pp. 231–256). Kastaniotis Editions: Athens.

Desio, A. (1924). *La potenzialità agricola delle isole del Dodecaneso e i suoi rapporti con la constituzione geologica*. Florence: Istituto Agricolo Coloniale Italiano.

Doumanis, N. (1997). *Myth and memory in the Mediterranean: Remembering fascism's empire*. Basingstoke: MacMillan.

Elia, V. (1918a). *Rapporto a MAE. [Report to the Ministry of Foreign Affairs, 26 June 1918, signed Elia]. Archivio di Gabinetto 1915–1918 (box 56, file 4)*. Rome: Diplomatic Historical Archive of the Ministry of Foreign Affairs.

Elia, V. (1918b). *Rapporto a MAE. [Report to the Ministry of Foreign Affairs, 6 October 1918, signed Elia]. Archivio di Gabinetto 1915–1918 (box 56, file 4)*. Rome: Diplomatic Historical Archive of the Ministry of Foreign Affairs.

Franghiadis, A. (2009). La politica ecnomica del fascismo nel Dodecaneso: il periodo del governatore Mario Lago (1923–1936). In M. Peri (Ed.), *La politica culturale del fascismo nel Dodecaneso: atti del convegno Padova 16–17 november 2007* (pp. 51–61). Padova: Esedra.

Gayda, V. (1928). L'economia del Dodecaneso. *L'Oltremare, 4*, 146–149.

Grassini, G. (1937). *Situazione del comune di Patmo. [Report on the situation of the community of Patmos, from Grassini to De Vecchi, 18 March 1937] Affari Politici 1931–1945, Dodecaneso-Egeo (box 13, file 7)*. Rome: Diplomatic Historical Archive of the Ministry of Foreign Affairs.

Guidoni, U. (1922). *Il problema doganale di Rodi. [Attachment to a report of Count De Bosdari, governor of Rhodes]. Affari politici 1919–1930 (box 985, file 2410)*. Rome: Diplomatic Historical Archive of the Ministry of Foreign Affairs.

Hobbs, D. (1998). Going down the glocal: The local context of organised crime. *The Howard Journal, 37*(4), 407–422.

Hobbs, D. (2013). *Lush life: Constructing organised crime in the UK*. Oxford: Oxford University Press.

Inalcik, H., & Quataert, D. (Eds.). (1997). *An economic and social history of the Ottoman Empire, volume 2: 1600–1914*. Cambridge: Cambridge University Press.

Istituto Coloniale Fascista. (1932). *Annuario delle colonie Italiane e paesi vicini*. Rome: Castaldi.

Jaja, G. (1913). *L'isola di Rodi*. Rome: Società Geografica Italiana.

Labanca, N. (2002). *Oltremare: storia dell'espansione coloniale italiana*. Bologna: Il mulino.

Lago, M. (1924). *Commercio del porto di Rodi. [Report to the Ministry of Foreign Affairs, telespresso n. 8227, 7 September 1924, signed Lago]. Direzione Generale Affari Commerciali, Egeo 1924–1926 (category 4, fiile 2)*. Rome: Diplomatic Historical Archive of the Ministry of Foreign Affairs.

Martinoli, S., & Perotti, E. (1999). *Architettura coloniale italiana nel Dodecaneso*. Torino: Fondazione Giovanni Agnelli.

Mastrolia, F. A. (2003). *La pesca delle spugne nel Mediterraneo del secolo XIX*. Napoli: Edizioni Scientifiche Italiane.
Ministero degli Affari Esteri. (1935, 23 October). *Contrabbando di armi e spionaggio per il Dodecaneso. [Transcript of a communication from the Italian consulate of Piraeus to the Ministry of Foreign Affairs, Telespresso n 237891, 23 October 1935].*
Myres, J. L. (1920). The Dodecanese. *The Geographical Journal, 56*(5), 329–347.
Myres, J. L. (1941). The islands of the Aegean. *The Geographical Journal, 97*(3), 137–156.
Pignataro, L. (2011). *I: Il Dodecaneso italiano 1912–1947: i lineamenti giuridici l'occupazione iniziale: 1912–1922*. Chieti: Edizioni Solfanelli.
Pignataro, L. (2013). *II: Il Dodecaneso italiano 1912–1947: il governo di Mario Lago 1923–1947*. Chieti: Solfanelli.
Stefenini, G., & Desio, A. (1928). *Le colonie, Rodi e le isole Italiane dell'Egeo*. Torino: UTET.
Tsirpanlis, Z. (1998). *Italokratia sta Dodecanisa*. Rhodes: Office of the Medieval Town of Rhodes.
van Duyne, P. (1996). The phantom and threat of organised crime. *Crime, Law and Social Change, 24*, 341–377.
Vannutelli, L. (1909). L'isola di Rodi. *Bolletino della Società Geografica Italiana, 46*.
Zervos, S. (1919). *The Dodecanese: The history of the Dodecanese through the ages, its services to mankind and its rights*. London: A. Page.

Chapter 12
"The Big Scare": Bikers and the Construction of Organized Crime in Norway

Paul Larsson

Introduction

Criminal 1 % clubs are among the networks that represent the gravest threat in organized crime in Norway today Norsk politi (2012)

This chapter deals with a central question in Hobbs (2013) book "Lush Life," the construction of organized crime. I will argue for the central importance of the biker groups, especially the Hells Angels and Bandidos, as the archetype of organized crime in the Nordic countries. In one sense this is ironic since biker clubs seem to fall outside the legal definitions of "organized crime,"[1] as proven in a series of court cases and appeals to the Norwegian Supreme Court. Whether these groups should be defined as OC groups is also debated in international studies. That such controversies exist is not surprising since the term OC is vague, and much is at stake in the process of defining groups in or out. For many police officers the term in itself is of less interest, since what matters is the use of it to get resources and to call for secret and extraordinary investigative methods.

The chapter deals with the processes whereby biker groups have been selected for attention by the police and media. There are two periods of focus, from 1992 until 1997, and from 2011 until today. In the intertwining years other "evils," like the robber networks, the ethnic OC groups and the mobile offenders were conceived as the main threat.[2]

---

[1] "An organized criminal group is here defined as an organized group of three or more persons whose main purpose is to commit an act that is punishable by imprisonment for a term of not less than three years, or whose activity largely consists of committing such acts" (The General Civil Penal Code of Norway §60a).

[2] Not to mention terrorism and the so-called radicalization that since the attack in Oslo and Utøya in 2011 has been on top as a threat.

P. Larsson (✉)
The Norwegian Police University College, Oslo, Norway
e-mail: paular@phs.no

G.A. Antonopoulos (ed.), *Illegal Entrepreneurship, Organized Crime and Social Control*, Studies of Organized Crime 14, DOI 10.1007/978-3-319-31608-6_12

The Concept Is Established

Organized crime did not exist in Norway before 1992. The phrase was rarely used by media and police or in official publications. Whenever it was used, it meant large-scale drug trafficking. In fact, Norway has had organized crime of the "classic" brand at least since 1916, when liquor and strong wine were prohibited. The partial prohibition lasted until 1927 and left a heritage of traffickers and bootleggers who have kept busy in the trade until today (Johansen, 2004).

Changes were on the way. In the early 1990s new enemies surfaced. Homegrown ethnic gangs, mainly of Pakistani origin, had been around for some years. Then there were the Chinese triads, the ex-Yugoslavian networks, the Russian "Mafia," and last but not least the bikers. The triads or the red Mafia, even when it was stressed that they were now "established" in Norway, never caught on. A police report on Russian organized crime groups in Oslo stated that there were no traces of such, except maybe some connections to a cheese shop in Bogstadveien on the west-end of Oslo. Not the scariest scenario! But when the local toughs of the Rowdies in Trondheim put on a new tag on their vests saying "MC[3] Norway" in 1992, panic was in the air. This change signaled that the club had made contacts with the big boys down in Denmark. In this process, the "good old boys" turned into serious criminals in the eye of the public. Hells Angels was nothing but a band of criminals that should be chased out of town according to the Police Chief of Trondheim. He went on in the newspapers to say, "Membership, as we know it from other countries, requires criminal activity like theft, robbery, violence and murder in order to finance the operation of the clubs" (Larsson, 2008: 11). Robbery and murder, no less!

The same process happened in the other Nordic countries. Both in Denmark and Sweden the term organized crime was, for some reason, linked to the clubs Hells Angels and Bandidos in the early 1990s (Korsell & Larsson, 2011). There have been periods of fights between these main clubs, especially in Denmark. The first period of open violence was in the 1980s between the club of rockers, the Bullshits and Hells Angels. Hells Angels "won" this battle but things got worse. The mainly Danish feud between Bandidos and Hells Angels spread to Sweden, Finland, and Norway in 1996. This is known from the media as the Nordic biker *war*; but it was not a war; rather, the term feud is more correct (Bay, 1998). Open hostility between members of the clubs led to an escalation that ended in the use of rocket launchers, bombings, hand grenades, and automatic rifles. The 2-year conflict cost 11 lives and approximately 100 casualties, and ended with the signing of a peace treaty between the clubs in 1997.[4] This conflict was a confirmation of our worst nightmares. These groups were not to be trusted; they were outright violent and the war was presented as nothing more than a fight over the control of the illegal drug markets; such was the media explanation of what happened.

---

[3] Motorcycle Club.

[4] The main element of the treaty was a division of territories of interest between the two groups (Høyer, 1998).

1997–2011, All Quiet on the Northern Front

After the peace treaty in the fall of 1997 (Høyer, 1998) there were few signs of trouble involving the bikers in Norway for a long time. Other groups caught the attention of police and media, such as mobile criminals from the Baltic states and former eastern bloc countries stealing in volume, the activity of the network of robbers that culminated in the Nokas[5] bust in 2004, and the criminal ethnic gangs of Oslo.

The "one-percenters" started to lose their status as media villains. The police still used resources on surveillance and followed movements in the clubs but they were not considered dangerous or a threat to Norwegian society. This was reflected in the threat assessments made by the Oslo police and action plans on bikers by the National Police Directorate. There was criminal activity in relation to the groups, and especially the supporter groups, but the general level of violence between the clubs was low and seemed to be stable. The fear was always the outbreak of a new conflict between Hells Angels and Bandidos. When the Oslo police established good channels of communication, especially with the Hells Angels, they received valuable intelligence to prevent future feuds and open hostility. It seemed like all was quiet on the northern front.

From Bikers to Criminal 1 % Clubs

> "*This is the 1 % clubs:*
> *- The clubs who define themselves as outside the Norwegian society, and have their own laws and regulations. They consider themselves a fraternity, and 2/3 of the members are convicted.*
> *- Of the 115 who were members of the Hells Angels in the period 2010-2012, 71 per cent were convicted of crimes. 62 per cent of the members of the Bandidos are convicted. In Coffin Cheaters 56 percent are convicted of crimes.*
> *- According to POD[6] members of 1 % clubs are often involved in serious crime, particularly the trafficking of drugs, as torpedoes,[7] and in violence*" (Norsk politi, 2012: 8)

Something unexpected happened in 2011. The citation above illustrates well the aggressive tone adopted by central actors in the Norwegian police with regard to bikers. These views were not new. Since the early 1990s there had been a handful of police experts painting this bleak picture, but there were also other voices inside the police presenting different perspectives on the scope of the problem. The unexpected was that the hawk's perception came to be adopted as the official view of the police and other strategies was forced to the background. This resulted in a heavy focus on the clubs and a sharpening of language and methods used.

[5] The Nokas robbery was conducted like a military operation. It is without doubt the most sensational robbery in modern Norwegian history. All of the robbers were convicted and sentenced to long prison terms.

[6] Politidirektoratet—The National Police Directorate of Norway.

[7] A Torpedo is a money collector of the more aggressive type, the ones that use threats, fear, and ultimately violence.

Since the end of the conflict in 1997 two different approaches were developed as to how the police would manage the *biker problem*. One was by zero tolerance and confrontation, represented by Kripos[8]; the other was by the use of dialogue with the clubs, backed up by surveillance and other police methods by the Oslo police. In 2011 the confrontation line won. Police officer Eirik Jensen, representative of the dialogue approach, pointed this out: "the MC gangs have developed into a 'suitable enemy' in the eyes of the police. It is nearly like a religious fever, and there are no other groups that raise such strong feelings among police officers as the MC gangs" (Jensen, 2015: 121).

Many in the police were surprised and questioned how such a change could take place. A majority of experts on bikers in the police did not see any signs that such a change of strategy was necessary. There are different explanations to the shift. The official story states that not all was quiet on the northern front; indeed the absence of conflict and the peacefulness was perceived as a problem in itself. It was seen as a sign that the clubs were cementing their positions and expanding their criminal activity by the use of supporter clubs and others. In 2010–2011 there had been a growth in biker clubs that the police associated with the main "1 % clubs." Old clubs put on the colors of Gremium, Gypsy Jokers, Devils Choice, Coffin Cheaters, and Gladiators, to name a few. This was interpreted as a clear sign of especially Hells Angels consolidating their power.

However, there were other explanations presented by both representatives of the police and the bikers themselves. The shift could be interpreted as an opportunity to acquire resources, status, and a wider array of investigative methods by sections in the police. There had been a buildup of resources in the field of organized crime since the late 1990s (Larsson, 2008). A substantial part of this had gone to the central investigative agency, Kripos, and Oslo Police Department. The resources used on the robber networks and the ethnic gangs had been tremendous.[9] These problems seemed to be of less importance since the most active robbers were serving time and the gangs seemed to age and change their ways of doing business. The biker groups, colorful, highly visible, and loud, were well suited for a comeback. It would not be an exaggeration to claim that there were sound reasons on the organizational plan for such a reorientation.

Of great importance was the action plan against criminal biker clubs 2011–2015 (Politidirektoratet, 2012) and the preventive handbook on prevention of criminal biker clubs by the police and the municipalities (Politidirektoratet, 2014). The volume of police raids against clubs labeled as bikers accelerated in 2011. These busts were characterized by massive use of force, police in bulletproof vests, shields, and helmets.[10] The number of officers in these raids was high, and there was use of armored cars and helicopters on clubs with a handful of members.

[8] The National Criminal Investigation Service (KRIminalPOlitiSentralen).

[9] The bill on the NOKAS case was tremendous, approximately 30 million pounds, while the robbers got away with 5 million pounds.

[10] The Norwegian police has until recently been unarmed and have a proud tradition of civil ideals in policing. The massive use of force is not representative of the ideals of policing in the country.

The logic behind this was proactive policing, crime prevention, and zero tolerance. The idea was to scare existing and potential members. A police chief in Bergen, where there had been a number of raids on both Hells Angels and Devil's Choice, commented on the use of force in this way: "I realize that some actions may have seemed violent but they have been implemented to prevent crime" (Bergensavisen, 2013). The message was clear. Hells Angels, Bandidos, Outlaws, and other that "take the side" of such clubs are so different from the normal population, so dangerous that zero-tolerance policing is seen as legitimate and indeed fruitful strategy. One might ask, how did we arrive at this point?

The Creation of the *Criminal* "One-Percenter"

In hindsight it is clear that there was a conscious strategy to construct the bikers as "serious criminals." In this process crusaders in the police played a pivotal role. Below I will analyze the way intelligence reports and analyses have been used to document the seriousness of the problem. Media reports on the clubs have always been good news. From a media point of view, the clubs have everything: sex, drugs, rock and roll, and violence. They are flamboyant and highly visible, while at the same time being closed and secretive; so everyone can read whatever they want into them.

In the last decades the importance of the use of police intelligence and analyses has been central to policing organized crime, terrorism, and a wide array of other social problems (Rønn, 2012). The idea to use information sources to try to prevent and solve crime problems seems sound. To do this the police are dependent on knowledge not only about the scope and the seriousness of certain crimes, but also on *why* they occur. Police intelligence is especially important when dealing with closed and secret networks or organizations and crimes not reported by the public. So far so good, but there are problems, and some of these are well illustrated in the case of the bikers in Norway.

First of all, threat assessments are not scientific reports, even if some of them have a certain academic air. In many aspects they are fundamentally different. The data for threat assessments are often unsorted. It is a mix of information from different sources, such as informers, undercover agents, bugging and surveillance to police registers, court cases, police reports, and open sources. Data from hidden sources have proven to be unreliable (see Billingsley, 2009; Rosenfeld, Jacobs, & Wright, 2003) and range from outright bluffs and lies to more trustworthy information. Informers often use information to take other criminals out of business or to get "off the hook" and improve their own situation (Natapoff, 2009). In many cases the assessments rely heavily on information drawn from Europol, Interpol, UN reports, or other international agencies; what happens in Germany or the Netherlands will soon come to our shores. This could be seen in the first action plans against bikers in Norway by the National Police Directorate where facts, examples, and pictures often were from the USA, without mentioning this in the text or without trying to interpret the information from a Norwegian viewpoint. These international reports are usually struggling with the same data problems as the locals but on a bigger scale. Even if the police have systems of assessing the quality of the sources, these are in no way close to scientific standards. There is rarely any information about the quality of the sources in the reports. Data are often used in such a way that it is close to impossible to decide the level of accuracy of the statements of the reports. The assessments are in many cases made not to document or explain the "facts" but to warn of problems that *might* surface, or to "prove" that something—drugs, beggars, bikers, and so on—actually is a "serious problem" and should be given more attention.

This process is often spurred on by international processes whereby some evils are presented as a global problem; this is often backed by US pressure to introduce new legislation or co-operative efforts within the EU. In the case of the bikers, not only does it seem that the clubs Hells Angels and Bandidos are foreign imports but so do the measures, reactions, and "understanding" of the problem. Norwegian police is co-operating with police on a global scale adopting ready-made perspectives and "facts" to feed the media and the politicians.

Not only are the data shaky but the definitions and the use of the terms are particularly vague and in many cases not problematized at all. Terms such as "organized crime," "money laundering," and "biker groups," to mention some, are all shifting and opaque, and vary in meaning over time and between countries. This actually means that we often talk about different phenomena or have no common understanding of what we talk about. The case of organized crime is a good example. If the Norwegian threat assessments and intelligence should be trusted as a reliable source on the extent of organized crime there is more or less no organized economic crime or smuggling of alcohol, while bikers and narcotics are a huge problem (Politidirektoratet, 2005). This information tells us more about the perspectives and priorities of the Norwegian police than the actual crime problems. There are good reasons to believe that there are plenty of organized economic crimes but they are not seen as such while the bikers and the traffickers are the ones associated to the term "organized crime" and, therefore, over-reported. The attempts to measure the scope of, let us say, money laundering or the drug trade are, therefore, built on sand (see Naylor, 2002; Young, 2011).

The last point to be mentioned about the reports and assessments is the challenges concerning the analysis of the data. Below I will take a closer look at the "secret" report on the crimes of Hells Angels in Norway. The main problem is not always the uncertain quality of the data; as social scientists analyzing organized crime we face the same problem. The problem is rather the use and interpretation of the information. When more or less all data are used as a confirmation of a perspective, that Hells Angels Norway are highly criminal and there are no other possible or alternative explanations, we have a problem. Bias is never discussed in these reports but rather certain interpretations are presented as obvious and true. In the same reports there is a problem of having no comparative point. The bikers may be a "serious curse" but compared to what, one might ask.

The readers outside the justice system, and most inside, will have limited possibilities to judge the quality of what they read. This is also the case when international reports are used to document trends and threats. We do not know *who* has provided the information, the quality, and the background of the data, as well as their interpretation and use. The process is not open to scrutiny since sources are often secret. There seems to exist a process whereby truth and information are validated by the process of circulation and reference.[11] Thin data and analysis are quoted, not only by other assessments and reports, but also by media and academia. After some rounds in this system any original assertion will emerge as something everybody knows as a "fact." I have seen examples where intelligence officers have quoted information they have delivered anonymously in reports as facts (not mentioning that they themselves are the source). In this way they have "laundered" their own information. Intelligence officers and analysts know about these issues but are the media, the police leaders, academics,[12] or the politicians aware of them? The problem becomes acute when intelligence reports and other police information are used as data, often with little reservation, to document or prove the seriousness of a certain threat.

The Hells Angels Report[13]

The goal of the report was to document that Hells Angels Norway is a "criminal MC gang." The term organized crime is rarely used in the report. The reason for this omission is probably the fact that the police are well aware that no member of the club or the club itself had been sentenced by the special law concerning organized crime at the time of writing. The aim was to present the club, supporters, and hangarounds as heavily involved in "serious crimes." The data collection in the report is done by police registers. These are of quite varied nature. There are intelligence registers, where all sorts of qualitative information on persons is gathered; others are case registers in connection to reporting, investigation, and sanctions. Some sources have no time limit. In one case a speeding ticket from 1973 was counted.

Wide categories, like drugs,[14] violence, and theft, are used so the tables and presentations are hard to make sense of. One table sums up: *Sentenced, charged, arrested/apprehended*, and *suspected*. This makes it near impossible to figure out

[11] Something that often happens in academia too.

[12] Parts of academia working in the field of organized crime still relies heavily on police and official information. Without a critical understanding of the process of information gathering and use in the police this can easily end up with reproducing taken for granted biases.

[13] Since this Kripos report from 2012 is secret, no direct references will be made. The report was leaked to the public by the TV channel TV2 and is now available on the net as "The secret report."

[14] 97.5 % of all drug cases in Norway are minor cases such as use, possessing, or buying. Often a person is charged for both buying *and* possessing.

what the presentation is trying to say. The problem is acute when we know that these groups are heavily supervised and monitored. The wide category of *infringements*, not normally used in Norwegian statistical presentation, is used and it covers violations of penal and civil laws, crimes, and misdemeanors.

There is a presentation of the total numbers of infringements of the penal law. But it does not have any time limits. It is sorted by extremely wide categories of infringements. The five most frequently reported categories are theft, drugs, violence and threats, fencing stolen property, and vandalism. Minor and grave theft cover a wide range of acts from taking something of more or less no value without breaking or entering to large-scale theft of valuable property. Drugs and violence cover a very wide array of acts. From the tables included in the report one can see that the drug cases reported are—with few exceptions—use and possession of small quantities. Since violence and threats are aggregated in the same category, this can be anything from using offensive language to the use of knives, guns, and seriously wounding people. Without more information it is hard to say what these infringements are and we have no way of knowing when they happened.

The overwhelming majority of the cases are traditional crimes. Even when the report presents more recent crime cases, much of these are either drug related (buy and sell of amphetamines) or traditional cases of violence. When someone in Hells Angels is sentenced for, let us say, violence against a partner, this is presented as related to his identity as member of Hells Angels. Medium scale, from a Norwegian perspective, cannabis cases that in no other circumstances would get much media attention, are presented in media in bold letters as Hells Angels members caught in a drug ring.

It is hard to judge the seriousness of the criminal involvement of HA Norway from the report. Since there are no other control groups that these figures are compared to, we actually do not know what to make of it. We do not know, for example, how the smuggling networks or street gangs would score in comparison. The figures are not comparable to other data. When the report tries to explain and interpret developments or events, these are described as connected to criminal activity. The spread of supporter clubs is a sign of HA taking control over wider territories. These groups are used to commit crimes, and criminal activity is presented as a way for them to get promoted in the HA hierarchy. HA is expanding to eastern Europe to open new criminal markets and/or to try to escape the control of the long arm of the law in the west, and so on. Other plausible explanations do not exist. All intelligence is treated as confirmation of criminal intent. Slogans and biker lore, full of bragging, and mythology are taken at face value. Supporter groups are not aspiring men that wish to associate and rub shoulders with Hells Angels; they are criminals used to commit crimes doing the dirty work for the "old men." The spread of the groups is not seen as a process whereby clubs and persons who associate with the lifestyle and ideals of bikers are disparate; it is organized crime seeking new markets.

To be sure, not all of this is fiction and spurious constructions. Some members of supporter groups do commit crimes that benefit members of Hells Angels. Sometimes they do the dirty work for the clubs, literally. Members of supporter teams sometimes commit serious crimes in order to be accepted as members. There are members of Hells Angels who commit serious crimes, often in connection to networks outside the club. The question is what does this mean. How do we understand and interpret this?

The Biker as the "Other"

In his *Vertigo of late modernity* Jock Young (2008) points out processes that can be observed every day. There is a process of liberation, tolerance, and inclusion on the one side of groups like the gay, while at the same time there is exclusion and othering of Muslims, immigrants, and groups of deviants. In this context the bikers, especially the Hells Angels, are an example of a group that is treated by *othering*.

> *... othering ... by its nature is a form of demonization. It is an inversion, a projection onto other groups of negative attributes, qualities of evil and depravity, which are set against the solid virtues of one's self and one's own kind* (Young, 2011: 63).

Since 2011, when the new action plan for the Norwegian Police was written, the bikers have been pictured as antisocial and a threat to society. They are presented as different. Not only are they serious criminals, experts in drugs and violence but they are also portrayed as outside the society, living in a closed secret world with norms that invert the ideals of "our" society. The description of the rules inside these groups and the initiation rituals that members must go through share similarities with the ones of secret societies like witches and sorcerers. The prospects and hang-arounds must prove that they are worthy as members of the club by committing crime. The clubs deny this. There circulates an oath[15]: "A one percenter is the 1 % of a hundred of us who have given up on society and the politicians one-way law. This is why we look repulsive. We are saying we do not want to be like you or look like you. So stay out of our face" (Politidirektoratet, 2014: 13–14).

This "oath" is open to interpretation. In the action plan, it is presented as evidence that these groups are hardened criminals beyond good and evil, outside society. But the "oath" is more likely seen as a positive confirmation inside the clubs. They do not want to be members of a "straight" society that treats them with no respect or understanding. It is a sore tone, "we don't want to be like you," so we retreat to our own world. This credo also confirms the myths in the clubs, that they are special, love freedom, and associate with values of the old west. The Bandidos slogan: "We are the people our parents warned us about" says it is "us" and "them." "Our parents" represents the square world, we are something else, in our eyes better. This is the romanticism of the outsider. The slogan of the Outlaws "God Forgives, Outlaws Don't—GFOD" is a reflection of the macho-myths, the hard man, the Outlaw. Such slogans should under no circumstances be taken literally. They sound like something from a spaghetti-western movie, the good, the bad, and the ugly.

---

[15] The source of this oath is not presented in the publication.

The preventive plan (Politidirektoratet, 2014) presents "facts" on the bikers. The following is on the use of vests with club signs/colors: "The vest signals to the world that members represent a world-wide criminal network that easily uses violence and threats if they do not get their will. The MC vest, therefore, is a tool that is used to create fear and respect, but also trust among criminal collaborators" (Politidirektoratet, 2014: 6). The vest is presented as nothing but a symbol of a criminal lifestyle. No words on the proudness of being in an elite club. Of becoming a member of a closed society, of belonging, of the importance of being part of something bigger. In a world where people feel alienated and lonely, clubs like these represent a home, friends, respect, and a "meaning of life." The vest as a symbol of these positive attributions has no place in the report. The possibility that some of these clubs are mainly lifestyle groups where crime *per se* is not an important thing, even if some of the members are criminally active, seems to be hard to fathom. The closed and often laborious process of recruiting in these clubs contributes to a homogenization of the members. Friends and acquaintances will normally share similarities. The presentation of such groups as tough criminals by the media and the police will also function as a strengthening of a belief that the groups really are so. This might easily strengthen the process of attracting members with deviant backgrounds and act as a self-fulfilling prophesy.

A Suitable Enemy?

The term *suitable* or *good enemy* is central in Nordic criminology. Nils Christie and Kettil Bruun (1985) coined the term the *good enemy* in the drugs scene. They stated that drugs are enemies because most people will agree that they are bad and will unite in the fight against them. Such enemies present some special conditions that are well suited to the bikers' case too. Seven conditions have to be fulfilled in order for a group to be called a good enemy:

1. Power is to get your will, regardless of others' interest. The first use of power is to define the enemy. Crime problems cannot be defined in such a way that it threatens the elite of society.
2. The enemy has to be defined as dangerous, possibly as diabolic or unhuman.
3. The ones that rages the war have to feel safe in their task. There is little room for critical voices.
4. Good enemies are the ones that never die. The enemy is so smart, clever, and ever changing that it is impossible to beat.
5. The enemy has to be defined in so vague terms that it is impossible to say if it is getting stronger or weaker by the war.
6. This vagueness has clear limits. The enemy has to symbolize the negative, the evil, and the opposite of established values in society.
7. The evil is not an absurd construction. There has to be a core of truth; it cannot be a presentation built on sand.

When Eirik Jensen (2015) stated that the biker groups have developed into a suitable enemy for the police he was on firm criminological ground. These groups seem to fit the seven terms well. These bikers have been defined, labeled, and re-labeled several times. How to decide which group is inside or outside the definition is usually up to the police. By now most of us have read and are well acquainted to the horror stories of the different biker groups; and there is more than a grain of truth: the presentation is not built on sand but it is blown totally out of proportion. If the problem gets better or worse is nearly impossible to say, not only because of vagueness in definitions but also because there are few measure rods in use and no research or serious evaluations done on the effects of the efforts.

Concluding Remarks

Police officers are not scientists; they are more interested in practical questions, such as what they are allowed to do and the use of police methods, not definitions. Since organized crime was declared a serious threat to society in the early 1990s, new laws have been passed, sentences are longer, and new secure prison wards have been built. There has been an improvement in police resources and, most importantly, "new" methods of investigation have proliferated. The concept of organized crime in its hopeless vagueness has been well suited for the spread of these methods (Larsson, 2014). Surveillance methods that used to be limited to drug-related crimes and threat against the national security are now used in cases of economic crime and illegal wolf-hunting, defined as organized crime.

In this process of giving meaning to the term organized crime, a term that felt foreign and un-Norwegian, the biker groups, especially Hells Angels and Bandidos, played an essential part as "role models." All discussion about the establishment of these American clubs on Norwegian soil seemed to forget that the boys were local, often well known to the police, and that the clubs had been around for years. They had been "1 % clubs" for a long time, sharing central aspects of the culture, lore, and mythology of the biker life. Becoming Hells Angels or Bandidos was a step up the ladder in the status system of the bikers. For many in the police this was a clear sign of organized crime. They came to represent something that had little to do with Norwegian culture and ideals. Their symbols, bikes, looks, and slogans were proving that they were antisocial, outside of society, not like "us" and heavily involved in criminal activity. The case was made worse by the fact that they were highly visible and often confirmed these prejudices in words and action. So, the threat from abroad was basically from locals, dressed in alien colors.

One of the most interesting questions is why the bikers got this role not once but twice. At a point, attention towards these groups started to slip away. Other networks and problems filled the gap. Then they were brought back to serve as manifestations of evil and danger in 2011. This comeback, as we have seen, was a result of a conscious strategy of presenting the bikers in negative terms by presenting "facts" and information to prove this. This process involved the production of reports, the use of media, and a political focus on the municipal level. Local authorities, hand in hand with the police, had a central role in the proactive work aiming at the clubs. Agreements to cooperate in the efforts against the clubs were signed, implementing measures to close down clubhouses (not allowing bikers to settle) and using regulatory laws concerning food and drink, fire regulations, and so on in a creative way. The police raided the clubs and used measures like controls of visitors, stop and detention of foreign visitors, and vehicle controls around the clubhouses. There were local variations in the use of methods of policing. Most raids and preventive measures produced meagre results, usually some grams of cannabis or amphetamines.[16] Today the hot air seems to slip out of the biker balloon once more. Few, if any, have questioned the resources used or whether the goals have been reached.

References

Bay, J. (1998). Konfliktar mellan mc-klubbar. In O. Sernhede (Ed.), *Krom och manlig gemenskap. En antologi om bikerkulturen*. Daidalos förlag: Göteborg.

Bergensavisen. (2013). Her sitter politiet og Hells Angels side om side. *Bergensavisen*. October 1. Retrieved from http://www.ba.no/nyheter/her-sitter-politiet-og-hells-angels-side-om-side/s/1-41-6894514.

Billingsley, R. (2009). *Covert Human Intelligence Sources. The "unlovely" face of police work*. Hampshire: Waterside Press.

Christie, N., & Bruun, K. (1985). *Den gode fiende: Narkotikapolitikk i Norden*. Oslo: Universitetsforlaget.

Hobbs, D. (2013). *Lush life: Constructing organized crime in the UK*. Oxford: OUP.

Høyer, T. (1998). *Den store nordiske rockerkrig*. København: Gyldendal.

Jensen, E. (2015). *På innsiden. Historien om mitt politiliv*. Oslo: Kagge forlag.

Johansen, P. O. (2004). *Den illegal spriten: fra forbudstid til polstreik*. Oslo: Unipub forlag.

Korsell, L., & Larsson, P. (2011). Organized crime the Nordic way. *Crime and Justice, 40*, 519–554.

Larsson, P. (2008). *Organisert kriminalitet*. Oslo: Pax.

Larsson, P. (2014). Normaliseringen av det unormale—utvidelsen i bruk av utradisjonelle politimetoder. *Nordisk politiforskning, 1*(1), 41–57.

Natapoff, A. (2009). *Snitching. Criminal informants and the erosion of American justice*. New York, NY: New York University Press.

Naylor, R. T. (2002). *The wages of crime. Black markets, illegal finance, and the underworld economy*. Ithaca, NY: Cornell University Press.

Norsk politi. (2012). *Énprosent mc kriminalitet*. Nr. 2. Retrieved from https://www.politi.no/vedlegg/lokale_vedlegg/politidirektoratet/Vedlegg_1853.pdf

Politidirektoratet. (2005). *Project organized crime*. Oslo: Politidirektoratet.

Politidirektoratet. (2012). *Politiets bekjempelse av kriminelle MC-gjenger i perioden 2011–2015*, Oslo. Retrieved from https://www.politi.no/vedlegg/rapport/Vedlegg_1706.pdf

[16] The information on the results of the busts is often presented as "Hells Angels caught in a drug raid" by the media, while there is no mention of the type or quantity of drugs. In one of the most famous busts on Hells Angels in Oslo (2011) 11 guns were seized. What is rarely mentioned is that many of the guns were from WW1 and WW2 and there were also shotguns. What seemed like a depot could easily be described, with some exceptions, as the lot of a nostalgic collector.

Politidirektoratet. (2014). *Forebygge og bekjempe kriminalitet fra énprosentmiljøet ogkriminelle MC-gjenger. Håndbok for politi og kommunale myndigheter.* Oslo. Retrieved from https://www.politi.no/vedlegg/lokale_vedlegg/politidirektoratet/Vedlegg_2456.pdf
Rosenfeld, R., Jacobs, B. A., & Wright, R. (2003). Snitching and the code of the street. *British Journal of Criminology, 43*, 291–309.
Rønn, K. V. (2012). *The Epistemology of Intelligence: A Dissertation on Epistemological Aspects of Intelligence-led Crime Investigations* (Ph.D. dissertation, University of Copenhagen, Denmark).
Young, J. (2008). *Vertigo of late modernity*. London: Sage.
Young, J. (2011). *The criminological imagination*. Cambridge: Polity Press.

Chapter 13
The Innovative Containment of Organized Crime Problems in Amsterdam's Inner-City, 1996–2015

Cyrille Fijnaut

The Starting Point: The Local Dimension of Organized Crime

One of the constant themes in the writings of Dick Hobbs is the local context of organized crime and its precursors. This is overwhelmingly present is his first book: *Doing the business. Entrepreneurship, detectives and the working class in the East End of London* (Hobbs, 1988) and in his testament in this field: *Lush life: Constructing organized crime in the UK* (Hobbs, 2013). Halfway this time span of 25 years—in 1998—he wrote the influential article titled 'Going down the "glocal". The local context of organized crime' (Hobbs, 1998), summing up his basic ideas on the local dimension of global organized crime problems and their precursors in London (and elsewhere). I always wholeheartedly agreed upon this glocal aspect of organized crime with Hobbs who I met for the first time in the 1980s at the Centre for Criminology at Oxford University and I have since stayed in close contact with. The reasons for my endorsement of his view on organized crime are manifold.

On the one hand it was based upon my personal experience as a police lieutenant in the Dutch City of Tilburg at the end of the 1960s and the beginning of the 1970s. In this capacity I observed that well-known underworld figures left their traditional businesses of stealing and cheating, and moved into the upcoming national and international black markets of cannabis and synthetic drugs, but Tilburg remained their biotope (Woodiwiss, 2014).

On the other hand I learned later on from the literature on the Italian mafia and the American *Cosa Nostra* how locally embedded their criminal enterprises in the end were. The 'families' of New York City did not build cartels in legitimate markets anywhere in the world but in the waste disposal markets and food markets of

C. Fijnaut (✉)
Tilburg Law School, Tilburg University, PO Box 90153, 5000 LE Tilburg, The Netherlands
e-mail: C.J.C.F.Fijnaut@uvt.nl

G.A. Antonopoulos (ed.), *Illegal Entrepreneurship, Organized Crime and Social Control*, Studies of Organized Crime 14, DOI 10.1007/978-3-319-31608-6_13

the Big Apple. Their involvement in the transnational illegal drugs business did not mean at all that they left the City. On the contrary, their biotope evolved into one of the key links in the whole chain form production to distribution (Jacobs, Friel, & Radick, 1999; Jacobs, Panarella, & Worthington, 1994). The heading of the related Palermo Convention 2000—the United Nations Convention against Transnational Organized Crime—therefore is fundamentally flawed. It spirits away the local dimension of organized crime and denies in this way the 'glocal' nature of very important manifestations of organized crime like drugs trafficking, the illegal trade in small arms and human trafficking.

The 'glocal' nature of organized crime problems—to the extent they are related to the delivery of persons, goods and services—has always been the starting point of my research in this field. It was the point of departure of the research with regard to organized crime in the Netherlands that was done by a group of criminologists under my direction—the so-called Fijnaut Research Group—in the framework of the parliamentary committee that in the years 1994–1996 investigated the abuse of undercover policing (Fijnaut, Bovenkerk, Bruinsma, & Van de Bunt, 1998; see also Kleemans, 2004). In addition, this research constituted the conceptual basis of the research concerning cross-border (organized) crime, in particular drug crime, I did together with Toine Spapens in 2004–2005 and with Brice De Ruyver in 2008 in the Euroregion Meuse-Rhine, the urban and densely populated crossing between The Netherlands, Germany and Belgium (Fijnaut & De Ruyver, 2008; Spapens & Fijnaut, 2005, 2010).

This perspective not only influenced my research on the nature, seriousness and development of organized crime in the Low Countries and elsewhere, however. It also had a decisive impact on my ideas on the containment of organized crime and my involvement in a number of policy initiatives. In my view, it is first and foremost the responsibility of local authorities—empowered by national legislation, national authorities and international treaties—to deal with this phenomenon. That is in any case the lesson one should deduct from the huge efforts the successive mayors of New York City, particularly Giuliani, have made to liberate its legal markets from the grip of organized crime through the introduction of rigorous screening procedures in the licensing systems and the bidding processes in the City. International organizations—particularly in the context of the European Union—like Interpol, Eurojust and Europol, can only play a supportive or, at best, a coordinating role in relation to the local and national authorities of the states concerned.

In order to demonstrate the impact of these ideas on research and policy with regard to organized crime in the Netherlands I limit myself in this contribution to the policy developments in the inner-city of Amsterdam (postcode area 1012) that took place in the wake of the report Bovenkerk and I—in the framework of the above-mentioned parliamentary committee of inquiry chaired by van Traa (Van Traa Committee)—wrote about the organized crime problems in the heart of the capital of the Netherlands.

The Impact of the Fijnaut–Bovenkerk Report on Policy Making in the Years 1996–1998

The research that the Fijnaut Research Group executed for the Van Traa Committee was undeniably not only heavily influenced by the findings of the New York State Organised Crime Task Force concerning the role *Cosa Nostra* families played in the legal and illegal markets of New York (Fijnaut, 2002a, 2002b; Fijnaut & Jacobs, 1991). It was also inspired by the fear in Dutch governmental circles that equally in the Netherlands organized crime groups, which already at that time were making huge profits in the drugs markets, would try to control important legal markets. The design of the research project and the report on its results clearly testify of these influences. Simultaneously, however, the Fijnaut Research Group stuck to the idea that organized crime problems had to be studied at the (inter)national level as well as in the local context because organized crime-related issues are very difficult to understand and contain in an effective manner if not in their local dimension. This is the reason why the members of the research group made a real effort to study organized crime problems in a number of Dutch cities and particularly in (the inner-city of) Amsterdam.

As far as the problems in the heart of Amsterdam are concerned, Bovenkerk and I—on the basis of police reports and other sources—came among other to the following conclusions:

- At least a fifth of all 4000 hotels, restaurants, nightclubs and pubs were directly and indirectly under the control of five large criminal groups.
- Quite a big number of criminal groups had half of the 6000 slot machines under their control and these groups were also thought to be active in the drug trade, the prostitution business and the arms trade.
- In particular in the Red Light District (also called the Wallen) 16 powerful individuals and groups with serious criminal records or clear criminal connections had acquired a considerable share in the hotel, restaurant, nightclub and pub business and in the gambling sector (Fijnaut et al., 1998: 137–139).

One can easily imagine that these findings were quite shocking for many people in Amsterdam. The Mayor at the time, Schelto Patijn, even asked me whether I would be willing to present and to defend these conclusions in an open meeting of the Town Council, which is what I did and—if I may say so—with success. The Mayor and the members of the Town Council accepted the outcome of our research and took directly two important measures. On the one hand they immediately appointed a special manager, Freek Salm, for the Red Light District, also called 'the Wallen manager', and ordered him to screen the licenses that over the years had been issued in relation to the prostitution business, the gambling sector, and the cafés and restaurants in the area. His activities not only led to a number of initiatives to come to grips with the lack of compliance by many businesses, such as the establishment of a reliable property database, the closure of non-operational limited companies, the stock-taking of escort services and the restructuring of the consultative mechanisms with the inhabitants of the Wallen. They also made crystal clear that a major comprehensive strategy was needed in order to restore law and order in this area. The development of this strategy was entrusted to a steering committee and an operational Wallen Team consisting of representatives of the City of Amsterdam, the Amsterdam Police Force, the Prosecution Service, the Internal Revenue Service and, of course, the Wallen manager himself.

The most difficult issue that had to be solved by these bodies before action could be taken was to make a legally sustainable arrangement for the open exchange of information between the related authorities and services. This problem was difficult because of the fact that the existing legislation offered very limited possibilities for such operational cooperation. This obstacle was to a large extent the result of two factors: serious concerns concerning the protection of personal data as well as the lack of experience with regard to the administrative, and definitely integrated, containment of organized crime problems. Only in June 1998 the authorities were able to conclude a formal arrangement that could make up a basis for common administrative, fiscal and judicial operations in the Red Light District.

On the other hand the Mayor and the Council appointed an official committee in order to define the role the local Amsterdam authorities should play in the fight against (organized) crime, alongside the police, the judicial and the tax authorities. This committee published its final report in the beginning of 1998. First of all this report clearly stated the general aims the City should try to achieve. These aims ranged from the advancement of awareness of the involvement of organized crime in the legal and illegal economy of the City to the consistent application of a number of policy instruments for combating this type of criminal activities. In addition, this report listed up 77 activities in order for these goals to be reached. These activities—called Van Traa activities—related, e.g. to the promotion of the awareness of the threat of organized crime among Town officials, the City-wide implementation of a Horeca (hotels, restaurants and cafés) Information System, the development of a coherent policy to keep the entertainment districts in control, the extension of the possibilities to refuse or to withdraw permits and subsidies, and the identification of 'frontmen' via in-depth information on property. On April 1, 1998 a coordinator for the administrative approach to (organized) crime all over the City was appointed (Jansen Schoonhoven, 2002: 46–49).

A year later, the coordinator published the first annual report. This report made clear that the implementation of the policy measures was not easy for a number of reasons. One of the reasons was that their implementation required a rather radical change of opinion within the local administration concerning the role the City had to play in the fight against (organized) crime. The general idea among the officials was that crime fighting was first and foremost the responsibility of the police and judicial authorities. Another reason was that—despite the agreement—the steady exchange of information between the related authorities and agencies remained a thorny issue. In particular the police and the tax authorities did not cooperate to the extent the representatives of the City had hoped for. The consequence was that the much-needed mutual flow of information did not take place and the City quite often was more or less forced to take on the problems without the support of the aforementioned named agencies (Varma, Köbben, Lacet, & De Graaf, 2013: 28–30).

A Picture of the Activities of the Van Traa Team in the Period 1998–2005

Apart from the measures that already had been taken at the instigation of the Wallen manager, the Wallen Team—in close cooperation with other departments of the City administration—undertook a number of other sub-projects in the inner-city. The most remarkable one was the purchase of premises in the Red Light District in order to gain again the upper hand in this area. This project was based on the conclusion of the report Bovenkerk and I wrote that criminal groupings bought these premises as investments of their criminal money and as the logistic bases of their illegal activities:

> *The criminals gain access to the legal "upper world" and one sees an undesirable mixing of legal and illegal activities. The buying of premises with criminal funds sends property prices upwards to a point that they are (almost) unaffordable for bona fide businesses. The premises largely house semi-legal and illegal businesses, occasionally linked with a nuisance factor and urban blight* (Fijnaut et al., 1998).

In order to counter this trend the city concluded a secret deal with the housing corporations to gradually buy the tainted premises and to transform them into self-contained residences, ordinary shops, guest houses, etc. In a number of cases the purchased premises were immediately leased to private businesses. These businesses were informed in advance that they would be screened in order to prevent the positioning of frontmen. In other cases the premises were redeveloped and—in terms of quality—enhanced before they were sold to bona fide purchasers in order to give a positive boost to the area. Between Spring 1998 and December 1999, 35 premises were bought, among others 11 brothels and 5 coffee shops. The purchase of premises proved to be effective in the framework of the general renewal of the area. In conjunction with this conclusion it is important to note that there was no profit made on the purchase and sale of these premises. Thanks to the cooperation with the housing corporations the municipality's costs were limited, totaling 2.6 million euros. For the rest, one has to observe that far from all premises offered were bought by the City of Amsterdam (Köbben, 2002: 79–85).

In the beginning of 2000s the Van Traa Team continued its efforts to further the administrative policy in order to limit the opportunities for serious (organized) crime all over the City. This meant that members of this team—usually in close cooperation with members of other departments of the City administration—prepared in-depth reports on a number of issues. These reports not only addressed the crime problems and/or potential crime risks in certain parts of the City, in certain economic branches and in certain public sectors. They also contained a series of recommendations with regard to the possibilities to deal with the problems and/or to limit these risks. The team coordinated, e.g. reports on Westpoort (an important part of the Amsterdam harbour), on a number of restaurants and bars in the City, on the business of phone shops, and on important segments of the public housing sector.

Parallel to this important advisory task the Van Traa Team got heavily involved in the development and the application (only in Amsterdam, of course) of an Act, the 2003 Public Administration (Probity Screening) Act (usually called in the Netherlands the 'BIBOB Act' after its heading in Dutch). This Act enables administrative authorities to refuse or to revoke permits as well as subsidies and tenders funded by the government if screening required by the Act has a negative outcome. The aim of this Act—that in itself must be seen as the embodiment of the idea that organized crime first of all has to be contained on a local level—is to prevent public authorities from unintentionally facilitating criminal activities in economic sectors that are vulnerable by the infiltration by organized crime, among others the Horeca sector, the sector of waste disposal and the sector of the coffee shops.

The screening under the BIBOB Act has both a repressive and a preventive aspect. The screening is preventive if the authorities refuse to grand a permit, a tender or a subsidy because of the serious risk that it will be used to commit or to facilitate criminal offences. It is repressive if they withdraw the permit, the subsidy or the tender on the basis of suspicion that criminal offences are being committed with the contribution of these means. With a view to the effective application of this Act the authorities can ask the BIBOB Bureau in the Ministry of Security and Justice for advice concerning the applicants they want to screen. This Bureau has access to all types of relevant police and judicial data, the data of the Internal Revenue Service and even the data of private parties such as the Chambers of Commerce. This means, of course, that this Act can only effectively be applied in cases wherein the police, the Prosecution Service, the Internal Revenue Service and other authorities have fulfilled their tasks, i.e. have made criminal investigations, collected fiscal data on natural as well as legal persons, etc. If their data systems are empty so to speak, the BIBOB Bureau has not that much to offer to administrative authorities that are looking for in-depth advice about applicants for a permit, a subsidy or tender (Peters & Spapens, 2015: 272–273).

Having said this, it is easy to understand that—as a consequence of the inadequate cooperation between the related authorities and services in (the inner-city of) Amsterdam—it was rather difficult for the Van Traa Team to apply the BIBOB Act in a fast and effective manner. Nevertheless, in the period 2003–2005 its Coordination Bureau BIBOB supported a large number of local authorities and other City departments with regard to the application of screening procedures on the basis of the BIBOB Act. This bureau itself was in this period heavily involved in the execution of such procedures in some 50 complicated cases in the Horeca sector, the gambling business and the prostitution sector among others.

In 2005 a group of researchers from the Free University of Amsterdam published an evaluation report on the Van Traa Team (Huisman, Huikeshoven, Nelen, van de Bunt, & Struiksma, 2005). In general terms the report concluded that this team indeed had delivered a number of reports, had executed a number of projects inside and outside the inner-city, and had played an important role in a number of screening procedures; however, for a number of reasons the *impact* of all these activities on organized crime problems in the Red Light District was not clear. One of the reasons was in the researchers' opinion that the team had focused more on criminal activities in legal markets than on the activities of criminal organizations in illegal markets. Another reason was that the team did not dispose of an in-depth view of the organized crime problems in this area because it did not get the relevant information from the police and the Internal Revenue Service. Therefore, the research group recommended among others that in the future the Van Traa Team should not define the scope of its projects; this should be done by the police and the Internal Revenue Service.

In my view this evaluation did not testify of an in-depth insight in neither the organized crime problems in the City of Amsterdam nor the problems of a multi-agency approach to contain them. The implicit idea, e.g. that the Van Traa Team on its own could fight organized crime problems in the City in an effective manner was rather astonishing, particularly because the researchers themselves had concluded that the police and tax authorities were not really willing to share information with this team. Equally the recommendation that in the future exactly these services, on the basis of the information they disposed of, should select the projects was quite mistaken. Do they really have a much better picture of the organized crime problems in the inner-city? Do they conduct the comprehensive in-depth investigations that are needed for a constant update of a solid picture of these problems? And if this is not the case, should the City administration then stop its efforts to contain organized crime? It was no surprise that the Mayor and the Aldermen of Amsterdam in December 2005 sent a rather devastating letter to the Council on the evaluation report (Fijnaut, 2010: 54–58; Van Daele, Kooijmans, Van der Vorm, Verbist, & Fijnaut, 2010: 369–372).

The Shift to a More Integrated and More Radical Approach of Organized Crime Problems in the Years 2006–2007

Against this background it was not that much of a surprise that the then Mayor of Amsterdam, Job Cohen, discussed with the minister of Justice at the time (August 2006), P-H. Donner, the necessity to get the State more involved in the fight against organized crime in the inner-city. They came to the conclusion that the mutual cooperation between the City and the state should, indeed, be reinforced in order to counter the mingling of the underworld and the upper world in a more effective manner. On the basis of this conclusion they organized a common project, called Emergo (in English: 'I will overcome'), in which the City, the ministries of Justice, Internal Affairs and Finance, the Prosecution Service and the Amsterdam Police

Force would closely cooperate to achieve this goal. In the agreement the parties signed on July 11, 2007, the aim of Emergo was formulated in Article 1 in a more or less operational manner:

- The parties involved should by close cooperation and on the basis of investigation and analysis develop insight in the concentrations of criminal power and the related opportunity structures in the inner-city.
- On the basis of the information they would collect, they should by means of concrete actions—consisting of a mix of administrative, penal and fiscal interventions—use the possibilities to fight and to prevent the named problems.

In the other articles it was stated that the parties not only should give each other access to their relevant databases but they should also support each other in other ways, among others by posting collaborators to the project and by actively participating in its actions. The overall direction of Emergo was entrusted to the minister of Justice, the responsibility with regard to administrative measures remained with the Mayor and the responsibility with regard to penal measures with the Chief Public Prosecutor of the City. A steering committee and a project group, supported by a handful of researchers and a scientific adviser (the author of this chapter), would take care of the practical execution of Emergo. The deadline of this project would be December 31, 2010 but later on was extended to July 1, 2011. In November 2011 the final report on Emergo was published (Projectgroep Emergo, 2011).

It may be clear that this project was a deliberate effort of the Mayor of Amsterdam to solve in a structural manner the permanent problem of cooperation between the related authorities and services at the level of the exchange of information as well as the level of concrete action. In addition, it has to be underlined that Emergo, in any case in the Dutch context, was a very innovative project: never before such a concentration of governmental power was organized in order to deal in a coherent manner with organized crime problems in a particular urban area. For this reason, this project was generally seen as an experiment, even a bold enterprise, that, if successful, could have a major impact on the way the Netherlands in the future generally would try to deal with organized crime problems. And this expectation has, indeed, gradually become true (see Spapens, Peters, & Van Daele, 2015: 505–686).

The establishment of Emergo, however, was only one side of the more integrated and more radical strategy that was developed in 2006–2007 in order to deal in a more effective manner with the organized crime problems in the inner-city of Amsterdam. The other side, its complement so to speak, was certainly as important: a new zoning plan for the heart of the City. The idea for such a plan was partly based on a report some members of the Van Traa Team published in the summer of 2007: *Grenzen aan de handhaving. Nieuwe ambities voor de Wallen* (*Limits to enforcement: New ambitions for the Wallen*). In this report they stated that it was impossible to contain organized crime problems in the town centre only by improving the enforcement of the law. According to them it was also necessary to take on the infrastructure of organized crime itself by reducing the criminogenic branches that made up its most important breeding ground: the hundreds of Horeca establishments, the 451 windows in the Red Light District, the 76 coffee shops, the 19 smartshops, the 38 head shops, the 10 gambling halls, the numerous phone shops, the 10 money transfer bureaus and the 19 mini markets. By reducing this infrastructure the multifunctional character of the inner-city could flourish again and Amsterdam would get the possibility to develop the qualitatively high standing, balanced and attractive entrance that would meet its high ambitions. (Projectgroep Emergo, 2011: 24–28). The authors demonstrated the criminogenic nature of the aforementioned economic sectors by referring among others to the fact that quite often criminals were the owners and/or the financiers of Horeca establishments. In fact, behind the coffee shops huge illegal cannabis production capacities had been found.

This idea to control organized crime problems by changing in a quite radical manner the zoning plan for the heart of Amsterdam was and still is a rather revolutionary concept. As far as I know nowhere in the world such a pioneering initiative has been taken. It meant that the local authorities were no longer satisfied with taking out, via often rather cumbersome and lengthy procedures, the clearly 'rotten apples' in these and other legal branches of the economy but that they were also willing—as a complement to this form of governmental piecemeal engineering—to restructure the economy of the inner-city as a whole. It goes without saying that this double-edged radical approach gave rise to a lot of public debate inside and outside of Amsterdam. The political parties, in particular the Social-Democratic PvdA which constituted the local government, did not yield to the criticism, however.

In November 2008, the Mayor and Aldermen of Amsterdam published a colourful panoramic view on the future of the town centre and invited inhabitants, businesses and opinion leaders in this area to take part in the discussion on this policy plan. The related reports presented general ideas about the redistribution of the main functions the different parts of the inner-city—the shopping and housing areas, the historic squares, the University of Amsterdam, the red light district, Chinatown and others—should fulfil in the future. The transformation of the main streets (Damrak, Rokin, Vijzelstraat, etc.) from the Central Station to the South Axis into a wealthy 'Red Carpet' would create a more contemporary impressive and attractive metropolitan backbone for the inner-city.

At the same time, however, The Coalition Project 1012—after the postcode of the area: 1012—indicated exactly the number of windows in the window prostitution that in some areas would be closed down and the number of coffee shops that in certain streets would obtain no permit. The number of windows would be reduced from 482 to 212 and the number of coffee shops would be reduced from 76 to 38 (Gemeente Amsterdam, 2008; Werkgroep Toekomstperspectief, 2008). One can easily imagine that these proposals provoked not only protest from the side of the owners of the related windows and shops, but they also inflamed a political and moral debate about the (self-)image of Amsterdam as the most 'progressive' and 'tolerant' city in the world. However, despite the reactions, on June 25 and on July 2, 2009, respectively, the Town Council and the Council of the inner-city endorsed the Coalition Project 1012. Its term was fixed at 10 years.

The Execution and the Result of Emergo in the Red Light District in the period 2007–2011

For various reasons it took some considerable time for the project to gain momentum. One reason was the project's organizational complexity. After all, the cooperating institutions and agencies are largely autonomous and none regarded Amsterdam's inner-city as a cause for common concern. An equally important reason was that the agreement they had concluded was in itself insufficient to facilitate the *immediate* exchange of information within Emergo; it took more than a year before a specific legal framework for the collection, exchange and use of information was established and the technical systems became available to support the informative collaboration. The third main reason was the absence of an up-to-date and well thought-out scientific or police-based analysis of the crime-related problems in the 1012 postcode area which targeted interventions could be focused on.

The project had to be realized more or less from scratch. This has led to the development of an explorative strategy in order to get the clearest possible picture of the state of affairs in the 1012 postcode area. The idea was to initially start a few pilot projects to gain experience with the integrated approach to organized crime problems. The experience and findings that emerged from these projects were then to be used to set up ICT projects to explore not only the extent to which the project findings could be computerized but also to produce a satisfactory problem scan of the entire Wallen area. The third and final phase was to be the production of this scan. The original set of pilot projects covered:

- The analysis of a street in the Wallen that in many respects was typical of the legal and illegal activities in this area.
- The study of trafficking in women associated with window prostitution, in particular on the basis of a number of criminal cases.
- The analysis of the 'cheaper' (1–3 star) hotels in the town centre.

Later on, the number of pilot projects was increased to include:

- The analysis of the coffee shops sector—the first analysis ever since they popped up in the 1970s—in relation to the illegal cannabis cultivation and the operations of the 'growshops'.
- The overview of key individuals and businesses in the criminogenic markets, in parallel with an analysis of the Amsterdam-based professional criminals operating in the area.

It is beyond the scope of this contribution to present details of the research method, the scale, and the findings of each pilot project. In general terms one has to underline the unprecedented opportunities Emergo generated for the participants to build close cooperation. Herewith, one may in the first place refer to the opportunity of direct information sharing with as few restrictions as possible—and in such project, information is the real life blood. In the second place one has to highlight that, whereas prior to Emergo any cooperation between institutions and services was fragmented, the teamwork between the direct participants of Emergo became deeper and more comprehensive as the project progressed. In the third place, the added value of ICT technology in Emergo should not be overlooked. The project provided an opportunity to develop a methodology for the large-scale linking of databases that initially appear incompatible. This methodology helped parties to gain a more extensive and clearer picture of the data they jointly possessed and enabled them to perform their duties better, both jointly and separately.

On the other hand, one should not hide away the complications in the execution of a project such as Emergo. First of all it has to be mentioned that—apart from the protracted process of developing the legal framework for the informational collaboration—the main problems were concerned with the legal powers of the parties concerned. One of these problems was the application of those powers by the institutions and agencies involved, and in particular the problem of defining the circumstances wherein the administrative powers of surveillance and control could be substituted by powers enshrined in the framework of criminal investigation. A weak starting point—in terms of facts and figures—meant that this transition sometimes was not feasible despite being absolutely appropriate, according to the officials involved. Another issue in this context was the lack of clear and specific administrative powers to control clandestine, and possibly illegal, activities such as sexual services in massage parlours. In this case, would it be acceptable to ask from a civil servant to act as a pseudo customer?

Secondly, one should not lose sight of the fact that Emergo formed 'a coalition of the willing' in its own way: the entire project actually revolved around the willingness of mutually independent organizations to realize a successful project by joining forces. The project, therefore, had no project leader with a mandate to run the project systematically and to take strong measures—if necessary against the will of the parties involved. The negative side of this construction was particularly acute in relation to the staffing of the project. Sometimes it was rather difficult to get the much-needed capacity from the participating organizations. Not just quantitative capacity but most of the time qualified or specialist capacity—tactical detectives or experienced analysts—to suit each specific case. Capacity of this kind is always scarce.

Finally, I would like to mention here the problems which relate to the ICT projects. Despite the general success of using ICT technology in Emergo, the application of this technology was not always plain sailing. For example, enormous efforts went into bringing together the databases on time and preparing them for the analyses.

Despite these and other complications, Emergo delivered in conformity with its objectives quite an important diverse output. We will focus on three of its results. Firstly, one has to remember that a few of the pilot projects, e.g. the pilot on the coffee shops in the town centre, were not designed for immediate action against specific businesses, buildings, groups or individuals, but were viewed as a vehicle for raising the level of knowledge about this sector to new heights. This pilot project demonstrated among others that quite an impressive part of the managers and executive personnel (145 from 560 in the sample) of the coffee shops had a rather serious criminal record and that many of them in one way or another maintained close relations with (other) heavy criminals in the City. In conjunction with this conclusion one may refer to the results of the sub-project with regard to the illegal production of cannabis. This sub-project demonstrated that cannabis production, inside and outside of the City, is huge—on an annual basis some 3900 indoor and outdoor plantations—in order to be able to serve all the coffee shops continually. This illegal business in particular makes up an important threat to the already socially and economically weak quarters of the City because of the fact that quite a large number of the youngsters living in these districts seek refuge in this illegal economic activity. Moreover, the growshops in their turn (these days those shops are forbidden to the extent they support the illegal cannabis industry) could easily be regarded as the 'spiders' in the criminal networks that are involved in the *whole* cannabis industry in the City. The sub-project demonstrated that growshops sold all the gear that was needed to grow cannabis, bought from the producers the harvest and sold a large part of it to the coffee shops again. To the extent the growshops were controlled by criminal groupings, these groupings in this way formed more or less of a monopoly in Amsterdam's cannabis sector. The conclusion of the Van Traa Team in 2007 that the coffee shop sector, in particular in the inner-city, had to be seen as a criminogenic sector was in other words fully justified.

Secondly, it is important to mention some of the interventions that were undertaken to demonstrate in which concrete manners more coordinated efforts to deal with organized crime in the City could be realized. In Spring 2011 six criminal investigations were initiated in areas including money laundering, the drugs trade and human trafficking. These interventions sometimes raised the question of what the connection may be with combating serious organized crime in the 1012 postcode area. In some cases, such as trafficking in women, the link was clear. In other cases the link was less conspicuous and less direct, but no less important, as the case of the actions against illegal and legal hotels, against bars and massage parlours demonstrated. The opportunities for serious organized crime in the related sectors, and for plucking the fruits of such crime, were curtailed in this way.

Thirdly, the criminography of the heart of the City that could be put together before 2007 showed that Amsterdam had no criminal groups with a 'mafia-style' grip on social and economic life. The picture tended to be one of individuals and groups that play key operational and infrastructural roles in the organized crime problems that manifest themselves in the town centre. This general picture of the situation was clarified and specified in the Emergo projects and investigations. Emergo showed that organized crime in the 1012 postcode area takes many forms and is embedded in a number of business sectors. If organized crime is viewed from the perspective of its perpetrators, Emergo showed that it is mainly committed by individuals and groups of Dutch origin or at any rate by people who have lived for some considerable time in the Netherlands. A number of them act as nodes in the criminal networks of Amsterdam, the Netherlands and elsewhere in the world. They are in other words the key players the policy makers should focus on. In this sense, Emergo was very helpful in defining an appropriate and applicable law enforcement strategy, not only into domains that were inside of the scope of Emergo but also outside of its scope, e.g. the gambling sector.

In conjunction with this summary it should be underlined that it is beyond any doubt that in the wake of Emergo the City step by step has done a lot in the last years to deal in an effective manner with the organized crime problems in the town centre. First of all, the Regional Information and Expertise Centre (RIEC), which was established as the successor of the Van Traa Team in 2013, supported a large number of BIBOB procedures relating to applicants for a permit in the inner-city. Secondly, one may not lose sight of the fact that in the last years a number of remarkable criminal and fiscal cases in the field of prostitution, drugs, gambling and money laundering as well as in the sector of the Horeca testify of the important efforts of the local administrative, police, judicial and fiscal authorities to curb organized crime problems in the heart of Amsterdam (Gemeente Amsterdam, 2014, 2015a; RIEC, 2015).

The Ongoing Adventures of the Coalition Project 1012 in the Heart of Amsterdam Until 2015

It is self-evident that Emergo was an important pillar in the strategy of the City government to redress the entrance of Amsterdam. Its output, indeed, was one of the important arguments to reduce the criminogenic industries in the town centre with the help of a new zoning plan that has already been mentioned in this contribution. However, the execution of this zoning plan in its turn is equally not an easy job for a number of reasons. First of all one has to acknowledge that from time to time not only interest groups and opinion leaders but also members of the Council questioned and still question the foundation, the content and the execution of key components of the Project. In the meeting of the Council on July 2, 2015, for example, one of its members raised the issue whether a rather small number of windows in the prostitution sector were closed down as this development limited in several ways the possibilities for sex workers to make money.

Secondly, one should not underestimate in this context the financial and banking crisis and its negative impact on the investments in cities like Amsterdam. This crisis definitely affected the possibilities of people to get the loans that are necessary to start new businesses (restaurants, design shops, etc.) in the cleared parts of the Wallen.[1]

Thirdly, one has to take into account that not only in the wake of the financial and the banking crisis but also as the consequence of a series of scandals in the sector of the housing corporations all over the country, the possibilities of the Amsterdam corporations to support in a structural manner the renewal of the inner-city, were seriously reduced by the national government. Nowadays, housing corporations have to limit themselves to their traditional core business: social

[1] One should not be too pessimistic about this problem, however. See the investments in the 'Red Carpet': the Rokin has become the place-to-be for among others a leading national newspaper (NRC-Handelsblad), a great bookshop (Scheltema) and top-level department stores (Marks & Spencer; Hausmann).

housing. For this reason it has become difficult, if not impossible, for them to purchase, e.g. former prostitution houses and to allocate them to completely different purposes.

Last but not least one should not lose sight of the fact that the implementation of a zoning plan under the rule of law takes a lot of time, i.e. a number of years. The reduction in the number of coffee shops is a good example to demonstrate this complicated and time-consuming problem. On July 10, 2009 the Mayor sent a letter to the owners of the related coffee shops[2] and informed them—in accordance with the principles and provisions in the field of administrative law—that the permits, which on the basis of the new policy regarding the inner-city *in principle* could not be extended anymore between September 1, 2012 and July 1, 2013, would nevertheless be extended until July 1, 2013; and finally that the other permits would ultimately remain valid until June 1, 2015. A number of them protested in September 2013 against this policy before the Amsterdam Court and, when they lost their case, appealed to the Council of State. This Council came—on February 25, 2015—to the conclusion that the policy of the Mayor was in no way in contradiction with those principles and provisions, however (Raad van State, 2015). In other words, it took nearly 6 years to clear the way for the full execution of this important component of the Coalition Project 2012.

A similar story can be told about the reduction of the window prostitution. In May 2015, 115 of the 482 windows (in 2007) were in a number of ways closed down. According to the related report, at that moment still 94 windows in 25 houses (outside of the newly established prostitution zones) in one way or another had to be removed from this segment of the prostitution market. It is equally important to note here that in the last years the municipal by-laws—as part of a comprehensive program with regard to prostitution—have become much more demanding for the remaining brothel keepers in order to take on women trafficking and to prevent all conceivable kinds of abuse. Recently—on October 1, 2015—the Court of Justice in Luxemburg ruled that the requirement that these service providers should be able to communicate with the prostitutes in a language which these sex workers understand is appropriate for achieving its objective: to strengthen the monitoring of criminal activities related to prostitution by the operators of prostitution businesses (Court of Justice, 2015; Gemeente Amsterdam, 2015b: 26, 2015c).

Against the background of these and other problems it is astonishing what has been achieved in the last years in the Wallen. Referring to the progress report from May 26, 2015, and related reports on the current situation in the postcode area 1012 one can mention here:

- That the number of 'normal' businesses in key areas has increased quite significantly (retail shops and horeca, in particular restaurants).

[2]This letter was a sort of pre-warning to the coffee shop owners in order to give them sufficient time to look for other business endeavours.

- That equally the number of houses and apartments across the inner-city has increased considerably.
- That a quite large number of companies, department stores and hotels all over the place have invested seriously in the enlargement and renovation of their buildings.

The total amount of private investments in the inner-city for the period 2008–2018 is estimated at 950 million euros and the total amount of public investments in this period of time at 100 million euros. In these years, all in all some 370,000 m^2 will be redeveloped.

Considering all these changes it is not that astonishing that despite the critical discussion, the setbacks and the lengthy procedures, more and more parts of the Wallen (Geldersekade, Zeedijk, Rokin/Nes, Warmoesstraat a.o.) and the 'Red Carpet' (Damrak and Rokin) completely or partially meet the ambitions and the expectations of the drafters of the Coalition Project 2012: on the one hand to contain organized crime by reducing the criminogenic branches and to clear the related one-sided low-quality retail businesses in the inner-city and, on the other hand, to transform the postcode area 1012 into a much more multifunctional, balanced and attractive heart of Amsterdam. This challenging task has not yet been finalized: there are still streets and squares that need to be redeveloped in the years ahead. In addition, one may not lose sight of the fact that parallel to this major task the local authorities are confronted with another difficult challenge: to keep street crime and anti-social behavior under control in postcode area 1012 and to increase the safety feelings of its inhabitants. Generally speaking, these problems are not on the rise but the police data as well as local surveys reflect an increasing concern about the sale of (fake) drugs and about nuisance by the steadily increasing number of tourists and visitors. This is, of course, the other side of the success of the Coalition Project 1012 (Gemeente Amsterdam, 2015d).

Concluding Remarks

A few years after he retired as Major of Amsterdam, Patijn told me that the report I wrote together with Bovenkerk was a shocking one, indeed, but that he, in fact, was really 'happy' with our analysis of the situation. For two reasons: it addressed in a convincing manner the serious organized crime problems in the inner-city he was since long aware of, and it equally legitimized a comprehensive and forceful strategy to diminish them in a fair and effective manner. This contribution demonstrates that his assessment has become true, although he certainly did not expect at the time that the Fijnaut-Bovenkerk report would become a stimulus for the long-term and large-scale renewal of the inner-city.

This does not mean that at this moment—some 20 years later—those problems have been solved by the execution of successive, cumulative and complementary projects and initiatives: the Wallen manager, the Van Traa Team, the

Emergo project and the RIEC, and the Coalition Project 1012. For a number of reasons this would also have been a very unrealistic expectation. One of them is that organized crime problems in the heart of Amsterdam since the 1960s are heavily embedded in the infrastructure and economy of the town centre and it is—as we have seen—in many ways a complicated and time-consuming challenge to reduce these problems to a manageable size. A number of policies, e.g. with regard to the coffee shops, can only these days be implemented to the full. It would be, in other words, quite nonsensical to ask at this moment for a definitive evaluation of the named projects and initiatives. It will take perhaps another 10 years before such an evaluation is possible.

Even at that moment, however, it will be difficult to prove the effectiveness or the impact of the strategies that in a more or less coherent and consistent manner have been used to fight organized crime problems in the postal area 1012. One of the most serious obstacles is that it is nearly impossible to compare openly and thoroughly the analysis of these problems in 1996–1997 and the impact of what has been done in the last decades to tackle them. Ultimately, this is the consequence of the fact that organized crime 'by nature' always is a rather hidden problem that never can be totally revealed. No less important, however, is that the data in relevant reports on individuals and individual businesses for security and privacy issues may not be published. This issue makes it in any case these days impossible to use press clips on administrative, criminal and fiscal cases for an in-depth comparative analysis of the organized crime developments in the heart of Amsterdam.

This is from an academic perspective as well as a political perspective a nasty problem. Its political maliciousness consists among others of the fact that in the world we live in these days, people find it very difficult to accept that a project like this even under a lucky star can take 30 years before it yields more or less definitive and to some extent transparent results. The consequence of this impatience is that at a given moment inevitably—also in connection with changing political and economic circumstances—the debate comes up whether the project should not be reviewed, revised or even stopped. In Amsterdam in the last 2 years this development crystallized in a debate about the recalibration of the Coalition Project 1012. Some of the discussants—as one could expect—question the necessity to stick to this project as it has been developed some years ago, because of the fact that many measures already have been taken to reduce the organized crime problems in the inner-city. Another issue concerns the financial constraints the City has to deal with, and this issue has after a lot of debate ended up in the question whether the further renewal of the inner-city should not be organized via public-private partnerships. Up to this moment, this discussion has not yet been rounded off, but one may hope that the Mayor, the Aldermen and the Town Council take into account what has been said before and keep their nerve (Andersson Elffers Felix, 2013; Gemeente Amsterdam, 2015e, 2015f).

References

Andersson Elffers Felix. (2013). *Evaluatie organisatie 1012*. Utrecht: Andersson Elffers Felix.

Court of Justice. (2015). *Joined Cases C-340/14 and C-341/14* (Third Chamber). October 1, 2015.

Fijnaut, C. (Ed.). (2002a). *The administrative approach to (organised) crime in Amsterdam*. Amsterdam: Gemeente Amsterdam.

Fijnaut, C. (2002b). The administrative approach to organized crime in Amsterdam: Background and developments. In C. Fijnaut (Ed.), *The administrative approach to (organized) crime in Amsterdam* (pp. 15–30). Amsterdam: Gemeente Amsterdam.

Fijnaut, C. (2010). Introduction of the New York double strategy to control organized crime in the Netherlands and the European Union. *European Journal of Crime, Criminal Law and Criminal Justice, 18*(1), 43–65.

Fijnaut, C., Bovenkerk, F., Bruinsma, G., & Van de Bunt, H. (1998). *Organized crime in the Netherlands*. The Hague: Kluwer Law International.

Fijnaut, C., & De Ruyver, B. (2008). *Für eine gemeinsame Bekämpfung der drogenbedingten Kriminalität in der Euregio Maas-Rijn*. Maastricht: Provincie Limburg.

Fijnaut, C., & Jacobs, J. (Eds.). (1991). *Organised crime and its containment. A transatlantic initiative*. Deventer: Kluwer Law and Taxation.

Gemeente Amsterdam. (2008). *Hart van Amsterdam. Strategienota Coalitieproject 1012*. Amsterdam: Gemeente Amsterdam.

Gemeente Amsterdam. (2014). *Jaarverslag Directie Openbare Orde en Veiligheid. Programma Van Traa/Coördinatiebureau Bibob 2013*. Amsterdam: Gemeente.

Gemeente Amsterdam. (2015a). *Coördinatiebureau Bibob Amsterdam. Jaarverslag 2014*. Amsterdam: Gemeente.

Gemeente Amsterdam. (2015b). *Voortgangsrapportage 2015 Project 1012*. Amsterdam: Gemeente.

Gemeente Amsterdam. (2015c). *Programma prostitutie Amsterdam. Bestuurlijke monitor 2014. Achtergronden en trends*. Amsterdam: Gemeente.

Gemeente Amsterdam. (2015d). *Gebied 1012 in beeld. Vijfde meting (2014). Ontwikkelingen volgens bewoners en statistieken*. Amsterdam: Gemeente.

Gemeente Amsterdam. (2015e). *Notitie herijking project 1012*. Amsterdam: Gemeente.

Gemeente Amsterdam. (2015f). *Beantwoording vragen herijking raadscommissie AZ van 9 april 2015*. Amsterdam: Gemeente.

Hobbs, D. (1988). *Doing the business. Entrepreneurship, detectives and the working class in the East End of London*. Oxford: Clarendon Press.

Hobbs, D. (1998). Going down the 'glocal'. The local context of organized crime. *The Howard Journal of Criminal Justice, 37*(4), 407–422.

Hobbs, D. (2013). *Lush life. Constructing organized crime in the UK*. Oxford: Oxford University Press.

Huisman, W., Huikeshoven, M., Nelen, H., van de Bunt, H., & Struiksma, J. (2005). *Het Van Traaproject. Evaluatie van de bestuurlijke aanpak van georganiseerde criminaliteit in Amsterdam*. Den Haag: Boom Juridiche Uitgevers.

Jacobs, J., Friel, C., & Radick, R. (1999). *Gotham unbound. How New York City was liberated from the grip of organized crime*. New York, NY: New York University Press.

Jacobs, J., Panarella, C., & Worthington, J. (1994). *Busting the mob. United States v. Cosa Nostra*. New York, NY: New York University Press.

Jansen Schoonhoven, N. (2002). Development of an effective set of tools for the executive control of organized crime. In C. Fijnaut (Ed.), *The administrative approach to (organized) crime in Amsterdam* (pp. 41–50). Amsterdam: Gemeente Amsterdam.

Kleemans, E. (2004). Crossing borders. Organized crime in the Netherlands. In C. Fijnaut & L. Paoli (Eds.), *Organized crime in Europe. Concepts, patterns and policies in the European Union and beyond* (pp. 303–332). Dordrecht: Springer.

Köbben, A.-C. (2002). The Wallen project. In C. Fijnaut (Ed.), *The administrative approach to (organized) crime in Amsterdam* (pp. 73–96). Amsterdam: Gemeente Amsterdam.

Peters, M., & Spapens, A. (2015). The administrative approach in the Netherlands. In A. Spapens, M. Peters, & D. Van Daele (Eds.), *Administrative measures to prevent and tackle crime. Legal possibilities and practical application in EU Member States* (pp. 265–306). The Hague: Eleven International.

Projectgroep Emergo. (2011). *De gezamenlijke aanpak van de zware (georganiseerde) misdaad in het hart van Amsterdam. Achtergronden, ontwikkelingen, perspectieven.* Amsterdam-Den Haag: Gemeente Amsterdam - Ministerie van Justitie. Emergo.

Raad van State. (2015). *Uitspraak 201306110/1/R1.* February 25, 2015.

RIEC. (2015). *Jaarverslag 2014 Amsterdam Amstelland.* Amsterdam: RIEC.

Spapens, A., & Fijnaut, C. (2005). *Criminaliteit en rechtshandhaving in de Euregio Maas-Rijn. De problemen van transnationale (georganiseerde) en de grensoverschrijdende politiële, justitiële en bestuurlijke samenwerking.* Antwerpen: Intersentia.

Spapens, A., & Fijnaut, C. (2010). The Meuse-Rhine Euroregion. A laboratory for police and judicial cooperation in the European Union. In F. Lemieux (Ed.), *International police cooperation. Emerging issues, theory and practice* (pp. 101–125). Willan: Cullompton.

Spapens, A., Peters, M., & Van Daele, D. (Eds.). (2015). *Administrative measures to prevent and tackle crime. Legal possibilities and practical application in EU Member States.* The Hague: Eleven International.

Toekomstperspectief, W. (2008). *Toekomstbeeld 1012.Hart van Amsterdam.* Amsterdam: Gemeente Amsterdam.

Van Daele, D., Kooijmans, T., Van der Vorm, B., Verbist, K., & Fijnaut, C. (2010). *De bestuurlijke aanpak van georganiseerde criminaliteit in Nederland en België.* Antwerpen: Intersentia.

Varma, B., Köbben, A.-C., Lacet, K., & De Graaf, B. (2013). De gemeente Amsterdam en de Wet Bibob. De Amsterdamse lessen. In M. IJzerman, L. Kneppelhout, & N. Romijn (Eds.), *Zuiver zaken doen. Tien jaar BIBOB belicht* (pp. 26–37). Den Haag: Ministerie van Veiligheid en Justitie.

Woodiwiss, M. (2014). The analysis and containment of organized crime in Europe. An interview with Cyrille Fijnaut. *Trends in Organized Crime, 18*(1–2), 94–106.

Chapter 14
Trafficking and the "Victim Industry" Complex

Paraskevi S. Bouklis

Introduction

This chapter visits the Greek antiorganized crime narrative entwined with antitrafficking in women and interrogates the conditions under which trafficking was constructed as a phantom threat that required an immediate legislative response (Antonopoulos & Papanicolaou, 2014; Edwards & Levi, 2008; Hobbs, 2013; Levi, 1981). Commonly perceived as a rupture of Greek "law and order," trafficking in women emerged from its former invisibility during the years 2002 and 2003, and invoked extraordinary levels of hype, excitement, and anxiety, gaining journalistic and legal prevalence in the public domain (Papanicolaou, 2008b, 2011; Papanicolaou & Bouklis, 2011; Triantafyllou, n.d.; Triandafyllidou, 2000).

New antitrafficking discourses and technologies emerged to counterpose national security as well as human security threats. Namely, the threat posed by organized crime and its dominance in the Greek sex industry (Lazaridis, 2001; Papanicolaou, 2008a), the threats posed by domestic terrorism (Bouklis, 2012; Xenakis, 2011) and its constructed links with trafficking, and the unregulated migration threat amplified by trafficking networks violating Greece's migration policies and justice system. The dominant narrative explored here reaffirms that human security, victim, and human rights have been mobilized as a tool for meeting punitive targets against phantom amplified threats.

To respond to these threats, an initial criminalization response focusing on national security measures, border controls, and retaliatory punitiveness was deemed inefficient as it was leaving victims unsupported (YPES Ministry of Foreign Affairs, 2008). In its place, and with the aim to improve previous weaknesses, global human rights governance, interagency coordination, and intergovernmental projects

P.S. Bouklis (✉)
Open University, Milton Keynes, MK6 7AA, UK
e-mail: avi.boukli@open.ac.uk

G.A. Antonopoulos (ed.), *Illegal Entrepreneurship, Organized Crime and Social Control*, Studies of Organized Crime 14, DOI 10.1007/978-3-319-31608-6_14

repositioned the victim industry at the core of antitrafficking (YPES Ministry of Foreign Affairs, 2008: 1). With this constructed antagonism between a criminalization and a human rights approach, the range and ambition of the specter of "trafficking" spread much wider and deeper. "Trafficking in women" is far from a "malady of modernity" and a globalized mutation of "violence against women" (Back, 2014).

Rather, following Hobbs (2013), the specific sociolegal and operational changes examined in this chapter constitute a prime example of "domain expansion" in which the parameters of a previously accepted problem expand far beyond all forms of social recognition (Back, 2014: 1; Best, 1990: 15). Namely, the expanding construction of "organized crime" transmogrifies the operation of the victim industry initially engaged in fighting trafficking. As the phantom threat of transnational trafficking ideologically transformed key institutions in Greece, it created a victim industry—a set of social arrangements that now aims to support the identification of large numbers of victims (Best, 1997: 9). These victims' services emerged with a pivotal role: not only did they cooperate with law enforcement and assist in victim protection, but they also offered secure accommodation, enabling medical care and securing public health. As an assemblage of powers, this newly formed victim industry mobilized elements from the surveillance and the medical–industrial complex to engage in a metamorphosis of antitrafficking (see Framework program concerning police and judicial cooperation in criminal matters (AGIS) 22 July 2002). Relying mostly, however, on exogenous, discontinuous, and opportunistic funds, the financialization of victims' services, and its primary competitiveness in a *social problems marketplace* (Best, 1990: 15) leads to fluid and often unpredictable interchanges beyond criminalization and human rights logics.

'Starting the Business': A Methodological Note

Funded by the Onassis Foundation and under the guidance of Frances Heidensohn and Dick Hobbs, I preliminarily investigated trafficking in Greece in 2006 and 2007 (Bouklis, 2007). Over the years, antitrafficking discourses and technologies entered the core investigation in full force. To investigate this powerful discursive domain, a tripartite "antitrafficking promise" that aims to eliminate trafficking through criminalization, security, and human rights was located. In grappling with these questions, I undertook both empirical and theoretical enquiries. The empirical part is based on research I conducted in the Greek antitrafficking mechanisms during 2008–2009 and during follow-up visits in 2015, as well as on analysis of media representations of trafficking in women (Bouklis, 2012).

The initial selection of Greece as a case study was not merely dictated by geopolitical considerations. It is well documented, for instance, that Greece has been both a destination and a transit European country for female victims of trafficking (US 2002, 2003). It is also well established that Greece is the external southeastern European border, at the crossroads of east and west, with a rugged coastline and a multitude of islands. Since the 1990s, Greece has been well known as a popular attraction for illegalized migrants (Pavlou, 2004; Triandafyllidou, 2000). During the same period, Greece has been frequently represented as the "centre of trafficking in Europe" (Hötzeldt, 2003).

Neoliberalism: Crime Control and Victim Industries

To trace the shifts that are presented in the following sections, I provide here a brief tripartite reference to neoliberalism in order to establish connections between (a) the logic of finance capital, (b) the financialization of agencies, and (c) the victim industry. First, neoliberal state institutions have evolved over the last 30 years on the premise of "strong individual private property rights, of freely functioning markets and free trade" (Harvey, 2005: 64). Essentially, this evolution lies in the liberation of capital from its Fordist institutions, in the transition from the hegemony of industrial capital to that of finance capital, which "unifies industrial and commercial capital into a coherent whole" (Lazzarato, 2015: 139). Within this framework private enterprise and entrepreneurial initiatives are considered fundamental to innovation and wealth. Based on the assumption that continuous increases in productive and capital accumulation should deliver higher living standards to everyone, competition is held to be a primary virtue. Be it competition between individuals and institutions, firms, nations, or cities and regions, neoliberal reforms are aligned with the formation of competitive agencies in the world market (Harvey, 2005).

Second, neoliberalism is a loose and shifting signifier (Brown, 2015). Its discursive formulations, policy entailments, and technologies are not fixed or settled. Extending beyond the limits of economic policy, neoliberalism is a modality of governance expanding through diverse portals and agents. Not only does it produce financial institutions, but it also generates subjects and practices of financialized spheres and activities "heretofore governed by other tables of value" (Brown, 2015: 21; Whitehead, 2015). With its variant instantiations, neoliberalism's plasticity often resides in progressive remedial narratives. From progressive tax reform and increasing investments in pharmaceutical, energy, and technology research, to profitable immigration and counter-crime reforms, each of these issues has been framed in terms of its contribution to innovation, economic growth, and market competitiveness (Brown, 2015).

Third, driven by private profit incentives and the economization of agencies, a new form of victims' services is emerging in the second decade of the new millennium, which borrows components from two fields. On the one hand, it borrows components from the crime control industry. Following Nils Christie (2000), crime control has been transformed by a silent revolution. Industrial drive, innovation, private profit, and capital accumulation have been at the core of the crime control commercial expansion. Replaced by the ethics of profit, a neoliberal political economy argument asserts that pressures toward a flexible economy create a large underclass of unnecessary labor. This new underclass is, in effect, "warehoused"

(Lacey, 2008: 131) in the penal and crime control industry. Considering the fiscal implications of this shift, penality and social welfare strategies are deployed for managing social marginality and maximizing private profit (Beckett & Western, 2001; Lacey, 2008).

On the other hand, these new victims' services borrow components from an ever-expanding victim industry. Analogously to the crime control industry, Joel Best (1997: 16) identifies the victim industry as an "industry mass producing victims." Best argues that due to the absence of institutional restraints, most external agencies like legal institutions, mass media outlets, as well as crime control agencies endorse the victim industry. Accepting that increasingly more individuals should be recognized as victims, the victim industry also internally expands an ideological trend, according to which experts have a right and obligation to "label individuals as victims and guide them into accepting that label" (Best, 1997: 16). Lastly, participants in the victim industry often have vested interests in the identification of victims, including enhanced prestige, influence, validation, increased income, and popularity (Dunn, 2010). Ultimately, these interests are weighted within a purported balance that needs to be achieved between the recognition and protection of victims, and the protection of offenders' rights in the penal and crime control industry. As a result, convivial dynamics sustain crime control and victim industries (Lacey, 2008; Mythen, 2007; Walklate, 2005).

To further complement this analysis, I suggest that it is useful to discuss key institutional changes in national victims' services by including two main factors: (1) The growing coalescence of crime control and victim industries as a concurrent "domain expansion" (Best, 1990: 85); and (2) the subordination of agencies to new forms of financialization and valorization via emerging mobility, flexibility, evaluation, and debt debates. With the former, while there might be a consensus about the core images of sex-trafficking victimization, the problem's periphery features active debates over what should be considered victimization (e.g., sex work), and what are the accepted solutions to the problem (e.g., vocational training, residence permits) (see, for instance, Agustín, 2007; Doezema, 2005; Kara, 2009; Obokata, 2006). In these peripheral debates, crime control and victim support are part of the claims-making rhetoric. As the victim industry is transformed through the examined debt-stricken period, various mutations occur in the interaction and convergence with phantom threats. Sensational media representations suggest that the national mutations of the victim industry discussed in the paragraphs that follow supposedly have direct involvement in trafficking, organized crime, and corruption (Tsaldaris & Psarra, 2015). Thus, a new model for the perpetuation of "organized crime" is generated.

Core Claims: The Emergence and Growth of Victims' Services

Beyond these prevalent elements, the Greek case study is important for the frame that it provides. From a legal perspective, the birth of the Greek antitrafficking mechanisms with their "victim industry complex" had a firm legal basis, with strong antiorganized crime sentiments, often described as efforts against "chameleon crime" (Micha, 2015: 8). Major external developments that influenced the core claims of the Greek victim industry were the Annual US Trafficking in Persons (TIP) Reports (US 2001) and the 2000 United Nations Protocol to Prevent, Suppress and Punish Trafficking in Persons Especially Women and Children, Supplementing the United Nations Convention Against Transnational Organized Crime. Also, the 2005 Council of Europe's Convention on Action against Trafficking in Human Beings, celebrated for its gender and equality imagery, set out the frame or model of victimization articulations, especially with its requirement for member states to identify and protect victims.

Influenced by these developments, Law 2928/2001 (Modification of Provisions of the Penal Code and Code of Penal Procedure and for the Protection of Citizens from Punishable Acts of Criminal Organizations) stipulated protection measures granted to crime witnesses later to be applicable to the establishment of a Witness Protection Department, at the sub-division against Organized Crime of the Security Directorate of Attica and Thessaloniki (United Nations Security Council, 2006). Further, the formation of the antitrafficking task force of the Hellenic Ministry of Public Order (merged in 2007 with the Ministry of Interior, and renamed in 2009 as the Ministry of Citizen Protection), combined with a network of NGO elements, was founded upon the enactment of the antitrafficking legislation, Law 3064/2002 (ΦΕΚ Α′248/15-10-2002). In fact, the implementation of L.3064/2002, subsequently supplemented by delegated legislation and other specific provisions contained in L.3386/2005 (ΦΕΚ Α′212/23-08-2005) on the status of third country nationals, amended Chap. 19 of the Greek Penal Code. The new legal framework added a new paragraph to Article 323 (slave trade) of the Penal Code, entitled "Trafficking in Human Beings" (Article 323A). Article 323A criminalized contemporary forms of trafficking, *inter alia*, for the purpose of sexual exploitation and the economic exploitation of sexual freedom. This first legislative response has been criticized for its disproportionate focus on punitive and criminalization measures over preventive and protective measures (Micha, 2015). It was also criticized for the underlying assertion that the sex industry was a prioritized target over other forms of labor violations (Papanicolaou & Bouklis, 2011). Its executive Presidential Decree 233/2003 on arrangements for victims' protection (relevant to the Penal Code articles 323, 323A, 349, 351, and 351A) defined trafficking victimization while listing in its Annex authorized victims' services.

It is within this framework that competitors in the social problems market place (Best, 1990: 17) engage in antitrafficking claims-making. An important core element of this rhetoric constitutes the ongoing renewal of counter-trafficking developments. For instance, L.3386/2005 inserted the provision of victims' protection on humanitarian grounds within a broader border control context. To strengthen that front, a few years later L.3875/2010 (ΦΕΚ Α′158/20-09-2010) ratified the UN Convention against Transnational Organized Crime and the Protocols Thereto, inserting both harsher criminalization provisions as well as broader victim protection. Broadening the possibility of victim protection to victims who do not cooperate with prosecution, and extending the "reflection period" available to victims for considering their options from 1 to 3 months was meant to bargain for a more victim-centered approach. Further, following the "gendered and victim-centered approach" of the European Parliament and Council (Directive 2011/36/EU), the Greek Law 4189/2013 (ΦΕΚ Α΄215/11-10-2013) offered provisions against the criminalization of victims for more "rigorous prevention, prosecution and protection of victims' rights" (par.7 Directive 2011/36/EU).

For instance, it introduced a temporary suspension of prosecution for violations relevant to sex work and illegal entry against victims of human trafficking, where victims cooperate with the authorities against their traffickers. It also introduced a temporary suspension of deportation for those testifying against organized crime groups. Crucially, L.4198/2013 introduced harsher punishments for offenders, and amending provisions of L.3811/2009 (ΦΕΚ Α΄ 231/17-12-2009) linked the Hellenic Compensation Authority, under the auspices of the Ministry of Justice, Transparency and Human Rights, with trafficking victimization by adding victim compensation as part of victim support provisions. Most recently, the codified current legislation was presented in L.4251/2014, Immigration and Social Integration Code and Other Provisions (ΦΕΚ Α΄80/01-04-2014), replacing and codifying all current provisions, and simplifying procedures for access to justice and victim support. After all these ongoing changes, a system of "cooperation in exchange of protection" is still in place, where in practice the granting of residence permits to victims presupposes cooperation with the competent authorities (Micha, 2015: 32; L.4251/2015, arts. 49–56).

Operationally, since 2001 the interministerial committee OKEA (Group Combating Human Trafficking) has been involved in counter-trafficking efforts, and since 2004 Greece has been implementing an integrated National Plan of Action against trafficking in human beings, aiming to screen, identify, protect, and assist victims, as well as establishing repatriation support avenues (KETHI, n.d.). To strengthen efforts, in 2006 the action plan ILAEIRA was introduced. Meanwhile, in 2007 the first case was established attesting to the dynamic participation of NGOs in counter-trafficking and victim support during the operation Vitrine (Onisenko, 2007). In 2013 the National Rapporteur Office for Combatting Human Trafficking, head of the Office for the Combatting of Human Trafficking, was established (Ministry of Foreign Affairs, 2013). The Rapporteur was to play an important role by representing Greece in the EU network of National Rapporteurs against trafficking in human beings set up by the European Council. At the national level, in line with Directive 36/2011, the Rapporteur's role involves monitoring the implementation of antitrafficking policy and strengthening data collection. Its aim was the "integration of the National Reporting Mechanism for the identification of victims, the creation of a national database, the training of agencies and the deepening of cooperation" between competent services (Ministry of Foreign Affairs, 2013). As a result, convivial rather than antagonistic relations between the criminalization and human rights approaches have been continuously implanted.

Hellenic Victims' Services and the Financial Crisis

Genealogies of the "victim industry" can be discerned in the diverse commentaries focused on trafficking in Greece as a phenomenon linked to prostitution and the exploitation of migrant women in this specific social context (see, for instance, Lazaridis, 2001; Lazos, 2002a, 2002b; Lazos & Zanni, 2003; Papanicolaou & Bouklis, 2011). Clandestine activities and phantom threats linked to transnational organized crime (Antonopoulos, 2009; Antonopoulos & Winterdyk, 2005) triggered ongoing legislative changes (Bouklis, 2012; Bouklis & Chatzopoulos, 2015; Dimitrainas, 2003; Papanicolaou, 2011; Papathanasopoulos, 2007; Sykiotou, 2009; Symeonidou-Kastanidou, 2003). Once antitrafficking was understood as investing not only in criminalization but also in the victim protection dimension, the lack of a national victim support service generated a gap in the wider design.

Gabriella Lazaridis' research, conducted between winter 1998 and spring 1999 (Lazaridis, 2001), concludes that very few organizations gave support "to prostitutes" and victims of trafficking in Greece. According to Lazaridis (2001), the support network reflected the way women, sex, women's rights, and women's bodies are (de)*valued* in Greece. Simultaneously, Lazaridis focuses on a very specific instance of this devaluation and maintains that a barter system "where sex is exchanged for non-deportation" exists (Lazaridis, 2001). Based on this, the success or "failure to protect victims and punish perpetrators" is often an intricate system of social reproduction.

Only a few years later, in 2004–2006, Georgios Papanicolaou's research mapped out a diverse and interconnected field of specialized antitrafficking actors. With particular reference to sex work, however, his account contends that the Greek antitrafficking structures were constituted time and time again under the influence of the abolitionist and "client-hostile" overtones of the US TIP Reports. Hence, the demands for creating a policing antitrafficking core that would cooperate with ministries and NGOs—the latter being at the periphery—with the target to eliminate trafficking in women, have been a US TIP Report conceptualization imposed on Greek structures (Papanicolaou, 2008a).

In line with Papanicolaou's findings, at the time of my research into antitrafficking structures and victims' services, the civil society actors involved in pertinent services had already achieved a high level of organization, as an interconnected field of actors with both nationally and transnationally recognized social action. This evolution of a network of services, with their potential for interconnected actions, was remarkable as a sign of adaptable national structures and a clear indication of the force of international antitrafficking discourses and technologies. To some extent, however, the first signs of a "crisis" were evident since 2009. Complaints about "strategic funding" and "underlying nepotism" had already been acknowledged as the underlying reason for many inconsistent initiatives and for organizations that were "breaking under pressure" (see, e.g., Koukouzikis, 2011; Matsi, 2011; Papadopoulos, 2014).

Worse, in 2012, important changes took place relevant to the financial support of victims' services because the financial crisis was having a domino effect on the funds made available to services for the victims of crime. Announcing the establishment of long- and short-term shelters for women victims of domestic violence and trafficking in 14 municipalities across Greece, scheduled to be set up in May 2012, the Greek Prime Minister, Loukas Papademos—leading a provisional government to come to an agreement with the Troika—described the situation as a battle.

In the years 2013–2015 important changes took place in the Greek trafficking landscape. From being predominantly a country of destination and transit, Greece gradually succumbed to source country trends (U.S. Department of State, 2013, 2014, 2015). This was a putative shift attributed to the stark impact of the financial crisis on all the three areas of prosecution, prevention, and victims' support, exacerbated by "severe budgetary constraints" (U.S. Department of State, 2015: 170). Widespread unemployment and a drastic decline in opportunities resulted in what was often described as "desperate situations … where people are prone to take risks and have few viable alternatives" (European Commission, n.d.). Echoing these concerns, voices from NGOs suggested that "we are all victims of the financial crisis now." This statement was taken up by the wider media, suggesting that all Greeks are now victims of trafficking due to the economic exploitation inflicted by European economic policies (Karteros, 2011). Amid these reconfigurations a further counter-trafficking development took place. From the initial introduction of the National Rapporteur's post and its foundation in the Ministry of Foreign Affairs, two key incentives became clear.

First, the connection between criminalization and human rights antitrafficking models was now taking a "penal populist" turn (see Garland, 2002), the target of the Rapporteur being to "promote zero tolerance for the exploitation and trafficking of persons" (Ministry of Foreign Affairs, 2013). Mirroring the often circulated "zero tolerance" discourse toward promise breaking in relation to the repayment of the Greek debt to creditors, antitrafficking was gradually elevated to a matter of national survival (Zilibotti, 2015). This created a dynamic claim-making that linked economic collapse and trafficking, and packed a "powerful rhetorical punch" (Best, 1990: 18), suggesting that the financial crisis arguably placed Greece "closely alongside other poor European countries, which have supplied the worlds brothels and demand for free labour in the last two decades" (Cross Border Initiatives, 2015).

Second, the financialization of the relevant initiatives enforced in the debt-sinking context a discussion about the cost of these services in various forms (Freitas, 2015). Within the role of the Rapporteur, a disconnection of these services from the spread and proliferation of debt was attempted. Specifically, it was reported by the Ministry that "[t]he founding and operation of the Office will not incur any expenditure, because the Office will be staffed exclusively by Foreign Ministry personnel" (Ministry of Foreign Affairs, 2013). This introduced the debatable assertion that as a progressive change, justice, crime control, and victim support goals should be paired with financial and economical goals.

Under financialization and connected to the newly found reverence for innovation, the Rapporteur expressed the commitment to engage with the private sector and the "political economy of trafficking" by offering "innovative," "out of the box" thinking (Rapidis, 2015). For the Rapporteur to achieve "demand reduction" was also set as core target in order to achieve a chain reaction: "sustain growth and responsible business and consumer behavior and durable employment generation" (Moskoff, 2014: 3). In this market-driven account, making businesses responsible also included the creation of responsible consumers, according to the Rapporteur, by which "'responsible consumers' are prepared to pay a premium for products bearing a socially responsible 'footprint'" (Moskoff, 2014: 4). In fact, the Office aimed to also "create conditions for better absorption of European funding and the realization of relevant" programs (Ministry of Foreign Affairs, 2013), including: funding for the setup of the National Coordination Mechanism for all state agencies; the setup of a National Referral Mechanism (NRM), following the UK model, for swift victim identification, referral, and support; the setup of a National Database for victim assistance as well as for prosecutions; the provision of training, and the establishment of awareness-raising campaigns (Rapidis, 2015). From the above, it becomes evident that also at the core of antitrafficking claim-making a new neoliberal citizenship is being reworked as responsibilized entrepreneurialism and self-investment as a "shared sacrifice routinely solicited by heads of state and heads of businesses" (Brown, 2015: 210), working together for innovative solutions to prevent professed imminent catastrophes.

Periphery: Rights, Faith, and Security Claims

To facilitate this discussion, the specific composition of the victim industry is explored in further detail. The complex orientation of the diverse agencies can be broadly classified into three groups: (1) rights based, (2) faith based, and (3) security led. These groups often have overlapping rhetoric and ideologies that cut across the imposed artificial borders. The idea of multidisciplinary agencies that cooperate, mobilize, and engage a complex group of actors is rooted in July 2001, when Human Rights Watch (HRW) issued its Memorandum of Concern: Trafficking of Migrant Women for Forced Prostitution into Greece (US 2001, 2002; Amnesty International, 2007b). The HRW Memorandum acknowledged the joint ministerial decision by the ministers of public order and interior signed in May 2001 as a positive development to create a "work management group on trafficking" to develop, coordinate, and implement antitrafficking policy in Greece. The working group had a policing core and consisted of police officials, representatives from the Ministry of Foreign Affairs, the General Secretariat for Equality and the International Organization for Migration (IOM), as well as the national representative from the European Observatory on Trafficking, and a sociologist (Human Rights Watch, 2001).

This work management group had a difficult target ahead due to: (1) the absence of comprehensive antitrafficking legislation; (2) the low number of prosecutions for trafficking under existing criminal law; (3) the lack of witness protection programs for trafficking victims to facilitate their participation in prosecutions; (4) the absence of government-sponsored services for all trafficked women, including shelter, medical care, psychological support, and assistance with other basic needs; (5) the ongoing detention and deportation of trafficking victims; (6) the complicity of police officers in the trafficking in women (Human Rights Watch, 2001).

Gradually, by August 2004,[1] a high political-level Inter-ministerial Committee was formed, which prepared the integrated National Action Plan against trafficking in human beings. By attempting to cover the whole spectrum of actions related to trafficking, from locating, recognizing, fully supporting, and offering shelter to victims, issuing a temporary residence and work permits, or granting voluntary repatriation on the merits of each case (Hoyle, Bosworth, & Dempsey, 2011), to education and labor integration, a broad array of measures were brought to the negotiations table (Hellenic Police, 2008a). From early on the General Secretariat for Gender Equality of the Ministry of the Interior, Public Administration and Decentralization placed issues affecting women victims of trafficking in the claim-making rhetoric of the domain.

With reference to nongovernmental elements, the investment in civil society organizations gained official recognition in 2005. The establishment of a "permanent forum" for the exchange of information and best practices between the competent ministries and NGOs was institutionalized after the enactment of L.3064/2002. This was based on the principles of victims' rights and the recognition of a set of entitlements applicable to trafficking victims, as laid down by the Presidential Decree 233/2003. In this framework, the Memorandum of Cooperation on Combating Trafficking in Persons and for Providing Aid to the Victims was signed by the jointly competent Secretaries (Justice, Interior, General Secretariat for Gender Equality, Foreign Affairs, Employment and Social Protection, Health and Social Solidarity, Public Order), 12 NGOs, and the IOM. According to the views expressed at the time, this institutionalization was vital, as it "lifted many coordination problems" and facilitated NGO access to the screening and referral process (see, e.g., Panouris, 2007).

The NGO component included a multifaceted group of diverse organizations: the NGOs Arsis and Solidarity, the Center of Rehabilitation of Victims of Torture and Other Forms of Abuse, the Center for Defense of Human Rights (KEPAD), the Greek Council for Refugees, the European Network of Women, the International Company of Family Support (DESO), the NGO KLIMAKA, the StopNow program, and the organization Smile of the Child. Additionally, in the Memorandum, the participation of IOM was also institutionalized. In subsequent collaborations between civil society organizations more actors also participated, such as the Greek Section of Amnesty International and international organizations with a long-standing presence in Greece such as Doctors Without Borders and Doctors of the World (Papanicolaou & Bouklis, 2011).

[1] In 2004, the Olympic Games were hosted in Athens, Greece. The organization of the Games promised to transform Athens in many different ways (Bouklis, 2012, Chap. 6). According to special reports regarding high security measures imposed by "Olympic security," the main priority was to strengthen protection against terrorism and organized crime (see Tsenes, 2006).

Revisiting the above victim–industry complex in 2015, it is evident that the engagement with civil society has been renewed and new synergies have emerged. Informed by the rapid abandonment of the welfare-oriented paradigm, and the adoption of the neoliberal financialization project, the establishment of the Office of the National Rapporteur replaced the previous Coordination Mechanism of competent Ministries, International Organizations, and accredited NGOs. This aimed to promote better cooperation between the competent authorities and stakeholders. By directly applying for National Structural Funds (ESPA), and other EC funds for "smart, sustainable and inclusive growth" (European Commission, 2013) the Rapporteur now acquired a coordinating mandate, "[c]oordinating competent State, NGO, private and cultural sector stakeholders, towards a large-scale, multi-disciplinary anti-THB Action Plan in Prevention, Prosecution, Protection and Partnership" (National Rapporteur, 2014). As a result, in the sections that follow I explore the changes reshaping this victim–corporate complex, implicitly fostering the institutionalization of relations of dominance, and filling up the space left by the decline of the welfare state (Gürcan 2015).

Rights-Based Actors

The main organization that has been defining trafficking as a gender equality and human rights issue is the General Secretariat for Equality and its research center, the Center of Research For Equality Issues (KETHI—*ΚΕΘΙ*). KETHI's role has been vital in many respects. In 2001, KETHI issued an important overview of legal definitions related to what constitutes trafficking, how victims of trafficking are defined, how victimization occurs in this context, and also what the human rights issues at stake are (see Tsaklagkanou, 2001). Also in 2001, an overview of the trafficking in women literature and the links between trafficking in women, sex work, and sexual exploitation, as presented in national and international literature was compiled (Lazari & Laliotou, 2001). Focusing on violence against women, the first national epidemiological research project on domestic violence was published by KETHI in 2003, and its results portrayed a rather alarming picture. According to the research, 56 % of the women who participated had been experiencing violence (psychological, physical, or sexual) (Artinopoulou et al., 2003). Moreover, and with a view to engage with issues linked to trafficking in women, during the years 2007 and 2008 KETHI issued a number of publications relevant to migration and trafficking, and to women refugees and asylum seekers in Greece (Apostolaki, Paraskeva, Prepoudis, & Tataridis-Pallas, 2008; Drouga, 2008; Maratou-Alipranti et al., 2007).

In the years 2011–2014, the General Secretariat for Gender Equality took a more innovative direction. In cooperation with municipalities all over Greece it launched the establishment of shelters for women victims of violence and, *inter alia*, victims of trafficking. Funded by the National Strategic Reference Framework (NSRF 2007–2013), 16 shelters initiated operation, and three more were operated by the National Center for Social Solidarity (EKKA), "offering assistance to 15 new cases in 2013" (National Rapporteur, 2014: 8). Designed to restructure the operation of shelters, KETHI also engaged in dynamic synergies with IOM, with the aim of organizing public awareness campaigns and engaging with the private sector to enhance "corporate social responsibility" (European Commission, n.d.), and in cooperation with local Bar Associations in Greece developed action to help the legal representation of trafficking victims (National Rapporteur, 2014: 9).

Of equal importance, at the level of civil society, the Center for Research and Action on Peace, (KEDE—*ΚΕΔΕ*), founded in 1988 (KEDE, n.d.) and operating as a women's organization since 1999, launched in December 2002, until December 2004 the project StopNow I, and from October 2004 until September 2006 the project StopNow II, funded by YDAS (Hellenic Aid) of the Greek Ministry of Foreign Affairs. Instilling a rhetoric of efficiency and accountability, the projects have provided highly influential accounts in the official formation of Greek antitrafficking claims (Papanicolaou, 2008a; Papanicolaou & Bouklis, 2011). In particular, the alarming statistical data provided by StopNow have been repeatedly quoted in the years following the research, reporting that from 1990 to 1997 the number of foreign women forced into prostitution in Greece multiplied tenfold from 2100 to 21,750, and fell to 17,200 by 2002 (Lazos & Zanni, 2003: 7). An equally active project spawned by KEDE, with a view to empower women, has been the Women's Initiative for Peace (WINPEACE) project, an initiative led by Margarita Papandreou (Van Steen, 2003).

The study of the Greek sex industry and trafficking in women for the purposes of sexual exploitation, funded by StopNow and the Greek state, was based on prostitution, migration, and sex trafficking victims as inseparable categories (Lazos, 2002a; Lazos & Zanni, 2003). The demand for sexual services was described as the underlying factor behind the commodification of women and the (modern-day) sex slave trade (Papanicolaou, 2008a). In these descriptions, constructions of gender and sexuality were evoked: "one million men—about 30 percent of the nation's sexually active population—call on these women regularly (about twice a month) to satisfy their erotic whims and impulses" (Tzilivakis, 2009). These representations certainly enforce associations between trafficking, sex work, and the "nation's sexuality." Meanwhile KEDE was mentioned as an active participant in the ILAEIRA Anti-Trafficking Interagency-Operational Action Plan in July 2008 (Hellenic Police, 2008a, 2008b).

Moreover, the Galatsi Group has been enforcing the antitrafficking campaign in Greece (Sotiropoulos & Karamagioli, 2006). The Galatsi Group emerged in 2001–2002 and involved a range of organizations from different cities and diverse activist fields (Papanicolaou & Bouklis, 2011). From the Greek section of Amnesty International, the Center of Support of Victims of Ill-treatment and Social Exclusion, the Center for the Rehabilitation of Victims of Torture and Other Forms of Ill-treatment, to the Center for Support of Families of the Holy Archdiocese of Athens, the Galatsi Group has been comprised of diverse actors. A few have been officially included in the Memorandum of Cooperation, while others preserve a level of independence in terms of official cooperation with the Greek antitrafficking authorities.

There is also the European Network of Women, a women's organization that is interconnected with groups and individuals throughout Europe. During the years of my investigation, The European Network of Women was offering accommodation (shelter) for time periods ranging from 1 week to several months, and psychological support to victims (European Network of Women, n.d.). The Network also operated an SOS Hotline, which came to fill an important gap in the area of support for trafficking victims in Greece. In 2011, due to the lack of funds and debt accumulation, only the "SOS line survived with the help of volunteers" (Reinventing Greece, 2012).

Importantly, the Greek Council for Refugees (GCR), founded in 1989, has been crucial in the areas of trafficking, refugee, and asylum in Greece. Their legal department specializes in humanitarian assistance and the legal representation of refugee and asylum applicants in Greece (Greek Council for Refugees, n.d.). For victims of trafficking, GCR has been cooperating with the Anti-trafficking Directorate of the Greek Police and the competent judicial authorities in order to facilitate the process of victims' identification and contribute to the provision of both legal and social assistance.

Lastly, the Greek Helsinki Monitor (GHM) was founded in 1992 and has since been affiliated with the Minority Rights Group—International (Greek Helsinki Monitor, n.d.-a; Minority Rights Group—International n.d.). GHM monitors, publishes, and lobbies on human rights issues in Greece, and occasionally in the Balkans, as part of a wider human rights network. Based on GHM's affiliations and memberships, this network has been comprised of the International Helsinki Federation, which was forced to close down in November 2007 due to bankruptcy caused by fraud (see International Helsinki Federation, n.d.), the International Freedom of Expression Exchange (IFEX), the Euro-Mediterranean Human Rights Network (EMHRN), the Southeast Europe Media Organization (SEEMO), OneWorld.Net and the World Organization Against Torture (OMCT) (International Freedom of Expression Exchange n.d.; Euro-Mediterranean Human Rights Network n.d.; South East Europe Media Organisation n.d.; OneWorld.Net n.d.; The World Organisation Against Torture n.d.). It is best known for its anticonformist discourse in defending the rights of minorities in Greece, including ethnic, religious, and sexual minorities, and for its aggressive critique of discriminatory institutional practices, hate speech, and state violence (Greek Helsinki Monitor, n.d.-c).

With regard to trafficking in women, insofar as trafficking is conceptualized as a gender violence and illegalized migration problem, GHM situates the issue in structural root causes, namely, institutionalized xenophobia and sexism (see, e.g., Greek Helsinki Monitor, n.d.-b; Greek Helsinki & The World Organisation Against Torture, 2002). With specific reference to Greek antitrafficking developments, two main points commonly appear in GHM's criticism. The first is related to victims' treatment: "[v]ictims of trafficking in Greece continue to be treated like criminals. As individuals without papers, they are detained in prison pending deportation for working illegally in Greece" (Greek Helsinki Monitor, 2009; Greek Helsinki & The World Organisation Against Torture, 2002). The second pertains to the judicial mechanisms and the effectiveness and accountability of the broader criminal justice system: "[a]lthough Greece has incorporated the term 'trafficking in human beings' in Law 2605/98 with which Greece has ratified the Europol agreement, the term has never been invoked officially before the Greek court of law" (Greek Helsinki & The World Organisation Against Torture, 2002). In this respect, GHM has been the source that fed a series of interventions by transnational NGOs in the Greek trafficking situation, on the basis of its fierce and consistent human rights criticism and activist action (Human Rights Watch, 2002). Ultimately, GHM's insistence on the question of the root cause of xenophobia and racism has been underpinned by an awareness of the fact that the Greek government's response to the problem has been intricately conditioned by the need to defuse international interventions, which did press toward more police action (Papanicolaou, 2008a).

An important entrepreneurial initiative aimed at providing temporary shelter services in the Attica district, Central Macedonia and Lesvos, is the STEGI project, implemented by the NGO PRAKSIS set up in 2005, and funded by the EEA SOAM[2] program. Offering services to unaccompanied minors, asylum seekers, and vulnerable women, PRAKSIS has been collaborating with IOM in order to "facilitate the voluntary repatriation of unaccompanied minors … and achieve family reunification in case their parents have already settled and live in a European country (Dublin II)" (PRAKSIS, n.d.-b). With an extensive track record of collaborations, e.g., with KLIMAKA, Doctors of the World, ARSIS and various municipalities, as well as fund generation (e.g., European Social Fund), PRAKSIS has been addressing poverty and social housing (PRAKSIS, n.d.-a).

Lastly, the Family and Childcare Center KMOP, with an extensive repertoire of diverse claim-making from BeatBullying to Delete Cyberbullying and Mingle (lifelong learning), gradually became by 2013–2014 the leading organization of the international partnership between Greece, Italy, France, and Portugal, leading the project Resiland: Participation, Capacities and Resilience of Children on the Move against Trafficking and Exploitation, funded by the program Prevention of and Fight against Crime (ISEC) (European Commission, n.d.). Commencing on 1 November 2013 for 24 months, this project was based on "an innovative human rights-based approach" putting "children and their histories at the centre in order to identify effective protection measures," and contributing to the EU antitrafficking debates (Resiland, 2013).

Faith-Based Actors

The nineteenth-century antislavery campaign against the "white slave trade" has influenced contemporary "moral crusaders," whose impact on the establishment of antitrafficking initiatives is significant. Contemporary antitrafficking public letters have been generated by increasing Evangelical involvement, and by celebrities, activists, and

[2] "SOAM Program - Supporting Organizations that assist migrant asylum seeking population in Greece".

academics who have been seeking to put pressure on world leaders for tough measures on prostitution (Elliott, 2004). In Europe, faith-based organizations have been active in antiprostitution crusades. The international Catholic charity Caritas, for instance, "organizes prevention campaigns, operates safe houses, and assists in the repatriation of trafficked women" (Elliott, 2004; Caritas Internationalis, 2015).

Typically, faith-based types of assistance to victims may include, among other types of support: (1) shelter, medical assistance, food, and clothing; (2) social, psychological, and spiritual assistance; (3) legal and financial help; (4) moral support for victims in legal proceedings and meetings with police; (5) help in contacting other services, doctors, and advice centers (Elliott, 2004). Arguably, the main dimension that faith-based initiatives can add to aftercare is "compassion based on the conviction that the spiritual healing of the Great Physician is the best hope for overcoming the pain, brokenness, and trauma suffered by trafficking victims" (Elliott, 2004). Along these lines of faith-based intervention, Caritas Hellas has contributed to antitrafficking knowledge production. According to its estimates, up to 90,000 people were believed to have been trafficked into Greece in 2000, mainly from Eastern Europe (Elliott, 2004).

In terms of similar claims missions, Nea Zoi is a distinguished organization, internationally recognized for its contribution to Greek antitrafficking structures. It defines its work as "support and restoration of individuals in prostitution" (US 2008: 42). These initiatives have arguably focused on victims' rights. Nea Zoi was founded as a nonprofit organization in 2006 and has been based in the center of Athens. Its mission has been to "rehabilitate individuals involved in prostitution by addressing their physical, emotional and spiritual needs through outreach work and relationship building by developing exit strategies in partnership with local churches and local and governmental initiatives" (Nea Zoi, n.d.-c). Nea Zoi focuses on reaching out to men and women working in prostitution (mostly in street prostitution) and offers "hope, assistance, support and alternatives, desiring to see men and women empowered by God for a new life" (Nea Zoi, n.d.-b):

> *Motivated by God's love, Nea Zoi visits red light districts of Athens where they offer friendship, advice and opportunities for a change, believing that a relationship with a loving God is the foundation for lasting transformation* (INV.gr, n.d.).

Importantly, and similarly to Caritas, Nea Zoi has identified specific socioeconomic factors that have been increasing the risk of trafficking, such as poverty, unemployment, corruption, the degradation of cultural values (work ethic and gender roles), and global economic factors (Nea Zoi, n.d.-a). To achieve the rehabilitative and healing potential of the exit strategies it promotes in the context of trafficking, Nea Zoi has been working with "ALL people in prostitution" as what "often begins as trafficking ends as 'choice'" (Nea Zoi, n.d.-a). Among its actions, a prominent initiative has been funded by the Stavros Niarchos Foundation. According to this, Nea Zoi has been working toward the implementation of a vocational day program with a job placement/creation component for "exploited women to exit prostitution" (Nea Zoi, n.d.-c). In line with the entrepreneurial changes of 2011–2014, Nea Zoi has been involved in partnerships with Love 146 UK, the Ratiu Center for Democracy, and the National Agency Against Human Trafficking in Persons (Romania). It also led the preparation of a handicraft business for women victims of trafficking "in order to make and sell handbags" (European Commission, n.d.).

Moreover, the Center for the Support of the Family, KE.S.O. (*Kentro Stiriksis Oikogeneias*), which was established by the Archdiocese of Athens and the Church of Greece in 1999, has been operating as a service of the Archdiocese of Athens with a view to conduct campaigns on issues such as the "crisis of the Greek family, the foundation of the conservation and growth of the Nation" and the "biological annihilation of the Greek nation," as well as to offer charitable support to diverse vulnerable groups (Papanicolaou, 2008a). From drug users, "victims of abortions," victims of domestic violence and their children, to victims of trafficking, KE.S.O. has synthesized humanitarian and religious discourses (KE.S.O., n.d.). Notably, it has maintained that trafficking is a national issue. As in national economic disasters, KE.S.O.'s claim-making revolves around the empowerment of the Greek heterosexual family as the antidote to crises and catastrophes (KE.S.O. 2013).

Beyond the ideological importance of KE.S.O.'s institutional motives, its intervention developed a practical relevance from an early stage, as the organization was in a position to mobilize the Church's already well-established infrastructure and draw additional funds in order to provide shelter and support to women. These actions were often executed in cooperation with other organizations, including IOM (Papanicolaou, 2008a). Similarly, the NGO 'Solidarity' of the Church of Greece, based in Athens, played a prominent role in the area of victims' services. Accommodation, legal advice, medical treatment, psychosocial support, assistance to find work, in-house language courses, and support from IOM for victims' repatriation are among the services provided. Further, in 2015 Solidarity signed a memorandum of cooperation with Aegean Airlines, to offer support to vulnerable social groups (Solidarity, 2015). In 2014, however, this NGO was repeatedly characterized as a "sinful" organization by the media, with millions of "corrupt" funds drawn from the Ministry of Foreign Affairs (YDAS) (Avgi, 2014; Iefimerida, 2014). Lastly, a reference should also be made to the action of Kivotos, "a multi-ethnic youth center, run by a Greek Orthodox priest and dedicated to rescuing youngsters from the brink of social exclusion" (INV.gr, n.d.).

Security-Led Initiatives

In the emergence of security-led initiatives, an assemblage of intelligence, securitization practices, and rights discourse has bridged victims' services (rights claims) and intelligence. This assemblage has dictated that victims' services are to be read in conjunction with existing security discourses and technologies. NGOs such as PRAKSIS, Smile of the Child, ARIS, KMOP, GCR, the NO Project, and the governmental IOM and General Secretary of Gender Equality have been participating in partnerships in order to reconcile victim-centered and security-centered approaches.

For instance, the EU and IOM project AGIS started in 2003 and comprised multiple phases with diverse objectives and European Commission funds. Specifically, AGIS 2003 (Phase I) established a network of partners involved in counter-trafficking training. Phase II in 2005 extended the cooperation through a multidisciplinary training process, bringing together law enforcement, judicial practitioners, and NGO partners, in identifying and providing assistance to victims of trafficking. Phase III facilitated the implementation of security training courses at national levels, via (1) translation of training materials, (2) implementation of pilot training courses by EU experts, (3) promotion of best practices and knowledge exchange, (4) publication of conclusions and recommendations (IOM, n.d.). In Greece, this initiative had crucial implications, such as the establishment of the Law Preparatory Committee. In cooperation with the competent ministries and the Hellenic Police, this Committee was appointed to introduce to the Greek Parliament a bill for the ratification of the UN 2000 Anti-trafficking Protocol. The bill aimed to introduce a holistic framework, with the establishment of shelters and victims' identification and support services at its core (IOM, n.d.). To this, a bilateral agreement between Albania and Greece, signed in 2005 and focused on the transnational protection and humanitarian repatriation of children, was ratified on 25 August 2008, with the new Law 3692/2008 (Shuteriqi, Pippidou, & Stoecklin, 2006). The implementation of L.3692/2008 includes prosecution and prevention activities in both countries, as well as cooperation for the identification of victims, for the individual assessment of each case, and for repatriation and reintegration in the country of origin. In this respect, the reference to victims throughout the security-led initiatives reflects a very specific and rather narrow conceptualization of which actions are to be taken with the aim to protect victims.

With specific reference to securitization (Aradau, 2004), and while it has been presented as an issue of prevention within the broader framework of "protective measures," the Ministry of Foreign Affairs has been exclusively responsible for cases that involve third-country nationals, particularly those who are in need of Schengen visas to enter Greece. In this respect, any actions taken by the Ministry of Foreign Affairs have been portrayed as sensitive to preventing human rights violations. This applies to actions that involve the implementation of increased controls and the launch of investigations to determine whether visas have been obtained in fraudulent ways, as by enacting stricter controls the pertinent authorities have claimed that victims' identification is facilitated.

Since the establishment of the National Rapporteur Office mentioned earlier, key guidelines were to be developed for the identification, compensation, and safe repatriation of victims falling now under the remit of the NRM. As a result, for the period 2014–2020 funds from EU structural funds (ESPA) and the Internal Security Fund (ISF) are to sustain the National Rapporteur Office's assuming a lead role in compiling information and coordinating all stakeholders and partners of the NRM. Again, these developments were deemed efficient as, in line with a "victim-centered approach, the NR Office will opt to participate in a larger EU Transnational Referral Mechanism which links national referral mechanisms to better identify, refer, protect, and assist victims." Additionally, these developments were deemed economical as they succeed with a "considerable economy of resources" (European Commission, n.d.).

It is also worth mentioning at this stage that IOM Athens has been involved in a rather diverse set of activities: from being an important partner in the resolution of victims' identification and repatriation, to organizing educational seminars for raising awareness among students in Greece, and raising wider awareness and promoting the rights of migrant women and the rights of women victims of trafficking in Greek society (funded by Hellenic AID, of the Greek Ministry of Foreign Affairs). In this context, under the European Initiative EQUAL, and in cooperation with the Development Partnership to Promote Equal Rights for Trafficked Persons (ASPIDDA), IOM Athens has organized information seminars on the issue of trafficking in women. IOM's involvement in raising awareness and participation in the broader antitrafficking structures and, more specifically, the ongoing cooperation between IOM Athens and the Greek Ministry of Foreign Affairs in the issues of trafficking in women, serves as a constant reminder that the underpinning elements of the rights language have been used to deliver policy results pertinent to illegalized migration (Bouklis, 2012: Chaps. 1, 2, and 4).

With trafficking victimization becoming more elusive and harder to identify as "more and more victims turn into perpetrators," IOM identified a tactic that relies on coercion, perversely referred to as "happy trafficking" (Kitsantonis, 2008), and adapted their efforts based on these emerging trends. To this end, in the years 2011–2014, IOM Greece intensified their actions in cooperation with NGOs and state organizations (Anti-Trafficking Unit of the Hellenic Police, EKKA, the A21 Campaign), and with IOM missions in origin countries (Russia, Romania, Bulgaria) (National Rapporteur, 2014: 8). This is significant as it shows that the "new" antitrafficking conceptualization has been counting on the previously established structures and yet it has been attempting to improve or correct them without offering, in practice, a clear sense of what exactly needs to be improved.

Shelters

Under Greek law, trafficked victims are entitled to free medical, pharmaceutical, and hospital care throughout the period they are entitled to protection and assistance, i.e., throughout the period they cooperate with law enforcement. This exceeds the minimum requirement for emergency care outlined in the Council of Europe Convention on Action against Trafficking in Human Beings. However, it has been widely acknowledged that many women have difficulty accessing health care in state hospitals because of the lack of awareness among hospital staff of the social aspects of trafficking and antitrafficking legislation. According to the testimony of NGO representatives:

> *Only when we accompany the victims in the hospital and explain to the personnel there what the situation is, what the [2003 Presidential] Decree stipulates, as well as the fact that our organisation, although not on the list of organisations mentioned in the Decree, has a memorandum of cooperation with the authorities in assisting victims of trafficking, do they agree to look at the case. In effect, we need to carry a big file with the relevant paperwork to the hospital each time.* (Amnesty International, 2007a)

The issue of shelters is then highly important, and yet extremely underrepresented in the literature. Between the years 2004 and 2015 two key developmental stages have been identified. The first stage started with the mobilization of antitrafficking imported discourse and technologies and the operation of existing shelters until 2008. For this first stage, the establishment of the Group against Human Trafficking led the way in setting up and potentially monitoring shelters in Greece. This interministerial composition initially promoted the change of the legislative framework and coordinated information about and the sensitization of the public to the phenomenon of trafficking. However, this committee set up only an informal referral system coordinated by the National Center for Social Solidarity (EKKA), under the Ministry of Labor, Social Insurance and Social Solidarity (Ariadne Network, 2007; EKKA, n.d.). In this respect, EKKA has been the main governmental entity responsible for providing protection and accommodation to trafficking victims. In 2008, EKKA operated two shelters for trafficking victims, one in Athens and the second in Thessaloniki.

However, by 2008, due to what appears to be a lack of sufficient regulation and funding, most of the shelters that became operative during the first few years were gradually closing down. For instance, the NGO KLIMAKA for women victims of human trafficking (Klimaka NGO, n.d.), supported by the Ministry of External Affairs (YDAS), operated the shelter CHLOE in Athens, with the capacity to host 12 women and children. Between the years 2005 and 2008 the shelter reportedly hosted 110 survivors (Klimaka Policy Blog, 2010). In 2008, the functioning of the shelter was interrupted (Kantouris, 2009). Similarly, the NGO CVME's (or EKYTHKA in Greek) Center for Research and Support of Victims of Abuse and Social Exclusion was among the projects initially funded by Hellenic Aid and YDAS (Wikileaks, 2006). CVME run a shelter in Ioannina, which was reportedly facing operational problems due to budgetary problems in 2009. Further, in Thessaloniki, the shelter run by the Medical Center for the Rehabilitation of Victims of Torture and Other Forms of Ill-treatment stopped receiving regular funds since 2004 and has stopped cooperating with the interministerial commission. Meanwhile, again in Thessaloniki, the shelter operated by the National Center of Social Solidarity, funded by the Ministry of Health, primarily hosted victims of domestic violence but not victims of sex or labor trafficking (Kantouris, 2009). Lastly, reference should be made to the NGO International Company of Family Support (DESO), as it was set up in 2004 and operated a shelter in Athens, administered by the Ministry of Health and Social Solidarity. In the years that followed the economic crisis, DESO was also among the organizations that sought private funds to sustain their work, specifically their shelter Care (Frontida) (Kleva Pharmaceuticals, 2009).

The second stage in the shelter claim-making domain involved key changes that took place in 2008–2015. A notable NGO that reflects these changes is the A21 Campaign established in 2007–2008. In the first stage of claim-making A21 was not mentioned in the Memorandum of Cooperation. From the end of 2008 onward, however, A21 has been operating a shelter in Thessaloniki and has been involved in research, planning, and fund-raising. The A21 Campaign is a team comprised of individuals, organizations, government officials, and "people committed to abolish injustice in the 21st Century," with the goal to "raise awareness, take legal action and offer rehabilitation services to rescued victims of human trafficking in order to fight this injustice by using a comprehensive approach" (The A21 Campaign, n.d.-a, n.d.-b). In the years 2013–2015, the A21 Campaign has been involved in new collaborations and enterprises. Specifically, a social enterprise called Renew Boutique involves second-hand clothes being donated and then sold. Their entrepreneurial activities also involve the operation of an online shop. The shop has commercialized core claims of the campaign, with t-shirts, wrist bands, and prayer guides offering "specific verses and topics that relate to human trafficking, as well 21 ideas on how you can take action to abolish injustice" (The A21 Campaign, n.d.-c).

In the years 2013–2014 EKKA also operated five short-term shelters (EKKA 2015). Influenced by the financialization changes, since 2011 EKKA has been engaged in the "innovation and coordination" of housing projects. For instance, EKKA has been managing housing applications for asylum seekers in Greece, achieving "a much better coordination of all housing projects that are financed by the European Refugee Fund" (European Commission, n.d.). The changes undergone by EKKA have arguably increased the national ability to support vulnerable victims of trafficking by adjusting the protection offered by state or nongovernmental organizations under the existing web platform—called ESTIA. The introduction of the new National Referral System aims to cover victims' needs and provide a "road map and a real-time response to each incident that is reported" (European Commission, n.d.). Further, funded by the National Strategic Reference Framework (NSRF 2007–2013), the General Secretariat for Equality in cooperation with municipalities all over Greece has launched the establishment of shelters for women victims of violence, including trafficking. It was reported that in 2014–2015 16 shelters were in operation and three were operated by EKKA, "offering assistance to 15 new cases in 2013" (EKKA 2015).

During these two stages, some initiatives raised important questions pertinent to their ability to provide safe services to victims, due to alleged links to trafficking networks (Linardou, 2007). Opening up a gray zone between criminality and victimhood, the use of shelters is also connected to a wider discussion about immigration detention centers and their suitability for "protecting" victims (Greek Helsinki & The World Organisation Against Torture, 2002). From the above it is evident that a quasi-autonomous and rather fragmented NGO sector has been mobilized in Greece (Frangonikolopoulos, 2014). With the majority of NGOs being governed by self-perpetuating boards, without proper oversight of their activities and more importantly their finances, and with a "growing number of scandals regarding irregularities in the allocation and management of state funds by NGOs" (Clarke,

Huliaras, & Sotiropoulos, 2015; Frangonikolopoulos, 2014: 5), the initially observed trafficking phantom threat expanded via corruption and clientelism within antitrafficking and victim support.

The Trafficking Victim Industry: A Tentative Conclusion

After more than a decade of public discussion and domain expansion, trafficking's periphery features active debates about what should be considered abuse and what the available solutions to this are. By considering rights, religious and security claims, and their interconnections, in the years 2002–2015 changes in the funding opportunities due to financial crises have led to a core claim toward neoliberal reforms, characterized by increased managerialism and entrepreneurialism. Rather than mobilizing local communities against neoliberal policies and structural inequalities, mainstream NGOs act as "charity intermediaries" for intensifying neoliberal shifts (Gürcan 2015: 48).

Domain expansion efforts are not always validated and, in their claim-making (in)capacity, initiatives have been accused of direct participation in trafficking (Tsaldaris & Psarra, 2015). Divided between progressive reformers versus corrupt organizations, the initiatives have been reliant on the international capacity to transit project design and generate funding: "[t]here cannot be national strategies and policies with occasional funding given by the EU. When this funding stops the structures stop working as well" (Lazaros Petromelidis, Director of Greek Council for Refugees, quoted in Amnesty International, 2010). As a result, contemporary changes, marked by the increasing financialization and neoliberalization of the world economy, tend to perpetuate and generate new phantom threats.

References

Agustín, L. M. (2007). *Sex at the margins. Migration, labour markets and the rescue industry.* London: Zed Books.

Amnesty International. (2007a). *Greece: Health professional action: Trafficked women: Inadequate time for psychological recovery. EUR 25/005/2007.* London: Amnesty International.

Amnesty International. (2007b). *Greece: Uphold the rights of women and girls trafficked for sexual exploitation. EUR 25/002/2007.* London: Amnesty International.

Amnesty International. (2010). *Greece: The Dublin II trap: Transfers of asylum-seekers to Greece. EUR 25/001/2010.* London: Amnesty International.

Antonopoulos, G. (2009). 'Are the "others" coming?': Evidence on 'alien conspiracy' from three illegal markets in Greece. *Crime, Law and Social Change, 52*(5), 475–493.

Antonopoulos, G., & Papanicolaou, G. (2014). *Unlicensed capitalism, Greek style: Illegal markets and 'organised crime' in Greece.* Nijmegen: Wolf Legal Publishers.

Antonopoulos, G., & Winterdyk, J. (2005). Techniques of neutralizing the trafficking of women. A case study of an active trafficker in Greece. *European Journal of Crime, Criminal Law and Criminal Justice, 13*(2), 136–147.

Apostolaki, S., Paraskeva, M. I., Prepoudis, H., & Tataridis-Pallas, G. (2008). *Guide for women refugees: Rights and obligations*. Athens: KETHI.

Aradau, C. (2004). Security and the democratic scene: Desecuritization and emancipation. *Journal of International Relations and Development, 7*, 388–413.

Ariadne Network. (2007). *Greece*. Athens: Human Rights Defence Centre—KEPAD and the Association for the Social Support of Youth—ARSIS.

Artinopoulou, V., Farsedakis, I., Papagiannopoulou, M., Zoulinaki, A., Katsiki, G., & Xydopoulou, E. (2003). *Domestic violence against women: First national epidemiological research*. Athens: KETHI.

Avgi. (2014, February 23). Amartoles NGO: The blue 'civil duty' and the holy 'Solidarity' (Amartoles NGO: To galazio "Ergo Politon" kai h ieri "Allileggih"). *Avgi*.

Back, L. (2014, July). Book review: Lush life: Constructing organised crime in the UK, by Dick Hobbs. *Internet Journal of Criminology*. Retrieved October 22, 2015, from http://www.internetjournalofcriminology.com/book_review_back_lush_life_constructing_organised_crime_in_the_uk_july_2014.pdf

Beckett, K., & Western, B. (2001). Governing social marginality. In D. Garland (Ed.), *Mass imprisonment: Social causes and consequences* (pp. 35–50). London: Sage.

Best, J. (1990). *Threatened children, rhetoric and concern about children victims*. Chicago, IL: University of Chicago Press.

Best, J. (1997). Victimisation and the victim industry. *Society, 34*(4), 9–17.

Bouklis, P. S. (2007). *Female sex trafficking in Europe and the feminist debate. Greece as a case study on policy implementation and the role of feminists*. MSc Dissertation, London School of Economics, London.

Bouklis, P. S. (2012). *Imaginary penalities: Reconsidering anti-trafficking discourses and technologies*. London: London School of Economics and Political Science.

Bouklis, P. S., & Chatzopoulos, G. (2015). Imaginary counter-trafficking penalities: A comparative analysis of Greece and the United Kingdom. *Journal of Trafficking, Organised Crime and Security, 1*(2), 76–90.

Brown, W. (2015). *Undoing the demos: Neoliberalism's stealth revolution*. New York: Zone Books.

Caritas Internationalis. (2015, August 6). Migrants and asylum seekers are vulnerable to modern slavery. Retrieved October 22, 2015, from http://www.caritas.org/2015/08/migrants-and-asylum-seekers-are-vulnerable-to-modern-slavery/

Christie, N. (2000). *Crime control as industry: Towards gulags, western style*. New York: Psychology Press.

Clarke, J., Huliaras, A., & Sotiropoulos, D. (2015). Introduction. In J. Clarke, A. Huliaras, & D. Sotiropoulos (Eds.), *Austerity and the third sector in Greece* (pp. 1–6). Aldershot: Ashgate.

Cross Border Initiatives. (2015, January 18). Prevention Greece. Retrieved October 22, 2015, http://www.crossborderinitiatives.org/portfolio-item/prevention-greece/ - story

Dimitrainas, G. (2003). Combating human trafficking after L.3064/2002. In E. Symeonidou-Kastanidou (Ed.), *The new Law 3064/2002 on human trafficking* (pp. 87–156). Athens: Sakkoulas Publications.

Doezema, J. (2005). Now you see her, Now you don't: Sex workers at the UN trafficking protocol negotiation. *Social & Legal Studies, 14*(1), 67. doi:10.1177/0964663905049526.

Drouga, K. (2008). *Guide for consultants: 'Trafficking in women'*. Athens: KETHI.

Dunn, J. (2010). *Judging victims: Why we stigmatise survivors, and how they reclaim respect*. London: Lynne Rienner Publishers.

Edwards, A., & Levi, M. (2008). Researching the organization of serious crimes. *Criminology and Criminal Justice, 8*(4), 363–388.

EKKA. (2015, October 23). A brief account of the National Centre for Social Solidarity. Retrieved October 20, 2015, from http://www.ekka.org.gr/EKKA!show.action?lang=en

EKKA. (n.d.). A brief account of the National Centre for Social Solidarity. Retrieved October 20, 2015, from http://www.ekka.org.gr/EKKA!show.action?lang=en

Elliott, M. R. (2004, November 13). *Faith-based responses to Trafficking in Women from Eastern Europe*. Paper presented at the The Lilly Fellows Program National Research Conference, 'Christianity and Human Rights', Samford University, Birmingham, Alabama.

Euro-Mediterranean Human Rights Network. (n.d.). Euro-Mediterranean Human Rights Network. Retrieved March 1, 2012, from http://www.euromedrights.org/en/

European Commission. (2013). European structural & investment funds. Retrieved October 22, 2015, from http://ec.europa.eu/contracts_grants/funds_en.htm

European Commission. (n.d.). Greece: Together Against Trafficking in Human Beings. Retrieved March 23, 2016, from https://ec.europa.eu/anti-trafficking/ec-world-countries/greece_en

European Network of Women. (n.d.). European Network of Women Actions. Retrieved August 5, 2009, from http://www.irini-equal.gr/dge.htm

Framework programme concerning police and judicial cooperation in criminal matters (AGIS) (2002, July 22). Council Decision 2002/630/JHA.

Frangonikolopoulos, C. (2014, February). Politics, the media and NGOs: The Greek experience. *Perspectives on European Politics and Society,* 1–14.

Freitas, J. (2015, July). The tragedy of young migrants in austerity-hit Greece. *New Internationalist.*

Garland, D. (2002). *The culture of control: Crime and social order in contemporary society.* Oxford: OUP.

Greek Council for Refugees. (n.d.). Greek Council for Refugees. Retrieved March 1, 2012, from http://www.gcr.gr/en/node/52

Greek Helsinki Monitor. (2009). Press Release 13 February 2009, Dysfunctional the Response to Trafficking by the Police and the Judicial in Greece.

Greek Helsinki Monitor. (n.d.-a). Greek Helsinki Monitor. Retrieved March 1, 2012, from http://www.greekhelsinki.gr/bhr/english/profile.html

Greek Helsinki Monitor. (n.d.-b). Greek Helsinki Monitor & Minority Rights Group—Greece—1995 Activity Report. Retrieved March 1, 2012, from http://www.greekhelsinki.gr/english/profile/annual-activities1995.html

Greek Helsinki Monitor. (n.d.-c). Greek Helsinki Monitor Reports on Greece. Retrieved March 1, 2012, from http://www.greekhelsinki.gr/english/reports/GHM-Reports-Greece.html

Greek Helsinki Monitor, & The World Organisation Against Torture. (2002). Violence against women. Report Prepared for the Committee on the Elimination of Discrimination against Women at its Exceptional Session of 5–23 August 2002 Considering Greece's Compliance with Its Obligations Under the UN Convention on the Elimination of All Forms of Discrimination Against Women, July 2002. GHM/MRG-G.

Gürcan, E. C. (2015, April). The nonprofit-corporate complex: An integral component and driving force of imperialism in the phase of monopoly-finance capitalism. *Monthly Review*, 37–53.

Harvey, D. (2005). *A brief history of neoliberalism.* Oxford: Oxford University Press.

Hellenic Police. (2008a). *National action plan on the response and fight against the economic exploitation of the sexual life of women and minors—Ilaeira.* Athens: Hellenic Police.

Hellenic Police. (2008b). *Informational note: Actions of the Ministry of Interior and the Hellenic Police for the Combat and Prevention of Human Trafficking.* Athens: Hellenic Police, Attica Department, Vice Division.

Hobbs, D. (2013). *Lush life: Constructing organised crime in the UK.* Oxford: Oxford University Press.

Hötzeldt, A. (2003). Prevention and fight against trafficking: Institutional developments in Europe, Greece Report. Retrieved March 1, 2012, from http://ec.europa.eu/justice_home/daphnetoolkit/files/projects/2002_010/int_fight_against_trafficking_greece_report_2003.pdf

Hoyle, C., Bosworth, M., & Dempsey, M. (2011). Labelling the victims of sex trafficking: Exploring the borderland between rhetoric and reality. *Social & Legal Studies, 20*, 313–329. doi:10.1177/0964663911405394.

Human Rights Watch. (2001). Memorandum of concern: Trafficking of migrant women for forced prostitution in Greece. Retrieved March 1, 2012, from http://www.hrw.org/en/news/2001/07/23/trafficking-migrant-women-forced-prostitution-greece

Human Rights Watch. (2002). Greece: Recommendations regarding the draft law for the 'fight against trafficking of human beings and the provision of aid to the victims of crimes related to the financial exploitation of sexual life'. Retrieved March 1, 2012, from http://www.hrw.org/legacy/backgrounder/eca/greece/greece_law.htm

Iefimerida. (2014, February 27). The state is asking back mondey: Church NGO "Solidarity" Received 23 Million Euros from the State Only Completed 10 Programmes Out of 32., *Iefimerida.*

International Freedom of Expression Exchange. (n.d.). International Freedom of Expression Exchange. Retrieved March 1, 2012, from http://www.ifex.org/

International Helsinki Federation. (n.d.). International Helsinki Federation. Retrieved March 1, 2012, from http://www.ihf-hr.org/

INV.gr. (n.d.). Selected charities and NGOs in Greece. Retrieved June 1, 2011, from http://www.invgr.com/ngos_greece.htm

IOM. (n.d.). Counter-trafficking. Retrieved October 22, 2015, from http://www.iom.hu/counter-trafficking

Kantouris, S. (2009, March 8). Unprotected victims of trafficking' (Aprostateuta ta thymata somatemporias). *Makedonia.*

Kara, S. (2009). *Sex trafficking: Inside the business of modern slavery.* New York: Columbia University Press.

Karteros, S. (2011, July 29). Solidarity or trafficking? *TVXS News.* Retrieved October 22, 2015, from http://www.tvxs.gr/

KE.S.O. (2013, March 11). The Greek Family is global example of resilience and solidarity during the economic crisis. Retrieved October 22, 2015, from http://www.kesoiaa.gr/

KE.S.O. (n.d.). Centre for the Support of the Family. Retrieved March 15, 2012, from http://www.iaath.gr/index.php?option=com_content&view=article&id=219&Itemid=491

KEDE. (n.d.). STOPNOW 1 and STOPNOW 2. Retrieved January 7, 2012, from http://www.kede.org/index.php?do=article&pcid=134

KETHI. (n.d.). Human trafficking. Retrieved October 22, 2015, from http://www.isotita.gr/index.php/docs/c30/

Kitsantonis, N. (2008, January 29). In Greece, female sex victims become recruiters. *The New York Times.*

Kleva Pharmaceuticals. (2009). News: Visit in the shelter for abused women "Frontida". Retrieved October 20, 2015, from http://www.kleva.gr/index.php?language=greek&news=65

Klimaka NGO. (n.d.). Klimaka NGO—News. Retrieved October 20, 2015, from http://www.klimaka.org.gr/newsite/

Klimaka Policy Blog. (2010, January 8). NGO Klimaka—Policy and Strategy. Retrieved October 20, 2015, from http://klimakapolicy.blogspot.co.uk/2010/01/k-2432008.html

Koukouzikis, K. (2011). Xenelasia vs Philoxenia: 1-0. Retrieved August 14, 2011, from http://blogs.eliamep.gr/koukouzikis/xenilasia-vs-filoxenia-1-0/

Lacey, N. (2008). *The prisoners' dilemma: Political economy and punishment in contemporary democracies.* Cambridge: Cambridge University Press.

Lazari, D., & Laliotou, I. (2001). *Trafficking in women, prostitution, sexual exploitation. Overview of Greek and international literature.* Athens: KETHI.

Lazaridis, G. (2001). Trafficking and prostitution: The growing exploitation of migrant women in Greece. *European Journal of Women's Studies, 8*(1), 67.

Lazos, G. (2002a). *Prostitution and transnational trafficking in modern Greece 1. The prostitute.* Athens: Kastaniotis.

Lazos, G. (2002b). *Prostitution and transnational trafficking in modern Greece 2. The client.* Athens: Kastaniotis.

Lazos, G., & Zanni, M. (2003). *Trafficking in Greece in 2002.* Athens: StopNow - KEDE.

Lazzarato, M. (2015). *Governing by debt.* Pasadena, CA: Semiotext(e).

Levi, M. (1981). *The phantom capitalists: The organisation and control of long-firm fraud* (Vol. 44). London: Heinemann.

Linardou, G. (2007, July 15). The international business of red lights. *Eleutherotypia.*

Maratou-Alipranti, L., Papatzani, K., Vonda, E., Iordanidou, A., Kapetanopoulos, A., & Porfyri, I. (2007). *Women's migration in Greece. The findings of the national research conducted by KETHI.* Athens: KETHI.

Matsi, A. (2011, February 15). 528 NGOs on the table: Elusive framework of the active Greek NGOs. *Eleutherotypia.*

Micha, E. (2015). *Practical legal guide for the combat of human trafficking (in Greek)*. Athens: Stop Trafficking.
Ministry of Foreign Affairs. (2013, December 2). Dr Iraklis Moskoff appointed National Rapporteur for Combatting Human Trafficking. Retrieved October 22, 2015, from http://www.mfa.gr/en/current-affairs/news-announcements/dr-iraklis-moskof-appointed-national--rapporteur-for-combatting-human-trafficking.htm
Minority Rights Group - International. (n.d.). Minority rights. Retrieved March 1, 2012, from http://www.minorityrights.org/?lid=326
Moskoff, I. (2014, July). Cooperation with the private sector to reduce "demand" for human trafficking. *British Hellenic Chamber of Commerce,* 2–5.
Mythen, G. (2007). Cultural victimology: Are we all victims now? In S. Walklate (Ed.), *Handbook of victims and victimology*. Devon: Willan Publishing.
National Rapporteur. (2014). *Assessment report 2011–2014*. Athens: National Rapporteur.
Nea Zoi. (n.d.-a). *Power point presentation 'Take a stance against trafficking, help a prostituted person to change his/her life'*. Athens: Nea Zoi.
Nea Zoi. (n.d.-b). *Greece—Athens (Nea Zoi)*. Retrieved February 1, 2012, from http://www.iteams.org/wws/europe/athens_neazoi.shtml
Nea Zoi. (n.d.-c). *Nea Zoi Program Support*. Retrieved August 6, 2009, from http://www.snf.org/index.php?ID=grants_EN&Rec_ID=886
Obokata, T. (2006). *Trafficking of human beings from a human rights perspective: Towards a holistic approach*. Leiden: Koninklijke Brill NV.
OneWorld.Net. (n.d.). OneWorld.Net. Retrieved March 1, 2012, from http://uk.oneworld.net/guides
Onisenko, K. (2007, July 15). Non-governmental organisations in the fight against trafficking. *Kathimerini*.
Panouris, P. (2007). Speech of the Secretary General of the Greek Ministry of Justice, Mr. Panagiotis Panouris, event held at the American Congress with the Subject: 'Trafficking in Persons: Modern Day Slavery', 13 March 2007. Hellenic Ministry of Justice.
Papadopoulos, Y. (2014, March 11). Cloudy landscape for NGOs: An Odyssey the attempt to record them. *Ta Nea*.
Papanicolaou, G. (2008a). *Policing sex trafficking in southeast Europe. A theoretical case study of transnational policing*. Edinburgh: University of Edinburgh.
Papanicolaou, G. (2008b). The sex industry, human trafficking and the global prohibition regime: A cautionary tale from Greece. *Trends in Organised Crime, 11*(4), 379–409.
Papanicolaou, G. (2011). *Transnational policing and sex trafficking in southeast Europe: Policing the imperialist chain*. London: Palgrave Macmillan.
Papanicolaou, G., & Bouklis, P. S. (2011). Sex, trafficking and crime policy in Greece. In L. K. Cheliotis & S. Xenakis (Eds.), *Crime and punishment in contemporary Greece: International comparative perspectives* (pp. 307–338). Oxford: Peter Lang Publishing Group.
Papathanasopoulos, E. (2007). Human trafficking and the reflection period under L.3386/2005. In L. Kotsalis & G. Triantafyllou (Eds.), *Human rights and criminal law* (p. 403). Athens: Sakkoulas Publications.
Pavlou, M. (2004). The migrants 'like us': Responses to the migratory phenomenon in Greece and in Europe. In M. Pavlou & D. Christopoulos (Eds.), *Greece of migration. Social participation, rights and citizenship* (p. 39). Athens: Kritiki.
PRAKSIS. (n.d.-a). Current interventions. Retrieved October 22, 2015, from http://www.praksis.gr/en/our-programs/current-interventions
PRAKSIS. (n.d.-b). STEGI PLUS (+). Retrieved October 22, 2015, from http://www.praksis.gr/en/our-programs/current-interventions/item/%C2%AB%CF%83%CF%84%CE%B5%CE%B3%CE%B7-plus-%C2%BB
Rapidis, D. (2015, March 17). The most demanding challenge concerns our endeavour to address demand reduction and engage the private sector—Interview with Heracles Moskoff. *Bridging Europe*.
Reinventing Greece. (2012). Profile of the European Women Network. Retrieved October 20, 2015, from http://www.reinventinggreece.org/2012/06/profile-on-the-european-women-network-enow/

Resiland. (2013). The Resiland Project starts on 1st November 2013. Retrieved October 22, 2015, from http://www.resiland.org/the-project.html

Shuteriqi, M., Pippidou, D., & Stoecklin, D. (2006). *Transnational protection of children: The case of Albania and Greece: 2000–2006*. Lausanne: Terre des Hommes.

Solidarity. (2015). Allileggii. Retrieved October 20, 2015, from http://www.solidarity.gr/

Sotiropoulos, D. A., & Karamagioli, E. (2006). Greek Civil Society: The long road to maturity (2005). Civicul Civil Society Index shortened assessment tool report for the case of Greece. http://www.civicus.org/new/media/CSI_Greece_Executive_Summary.pdf

South East Europe Media Organisation. (n.d.). The South East Europe Media Organisation. Retrieved March 1, 2012, from http://www.seemo.org/

Sykiotou, A. (2009). Gendered criminality: An attempt towards a critical approach. In N. Kourakis (Ed.), *Gendered criminality: Penal and criminological approaches to gender* (p. 83). Athens: Sakkoulas Publications.

Symeonidou-Kastanidou, E. (2003). Human trafficking in the international context and the criminalisation approach to it under the Greek law. In E. Symeonidou-Kastanidou (Ed.), *The new law 3064/2002* (p. 9). Athens: Sakkoulas Publications.

The A21 Campaign. (n.d.-a). The A21 Campaign. Retrieved August 11, 2012, from http://www.thea21campaign.org/

The A21 Campaign. (n.d.-b). The A21 Campaign, Our Strategy. Retrieved June 5, 2010, from http://www.thea21campaign.org/index.php/en/home/our-strategy

The A21 Campaign. (n.d.-c). Shop A21 Prayer Guide (25 Pack). Retrieved October 20, 2015, from http://www.a21.org/offer.php?intid=173

The World Organisation Against Torture. (n.d.). The World Organisation Against Torture. Retrieved March 1, 2012, from http://www.omct.org/

Triandafyllidou, A. (2000). The political discourse on immigration in southern Europe: A critical analysis. *Journal of Community & Applied Social Psychology, 10*(5), 373–389. doi:10.1002/1099-1298(200009/200010)200010:200005<200373::AID-CASP200595> 200003.200000.CO;200002-R.

Triantafyllou, M. (n.d.). A conversation with Professor Grigoris Lazos from Panteion University. Forced Prostitution of Foreign Women in Greece. Retrieved January 2, 2012, from http://www.epohi.gr/triandafyllou_lazos_interview_issues 2762004.htm

Tsaklagkanou, G. (2001). *Transnational trafficking*. Athens: KETHI.

Tsaldaris, M., & Psarra, A. (2015, March 29). White slave trade and white bread. *EFSYN*.

Tsenes, S. (2006). *Olympic security 2004: Terrorism and organised crime*. Athens: Hellenic Police.

Tzilivakis, K. (2009, September 25). New fight to stop sex trade: Protagonists in the fight to end sex slavery in Greece say public awareness of the matter must go hand in hand with law enforcement efforts. Retrieved September 25, 2011, from http://www.helleniccomserve.com/archivedgreeknews33.html

U.S. Department of State. (2013). Trafficking in persons report 2013. Retrieved October 22, 2015, from http://www.state.gov/j/tip/rls/tiprpt/2013/

U.S. Department of State. (2014). Trafficking in persons report 2014. Retrieved November 20, 2014, from http://www.state.gov/j/tip/rls/tiprpt/2014/?utm_source=NEW+RESOURCE:+Trafficking+in+Persons+R

U.S. Department of State. (2015). Trafficking in persons report 2015. Retrieved October 22, 2015, from http://www.state.gov/j/tip/rls/tiprpt/2015/

United Nations Security Council. (2006, December 28). Letter dated 26 December 2006 from the Chairman of the Security Council Committee established pursuant to the resolution 1373 (2001) concerning counter-terrorism addressed to the President of the Security Council.

US. (2001). Victims of Trafficking and Violence Protection Act of 2000: Trafficking in persons report. Retrieved October 26, 2008, from http://www.state.gov/j/tip/rls/tiprpt/2001/

US. (2002). Victims of Trafficking and Violence Protection Act of 2000: Trafficking in persons report. Retrieved August 7, 2008, from http://www.state.gov/j/tip/rls/tiprpt/2002/index.htm

US. (2003). Victims of Trafficking and Violence Protection Act of 2000: Trafficking in persons report. Retrieved November 10, 2011, from http://www.state.gov/j/tip/rls/tiprpt/2003/index.htm

US. (2008). Trafficking in Persons Report 2008. Retrieved March 1, 2012, from http://www.state.gov/j/tip/rls/tiprpt/2008/index.htm%5D

Van Steen, G. (2003). Margarita Papandreou: Bearing gifts to the Greeks? *Journal of Modern Greek Studies, 21*(2), 245–282.

Walklate, S. (2005). Researching restorative justice: Politics, policy and process. *Critical Criminology, 13*, 165–179.

Whitehead, P. (2015). *Reconceptualising the moral economy of criminal justice: A new perspective*. London: Palgrave Macmillan.

Wikileaks. (2006). Greece Part 2: TIP report submission 2006. Retrieved October 20, 2015, from https://wikileaks.org/plusd/cables/06ATHENS570_a.html

Xenakis, S. (2011). Organised crime and political violence. In L. K. Cheliotis & S. Xenakis (Eds.), *Crime and punishment in contemporary Greece* (p. 241). Oxford: Peter Lang Publishing Group.

YPES Ministry of Foreign Affairs. (2008). *National report "Actions to monitor and combat trafficking in human beings"*. Athens: YPES.

Zilibotti, F. (2015, February 13). The Greek debt crisis: Pragmatism as a matter of principle. *Finanz und Wirtschaft*.

Chapter 15
Bred and Meet: Gangs and God in East London

Gary Armstrong and James Rosbrook-Thompson

Omertá Before God[1]

For centuries religious belief has been credited with the ability to keep in check propensities to criminal behaviour. Be it the stake in conformity religious observance usually brings or fear of the wrath of God, religious faith has been held to keep believers on the societal straight and narrow. In recent decades scholars have shown an interest in the relationship between organised religion and organised crime. Perhaps unsurprisingly, it is the various connections between the mafia and the Catholic Church that have attracted their attention—both are notoriously hierarchical and have a penchant for excommunication. The role of religious ritual and performance in the formation and sustenance of mafia identities has been examined by Merlino (2014), while previously researchers examined the Catholic Church's attitude to mafia activities (Sales, 2010) and the relationship between theology and mafia ethics (Cavadi, 2009; Dino, 2008). The latter exhibited a two-way dynamic between *Cosa Nostra* and the Church, which allowed people to possess mafia affiliations while at the same time cleaving to traditional Catholic values. Good and Evil were not always apparent.

[1]The authors are indebted to Sheldon and Michelle Thomas and all the sessional workers who facilitated this research and provided answers to our questions. Thanks are also due to various people who constitute the Newham MPS (Metropolitan Police Service) Gangs and Firearms Unit and all the members of the forums held under the banner of Newham MPS and Newham Council seeking to address SYV/gangs between 2011 and 2013.

G. Armstrong
College of Business, Arts and Social Sciences, Brunel University, London, UK
e-mail: gary.armstrong@brunel.ac.uk

J. Rosbrook-Thompson (✉)
Department of Humanities and Social Sciences, Anglia Ruskin University, Cambridge, UK
e-mail: james.rosbrook-thompson@anglia.ac.uk

G.A. Antonopoulos (ed.), *Illegal Entrepreneurship, Organized Crime and Social Control*, Studies of Organized Crime 14, DOI 10.1007/978-3-319-31608-6_15

Mafiosi at times sought to legitimise their power and prestige in the eyes of the wider community through religious involvement. This relationship is nothing new (Merlino, 2014). In July 1937, during an annual procession through the centre of Riesi, Sicily, which carried in train a statue of the province's patron saint, Saint Joseph, proceedings came to a halt. The procession idled in front of the home of the local mafia boss. On this occasion the ritual had added importance. As the procession drew to its customary halt, the boss moved away from the crowd, approached his son, and kissed him three times. In response, the son bowed to his father and to the statue of Saint John. In so doing he had—in a silently recognised, unofficial tradition—been consecrated as the new head of the Caltanissetta mafia.

Transitions of a different kind also have a religious-criminal dimension. In 1954 the people of Villalba gathered to commemorate the death of a mafia boss. While an elegy praising his "respect of the law" and "defence of all rights" was pinned to the door of the local church, his links to organised religion were less abstract. O the face of it, it might be surprising to learn that the man charged with 39 murders, 6 attempted murders, and myriad other charges including theft and extortion, was the brother of two priests and nephew and cousin to the Bishops of Muro Lucano and Noto, respectively (Farrell, 1997; Merlino, 2014). God's mercy might be integral to such relationships; a motto appeared alongside his funeral photo which read: "Vedi giudizio umano, come spesso erra!"—"How often human judgement wanders wide!"

For some wanderers and fugitives, religious practice must necessarily be brought closer to home. Despite links between Catholic ritual and mob status, Merlino (2014) notes how, over time, the Church has sought to distance itself from the mafia—a trend which culminated in June 2014 with Pope Francis' excommunication of all *Mafiosi*. This came at a time which had seen the privatisation of religious ritual among high-ranking mafia officials. Because church attendance heightened their risk of arrest, where money allowed and/or circumstances dictated, mafia *latitanti*—members in hiding—sought spiritual guidance in their houses and hideouts. After being accused of numerous murders, including the high-profile homicides of journalist Giuseppe Fava and General Carlo Alberto Dalla Chiesa, mafia boss Benedetto "Nitto" Santapaola hid out in a Catania farmhouse for 11 years. Unwilling to disrupt his weekly pattern of religious observance, he commissioned the building of a chapel within the bounds of the farm which included an altar, statue of the Virgin Mary and red-brick benches. A similar altar was found in the hideout of Santa Maria di Gesú mafia boss Pietro Aglieri when it was raided by police in 1997. However, withdrawal from public life is not an option available to everyone involved in nefarious activities, and not all strands of Christianity have links with organised crime like some branches of the Catholic Church.

Shaming the Chosen

Gang life and religion of a different type have occupied another set of scholars. Anti-gang programmes in the USA and Latin America rooted in various branches of Protestantism have been designed to address a clutch of "gang-related" issues including drug and alcohol addiction (Brennerman, 2011; Leon, 1998; Sanchez-Walsh, 2003; Wolseth, 2010). These programmes aim to address criminal behaviours through a combination of religious practice, self-monitoring and prescribed patterns of scripture-inspired interaction. The 12-step model of Alcoholics Anonymous—beginning with the admission of addiction and ending with assistance of fellow group members—directly informs the work of organisations such as *Criminal and Gang Members Anonymous*.[2] The model is underpinned by latent religiosity and explicit negotiations of (hyper)masculinity (Flores & Hondagneu-Sotelo, 2013, p. 4)[3] According to their proponents, programmes incorporating the 12-steps have enjoyed considerable success (Toft, 2000). However, such interventions have also been subject to criticism. Some have claimed that the model imposes neoliberal governance by forcing subjects to accept fault and accountability (Bourgois & Schonberg, 2009). Others have argued that such methods disempower adherents by forcing them to follow a linear narrative of recovery from a regrettable past, to rock bottom, to clean future (Carr, 2010; Flores & Hondagneu-Sotelo, 2013)—thereby extending and reinforcing state power.[4]

A different approach (which also emerged in the USA and Latin America) has aimed at "setting gang members free" via Pentecostalism. With its focus on the experiential dimension of faith, especially around worship, Pentecostalism offers gang members a path to redemption punctuated by expressive, energetic and interactive church services. Many schemes inspired by this denomination of Protestantism also utilise "reintegrative shaming" (Braithwaite, 1989). As we learn from Brennerman's (2011) study of both Pentecostal and (Catholic) Jesuit-based intervention programmes in Central America, this shaming forged bonds between recovering gang members and a sympathetic church congregation through the joint denunciation of gang activity. Men confessing in such scenarios were encouraged to weep in the presence of church attendees, the idea being that the hypermasculine status of gang members is undermined via displays of vulnerability and a new sense of trust cultivated beyond the gang setting. The use of so-called disintegrative shaming in mainstream institutions such as schools and prisons has been criticised (Rios, 2011). For critics (Braithwaite, 1989; Flores & Hondagneu-Sotelo, 2013; Hagan &

[2] *Criminals & Gang Members Anonymous* was founded in 1997 by Richard Mejico, a gang member and prisoner of Mule Creek prison in Ione, California. Sentenced to death for murder, while on death row Mejico was visited by a nun who gave him a copy of the Big Book of Alcoholics Anonymous. In examining the book's teachings he realised that many could be applied to criminal gangs. The organisation's mission is to assist gang members in overcoming addiction to the criminal activities typically associated with gang life.

[3] Though largely considered to be couched in the terms of Protestant Christianity (Rudy and Greil, 1989), the exact religious orientation of Alcoholics Anonymous strategies seems to be context-dependent. In his study of young alcohol-dependent men in Mexico City, Brandes (2002) noted how the core values of Mexican Catholicism—guilt, confession and salvation—figured frequently in AA programmes' narratives.

[4] These criticisms draw on wider debates about structure and agency and whether the former—patterned and/or institutionalised arrangements/assemblages which delimit human action—or the latter—the ability of individuals to act independently—has primacy in shaping human behaviour (Giddens, 1976).

McCarthy, 1997), this method targets the deviant individual rather than his or her behaviour and, therefore, lacks rituals of reacceptance and reintegration, meaning deviant behaviour continues.

In the Name of the Father

The methods used in these interventions thus raise many issues. Aside from pointing to the basic contradiction between its rhetoric of "freedom" and its ascetic codes (O'Neill, 2011; Pine, 2008), critics have pointed to Pentecostalism's perpetuation of patriarchal ideals. In the majority of Pentecostal churches in the USA, leadership positions are reserved for men. One might therefore argue that the church's appeals to recovering gang members are predicated on trading one male code of honour for another (Leon, 1998; Sanchez-Walsh, 2003). These young men may be encouraged to forgo extreme acts of machismo, such as drug and domestic abuse, but do so in exchange for the less exaggerated masculine dominance of the household—or, in other words, the privileges of so-called "soft patriarchy" (Wilcox, 2004). Interestingly, some researchers have praised this adaptation of masculinity because of its facilitation of upward social mobility through the deflection of resources from the street to the domestic family unit (Brusco, 1995).

Some faith-based gang interventions also have a captive congregation. The literature analysing the role of religion in prisons reveals increasing diversity in terms of the religious orientation of inmates and those seeking to reach them via spiritual rehabilitation. However, Thomas and Zaitzow (2006) assert all the same that Christianity is still the dominant religious influence in prisons and cite Florida's faith-based prisons[5] and the embedding of denominational precepts therein, and the work of Prison Fellowship Ministries,[6] which has implemented Christianity-based programmes in prisons across four US states. They also discuss Brazil's Humaita Prison, which has been successful in turning a penal institution into a religious community (Johnson, 2002), and the *Baptist Experiencing God* programme in Angola Prison, Louisiana, which has been credited with reducing violence and escape attempts, and generally serving to stabilise inmate culture (Frink, 2004). In the UK, the *Alpha Course* has been successful in aiding the rehabilitation of prisoners and offenders (Hunt, 2005). Described as "a contemporary proselytising programme … designed for the contemporary post-Christian age", the Course, pioneered by members of an Anglican church in Brompton, London, is advertised as a "ten week

[5] The number of faith-based prison facilities in the USA has grown rapidly since the Carol Vance Unit opened in the outskirts of Houston in 1997. Staffed by devout volunteers, these facilities now cater for a range of faiths and claim to foster an environment which reduces the number of prisoner infractions and recidivism (Crary, 2007)—though this and related claims are contested (Volokh, 2011).

[6] Prison Fellowship is an organisation based on prison outreach and criminal justice reform. Based in Washington, DC, it was formed in 1997 by ex-offender Chuck Colson and now operates in 112 countries worldwide.

practical introduction to Christianity" (Hunt, 2005, p. 2). Its prison missions are based on the booklet, *Caring for Ex-Offenders* (Gumbel, 2001).

If God works in many ways and via many people, the Criminal Justice System would be failing in its purpose if it did not utilise the words and teachings of religious protagonists. How the message of God is delivered together with its effects on recipients are thus worthy of academic analysis.

The Opium of the People?

The research described in what follows took place between 2011 and 2013 in the east London Borough of Newham (LBN). Situated north of the River Thames, around 5 miles from the City of London, Newham is one of the poorest boroughs in the UK. It is also the second most diverse in terms of the ethnicity of its residents. According to the results of 2011 Census, 29% of Newham's estimated 307.000 population is White (16.7% White British, 0.7% White Irish, 0.2% Gypsy or Irish Traveller, 11.4% Other White), 4.6% of mixed race (1.3% White and Black Caribbean, 1.1% White and Black African, 0.9% White and Asian, 1.3% Other Mixed), 43.5% Asian (13.8% Indian, 12.21% Bangladeshi, 9.8% Pakistani, 1.3% Chinese, 6.5% Other Asian), 19.6% Black (12.3% African, 4.9% Caribbean, 2.4% Other Black), 1.1% Arab and 2.3% of other ethnic heritage. With the highest fertility rate in the country (LBN, 2014), this incredibly diverse populace is set to grow rapidly in coming years. In terms of religion, the population of Newham is 40.0% Christian, 32.0% Muslim, 9.3% No religion, 8.8% Hindu, 2.1% Sikh, 0.8% Buddhist, 0.1% Jewish (LBN, 2014), with the borough being home to some 35 mosques, 26 Anglican churches, 16 Baptist churches, 12 Catholic parishes and 4 synagogues. Religious diversity is a lived reality, and this diversity has a long and political history.

Diasporas have long existed in this locale as a consequence of religious schism and attempts at self-preservation. Many Huguenots (French Protestants) settled in the area in the decades following the Revocation of the Edict of Nantes (1685)—by 1700 there were nine Huguenot churches in the Spitalfields district (BBC, 2015). Though many Irish Catholics had come to London in the eighteenth century as economic migrants, the Irish Famine of the mid-nineteenth century created a much larger Irish diaspora in the East End—by 1850 the Irish-born population of London numbered 109.000, many of whom sought work (on the docks, canals, railways, and roads) and residence in the east of the city (Hobbs, 2013). Bringing Catholicism with them, they strengthened the influence of the Catholic Church in East London (Jackson, 1963; Lees, 1979). Between 1881 and 1914, more than two million Jews fled Eastern Europe in the face of *pogroms* and economic hardship.[7] Many arrived

[7] A smaller influx had occurred after the provinces of Astrakhan and the northern Caucuses were excluded from the Russian Pale of Settlement in 1835, which saw Jews barred from trades and professions.

in Britain expecting to use it as a way station, with America being their ultimate destination. However, more than 100.000 decided to remain in the UK, with a large number settling in East London—by 1900 Jews constituted approximately 95% of the population in the Wentworth Street district of Spitalfields (BBC, 2015). Others would arrive from the West with a different take on redemption.

Following the passing of the British Nationality Act of 1948 (which created the status of Citizen of the UK Colonies), people from the Caribbean came to settle in East London (particularly in Hackney), bringing with them religious traditions rooted in Evangelical Christianity. The same Act would see Africans from Commonwealth nations settle in the UK, albeit later and in smaller numbers. Meanwhile Muslims from the Indian subcontinent also began to settle in the East End. The East London Mosque and Islamic Centre opened on Commercial Road in 1941, while from the late 1950s the area saw waves of immigration from the Sylhet region of East Pakistan (the latter seceded in 1971, becoming Bangladesh). Religious observation was in many instances crucial to an industrious and exemplary lifestyle premised on seeking a better existence in the here and now.

The Word and the Receiver

Not all who arrived in East London made good. Consequently the neighbourhoods which constituted the east of the capital also witnessed their fair share of religion-based interventions in the lives of the poor. The London City Mission was founded in Hoxton by former Secretary of the Religious Societies in Glasgow, David Naismith. Having already founded the Young Men's Society for Religious Improvement (1924) and City Missions in Glasgow (1926) and Edinburgh (1932), Naismith wanted the Missions to assist the East End's poor and destitute, while also providing aid to Ragged Schools.[8] The Salvation Army (originally the Christian Mission) was also founded in the East End in 1865 by former Methodist minister William Booth. With its officers ordained as Ministers of Religion, the Salvation Army sought to provide shelter for the destitute and help other vulnerable members of the community such as the elderly, newly released offenders, the disabled and the alcohol- and drug-dependent. London's East End was for millions a haven in a heartless world. But for many residents, eking out a living was a constant battle for survival. Violence and intimidation were no strangers to those who called Newham "home".[9]

In the contemporary Newham setting, SYV/gangs is one of the main concerns of those tasked with policing, community-relations and all manner of related

[8] Created in the nineteenth century amid the rapid industrialization of British towns and cities, Ragged Schools were charitable institutions which provided free education, lodging, clothe and food to destitute children. Bible study formed an integral part of the school curriculum.

[9] The name "Newham" was coined in 1964 when the former boroughs of East Ham and West Ham were integrated to become Newham (see Armstrong, Hobbs, and Giulanotti, 2016).

public-spirited interventions. The contexts that violence occurs in were not easily accessible to the multiple agencies which set out to address the issue nor, indeed, to the researchers. Despite this, an ethnographic approach was adopted, with observation, participant observation and in-depth interviews used in combination. Ethnography is particularly relevant as a methodology to facilitate an understanding of marginalised communities (Kearns & Smith, 1994). Others exploring the complex social issues associated with crime have recognised the method's potential to give a voice to society's most peripheral groups (Robinson, 2002; Emirbayer & Williams 2005; Bourgois & Schonberg, 2007; Magee, 2011). The ethnographic method is both a process and a product (Milgate, 2007). Making sense of that witnessed is thus not a simple task. While there are a number of definitions of "ethnography", there is broad consensus that the method requires the researcher to understand and articulate the meanings through which social agents encounter the world (Atkinson, Coffey, Delamont, Lofland, & Lofland, 2002). In what follows the predominant voice is that of 50-year-old Sheldon Thomas. That said, in his company young men also spoke.

The fieldwork was carried out within three institutions, all of which had a stake in combatting SYV/gang-related activity in Newham: the local council, the Metropolitan Police Service (MPS), and "TAG". While the chapter focuses principally on the latter, the nature of the problem was to large extent defined by the former two organisations, and the way in which they engaged with Third Sector organisations[10] such as TAG is an important part of the account provided here and will be explained in greater detail in future publications (Armstrong et al., 2016).

Preaching and the Converted

In the politics of crime control, solutions sometimes precede problems, or at least definitional clarity. According to the Mayor of London (2014),[11] 250 youth gangs—together comprising 4800 individuals—were active in the capital in 2012.[12] The behaviours and tactics used by those perpetrating such violence in the collectives known colloquially as "gangs" and the personnel tasked with preventing their offending behaviours differ from borough to borough.[13] The governance of "gang"

[10] The Third Sector includes organisations that are not-for profit and non-governmental, as distinguished from the public and private sectors. It is also referred to as the voluntary, community, non-profit or civic sector. There are currently over 180,000 charities in the UK today, employing around 778,000 paid workers (TPP, 2015).

[11] The current Mayor of London is Conservative Party member, Boris Johnson. Together with the 25 elected members of the London Assembly, the Mayor is responsible for the strategic government of Greater London.

[12] In 2007 youth gangs became the focus of a Home Office specialist subgroup, the *Tackling Gangs Action Programme*, chaired by the Home Secretary and overseen by the *Task Force on Gangs and Guns*.

[13] These personnel also face fundamental issues relating to the definition of gangs and consequently gang membership and gang crime.

crime is thus crucial to the issue but one deserving of far greater analysis than is possible here (for an extended analysis see Hallsworth & Brotherton (2011) and Armstrong et al. (2016)). For now, suffice it to say that according to MPS intelligence in 2010 the London Borough of Newham contained a dozen known youth gangs, five of which were "violently active". According to MPS intelligence, in 2011 Newham was home to three individual "gang nominals"—those suspected by police of gang involvement (Pitts, 2014, p. 51)—who were among the top 10 in London in terms of violent potential. In 2012 the same source identified one of the borough's gangs as among the most notorious in the whole of the capital. For Newham MPS, the objective for the year 2012–2013 was to target such groups that gathered within its boundaries.

We would not wish to challenge the violent potential represented by such individuals and collectives. The violent feuding carried on between such groups is consequential; at worst people die.[14] At other times the wounds inflicted change lives. Significantly, many considered big players in "Road life" are also deemed to be most "at risk" of violent attack. As well as posing a real and present physical threat, mainly to like-minded peers, for the (non-combatant) residents of Newham these encounters bring reputational risk; housing estates are tarnished by the actual violence and by SYV/gang association. Local businesses face declining profits when customers decide to spend their money elsewhere and insurance cover is only available at premium rates. When altercations occur in-and-around schools, the educational system is challenged to its core and the teaching profession becomes preoccupied with its protective, rather than pedagogic, responsibilities.

The Newham MPS recognised that the term "gang" was emotive. It suggested an established, quasi-military structure, which police knew was not the case. The dedicated SYV/gang police personnel, therefore, employed a suite of terms such as "organised chaos" and "loose-knit neighbourhood gatherings", signalling a recognition that, in reality, the entities they dealt with were fluid in membership and prone to fracture, fissure and re-branding. However, once framed, the police sought to stop their SYV/gang activities and worked with the metaphor of "the gang" in the absence of a more accurate descriptor.

The Gangs and Firearms Unit (GFU) of the Newham MPS (formerly the Serious Youth Violence Team existing between 2009 and 2011) was established in early 2012. The 12-strong unit had overall responsibility for gang-related violence and gun crime in the borough. Such offences were often the most delicate and demanding of police resources, and represented the highest risk to the safety of young people and other borough residents. The Unit was formed in response to a 70% increase in reports of street robbery and a 17% rise in firearms offences; officers were aware that a number of young men in the borough had access to automatic weapons capable of discharging rounds of ammunition at the rate of 200-per-minute. That said, incidents involving such weapons were exceptional. More routinely, the violence which took place among young people was drug-related; those engaged in

[14] Between 2005 and the present day (November 2015), 181 teenagers have been murdered in London (Citizens Report, 2015).

acquisitive crime were also users and dealers of class A drugs. There were drug profits to make and drug markets to protect. Violence could be crucial to the settling of debts and the reputation of the dealer. At other times the issue was internecine and related to notions of personal dispespect (real or perceived), trespassing on territory "belonging" to another entity and "riding out" (small groups travelling in vehicles on targeted missions to attack those perceived as enemy gatherings). At times the monies fought over were minimal. The personal slights were at times unintended. The level of violence provoked by these debts and encounters was mystifying.

The Roots of—Addressing—Evil

The search for causation and prevention was wide-ranging. The enforcement side of the policing of SYV/gangs was combined with prevention and diversion strategies. This reflected a recognition in MPS circles that enforcement alone, i.e. applying the law and seeking conviction and custodial sentences, could not solve the issue. This triad of approaches to the problem saw the MPS form partnerships with a variety of officers from Newham Council, notably Housing, the ASBO[15] and Youth Offending Teams, Community Safety, Child Protection, Health, Education and Training. These partnerships aimed to provide a variety of interventions and programmes for identified SYV/gang members and those considered vulnerable youths.[16] Local police had also turned to charities and non-governmental organisations, one of which was TAG.

The employment of TAG personnel in Newham was situational and fortuitous. Situational in that Sheldon Thomas lived in the borough and fortuitous in that a speech he gave in a Midlands town so impressed a police officer in the audience that he referred Thomas to his colleague in Newham tasked with addressing SYV/gangs. The Chief Inspector of the Newham GFU was forthright in his belief that enforcement alone could not address the issue. After a meeting with TAG personnel he thus signed an agreement which allowed them to work on the issue of diversion among the police's target groups and also gave TAG the freedom to intervene with others they came across whom they considered at risk of offending. In so doing the Newham MPS was following other forces who realised that the task of reaching out to young (overwhelmingly) black youths was one they were not particularly good at.

[15] The Anti-social Behaviour Order (ASBO) was introduced in the UK in 1998. It is a civil order made against an individual who, on the balance of evidence, has been shown to engage in anti-social activities such as spitting, mugging and intimidation.

[16] The constant—and unresolved—issue in all such multi-agency approaches to the issue of SYV/gangs was agreeing on what constituted a gang. There were academic and police attempts at definition but none that were universally accepted in the Newham context.

TAG began life in 2007 as "Gangsline", a 24-h helpline for youth "gang" members or those fearful about the involvement of friends or family members in youth gang-related activity. The organisation grew from an information/advice service—primarily a phone-line which also produced leaflets and distributed them in fast-food outlets and wherever its outreach workers could find groups of young people "hanging out"—to an intervention-based organisation that was both reactive (with a specialist Outreach Response Team) and proactive in utilising various expertise, and in so doing became TAG. The result was a Gangsline/TAG educational and counselling service prepared to work amid hardened offenders. From its inception, TAG sought to address the root causes of SYV/gang membership, a task which Thomas believed required an understanding of psychosocial issues including family breakdown, anger problems, the consequences of rejection, emotional hurt, unresolved conflict, a (missing) sense of belonging, the dangers of the disillusioned and the despair of struggling parents. Crucially, the TAG mission was underpinned by a faith-based framework that focused on notions of responsibility, morality, humanity, positive thinking, cognitive behaviour and self-esteem. Its training programmes were delivered in diverse settings to individuals or groups and did not follow a set format. Sessions were adaptable in order to meet the needs of young men and women at times too frightened or lacking in confidence to leave their known and "safe" environment. Thomas led the sessions and utilised his major strength—his charisma. The organisation *was* Sheldon Thomas.

Speaking in Tongues

TAG's literature described Thomas as "[a]n inspirational speaker and a pioneering individual with an unrivalled insight into gangs through his own experience as a leading gang member in the 1970s who uses a 'no holds barred', yet spiritual, approach to changing people's lives". His expertise saw him act as advisor to the Home Office on youth gang culture and violence, and consult with the MPS specialist Trident Command Unit.[17] With a BSc in Marketing Management, Thomas was not shy in stressing that TAG was a business, as well as a Christian charity; inspired by God but also by values of entrepreneurship.

At other times Thomas had obtained funds through intimidation. The Divine, he believed, had saved him from death. In the 1970s and 1980s Thomas was a leading player in a notorious Brixton-based street gang. After becoming involved in the provision of "sound systems",[18] his life spiralled out of control when he

---

[17] Operation Trident (known in the MPS colloquially as "Trident") was established by the MPS in 1998 in response to a spate of shootings in the London boroughs of Lambeth and Brent. Though originally conceived to address gun crime and homicide in the "black communities" of London, Trident's task has grown to encompass the investigation of non-fatal shootings and "gang crime".

[18] Sound systems consist of a group of MCs, DJs and sound engineers, and typically play reggae, dancehall, ska and/or rocksteady music. The concept emerged in the ghettos of Kingston, Jamaica

became embedded in the London-Jamaican criminal networks which controlled the distribution of crack cocaine in parts of the capital. He had first-hand experience of several killings that took place in-and-around the dance halls of South London. However, he decided to change his life after being shot at and seeing a young man standing next to him in a nightclub die after being shot in the head several times.

Redemption for Thomas was partly found in politics and politicians. From 1989 to 1993 Thomas was mentored by the former Brent MP Bernie Grant[19] who took him on a tour of inner-city USA. There Thomas met with one-time black Presidential hopeful Rev. Jesse Jackson, who showed him around the drug- and gun-infested underground economies of the American inner-city. Crucially, Jackson would also introduce Thomas to the teachings of the Bible. On his return to the UK Thomas began working in inner-city areas such as Moss Side (Manchester), Handsworth (Birmingham), Peckham, Harlesden, Brixton and Hackney (London). In such places he sought to bridge the gap between the black community and the police and pioneered the Brother Movement, a scheme designed to unite the community in confronting black-on-black violence through music. This saw him sign a recording contract with the world-renowned record label, Island.[20] Some music was made, with records sold and events staged. This was, however, a competitive market and one which Thomas left behind to a degree.

In founding Gangsline/TAG, Thomas was seeking to address not only the key factors in the decision to become involved in SYV/gang culture, but offer credible support through a series of specially designed programmes and workshops that focused on developing the hitherto submerged and unrealised talents of young people. The interventions were structured according to curricula and programmes based in conflict resolution, counselling and psychotherapy. The TAG programmes were delivered on an individual basis, usually over a 12-week period and aimed to equip individuals with the necessary tools to bring about responses around various emotional, physical, financial and spiritual factors which—ideally—would allow them to break free from distorted thinking and destructive life-cycles. The TAG programmes concomitantly promoted the development of leadership skills, seeking ways out of the "gang mentality", "breaking the chains" of anger and addressing past hurts/emotional pain and family dysfunction, be it based on absent fathers, attitudes to women, or aberrant sexual behaviours.

---

in the 1950s and have since become an important part of Jamaican history and culture (Henriques, 2003).

[19] Grant was born in Georgetown, Guyana in 1944 but moved to London with his parents in 1963. After studying mining engineering at Heriot-Watt University, he joined the Labour Party and was elected as a councilor of Haringey Council in 1978. He became leader of Haringey Council in 1985 and in 1989 formed the Parliamentary Black Caucus (inspired by the Congressional Black Caucus in the USA) with a view to increasing the number of ethnic minority MPs in parliament.

[20] Island Records was founded by entrepreneur Christopher Blackwell in 1959. A former Major in the Jamaican Regiment of the British Army, Blackwell is credited with bringing the Jamaica-originated Ska music to the UK and produced iconic reggae albums such as Bob Marley's *Catch a Fire*.

The motivation to intervene was underpinned by the precepts of Christianity. Both Sheldon and his wife Michelle sought to reach inner-city youths involved in a life of drugs, prostitution, guns, and knife crime with a message of hope derived from the Gospels and channelled through the assemblies of Pentecostal Christianity.[21] His faith was most evident in his phone conversations which were smattered with words such as "bred" (short for brethren) and "bless" (the sign-off: God bless).

Devil Takes the Hindmost

Thomas spun his narrative in the homes of the young and aspiring gang members and sometimes in a room hired in a Methodist church complex in the Beckton neighbourhood in the south of the borough. Entering the latter premise, Thomas explained how many of the teenage boys TAG worked with in this area knew the location well: "They once came here as little kids on Sunday mornings, dragged by their Mums." Invited to the church to meet with the TAG team in March 2012—which consisted of Thomas and Paul[22]—is Danny, who had recently completed a 3-year custodial sentence for discharging a shotgun. He was also charged with murder but the charge was dropped because of a technicality. In Thomas' words, Danny is "in limbo". Now aged 23, he is unsure whether he will ever return to the "gang" friends he left for custody, or whether he will seek new arenas to live in and careers to pursue. The wait for the newly released is lengthy; Danny is taking driving lessons and has a daily routine at a gymnasium. The pursuit of the muscular body beautiful annoys those awaiting him. His desire for ever-increasing strength seems to take precedence over his longer-term future. Some comfort is found in his learning to drive: an endeavour which suggests the search for new horizons and meaningful employment.

There are urgent issues to resolve. Recent trouble in the neighbourhood saw a young man stabbed and shot in public during the daylight hours. The wounds inflicted were potentially life-changing, if not life-threatening. The identity of the perpetrators was suspected but not confirmed. The potential for revenge attacks was considered high and in MPS circles considered inevitable. Inquiring police officers had met with the proverbial wall of silence as to who did what and why. With his ear to the ground and as a man trusted by the main players in these dangerous disputes, Thomas has a "take" on events few would dare to challenge. He explains to the curious that the Beckton Boys (BB) are the same people who constitute the Black Gang

[21] A similarly committed Christian, black British Michelle was integral to the TAG enterprise. Her tasks included speaking with female victims of SYV/gangs and contacting the mothers of the young men who constituted TAG's client base. Michelle came from a highly respectable Christian family and had no claims to a previous criminal life.

[22] Recently released from a 10-year prison term for Armed Robbery, 40-year-old Paul was of dual Anglo-Jamaican heritage and spoke with a strong Midlands accent. He was renowned in his home town for the leading role he played within local football hooligan gatherings.

and that all of the BB are aged between 15 and 18. While revealing this he also phones Danny and, when his call is answered, launches into questions about the current climate of hostility without any preliminary formalities:

> ST: The Beckton Youngsters Asa and Trump—who's controlling them? ... How do you fit into the equation? (The listener then tells of his recently-completed jail term and explains the circumstances behind the dropping of the murder charge) ... So, at the moment, who's the driving force?
>
> A: (Thomas turns the mobile phone onto loudspeaker) I'm not too sure... it's got the music thing 'innit? They're calling each other names and lyrics. It's along those lines ... that's just what happens.
>
> ST: What about the attacks on Roby—why?
>
> A: Someone told them to do it...

Ending the conversation with the word "bless" and promising to phone back soon, Thomas takes an incoming call. This is a police officer from Scotland Yard who wants to talk about the recent shooting of a black youth. The officer and Thomas are, however, at cross purposes for a minute. According to Thomas, the shooting in a neighbouring borough of a black youth by police was unnecessary. His reasoning is that the shots were fired at the youth after he had been tasered.[23] Why, Thomas asked the police contact, was such force needed? It took a minute for both to register that the call was really about a black-on-black shooting in the South London borough of Peckham and the officer was calling to ask Thomas to attend an Independent Advisory Group[24] meeting to discuss it. The conversation illustrated that police saw the necessity of having Thomas in their forums. In turn, Thomas was quick to remind police that he was not cowed by them and could be blunt in his criticism of their handling of incidents.

Thomas turns his attention to the aforementioned circumstances and causal factors of the Beckton shooting, and in so doing elaborates on the structure of criminal networks and the incompetence of their protagonists:

> Forget the 'Big Man' gangster stuff around here, because once you have a gun, you are your own man and no-one gives you orders. Guns come from all over down this end: Bosnians, Lithuanians, white criminal networks. Black guys don't have structures like them. Neither do they have the markets for the straps (guns) so they have to buy second-hand. A 9mm cost £300, a Glock £450, a MAC 10 £800, an Eagle Eye £600. The ammo (ammunition) comes with the guns. The thing is, there's no target practice or training ... that's the reason why these black youths can't really shoot straight; they buy a piece (gun), and use it the next day but can't control it and that's how innocents get killed or maimed. These black kids need telling they are not 'gangsters', because unlike their white counterparts, they don't make money. White gangs don't live with their Mums. White gangsters don't live in blocks with

[23] A Taser—also known as a conducted electrical weapon (CEW)—is an electroshock weapon manufactured and sold by Taser International to security services around the world. The device delivers electric current via two electrodes, which are fired from (and remain connected to) the main unit, causing neuromuscular incapacitation.

[24] Since 2000 "Independent Advisory Groups (IAGs) have developed nationally within both police forces and police authorities to assist the police service in understanding the role and impact it has within diverse communities". These groups were formed in response to the Macpherson Inquiry into the murder of Stephen Lawrence, and encompass issues such as Race, Disability and Age.

piss-filled lifts and their children don't go to no-hope comprehensive schools … Where does this all begin? It's not parenting *per se*, some of their homes are nice and some have a good family network, but it's too female-centred for many of these boys. I would put family breakdown as a major cause. There's a common denominator in these boys' lives, and that is the absence of a father. A good father would make all the difference and go a long way to stopping all this. As it is, some of them are in their mid-teens and end arguments about their behaviour with their mums by punching them … They could look to religion as well. Danny has come out of prison. He's 'got' Islam. But for some it's a fashion because a true Muslim wouldn't have a tattoo or fornicate or make music or provoke violence.

Seeking local specificity, Thomas responds to questions about another shooting in the Beckton district which happened 10 days before. Thomas' knowledge of both the feud and the individual are crucial in revealing the fractious entities that continue vendettas and the vagueness of the issue being fought over.

It's a seven-year 'beef' (vendetta/feud) between the Cathall (a housing estate in the neighbouring borough of Waltham Forest) Gang and Woodgrange (a district of Newham). The beef goes back to sometime before the shooting when a Cathall man got stabbed. The Cathall come down mobbed out looking for Ellem; he's 'big time' in Woodgrange. They shoot him but only hit him once … I went to a school in Newham the day after the shooting and chatted with a few and told them to squash it (end it) with Waltham Forest … I told the Youngers not to go looking (for revenge). The Cathall was controlled by Russ but he's in prison and this leaves a hole and means it's breaking into factions, and the Youngers have got their own men. The shooting occurred because there's more than one clique involved … we don't know which way it will go.

With that, Thomas phones "A", one of the Cathall Gang, asking for elaboration as to the current situation. His discussant has no reservations in describing matters, which only serves to confuse the issue further:

A: It's all gone different, man. The Youngers have got more influence than Russ. There's beef between the Youngers, Russ was a link between the Youngers and Elders, that's all. But the groups do their own thing. The man you should talk to is Rodger (mixed-race, aged 21).

Thomas: What about [names a youth]?

A: He's not allowed in the borough 'cos of an ASBO. He lives out of the borough and no-one knows for sure where he is right now.

Thomas: What power does Russ have?

A: It's down to your own crew. You might have 10 men who've 'got' the area, who 'ride out' (support—with violence if need be) and roll up for each other. The Youngers have their own issues, their own beef. Factions are growing. It's all factions. Those accusing are willing—it's all crew-on-crew. More crews, you've now got the ACG—Anyone Can Go (a newly-named collective of the area).

Thomas: So who in Waltham Forest can speak to anyone?

A: You'd have to befriend each faction of a crew—got to permeate each side, reason with all sides. I don't want to say 'put down your arms' and then find one side are still banging (prepared to shoot). You see Waltham Forest is a small neighbourhood and they're falling out and riding into Newham. The Newham crews though have been going at it for years. There's a lot of history. It's hard to squash, but you can slow things down. Things like the riding out, you slowed it down a bit.

Thomas: One of the Elders has just come out of prison. He doesn't want it anymore; can this influence things?

A: They are different cliques now. You can reason with me man, but there are cliques without a main man. There's no 'gang strategy' on the streets. The nature of the beast is not understood …

As the conversation ends, Thomas suggests the respondent, "stay blessed and keep me in your prayers."

At times Thomas responds to phone calls to his organisation. The previous day, Thomas had been in the home of a 13-year-old by the name of Brian who in the words of Thomas is "in above his head". In the presence of Brian's Mother, Thomas has told Brian that he fears for his future, and worries that he could end up dead, a victim of SYV/gang killing. His mother must have thought the same because she had contacted Gangsline and requested that Thomas visit the home and speak with her. In the well-kept Forest Gate council flat, the white working-class mother described her despair at Brian's behaviour. His Jamaican father was long gone from the marital home, Brian is not attending school and his main focus of activity was hanging out with youths from the Woodgrange district of Newham and at the age of 13 is the youngest in this gathering that regularly numbers over 60. Brian is distinguishable by virtue of being one of just two mixed-race boys in this entity. Such a detail is quite evident in a recent YouTube video produced by the Woodgrange Gang titled "The Clique". This footage was slickly produced but also antagonistic, urging violence on the Custom House Gang.[25] The latter were the most notorious in the borough in terms of propensity to violence and were rumoured to have sent word that they were not taking this online insult lightly. Thomas knew Custom House would respond with violence and in his opinion, being both young and recognisable Brian was an obvious target. Thomas pulled no punches imparting such knowledge and in a long conversation warned Brian that his involvement in the video would bring retribution. On learning this Brian choked back tears of fear as his mother openly wept. The warning did not come with a solution. Privately Thomas believed he could convince the Custom House Gang to forgive Brian on account of his young age.

The Truth and the Light

At the Methodist church at 4.30 pm on a wet Thursday afternoon, six young black men sit around a table in the meeting room of the church complex with Thomas and Paul. Three of the six are new to the premise (by virtue of living some miles away), and indeed the work of TAG, but have arrived because they respect the word of Danny—he has told them that Thomas is worth listening to. Danny has yet to arrive. Among the six is Thorp who has a notoriety in the area and who recently received stab wounds during an altercation with a neighbouring gang. Initially, the room is quiet, most probably because of the slight embarrassment felt by the youths present given the incongruity of the situation. They hail from three different areas and represent three named gangs; they have all participated in altercations with one another.

[25] Custom House is a district of the London Borough of Newham. It is named after the custom house of Royal Victoria Dock where government officials would oversee the completion of paperwork relating to imported and exported goods and collect import duties.

They are soon at ease with Thomas who begins by asking for a basic level of respect from all present, which requires them to turn their mobile phones to silent and avoid answering any calls for the duration of the meeting.

Then, thanking them for attending, Thomas launches into a narrative as to his "ting" (purpose) and background. The young men absorb these facts and quickly get a sense of what is and is not authentic:

> In the last three years there's been 40 youth murders in London with one common characteristic: the victims and perpetrators are all black, all of an age range of 15 to 20. You gotta ask: Why is that? And who killed them? You might know the answer—some of youse have been close to death. The victims are the same profile as the perpetrators … You lot can't even blame racists for the violence on youse and the deaths. Those of us on the streets in the 70s, we had to put up with racism from white police and NF (National Front)[26] gangs—it wasn't black-on-black then. Mine was a time with proper gangsters—you're not. [This assertion elicits a nervous chuckle from the five]. Let's have the bare truth: None of you are big time gangsters out there … Why? Gangsters don't make YouTube videos. YouTube videos are for black kids. Now that's real talk for you isn't it? (All five nod and stifle smirks). Let me tell you this: in my day there was no guns, no 16-year-old had a gun. You were too irresponsible to angle one—you still are. If there was a gun, it was an M16. My land was Peckham, Brixton and the PDC.

At this point, ten minutes into the talk, Danny arrives with another youth who has not previously attended. After introductions Thomas continues his tirade. "Do you really believe you are gangsters?" (No answer is forthcoming from those questioned.) Another question is posed: "How "real" are you?"[27] One answer comes from Asa: "Not real" (a response that no one challenges). "So why do it?" asks Thomas. An answer to that question is hard to come by. In the uneasy silence Thomas reflects on the winners and losers in their lifestyle:

> I can understand the YouTube stuff … you're all cussing and laughing, maybe trying to sell some videos. But you could end up being pathetic (citing the name of a local man the group is familiar with). Look at him: 33 years old, just out (of prison), now gone back in, and wants to but can't even gang-bang at that i.e. has no street reputation and makes no income (the room laughs at the tragicomedy of the scenario that they all recognise).

The denigration of those similar to them does not offend the young men present. Their meagre incomes only highlight the bind they are in. Having decried their lifestyle the task is now to explain why their position is futile—and then to suggest an alternative.

[26] Founded in 1967, the National Front (NF) is a far-right, "whites-only" British political party which opposes non-white immigration and endorses a programme of repatriation. Its support reached a high point in the 1970s—it fielded 303 candidates at the 1979 general election (none were elected)—but since then its popularity has waned. In the 2010 general election the NF fielded just 17 candidates.

[27] One moment of genuine hilarity occurred when Thomas asked a group of youths if they were "On the Road". One misunderstood the question, admitting by way of response that he was, "On the Rail". This was true, he was in the employment of a railway company. The congregation realised this misunderstanding with uproarious laughter.

Out of Darkness

Thomas then directs his ire at another demographic, asking who brings "it" (drugs) into the country? He has the answer to his question:

> The big white gangs and big men like (names a big white player in drugs distribution in the borough). The Feds (police) can't touch him so they go after you lot. His income is worth more than all of us in this room put together. If he wanted to he could 'drop' £100k to a police friend, some of them are on £35k so his money is good for them. He's virtually untouchable—and you can't match him. You've got to understand this: real gangsters don't feud over a £5 debt, and they don't live in Newham. What you're doing is feeding The Man (those in authority intent on keeping others in a subordinate position) by carrying little bags, and then you make YouTube chat and think you're All That.

Thomas has discomforted the room—the faces are grim, dejected even—but his words have hit home. A couple of his lines elicit the approving response of "serious" from Asa, while others nod silently in approval at what they are hearing. Then, as if to apologise for his tirade, Thomas continues: "Check my colour (pinches his left forearm with two fingers of his right hand). I'm not knocking you and this talk ain't a putdown, but I lived the life."

And with that Thomas plunges into Jamaican patois which causes mirth among the Caribbean-born in the room and incomprehension among the African-born. He continues, referencing notorious black youths whom they all know and itemises their preposterous claims of making big money "On the Road". He tells of the London Fields[28] Gang which is not making any money. He speaks of one of the main players in another group living a pack of lies and another who has been "griming" (attempting to make money through low-level crime) for 12 years with nothing to show for it. He then goes round the table, asking everyone present if they are currently making money. They laugh at the question: only two admit to making a few hundred pounds in the last few months via drug dealing which elicits from Thomas the comment—"if they could see you, the white man would just be saying 'Jiggaboos…cheap change. They're (black youths) making no money and meanwhile shooting each other, and I'm sat on my seven-million-pound boat.'"

Keen to impress upon them the futility of their activity and the preposterousness of their existence, Thomas explains the following:

> You're involved in random shooting and stabbing, and that's not 'gangster'. You've got no one to answer to and you're just looking to go to jail. You've got no order or structure, you do what you want to do. Things were different when I was 14—I was approached by the (names a South London Crime syndicate). Among other things, they did diamonds. They said I could work for them and—hear me out—they said to me, you bring 'heat' (i.e. trouble with other gangs and/or police attention), we will kill you".

---

[28] London Fields is a district of the London Borough of Hackney which has gained a notoriety over the past decade because of SYV/gang issues which culminated in Upper and Lower Clapton Road being labelled "Britain's Murder Mile" (Mendick and Johnson, 2011).

The room falls silent. This scenario is one way above their heads. Breaking the silence, Thomas continues:

> You mess up your life based on a lie. I and others in this room have come through the pain barrier. I've been 'played', and I reckon I've been a dickhead. All you're doing is beefing with Woodgrange who look like you: same colour, same background. And what's the issue? Can anybody remember? Cos I think it's something to do with one of you being rude to another three years ago. I think this is a stupid existence because success in life is hanging around people who are real and asking yourselves: Where is this going to lead? Is losing a career or a life more important than backing down from an insult? Let me tell you how I got out. My game was extortion. I had a big reputation and I was a Rasta. I didn't look normal and I could walk around alone in any borough South and East (London). I could and did pull up any man without a gun. Was I a good fighter? No, but if I got 'marked-up' (injured at the hands of a rival gang) cars would have ridden up and shot down the street. I took money. I could approach a Bred (friend) and if he was rude, and I had to ask again, he got a gun put in his face. I got out because of a 'West' (West London versus South London) issue—Notting Hill and Shepherd's Bush booked a rave on Brixton. This was rude, they didn't ask our permission. Me and others were asked to ride up in a car. As we did, I got an unease. I said 'Stop the car, something's not right'. In the boot of the car were five guns. I ducked out. I never killed anybody. In those days, you didn't kill your own: it wasn't black-on-black. I got called everything (in patois he recites the insults he received from his associates). The next day I read about 20 people being shot that night in the venue.

He recounts a character he grew up with, Little A, who unlike him could not get "Off the Road", and eventually died in an attack which saw his body riddled with bullets. The moral of this and all preceding stories according to Thomas is: "You've got to break the mentality. You think you're 'bad' and want to kill people who look like you. Your number's going to come up, and where in actuality has this got you?"

Forgiveness and Beginnings

Thomas lightens the mood, asking: "So, can we come together?" The immediate response is from Asa and consists of two short statements. "Too stubborn. Too much pride." Everybody seems to know what is meant. Aware of Asa's skills in penning lyrics, Thomas explains a business model whereby Asa's undoubted ability as a "lyricist" and singer could be promoted by those in rival areas who had skills and the show transported by those from yet another area—in a sense, a business model where everybody wins, i.e. makes money. While on the topic of income, Thomas asks: "How will you make money? Do you fancy being broke at 23? (23-year-old Danny, aware of his own predicament, laughs). There's so much "beef" (i.e. potentially violent hostility) around here you can't even earn. To go 4 miles to Stratford you have to take a cab there and a cab back "cos you can't take the tube" (an admission that entering areas "belonging" to enemies necessitates cab rides rather than journeys via public transport at a tenth of the price). All recognise this dilemma and laugh. "You're stopping the flow of money and you can't even move in your own neighbourhood."

At this point Danny interjects, explaining "This is so real … I recently promoted a 'rave' in Stratford and I lost money. Why? Because the club security wanted extra security as they'd heard some of the others were going to turn up and fight which means many people, fearing the beef, didn't turn up. If there'd been no beef, I would have made money and I would have invested in other areas. All could have eaten nice (made some income)."

Thomas then elaborated on the issue of respect: "'Respect' is actually not about fighting, but is based in how you can help people. You've got to put down noise (fracas between members of rival groups) and guns and get off the road. In a few years you'll be lucky to have wives and kids (only one individual in the room has a child—he is aged 17). Who's gonna pay for your kids food and school? Are you going to settle down with a girl with that life? Are you gonna be 29-years-old sticking up people (robbing people at knife- or gunpoint), thinking you're bad? (All nod approvingly.) And that's why I'm here; squashing the beef." The enormity of the task is then brought home as Asa explains that the problem is their Woodgrange equivalents. According to Asa, who was a victim of a recent beating at the hands of the Woodgrange, they must strike up the first apology to end matters: "They rushed me first—they have to say sorry." The silence is broken by Thomas asking: "How do we stop all this?" Thomas looks around the room as he asks that question. One youth ventures the following argument, stating: "If we (Beckton) come off, the rest have to do the same. Trust is needed. We need to know we're all on the same thing". Another youth chips in: "There's six groups on Newham—so which crew do we start with? I agree, I don't want my kids going down this road, and I don't want my daughter taking a bullet from a stray shot." Thomas responds: "This may sound superficial, but I'm mainly interested in stopping innocent people getting killed."

Sensing no way out, Thomas moves the debate to the coming few months and how Newham will be under virtual police lockdown. Explaining how the Olympics will give an excuse for police, if so motivated, to do just about anything they want to keep the peace around the event, Thomas warns them they will be "treated like terrorists, not street kids", then in defence of the tactics of the MPS recounts a visit to Jamaica where the Jamaican police shot a nominal in the leg because he refused to answer their question when stopped in the street. As Thomas says, "one bad look, you're going down for the whole of the Olympics. It's gonna be military-style and they're not joking. If you don't change your ways, you'll be behind bars. Let me, as an Elder, help you."

After 70 min the meeting comes to a close, and asking the room who is a Christian Thomas gets a 100% show of hands. And so, with eyes closed and hands clasped in prayer, the group listens to the words of Thomas, who thanks the Lord for "a wonderful meet for the young men, for their heart, for peace, to opening their hearts to receive life changes, for business opportunities and for improving circumstances." The group leaves with handshakes and clasps and promises to return to the same venue in 2 weeks' time.

Informing them of the futility of their ways is one thing, but Thomas has to offer an alternative existence which for all requires gainful employment. He tells them he has a business model which requires three things of them: a commitment to accept week-by-week help, that they join the TAG programme, and that they "work with what you've got" The latter requires those in school to study, those out of school to consider business opportunities and from all regardless of their age and status: "put the community above self, get out of the ghetto mentality, forget the bling (jewellery and expensive branded accoutrements), and stay out of the game". Before the group depart, Thomas exhorts them to come again, to bring their friends, but in the meantime warns them that if anyone in the interim "beefs" (continues gang-based vendettas) they are not to come back. The words seem to register and the departing Asa states aloud: "I'm squashing the beef" (i.e. ending hostilities).

God, the Father and the Son

In examining the role of religion in the work of TAG, a number of themes come to the fore. The first interesting phenomenon—and in the case of TAG, this seems the only place to start—relates to its founder and leader. Even though his days as an enforcer were behind him, Thomas' overtures to young people relied heavily on his past exploits, many of which involved violence and intimidation. His status was underpinned by large amounts of social and cultural capital—best represented today by his network of contacts and his reputation, respectively. His current involvement in the rehabilitation of young people, and his role within the London Pentecostal community more broadly, saw these forms of capital transposed to a different setting. A one-time leading figure in South London's organised crime scene could change his ways and become the leading figure in a London-based Christian charity. In both contexts Thomas was listened to. He was authentic and legitimate in the eyes of young men involved in SYV/gangs because he had "been there" and had lived to tell the tale. He offered them a narrative of redemption arising out of his own experiences. His message is: "Don't follow my path". But the path is seductive to those listening. Many would like to walk it in order to possess Thomas' store of anecdotes.

His exhortations to young people are shot through with notions of masculinity and masculine ideals. He lamented the fact that few of the young men he sought to rehabilitate had grown up in households where a father was present. In some instances this had seen them develop a sense of hypermasculinity fed by violence and the celebration of machismo. Rehabilitation via TAG offered the prospect of a different set of masculine norms; those rehabilitated would lead a settled family life, possibly as the male head of the household. Through religious observance the same young man may also amass the spiritual capital which could see him enjoy a more elevated status in other neighbourhood groups. This road to salvation is reminiscent of debates surrounding the Pentecostal movement. Specifically, the contention that, in relinquishing gang activity via religious conversion, Pentecostalism offers young men the chance to trade gang hypermasculinity for the "soft patriarchy" of heterosexual domesticity.

As well as being allied to a traditional model of family structure, the notions of masculinity promoted by TAG were related to the ideals of enterprise. It could also be seen in the "business model" he spoke of and the threat of "being broke at 23". The alignment of religion (particularly Calvinist Protestantism) and the acquisitive spirit is well known (Weber (2010) [1905]; Tawney (1953) [1926]). More narrowly, TAG's championing of entrepreneurship is consonant with the teachings of Pentecostalism. Indeed, sociologist of religion Bernice Martin contends that the movement encourages a radically individualised self-consciousness which acts as a fitting primer for the realities of neoliberal capitalism. For Pentecostalism, she argues, "business is the business of selfhood" (Martin, 1998, p. 129). Thomas would not argue with this. But debates about selfhood were shot through with issues of "race". The "white man" was characterised as "The Man", someone occupying a superior position within the hierarchies of both acquisitive enterprises and organised crime. The same man raked in the profits from both contexts while remaining aloof from day-to-day criminal activities. He enjoyed the proceeds of neighbourhood-level crime while devolving the risk to young black men. Where God stood on this matter was not known.

In some ways this interracial dynamic has parallels with the early twentieth-century beginnings of the Pentecostal movement. The man credited with organising the first institutionalised practice of Pentecostalism, William Seymour, the son of former slaves, learned the doctrine that *glossolalia* (or speaking in tongues) was evidence of a Christian being infused with the Holy Spirit from white preacher Charles Parnham. Seymour was given permission to listen to Parnham's lectures but only through an open door while sat in the corridor of a Bible School in Houston, Texas. Though Parnham was initially supportive of Seymour's attempts to spread the word of Pentecostalism,[29] as a sympathiser of the Ku Klux Klan he disapproved of the co-presence of whites and blacks at religious gatherings, and the two became dissociated, forming the (black) Church of God in Christ and the (white) Assemblies of God, respectively. There was, therefore, a religious precedent for the racial division of labour in the drug-distribution market so lamented by Thomas.

TAG's broader appeals to the Christian tradition were also noteworthy. Given Pentecostalism's emphasis on the experiential dimension of worship—the personal experience of God through baptism with the Holy Spirit—the ritual elements of TAG's work come as no surprise. However, many of these were subtler than one might expect. For example, in many cases the conversion which began a young person's rehabilitation was not necessarily marked as a radical disjuncture in their lives. For many, rehabilitation involved a return to, rather than discovery of, the religious life. As Thomas observed, most young men had attended church regularly as youngsters, so involving themselves in religious life represented a gathering up of slackened spiritual reins, rather than something wholly new. That said, there were some performative elements of ritual on show via TAG.

---

[29] Seymour began preaching the gospel of Pentecostalism in a run-down, disused stable on Asuza Street, Los Angeles in 1906. The Azusa Street Revival, as it became known, lasted for 3 years and attracted Christians from across the world (Sack, 2000).

As well as the fact that many of TAG's programmes were staged in a local church, the exchanges overseen by Thomas had a ritualised quality. The lengthy appeals to his young charges were sermon-like in both their intensity and moralising force. In most cases dialogue was limited to call-and-response. Indeed, the dialogue which took place during TAG programmes resembled the antiphonal exchanges common within various evangelical denominations of Christianity (Flores & Hondagneu-Sotelo, 2013). Whereas churchgoers may signal their approbation by yelling "preach!", the young men who together constituted the congregation at TAG would register their approval by the more understated "serious". At other moments youngsters were asked for explanations or descriptions pertaining to various gang-related events, another phenomenon with a direct equivalent in the Pentecostal movement—the public testimony of past sins commonly used in worship services (Flores & Hondagneu-Sotelo, 2013). In the case of TAG this took the form of reintegrative than disintegrative shaming, with criminal acts cast as errant behaviour rather than being the function of deviant personalities. That said, Thomas was not averse to unsettling the young men among whom his work was carried out. At times his tone was accusatory and belittling, creating the remorseful environment he thought conducive to rehabilitation.

These ritualised elements were punctuated by the use of Christian vocabulary—notably "bless", "bred" (brethren), the repeated invocation of "God"—and sessions were brought to a close by prayer. Taken collectively, and given that they were geared to the rehabilitation of young people, these elements certainly tally with Victor Turner's (1982, p. 89) famous explication of ritual: "I like to think of ritual essentially as a performance, enactment … To perform is thus to bring something about, to consummate something, or "to carry out" a play, order, project". For TAG, "squashing the beef" is a ritualised process shaped by the patterns of Pentecostal Christianity. The performance was meant not just to entertain but to connect with hearts and minds.

Conclusion

The teaching of TAG utilised what might best be termed a *realpolitikal* commentary on the contemporary existence of young minority-ethnic males from lowly social backgrounds, wrapped in Bible-inspired pastoralism. In this latter lay hope—even faith—that today's sense of failure and futility could—with a change of heart and mind—be tomorrow's success story. The imminent and the immediate reality took precedence over contemplation; as such Thomas used words rather than religious texts, realising that in interventions of this nature the quoting of psalms and parables was a waste of time. TAG meetings thus avoided engagement with religious scripture, even if young men admitted their past misdeeds via forms of quasi-religious confession. Notions of redemption were limited to the here and now. No mention was ever made of an afterlife. Salvation consisted of being saved from premature death via SYV/gangs. Ideally the Youngers and Elders were converted, their inner moral change best reflected by their charting a new course in life which, if successful, could lead to material improvement. In doing so, they might also realise the futility of fighting not just their peers and equivalents but also the system, i.e. the state, and with it a recognition that its propensity for violence and corruption favoured individuals with far greater resources than those gleaned "On the Road".

The words of Thomas evidently hit home to many listening. Some of the young men Thomas spoke with were rehabilitated. Asa, for example, got a job and left the area. The violence that Brian feared was not visited upon him: Thomas's quiet words with those posing a threat defused the issue and dried the tears of Brian's mother. Some, having listened to Thomas, attempted to change only to lapse. Yet others illustrated how faith could be synchronised with the ways of the world; Danny, for all his approval of Thomas' words and efforts, continued the "Road Life" and in 2013 was sentenced to 6 years in prison for possession of firearms and sexual assault. The messages of others could be suppressed; the offending "Woodgrange Clique" video received nearly 300,000 hits before being removed in 2012 from YouTube by a joint MPS-LBN operation.

In 2013, monies from various budgets that funded the work of TAG were not renewed. The remaining budget was redirected to other agencies tasked with addressing SYV/gangs. Meanwhile, videos disrespecting peers continued to be posted on social media by named youth entities. The GFU saw its numbers increase. The local authority personnel continued their work in schools and among families. Meanwhile stabbings and shootings in Newham continued. How effective the words and interventions of TAG were remains unquantifiable. The belief that one soul might be saved was (and remains) a cause for rejoicing in both the Kingdom of Heaven and the borough of Newham. But in measuring the effectiveness of TAG, funding bodies did not factor in the words of God.

References

Armstrong, G., Hobbs, D., & Giulanotti, R. (2016). *Policing the 2012 olympics: Legacy and social exclusion*. London: Routledge.

Atkinson, P., Coffey, A., Delamont, S., Lofland, J., & Lofland, L. (Eds.). (2002). *Handbook of ethnography*. London: Sage.

BBC. (2015). *The Huguenots*. Retrieved from: http://www.bbc.co.uk/legacies/immig_emig/england/london/article_1.shtml.

Bourgois, P., & Schonberg, J. (2007). Ethnic dimensions of *Habitus* among homeless heroin injectors. *Ethnography, 8*(1), 7–31.

Bourgois, P., & Schonberg, J. (2009). *Righteous dopefiend*. Berkeley, Ca.: University of California Press.

Braithwaite, J. (1989). *Crime, shame and reintegration*. New York: Cambridge University Press.

Brandes, S. (2002). *Staying sober in Mexico City*. Austin, TX: University of Texas Press.

Brennerman, R. E. (2011). *Homies and hermanos: God and gangs in Central America*. Cambridge, MA: Oxford University Press.

Brusco, E. E. (1995). *The reformation of machismo: Evangelical conversion and gender in Colombia*. Austin, TX: University of Texas Press.

Carr, E. S. (2010). *Scripting addiction: The politics of therapeutic talk and American sobriety*. Princeton, NJ: Princeton University Press.

Cavadi, A. (2009). *Il Dio dei mafiosi: attualitá e storia*. Milan: San Paolo.

Citizens Report. (2015). 'Mapping the Location and Victim Profile of Teenage Murders in London from 2005 to 2015'. Retrieved from: http://www.citizensreportuk.org/reports/teenage-murder-london.html.

Crary, D. (2007). Faith-based prisons multiply. *USA Today*(October 13).

Dino, A. (2008). *La mafia devote: Chiesa, religione, Cosa Nostra*. Rome: GLF editori Laterza.

Emirbayer, M., & Williams, E. M. (2005). Bourdieu and social work. *Social Service Review, 79*, 679–724. December.

Farrell, J. (1997). *Understanding the mafia*. Manchester: Manchester University Press.

Flores, E. O., & Hondagneu-Sotelo, P. (2013). Chicano gang members in recovery: The public talk of negotiating chicano masculinities. *Social Problems, 60*(4), 1–15.

Frink, C. (2004). Breaking into prison. *[Electronic version]. Christianity Today*(May 7). Retrieved from: http://www.txcorrections.org/article.pdf.

Giddens, A. (1976). *New rules of sociological method*. Cambridge: Polity.

Gumbel, N. (2001). *Caring for ex-offenders*. Eastbourne: Kingway.

Hagan, J., & McCarthy, B. (1997). *Mean streets: Youth crime and the homeless*. New York: Cambridge University Press.

Hallsworth, S., & Brotherton, D. (2011). *Urban disorder and gangs: A critique and a warning*. London: Runnymede Trust.

Henriques, J. F. (2003). Sonic dominance and the reggae sound system session. In M. Bull & L. Back (Eds.), *The auditory culture reader* (pp. 451–480). Oxford: Berg.

Hobbs, R. (2013). *Lush life: Constructing organised crime in the UK*. Oxford: Oxford University Press.

Hunt, S. (2005). The alpha course and its critics: An overview of the debates. *PentecoStudies, 4*, 1–22.

Jackson, J. A. (1963). *The Irish in Britain*. London: Routledge.

Johnson, B. R. (2002). *Assessing the impact of religious programming and prison industry on recidivism: An exploratory study*. Retrieved from http://web.archive.org/web/20030408001536/http://www.txcorrections.org/article.pdf.

Kearns, R. A., & Smith, C. J. (1994). Housing, homelessness, and mental health: Mapping an agenda for geographical inquiry. *Professional Geographer, 46*, 418–424.

Lees, L. (1979). *Exiles of Erin: Irish migrants in Victorian London*. Ithaca, NY: Cornell University Press.

Leon, L. D. (1998). Born again in East LA: The congregation as border space. In R. S. Warner & J. G. Wittner (Eds.), *Gatherings in Diaspora* (pp. 163–196). Philadelphia, PA: Temple University Press.

London Borough of Newham (LBN). (2014). *Local economic assessment*. London: Regeneration Planning and Property Directorate.

Magee, J. (2011). Disengagement, de-motivation, vulnerable groups and sporting inclusion: A case study of the homeless World Cup. *Soccer & Society, 12*(2), 159–173.

Martin, B. (1998). From pre- to postmodernity in Latin America: The case of Pentecostalism. In P. Heelas, D. Martin, & P. Morris (Eds.), *Religion, modernity and postmodernity*. Oxford: Blackwell.

Mayor of London. (2014). *Strategic ambitions for London: Gangs and serious youth violence*. London: The Mayor's Office.

Mendick, R., & Johnson, A. (2011). Eight men shot dead in two years. Welcome to Britain's Murder Mile. *The Independent*(September 18).

Merlino, R. (2014). Sicilian mafia, patron saints, and religious processions: The consistent face of an ever-changing criminal organization. *California Italian Studies, 5*(1), 109–129.

Milgate, M. (2007). Book review: Handbook of ethnography. *Australasian Journal of Market & Social Research, 15*(1), 43–47.

O'Neill, K. (2011). *City of God: Christian citizenship in postwar Guatemala*. Berkeley, Ca.: University of California Press.

Pine, A. (2008). *Working hard, drinking hard: On violence and survival in Honduras*. Berkeley, California: University of California Press.

Pitts, J. (2014). Who dunnit? Gangs, joint enterprise, bad character and duress. *Youth & Policy, 113*, 48–59.

Rios, V. M. (2011). *Punished: Policing the lives of black and latino boys*. New York: New York University Press.

Robinson, C. (2002). *Being somewhere: Young homeless people in inner-city Sydney*. Sydney, NSW: School of Sociology, University of New South Wales. Unpublished dissertation.

Rudy, D. R., & Greil, A. L. (1989). Is alcoholics anonymous a religious organization?: Meditations on marginality. *Sociology of Religion, 50*(1), 41–51.

Sack, K. (2000). The Pentecostal Church in America. *New York Times* (June 4).

Sales, I. (2010). *I preti e i Mafiosi: storia dei rapport tra mafie e Chiesa cattolica*. Milan: B.C. Dalai.

Sanchez-Walsh, A. (2003). *Latino Pentecostal identity: Evangelical faith, self, and society*. New York: Columbia University Press.

Tawney, R. (1953). *[1926] Religion and the rise of capitalism*. London: Mentor.

Thomas, J., & Zaitzow, B. H. (2006). Conning or conversion? The role of religion in prison coping. *The Prison Journal, 86*(2), 242–259.

Toft, D. (2000). Recent research offers compelling support for the effectiveness of twelve Step-based treatment. *The Voice*(Summer). Retrieved from https://www.hazelden.org/web/public/vcsum0research.page.

TPP. (2015). *Getting into the charitable sector*. Retrieved from: http://www.tpp.co.uk/jobseekers/career-advice/change-of-career/getting-into-the-charitable-sector.

Turner, V. (1982). *From ritual to theater: The human seriousness of play*. New York: PAJ Publications.

Volokh, A. (2011). Do faith-based prisons work? *Alabama Law Review, 63*(1), 43–95.

Weber, M. (2010). *[1905] The protestant ethic and the spirit of capitalism*. Oxford: Oxford University Press.

Wilcox, W. B. (2004). *Soft patriarchs, new men*. Chicago, Il.: University of Chicago Press.

Wolseth, J. (2010). Safety and sanctuary: Pentecostalism and youth gang violence in Honduras. *Latin American Perspectives, 35*, 96–111.

Chapter 16
EU Fraud and New Member States: Is It a Case of the Curate's Egg?

Brendan Quirke

Introduction

"The curate's egg" which forms part of the chapter title is a reference to the famous cartoon from the British satirical magazine, "Punch", published in November 1895. A visiting Bishop remarks to his clergyman host at dinner that it appears he has got a bad egg, and the clergyman replies: "It is good in places". The purpose of this chapter is to consider the experience of two relatively new member states in seeking to establish and strengthen anti-EU fraud structures and measures, the problems they encountered and how they sought to overcome them as well as the wider lessons that can be drawn for those countries that wish to join the European Union and whether the problems of fraud and corruption outweigh the positive contributions made by both countries—the "bad egg" analogy.

The EU has been viewed in the past as an organisation that is prone to corrupt and fraudulent activities because it has poor financial control systems and a corruptible bureaucracy as well as a somewhat peculiar accountability structure which in agency terms means that member states as principals have delegated to themselves the collection and distribution of an enormous percentage (over 80 %) of the EU's budget and have also delegated to themselves the operation of most of its regulatory structure. So for much of the time, the agent is also the principal. If combating corruption involves policing the agents, then it is member states which must be controlled. If those member states have joined the EU when they are facing serious problems of corruption then this problem of weak monitoring and control structures, and member states policing themselves can only be exacerbated.

B. Quirke (✉)
Business School, Manchester Metropolitan University, Manchester, UK
e-mail: B.Quirke@mmu.ac.uk

G.A. Antonopoulos (ed.), *Illegal Entrepreneurship, Organized Crime and Social Control*, Studies of Organized Crime 14, DOI 10.1007/978-3-319-31608-6_16

The methodology employed in this study includes a review of secondary materials such as European Commission reports, academic articles, government documents as well as semi-structured interviews with government officials of the Czech Republic and Romania and with Czech academics.

Background

The Czech Republic joined the European Union as a fully fledged member in 2004, along with nine other states, the majority of them having made the rapid transformation from communist states to democratic market economies within a very short period of time. Romania joined in January 2007, along with its neighbour Bulgaria. As with any club or society, whether it is the European Union, the Freemasons or the local tennis club, every new member has to abide by the rules of the club, but in order to be able to abide by the rules and also to make a positive contribution, the new member needs help and support from both existing members as well as from the senior officials of the club or society. What kind of support did the Czech Republic and Romania receive? This chapter will attempt to make an assessment.

It is not possible or appropriate to study the phenomenon of EU fraud in isolation, but also to consider the broader context within which it operates such as the political, economic, social and historical circumstances (Scheinost, 2006). The Czech Republic having joined the EU in 2004, presumably with some enthusiasm, very quickly adopted a somewhat Euro-sceptic attitude towards Brussels. For example, it was opposed to the EU Constitution and has serious concerns about the threats posed to national sovereignty with respect both to policymaking and with the primacy of EU law and decision making. This scepticism emanated from President Klaus and cascaded downwards through the Civic Democratic Party of which he is a former leader, to sections of the population at large. Such an attitude is potentially damaging to a nascent EU anti-fraud service, when that service is in need of support from its national government in the form of lobbying in Brussels for more training and assistance from the anti-fraud office and the rest of the European Commission. Romania, on the other hand, has had a more positive attitude towards the European Union, both before and after accession, yet by 2008 she was the subject of a highly critical report from the European Commission regarding the progress she had made to address corruption which reflected continuing concern as to how she would address potential abuse of EU funds.

In seeking to understand any form of economic crime, such as EU fraud, it is essential as Scheinost (2006) explains, under the communist regime of Czechoslovakia, as it was then, all property apart from personal belongings, was owned by the state. It was regarded as so-called property in socialist ownership and it was afforded a greater protection under law than personal belongings and as a consequence, punishment for crimes committed against state property was far more severe. Despite this sanction, in the opinion of the general public, to take something from the state was considered to be a relatively minor offence and such behaviour tended to be tolerated by the general public (Scheinost, 2006). Jordan (2002) quotes a Communist era Czech axiom: "If you do not steal from the state, you rob your family".

When a society is in transition, values, norms and practices from a previous period interact with emerging norms and values of a free market economy. As Scheinost (2006: 77) comments: "*...Toleration of theft of state property together with disrespect for the private property that has been nourished for so many decades, encountered the appetite to get rich quickly, to achieve speedy success (expressed in money and social status) and exploit favourable opportunities. The speed of the transition process and ability of the entrepreneur to make headway in the new conditions was regarded more highly than strict observance of the law*". Jordan (2002) observes that during this period, administrative corruption persisted just as it did under the communist period. Poorly paid bureaucrats demanded bribes to supplement their incomes and bribe payers came to regard the practice as a normal business cost. When this coincides with market reforms and privatisations, there are opportunities to make massive profits and gains. Barnes (2003) notes that the Czech government in the early 1990s was able to pursue sweeping economic reforms including mass-voucher privatisations. This swashbuckling period of economic reform and transition did influence the extent and forms of economic crime. As Scheinost (2006) explains, it was very easy to acquire bank loans on the basis of entrepreneurial projects which were somewhat "thin" to say the least. The quality of these projects would not be closely scrutinised and the state would not allow key banks to become bankrupt. It was also of advantage to know that the courts could not cross-check the decisions of the privatisation committee which played a key role in the privatisation process. Whilst all transgressions were not necessarily unlawful, some were at least unethical and involved looking for opportunities often on the edge of legality, in the knowledge that economic crime and commercial sharp practice were not at the top of the list of priorities for investigation.

As Burduja (2006) outlines, the legacy of the Ottoman Empire has some significance when one considers present-day Romania. The Ottomans ruled over the Romanian provinces of Moldavia and Walachia which comprise almost two-thirds of Romania's territory, for several centuries until 1877. The Ottomans presided over a regime which tolerated corrupt practices such as bribing public officials. This became most severe in the nineteenth century when what was perceived as the extreme corruption of Ottoman appointed rulers led to popular uprisings. As Burduja (2006) observes, during the years of Communist dictatorship from after the Second World War until 1989, norms and mores developed whereby corruption became endemic in Romanian society: "*At the top level, the dictator practised "sultanism" or "dynastic communism", by appointing close friends and relatives to positions of power. These exclusive elites were extremely powerful and had a privileged status in society, as did other members of the nomenklatura. Considering the chronic shortages during the 1980s in Romania, normal citizens were trying to win the favour of these elites in order to have access to better goods and services; thus, corruption and bribery became deeply rooted as an everyday affair at all levels of society...*" (Burduja, 2006: 57).

As Burduja (2006) has commented and indeed Henshaw (2006) confirms, whilst corruption did not begin with Romania's transition from a communist to a democratic state, the change to a democratic system did create new opportunities for corruption. After the Communist Party was pushed from power, "*it did not take long until a number of people identified the lack of legal regulations in certain areas—such as banking, commerce, foreign trade and so on—and started to exploit this vacuum for their own benefit*" (Ghitescu cited in Henshaw, 2006: 644). Henshaw (2006) observes that the immediate aftermath of the transition to democracy created an environment in which what can only be described as institutionalised theft became the norm rather than the exception. A minor example, although not for the victims of this particular crime, was the disappearance of a government bank account containing donations from millions of Romanians which had been earmarked to support victims of the Revolution.

An area that was heavily exploited for the purposes of corruption after the transition to democracy was the privatisation of state-owned enterprises. Privatisation was regarded as essential to transform the country from a communist centralised command economy to a market economy. As Gheorghe (2005) comments, there are standard and non-standard means of privatisation. The standard means used in Eastern Europe were public auction, public tender and direct sell. The non-standard means are employed in general mass privatisation schemes like the voucher scheme employed in the Czech Republic or the manager employee buyout scheme applied to some extent in Romania. In Romania the preferred method of mass privatisation was the manager employee buyouts method (MEBO) for small- and medium-sized enterprises combined with standard methods for big size industrial giants.

Given that, privatisation occurred during a period when Romania was ranked very poorly in terms of perceptions of corruption by Transparency International. In 1997, Romania was in 37th position with a score of 3.44 whilst in 2001 she had fallen to 69th position with a score of 2.8. In addition, at this time, according to Gheorghe (2005), Romania had the highest level of administrative corruption in Central and Eastern Europe, excluding the former soviet states. When this situation was combined with the most widespread method of privatisation applied in Romania, namely the MEBO, then this favoured in the view of Gheorghe (2005), further corruption since favoured individuals could gather large blocks of shares which would enable them to take control. This could be achieved by paying bribes, for example, to officials of the government agency which oversaw the privatisation—the State Ownership Fund (SOF). The large privatisations of the big industrial enterprises were overseen by the SOF. This organisation was ranked in the World Bank Report on Corruption in 2001 as the third most corrupted institution after the customs authorities and the judicial and prosecution authorities. According to Gheorghe (2005), it was perceived as corrupt by 57 % of enterprises, 52 % of public officials and 44 % of households.

Gheorghe (2005) comments that it was not difficult to understand why this fostered or favoured corruption, because putting the privatisation process under the control of a state institution suffering from the general weaknesses of many Romanian institutions was at best ill-advised. Moreover, the privatisation agency only dealt with the privatisation process leaving the investor afterwards alone in a jungle of bureaucratic institutions that asked for many different kinds of permits and authorisations. During 1999, a typical firm had to obtain between 23 and 29 different approvals, authorisations, licences, permits and so on. To complete the paperwork it needed 42–102 working days and to receive the results a further 34–101 working days. Inevitably, the investor would look to informal networks in order to speed the process up—thus creating opportunities to indulge in corrupt behaviour.

In addition to privatisation, another area of the economy which saw major corruption was the banking sector. Henshaw (2006) states that the standard pattern of corruption in this sector was for well-connected individuals to use weak regulations, personal and political influence and/or bribery to obtain sufficiently secured or unsecured loans from state banks, default on them and use their connections to avoid legal punishment. In the views of some commentators, corruption in the banking sector was so widespread that, even as late as 2004, *"insider-trading, self-loans, and theft appear more as systemic features rather than isolated incidents"* (Cernat, 2004 cited in Henshaw, 2006: 453).

There has also been major high level corruption with a former prime minister under investigation for his general business affairs and suspected corruption such as paying/ taking bribes and the peddling of influence. Another questionable occurrence was the awarding of billions of dollars contract to the US Bechtel and a Franco-German-Spanish EADS consortium in a no bid, no public tender contracts issued in 2003 and 2004 to expand the road network.

All these incidences of corrupt behaviour together with all the numerous and often unreported incidents of low grade corruption involving ordinary citizens and officialdom have had unfortunate consequences for Romania's reputation abroad. Henshaw (2006, p. 6) makes the point that *"the EU has every reason to be wary about bringing Romania into the organisation and giving Romania's corruption an opportunity to waste EU funds, or worse, become an infectious seed to spread corruption elsewhere within the EU"*. Surely, a honeypot of EU funds would prove to be very attractive to fraudsters and corrupt officials.

In such a sea of corruption, can there be islands of honesty, probity and good practice? The fact is that Romania's efforts to join the European Union and to be seen as a "good citizen" in terms of how it manages EU funds and how seriously it tackles fraud and irregularity against them has had positive spin-offs. Romania's EU anti-fraud office (DLAF) is respected by officials in Brussels[1] and has been publicly praised by the Director-General of OLAF as providing an example of good practice for other countries to learn from (European Commission, 2005, 2006, 2010). So, it does appear to be possible. Romania and its anti-corruption and anti-fraud efforts have not been subjected to the same criticisms and sanctions as have those of its neighbour and fellow recent entrant—Bulgaria. This is perhaps a sign of some progress having been made. The efforts of Romania to construct effective anti-fraud structures will be considered below.

---

[1] Interview with OLAF Officials 2007.

Now that this 'swashbuckling' period of transition is over, economic crime has become established as a feature of criminal activity and given the entry of the country into the European Union, then a "honeypot" of EU funds must be an attractive opportunity for fraudsters. Criminals want to make money and they do undertake their own form of risk analysis—if the risks of detection appear to be low and the rewards are attractive, then it appears inevitable that they will direct their attention towards EU funds. In the late 1990s as the process of preparing for enlargement gained pace, officials of the then anti-fraud unit of the European Commission—UCLAF, were very worried about organised economic criminals in Central and Eastern Europe getting their hands on EU funds: 'Officials here are worried sick about EU money disappearing into a black hole".[2] How 'organised' these criminals are, is a matter of some debate both within and without the academic community. van Duyne (2003) and Spencer (2007) have both noted that organisation can be very loose and local, and consist of entrepreneurs looking for opportunities in a very enterprising way. There may well not be a "Dr Evil" directing hierarchical criminal networks which are hell-bent on swindling the European Budget and taxpayer. This does not mean that EU funds are not under threat; even locally based fraudsters can still swindle the EU out of thousands of euros and even more. In order to counter this threat, a system of financial aid and technical support to candidate countries was introduced.

Impact of the Expansion of the EU on the Fight Against Fraud

Prior to the expansion of the EU in 2004, fraud has been a major issue. Academic commentators such as Tutt (1989), Sherlock and Harding (1991), Passas and Nelken (1993), Sieber (1998) and Quirke (2006), amongst others, have all highlighted the issue and problem of fraud. When there were just 15 member states, the fight against fraud was dogged by the fragmented response from a multiplicity of member state agencies operating within 15 separate legal systems, all of which defined fraud differently, investigated it differently and reported it differently. The true extent of fraud has never been quantified; given that fraudsters like to keep their activities secret, this is not surprising. Estimates have ranged from 2 to 10 % and above (Ruimschotel, 1994). Now that EU membership has increased, first to 25, and now to 28, this problem of fragmentation can only be exacerbated. For example, Community institutions have now to cope with 13 new legal systems—this is unlikely to improve the existing situation.

Fraudsters exploit differences in legal systems and procedures, they operate in "real time", they do not have to comply with legal protocols and agreements. There were attractive sums for the fraudsters to consider focussing their attention upon, as Murawska (2004) outlines, the candidate countries received on average about 3 billion euros per year and from 2004 to 2006, the new member states received about 16 billion euros. In order to minimise the risk of fraud, the European Fraud

[2] Interview with UCLAF Official 1998.

Prevention Office (OLAF) which administratively is part of the European Commission made checks and investigations in the candidate states and sought to ensure good co-operation between itself and the administrations of the new member states (Murawska, 2004). The role of OLAF is to protect the finances of the European Community and to support and liaise with national investigative bodies particularly where investigations have a cross-border dimension (Illett, 2004).

Prospective member states made efforts to adopt the acquis communitaire in the protection of the Communities financial interests and the candidate countries were required to "create an efficient anti-fraud protection system with respect to funds provided in the framework of the Accession Partnership such as the programmes PHARE, ISPA or SAPARD" (Murawska, 2004: 3).

Efforts of the Czech Republic and Romania to Prepare for Accession

The Czech Republic and Romania were obliged to comply their legal systems with the acquis communitaire, under the first pillar of the European Union, as part of its preparation for accession. As Murawska (2004) comments, the Community measures about protection of the Community's finances are fairly modest. These consist of three EC Regulations:

- Council Regulation (EC Euratom) No. 2988/95 of 18 December 1995 on the protection of the European Communities financial interests.[3]
- Council Regulation (EC, Euratom) No. 2185/96 of 11 November 1996 concerning on-the-spot checks and inspections carried out by the Commission in order to protect the European Communities financial interests against fraud and other irregularities.[4]
- Regulation (EC) No. 1073/99 of the European Parliament and of the Council of 25 May 1999 concerning investigations conducted by the European Fraud Prevention Office (OLAF).[5]

In addition, the Czech government and the Romanian government were expected to incorporate into their legal system the Convention on the Protection of the European Communities Financial Interests (the PFI Convention) together with its associated protocols. The PFI Convention is intergovernmental and lies within the

[3] Official Journal of the European Communities, 312, Council Regulation (EC, Euratom) No. 2988/95 of 23/12/1995, On the protection of the European Communities financial interests, pp. 1–4.

[4] Official Journal of the European Communities, 292, Council Regulation (EC, Euratom) No. 2185/96 of 15/11/1996 Concerning on the spot checks and inspections, pp. 2–5.

[5] Official Journal of the European Communities, 136, Council Regulation (EC) No. 1073/99, Concerning Investigations conducted by the European Fraud Prevention Office (OLAF), pp. 1–7.

third pillar of the European Union.[6] The convention, as Fenyk (2007) details, requires that member states shall incorporate frauds against the European Communities' financial interests into their criminal code and should take the necessary steps to ensure that fraudulent behaviour and conduct is punishable by criminal penalties that are effective and reasonable, and also that heads of businesses and other senior executives that have the power to take decisions or exercise control "to be declared criminally liable in accordance with the principles defined by national law in cases of fraud affecting the European Community's financial interests…" (Fenyk, 2007: 2).

The First Protocol to the PFI Convention requires that definitions on what is termed corruption, both active and passive (Articles 2–3), be assimilated into the criminal law and the Second Protocol to the PFI Convention requires national law to provide that legal persons can be held liable in cases of fraud or active corruption and money laundering committed that damage or are likely to damage the European Communities' financial interests (Fenyk, 2007).

In order to ensure effective co-operation between OLAF and the national administrations in the candidate countries as well as seeking to have in place organisational arrangements which would be capable of preventing and detecting frauds and irregularities, OLAF supported the creation of independent anti-fraud structures at a national level in the then candidate countries. These structures were termed AFCOS—Anti-Fraud Co-ordination Service. The rationale behind such structures was to ensure effective co-ordination between legislative and administrative measures dealing with EU fraud policy (Murawska, 2004). OLAF provided training and support although it has been acknowledged by academic commentators such as Murawska (2004) and by national officials that such support was not sufficient and in some cases was regarded as being fairly minimal.[7] This is an important consideration, given the complexity of EU programmes and fraud investigation, and there was an obvious need for substantial and substantive support both from OLAF and from the Commission as a whole.

Assessment of the Anti-fraud Co-ordination Arrangements Prior to Czech Accession

Prior to accession, a mission to the Czech Republic was carried out by a consultancy firm—Investment Development Consultancy (IDC) working for the Directorate General-Enlargement in late 2002. Its goal was to examine the anti-fraud co-ordination and investigation arrangements. The subsequent report identified a number of problem areas:

- There were gaps in the level of understanding of anti-fraud topics and areas. All the relevant rules, legislation manuals, etc. needed to be gathered together in order to achieve a common understanding by officials.

[6] Official Journal of the European Communities, C316, 27/11/1995, Convention on the Protection of the European Communities Financial Interests, pp. 1–8.

[7] Interview with Czech Officials 2006.

- There was an absence of practical insight and training into the different types of EU fraud cases, detection and investigation practices.
- There was a lack of knowledge of computer audit techniques and risk analysis techniques.
- Information technology support in terms of databases and case management systems, data encryption and security was also found to be poor.

In terms of the anti-fraud structures themselves, the consultants found there to be a skills gap in terms of being able to cope with the complexities of fraud investigation as well as there being a lack of strategic objectives so that all interested parties would be aware of the long-term objectives of AFCOS and their role in helping them to be achieved. This led to delay in responding to requests from OLAF for assistance and a lack of co-ordination with respect to the conduct of investigations into suspected fraud and irregularities. There was a need for a comprehensive training programme for all interested parties. These findings beg the question as to why these difficulties and gaps in knowledge and operational skills, particularly on the administrative side of the investigation and reporting process, could not have been foreseen and measures put in place to address these issues. The European Commission and OLAF should have been far more proactive during the early period of the accession process and negotiations in order to ensure that the Czech AFCOS regime and constituent parts had the necessary skills and expertise in order to fully meet its responsibilities and commitments.

In mid-2003 the European Commission asked Sigma, the consulting arm of the OECD, to assess the anti-fraud structures in candidate countries. The objective of Sigma's assessment in the Czech Republic was to: "*evaluate the operational and administrative capacities of AFCOS and its partner institutions in the protection of the Community's financial interests and, where needed, to put forward proposals and recommendations for strengthening these capacities*" (Sigma 2004a: 2). The main findings of the report were that despite the strong legal position of AFCOS which was an advantage of having the SPPO[8] at its head, the following had yet to happen:

- AFCOS had not carried out a risk assessment of pre-accession funds and a National anti-fraud strategy had still not been developed.
- The relevant ministries had not been given the OLAF reporting guidelines and the reporting format on suspected cases of irregularity.
- No training had been given on the use of these guidelines.
- The OLAF anti-fraud system (AFIS), which enabled constituent parts of AFCOS to securely communicate with each other and with OLAF, had yet to be installed in the Directorate-General of Customs and linked by terminal to the relevant ministries.
- No irregularities had been filed by AFCOS with OLAF (Sigma 2004a: 2).

[8] Supreme Prosecutor's Office of the Czech Republic.

The Supreme Prosecutors Office as the lead agency in the AFCOS structure, needed to take a more proactive role in seeking more support from Brussels in terms of training and expert advice also in seeking the assistance of the private sector in terms of training in techniques of risk analysis, for example. There could also have been contacts with AFCOS in other candidate countries to share experiences and also perhaps to share expertise and knowledge, which may well have helped to bridge some of the gaps identified. The fact that the national anti-fraud strategy had not been developed was a weakness because the AFCOS role needed to be highlighted and publicised and the emphasis on prevention needed to be highlighted because, as the Sigma Report notes, it is a far more cost-effective way of controlling fraud than investigation and prosecution and also improvements in control mechanisms and institutional co-operation reduce the potential for frauds to be successfully committed (Sigma 2004a). Although to obtain convictions is very useful because it shows results are being achieved and it can also serve as a deterrent "pour encourager les autres".

Upon Accession in 2004 it can be seen that, although significant progress had been made, there were gaps and problems in the response of the Czech Republic to the problem of EU fraud. The national anti-fraud strategy had not been completed by the designated deadline of December 31, 2003, but by May 2004, the Czech Government adopted Resolution 456 to the National Strategy against Fraudulent Activities Damaging or Threatening the Financial Interests of the European Communities. The Strategy includes: "*the system of internal control of the management of financial funds of the individual programmes from the European Union total budget, the AFCOS system and the internal communications network, announcement of ascertained discrepancies and legislation relating to the protection of the EU's financial interests*" (Ministry of the Interior 2005: 34). In addition, in 2004, in order to strengthen the position of AFCOS in both legislative and operational terms, an AFCOS section was created within the Department of Serious Economic and Financial Crime which would be supervised by the First Deputy Prosecutor General and would be composed of prosecutors experienced in the area of fighting against fraud and supported by administrative staff with managerial, organisational and language skills (SPPO 2005).

To have structures in place which appear to have the necessary expertise and capacity to carry out and fulfil particular missions is reassuring, but it is how these structures operate in practice that is the acid test of their effectiveness. The results to date are mixed to some extent. The Director-General of OLAF in 2006 in his foreword to the 2005 OLAF Annual Report commended the Czech authorities for always meeting their reporting deadlines and stated that OLAF has good co-operation from the Czech tax authorities in the fight against VAT fraud; however, he did say that there was room for improvement in the Czech administration as a whole as far as communication about irregularities was concerned.

One area of irregularities communication that needs to be examined concerns the number of departments that communicate irregularities directly to OLAF. Each Ministry communicates irregularities to OLAF on a quarterly basis, despite officially there being only one contact point with OLAF, namely the Supreme Prosecutor's Office.[9] This is one of the important principles which

[9] Interview with Czech Officials 2006.

underpins the AFCOS system, yet this principle has been undermined with the full co-operation of OLAF. A common theme in the academic literature emphasised by commentators such as Passas and Nelken (1993), Doig (1995), Sieber (1998), Pujas (2003) and Quirke (2006, 2007) is that fragmentation with a multiplicity of agencies involved in the fight against and reporting of fraud, complicates, and in fact dilutes the response to the problem of fraud. The Supreme Prosecutor's Office should be provided with information before the regularities are reported to OLAF, but it is not clear that this always happens.[10] If the AFCOS system is to operate as it surely was intended to operate, then all irregularities should be reported to OLAF through the SPPO and not around it.

Since accession there have been problems with a lack of political support from the current Czech government which does not favour overt co-operation with Brussels at the present time[11] with issues of national sovereignty complicating matters. When an organisation is in its infancy, and should be seeking support from Brussels in terms of training and even secondment of experts and so on, the fact that the government has a negative attitude in this respect, severely complicates matters and handicaps the development of the infant organisation.

The duplication of requests for information from Brussels is frustrating for the Czech authorities. OLAF asks for information at one point in the year and then some time later, and the Commission asks for the same information—this is inefficient and time consuming.[12] The SPPO has also been disappointed by a lack of support from OLAF, a particular example of this being in a case involving possible fraud and irregularity with respect to PHARE funds which funded specific projects in the run up to Accession. Eight officials entrusted with the process of transferring money from the PHARE fund to the Czech Republic were suspected of having tried to siphon off millions of Czech crowns into their own accounts. Two of these people were senior officials at the Ministry of Regional Development and were placed under investigation for fraud and embezzlement (www.radio.cz/en/article72526). OLAF officials many of whom were on temporary contracts and were perhaps unsure of their long-term future with the organisation were reluctant to get involved when the SPPO sought support.[13] The Czech government did not want an investigation to take place,[14] no doubt concerned about political embarrassment which could have tarnished its reputation with the authorities in Brussels. The issue of the high proportion of OLAF staff on temporary contracts has been raised repeatedly, both by the European Court of Auditors and academic commentators such as Quirke (2007). The issue of political interference into criminal investigations was a factor involved in the resignation of the head of the AFCOS system—the Deputy Chief Prosecutor.[15]

[10] Interview with Czech Officials 2006.

[11] Interview with Czech academic colleagues 2015.

[12] Interview with Czech Officials 2006 and 2015.

[13] Interview with former Czech Official 2006.

[14] Interview with former Czech Official 2006.

[15] Interview with former Czech Official 2006.

Another high profile case is where senior government officials have been implicated in a situation where there was a plan to renovate the state-owned Budisov chateau. The cost of the renovation was deliberately inflated to almost 70 million crowns which was around 30 million crowns higher than the real cost. This "difference" was then to be shared between three officials (www.radio.cz/en/article)—this is a classic structural funds fraud—over inflation of the cost of works and no doubt a siphoning off of interest earned on the funds as well. Such cases whilst embarrassing for the authorities are also useful in demonstrating that no one is above the law and providing an opportunity to show that cases of EU fraud will be vigorously investigated and prosecuted if the evidence warrants it.

More recent examples from the Czech Republic include the use of counterfeited documents giving "paper proof" that projects funded by EU money have been completed successfully; misuse of grant monies—not used for their intended use; collusion in public procurement—favoured beneficiaries and misuse and abuse of the tendering process; and false declaration of beneficiaries' own resources in projects that are supposedly co-funded.[16]

The Experience of Romania

In terms of establishing an effective AFCOS network, a country like Romania which is one of the poorest in the EU, with a nascent anti-fraud office, with officials who did not have the experience of dealing with the complexities of EU policy regimes as well as perhaps not having the experience of investigating transnational frauds, obviously were in need of support and nurturing.

In Romania the designated AFCOS body in 2002 was the Prime Minister's Control Department. It was established as the sole liaison institution with OLAF. The reorganisation of the government in 2003 included the transfer of this liaison function to the newly established Government Control Department. Within the Government Control Department, fulfilment of the Anti-Fraud Co-ordination Service (AFCOS) function was delegated to the OLAF division (Sigma, 2004b). This division was subordinate to the head of the Government Control Department, but for issues related to the protection of EU financial interests, the reporting line ran directly from the Director of the OLAF division to the Prime Minister.

Sigma, the consulting arm of the OECD in Paris, was commissioned by the European Commission to undertake an assessment of the anti-fraud structure in Romania and it reported in 2004. The objectives of Sigma's assessment in Romania were to "*evaluate the operational and administrative capacities of AFCOS and its partner institutions in protecting the European Union's financial interests and, where needed, to put forward proposals and recommendations for strengthening these capacities*" (Sigma, 2004b: 7). Sigma's evaluation of the operational and administrative capacities of AFCOS and its partner institutions was made on the

[16] Interview with Czech officials 2015.

basis of AFCOS's basic functions which were and are: co-ordination, co-operation and communication (the 3 C's). These signify the ability:

- To co-ordinate within Romania, all legislative, administrative and operational obligations and activities related to the protection of the Community's financial interests.
- To co-operate with OLAF and its partner institutions whenever OLAF requires investigation assistance or, on the other hand, whenever OLAF assistance is required.
- To communicate with OLAF and its partner institutions with regard to mandatory reporting and information exchange.

The main findings of the Sigma report were as follows:

- There was an improving situation in Romania. Several laws had either been passed or had been drafted which were aimed at improving overall financial management and control to protect EU financial interests.
- Although the Government Control Division of which AFCOS—the OLAF Division—was an integral part, had its own budget and a high degree of operational independence, it was still subordinate to the National Control Authority which was headed by a deputy minister and was responsible for initiating and ensuring implementation of the legal framework within which it co-ordinated control plans and exercised quality control functions throughout the public sector. The National Control Authority still took decisions on recruitment, appointments and dismissals with record to AFCOS and the Government Control Department, so independence was compromised to some degree.
- Neither a national anti-fraud strategy nor a more specific strategy for protecting the financial interests of the European Union in Romania had been implemented.
- There was no training programme to support the OLAF division of the Government Control Department.
- A network of contact officials in partner institutions had not been developed.
- The relevant ministries had not been given the OLAF reporting guidelines and the reporting format on suspected cases of irregularity detrimental to Community funds. No training had been given on the use of these guidelines.
- The OLAF Anti-Fraud Information System (AFIS) had yet to be installed and linked by terminal to the relevant ministries.

The fact that there was no national anti-fraud strategy in place was problematic. As the Sigma experts noted, a strategy for fighting fraud in Romania would be useful in harmonising the various efforts undertaken by different ministries and bodies to protect both national and international financial interests, including the EU budget and own resources. Such a strategy would have emphasised Romania's commitment to take action in this respect. Romania did have a draft "National Strategy for Protecting the Financial Interests of the European Union" in the country, and this could serve as a starting point for the elaboration of a national anti-fraud strategy.

The lack of training for staff of the OLAF division of the Government Control Department (GCD) was very worrying. Fraud investigation is a complex process at the best of times, and when this is coupled with the complexities of EU policy programmes such as the Common Agricultural Policy and the Structural Funds then such complexities can only be compounded. The AFCOS structure should have recognised this and asked for more help from Brussels in this respect. It should also have been obvious to the authorities in Brussels that a nascent anti-fraud service was going to have problems in terms of deficiencies in the skills set and expertise, and the commission should have been far more proactive in terms of addressing this issue. It is not always up to the member state to come with the "begging bowl" to Brussels. It is not the first time that this problem of inadequate training has been recognised. The same was true of the AFCOS structures of the Czech Republic. It appears that no lessons were learned from that particular experience.

The Government Control Department also had not developed written and structured procedures for disseminating information to the national authorities responsible for the management of EU funds and revenue. The Sigma experts found that fraud and irregularities were defined in law but not understood in practice, and the difference between an error and an irregularity had not been defined.

Moreover, there were no formal co-operation agreements with partner institutions. This was a major weakness. All the experience and analysis to date both from academic experts and practitioners has indicated that this whole area is bedevilled by the issue of fragmentation. As Quirke (2008) identified, in a small country like the Czech Republic, there were at least ten different agencies with an involvement in EU fraud investigations. The situation was not likely to be any less fragmented in a country like Romania. The potential for overlap and duplication of effort was enormous. This was a problem that needed to be addressed urgently.

Response of the Romanian Authorities

In response to these deficiencies, initially in 2004, the AFCOS role was taken over by the Prime Minister's Department for Inspection and Monitoring of the Transparent Use of Community Funds (DIPM) in 2004. This department had responsibilities outside of the European funds dimension, as it carried out controls, and checks at the request of the Prime Minister and its operational competences regarding the control of European funds were limited, since the department's representatives could only request documents and information and its control report had the value of a simple notification. There was no strategy, no clear vision and no concrete action plan as regards the fight against fraud (DLAF, 2007).

The European Commission in its Monitoring Report of October 2004, which dealt with the progress made by Romania towards accession, said that special attention must be paid to the protection of the Communities financial interests by means of:

- Creating and implementing the legislative framework.

- Establishing effective mechanisms for carrying out anti-fraud investigations.
- Drafting and implementing an anti-fraud strategy (European Commission, 2004).

In response to these recommendations, the Romanian government in 2005, created a new department—the Fight against Fraud Department—DLAF, which was placed within the Prime Ministers office and would report directly to him/her. Also, the task of controlling Community funds was separated from investigations and the new department's role was exclusively in the field of protecting the Communities' financial interests and DLAF investigators were given the powers of conducting on the spot investigations, taking statements and retaining evidence. There are some police type powers here, yet DLAF is not a criminal investigation body, it conducts administrative investigations. There is the potential for confusion as well as the potential for errors and mistakes in the collection of evidence, which could potentially compromise subsequent legal cases.

As noted in DLAF's Annual Report of 2006 (DLAF, 2007), the number of members of staff was increased from 26 to 45, the majority of which were young—well under the age of 40. This could have been a conscious attempt to avoid employing older investigators who may have been compromised by a culture of corruption—Romanian officials were somewhat enigmatic when asked to confirm if there was any substance to this observation.[17] It may be the case that younger investigators do not possess the skills borne out of and honed by years of experience, although this is not perceived to be a problem by the Romanian authorities.[18] Moreover, there was and still is a substantial difference in salary between DLAF investigators and other civil servants—DLAF investigators are paid around 75% more. Romanian officials admitted that this was a conscious attempt to ensure that they would not be tempted by offers of bribes or to engage in other corrupt activities.[19] It is unfortunately a fact of life that low paid public servants are more likely to take the offer of a bribe than higher paid public servants.

As well as establishing this new anti-fraud office, the government also adopted the National Anti-Fraud Strategy for the protection of the Communities' Financial Interests in Romania (SNLAF). The strategy emphasised:

- The necessity to harmonise Romanian legislation with European regulations in the area of protecting EU financial interests and to prepare the institutional, legal and operational framework for EU accession.
- The need for effective financial control regarding EU funds.
- Strengthening DLAF's role as operational and communications co-ordinator for the institutions involved in the fight against fraud (DLAF, 2007).

The overall objectives of the strategy were the development of an integrated system for co-ordination of the anti-fraud fight and the strengthening of administrative capacity of those institutions involved in preventing, identifying, investigating fraud and seeking recovery of funds fraudulently obtained.[20]

---

17 Interview with Romanian Officials 2008.

18 Interview with Romanian Officials 2008.

19 Interview with Romanian Officials 2008.

20 Interview with Romanian Officials 2008.

The new anti-fraud office, DLAF, has agreed a number of co-operation protocols with bodies/agencies which have a role in the investigation and prosecution of fraud cases. These range from the national Anti-Corruption Office (DNA) which would actually prosecute any alleged fraudsters to the General Inspectorate of the Romanian Police, to the Customs Service, to the Central Unit for the harmonisation of the Public Internal Audit (UCAAPI) as well as those bodies which manage funds such as CAP funds, and which have their own units for carrying out investigation of irregularities. These services are obliged to notify DLAF with respect to any identified irregularities. From this brief overview it is clear that there are many agencies involved in detecting/investigating EU frauds in Romania. It is possible to identify two sub-groups in these arrangements. In one, which could be called criminal investigation groups, there are well-established arrangements for contact and co-ordination between the DNA, and the Police and Customs. In the other sub-group, there are organisations which tend to undertake non-criminal investigations such as the Internal Audit Service, and these have no practical experience of liaising with the criminal investigative bodies. Just as Quirke (2008) identified in the case of the Czech Republic, in Romania there is potential for confusion, inefficiencies, duplication and misunderstandings.

A potential difficulty for any of the above agencies in terms of a fraud investigation is when there is a suspicion that politicians could be involved. The Romanian parliament has passed a law which would protect politicians from investigation and prosecution, as this would be contrary to the constitution, in their view. The view of DLAF is that because they are based within the Prime Minister's office and have the status which this placement confers, they would not be inhibited from pursuing any such investigations; there could be a problem though in terms of co-operation and access to documentation and so on. This issue needs to be addressed as a matter of urgency. It is surely axiomatic to say that no one is above the law.

Wider Lessons That Can Be Drawn from the Czech and Romanian Experience

There are a number of lessons that can be drawn:

- There is a need for wholehearted support from the national government in terms of dealing with the Brussels authorities in seeking to gain material support and operational expertise and training.
- The AFCOS organisation must be proactive in analysing its strengths and weaknesses and using this analysis to put a case forward to OLAF and the European Commission for help, support and training in order to strengthen the organisation.
- The issue of fragmentation has to be tackled. Having a multiplicity of organisations involved in both investigation and reporting is difficult to co-ordinate and can lead to mixed messages being sent to the authorities in Brussels with some authorities investigating on an administrative basis and others on a criminal investigative basis.

- The authorities in Brussels need to actively support the lead institution in the AFCOS structure, and there should not be separate reporting of irregularities by individual ministries as this undermines the authority and position of the lead institution.
- The duplication of information requested by Brussels also needs to be considered. Member States should not be asked to provide the same information both to OLAF and also the Commission—this duplication is costly, inefficient and time consuming.
- OLAF officials should be based in the candidate countries as in the OLAF Poland project; this leads to a wider understanding of the issues facing national authorities on the part of OLAF, as well as experience for national officials of working and liaising with a transnational body like OLAF.
- There should be a regular system of seconding national officials to OLAF in order for them to gain experience of the Europe-wide perspective which OLAF has.

Conclusions

The Czech Republic has been able to establish an AFCOS structure which appears to be respected by the anti-fraud office in Brussels, OLAF, but which nevertheless has faced problems such as a lack of knowledge and operational expertise on the part of some of its officials which need to be addressed by actively seeking the assistance of the Brussels authorities and perhaps also the expertise of the private sector where appropriate in order to bridge the skills and knowledge gap. This effort needs to be actively supported by the Czech government which will enable the AFCOS structure to develop and enhance its expertise and efficiency as well as by the European Commission which should be more proactive in seeking to assist new member states and should not always expect them to come to Brussels with a "begging bowl". The recent history of the country with the rapid transformation from communism to capitalism has provided opportunities for both sharp commercial practice and outright financial and economic crime, and it would be naïve to assume that EU funds will not attract attention from such criminals; in fact there have been high profile instances of this. The experience of the Czech Republic provides lessons for other candidate states in terms of seeking to reduce the level of fragmentation in the investigative and reporting dimensions as well as seeking the active support of the national government in dealing and co-operating with the Brussels authorities.

The entry of Romania to the EU was viewed with suspicion by some member states and by some commentators, yet she appears to have made genuine efforts to address those suspicions and concerns. Romania has been able to establish an AFCOS structure which has been lavishly praised by the Brussels authorities as offering a model for other new member states to follow. Despite this, it does appear to suffer from certain problems such as fragmentation and also a skills and knowledge gap which needs to be addressed by the national authorities working in conjunction with Brussels. The perceived high level of corruption in the country does mean that EU funds will be vulnerable to the nefarious acts of corrupt officials, and DLAF and the other agencies will need to be on their guard. There does appear to be a genuine pocket of non-corruption in an environment which looks problematic.

This situation is not helped by the attempt to protect politicians from fraud investigation and prosecution which does undermine the independence of the anti-fraud agencies and needs to be addressed as a matter of urgency. The relationship with Bulgaria is also fraught with difficulty. A good deal of effort will have to be expended in order to foster a more harmonious and productive working relationship. There are lessons to be learned by other candidate countries in terms of reducing the degree of fragmentation and building productive working relationships with their neighbours.

Yet, a cynic might comment that Romania has had to make strenuous efforts to "get its house in some kind of order" because the eyes of the Brussels authorities and the other member states have been upon it, and it could not afford to be seen to be lacking in this respect, as EU funds may have been suspended or withdrawn. When the eyes of the EU authorities turn elsewhere to other prospective member states, perhaps the shores of this island of non-corruption, DLAF, may well be swamped by a "tsunami" from the ocean of corruption surrounding it. Time will surely tell.

Both countries have suffered from self-inflicted wounds such as not ratifying the PFI Convention on the protection of the EU's Financial Interests, as they were supposed to do, prior to accession; however, they could have been supported more fully by OLAF in terms of basing OLAF officials there in the post-accession period during the "nurturing phase" of the development of anti-fraud capabilities and expertise.

Is it a case of the curate's egg? Well, there are certainly some examples of good practice and the accession of countries such as the Czech Republic and Romania has not been the disaster that some observers predicted it would be. So, to describe these accessions as being akin to the curate's egg is perhaps not wholly accurate.

References

Barnes, A. (2003). Comparative theft: Context and choice in the Hungarian, Czech and Russian transformations, 1989-2000. *East European Politics and Societies, 17*(3), 533–565.

Burduja, S. I. (2006). Assessing corruption in Romania. An integrationist story. *Stanford's Student Journal of Russian, East European and Eurasian Studies, Spring*, 51–69.

Convention on the protection of the European Communities Financial Interests. *Official Journal of the European Communities*. C316, 27/11/1995, 1–8.

Council Regulation (EC). No. 1073/99. Concerning Investigations conducted by the European Fraud Prevention Office (OLAF). *Official Journal of the European Communities, 136*, 1–7.

Council Regulation (EC, Euratom). No. 2185/96 of 15/11/1996. Concerning on the spot checks and inspections. *Official Journal of the European Communities, 292*, 2–5.

Council Regulation (EC, Euratom). No. 2988/95 of 23/12/1995. On the protection of the European Communities financial interests. *Official Journal of the European Communities, 312*, 1–4.

DLAF. (2007). *The fight against fraud: 2006 annual report*. Bucharest: DLAF.

Doig, A. (1995). A fragmented organisational approach to fraud in a European context. *European Journal on Criminal Policy and Research, 3*(2), 48–64.

European Commission. (2004). *Monitoring report on Romania*. Luxembourg: Office of Official Publications of the European Communities.

European Commission. (2005). *Monitoring report on Romania*. Luxembourg: Office of Official Publications of the European Communities.

European Commission. (2006). *Monitoring report on Romania*. Luxembourg: Office of Official Publications of the European Communities.

European Commission. (2010). *Report of the European Anti-Fraud Office, tenth activity report for the period 1 January 2009 to 31 December 2009*. Luxembourg: Office of Official Publications of the European Communities.

Fenyk, J. (2007). The level of implementation of the convention on the protection of the EC's financial Interests and of the Follow-up Protocols in the Czech Republic. *European Law and National Criminal Legislation, 1*, 116–121.

Gheorghe, L. (2005). *Privatisation, institutional culture and corruption in Romania*. Retrieved from www.10iacc.org/download/ml-02.pdf

Henshaw, C. (2006). *Corruption in Romania*. Retrieved from www.talis.ca/essays/Corruption in Romania.pdf

Illett, N. (2004). The European Anti-Fraud Office (OLAF). *Journal of Financial Crime, 12*(2), 120–122.

Jordan, J. M. (2002). Patronage and corruption in the Czech Republic. *SAIS Review, 22*(2), 19–52.

Ministry of Interior. (2005). National strategy against fraudulent activities damaging or threatening the financial interests of the european communities. Prague: Ministry of Interior.

Murawska, A. (2004) *Impact of the Enlargement on the Protection of the Financial Interests of the European Community against fraud*. Paper presented at the second Pan-European Conference Standing Group on EU Politics, Bologna, Italy, June 24–26.

Passas, N., & Nelken, D. (1993). The thin line between legitimate and criminal enterprises: Subsidy frauds in the European Community. *Crime, Law and Social Change, 19*, 223–243.

Pujas, V. (2003). The European anti-fraud office (OLAF): A European policy to fight against economic and financial fraud? *Journal of European Public Policy, 10*(5), 778–797.

Quirke, B. (2006). Economic crime and legal competence in the EU. In P. C. van Duyne, A. Maljevic, M. van Dijck, K. von Lampe, & J. L. Newell (Eds.), *The organisation of crime for profit* (pp. 91–107). Nijmegen: Wolf Legal Publishers.

Quirke, B. (2007). OLAF: The fight against EU fraud. *Journal of Financial Crime, 14*(2), 178–189.

Quirke, B. (2008). EU fraud and new member states: The case of the Czech Republic. In P. C. van Duyne, J. Harvey, A. Maljevic, K. von Lampe, & M. Scheinost (Eds.), *European crime markets at cross-roads* (pp. 221–236). Nijmegen: Wolf Legal Publishers.

Ruimschotel, D. (1994). The EC Budget: Ten per cent fraud? A policy analysis approach. *Journal of Common Market Studies, 32*(3), 319–342.

Scheinost, M. (2006). Some reflections on researching financial and economic crime. In P. C. van Duyne, A. Maljevic, M. van Dijck, K. von Lampe, & J. L. Newell (Eds.), *The organisation of crime for profit* (pp. 69–90). Nijmegen: Wolf Legal Publishers.

Sherlock, A., & Harding, M. (1991). Controlling fraud within the European Community. *European Law Review, 16*(1), 20–36.

Sieber, U. (1998). Eurofraud: Organised fraud against the financial interests of the EU. *Crime, Law and Social Change, 30*(1), 1–42.

Sigma. (2004a). *Draft report of the assessment of the Anti-Fraud system in the Czech Republic*. Paris: OECD.

Sigma. (2004b). *Draft report of the assessment of the Anti-Fraud system in Romania*. Paris: OECD.

Spencer, J. (2007). The illicit movement of people across borders. In P. C. van Duyne, A. Maljevic, M. van Dijck, K. von Lampe, & J. Harvey (Eds.), *Crime business and crime money in Europe* (pp. 111–129). Nijmegen: Wolf Legal Publishers.

SPPO (Supreme Prosecutors Office of the Czech Republic). (2005). *Position of the Supreme Prosecutor's Office of the Czech Republic in the AFCOS System*. Brno: SPPO.

Tutt, N. (1989). *Europe on the fiddle: The common market scandal*. London: Croom Helm.

van Duyne, P. C. (2003). Greasing the organisation of crime markets in Europe. In P. C. van Duyne, K. von Lampe, & J. L. Newell (Eds.), *Criminal finances and organising crime in Europe* (pp. 1–19). Nijmegen: Wolf Legal Publishers.

Chapter 17
Where There's Muck, There's Brass—and Class: Financial Market Regulation and Public Policy

Nicholas Dorn

Introduction

Taking as its point of departure the financial market crises from 2007 onwards and the misconduct revealed, this chapter proposes that a conceptual and governance shift is needed: from regulation, which is past- and present-focused and concerned with *means*, to policy, which is future-orientated and concerned with *ends*. Whilst debates on regulation have been much concerned with distinctions and balances between its public and private forms, debates on policy have increasingly turned to more fundamental questions about the structure of finance and how to transform it. The chapter summarily reviews new cross-disciplinary understandings of money creation and of the manner in which finance projects losses into the future, corresponding to the rake-off of profits today. Accordingly, it has been proposed that such financiers constitute a "risk class" (or risk stratum or faction), which manages and benefits from such transfers. In conclusion, the chapter eyes policies of suppression, polluter pays and right-sizing of finance.

In 1925, British Chancellor of the Exchequer, Winston Churchill, declared as follows: "I would rather see Finance less proud and Industry more content" (Best, 2001: 119). That was "shortly before he took the fateful decision to subject Britain's northern manufacturing heartland to an overvalued pound by returning to the gold standard" (The Economist, 2007), provoking John Maynard Keynes' to ironically entitle his book, *The Economic Consequences of Mr Churchill*. Churchill's words were repeated almost a century later by Christine Lagarde (2014), Managing Director of the International Monetary Fund (IMF). Presumably her statement was made without irony, although it could have been interpreted as an unkind and

N. Dorn (✉)
Institute of Advanced Legal Studies, University of London, London, UK
e-mail: nicholas.dorn@sas.ac.uk

G.A. Antonopoulos (ed.), *Illegal Entrepreneurship, Organized Crime and Social Control*, Studies of Organized Crime 14, DOI 10.1007/978-3-319-31608-6_17

disparaging remark about the design of the Eurozone (the modern-day Gold Standard, albeit with Britain this time outside it).

Clearly, in the long period between Churchill and Lagarde, the financial sector first became more proud, then less, as the financial crisis brought finance into disrepute, heaping upon "bankers" the double humiliation of appearing both incompetent and corrupt. What had been a closed-off policy area was suddenly less so. One of advantages of crises is that they can raise fundamental questions. The financial crisis—and the continuing stream of malpractices and manipulations that now constitute the financial sector in the eyes of the public—opened up some intellectual and political space for debate. No longer is finance accepted as being a benign matter, to be governed in a politically neutral and technocratic matter. Indeed it is now widely understood that financial markets have as much power for evil as for good and that, rather than being allowed to rule the roost, they must themselves be shaped according to some notion of the public good. The big question is, *what and whose* notion of public good?

This chapter seeks to contribute to that debate. The notion of protecting the future from the deprecations of the present is not considered bizarre when thinking of the environment, where precautionary action is at least understood, if hard to implement. For some time now, public policy on financial markets has been hovering on the brink of its own precautionary moment of truth. This chapter seeks to advance that discussion.

Where There's Muck

"Where there's muck, there's brass" is a traditional English (north-eastern) saying that has wider applicability than its specific origins suggest. Following the realisation that conflicts of interest, unfair market practices, fraud, manipulation and all manner of wrongdoing were at the core of financial markets prior to the financial crisis that began in 2007—and that such practices continued even when many of firms involved had been rescued by the public assistance and sometimes public ownership—these practices are taken more seriously than hitherto. The deeper that one digs, the more cases come to light, amounting not only to specific cases of market unfairness but also to wholesale, systematic and indeed systemic rigging of markets: Libor cases concerning "fixing" of interest rates (O'Brien, 2015) being followed by investigation into other benchmarks, for example currency exchange rates. Benchmark manipulation, high frequency trading and spoofing (a form of price manipulation in which markets are bombarded with orders that are quickly withdrawn) are among newly recognised forms of market misconduct, alongside the familiar ones such insider trading, misrepresentation, deception and fraud. In all of these areas there been has a glut of cases, due possibly partly to an upsurge in malfeasance but also and more credibly to a stepping up of regulatory enforcement since the financial crisis. This currently is resulting in market learning "how not to get caught", which can be expected to change the profile of misconduct.

What makes these cases seem so egregious is not only their scale and repetitiveness, and the gleeful tone of the perpetrators, but also that some of the firms involved were enjoying public support at the time. This has made such cases appear more scandalous than earlier cases, in which market perpetrators "only" defrauded each other—such as the infamous ABACUS manoeuvre that was midwifed by Goldman Sachs. Goldman Sachs brought together sellers of financial packages that were designed to be loss-making with purchasers who, whilst being tremendously more "sophisticated" in investment terms than the present author, nevertheless did not realise the following three things. The packages were designed to be loss-making. These characteristics were well known both to the seller and to Goldman Sachs, since they had collaborated on designing them, so that they could be "shorted" in the market. Any buyer was destined to be greatly disadvantaged.

However, viewing the broader canvass, losses do not only fall within financial markets.

Fraudulent by Design?

An understandable reaction to copious evidence of financial markets' *malfeasance* (Elliot Spitzer interview, cited in O'Brien, 2005: 459) could be to assert that they inherently follow a fraudulent design. This chapter argues that such a reaction gestures in the right direction, although it does not dig deep enough.

The issue is indeed one of design, which has been shown to be flawed. Following the collapse of the so-called "great moderation" and recognition of crisis from 2007 onwards, it is clear that finance is not stable. Quite the opposite: it is prone to wild swings, with unjust enrichment of financial market participants occurring in the upswings, followed by unjust impoverishment of others in the downswings. This means that, not only is there *contemporaneous* re-distributional effects, from particular occupational strata to less favoured social strata, but also *temporal* transfers. Evidently, those who in the future will feel the brunt of losses—through the socialisation of bailout costs and through concomitant austerity policies—are not in a good position to raise these issues in advance, since they do not know what is brewing. They will become fully aware only when it is too late, insofar that all there that will be left to discuss will be how to socially distribute the losses and/or how to try to push some of them further on to the *next* future (cf. Nesvetailova, 2015; Palan, 2015).

In this perspective, the illegalities that occur in financial markets, and which from time to time attract action and indignation, quite pale in comparison with what is perfectly legal. "Lawful but awful", to borrow the memorable phrase of Passas (2005). How are these issues to be grasped in a way that takes policy makers further than indignation? They can be grasped only partially in terms of capture and corruption. Of course, policy connivance and regulatory forbearance are much encouraged by industry lobbying (Corporate Observatory Corporate Observatory Europe, 2014) and, in many countries, political contributions. Certainly, many aspects of financial markets, often "innovations", were tolerated by policy makers. For example, pre-crisis, UK policy makers welcomed all comers, whilst US policy makers turned a blind eye to US firm's excessive leverage and their activities in "offshore" spaces (Hellwig, 2009: 54-55)—which from a US perspective included London, hosting Lehman Brothers International (Europe) and the AIG Financial Products Division.

It was not that policy makers had thought that there was no risk—rather, as some interesting post-crisis testimony shows, senior responsible people thought that risk had been shifted elsewhere. For example, the US financial industry and its regulators had imagined that risks inherent in the products that multiplied in the run-up to 2007 had been "spread" away from the originators, to other firms, sectors and indeed countries, only to find out that "the spreading of risk that was one of the supposed benefits of the originate-to-distribute model proved to be much less extensive than many believed" (Bernanke, 2008). Although some of the risk had indeed been so shifted, blowback was greater than anticipated, due not only to the nature of the financial instruments but also to the interconnectedness of international financial circuits (Dorn, 2015).

Nevertheless, the possibilities for risk-spreading seemed to retain some intellectual appeal following the crisis. For example in 2011 the then head of the UK Financial Services Authority, Lord Turner, mused that the financial system might be made safer if certain risky instruments could be "held outside the banking system [and] are held by investors who have so arranged their assets and liabilities that they could face the imposed losses without that in turn inducing systemic effects [today]" (Turner, 2011: 9). Indeed that might be convenient for the financial industry, removing from it the stigma of too often being, in Turner's words, a source of "economic pollution" (Turner, 2015: 4). Alas, the default *modus operandi* of the financial markets is to propel economic loss/pollution into the future, rather than into nowhere. Regulation is not a big enough tool to avert this.

Content and Plan of the Chapter

In the first half of the chapter, regulation is unpacked as a bundle of public (state) and private (market) initiatives, which take the promise of finance at its word, intervening to moderate its imperfections, not to question its purpose or transform it. The concern with misconduct provides an example: financial markets are berated for past manipulation, fraud and unfair dealing and are bidden to behave with more integrity (more on this below and on the regulatory engagements of public and private actors with these issues).

Four regulatory modes are discussed here, which can be summarised as follows: (i) Public regulation and enforcement in its strong form, often called "command regulation", where for a while the US and particularly the New York authorities were in the lead, shaming others into action. (ii) The current attenuation of (if not backing-off from) public enforcement, the latter being "recalibrated" in order to be

← **More public**		**More private** →	
Command regulation: imposed via state power, visible.	*Public-private*: negotiated, hence complex, not always clear	*Private regulatory orders*: rules and determinations are publicised	*Arbitration*: individualised, confidential, with determinations typically hidden.

Fig. 17.1 Varieties of publicity

more "proportionate" from the perspective of regulatees, who become, once again (somewhat as before the crisis), *partners* in regulation rather than *subjects* of it. (iii) The persistence and increasing pertinence of private regulators, such as sectoral associations—notably the International Swaps and Derivatives Association (ISDA). (iv) Arbitration, which currently seeks to expand its footprint within financial markets, providing what here we characterise—by analogy with certain trading venues—as a "dark pool" of private justice, within which matters of dispute can be settled in privacy, potentially inviting some risks.

These four forms of market governance correspond respectively to points along a public–private regulatory dimension, as illustrated in Fig. 17.1. The characterisations of public and private here refer both to "ownership" of regulation (by the public power or by private parties) and to its visibility (ranging from wide publicity to impenetrable privacy).

Historicizing Public and Private Regulation

Has there ever been, within capitalist countries, robust policy action to transform financial markets? The USA provides a possible example, as President Franklin Roosevelt brought in the New Deal in response to the 1930s depression, including serious reform of the financial sector and the appointment of a robust regulator (O'Brien, 2014). Policy action included passage of the Glass–Steagall Act which, amongst other provisions, largely separated commercial (retail) banking from more speculative investment activities. This provision was repealed in 1999, being partially reinstated in 2010 by the Dodd-Frank Wall Street Reform and Consumer Protection Act, over which implementation struggles continue to date (Williams, 2015).

The history is less robust for Europe, in particular for the UK, where there never has been public regulation of financial markets. London today provides the largest international platform for financial markets; up until 2008, it defended its international position by offering offshore-like self regulation within a classy wrapper; and London has been centrally involved in the formation of international and European regulatory architectures and cultures. The history of this city illustrates the core problem: the internationalisation and interlinking of occupational "status groups" and "closed clubs", as Max Weber (2000) called them.

Weberian Clubs

Up until the twentieth century, market rule making and enforcement in Europe were rooted in direct social contacts between traders, within geographically and culturally specific communities. Each of these economic communities had its own cultural, moral and (self)regulatory coherence. Such self-organisation served practical purposes within economic communities (resolution of disputes etc) and it also had political boundary-maintaining purposes, in two senses. The economic activities in question were reserved for those who had been accepted into the group (guild, club, cartel). Moreover, club regulation or private regulation (as we would call it today) kept at bay outside interference in the rules of the game.

Financial markets, in particular, "were regarded as being beyond the realm of party politics" (Cain & Hopkins, 1987: 6). The governance arrangements in place in London for many centuries, right up until the post-Second World War period, were strongly inward-facing. As Daunton (1989: 154) put it, "The [City] corporation and the guild companies had managed to avoid reform, so that they still remained largely beyond government control. The ancient right that the monarch could not enter the City without the permission of the lord mayor survived and this privilege had, in a sense, been inherited by the commercial and financial institutions of the City". The general franchise of 1918 did not touch these arrangements: democracy had arrived, yet financial market self governance carried on as before, the two running in parallel universes.

We now come to the 1980s when—according to the orthodoxy—financial market self regulation was swept away and public regulation began, with the formation of an "independent" regulator, the Financial Services Authority (FSA). However, did the birth of the FSA really mean the end of self regulation—can it really be counted as an Independent Regulatory Agency (IRA), in the sense of being independent of both state and market? No, say Michael Moran, Karel Williams and their colleagues, who in a series of important works culminating in Engelen et al. (2011), have explored the ideational and structural conditions in which crisis was brewing. They suggest that regulatory arrangements in the UK constituted a Potemkin village, meaning that it was meant to deceive: bureaucracy was introduced in the form of an apparently public regulator, yet one retaining a market mentality. Moreover, the FSA was funded by the industry, hardly a recipe for independence of spirit (Engelen et al., 2012: 374). George Gilligan's deployment of the notion of "relative autonomy" to describe UK financial market regulation goes in a similar direction, without implying bad faith (Gilligan, 1997). Either way, the UK ended up with "private regulation behind a public façade" (Dorn, 2015: 6).

Pseudo-public regulation is both a normative problem and a functional one. Normatively, it must be unacceptable that such a core aspect of governance should be convened outside the arena of common politics. We need to re-visit the political separation between democratic politics and markets—and the parallel disciplinary separation between economics and politics. We need to challenge the political structure within which basic assumptions are shaped, knowledge is constructed and the broad lines of policy are negotiated. Looking at the contexts within and levels at which financial market regulation occurs—the restricted, technocratic circles involved and the upward, elitist drift of networking—one notices the lack of wider political debate in the run-up to the crisis. Did we see widespread and vigorous contestations, through which not only politicians but also political parties and citizens might get engaged? Not really, nor even that much today. Even in the "periphery" of the Eurozone, where the lives of many have been deeply touched by down-turns in investment and by the austerity measures that are the flip side of bank bailouts, responses have been muted. There has been public anger, yet this has taken the form of widespread cynicism over elites, alongside displacement of anger unto foreigners and marginal groups—rather than attempts to move banking and other financial services into the centre of political debate and democratic decision-making. If the recent stirrings of democracy in some parts of Europe result in financial markets policies and regulation being politicised—in the vulgar meaning of the word—then that would be momentous. The odds, of course, are against.

Public Regulation: Signs of Roll-Back

For a while after the beginning of the financial market crisis, there was an unprecedented ramping up of public regulation in Europe. It was a shock for the industry to have command regulation imposed in the wake of the financial crisis. In the USA also, in the years following 2007, there was a reversal of pre-crisis de-regulatory trends. Enforcement also increased in the USA, the New York State authorities for a while being in the lead and shaming federal agencies into action. However, by the mid-2010s there were clear signs of regulatory roll-back, in illustration of which the chequered history of bank ring-fencing and the agenda for EU Capital Markets Union are now briefly mentioned.

Attempts to "ring-fence" the riskier bits of banking from retail banking (Independent Commission on Banking, 2011; High Level Expert Group, 2012) have been met by determined resistance, both in Eurozone countries (Hardie & Macartney, 2015) and in the UK (Binham & Dunkley, 2015, commenting on Prudential Regulation Authority, 2015). For the European Union, Capital Market Union (CMU) is a very broad policy package seeking to dismantle the remaining obstacles to free movement of capital within Europe. As part of CMU, a European Commission consultation exercise from 2015 onwards invites views about fine-tuning financial market regulation, on the grounds that some of the considerable amount of regulation that followed the crisis might be disproportionate (as the industry generally maintains) and/or that specific elements might interact in "unintended" ways (a much more subtle way of framing deregulatory questions: European Commission 2015). In short, CMU seeks, through new legislation in some areas and some roll-back in others, to revitalise finance and to extend its reach.

As those two examples illustrate, arguably the tide has turned and is now flowing in the direction of "less burdensome" forms of governance. There is once again negotiation between public and private, and consolidation of forms of private regulation outwith the state.

Negotiating Regulation

> Financial services risk and regulation—many see it as a problem, we see it as an opportunity. An opportunity to shine. An opportunity to grow. An opportunity to build trust. The company that overcomes risk and adversity is the company that people remember. The organisation that understands how to protect itself is the one that customers will turn to. At PwC, we work with you to redefine the way risk and regulation is seen. [...] With our help, you won't just navigate around potential problems, you'll also be positioned to get ahead. (Wardley, Leitch, Cable, & Steinhage, 2015: 11)

The above quote is taken from a PriceWaterhouseCoopers (PWC) publication entitled *Stand out for the right reasons*: *why you can't scare bankers into doing the right thing*. This publication does not follow the instrumental and possibly cynical analysis of some commentators, who say that many traders (and their managers) in the financial sector are so driven by incentives that they will continue to do wrong, just being more careful about how they do it, for example not using traceable communications systems (Partnoy, 2015). Rather, PWC offer an affective analysis, according to which making bankers anxious by threatening sanctions only makes them worse—whilst promises of rewards would be more likely to elicit behaviours that are innovative yet ethical (Partnoy, 2015: 4-8). Clearly this is something that many in the financial markets would like to hear; and it is in line with the UK policy trend from 2015 onwards.

Indeed, during the first half of the 2000s, command regulation seemed to have run its course. There has been a backing-off from public enforcement, in favour of public regulation being "recalibrated", in order to be more "proportionate" (in the sense of being less onerous for regulatees). However, both the industry and the public regulators have found it difficult to assemble appropriate presentational rationales for this, lest it appear too soft. In the face of the financial crisis (still within popular memory) and the aforementioned scandals (which re-ignite awareness, if not indignation), any proposal that seemed simply to be going back to pre-crisis versions of self-regulation would not be politically sellable.

In 2015, the UK Treasury, Bank of England and Financial Conduct Authority proposed a compromise, in terms of a partnership between public and private actors, with the latter taking a hand in crafting standards and rules—thus hopefully then they might better understand and more frequently abide by them. So goes the logic of the Fair and Effective Market Review (FEMR) (HM Treasury, Bank of England, & Financial Conduct Authority, 2015).

Some commentators have questioned the extent to which this proposal differs from the pre-crisis arrangement (Binham & Dunkley, 2015). Others, however, have seen it as potentially effective on the grounds that (this time) the public regulator will be more proactive (O'Brien, 2015). This softer line was underlined by the non-reappointment of Martin Wheatley as chief executive of the FCA (Fortado, Parker, Arnold, & Binham, 2015).

Trade Guilds, Modernised and Internationalised

Here, for reasons of space and manageability, discussion focuses on the International Swaps and Derivatives Association (ISDA). ISDA is the predominant sectoral association for traders in derivatives. It acts as a private regulator in the two key senses of making rules (model contacts) and effectively adjudicating uncertainties and disputes for its members (through its Determinations Committees, abbreviated to DCs). The workings of the DCs are sometimes complex and, according to some irreverent commentators, are made by markets participants with conflicts of interest (Durden, 2015). Nevertheless, whereas some aspects of private regulation, such as the credit rating agencies, came through the financial crisis with greatly impaired reputational profiles, ISDA has come through smelling of roses. Both before and after the crisis, it seems to have been valued by public regulators, on the grounds that it fills what would otherwise be regulatory gaps. On this score, John Biggins and Colin Scott have made a number of very interesting studies of ISDA and they say as follows:

> Whilst continuing events associated with the global financial crisis (GFC) encourage stronger scrutiny by national and supranational governmental bodies of private governance arrangements such as ISDA, it is striking how embedded private governance arrangements remain. Indeed, the crisis was a key factor in further crystallising ISDA's role [...] At the same time, whilst the function remains privately organised, it is nonetheless capable of exerting 'socially significant' third party effects in certain circumstances. This may continue to raise certain legitimacy and transparency issues, especially in cases where sovereigns and publicly supported financial institutions are at issue. (Biggins & Scott, 2013: 29)

On that reading, guild-like regulation has internationalised and institutionalised itself in the derivatives sector. ISDA has managed to steer away from competition with public regulation, indeed it positions itself to take what might otherwise be donkey work from the later, and sometimes receives respectful invitations to take up issues (Biggins & Scott, 2013, 2016). Clearly, ISDA is not a closed book in the eyes of public regulators, even if the gaze of the public *per se* does not penetrate far into such trade associations.

Arbitration: "Dark Pools" of Private Justice

Proceeding further along the path from public to private, we arrive at the most private—particularly in terms of its visibility. One option in private law is for contracting parties to write into their relationship the provision that any disagreement of dispute arising from their contract is to be settled by an arbitrator.

Arbitration is private in two senses: it is a matter of private law (the parties to the contract pre-designating the private regime under which they would like disputes settled); and in some caces it is also private in the sense that the parties may agree on standard clauses to the effect that arbitral proceedings and outcomes will be without publicity. Nevertheless, arbitration has attracted public and political scrutiny—and some controversy—insofar as states may enter into treaties making them subject to arbitral decisions (for background see Cremona, 2015). In such cases, commercial rights-holders may allege that they have been damaged by public policies vis-à-vis, for example, tobacco policies, farming products and practices, or wider environmental and energy markets. Were public policy on financial markets to be subject to arbitral decision then the consequences could be non-trivial; for example states might be required to set aside regulation that restricts certain financial products or practices. However, the merits or otherwise of such possibilities are not the concern here, where the focus is the implications for public policy of arbitration between private parties.

The private system of arbitration *arguably* shapes private conduct and curtails public enquiry and policy making. Crucially, arbitration provides opportunities for participants in financial markets to develop their contractual relations in such a way that deepens the private nature of such relations and shuts out public law. With what potential consequences? This is an unrehearsed field and all we can do here is offer *some hypotheses*.

Firstly, if there is a public interest in policy makers, regulators and citizens having information about what is going on in a sector—for reasons of sectoral monitoring, prudential regulation or policy renewal, for example—then the privacy instituted by arbitration cuts across that public interest. Reporting of wrong-doing is outside the scope of arbitration: it is not a duty of an arbitrator to make even an anonymised report to public authorities. One can only speculate whether we would have known of the Goldman Sachs ABACUS case (above), had the parties had an agreement to go to arbitration. Maybe the facts would have become known, because they were so juicy, on the other hand perhaps not.

Similarly, if investors in a firm, counterparties in its transactions, trading exchanges or other conduits that it uses have any interest in knowing about failures in the firm's procedures or management, then such an interest will be blanked by the privacy afforded by arbitration. This could be comforting for particular senior executives but potentially worrying for those kept in the dark—who might take a sceptical view of arbitration or least of its privacy clauses—were they to consider the matter.

Thirdly, arbitration might increase willingness to take risks insofar as, if things go wrong, at least resolution can be private, thus safeguarding the reputations of firms and their senior staff. This could, for example, allow firms with high levels of reputational capital to risk doing business with firms with less high reputation. Arbitration brings with it speed and finality, as well as privacy, all of which could be considerations for firms when assessing their risk appetites.

To summarise issues of public and private regulation: sometimes public power is in the ascendancy (as seen in the years immediately following the financial crisis of 2007-9). Sometimes the regulatees get their hands back on the reigns (clearly the case from the mid-2010s onwards). But to complicate the picture and to make it less "either-or", there are many regulatory intermediaries, partners and cut-outs (mentioned here: compliance consultancies and contractors, audit and law firms, arbitration).

Conceptions for Policy Making: Money, Risk, Class

Limitations of Analysis in Regulatory Terms

So far, this chapter has identified some historical and contemporary processes—the clubby evolution of financial market regulation, the quite wide variety of private regulatory arrangements, and a dynamic between public and private regulation that favours the former following crises, the latter in "normal times". Even though public regulation is positively obliged to up its game at times of manifest crisis, as that moment fades there is a tendency to for the public form once again to cede ground, through processes of cognitive capture by the industry and support for "our" firms. Guild-like structures and processes then quite quickly resume their evolution both *within* and *beyond* public regulation.

This preoccupation with public and private is a paradigm within which the present author has worked for some years now. However, it may be a rather self-limiting paradigm for two reasons. First, whilst it is soundly based in historical terms—the "post crisis" swing back in favour of regulation that, whatever its institutional home and formal "ownership", is *functionally* private, nicely points up the historical dynamic—that historical evidence base might result in a sense of inevitability. Thus, TINA (There Is No Alternative): except during exceptional times, there is no alternative to regulation being in the sway of the market. Command regulation has its moments but it then collapses. Second, the regulatory paradigm may be too limiting. In order to move forward, regulation theory may need to displaced, or at least aided, by a different theoretical locomotive. That is what is sought in the remainder of this chapter.

Policy—as here distinguished from and indeed counterposed to regulation—is a form of intervention that shapes social, economic and geo-political relations, by addressing the question of purpose(s): what sort of financial markets are desired, to what ends? Examples of policy-making in this sense vis-à-vis include the 1970s opening up of the City of London to international competition (provoking the Wimbledon analogy that even if Britain hardly ever won, at least she staged the event); the creation of the Eurozone (a huge and also hugely flawed experiment); and current attempts to create a Capital Market Union (seen by elites as an overdue opening up of European niche markets, societies and cultures to the free movement of capital: Dorn, 2016). To be clear, this chapter does not champion those particular policy moves—each of which sought to extend the scale, scope and power of financial markets—rather the chapter takes them as exemplary of clarity and determination of transformative thinking.

The challenge for policy analysis going forward, discussed in the conclusion of the chapter, is to identify some options for reconstructing finance. Such an analysis can make use of recent work on the appeal, power and danger of financial markets, in terms of their extraction of wealth from the present, by pushing the corresponding debt into the future, causing episodic crashes and impoverishment.

Here we come to the crux of the political question of financial markets: what do financial markets actually do and how do they do it? The industry-standard and politically plain vanilla answer to that question has long been as follows. Banks and other financial traders serve the real economy and citizens, by making available investment and hence prosperity, employment and enjoyment. The banks do this by lending out the deposits of other customers who had previously deposited their money with the bank for reasons of safekeeping, accrual of interest over time, and transactional ease though the banking system (payments in from employers, payments out by cheque, plastic card, direct debit, Internet etc).

In that story, banks are simply *intermediaries*—they recirculate money that already exists. However, the intermediary story of banking is now widely thought to be at best incomplete and possibly plain wrong. As a Bank of England paper puts it:

> One common misconception is that banks act simply as intermediaries, lending out the deposits that savers place with them. In this view deposits are typically 'created' by the saving decisions of households, and banks then 'lend out' those existing deposits to borrowers, for example to companies looking to finance investment or individuals wanting to purchase houses (McLeay, Radia, & Thomas, 2014: 2).

The impact of the financial crisis and the global recession has undermined the credibility of the intermediary story of banking—or at least rendered it an incomplete account. Clearly, the money machine does not always work as advertised: sometimes it precipitates massive losses. How can such variations be explained?

Finance and Money Creation: A Raid on the Future

According to the new narrative, banks do not simply re-circulate existing money; they create new money, by making loans over and above their deposits.

> When a bank makes a loan, for example to someone taking out a mortgage to buy a house, it does not typically do so by giving them thousands of pounds worth of banknotes. Instead, it credits their bank account with a bank deposit of the size of the mortgage. At that moment, new money is created. For this reason, some economists have referred to bank deposits as 'fountain pen money', created at the stroke of bankers' pens when they approve loans (McLeay et al., 2014: 3; for various analogies, see Ravn, 2015)

This new understanding—which has been facilitated by our collective experience of crisis—is that the financial markets *create* money, or at least give the appearance of doing so. Commercial banks, meaning the ones on the high street, agree a loan: by which is meant they extend credit (quite often over and above any deposits they have previously taken in). Investment banks and other financial vehicles (sometimes called "shadow banks") similarly create so-called market liquidity through chains of transactions involving for instance securitisation products (e.g. futures and options) or repurchase agreements (basically similar to the business of a pawnshop). Through such operation money is created at least in the short and medium term.

One might ask, where does such money-like credit "come from"? The answer is that that it is not a material thing but a social and legal construction: a promise, against which the borrower is conventionally entitled to spend. As a promise it references the future. However, as Ravn (2015) has summarised in a useful explainer, its origins are historical.

> In the mid-1600's, many wealthy Londoners began storing their gold with goldsmiths, and they were given deposit receipts in return. These 'goldsmith's notes' began to circulate as money, as they were easier to carry and keep than the gold. Meanwhile, other people borrowed gold from the goldsmith's ample supplies. At some point, a goldsmith persuaded a prospective borrower to take a (fake) deposit receipt instead, since it was as good as gold. The goldsmiths wrote them out in increasing numbers, pretending the gold backing the receipts was actually in their vaults. (Ravn, 2015: 101)

Fast forward now to modern times. In the centuries from the seventeenth onwards, finance increasingly gained the upper hand over other parts of the economy and other social strata. By the twentieth century, there were insufficient counterweights to restrain its "infectious greed", to use Frank Partnoy's (2009) phrase. By the twenty-first century, the very large amounts that were being taken out of the financial markets in terms of profits and remunerations created the potential for an eventual painful denouement. As for the intellectual arena, there was a failure to recognise this profit-taking as a form of asset stripping. Finance theory held to a model of banking that was silent on such extractions, whilst maintaining that finance markets tended to equilibrium. Taking the relatively simple case of banking, theory had it that banks (and other financial entities) extend loans out of money which they already have taken in as deposits. No deposits taken in?—then no loan to give out: that was the dominant conception of banks' activities, until recently.

However, the financial crisis provided an intellectual shock, as well financial and political shocks, and the intermediary theory of banking is no longer found credible. Indeed, since the 1600s (Ravn, 2015), banks may give out money that they do not have. Banks *extent to their borrowers a promise* that they will pay them—and, crucially, those whom the latter need to pay (suppliers, workers etc)—as the costs arise in the future. The whole thing crucially depends on the credibility of the bank (or other credit-extender) and its promise. If and when confidence is dented and there is a run on the banking sector, then payment may not possible. The availability of money, indeed the very concept of money, depends on not everyone calling for it all at once. Put simply, contemporary financial markets involve a temporal splitting, such that profits may be defined and realised in T1, the here-and-now, whilst uncertainty and profit or loss is pushed into the future, to T2. The show stays on the road only insofar as the same (and more) splitting can be accomplishes at T2, referencing T3 and so on. The show stops and much consternation ensues when and if the perception develops that things might be amiss, as arose from 2007 onwards. Then the credit chain collapses and what is left is debt.

Whether profit, break-even or loss is crystallised *at any particular point in time* is a highly contingent matter. However, one factor that either hastens or delays the eventually inevitable crystallisation of loss can be identified: the level of remuneration within the financial sector. The greedier the culture of finance at a particular time, the faster is the extraction of benefit for (at least some of) those within the sector, and the faster is the piling up of losses, which have to go somewhere. This loss splits two ways, partly into private loss and partly into public loss:

(i) Some of the loss stays within the private sector—although typically not around the necks of its creators, most of whom have moved on quite smartly, taking with them their fees. In this sense, financial speculation is like a game of musical chairs: whoever is holding a chunk of junk when the music stops, then owns it. The impacts on the real economy are not just a sudden reduction in working capital but also a boomeranging of sentient into extreme caution; so, credit boom gives way to recession. As Andrew Haldane and his Bank of England colleagues put it: "much of the growth reflected the effects of higher risk-taking [...] risk-taking strategies generating excess returns to bank shareholders and staff. Subsequently, as these risks have materialised, returns to banking have reversed. In this sense, high pre-crisis returns to finance may have been more mirage than miracle" (Haldane, Brennan, & Madouros, 2010: 87).

(ii) Turning to the public sector, some of the private loss is socialised, meaning that it is transformed into public debt. This is done as a crisis management measure, in order to rescue the financial sector and all those who relay upon it. The undesirability of the moral hazards that are repeatedly created by public policy—tacit governmental support for the private creation of a wall of money, followed by crisis and bailouts, then by yet more money creation, this time by the public authorities—is widely recognised. Given the dual recessionary impacts—upon private and public finances—central banks then seek to ameliorate the situation. They take over the role of the commercial banks and shadow banks, creating new stocks of money: quantitative easing (QE) and its variants. This is warmly welcomed by the financial sector, re-inflating speculation, whilst doing little for the real economy, which is traumatised. As regards the productive economy such measures are, in the words of John Maynard Keynes, like "pushing on a string": most of the value largely stays within financial circles. This refuels the overall process.

Implications More Bleak than Minskian Analysis

The above (revisionist) view of finance as an inherently fragile process of money creation co-exists with—and to some extent builds upon—Hyman Minsky's work on Ponzi finance, Minsky, 2003; Dorn, 2010). Minsky refers to market confidence, with overconfidence building up in good times, fuelling an upswing, drawing in many "wannabe" investors and entrepreneurs, thus floating a raft of unsustainable businesses, as is eventually realised, causing a collapse.

Thus, Minsky could be taken to imply that—if only market actors themselves or, failing restraint on their part, governments could prevent or at least reduce the irrational exuberance of upswings and the panic and pessimism of downswings—then, theoretically at least, financial booms and busts could be ameliorated. However, the post-Minskian conceptualisation of finance as *inherently* temporal is bleaker. It implies that the problem is not only one of sentiment (behavioural economics, mass psychology, market herding) but also, and more importantly, is structural. Financial markets look to the future and push potential losses into it, in order to release profit in the here and now: that is what they are and what they do. When not only have loans been made incautiously, with money being created in order to do so, but also high profits having been taken out over the years, then the implied loss that has to be realised at some point is greater than "just" the amount of incautious loans made. Money creation, extraction and destruction are strongly tied together in a zero sum game. Thus, booms and crashes are thus inherent in financial markets, with change of sentiment not causing cycles but resulting from them, as symptom rather than cause.

From Risk Society to a Financial "Risk Class"

The question about money creation can be addressed by taking up and refining the currently deeply unfashionable concept of class. Traditionally, class has been thought about in terms of the political, social and economic relations between groups which co-exist contemporarily: landowners versus tenants, mill-owners versus proletarians and recently finance capital versus the rest. Such relations are between contemporaries. Going beyond this, some scholars are looking at class and finance in temporal terms.

Notably, Dean Curran, a Canadian sociologist, re-reads Ulrich Becks' "Risk Society" in social class terms, coming up with the idea of financiers as constituting a "risk class" (Curran 2015a, 2015b, 2016). What is risk class? According to Curran, it is not a class as such but rather a sub-set of the elite, with which it shares a general position of privilege, yet within which it is differentiated by its particular relationship to risk. The risk class gains massively on the upswings but loses comparatively little on the downswings.

> This mismatch between the benefits and costs of systemic financial risk vis-à-vis others leads to what might be called a type of risk arbitrage in which their private benefits from ratcheting up risk are greater than the private costs of these risks, whether these risks manifest themselves in actual losses or not. [...] In thinking through the transformations engendered by contemporary finance, it may be concluded that, rather than risk society and systemic financial risk spelling the end of class, the processes associated with risk society are actually serving to intensify existing class inequalities. (Curran 2015a: 20 & 21)

Credit creators push risk into the future, by creating a bridge of credit that, not only in terms of a few isolated instances but as a whole structure, may fall down at any moment. Neither they nor anyone else knows exactly when the risk will crystallise. Hence for Curran (2015a), financiers form a specific stratum within global elites, which can be designated in terms of "risk class" (though there may also be others, such as owners and operators of coal mines and power stations). Note that Curran is not saying that financiers constitute a class as such: risk class is more of a stratum or (as the present author prefers) a faction. The difference between this risk class/stratum/faction and economically dominant classes is that the former's activities extract value from the future, rather than from the present or the past. The future, when it arrives, is thus already impoverished.

Conclusion: Reframing Policy

Two forms of analysis of financial market regulation have been summarised here, concerning two dimensions of finance: public/private and present/future. The question with which this chapter concludes is whether analysis of public and private manifestations of regulation (command regulation, public–private negotiation, market association's rule-making, arbitral dispute resolution etc) can be taken into a future-aware, "risk class" analysis. This requires an exploration of the overall or meta-objective that may be desired for financial markets vis-à-vis their tendency to shift risks not only socially but also temporally. We briefly mention three meta-objectives: to partially or entirely suppress social and temporal and social risk-shifting; to apply the "polluter pays" principle to financial markets; or to attempt some "right-sizing" of finance.

If the policy objective would be to partially or entirely *suppress* such temporal and social risk shifting, then this would require curtailing the conditions for reproduction of the financial risk class. In such an endeavour, not only public regulation, but also the various modes of private regulation, might be assessed for their potential to assist or impede such suppression. Command regulation would become the dominant form of public regulation, with public regulators loath to slip back to the pre-crisis situation of setting out principles or broad rules and trusting financial markets to implement them in the spirit intended. Existing and well established zones of private regulation would be respected by public regulators only to the extent that such private regulation facilitated "patient capital" and long term investment. So, for example, private equity and crowd-sourcing might be encouraged, and their private regulation tolerated or even encouraged, insofar as they facilitate long term capital lock-in, with financiers having "skin in the game" (they carry substantial risk, rather than passing it to others). By contrast, derivatives trading, securitisation and their private regulators (such as ISDA, see above) would required to demonstrate that they do not facilitate the shifting of risk into the future. As for high frequency trading (HFT)—which operates for example by opening and closing a multitude orders, and has been blamed by some for triggering or deepening some serious market flash-crashes—such activities would be subject to much greater restrictions than is the case to date. Note, however, that HFT attracts not only withering criticism (Lewis, 2014) but also strong support (Benos, 2015).

Alternatively, should the meta-objective be to allow some, most or all forms of financial risk shifting but strictly on a "polluter pays" basis? Such an approach was quite widely discussed in public regulatory circles in the immediate aftermath of the crisis from 2007 onwards (Ferran, Moloney, Hill, & Coffee, 2012; Haldane, 2015; Turner, 2015), however, as of 2015, EU proposals for a Financial Transaction Tax were partially stalled (Gabor, 2015). One impediment is that, whilst producers of pollution (environmental or financial) may admit to such pollution, they also argue that the private and public goods that they facilitate, such as economic growth and popular enjoyment, are so desirable as to render the pollution acceptable. To the extent that policy makers buy that argument, they tend to ease restrictions on the associated risks—as evidenced by developments in the UK and the rest of the EU from the mid-2010s onwards (notably, support across most of the political spectrum for EU Capital Markets Union, the re-starting of securitisation and so on: Dorn, 2016). The attempt to push more risk into the future, in order to get out of a recession caused by past risk shifting, represents not so much the failure of policy learning—one respects policy makers sufficiently to consider that they do appreciate the implications of their strategies—but rather a perceived lack of palatable policy alternatives. The question addressed here, however, is not how to persuade policy makers, but what practical tools might be employed by public and private regulators, in order to raise sufficient funds from the industry today, so that such sums would be available in order to offset harms tomorrow. Judging from past crises, rather large contingency funds would be required. Yet to raise such contingency funds from the financial markets (as opposed from public sources) could presumably render swathes of modern financial markets unprofitable: after all, they *depend* on shifting risk into the future, in order to generate profit today. The industry would be in favour, if at all, only if the precautionary funds to be raised were very minor, rather than corresponding to future risks. However, the industry broadly is unhappy in principle about a tax based on a "polluter pays" rationale, since it goes against the preferred story of finance as a social good. Thus, the "polluter pays" approach may become indistinguishable, in practice, from the suppression model, above.

Finally, by way of practical example of the potential implications for public and private regulation, consider the concept of "right-sizing" finance. This means identifying the proportion of the economy that it should represent. There are at least two issues here. First, in the globalising space, it is not easy to identify the geo-political reference point for right-sizing: in the case of the City of London, for example, is the most appropriate reference point metropolitan London, the south east of England, the UK, the EU or possibly (see Davies, Richardson, Katinaite, & Manning, 2010) the world? Second, on what basis would the optimal size of finance—and sectors thereof—be judged? Explicit in right-sizing perspectives is the sense that the industry is too big; implicit is some historical frame of reference, when the industry was a smaller proportion of national (and indeed international) economies. By contrast, and from the perspective of the present chapter, the danger of historical nostalgia can be avoided if one shifts from the past to the future—concerning oneself not with a supposedly golden age, but rather with construction of scenarios about how *current* risk shifting strategies might "blow up" in future years, as today's gains crystallise as tomorrow's losses. Regulators would then seek to develop tools to manage such losses. That would require an assessment of the scale of future losses that *could* be managed, and of the political acceptability of doing so (as explicit public policy rather than technocratic contingency). Financial markets would then be right-sized accordingly. This might seem quite a minimal ambition.

All of this—the prospects for suppression, polluter pays or right-sizing—is a far cry from the image of finance as a golden goose, which can be fattened to everyone's eventual benefit. Clearly there is a normative dimension here as well as an analytical one.

Finally, it has to be underlined that it is still early days in the generation of a policy agenda drawing upon finance, time and risk-transfer. The key point is that, increasingly, regulators and scholars are once again thinking about financial markets in *social terms*: not just in terms of "machinery" that needs to be fine-tuned, but as something to be transformed. At the very same time, finance is escaping the straightjacket that was (temporarily it seems) placed on it as a response to the financial crisis. The upshot is a sense of discontinuity, when the policy intellect has become aware of something big, then shaken the idea aside in the spirit of business as usual.

References

Benos, W. (2015). *High-frequency trading and market quality: What's the deal?* Bank Underground blog, 6 November, London Bank of England, http://bankunderground.co.uk/2015/11/06/high-frequency-trading-and-market-quality whats-the-deal/#more-738.

Bernanke, B. (2008). *Addressing weaknesses in the global financial markets: The report of the President's working group on financial markets, April 10, Washington DC: Federal Reserve System.* http://www.federalreserve.gov/newsevents/speech/bernanke20080410a.htm.

Best, G. (2001). *Churchill: A study in greatness*. London: Hambledon.

Biggins, J., & Scott, C. (2013). *Private governance, public implications and the tightrope of regulatory reform: The ISDA credit derivatives determinations committees*. http://digitalcommons.osgoode.yorku.ca/cgi/viewcontent.cgi?article=1299&context=clpe.

Biggins, J., & Scott, C. (2016). Resolving the gaps: Embedding ISDA in states' responses to systemic sisk. In N. Dorn (Ed.), *Controlling Capital: Public and private regulation of financial markets*. Abington: Routledge.

Binham, C., & Dunkley, E. (2015). Banks score victory on ringfencing rules. *Financial Times*(15 October). http://www.ft.com/intl/cms/s/0/53986f2e-7317-11e5-bdb1-e6e4767162cc.html.

Cain, P. J., & Hopkins, A. G. (1987). Gentlemanly capitalism and British expansion overseas II: new imperialism, 1850-1945. *The Economic History Review, 40*(1), 1–26.

Corporate Observatory Europe. (2014). *The fire power of the financial lobby*. Brussels: Corporate Observatory Europe. http://corporateeurope.org/sites/default/files/attachments/financial_lobby_report.pdf.

Cremona, M. (2015). Guest editorial: Negotiating the transatlantic trade and investment partnership (TTIP). *Common Market Law Review, 52*(2), 351–362.

Curran, D. (2015a). Risk society and Marxism: Beyond simple antagonism. *Journal of Classical Sociology, 64*, 44–62. doi:10.1177/1468795X15600929. 10 September.

Curran, D. (2015b). Risk illusion and organized irresponsibility in contemporary finance: Rethinking class and risk society'. *Economy and Society, 44*(3), 392–417.

Curran, D. (2016). *Risk, power, and inequality in the 21st century*. New York, London: Palgrave Macmillan.

Daunton, M. J. (1989). "Gentlemanly Capitalism" and British Industry 1820-1914. *Past & Present, 122*, 119–158.

Davies, R., Richardson, P., Katinaite, V., & Manning, M. (2010). Evolution of the UK banking system. *Bank of England Quarterly Bulletin, 50*(4), 321–332.

Dorn, N. (2010). The Governance of Securities: Ponzi finance, regulatory convergence, credit crunch. *British Journal of Criminology, 50*(1), 23–45.

Dorn, N. (2015). *Democracy and diversity in financial market regulation*. Abingdon: Routledge.

Dorn, N. (2016). Capital cohabitation: EU capital markets union as pubic and private co-regulation. *Capital Market Law Journal, 11*(1), 84–102.

Durden, T. (2015). *ISDA Determinations Committee's "External Review", An Inside Job*. New York: ZeroHedge.com/ABC Media Ltd.. Blog page. New York: ZeroHedge.com/ABC Media Ltd. http://www.zerohedge.com/news/2015-01-12/isda-determinations-committee's-external-review-inside-job.

Engelen, E., Ertürk, I., Froud, J., et al. (2011). *After the great complacence: Financial crisis and the politics of reform*. Oxford: OUP.

Engelen, E., Ertürk, I., Froud, J., et al. (2012). Misrule of experts? The financial crisis as elite debacle. *Economy and Society, 41*(3), 360–382.

Ferran, E., Moloney, N., Hill, J., & Coffee, J. (2012). *The regulatory aftermath of the global financial crisis*. Cambridge: CUP.

Fortado, L., Parker, G., Arnold, M., & Binham, C. (2015). Martin Wheatley resigns as chief of Financial Conduct Authority. *Financial Times*(17 July). http://www.ft.com/intl/cms/s/0/61f867fa-2c76-11e5-8613-e7aedbb7bdb7.html.

Gabor, D. (2015). A step too far? The European financial transactions tax on shadow banking. *Journal of European Public Policy*. doi:10.1080/13501763.2015.1070894.

Gilligan, G. (1997). The Origins of UK Financial Services Regulation. *The Company Lawyer, 18*(6), 167–176.

Group, H. L. E. (2012). *High-level Expert Group on reforming the structure of the EU banking sector*. Brussels: European Commission. Chaired by Erkki Liikanen, 2 October. http://ec.europa.eu/finance/bank/docs/high-level_expert_group/report_en.pdf.

Haldane, A. (2015). *Who owns a company?* London: Bank of England. Speech given at the University of Edinburgh Corporate Finance Conference on 22 May. http://www.bankofengland.co.uk/publications/Pages/speeches/2015/833.aspx

Haldane, A., Brennan, S., & Madouros, V. (2010). What is the contribution of the financial sector: Miracle or mirage? In A. Turner (Ed.), *The future of finance: The LSE report* (pp. 87–120). London: LSE. http://www.lse.ac.uk/newsAndMedia/publications/books/2010/TheFutureOfFinance.aspx

Hardie, I., & Macartney, H. (2015). *Too Big to Separate? A French and German defence of their biggest banks*. Brussels: Finance Watch. Blog, 26 March. http://www.finance-watch.org/hot-topics/blog/1067.

Hellwig, M. (2009). Systemic risk in the financial sector: An analysis of the subprime-mortgage financial crisis. *De Economist, 157*(2), 129–207.

HM Treasury, Bank of England, & Financial Conduct Authority. (2015). *Fair & effective markets review: Final report*. Bank of England: London.

Independent Commission on Banking. (2011). *Final Report [and] Recommendations*. London: National Archives. September.

Lagarde, C. (2014). *Economic inclusion and financial integrity—An address to the conference on inclusive capitalism, London, 27 May*. Washington: IMF. https://www.imf.org/external/np/speeches/2014/052714.htm.

Lewis, M. (2014). *Flash boys: A wall street revolt*. New York: Norton.

McLeay, M., Radia, A., & Thomas, R. (2014). Money creation in the modern economy. In *Bank of England Quarterly Bulletin Q1*. London: Bank of England. 1–14.

Minsky, H. (2003). The financial instability hypothesis'. In G. Argyrous & F. Stilwell (Eds.), *Readings in political economy: Economics as a social science* (pp. 183–185). Melbourne: Pluto Press.

Nesvetailova, A. (2015). A crisis of the overcrowded future: Shadow banking and the political economy of financial innovation. *New Political Economy, 20*(3), 431–453.

O'Brien, J. (2005). The politics of enforcement: Eliot Spitzer, state-federal relations, and the redesign of financial regulation. *Publius: The Journal of Federalism, 35*(3), 449–466.

O'Brien, J. (2014). *The Triumph, Tragedy and Lost Legacy of James M Landis*. Oxford: Hart.

O'Brien, J. (2015). Turning the building blocks into a powerhouse: The global implications of the Fair and Effective Markets Review. *Law and Financial Markets Review, 9*(2), 87–89.

Palan, R. (2015). Futurity, pro-cyclicality and financial crises. *New Political Economy, 20*(3), 367–385.

Partnoy, F. (2009). *Infectious greed: How deceit and risk corrupted the financial markets*. New York: Public Affairs.

Partnoy, F. (2015). *Few traders are likely to be deterred by verdict on Tom Hayes*. Financial Times, 4 August. http://www.ft.com/intl/cms/s/0/9a1019b8-3a94-11e5-bbd1-b37bc06f590c.html.

Passas, N. (2005). Lawful but awful: "Legal corporate crimes". *Journal of SocioEconomics, 34*(6), 771–786.

Prudential Regulation Authority. (2015). *The implementation of ring-fencing: Prudential requirements, intragroup arrangements and use of financial market infrastructures, consultation paper CP37/15*. London: Bank of England.

Ravn, I. (2015). Explaining money creation by commercial banks: Five analogies for public education. *Real-World Economics Review, 71*, 92–111.

The Economist. (2007). *After the fall*. 29 November, London. http://www.economist.com/node/10208311.

Turner, A. (2011). *Reforming Finance: Are We Being Radical Enough? 2011 Clare Distinguished Lecture*. London: Financial Services Authority. February 18. http://www.fsa.gov.uk/pubs/speeches/0218_at_clare_college.pdf.

Turner, A. (2015). *Between debt and the devil: Money, credit, and fixing global finance*. New Jersey: Princeton University Press.

Wardley, D., Leitch, J., Cable, D., & Steinhage, A. (2015). *Stand out for the right reasons. Why you can't scare bankers into doing the right thing*. London: PwC and London Business School. http://pwc.blogs.com/files/why-you-cant-scare-bankers-into-doing-the-right-thing.pdf.

Weber, M. (2000). 'Stock and Commodity Exchanges' [re-printing of Die Börse (1894)]. *Theory and Society, 29*(3), 305–338.

Williams, J. (2015). Dodging Dodd-Frank: Excessive speculation, commodities markets, and the burden of proof. *Law & Policy, 37*(1-2), 119–152.

Part IV
Dick Hobbs' Influence on Theory and Methods

Chapter 18
"Keeping It Real": Dick Hobbs' Legacy of Classic Ethnography and the New Ultra-realist Agenda

Steve Hall and Simon Winlow

Having known and worked with Dick Hobbs for over three decades, it seems to us that in most of his work he was very keen to expose the vast chasm between the fleeting fragments of reality about which we can claim to have knowledge and the socially constructed fantasies that litter the pavements of both popular culture and academia. Dick utilized symbolic interactionism early on his career but he quickly moved beyond this tradition to develop a gritty realist approach that cut underneath the symbolic interactionist concerns with the conversational self and the structures of symbolic definitional power. He sought explanations of cultures, emotions, and subjectivities in the socioeconomic and geographical contexts in which ordinary people spend the bulk of their lives. It is this realist turn that we want to focus upon and present as the pinnacle of Dick's work. At a time when left idealism was dominant and in career terms it was dangerous to move beyond weak social constructivism, Dick forged ahead to reveal uncomfortable truths about working-class culture, crime, and business. At the very moment cultural theorists were instructing legions of eager graduate students to regard all representations of reality as mere social constructs, outcomes of the ability of powerful groups to utilize language in order to construct a narrative that can pass for truth, Dick presented to the pious liberal philanthropists of the university mainstream an image of reality that was authentic and born of an intimate relationship with the research field. His descriptive ethnographic work immediately grabbed us and demanded we pay attention. Here was a world that we both knew well, a world in which working-class conservativism exists in abundance, a world of shady business and occasional violence, a world of proletarian entrepreneurs on the lookout for a deal, a world of belly laughs, hangovers, and short-termism, but also a world of danger, sadness, and retreat. It was the kind of depiction of working-class life that only a true native can produce.

S. Hall • S. Winlow (✉)
School of Social Sciences, Business and Law, Teesside University, Middlesbrough, UK
e-mail: steve.hall@tees.ac.uk; s.winlow@tees.ac.uk

G.A. Antonopoulos (ed.), *Illegal Entrepreneurship, Organized Crime and Social Control*, Studies of Organized Crime 14, DOI 10.1007/978-3-319-31608-6_18

Dick developed a hugely successful career, but he did this against the odds. The liberal mainstream never really forgave him for moving beyond language and representation, or for ignoring the injunction to portray the working class as a collection of beautiful souls fighting the good fight against capitalist authoritarianism. In our view, if Dick had discovered cultural resistance to capitalism in working-class neighborhoods, rather than the working class's incorporation into capitalist dreams and adoption of capitalist dynamics, he would have found himself at the very top of the discipline in Britain far sooner, and his stay there would have lasted far longer. Too often his work was treated as an entertaining curiosity. As the liberal elite that dominates our discipline remained keen to bolster the myth of diversity in university life, Dick was figuratively assigned a pigeonhole and invited in. He was one of very few genuinely working-class sociologists working at an elite university during the 1980s. His career and reputation developed, but he was never really invited into the inner sanctum, and his work did not receive the broad recognition that contributors to this collection are certain it deserved.

Dick has now retired from the fray of British university life. No longer is he surrounded by the ideological policing, blatant careerism, and competitive instrumentalism that afflict our institutions. He will, thankfully, no longer have to cope with petty bureaucracy and the increasingly desperate scramble for research funding. He will no longer have to work in a discipline dominated by the liberal middle classes, who have little knowledge or understanding of the reality experienced by the vast majority of people, and, since the arrival of the cultural/linguistic turn, even shy away from the broader political and economic contexts in which it is embedded. No longer will he have to comment on new ethnographic work conducted in marginalized social locations by well-meaning elites keen to spend a few weeks among the proles of the revanchist city. He can watch the descent of the university from the side lines, secure in the knowledge that he made a huge contribution to our understanding of the British working classes and their involvement in crime and deviancy. Our great hope is that, in retirement, his work will attract the attention of a new generation of social scientists keen to throw off the shackles of the cultural turn in order to explore the real world and its manifold pathologies.

Realism—The Heart of Hobbs' Oeuvre

Dick would be the first to admit that he was never one for philosophy, especially the arcane metaphysical obscurantism of the great continental philosophers. He was too grounded in an analysis of everyday experience to waste time on such indulgences. However, he knew very well that cognate disciplines are interconnected whether their specialist practitioners like it or not, so it would not come as too much of a surprise to him that he presaged the current realist turn, now developing into *speculative realism* in continental philosophy. Or at least he presaged a particular strand of it—not the Latourian-influenced object-orientated ontology of Graham Harman but, to us, the more credible and tractable strand of Žižek-inspired transcendental materialism championed by Adrian Johnston (Johnston, 2008; see also Hall, 2012). In this short chapter there is no space to present a summary of this complex position, but suffice it to say that its thesis on how the subject postpones moral agency and political struggle as it becomes caught up in prevailing ideologies and practices has furnished us with an ontological platform for the ultra-realist agenda proposed by us in the field of criminological theory (Hall & Winlow, 2015; see also Raymen, 2015). Speculative realism enjoins us to move beyond phenomenology, to escape the fetid atmosphere of endless, misleading, and often pointless intersubjective to- and -froing in the interpretive field and head back out into the *great outdoors* (see Meillassoux, 2009) of the current capitalist world, with its proliferating material objects, abstract financial system, ubiquitous markets, and apologetically cynical humans trying each day with every fiber of their being to avoid the snakes and climb the ladders.

In his ethnographic work Dick has always headed for the *great outdoors* (ibid.); yet he did not need the headache-inducing metaphysics of new realist philosophy to persuade him. "Instinct" is not the sort of word we are encouraged to use in the social constructionist ghetto in which we have voluntarily trapped ourselves, but it does seem that something unarticulated was driving him out there. Sheer curiosity, well known as the lifeblood of philosophy and science, but perhaps not encouraged to circulate too freely these days. Whatever it was, the *great outdoors* is where he was comfortable, not trapped in the internal struggle to achieve moral and ideological purity in a politically neutralized and increasingly insular and unworldly liberal academia. Too much energy is currently devoted to the production of ethically pristine and ideologically sound ideas that are too beautiful to represent the world outside with any integrity or clarity. Thus we constantly fail to capture the disintegrating world of late capitalism with its surreal complexity, and therefore fail in our efforts to construct a reliable platform, as an assemblage of experiences and parallax views, on which we can build convincing theory.

Dick always showed a healthy disrespect for an academic world currently dominated by a rather traditional middle-class liberal agenda replete with its myriad turd-polishing activities. Western intellectuals have largely accepted the dominance of the market in every dimension of our lives (see Winlow & Hall, 2013). To many of them, telling truths about its consequences as inevitable, if not always predictable, products of its internal logic seems pointless. As long as we have known him he showed a keen awareness of the Darwinian competition for status and money that is disavowed and masked by faux radicalism and some of the most comically transparent hypocrisies one could find. He was consistently critical of liberal societies' theatrical benevolentism, which in basic socioeconomic terms is always *ex post facto* and never structured into the icy logic of the business transactions that dominate our everyday lives. Dick was aware that the market was eating away and replacing all alternative human institutions, a vital insight he shared with the new Mertonians and social democrats (Messner & Rosenfeld, 2000; Reiner, 2007).

Dick was able to accept this rather daunting reality of late capitalism *as it is*, in the cold light of day rather than the dense fog of defunct and deaptative ideology. One of the reasons he was able to make this vital move back to the real was his rejection of the extremes of the Thompsonite (Thompson, 1996) romance of timeless dissent, resistance, and political agency. This myth is prevalent—one might say dominant—on the radical side of criminology's fence. In place of what has proven itself to be a politically and intellectually debilitating romance (see Winlow, Hall, Treadwell, & Briggs, 2015) he substituted a keen eye for rich description of those people who were determined to survive and prosper in the conditions that late capitalism continues to lay down for them on evermore unforgiving terms. His work showed the absence of politics in these environments, and as such it is significantly more valuable because it prevents the false hope that in the long run produces nothing at all, and shows us—whether intentionally or unintentionally, it does not matter—how much work, and precisely what sort of work, politics has to do in order to return to a transformative mode.

One real transformative social process of which Dick was aware was the transition from the proletarian to the mobile entrepreneurial worker, which helped to loosen the sociocultural bonds that once promised political solidarity but never delivered. He expended a considerable amount of energy charting shifts in working-class criminal enterprise throughout history (see, for example, Hobbs, 1988, 2013). His work made it quite clear that this was not something that suddenly appeared out of the wreckage of Western industrial life but a tradition that in the postindustrial period spread more virulently and became more visible than it had been during the industrial period. His work was replete with sharp detail and analysis. To label Dick Hobbs an apolitical cynic, which one or two occasionally did under their breath, would be to shoot the messenger, a foolish move that betrays a far deeper cynicism based on the avoidance of any honest inquiry into the deep causes behind the bad news that the messenger brings. Without the understanding that such honest inquiry brings no real effective politics will ever return in our lifetime. The understanding that Dick's work brought to us was based on the resilience of the human being forced into circumstances he did not choose, combined with a deep understanding of the extent of the difficulties working-class people face and the tendency for so many to conform to prevailing ideology. Better that those of us intent on political transformation know what we are up against than continue to be trapped in an imaginary realm replete with forces of organic resistance that do not exist in any effective, substantive form (Hall & Winlow, 2007).

Dick's ethnographic work was served by an insatiable curiosity and a keen eye for the details of how cultures emerge in specific environments that are not of the subject's choosing. However, his work was not sullied by the sort of Kantian disinterestedness that often characterizes the work of ethnographers steeped in the anthropological tradition. He was painfully aware of how difficult it is for a community to survive in the midst of a capitalist world that sanctifies nothing other than the commodity and prioritizes and enforces its own fundamental exchange relation in most human transactions. The combination of curiosity and empathy allowed him to pick out the sort of fine details that others miss, details which prove essential for a convincing analysis that provides insights into the relationships between structural conditions, meaning, the human actor, and its motivations and daily practices. A lot of political work coming online these days is being far more honest and outspoken about the daunting issue of why the majority have acquiesced to a system that makes their lives far more difficult than they could be. Dick Hobbs helps us to answer that crucial question, and in the future, when current ideological dogmas dissipate and we can return to the task of explaining the world as it is and how it might be made better in tangible ways, it will prove to be invaluable.

In Dick's work we can often find the sort of brutal honesty that might make some of us flinch, or make others despair, but one thing we never find is stigmatization. Following the legacy of the original Chicago School ethnographers, whatever condemnation or questioning might be warranted is always balanced by empathy and appreciation. We are dealing with human beings whose practices do not always reflect their ethical being, and, even where this might be the case, could have been very different human beings in different circumstances. This balance helps us to understand just how flawed many of social science's concepts actually are, and it is achieved by combining selected Geertzian methodological principles with a far keener awareness and understanding that Geertz and his flowers had of the underlying economic conditions and logic that the less well-connected and educationally loaded precariat are forced to confront every day.

What he opens up is the working-class world after deindustrialization, but with none of the optimistic platitudes supplied by the community development industry, the threat of poverty and insignificance combined with cynicism and loss of solidarity to lumber the working class with a debilitating load to bear. He shares a deep sense of absence with the likes of Currie (2008), an understanding that sometimes evades middle-class liberal commentators whose lives have certainly changed but have not undergone the profoundly disruptive transformations that have resonated throughout the economic, social, and cultural dimensions of working-class life. Thus Dick furnished sociology with an essential and truthful working-class perspective in rich detail, complete with a well-developed analytical context. It should be central to the social scientific endeavor, but it is too often marginalized by a dominant Panglossian current that picks out aspects of progress but ignores the huge pile of socioeconomic and cultural wreckage in which large numbers of people are trapped and have little choice but to eke out a living and forge an identity. This is wilful ignorance of course, because nobody—least of all a professional social analyst—with even minimally functioning senses and sensibilities could fail to notice this very large elephant in the room.

Dick is one of the few sociologists to admit that the allure of consumer culture can more often than not displace the general conditions of alienation and apathy that exist amongst many of the deproletarianized working class. Even the more experienced and celebrated leftist intellectuals tend to distinguish categories of alienation, apathy, and consumer incorporation and thus fail to see the reproductive relations between them (see, for example, Lea, 2015). The orthodox and poststructural left in general (see, for example, Hall, 1988) seems to be unaware of consumerism's ability to act as a surrogate symbolic order, filling the vacuum left by the disappearance of traditional working-class culture and political organization in the post-political world and laying down the master signifier of symbolically competitive, hyper-individualized late-modern subjectivities. However, many amongst the new generation of sociologists and criminologists are beginning to acknowledge this difficult issue and produce a growing corpus of sophisticated analyses (see Buccellato & Reid, 2014; Hayward, 2012; Horsley, 2014a, 2014b, 2015; Miles, 2014; Raymen, 2015; Smith, 2014), which of course bodes very well for the future. The nuances of this relation were beautifully captured in Dick's latest book, *Lush Life* (2013), in which he marshaled a large amount of highly detailed data to quite firmly implant excessive consumer desire amongst the primary motivations to acquisitive crime.

Today's structural conditions are not a direct cause of crime. Crime is not new but a tradition embedded in the conditions and the mentalities of the past. For Dick, who left behind the worst excesses of social constructionism but retained the functional core to criticize truly inappropriate ideas, "organized crime" was a flawed concept we should leave behind. The concept was constructed by political and media institutions as an "other," something alien to our own way of life. Dick was not blind to this fundamental ideological maneuver, which attempted to remove everything bad about our own way of life before projecting it onto something else—something dark, mysterious, predatory, and threatening, something which should be met with repression. He also drew attention to the deeply xenophobic and racist connotations of such a way of thinking about the world (see, for example, Hobbs & Antonopoulos, 2013). However, defying the Derridean injunction not to reconstruct what has been deconstructed, and immediately reverting back to realism, Dick became one of the leading voices behind the sociological reconceptualization of contemporary criminal activity as loose, fluid networks of entrepreneurial individuals.

Throughout his career Dick was a consummate chronicler and analyst of the complex mutation and normalization of illegal markets and criminal activities in the wreckage of industrialism. At a deeper level he revealed the logical and subjective sources of (dis)organized crime in our own way of life, the dark heart of capitalism that destroys communities, solidarity, and its own thin moral crust in its remorseless quest for commodification and profit. His work revealed in great detail a dynamic logic that determines everyday practice and a subjectivity which internalizes and eventually solicits this logic, a subjectivity which desires its symbolic rewards and seeks them out with perhaps not quite as much care for the well-being of others that was once expected in many working-class communities. This economic logic itself is not a strict determinant, and of course individuals are not mere dupes, but, in the current postindustrial consumer-capitalist period of our history, it seems able to cultivate and solicit the subjective pleasure that individuals seek as they are incorporated into its shifting constellation of symbols and sensations. Hobbs was more aware of this than many others who still cling on to romantic notions of resilient subjective autonomy and organic resistance.

Whereas some rather purist commentators on the left defend the timeless virtues of the working class no matter what, and commentators on the right are all too keen to condemn large sections of the working class as feckless and immoral, Dick was aware of the connections between the "upperworld" and the "underworld." Specific individuals operating in both of these positions in the social structure seem to be driven by variations of the same predatory logic that energizes the capitalist system as a whole and drives it forward. In fact he was one of the first criminologists to understand the rather grim reality that crime and its motivations transgressed norms and laws, but not this central logic and subjective desire (see Hall, Winlow, & Ancrum, 2008). He never used the term "pseudo-pacification" (see Hall, 2012), but throughout his career he was describing and analyzing the forms, practices, and consequences of this socioeconomic and historical process in great detail.

It has to be said that Dick was never too explicit about his theoretical frameworks, apart from early discussions of symbolic interactionism and his later move, in *Bad Business* (Hobbs, 1995), to a more Baumanesque framework, but his work was so rich with data and analysis that he did not like to waste too much space discussing them. In conversations he often demonstrated that he was well aware of them, and his awareness of their limitations deterred him from carrying a torch for any particular theory. He found synthesis difficult and in many ways rather pointless because the proliferation of theories in criminology from various one-dimensional political and cultural standpoints had created what he called an "off-key karaoke" (Hobbs, 2013). He preferred to get away from this cacophonous noise and the fetid atmosphere of the karaoke joint, with its narcissistic punters pushing past each other to seek the limelight, to ground his thinking in the cold light of day. To us this was a good decision, which, had he not taken it, would have denied us all the legacy of rich data and analysis that will remain with the discipline for the foreseeable future.

This is not to say that Dick's work was atheoretical, though. As we have said, he had started with orthodox symbolic interactionism, but quickly recognized its limitations and moved quite organically through Bauman towards an unspoken critical realist approach, exploring below the superficial empirical level of phenomena through the actual level of events and interpretations to the real level of structures and processes, all the time making incisive connections between these levels. The richness of his data and the honesty of its presentation allowed him to make these intellectual connections in a convincing manner, which he did far more effectively than most other ethnographers. For this reason alone his work is a beacon for the younger generation to follow, not to mention a detailed picture of life out there for theorists to ponder as they select the corroborations and risk the falsifications that are necessary to construct more convincing explanations of the social world.

Above all, though, Dick's work provides us a seminal example of the sociological awareness of fluidity, mutation, and the fleeting and often volatile collaborations that melt away as quickly as they come into being, often quicker than can be observed, certainly by a sociological discipline that too often seems too reluctant to fund vital qualitative forays into the reality of our times. His work provides more evidence than we need to prove the assertion that the term "crime" is conceptually confused and not statistically mappable. This is the sort of honesty and unflinching detail that should make administrative positivists and critical criminologists alike more wary than ever about resting analyses of the consequences of structural change and human agency on such a nebulous concept. Dick rarely discussed the notion of harm and the fledgling subdiscipline of zemiology, but his work can be used to put forward a strong case for criminology to challenge its current ontological assumptions and move onto this more fertile territory (see Hall & Winlow, 2015).

In fact, when pointing to the usefulness of Dick Hobbs' work for future criminology we can risk going a little further. Because he stuck to his guns throughout the procession of philosophical and theoretical fads that have waylaid and distracted social science since the 1980s, he has bequeathed us with huge vat of rich empirical detail and sociological analysis, most of which—especially his mid-career and later work—was constructed in a way that was unaffected by the questionable concepts and ontological frameworks these fads foisted upon us. His work was rather like a lifeboat—durable enough to survive the storms and land its passengers alive on the shore. These passengers have vital stories to tell. Now, with a turn back to an unflinching realism in philosophy, which we hope will eventually—although we are under no illusion that in an intellectual world still trapped in the positivist and Kantian interpretivist paradigms this will be anything less than a tough struggle—inspire social science to move in the same direction.

For us, personally, as we try to break through the current meta-paradigm to argue the case for a new *ultra-realist* project that might move criminological theory forward (Hall & Winlow, 2015; Raymen, 2015), Dick's work will remain with us as a constant source of detail and analysis. Whether Dick will like this project or not we do not know, but we are sorry to tell him that, either way, he is partly to blame for it. Very briefly, though, the ultra-realist project rests on the ambition of:

> *[…] cutting through the prohibitions placed on research and theorization by criminology's current dominant and subdominant authorities—i.e. neoclassical realism and left idealism—ultra-realism can open up parallax views, or new perspectives from previously obscured angles that create changes in the observational positions and displacements of the objects in view. Both the powerful and the abject social classes experience important concrete universal truths in their social spaces; truths that have been denied prominent positions in criminology's research programmes and storehouse of knowledge. It is the task of ultra-realist criminological research and theorization to open up these spaces and throw some light on revealed truths as symptoms of underlying causes and contexts* (Hall & Winlow, 2015, p. 2).

In this way ultra-realism seeks to answer the crucial Gramscian and Althusserian question and move beyond critical realism—which tends to separate the autonomous moral agent from the "real" dimension of structures and processes—to theorize the subject's incorporation as a willing reproductive agent in the system, and its "refusal to refuse." As Thomas Raymen explains:

> *[…]ultra-realism as a theoretical position builds upon and moves beyond a left realist Mertonian position and draws upon Žižek's transcendental materialism to offer a more comprehensive conceptualization of harmful subjectivities and the tensions between psychosocial drives and cultural-economic conditions in liberal capitalism* (Raymen, 2015)

We have to admit that no total "God's eye view" of the world is possible, but neither should we adhere to the Kantian interpretivist injunction to remain trapped in the minds of others. This injunction has led to the subjective, cultural, and epistemological separatism that postmodern culturalists have attempted to popularize. We are convinced that an assemblage of parallax views, enriched concepts, sophisticated theory, and detailed observation and analysis of the *great outdoors* can move us forward as we try to connect the particular to the universal.

Dick Hobbs' work is saturated with such parallax views and concrete universals. This is not surprising, because it has always been driven by the avowed intent to get underneath orthodox perspectives and grapple with the complex realities of everyday life *as they are* in their social and economic contexts. It never presented the individual as a mere dupe of ideology, but neither does it swing the pendulum too far and naively separate the subject as a moral agent from the logic of practice demanded by the economic environments in which we are all compelled to live, and by the historical reproduction of cultural norms and subject positions that are not nearly as easy to discard as middle-class liberal thinkers might like to imagine. Above all, throughout his work he was at pains to remind us that when we abandon every dimension of human life to the brutal logic and unpredictable outcomes of the market, we should not be so naïve as to expect what the best of us wish for.

Before we finish this brief chapter, we should perhaps offer a personal note of gratitude. Dick Hobbs acted as Winlow's PhD supervisor, and he worked with both Winlow and Hall on an ESRC project investigating Britain's burgeoning nighttime economy and the occupational role of bouncers within it (Hobbs et al., 2003). On this project Hobbs and Hall also gave Winlow his first full-time academic job as a research assistant. Had Dick not chosen to take on the task of supervising Winlow's PhD, Winlow would have left academic life behind and drifted into God-knows-what. It is not too dramatic to say that Winlow is now a fully tenured and well-published academic specifically because Hobbs was willing to take a chance on a young working-class lad who did not fit the standard academic stereotype and did not at that time carry with him the standard academic skills and cultural capital. Given that Winlow is every bit as rough around the edges as his mentor, this brief observation may further encourage the liberal mainstream's opprobrium and the tendency of many of them to dismiss Hobbs' oeuvre. Of course, we see things very differently. As we have suggested above, his work will remain of considerable utility for generations of scholars keen to understand the reality of working-class life. His enduring realism and commitment to depicting the world as it is have ensured that he leaves a truly important legacy. While some of our colleagues in sociology and criminology departments across the country might remember Hobbs as a little rough around the edges, these characteristics represented his background and real-world experiences, and he was not willing to abandon them in order to curry favor among our disciplinary elites. We fitted together well, and we owe him a lot.

References

Buccellato, J. A., & Reid, I. D. (2014). Obscene remainders: Neoliberalism and the gang crisis narrative. *Journal of Theoretical and Philosophical Criminology, 6*(2), 129–144.

Currie, E. (2008). *The roots of danger*. New York: Prentice Hall.

Hall, S. (1988). *The hard road to renewal*. London: Verso.

Hall, S. (2012). *Theorizing crime and deviance: A new perspective*. London: Sage.

Hall, S., & Winlow, S. (2007). Cultural criminology and primitive accumulation: A formal introduction for two strangers who should really become more intimate. *Crime, Media, Culture, 3*(1), 82–90.

Hall, S., & Winlow, S. (2015). *Revitalizing criminological theory: Towards a new ultra-realism.* London: Routledge.
Hall, S., Winlow, S., & Ancrum, C. (2008). *Criminal identities and consumer culture: Crime, exclusion and the new culture of narcissism.* Cullompton: Willan.
Hayward, K. (2012). Pantomime justice: A cultural criminological analysis of 'life stage dissolution'. *Crime, Media, Culture, 8*(2), 213–229.
Hobbs, D. (1988). *Doing the business.* Oxford: Oxford University Press.
Hobbs, D. (1995). *Bad business.* Oxford: Oxford University Press.
Hobbs, D., Hadfield, P., Lister, S., & Winlow, S. (2003) Bouncers: Violence and Governance in the Night-time Economy. Oxford: Oxford University Press.
Hobbs, D. (2013). *Lush life.* Oxford: Oxford University Press.
Hobbs, D., & Antonopoulos, G. A. (2013). Endemic to the species': Ordering the 'other' via organised crime. *Global Crime, 14*(1), 27–51.
Horsley, M. (2014a). The 'Death of Deviance' and the 'Stagnation of Twentieth Century Criminology'. In M. Dellwing, J. Kotarba, & N. Pino (Eds.), *The death and resurrection of deviance: Current research and ideas.* Palgrave Macmillan: New York, NY.
Horsley, M. (2014b). Censure and motivation: Rebalancing criminological theory. *CrimeTalk (Online).* Available at: http://www.crimetalk.org.uk/index.php?option=com_content&view=article&id=933:censure-motivation&catid=38&Itemid=41.
Horsley, M. (2015). *The dark side of prosperity: Late capitalism's culture of indebtedness.* Farnham: Ashgate.
Johnston, A. (2008). *Zizek's ontology.* Evanston, Ill: Northwestern University Press.
Lea, J. (2015). Back to the future: Neoliberalism as social and political regression. *Journal on European History of Law, 1*, 109–117.
Meillassoux, Q. (2009). *After finitude.* London: Continuum.
Messner, S., & Rosenfeld, R. (2000). *Crime and the American dream.* New York: Wadsworth.
Miles, S. (2014). Young people, "Flawed Protestors" and the commodification of resistance. *Critical Arts, 28*(1), 76–87.
Raymen, T. (2015). Designing-in crime by designing-out the social? Situational crime prevention and the intensification of harmful subjectivities. *British Journal of Criminology.* doi:10.1093/bjc/azv069.
Reiner, R. (2007). *Law and order.* Oxford: Polity.
Smith, O. (2014). *Contemporary adulthood in the night-time economy.* London: Palgrave Macmillan.
Thompson, E. P. (1996). *The poverty of theory.* London: Merlin Press.
Winlow, S., & Hall, S. (2013). *Rethinking social exclusion: The end of the social?* London: Sage.
Winlow, S., Hall, S., Treadwell, J., & Briggs, D. (2015). *Riots and political protest: Notes from the post-political present.* London: Routledge.

Chapter 19
"In There Like a Dirty Shirt": Reflections on Fieldwork in the Police Organization

James Sheptycki

Introduction[1]

Long ago, sociologists of deviance propounded the "appreciative stance" in relation to their research subjects (Downes & Rock, 2011; Matza, 1969). This approach advocates that, even when studying deviant and criminal group behavior, academic researchers should seek to view the situation from the point of view of their research subjects. In the manner of Clifford Geertz, rather that condemning or condoning a particular manner of social life, the job of the ethnographer is to provide an authentic and appreciative "thick description." Since then, a variety of close observational studies of criminal life have adopted a naturalistic stance (e.g., Anderson, 2000; Goffman, 2014; Wacquant, 2004; Wright, Decker, & Shover, 1997), but few ethnographers of criminal life have sustained the required research access for an entire career (cf. Hobbs, 1988, 1995, 2013). On the other side of the fence, so to speak, there is also a tradition of naturalistic ethnographic inquiry, but instead looking at the lifeworld of police (eg. Hobbs, 1988; Hobbs, Hadfield, Lister, & Winlow, 2003; Leibling, 2000; Manning, 1980; Manning & van Maanen, 1978; Young, 1991). Reading this ethnographic research "from both sides of the fence" and bringing it together helps us to better understand the social and political construction of serious and organized crime. This chapter reflects on recent fieldwork undertaken in an intelligence unit in a large North American urban police department and places it in the context of this research tradition and in the context of my own biography. Specifically, it dwells on the dilemmas that the sociological researcher encounters in adopting an appreciative mode of enquiry when the social practices under

[1] The research upon which this paper is based has been supported by the Social Science and Humanities Research Council of Canada (Insight Grant No. 435-2013-1283).

J. Sheptycki (✉)
Faculty of Liberal Arts and Professional Studies, York University, Toronto, ON, Canada
e-mail: jshep@yorku.ca

G.A. Antonopoulos (ed.), *Illegal Entrepreneurship, Organized Crime and Social Control*, Studies of Organized Crime 14, DOI 10.1007/978-3-319-31608-6_19

consideration involve the police. The chapter is grounded in some very preliminary observations about the politics of policing gun-crime in Toronto and considers my own idiosyncratic fieldwork experiences from a personal and political point of view.

Some Background

The practice is *fieldwork* and it has been described by Hobbs and Wright as referring to the "research practice of engaging with others on their own turf, exotic or otherwise, in order to describe their cultural practices, understandings and beliefs" (2006, p. x). I wanted to "enter the field" when I became a graduate student at the London School of Economics in 1986, but was clueless about the reality of doing so. Enthused by reading Ned Polsky's *Hustlers, Beats and Others* (1967) as an undergraduate, I had some vague ideas about doing something similar. At the time I had a number of friends and acquaintances from my Essex University days living in London who were living the consequences described by Nick Dorn and Nigel South in *A Land Fit for Heroin* (1987). Via this network I had found my way into the social world of people living in several squatted buildings and low rent accommodations scattered between Gray's Inn Road near Rosebery Avenue, north westwards to Battlebridge Road near Kings Cross Station. From my safe perch in a 1920s Art Deco mansion block on Judd Street, I would foray out into the dark world of quasi-proto-anarchist squatters from time to time, and wonder about how to turn it all into a doctoral thesis. However, I was having trouble turning the everyday doings in these places into anything like sociology, not least because I found it difficult to turn my erstwhile companions into research subjects.

It was in this context that I first encountered Dick Hobbs who, despite having not yet then quite completed and published the results of his doctoral research, was already a highly regarded ethnographer with a promising future. Hobbs was unlike any other person that Paul Rock and David Downes brought into their graduate seminars at the LSE for the improvement of their would-be students. His big personality, tale-telling, confidence as a sociologist and, above all, his mastery of London street argot made for an unbeatable criminological persona. Hobbs was already the Clifford Geetrz of British criminology and he showed it with his sense of "deep play" and his ability to provide authentic "thick descriptions" of a shady lifeworld few academic criminologists ever directly encounter. I was beginning to realize that my very comfortable, white, middle-class existence made a great pretense out of my fruitless ethnographic forays into the field, a pretense which came close to validating Liazos' condemnation of the sociology of deviance (1972). It was during that time that the first edition of Robert Reiner's *The Politics of the Police* (1985) was published and "police studies" did not then exist, although policing would be a self-evident research field by the time I completed my studies at LSE in 1991. Along with my good friend Ben Bowling, during those years I gradually focused my academic thinking and research onto the police lifeworld and away from crime per se. Undoubtedly, we were influenced in our thinking by Paul Rock's efforts to define the history of British criminology (1988), as well as the then current left-realist *Aufhebung* as exemplified in the study of crime, victimization and policing in inner-city London (Jones, Maclean, & Young, 1986).

Years later, and with quite a lot of practical research experience behind me, I joined the Department of Sociology and Social Policy at Durham University. Hobbs had already been there for some years and a group of young researchers had gravitated there as well.[2] It sometimes felt like I had wandered into the plot of a Guy Ritchie film. Professionally speaking, my research work was strictly behind police lines, while Dick's was most certainly not. At the time I was involved in a project for the UK Home Office concerning strategic criminal intelligence and organized crime and job shadowing police liaison officers in Europe. Hobbs and his crew were focusing on the night-time economy. I remember conversations and vivid stories from that work (which usually took place in the Dun Cow pub on Old Elvet Street) besides which observations from my own fieldwork seemed rather prosaic and dull. His was the authentic academic voice theorizing organized crime in England. On the other hand, I was a rootless cosmopolitan who drew on globalization theory in order to better understand the trope of transnational organized crime. Still, we had something in common—even if I was more intrigued by James Clifford's (1997) anthropology of global flows and he remained more Geertzian; more interested in the ethnography of local places (Hobbs, 1998). The feature word in *Bouncers* was "liminality"—policing the threshold—a *space between* where bouncers controlled (sometimes with great violence) a "liminal space" between outside and inside. Thinking about it now, it strikes me that this is a really interesting metaphor describing the practice of ethnographic fieldwork that is especially salient when it comes to the worlds of crime and policing. Crossing the limen to the secret social worlds of either police or villains is tricky. It is easier to read about policing theory in the library and safer to stay at home and contemplate the drama of crime in the media. Ethnographic transgressions are a more interesting and certainly more challenging way to gauge the complexities of social control. Ethnography is all the more fascinating because, in the practice of fieldwork, we can discover as much about ourselves as we can about the social world we wake up in. Dick Hobbs is one of those important scholars who helped to create and sustain the conditions for people who believe that the answers to the most general questions—why? how? what?—to the degree that they have answers at all, are to be found in the fine details of lived life (Geertz, 2000, p. xi).

Another Town Another Project

I left Durham in 2004 looking for new horizons in Canada, while trying to maintain an active presence in British criminology. In 2007 I published an essay in a collection edited by David J. Smith and Alistair Henry concerning the practice of ethnography

[2] I well remember Stuart Lister, Phil Hadfield, Rob Hornsby and James Hardie-Bick, with whom I became close friends.

in "the house of serious and organized crime" (Smith & Henry, 2007). In that paper, I suggested that the doctrine of national security and the increasing climate of secrecy surrounding the practices of policing would make it very difficult to undertake anthropological-type studies of police, especially when it came to the more involved types of policework. At Durham, Hobbs and I had been discussing the creeping expectations that ethnographic fieldwork be subjected to the same sorts of ethical constraints as, for example, medical research. The demand for "informed consent" would, we thought at the time, pose considerable practical difficulties for us. In order to do ethnographic research inside the police organization, it is necessary for the researcher to overcome substantial bureaucratic hurdles designed to protect the institution. Conversely with observation of people and groups on the other side of the fence, the difficulties of obtaining the research access and social trust necessary for creating an accurate, credible and persuasive ethnographic description, would render signed consent forms totally counter-productive. Neither police nor villains are likely to agree to put their autographs on consent forms of the sort that sociologists in more conventional settings are now obliged to use—both groups are tainted (sociologically speaking) and, in such contexts, research consent forms feel rather like signing an admission of guilt. It seemed to me then, and it remains the case, that in studying powerful institutions such as large urban police organizations, the social power they wield is a more than sufficient brake on a research practice that is minimally invasive into the personal lives of people who are, in fact, public servants "on the job." With rising demands that ethnographers obtain written consent and increasing pressure on police institutions to tighten up in the name of "national security," it seemed at the time that the future of direct observational research on police institutions was less than auspicious.

I had moved to Toronto to take up a post at York University and was casting around for new research possibilities, but the situation in Toronto was not conducive. There had not been a sustained ethnographic study of police in the region since Richard V. Ericson conducted his fieldwork in the late 1970s. The published results of that research had been explosive (Ericson, 1981, 1982). In the ensuing decades there had been an ongoing war of words between local police and academic commentators of all sorts (e.g., Beare & Murray, 2007; Harvey & Liu, 2003; Jackson, 1994; McMahon & Ericson, 1984; Wortley & Tanner, 2003) and it had become unthinkable that a locally based scholar would undertake a naturalistic study of policing from the inside. There were then at least three good reasons why it was unlikely that I would be able to undertake an immersive ethnography in the police environment in Toronto. Firstly, the rise in national security concerns leant increasing emphasis to the perceived need for secrecy within policing institutions. Secondly, research ethics approval requirements had become impractical in the context of crime and policing. Thirdly, and perhaps the most salient in the context, relations between academic commentators and police agencies in the region were distinctly un-cooperative (not to say poisonous).

Despite the daunting challenges, I set about trying to make my way into the game. 2005 had been christened by the local media as Toronto's "year of the gun," due to a spike in gun-crime that lead to fifty-two deaths (Siciliano, 2010) and my thought was to use that issue as a point of entry into a project with the Toronto Police Service (TPS). Fieldwork did not commence until the summer of 2014 and is, as of this writing, still ongoing. In the intervening period there were many false starts and *cul-de-sacs* but in the end both research access and funding were secured and I was, like my mother used to say, "in there like a dirty shirt." There is a lot to this story, but those details will have to wait for another time. My research question is: "what is 'intelligence-led' about intelligence-led policing against gun-crime in Toronto?" I want to understand the social organization of policing with respect to a very serious form of crime and to provide a descriptive account concerning the "pistolization" of street-crime in Toronto (and, by extension Canada more widely). It is the case that street level drug markets and street level crime in Canada generally did not have a significant presence of firearms until the relatively recent past. Since 2005, gun-crime has become normalized as part of the policing landscape in Toronto. I want to observe the policing of gun-crime and understand its development over time in order to understand the phenomenon of "pistolization" (Sheptycki, 2009).

Background to the Current Project

The Toronto Police Service lists itself as the fourth largest municipal police agency in North America and is the largest such service in Canada. With a budget of approximately $1 billion Canadian dollars, it has slightly more than five thousand police personnel and close to three thousand civilian support staff. It is governed by the Toronto Police Services Board (TPSB), a seven member civilian body with purview over policing policy, but with no operational remit or control. From 1990 an independent civilian review body—the Special Investigations Unit (SIU)—has investigated cases involving death, injury or allegations of sexual assault when they involve police officers. The SIU is the first of its kind in Canada and Ontario remains one of the few places worldwide with an independent *civilian* agency with the power to both investigate and charge police officers with a criminal offense. The TPS jurisdiction covers 641 sq kilometers (247 sq miles), which is divided into 17 Divisions. Toronto is Canada's largest city and is considered to be North America's fifth most populous municipality—with a population of 2.7 million people. The city itself is one of the most multicultural in the world and, as of 2011, more than half its citizens were born outside of Canada. Slightly less than half of the population is classed as "visible ethnic minority" (i.e., non-white) with South Asian (12 %), Chinese (11 %), Black (8.5 %), and Filipino (5 %) being the four largest classifications. Less than half of 1 % are indigenous First Nations persons. Toronto is only part of the Greater Toronto Area (GTA) which has a population of more than six million people. Briefly, whereas New York has a population of roughly 8.3 million and Chicago 2.7 million (approximately the same as Toronto), the cop-to-pop ratio (the number of police officers per head of population) is: NYC 1:240, Chicago 1:226, Toronto 1:524—in other words Toronto has less than half the police per head of population as compared to these American cities. At present, the proportion of violent crimes per head of population in the three cities is roughly: NYC 1:156, Chicago 1:98, Toronto 1:98. The rate of recorded crime has been falling all across Canada for years and between 2012 and 2013 the national homicide rate was 1.44 per 100,000 while in Toronto it was 1.34 per 100,000 (in Chicago at that time is was approximately 15.65 per 100,000 and in NYC the homicide rate was about 7.0 per 100,000). In 2013, the overall rate of officially recorded crime in the Toronto Region was the lowest of any other metropolitan region in Canada. So Toronto is a relatively peaceable place and its policing is governed through processes of civilian review; and, if Robert Reiner is correct that a paradox of police legitimacy is that the less they are needed the more effective and legitimate they seem to be (Reiner, 2010), then one might have expected the politics of policing to be less fraught in Toronto than elsewhere.

However, the opposite is the case and policing has been hotly contested for some years. The underlying reasons for the vexedness of policing politics in Toronto are many and complex.[3] As Beare and Murray put it, "the relationships between the police and politics are deep, varied and sporadic" (Beare & Murray, 2007, p. 82). One issue stands out among several and that concerns the policing of black people. In London they have "stop and search" (Bowling & Phillips, 2007), in New York City they have "stop and frisk" (Ridgeway, 2007), and in Toronto the police do "carding" (Owusu-Bempah, 2014). All of these practices are held to be racist on the grounds of statistical prevalence of certain socioeconomic and ethnic variables in criminal justice statistics. So-called "carding" is the police practice of engagement with members of the public during which they enquire about personal identity and document the time and place at which the interaction occurred and the reasons for the police enquiry. Canadian criminologists have long insisted that the practice amounts to "racial profiling" (Wortley & Tanner, 2003). Carding is frequently equated with the more invasive practices of police in cities like London and New York. As US Senator Mobina Jaffer put it in the Huffington Post:

> In Toronto, the police have implemented a carding system where police forces stop, question and document people during non-criminal encounters on the streets. The program is akin to New York's notorious "stop and frisk" program (Jaffer, 2014).

To comparative criminologists, it is obvious that carding is a less intrusive police practice than what is done in London and New York. Hypothetically, carding could suppress pistolization. That being the case, it is worth taking seriously the police claim that "carding" offers a deterrent to gun-crime, by discouraging the casual adoption of firearms as an *accouterment* of male attire, since it is a lesser form of police "intrusion." In April 2014, the TPSB—the civilian governance body of the police service—voted unanimously to accept a new "carding policy" put forward in the Police and Community Engagement Review (PACER) limiting this policing practice. Very briefly, PACER was an internal police effort to develop policies and procedures aiming to confine "carding" to instances of legitimate public safety

[3] https://nowtoronto.com/news/the-5-real-reasons-bill-blair-was-canned/.

concern. Front-line police personnel disengaged from the practice as debates swirled around questions concerning what constitutes legitimate public safety concern. When I entered the field some months later, efforts to reform "carding practice" were in tatters amidst a moral panic about "over-policing" and public accusations that the Chief of Police had been insubordinate to the will of the Toronto Police Services Board. Since the policing of gun-crime and the practice of carding were intertwined it was clear that ethnographic observation of policing gun-crime in Toronto was likely to be highly politicized.

In Situ

In preparation for my fieldwork, I imposed upon myself a years-long media blackout on news concerning policing in Toronto. This was very difficult and, of course, the headlines did not escape my consciousness. The so-called "Danzig shooting" in the summer of 2012 (when rival criminal groups shot up a neighborhood block party), the police shooting of Sammy Yatim (an 18-year-old mentally ill person) on a streetcar a year later and the constant barrage of opinion regarding policing the city were difficult to ignore, especially given the incessant stream of telephone and email enquiries I receive from freelance journalists. However, I diligently ignored the extensive OpEd commentary on the subject of policing in Toronto. I did not want to start my fieldwork with a mind already filled with opinions formed by opinion formers. To a remarkable degree I was successful in ignoring the "Commentariate" prior to entering the field, but that only meant spending considerable time trying to pick up that knowledge while doing the fieldwork. From my position as an observer within the TPS, I became an avid consumer of police news but with the advantage of doing so in the company of serving police officers. This is helpful in understanding the news through police eyes because it does look different from the inside (Reiner & Newburn, 2008, p. 356).

In the conduct of this fieldwork I have attempted to adopt Alison Liebling's stance of "appreciative inquiry" (2000). My goal is to understand the lifeworld of police agents from their perspective, not as a means of justifying that worldview, but rather as a means of understanding it. I want to understand the practices of intelligence-led policing against gun-crime in Toronto, of which the practice of "carding" is only a part. The police in Ontario essentially have a "duty to protect" under Part IV of the Police Services Act, which stipulates they are required to preserve the peace, prevent crime, assist the victims of crime and apprehend persons suspected of committing criminal offenses. Offenses involving firearms are a high priority in this regard and it makes sense that police would try to be proactive and attempt to prevent crime before it occurs, assist the victims of crime when it does and aim to apprehend people who commit offenses with firearms. Gun-crime victimization overwhelmingly affects specific communities already suffering multiple dimensions of social deprivation. Unfortunately, policing in these communities is said by many not to be a *service*, but rather to be but one more facet of the problem of social disadvantage:

> The current practice in carding (sic) is a product of this long and violent history of police interactions with the Toronto's black community (sic) and it is embedded in a larger web of social relations that have consigned blacks to a limited form of quasi-citizenship that is marked by the presumption of their guilt in the name of maintaining public order. Carding is an inherently violent practice precisely because of the ways it both informally and formally tramples the rights of those who are targeted; police violence need not only be at the barrel of a gun (Walker, 2015).

From the perspective of police officers there is a seeming paradox in that police would be condemned for failing in their duty to protect people and communities were they not proactively involved in responding to gun-crime while they are vilified for the attempt to fulfill those duties. A variety of terms have been applied: under-policing, over-policing, de-policing, racial profiling, etc. but in the absence of any observational data on the organization of intelligence-led policing, such terms do little to clarify how police practice actually works. Public debate on the issue generates more heat than light. An observational study of the policing of gun-crime in Toronto could illuminate practices that are little understood and unappreciated.

The ethnographic study of policing raises a host of questions as Liebling well maintained (2001, p. 478). Echoing her thoughts: How does one do ethnographic research within institutions when the policies ascribed to it are felt to be worthy of personal disapproval? It is even proper to observe an institution "from the inside" when there is ample publically available evidence that violence and brutality are practiced? How does one respond when colleagues are critical of a research strategy likened to that of the "embedded journalists" of the second Iraq war? On the latter point, upon hearing my advocacy of the appreciative stance in police ethnography, one colleague asked me if I had not already "drank the Kool-Aid." No matter. I enjoy being in liminal spaces and the process of getting into difficult to observe social worlds. On a more principled level, I adhere to Robert Reiner's (1985) insistence that police have a necessary social role as "dirty workers," that they are "a necessary evil in any complex society" (p. 63), that policework is "inevitably thankless and ultimately Sisyphean" (p. 64) and that policing is "both inevitable and inevitably dirty work" (p. 65). While this tragic perspective is undoubtedly "heretical" for many criminologists "on the left" (ibid. p. 63) who like to think that the police are "over-mighty oppressors … grown far too big for their jackboots" (p. 64), as Reiner (1985) eloquently argued, what is really needed is to change society and policing and you can't do that by alienating the police as intrinsic enemies (p. 65). Anti-police sentiment is part of the predicament of gun-crime in Toronto and those who hold steadfastly to such views may, albeit unwittingly, contribute to the pistolization effect.

I had not long been in the field when yet another media storm erupted concerning the issue of "carding." Subsequent to the PACER report, instances of carding fell dramatically and the internal documents I had access to confirmed this. Earlier in

2014 the Toronto Police Services Board (TPSB) had commissioned LogicalOutcomes, a nonprofit consulting firm, to evaluate the implementation of PACER policies. This was intended to respond to concerns that carding practice had a disproportionate impact on "racialized youth" (Law Union of Ontario, 2015). LogicalOutcomes was paid $75,000.00 (Canadian dollars) to conduct a community survey and the result was *A Community-Based Assessment of Police Contact Carding in 31 Division* (henceforth the CAPP Report). The *Toronto Star* quoted Neil Price, the lead author of the report, saying: "Unfortunately, as the findings of this report show, the current Community Contacts (ie. 'carding') Policy has effectively been ignored by police officers on the ground" (Winsa, 2014a). Sabrina Butterfly Gopaul, a community activist, was quoted as saying: "While the findings of the Community Assessment of Police Practices study have made news headlines throughout the GTA, they confirm what area residents know only too well: despite a revised carding policy designed to reign in police abuses, racially biased carding continues to be widespread" (Paul, 2014). The Toronto Police Accountability Coalition, a civilian pressure group, said the CAPP report was "a very serious blow to the Toronto Police Service" (TPAC, 2014). The study surveyed over four hundred respondents and it suggested that 62 persons interviewed had been "carded" in the summer months since the new policies had been put in place. The report maintained that 40 of the 62 people who said they had been carded during that period did not believe police had a valid public safety reason for engaging with them. According to internal TPS data, there were 83 officially recorded "carding" incidents for 31 Division, where the community survey took place, during the relevant period. Speaking to the public about the study's findings of "widespread noncompliance" of the new rules, the Toronto Police Chief Bill Blair noted that the methodology of the study was "somewhat suspect."

The week the CAPP report was issued I happened to be working in an intelligence unit based at Police Headquarters, on the same floor as the senior command offices and the office of the Chair of the Police Services Board, and was asked for my thoughts on the survey methodology. The solicitation raised contradictory feelings within me. On the one hand, it was quite pleasing because the request meant acceptance of my presence in the research environment. This signaled that the fieldwork had edged towards becoming a "participant observation study," to many a sort of "gold standard" for ethnographic work. On the other hand, the fieldwork had only recently begun and I was very reticent to become involved in a very public shooting match over the issue of police "carding." Up to that point, the fieldwork had only been in the environment of senior police management and there was still a lot of observations and interviewing at the Divisional level that lay ahead. Having had next to no experience with quantitative methods since my graduate school days, I sought advice and contacted quite a few colleagues asking them if they had any comments on the CAPP methodology. One responded saying that such commentary was "not a good idea," another suggested the request I had received was itself "extremely troubling" and when I mentioned this to another friend he said: "fools rush in where angels fear to tread."

Thus on the horns of a dilemma, I provided a short two-page memo based on my reading of the report which stated in part:

> On the face of it, the sample does appear to have some biases and so the degree to which the attitudes and perceptions recorded in the survey can be generalized to the population living in the area of 31 Division as a whole remains unclear. The report acknowledges that there "were two ways that the sample results diverged from the general population characteristics of the area" due to "an over sampling of young individuals and members of the Black population" (p. 60). The report's authors state "our canvassing method captured an oversampling of individuals with a unique racialized perspective of police-community interactions" (p. 60). The authors "believe that the oversampling of both groups [young people and people who self-identify as Black] is mainly due to the nature of the issue we were studying and, therefore a positive element of the study since there individuals who have either or both characteristics have an acute understanding and perspective on the issue of police-community interactions in 31 Division" (p. 61).

I went on to concur that "the sample bias is actually useful for gauging attitudes to the TPS policy and the practice of 'carding' among those people who are widely acknowledged to both experience this kind of activity and be resentful about it. The nature of the survey sampling method probably helps to ensure that a significantly high percentage of the sample population had had direct experience of 'being carded.'" Reading these words now, I think they seem mealy mouthed. I might have said that a statistically representative sample would have been preferable for reasons of representativeness and generalizability and been quite reasonably critical of the CAPP report. That was clearly what people on the inside thought was the case. From my position on the limen, I considered the first principle of medical ethics, *primum non nocere*—first, do no harm. By wading in with such a methodological critique the research I was engaged in could become publicly politicized almost from the start, and it would do nothing to shift the terms of public debate. In other words, it would harm the project and do no public good. Obviously fieldwork like this is political, but a public engagement on this level would transform my status as a neutral observer and I had yet to engage front-line personnel as a field researcher. The situation was already volatile and I chose observe rather than compete.[4] Offered the opportunity to become a "participant-observer," I opted to be an "observer-participant," or perhaps my standpoint is, in spite of best efforts at appreciative enquiry, even more ambiguous. For me, doing "public criminology" would have to wait (Loader & Sparks, 2010).

Alok Murkerjee, the Chair of the TPSB, remarked on the CAPP findings, calling them "extremely disturbing" and saying further that the Toronto Police Service faced "a crisis in confidence." Chief of Police Bill Blair stated publically that he thought "some of the chair's remarks were inflammatory and reckless" (Alder, 2014). Reportage in the local papers exaggerated the tone debate in TDSB meetings, with

[4] Taking my cue from Bertrand Russell's discussion of Pythgoras in his book *A History of Western Philosophy* (1961). There it is said that, "In this life there are three kinds of men, just as there are three kinds who come to the Olympic Games. The lowest class is made up of those who come to buy and sell, the next above them are those who come to compete. Best of all are those who come to simply look on." (p. 52).

headlines like "Blair slams negative survey"—but my observations of discussion between board members in those meetings has been that decorum prevails, although the words themselves can be pointed (Winsa, 2014b). The tone of the debate as presented in local media was extremely acerbic. Police Services Board meetings, the public forum for the democratic governance of police in the city, was sometimes interrupted by vociferous participation by members of the general public. In public discourse police were frequently characterized as overwhelmingly racist and anti-black and the official police rejoinder was a weak-sounding insistence that the Toronto Police Service was committed to "bias-free policing."

Watching a Youtube video of police carding with police personnel working at police HQ during this period was instructive and difficult.[5] The main point they wished to stress was that what they practiced was not "racial profiling" it was "crime profiling." They had examples to point to.[6] On Sunday November 16, 2014 not long after the club district had closed for the night, there was a shooting incident in a crowded downtown restaurant in which one man was killed and two women were injured. On October 24th that year police announced that they had seized guns and arrested two men in connection with gun-smuggling, across the US border. The year 2014 ended in Toronto with 57 persons dead in homicide incidents, including Adshir Hassan (a 31-year-old teacher shot dead outside his apartment building); Hamid Aminzada (a 19-year-old high-school student shot while at school); 15-year-old Michael Menjivar and 17-year-old Zaid Youssef (shot dead near their school at lunch hour), 33-year-old Andrea White (shot dead by 21-year-old Michael Vanai and 23-year-old former NCAA basketball player Alwayne Bigby, in a drive-by shooting incident not long after they attended the gravesite memorial service of Kwano Mensah who had been killed in 2013).[7] The police I was talking to wondered aloud (sometimes angrily) what it was they were supposed to do and who they were supposed to talk to in order to prevent crimes like this from occurring and to find out information after the fact. I appreciated their point of view.

The senior command officers in the Toronto Police Service are firmly committed to the language of community policing (Sillers, 2009). Based on my readings of internal reports concerning police policy and practice dating back to the early 1980s, I can attest that commitment to that language is long established. Peter Manning has called Community Policing a "rhetorical giant" (Manning, 1997), but rhetoric in the context of American policing is not the same as it is in the Canadian context. When it comes to gun-crime, one of Chief Blair's most often used aphorisms, which I have heard him use in public and private settings on several occasions, is that "we are not going to arrest our way out of this problem." To be sure, among the rank-and-file of the TPS a somewhat old-fashioned police professionalism remains very much in vogue and Blair himself has facilitated some major law enforcement operations against gun-crime in the city during his long career.

[5] https://www.youtube.com/watch?v=t6XDeIpjCcM

[6] http://tpsnews.ca/

[7] http://metronews.ca/news/toronto/1251373/toronto-homicide-count-at-57-for-second-straight-year/.

However, senior police officers in the TPS also recognize that major police operations cause fear and alarm in communities that is almost equal to the fear and alarm created by criminal shootings near schools and shopping malls. In the aftermath of major police enforcement operations, the TPS are very quick to mobilize police resources to reassure people in support of community safety. Blair himself has been characterized as a "thinking person's cop" who can "talk just as readily about social justice and Jane Jacobs as he can about surveillance techniques" (Lorinc, 2010).[8] In Toronto there are well-known incidents of bad policing and some communities do feel themselves to be unfairly policed. Looking at the situation as an appreciative observer of policing practice, one cannot help but think that the issues surrounding the so-called "carding" are amplified by moral entrepreneurs in the media as a way of boosting advertizing revenue in a time of falling newspaper circulation.[9]

Conclusions: Of a Sort

It is too early for me, or anyone else, to draw firm inferences or exacting interpretations regarding the policing of gun-crime in Toronto on the basis of my observations of the secret social world of the Toronto Police Service. The fieldwork remains ongoing, and conclusions are an end-point that must wait while many things yet remain to be considered. What I wish to emphasize here is the *between-ness* of my position as an observer of the police lifeworld and a participant in the social world more generally. Ethnographers who are interested in the meanings which people give to their own and others' behavior, observe dialectical, open and emergent qualities of social life and they do so in a "natural setting." Policing is similarly complicated, situated, evolving and interpretive, but police engage powerfully with aspects of social life labeled criminal or deviant, labels that are themselves empirically problematic, grounded in meaning, negotiated and emergent. Sociology is a language about power, policing is a language of power. In this short essay I have given an account of my biographical situatedness, if not my psychological configuration,

[8] Many examples can be cited that show sensitive community policing awareness in the TPS. The months-long Tamil protests of 2009 should be given equal mention alongside the much more often cited debacle surrounding the policing of the G20 security event in 2011, for example, but it is not. In the former instance, impassioned protesters disrupted city traffic and even occupied the city's main expressway, but the TPS's measured response struck the perfect balance between public safety and the preservation of the right to free speech. More importantly, nobody got hurt and there were only three arrests. Since there was no bad news, there was little to report and the policing of these large-scale protests in Toronto during the time of the Sri Lankan civil war is largely forgotten by media commentators.

[9] In 2013 *The Globe and Mail* reported "print advertising continues to decline at newspapers across North America." *The Globe* further reported that *The Toronto Star* was laying off 55 staff members, half of them in the editorial department: "Canada's largest newspaper is cutting dozens of jobs from its newsroom, outsourcing editing duties that are increasingly seen as too costly for cash-strapped dailies trying to cope with falling advertising revenue" (Ladurantaye, 2013).

and a consideration of my standpoint as an observer. In other words, this essay is an answer to the question: "who is the 'I' who observes and interprets?" (Liebling, 2001, p. 482). Echoing Paul Rock and Simon Holdaway, here I have tried to address the existential gap, the liminal space, between the seemingly impersonal domain of research and the personal domain of the researcher (Rock & Holdaway, 1998).

Noting that the observer, the observed, and the process of observation are part of a whole (*ibid.* p. 10), in my current research project I struggle to overcome the systemic presence of distrust notable among police as they tolerate me in their everyday surroundings and I do so by projecting an appreciative awareness of their lifeworld. This is ultimately an ambivalent posture and is not atypical of ethnographers, although it is striking to me that those observing the action on the other side of the fence have the *caché* of "underdogism" while it is difficult for anyone to describe police as, in any way, disadvantaged parties. How then to offer an ethical or political defense of an appreciative enquiry about policing when, perhaps more than any time during living memory, police are projected as singular oppressors on behalf of an unjust social order? Critical criminologists bemoan the regrettable nature of contemporary crime policy for its many injustices and an overwhelming foolishness. This is not only a matter of police practice—it is attributable to larger and deeply intractable political forces for which police, even those in positions of command and control, are neither responsible nor fully able to control. Wary of undertaking a sociological study that can all too easily be hijacked to the base aspects of agenda-setting and mindful of the possibility that observational data can be transformed through reductionist thought into administratively meaningful data, I still argue that it is worthwhile to look behind the façade established in media—be it on the Internet, in the cinema, on television and by news corporations—and into the everyday lifeworld of policing. It is socially useful because policing is both inevitable and inevitably dirty and, no matter what kind of social order we live in there will be policing in some form, so it is useful to have a grounded notion of what it is in practice. On a principled level, the point is to try to find ways to make policing humanistic. In order to do that, one has to appreciate the humans that make it up and one can only do that by talking to them.

However, life is moved by inner muses and passions as much as by clear-headed logical thinking, and I cannot pretend that the only motivation for doing sociology behind police lines stems from the *noblesse oblige* articulated by a would-be "public criminologist." Lonely prophet laboring for democracy, ambivalent policy advisor masquerading as a scientific expert, covert social activist, incognito governmental player, or just an ethnographer observing the action from the limen of a secret social world; regardless I have enjoyed the trip and have come some way from being a *flâneur* among fallen middle-class junkies. It is all very complicated—there are a lot of ins, a lot of outs, and a lot of what-have-yous and I enjoy being in there "like a dirty shirt." One of the abiding lessons learned in my long acquaintanceship with Dick Hobbs is that doing criminology is deadly serious, as well as hectic, irreverent and transgressive but that the best of it is done with a sense of fun. For that lesson, if for no other, I think everybody in British criminology should be grateful.

References

Alder, M. (2014). Police Chief Bill Blair disputes controversial 'carding' study, *North York Mirror*, Nov. 14, 2014.

Anderson, E. (2000). *Code of the street; decency, violence and the moral life of the inner-city*. New York, NY: W.W. Norton and Co.

Beare, M. E., & Murray, T. (2007). *Police and government relations; Who's calling the shots?* Toronto, ON: University of Toronto Press.

Bowling, B., & Phillips, C. (2007). Disproportionate and discriminatory: Reviewing the evidence on police stop and search. *Modern Law Review, 70*(6), 936–961.

Clifford, J. (1997). *Routes; travel and translation in the late twentieth century*. Cambridge, MA: Harvard University Press.

Dorn, N., & South, N. (1987). *A land fit for heroin, drug policies, prevention and practice*. London: Macmillan.

Downes, D., & Rock, P. (2011). *Understanding deviance; a guide to the sociology of crime and rule breaking*. Oxford: Oxford University Press.

Edwards, A., & Sheptycki, J. (2009). *Criminology and Criminal Justice, 9*(3), 379.

Ericson, R. V. (1981). *Making crime; a study of police detective work*. Toronto, ON: Butterworths.

Ericson, R. V. (1982). *Reproducing order; a study of police patrol work*. Toronto, ON: University of Toronto Press.

Geertz, C. (2000). *Available light; anthropological reflections on philosophical topics*. Princeton, NJ: Princeton University Press.

Goffman, A. (2014). *On the run; fugitive life in an American city*. Chicago, IL: University of Chicago Press.

Harvey, E. B., & Liu, R. (2003). *An independent review of the Toronto Star Analysis of Criminal Information Processing System (CIPS) Data provided by the Toronto Police Service*, (unpublished).

Hobbs, D. (1988). *Doing the business; entrepreneurship, the working class and detectives in the East End of London*. Oxford: Oxford University Press.

Hobbs, D. (1995). *Bad business; professional crime in modern Britain*. Oxford: Oxford University Press.

Hobbs, D. (1998). Going down to the glocal; the local context of organized crime. *The Howard Journal of Criminal Justice, 37*(2), 407–422.

Hobbs, D. (2013). *Lush life; constructing organized crime in the UK*. Oxford: Oxford University Press.

Hobbs, D., Hadfield, P., Lister, S., & Winlow, S. (2003). *Bouncers: Violence and governance in the night time economy*. Oxford: Oxford University Press.

Hobbs, D., & Wright, R. (2006). *The Sage handbook of fieldwork*. London: Sage.

Jackson, P. (1994). Constructions of criminality; police-community relations in Toronto. *Antipode, 26*(3), 216–235.

Jaffer, M. (2014). Toronto's carding system is basically a 'Stop and Frisk' Program, *Huffington Post* March 26, 2014.

Jones, T., Maclean, B., & Young, J. (1986). *The Islington crime survey; crime, victimization and policing in inner-city London*. London: Gower.

Ladurantaye, S. (2013). Toronto Star to cut jobs citing declines in ad revenue, *The Globe and Mail*, March 4, 2013.

Law Union of Ontario. (2015). *Law Union of Ontario submission to TPSB regarding the community-based assessment of police contact carding report, Dec. 15 2014*. Toronto, ON: Law Union of Ontario.

Leibling, A. (2000). Prison officers, policing and the use of discretion. *Theoretical Criminology, 4*(3), 333–357.

Liazos, A. (1972). The poverty of the sociology of deviance: Nuts, sluts and perverts. *Social Problems, 20*, 103–120.

Liebling, A. (2001). Whose side are we on? Theory, practice and allegiances in prisons research. *British Journal of Criminology, 41*(3), 472–484.
Loader, I., & Sparks, R. (2010). *Public criminology?* London: Routledge.
Lorinc, J. (2010). Force for change, *UofT Magazine*, Spring 2010, Toronto: University of Toronto.
Manning, P. K. (1980). *The Narcs' game; Organizational and informational limits on drug law enforcement*. Cambridge, MA: MIT Press.
Manning, P. K. (1997). *The social organization of policing* (2nd ed.). Prospect Heights, IL: Waveland Press.
Manning, P. K., & van Maanen, J. (1978). *Policing; a view from the street*. New York, NY: Random House.
Matza, D. (1969). *Becoming deviant*. Englewood Cliffs, NJ: Prentice Hall.
McMahon, M. W., & Ericson, R. V. (1984). *Policing reform; a study of the reform practices and police institution in Toronto*. Toronto, ON: Centre of Criminology.
Owusu-Bempah, A. (2014). *Black males' perceptions of and experiences with the police in Toronto*. University of Toronto, Ph.D. Thesis (unpublished).
Paul, G. V. (2014). Blair livid over carding report. *The Caribbean Camera*, No. 20, 2014.
Polsky, N. (1967). *Hustlers, beats and others*. Chicago, IL: Aldine Publishers.
Reiner, R. (1985). *The politics of the police*. London: Harvester Wheatsheaf.
Reiner, R. (2010). *The politics of the police* (4th ed.). Oxford: Oxford University Press.
Reiner, R., & Newburn, T. (2008). Police research. In R. King & E. Wincup (Eds.), *Doing research on crime and justice* (pp. 343–374). Oxford: Oxford University Press.
Ridgeway, G. (2007). *Analysis of racial disparities in the New York Police Department's stop, question and frisk practices*. Los Angeles, CA: RAND Corp.
Rock, P. (Ed.). (1988). *A history of british criminology*. Oxford: Clarendon.
Rock, P., & Holdaway, S. (1998). *Thinking about criminology*. Milton Keynes: Open University Press.
Russell, B. (1961). *A history of western philosophy*. London: Unwin.
Sheptycki, J. (2009) 'Guns, Crime and Social Order; A Canadian Perspective' in Criminology and Criminal Justice, Vol. 9 No. 3, pp. 307–336.
Siciliano, A. M. (2010). *Policing poverty; race, space and the fear of crime after the year of the gun (2005) in suburban Toronto*. Ph.D. Thesis, University of Toronto, Department of Geography (unpublished).
Sillers, S. (2009). Top cop emphasizes community policing, *The Toronto Observer*, Nov. 26, 2009.
Smith, D. J., & Henry, A. (2007). *Transformations in policing*. Aldershot: Ashgate.
TPAC. (2014). Toronto Police Accountability Coalition Bulletin No. 87, Nov. 20, 2014.
Wacquant, L. (2004). *Body and soul; notebooks of an apprentice boxer*. New York, NY: Oxford University Press.
Walker, B. (2015). Playing the race card: Policing Toronto the good, *Torontoist*, May 5, 2015.
Winsa, P. (2014a). Improper police 'carding' continues in Jane-Finch area, survey finds, *Toronto Star*, Wed. Nov. 12, 2014.
Winsa, P. (2014b). Police chief Bill Blair slams negative survey of officers in 31 Division as 'advocacy report', *Toronto Star*, Nov. 13, 2014.
Wortley, S., & Tanner, J. (2003). Data, denials and confusion: The racial profiling debate in Toronto. *Canadian Journal of Criminology and Criminal Justice, 57*(2), 367–390.
Wright, R., Decker, S., & Shover, N. (1997). *Armed robbers in action; stickups and street culture*. Lebanon: Northeastern University Press.
Young, M. (1991). *An inside job; policing and police culture in Britain*. Oxford: Oxford University Press.

Index

G.A. Antonopoulos (ed.), *Illegal Entrepreneurship, Organized Crime and Social Control*, Studies of Organized Crime 14, DOI 10.1007/978-3-319-31608-6

MIX
Papier aus verantwortungsvollen Quellen
Paper from responsible sources
FSC® C105338

If you have any concerns about our products,
you can contact us on
ProductSafety@springernature.com

In case Publisher is established outside the EU,
the EU authorized representative is:
Springer Nature Customer Service Center GmbH
Europaplatz 3, 69115 Heidelberg, Germany

Printed by Libri Plureos GmbH
in Hamburg, Germany